International Economics

Theory and Policy

Fourth Edition

Paul R. Krugman
Massachusetts Institute of Technology

Maurice Obstfeld
University of California, Berkeley

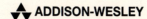 **ADDISON-WESLEY**

An imprint of Addison Wesley Longman, Inc.

Reading, Massachusetts • Menlo Park, California • New York • Harlow, England
Don Mills, Ontario • Sydney • Mexico City • Madrid • Amsterdam

For Robin and Leslie Ann

Senior Acquisitions Editor: Bruce Kaplan
Developmental Editor: Jane Tufts
Supplements Editor: Julie Zasloff
Project Editorial Manager: Melonie Salvati
Design Manager: John Callahan
Text Designer: EriBen Graphics
Cover Designers: Sarah Johnson and Scott Russo
Cover Photo: © The Stock Market, PhotoDisc
Art Studio: ElectraGraphics, Inc.
Electronic Production Manager: Su Levine
Desktop Administrator: Laura Leever
Senior Manufacturing Manager: Willie Lane
Electronic Page Makeup: Laura Leever
Printer and Binder: RR Donnelley & Sons Company
Cover Printer: The Lehigh Press, Inc.

Credits
Page 333, Table 13-1. "Currency Trading" from *The Wall Street Journal*, December 7, 1992.
Reprinted by permission of *The Wall Street Journal*, © 1992 Dow Jones & Company, Inc.
All rights reserved worldwide.
Page 414, "The Hamburger Standard" from *Big MacCurrencies*, November 10, 1990, pp.
77–78. © 1995 The Economist Newspaper Group, Inc. Reprinted with permission. Further
reproduction prohibited.

Library of Congress Cataloging-in-Publication Data
Krugman, Paul R.
　　International economics : theory and policy / Paul R. Krugman,
　Maurice Obstfeld. -- 4th ed.
　　　　p.　cm.
　　Includes index.
　　ISBN 0-673-52497-3
　　　1. International economic relations.　2. International finance.
　I. Obstfeld, Maurice.　II. Title.
　HF 1359.K78　1996
　337--dc20
　　　　　　　　　　　　　　　　　　　　　　　96-25542
　　　　　　　　　　　　　　　　　　　　　　　CIP

ISBN 0-673-52497-3
　45678910—DOC—999897

Brief Contents

Contents

9   THE POLITICAL ECONOMY OF TRADE POLICY   219

Part III Exchange Rates and Open-Economy Macroeconomics   299

Part IV International Macroeconomic Policy   533

18 THE INTERNATIONAL MONETARY SYSTEM, 1870–1973   535

19 Macroeconomic Policy and Coordination Under Floating Exchange Rates 571

20 Optimum Currency Areas and the European Experience 613

21   THE GLOBAL CAPITAL MARKET: PERFORMANCE AND POLICY PROBLEMS   649

Mathematical Postscripts   739

Index   I-1

Preface

The years since 1980 have brought a steady sequence of upheavals in economic relations among countries. Newly industrializing developing countries have seized from developed countries an important share of the world market for manufactured exports; a booming international capital market has forged new links among the world's financial centers but also raised new unease about global financial stability; wide swings in exchange rates and structural shifts in trade patterns have generated political pressures that gravely threaten the open international trading system built up so painstakingly after World War II; and, most recently, the countries of the former Soviet bloc have shaken off communist rule in the hope of establishing market economies open to international flows of commodities and capital. Even in the United States, which is more self-sufficient than nations with smaller economies, problems of international economic policy have assumed primacy and moved decisively to the newspapers' front pages.

Recent general developments in the world economy raise concerns that have preoccupied international economists for more than two centuries, such as the nature of the international adjustment mechanism and the merits of free trade compared with protection. As always in international economics, however, the interplay of events and ideas has led to new modes of analysis. Three notable examples of recent progress are the asset market approach to exchange rates; new theories of foreign trade and industrial location based on increasing returns and market structure rather than comparative advantage; and the intertemporal analysis of international capital flows, which has been useful both in refining the concept of "external balance" and in examining the determinants of developing country borrowing and default.

The idea of writing this book came out of our experience in teaching international economics to undergraduates and business students since the late 1970s. We perceived two main challenges in teaching. The first was to communicate to students the exciting intellectual advances in this dynamic field. The second was to show how the development of international economic theory has traditionally been shaped by the need to understand the changing world economy and analyze actual problems in international economic policy.

We found that published textbooks did not adequately meet these challenges. Too often, international economics textbooks confront students with a bewildering array of special models and assumptions from which basic lessons are difficult to extract. Because many of these special models are outmoded, students are left puzzled about the real-world relevance of the analysis. As a result, many textbooks often leave a gap between the somewhat antiquated material to be covered in class and the exciting issues that dominate current research and policy debates. That gap has widened dramatically as the importance of international economic problems—and enrollments in international economics courses—have grown.

This book is our attempt to provide an up-to-date and understandable analytical framework for illuminating current events and bringing the excitement of international economics into the classroom. In analyzing both the real and the monetary sides of the subject, our approach has been to build up, step by step, a simple, unified framework for communicating the grand traditional insights as well as the newest findings and approaches. To help the student grasp and retain the underlying logic of international economics, we motivate the theoretical development at each stage by pertinent data or policy questions.

THE PLACE OF THIS BOOK IN THE ECONOMICS CURRICULUM

Students assimilate international economics most readily when it is presented as a method of analysis vitally linked to events in the world economy, rather than as a body of abstract theorems about abstract models. Our goal has therefore been to stress concepts and their application rather than theoretical formalism. Accordingly, the book does not presuppose an extensive background in economics. Students who have had a course in economic principles will find the book accessible, but students who have taken further courses in microeconomics or macroeconomics will find an abundant supply of new material. Specialized appendices and mathematical postscripts have been included to challenge the most advanced students.

We follow the standard practice of dividing the book into two halves, devoted to trade and to monetary questions. Although the trade and monetary portions of international economics are often treated as unrelated subjects, even within one textbook, similar themes and methods recur in both subfields. One example is the idea of gains from trade, which is important in understanding the effects of free trade in assets as well as free trade in goods. International borrowing and lending provide another example. The process by which countries trade present for future consumption is best understood in terms of comparative advantage (which is why we introduce it in the book's first half), but the resulting insights deepen understanding of the external macroeconomic problems of developing and developed economies alike. We have made it a point to illuminate connections between the trade and monetary areas when they arise.

At the same time, we have made sure that the book's two halves are completely self-contained. Thus, a one-semester course on trade theory can be based on Chapters 2 through 11 and a one-semester course on international monetary economics can be based on Chapters 12 through 23. If you adopt the book for a full-year course covering both subjects, however, you will find a treatment that does not leave students wondering why the principles underlying their work on trade theory have been discarded over the winter break.

SOME DISTINCTIVE FEATURES OF *INTERNATIONAL ECONOMICS: THEORY AND POLICY*

This book covers the most important recent developments in international economics without shortchanging the enduring theoretical and historical insights that have traditionally formed the core of the subject. We have achieved this comprehensiveness by stressing how recent theories have evolved from earlier findings in response to an evolving world economy. Both the real trade portion of the book (Chapters 2 through 11) and the monetary portion (Chapters 12 through 23) are divided into a core of chapters focused on theory, followed by chapters applying the theory to major policy questions, past and current.

In Chapter 1 we describe in some detail how this book addresses the major themes of international economics. Here we emphasize several of the newer topics that previous authors failed to treat in a systematic way.

ASSET MARKET APPROACH TO EXCHANGE RATE DETERMINATION

The modern foreign exchange market and the determination of exchange rates by national interest rates and expectations are at the center of our account of open-economy macroeconomics. The main ingredient of the macroeconomic model we develop is the interest parity relation (augmented later by risk premiums). Among the topics we address using the model are exchange rate "overshooting"; behavior of real exchange rates; balance-of-payments crises under fixed exchange rates; and the causes and effects of central bank intervention in the foreign exchange market.

INCREASING RETURNS AND MARKET STRUCTURE

After discussing the role of comparative advantage in promoting trade and gains from trade, we move to the frontier of recent research (in Chapter 6) by explaining how increasing returns and product differentiation affect trade and welfare. The models explored in this discussion capture significant aspects of reality, such as intra-industry trade and shifts in trade patterns due to dynamic scale economies. The models show, too, that mutually beneficial trade need not be based on comparative advantage. We have also included in this chapter much of the material on regional economics that in the previous edition was placed in Chapter 8; reviews of that chapter indicated that a focus on agglomeration effects was helpful in explaining the nature of external economies but that the material did not seem to work well as a separate chapter.

POLITICS AND THEORY OF TRADE POLICY

Starting in Chapter 3, we stress the effect of trade on income distribution as the key political factor behind restrictions on free trade. This emphasis makes it clear to students why the prescriptions of the standard welfare analysis of trade policy seldom prevail in practice. Chapter 11 is focused on the currently popular notion that governments should adopt "strategic" trade policies aimed at encouraging sectors of the economy seen as crucial. The chapter also includes a theoretical discussion of strategic trade policy based on simple ideas from game theory.

INTERNATIONAL MACROECONOMIC POLICY COORDINATION

Our discussion of international monetary experience (Chapters 18, 19, and 20) stresses the theme that different exchange rate systems have led to different *policy coordination* problems for their members. Just as the competitive gold scramble of the interwar years

showed how beggar-thy-neighbor policies can be self-defeating, the current float challenges national policymakers to recognize their interdependence and formulate policies
cooperatively. Chapter 19 presents a detailed discussion of this very topical problem in the
current system.

THE WORLD CAPITAL MARKET AND DEVELOPING COUNTRIES

A broad discussion of the world capital market is given in Chapter 21, which takes up the
welfare implications of international portfolio diversification as well as recent problems of
prudential supervision of offshore financial institutions. Chapter 22 is devoted to the specific macroeconomic stabilization and liberalization problems of industrializing and newly
industrialized countries. The chapter places in historical perspective the interactions among
developing country borrowers, developed country lenders, and official financial institutions
such as the International Monetary Fund. In addition, students will find a structured approach to the recent efforts at inflation and budgetary control in the developing world.

INTERNATIONAL FACTOR MOVEMENTS

In Chapter 7 we emphasize the potential substitutability of international trade and international movements of factors of production. A feature in the chapter is our analysis of international borrowing and lending as *intertemporal trade,* that is, the exchange of present
consumption for future consumption. We draw on the results of this analysis in the book's
second half to throw light on the macroeconomic implications of the current account.

NEW TO THE FOURTH EDITION

For this fourth edition of *International Economics: Theory and Policy,* we have extensively redesigned several chapters. These changes respond both to users' suggestions and
to some important developments on the theoretical and practical sides of international economics. The most far-reaching changes are the following:

Chapter 4   The effects of international trade on income distribution have moved in
recent years from a largely academic question to an important policy issue: the simultaneous growth of exports from low-wage countries and income inequality in advanced countries has led to widespread concern that these phenomena are linked. The new version of
the chapter offers a new approach to the factor proportions model that is organized around
the debate over trade and income distribution.

Chapter 5   While the growth of newly industrializing countries has primarily raised
concerns about income distribution in the advanced nations, some observers have also argued that it has an adverse impact on overall real income. This dispute offers a useful way
to motivate the discussion of trade and growth.

Chapter 7   The policy discussion of international factor mobility has altered substantially in the United States, thanks mainly to two developments: growing concern about
immigration and the reemergence of large-scale capital movements to developing countries. The revised chapter emphasizes both issues.

Chapter 9   The most important development in trade policy since the third edition has been the completion of the Uruguay Round of trade negotiations. The chapter now contains an extended discussion of the round's achievements as well as its limitations. The chapter's discussion of the political economy of trade policy has also been updated to reflect the burgeoning theoretical literature in this area.

Chapter 10   Discussion of trade policy and development is increasingly dominated by two facts: the continuing extraordinary growth in East Asia and the equally extraordinary shift toward free trade policies throughout the developing world. The new chapter is thus oriented toward this "post-import-substitution" world.

Chapter 11   Both the language and, to a lesser extent, the content of calls for government intervention in trade have altered since earlier editions. The old debate over industrial policy has been replaced by a related but somewhat distinct debate about "competitiveness"; The debate has also to some extent shifted away from arguments about principles to a focus on the numbers. This chapter has been revised to reflect the changed language and tone of the discussion.

Chapter 12   The treatment of national income accounting has been reorganized and condensed to allow students to move immediately to the open-economy case without loss of comprehension.

Chapter 16   The chapter now describes how a government's attempts to exploit a short-run output-inflation trade-off can lead to an inflationary bias in its monetary policies. Also included is a new appendix linking the aggregate demand model in the chapter to the intertemporal analysis of borrowing and lending in Chapter 7.

Chapter 18   Now covered in depth is the role of the international gold standard in spreading the Great Depression worldwide.

Chapter 22   This heavily revised chapter puts less emphasis on the 1980s developing-country debt crisis than in previous editions. Instead the focus is on recent efforts by developing countries to restrain inflation, including the use of pegged exchange rates as "nominal anchors" in those efforts.

Chapter 23   Events have moved along considerably in the transition economies since our last edition. Surprise developments include the failure of large-scale capital inflows to materialize for most transition economies and the massive "dollarization" of the Russian economy. We offer analysis of these new phenomena, with an emphasis on the interaction between political uncertainty and economic disappointments.

In addition to these structural changes, we have updated the book in other ways to maintain current relevance. Thus we link the discussion of the Ricardian model to the critiques of free trade by influential writers like Sir James Goldsmith; we track the surprising results of European integration (French consumers buying English sliced bread!); and we have revised the discussion of the politics of trade policy to reflect the surge of interesting new research in that area. We discuss the effect of Mexico's 1994 peso devaluation on its trade with the United States (Chapter 16); and we look at the advisability of currency-board monetary systems for developing countries (Chapter 22).

LEARNING FEATURES

This book incorporates a number of special learning features that will maintain students' interest in the presentation and help them master its lessons.

CASE STUDIES

Theoretical discussions are often accompanied by case studies that perform the threefold role of reinforcing material covered earlier, illustrating its applicability in the real world, and providing important historical information.

SPECIAL BOXES

Less central topics that nonetheless offer particularly vivid illustrations of points made in the text are treated in boxes. Among these are the political backdrops of Ricardo's and Hume's theories (pp. 59 and 544); the surprising potential importance of NAFTA's effect on California's demand for water (p. 229); the astonishing ability of disputes over banana trade to generate acrimony among countries far too cold to grow any of their own (p. 244); the story of the Bolivian hyperinflation (p. 390); and the 1994 speculative attack on the Mexican peso (p. 470).

CAPTIONED DIAGRAMS

More than 200 diagrams are accompanied by descriptive captions that reinforce the discussion in the text and will help the student in reviewing the material.

SUMMARY AND KEY TERMS

Each chapter closes with a summary recapitulating the major points. Key terms or phrases appear in boldface type when they are introduced in the chapter and are listed at the end of each chapter. To further aid student review of the material, key terms are italicized when they appear in the chapter summary.

PROBLEMS

Each chapter is followed by problems intended to test and solidify students' comprehension. The problems range from routine computational drills to "big picture" questions suitable for classroom discussion. In many problems we ask students to apply what they've learned to real-world data or policy questions.

FURTHER READING

For instructors who prefer to supplement the textbook with outside readings, and for students who wish to probe more deeply on their own, each chapter has an annotated bibliography which includes established classics as well as up-to-date examinations of recent issues.

STUDY GUIDE, INSTRUCTOR'S MANUAL, AND READER

International Economics: Theory and Policy is accompanied by a Study Guide written by Linda S. Goldberg of the Federal Reserve Bank of New York and Michael W. Klein of Tufts University. The Study Guide aids students by providing a review of central concepts from the text, further illustrative examples, and additional practice problems. An Instructor's Manual, also by Linda S. Goldberg and Michael W. Klein, includes chapter overviews, answers to the end-of-chapter problems, and suggestions for classroom presentation of the book's contents. The Study Guide and Instructor's Manual have been updated to reflect the changes in the fourth edition.

Also recommended for use with *International Economics: Theory and Policy* is *Current Issues in the International Economy: A Reader,* compiled by Linda Goldberg and Michael Klein. Along with topical readings in trade and finance, this reader includes a valuable supplementary section that contains information on the Uruguay Round negotiations and international data on key macroeconomic variables.

ACKNOWLEDGMENTS

Our primary debts are to Jane E. Tufts, the development editor, and Bruce Kaplan, the economics editor in charge of the project. Jane's judgment and skill have been reflected in all four editions of this book; we cannot thank her enough for her contributions. Bruce has been a valued adviser and advocate through three editions. Melonie Salvati's efforts as project manager are greatly appreciated. We thank the other editors who helped make the first three editions as good as they were.

We owe a special debt of gratitude to Matthew Jones, who painstakingly updated data, checked art proofs, and critiqued chapters. Annie Wai-kuen Shun provided sterling assistance. For constructive suggestions we thank Jaime Marquez of the Federal Reserve Board, Larry Schembri of Carleton University, Federico Sturzenegger of UCLA, and Giuseppe Tattara of the University of Venice.

Very helpful comments were received from the following reviewers:

Jaleel Ahmad, Concordia University
Richard Ault, Auburn University
George H. Borts, Brown University
Francisco Carrada-Bravo, American Graduate School of International Management
Ann Davis, Marist College
Gopal C. Dorai, William Paterson College
Gerald Epstein, University of Massachusetts at Amherst
JoAnne Feeney, University of Colorado, Boulder
Robert Foster, American Graduate School of International Management
Diana Fuguitt, Eckerd College
Byron Gangnes, University of Hawaii at Manoa
Ranjeeta Ghiara, California State University, San Marcos
Bodil Olai Hansen, Copenhagen Business School
Henk Jager, University of Amsterdam
Arvind Jaggi, Franklin & Marshall College

Mark Jelavich, Northwest Missouri State University
Patrice Franko Jones, Colby College
Maureen Kilkenny, Pennsylvania State University
Corinne Krupp, Michigan State University
Bun Song Lee, University of Nebraska, Omaha
Francis A. Lees, St. Johns University
Rodney D. Ludema, The University of Western Ontario
Marcel Mérette, Yale University
Shannon Mitchell, Virginia Commonwealth University
Kaz Miyagiwa, University of Washington
Ton M. Mulder, Erasmus University, Rotterdam
E. Wayne Nafziger, Kansas State University
Donald Schilling, University of Missouri, Columbia
Ronald M. Schramm, Columbia University
Craig T. Schulman, University of Arkansas
Margaret Simpson, The College of William and Mary
Robert M. Stern, University of Michigan
Scott Taylor, University of British Columbia
Aileen Thompson, Carleton University
Sarah Tinkler, Weber State University
Arja H. Turunen-Red, University of Texas, Austin
Dick vander Wal, Free University of Amsterdam

Although we have not been able to make each and every suggested change, we found reviewers' observations invaluable in revising the book. Obviously, we bear sole responsibility for its remaining shortcomings.

Paul Krugman
Maurice Obstfeld

Introduction

The study of international trade and money has always been an especially lively and controversial part of economics. Many of the key insights of modern economic analysis first emerged in eighteenth- and nineteenth-century debates over international trade and monetary policy. Yet there was never a time when the study of international economics was as important as it is today. Through international trade in goods and services, and international flows of money, the economies of different countries are more closely linked to one another now than ever before. At the same time, the world economy is more turbulent than it has been in many decades. Keeping up with the shifting international environment has become a central concern of both business strategy and national economic policy.

A look at some basic trade statistics gives a first view of the increasing importance of international economics to the United States. Figure 1-1 shows the levels of U.S. exports and imports as shares of gross domestic product from 1965 to 1995. Two points are apparent from the figure. First, the United States exports much more of what it produces and imports much more of what it consumes than it used to: from 1965 to 1980 the share of both exports and imports in GDP more than doubled. Second, U.S. trade has gone through sharp fluctuations since 1980. From 1980 to 1987, exports plunged relative to GDP while imports did not. From 1987 to 1991 there was, by contrast, an export boom and then a surge in imports. Both the long-term trend toward increasing trade and the fluctuations in U.S. exports relative to imports have been crucial developments for the U.S. economy. By 1980, hardly any discussion of domestic economic policy, be it antitrust, regulation, taxation, or labor issues, could ignore the

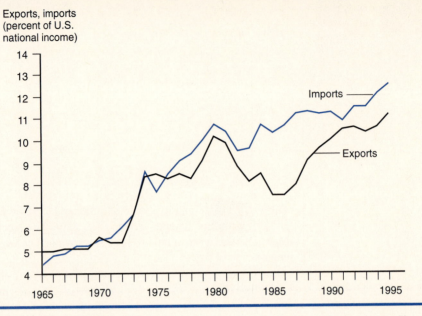

FIGURE 1-1

Exports and Imports as a Percentage of U.S. National Income

Exports, imports
(percent of U.S.
national income)

From the 1960s to 1980, both exports and imports rose steadily as shares of U.S. income. Since 1980, exports have fluctuated sharply.

role of international trade. Since 1980, the gap between imports and exports has been one of the most heated issues of U.S. economic controversy.

If international economics has become crucial to the United States, it is even more crucial to other nations. Figure 1-2 shows the 1994 shares of imports and exports in GDP for a sample of countries. The United States, by virtue of its size and diversity of its resources, actually relies less on international trade than almost any other country. This means that for the rest of the world, international economics is even more important than it is for the United States.

This book introduces the main concepts and methods of international economics and illustrates them with applications drawn from the real world. It is in large part devoted to the grand tradition of international economics; the nineteenth-century trade theory of David Ricardo and the even earlier international monetary analysis of David Hume remain quite relevant to the modern world. At the same time, we have made a special effort to bring the analysis up to date. The field of international economics has been in a creative ferment in recent years, with new views emerging on such issues as the political economy of trade policy, strategic trade policy, exchange rate determination, and the international coordination of macroeconomic policies. We have attempted to convey the key ideas of these new approaches while stressing the continuing usefulness of older ideas.

FIGURE 1-2

Exports and Imports as Percentages of National Income in 1994

International trade is even more important to most other countries than it is to the United States.

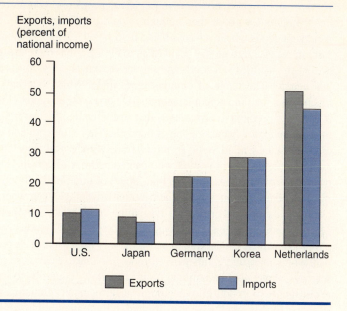

Exports, imports (percent of national income)

Exports Imports

WHAT IS INTERNATIONAL ECONOMICS ABOUT?

International economics uses the same fundamental methods of analysis as other branches of economics, because the motives and behavior of individuals and firms are the same in international trade as they are in domestic transactions. When a bottle of Spanish wine appears on a London table, the sequence of events that brought it there is not very different from the sequence that brings a California bottle to a table in New York—and the distance traveled is much less! Yet international economics involves new and different concerns, because international trade and investment occur between independent nations. Spain and the United Kingdom are sovereign states; California and New York are not. Spain's wine shipments to the United Kingdom can be disrupted if the British government sets a quota that limits imports; Spanish wine can become suddenly cheaper to British wine drinkers if the foreign exchange value of Spain's peseta falls against that of Britain's pound sterling. Neither of these events can happen within the United States, where the Constitution forbids restraints on interstate trade and there is only one currency.

The subject matter of international economics, then, consists of issues raised by the special problems of economic interaction between sovereign states. Seven themes recur throughout the study of international economics: the gains from trade, the pattern of trade, protectionism, the balance of payments, exchange rate determination, international policy coordination, and the international capital market.

THE GAINS FROM TRADE

Everyone knows that some international trade is beneficial—nobody would suggest that Norway should grow its own oranges. Many people, however, are skeptical about the benefits of trading for goods that a country could produce for itself. Shouldn't Americans buy American goods whenever possible to help save U.S. jobs? Probably the most important insight in all of international economics is the idea that there are *gains from trade*—that is, that when countries sell goods and services to one another, this is almost always to their mutual benefit. The range of circumstances under which international trade is beneficial is much wider than most people appreciate. For example, many U.S. businesspeople fear that if Japanese productivity overtakes that of the United States, trade with Japan will damage the U.S. economy because none of our industries will be able to compete. Some politicians charge that the United States is hurt by trade with less advanced countries, whose industries are less efficient than ours but who can sometimes undersell U.S. producers because they pay much lower wages. Yet the first model of trade in this book (Chapter 2) demonstrates that two countries can trade to their mutual advantage even when one of them is more efficient than the other at producing everything and producers in the less efficient economy can compete only by paying lower wages. Trade provides benefits by allowing countries to export goods whose production makes relatively heavy use of resources that are locally abundant while importing goods whose production makes heavy use of resources that are locally scarce (Chapter 4). International trade also allows countries to specialize in producing narrower ranges of goods, allowing them to gain greater efficiencies of large-scale production (Chapter 6). Nor are the benefits limited to trade in tangible goods: international migration and international borrowing and lending are also forms of mutually beneficial trade, the first a trade of labor for goods and services, the second a trade of current goods for the promise of future goods (Chapter 7). Finally, international exchanges of risky assets such as stocks and bonds can benefit all countries by allowing each country to diversify its wealth and reduce the variability of its income (Chapter 21). These invisible forms of trade yield gains as real as the trade that puts fresh fruit from Latin America in Toronto markets in February.

While nations generally gain from international trade, however, it is quite possible that international trade may hurt particular groups *within* nations—in other words, that international trade will have strong effects on the distribution of income. The effects of trade on income distribution have long been a concern of international trade theorists, who have pointed out that:

> International trade can adversely affect the owners of resources that are "specific" to industries that compete with imports, that is, cannot find alternative employment in other industries (Chapter 3).
>
> Trade can also alter the distribution of income between broad groups, such as workers and the owners of capital (Chapter 4).

These concerns have moved from the classroom into the center of real-world policy debate, as it has become increasingly clear that the real wages of less-skilled workers in the United States have been declining even though the country as a whole is continuing to grow richer. Many commentators attribute this development to growing international trade, especially the rapidly growing exports of manufactured goods from low-wage countries. Assessing this claim has become an important task for international economists and is a major theme of both Chapters 4 and 5.

THE PATTERN OF TRADE

Economists cannot discuss the effects of international trade or recommend changes in government policies toward trade with any confidence unless they know their theory is good enough to explain the international trade that is actually observed. Thus attempts to explain the pattern of international trade—who sells what to whom—have been a major preoccupation of international economists.

Some aspects of the pattern of trade are easy to understand. Climate and resources clearly explain why Brazil exports coffee and Saudi Arabia exports oil. Much of the pattern of trade is more subtle, however. Why does Japan export automobiles, while the United States exports aircraft? In the early nineteenth century English economist David Ricardo offered an explanation of trade in terms of international differences in labor productivity, an explanation that remains a powerful insight (Chapter 2). In the twentieth century, however, alternative explanations have also been proposed. One of the most influential, but still controversial, links trade patterns to an interaction between the relative supplies of national resources such as capital, labor, and land on one side and the relative use of these factors in the production of different goods on the other. We present this theory in Chapter 4. Recent efforts to test the implications of this theory, however, appear to show that it is less valid than many had previously thought. More recently still, some international economists have proposed theories that suggest a substantial random component in the pattern of international trade, theories that are developed in Chapter 6.

PROTECTIONISM

If the idea of gains from trade is the most important theoretical concept in international economics, the seemingly eternal battle between free trade and protection is its most important policy theme. Since the emergence of modern nation-states in the sixteenth century, governments have worried about the effect of international competition on the prosperity of domestic industries and have tried either to shield industries from foreign competition by placing limits on imports or to help them in world competition by subsidizing exports. The single most consistent mission of international economics has been to analyze the effects of these so-called protectionist policies—and usually, though not always, to criticize protectionism and show the advantages of freer international trade.

The protectionist issue is especially intense in the United States because of the trends illustrated by Figure 1-1. Since World War II the United States has advocated free trade in the world economy, viewing international trade as a force not only for prosperity but also for world peace. With the growing importance of international trade in the U.S. economy—and with growing concern that foreign competition might be driving down the wages of at least some American workers—this traditional free-trade position has come under growing pressure. The result has been a confused political picture. On one side, the United States has negotiated major free-trade agreements, such as the North American Free Trade Agreement with Canada and Mexico (approved in 1993) and the so-called Uruguay Round agreement (an agreement involving most of the world's economies, approved in 1994). On the other side, the United States has become increasingly aggressive in trade disputes with countries such as Japan, South Korea, and China; and frankly protectionist political statements have become increasingly common from politicians in both major parties.

As befits both the historical importance and the current relevance of the protectionist issue, roughly a quarter of this book is devoted to this subject. Over the years, international economists have developed a simple yet powerful analytical framework for determining the effects of government policies that affect international trade. This framework not only predicts the effects of trade policies, it also allows cost-benefit analysis and defines criteria for determining when government intervention is good for the economy. We present this framework in Chapters 8 and 9 and use it to discuss a number of policy issues in those chapters and in the following two.

In the real world, however, governments do not necessarily do what the cost-benefit analysis of economists tells them they should. This does not mean that analysis is useless. Economic analysis can help make sense of the politics of international trade policy, by showing who benefits and who loses from such government actions as quotas on imports and subsidies to exports. The key insight of this analysis is that conflicts of interest *within* nations are usually more important in determining trade policy than conflicts of interest *between* nations. Chapters 3 and 4 show that trade usually has very strong effects on income distribution within countries, while Chapters 9, 10, and 11 reveal that the relative power of different interest groups within countries, rather than some measure of overall national interest, is often the main determining factor in government policies toward international trade.

THE BALANCE OF PAYMENTS

In 1990 both Japan and Brazil ran large trade surpluses—that is, each sold more goods to the rest of the world than it bought in return. Japan's surplus of $56 billion brought complaints from many other countries that Japan was gaining at their expense; Brazil's surplus of $9 billion (which represented a much larger fraction of the country's national income) brought complaints from the Brazilians that *they* were being unfairly treated. What does it mean when a country runs a trade surplus or a trade deficit? To make sense of these numbers it is essential to place them in the broader context of the whole of a nation's international transactions.

The record of a country's transactions with the rest of the world is called the *balance of payments.* Explaining the balance of payments and diagnosing its significance is a main theme of international economics. It emerges in a variety of specific contexts: in discussing international capital movements (Chapter 7), in relating international transactions to national income accounting (Chapter 12), and in discussing virtually every aspect of international monetary policy (Chapters 16 through 22). Like the problem of protectionism, the balance of payments has become a central issue for the United States because the nation has run huge trade deficits in every year since 1982.

EXCHANGE RATE DETERMINATION

In February 1985 one U.S. dollar traded on international markets for 260 Japanese yen; in January 1988, a dollar was worth only 123 yen. This change had effects that reached far beyond financial markets. In February 1985 the average Japanese worker in manufacturing was paid a wage in yen that, converted into dollars at the prevailing rate of exchange, was only about half that of his or her U.S. counterpart. Three years later Japanese wages were about the same as U.S. wages. With their labor cost advantage vis-à-vis the United States gone, and in the face of competition from low-wage competitors like South Korea and Taiwan, Japanese manufacturers were initially forced into layoffs that drove the Japanese unemployment rate to its highest level since the 1950s, after which they began investing heavily in acquiring production facilities in other countries—especially in the United States.

One of the key differences between international economics and other areas of economics is that countries have different currencies. It is usually possible to convert one currency into another (though even this is illegal in some countries), but as the example of the dollar-yen exchange rate indicates, relative prices of currencies may change over time, sometimes drastically.

The study of exchange rate determination is a relatively new part of international economics, for historical reasons. For most of the twentieth century, exchange rates have been fixed by government action rather than determined in the marketplace. Before World War I the values of the world's major currencies were fixed in terms of gold, while for a generation after World War II the values of most currencies were fixed in terms of the U.S. dollar. The analysis of international monetary systems that fix exchange rates remains an important subject, especially since European nations have made a major effort to create a fixed-rate system in Europe. Chapters 17 and 18 are devoted to the working of fixed-rate systems, Chapter 19 to the debate over which system, fixed or floating rates, is better, and Chapter 20 to the workings of the European Monetary System. For the time being, however, some of the world's most important exchange rates fluctuate minute by minute and the role of changing exchange rates remains at the center of the international economics story. Chapters 13 through 16 focus on the modern theory of floating exchange rates.

INTERNATIONAL POLICY COORDINATION

The international economy comprises sovereign nations, each free to choose its own economic policies. Unfortunately, in an integrated world economy one country's economic policies usually affect other countries as well. For example, when Germany's Bundesbank raised interest rates in 1990—a step it took to control the possible inflationary impact of the reunification of West and East Germany—it helped precipitate a recession in the rest of Western Europe. Differences in goals between countries often lead to conflicts of interest. Even when countries have similar goals, they may suffer losses if they fail to coordinate their policies. A fundamental problem in international economics is how to produce an acceptable degree of harmony among the international trade and monetary policies of different countries without a world government that tells countries what to do.

For the last 45 years international trade policies have been governed by an international treaty known as the General Agreement on Tariffs and Trade (GATT), and massive international negotiations involving dozens of countries at a time have been held. We discuss the rationale for this system in Chapter 9 and look at whether the current rules of the game for international trade in the world economy can or should survive.

While cooperation on international trade policies is a well-established tradition, coordination of international macroeconomic policies is a newer and more uncertain topic. Only in the last few years have economists formulated at all precisely the case for macroeconomic policy coordination. Nonetheless, attempts at international macroeconomic coordination are occurring with growing frequency in the real world. Both the theory of international macroeconomic coordination and the developing experience are reviewed in Chapter 18 and 19.

THE INTERNATIONAL CAPITAL MARKET

During the 1970s banks in advanced countries lent tens of billions of dollars to firms and governments in poorer nations, especially in Latin America. In 1982 Mexico announced it could no longer pay the money it owed without special arrangements that allowed it to postpone payments and borrow back part of its interest; soon afterward Brazil, Argentina, and a number of smaller countries found themselves in the same situation. While combined efforts of banks, governments, and countries avoided a world financial crisis in 1982, the debt difficulties of less-developed countries remained in a state of periodic crisis through 1990. The debt crisis came to a surprisingly quick end in the early 1990s, as international investors began once again to put large sums of money into so-called "emerging markets," including the former debt crisis countries. And yet even this was not the end of the story: At the end of 1994 Mexico experienced a second crisis of confidence, which at least temporarily put a damper on the whole emerging market boom. This roller coaster history contains many lessons, the most important of which is the growing importance of the international capital market.

In any sophisticated economy there is an extensive capital market: a set of arrangements by which individuals and firms exchange money now for promises to pay in the future. The growing importance of international trade since the 1960s has been accompanied by a growth in the *international* capital market, which links the capital markets of individual countries. Thus in the 1970s oil-rich Middle Eastern nations placed their oil revenues in banks in London or New York, and these banks in turn lent money to governments and corporations in Asia and Latin America. During the 1980s Japan converted much of the money it earned from its booming exports into investments in the United States, including the establishment of a growing number of U.S. subsidiaries of Japanese corporations.

International capital markets differ in important ways from domestic capital markets. They must cope with special regulations that many countries impose on foreign investment; they also sometimes offer opportunities to evade regulations placed on domestic markets. Since the 1960s, huge international capital markets have arisen, most notably the remarkable London Eurodollar market, in which billions of dollars are exchanged each day without ever touching the United States.

Some special risks are associated with international capital markets. One risk is that of currency fluctuations: If the dollar falls suddenly against the Japanese yen, Japanese investors who bought U.S. bonds suffer a capital loss—as many discovered in 1995. Another risk is that of national default: A nation may simply refuse to pay its debts (perhaps because it cannot), and there may be no effective way for its creditors to bring it to court.

The growing importance of international capital markets and their new problems demand greater attention than ever before. This book devotes two chapters to issues arising from international capital markets: one on the functioning of global asset markets (Chapter 21) and one on foreign borrowing by developing countries (Chapter 22).

INTERNATIONAL ECONOMICS: TRADE AND MONEY

The economics of the international economy can be divided into two broad subfields: the study of *international trade* and the study of *international money*. International trade analysis focuses primarily on the *real* transactions in the international economy, that is, on those transactions that involve a physical movement of goods or a tangible commitment of economic resources. International monetary analysis focuses on the *monetary* side of the international economy, that is, on financial transactions such as foreign purchases of U.S. dollars. An example of an international trade issue is the conflict between the United States and Europe over Europe's subsidized exports of agricultural products; an example of an international monetary issue is the dispute over whether the foreign exchange value of the dollar should be allowed to float freely or be stabilized by government action.

In the real world there is no simple dividing line between trade and monetary issues. Most international trade involves monetary transactions, while, as the examples in this chapter already suggest, many monetary events have important consequences for trade. Nonetheless, the distinction between international trade and international money is useful. The first half of this book covers international trade issues. Part One (Chapters 2 through 7) develops the analytical theory of international trade, and Part Two (Chapters 8 through 11) applies trade theory to the analysis of government policies toward trade. The second half of the book is devoted to international monetary issues. Part Three (Chapters 12 through 17) develops international monetary theory, and Part Four (Chapters 18 through 23) applies this analysis to international monetary policy.

International Trade Theory

2

Labor Productivity and Comparative Advantage: The Ricardian Model

Countries engage in international trade for two basic reasons, each of which contributes to their gain from trade. First, countries trade because they are different from each other. Nations, like individuals, can benefit from their differences by reaching an arrangement in which each does the things it does relatively well. Second, countries trade to achieve economies of scale in production. That is, if each country produces only a limited range of goods, it can produce each of these goods at a larger scale and hence more efficiently than if it tried to produce everything. In the real world, patterns of international trade reflect the interaction of both these motives. As a first step toward understanding the causes and effects of trade, however, it is useful to look at simplified models in which only one of these motives is present.

The next four chapters develop tools to help us to understand how differences between countries give rise to trade between them and why this trade is mutually beneficial. The essential concept in this analysis is that of comparative advantage.

Although comparative advantage is a simple concept, experience shows that it is a surprisingly hard concept for many people to understand (or accept). Indeed, Paul Samuelson—the Nobel laureate economist who did much to develop the models of international trade discussed in Chapters 3 and 4—has described comparative advantage as the best example he knows of an economic principle that is undeniably true yet not obvious to intelligent people.

In this chapter we begin with a general introduction to the concept of comparative advantage, then proceed to develop a specific model of how comparative advantage determines the pattern of international trade.

THE CONCEPT OF COMPARATIVE ADVANTAGE

On Valentine's Day, 1996, which happened to fall less than a week before the crucial February 20 primary in New Hampshire, Republican presidential candidate Patrick Buchanan stopped at a nursery to buy a dozen roses for his wife. He took the occasion to make a speech denouncing the growing imports of flowers into the United States, which he claimed were putting American flower growers out of business. And it is indeed true that a growing share of the market for winter roses in the United States is being supplied by imports flown in from South America. But is that a bad thing?

The case of winter roses offers an excellent example of the reasons why international trade can be beneficial. Consider first how hard it is to supply American sweethearts with fresh roses in February. The flowers must be grown in heated greenhouses, at great expense in terms of energy, capital investment, and other scarce resources. Those resources could have been used to produce other goods. Inevitably, there is a trade-off. In order to produce winter roses, the U.S. economy must produce less of other things, such as computers. Economists use the term **opportunity cost** to describe such trade-offs: The opportunity cost of roses in terms of computers is the number of computers that could have been produced with the resources used to produce a given number of roses.

Suppose, for example, that the United States currently grows 10 million roses for sale on Valentine's Day, and that the resources used to grow those roses could have produced 100,000 computers instead. Then the opportunity cost of those 10 million roses is 100,000 computers. (Conversely, if the computers were produced instead, the opportunity cost of those 100,000 computers would be 10 million roses.)

Those 10 million Valentine's Day roses could instead have been grown in South America. It seems extremely likely that the opportunity cost of those roses in terms of computers would be less than it would be in the United States. For one thing, it is a lot easier to grow February roses in the Southern Hemisphere, where it is summer in February rather than winter. Furthermore, South American workers are less efficient than their U.S. counterparts at making sophisticated goods such as computers, which means that a given amount of resources used in computer production yields fewer computers in South America than in the United States. So the trade-off in South America might be something like 10 million winter roses for only 30,000 computers.

This difference in opportunity costs offers the possibility of a mutually beneficial rearrangement of world production. Let the United States stop growing winter roses and devote the resources this frees up to producing computers; meanwhile, let South America grow those roses instead, shifting the necessary resources out of its computer industry. The resulting changes in production would look like Table 2-1.

Look what has happened: The world is producing just as many roses as before, but it is now producing more computers. So this rearrangement of production, with the United States concentrating on computers and South America concentrating on roses, increases the size of the world's economic pie. Because the world as a whole is producing more, it is possible in principle to raise everyone's standard of living.

The reason that international trade produces this increase in world output is that it allows each country to specialize in producing the good in which it has a comparative advantage. A country has a **comparative advantage** in producing a good if the opportunity cost of producing that good in terms of other goods is lower in that country than it is in other countries.

TABLE 2-1		

Hypothetical Changes in Production

	Million roses	**Thousand computers**
United States	−10	+100
South America	+10	−30
Total	0	+70

In this example, South America has a comparative advantage in winter roses and the United States has a comparative advantage in computers. The standard of living can be increased in both places if South America produces roses for the U.S. market, while the United States produces computers for the South American market. We therefore have an essential insight about comparative advantage and international trade: *Trade between two countries can benefit both countries if each country exports the goods in which it has a comparative advantage.*

This is a statement about possibilities, not about what will actually happen. In the real world, there is no central authority deciding which country should produce roses and which should produce computers. Nor is there anyone handing out roses and computers to consumers in both places. Instead, international production and trade is determined in the marketplace where supply and demand rule. Is there any reason to suppose that the potential for mutual gains from trade will be realized? Will the United States and South America actually end up producing the goods in which each has a comparative advantage? Will the trade between them actually make both countries better off?

To answer these questions, we must be much more explicit in our analysis. In this chapter we will develop a model of international trade originally developed by the British economist David Ricardo, who introduced the concept of comparative advantage in the early nineteenth century.[1] This approach, in which international trade is solely due to international differences in the productivity of labor, is known as the **Ricardian model.**

A ONE-FACTOR ECONOMY

To introduce the role of comparative advantage in determining the pattern of international trade, we begin by imagining that we are dealing with an economy—which we call Home—that has only one factor of production. (In later chapters we extend the analysis to models in which there are several factors.) We imagine that only two goods, wine and cheese, are produced. The technology of Home's economy can be summarized by labor productivity in each industry, expressed in terms of the **unit labor requirement,** the number of hours of labor required to produce a pound of cheese or a gallon of wine. For example, it might require 1 hour of labor to produce a pound of cheese, 2 hours to produce a gal-

---

[1]The classic reference is David Ricardo, *The Principles of Political Economy and Taxation,* first published in 1817.

lon of wine. For future reference, we define a_{LW} and a_{LC} as the unit labor requirements in wine and cheese production, respectively. The economy's total resources are defined as L, the total labor supply.

PRODUCTION POSSIBILITIES

Because any economy has limited resources, there are limits on what it can produce, and there are always trade-offs; to produce more of one good the economy must sacrifice some production of another good. These trade-offs are illustrated graphically by a **production possibility frontier** (line PF in Figure 2-1), which shows the maximum amount of wine that can be produced once the decision has been made to produce any given amount of cheese, and vice versa.

When there is only one factor of production the production possibility frontier of an economy is simply a straight line. We can derive this line as follows: If Q_W is the economy's production of wine and Q_C its production of cheese, then the labor used in producing wine will be $a_{LW}Q_W$, the labor used in producing cheese $a_{LC}Q_C$. The production possibility frontier is determined by the limits on the economy's resources—in this case, labor. Because the economy's total labor supply is L, the limits on production are defined by the inequality

$$a_{LC}Q_C + a_{LW}Q_W \leq L. \tag{2-1}$$

When the production possibility frontier is a straight line, the *opportunity cost* of a pound of cheese in terms of wine is constant. As we saw in the previous section, this opportunity cost is defined as the number of gallons of wine the economy would have to give up in order to produce an extra pound of cheese. In this case, to produce another pound

---

FIGURE 2-1

Home's Production Possibility Frontier

The line *PF* shows the maximum amount of cheese Home can produce given any production of wine, and vice versa.

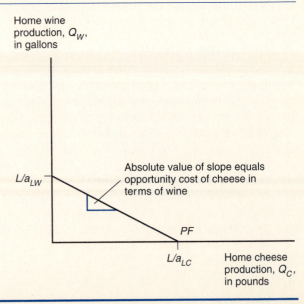

would require a_{LC} person-hours. Each of these person-hours could in turn have been used to produce $1/a_{LW}$ gallons of wine. Thus the opportunity cost of cheese in terms of wine is a_{LC}/a_{LW}. For example, if it takes one person-hour to make a pound of cheese and two hours to produce a gallon of wine, the opportunity cost of cheese in terms of wine is one-half. As Figure 2-1 shows, this opportunity cost is equal to the absolute value of the slope of the production possibility frontier.

RELATIVE PRICES AND SUPPLY

The production possibility frontier illustrates the different mixes of goods the economy *can* produce. To determine what the economy will actually produce, however, we need to look at prices. Specifically, we need to know the relative price of the economy's two goods, that is, the price of one good in terms of the other.

In a competitive economy, supply decisions are determined by the attempts of individuals to maximize their earnings. In our simplified economy, since labor is the only factor of production, the supply of cheese and wine will be determined by the movement of labor to whichever sector pays the higher wage.

Let P_C and P_W be the prices of cheese and wine, respectively. It takes a_{LC} person-hours to produce a pound of cheese; since there are no profits in our one-factor model, the hourly wage in the cheese sector will equal the value of what a worker can produce in an hour, P_C/a_{LC}. Since it takes a_{LW} person-hours to produce a gallon of wine, the hourly wage rate in the wine sector will be P_W/a_{LW}. Wages in the cheese sector will be higher if $P_C/P_W > a_{LC}/a_{LW}$; wages in the wine sector will be higher if $P_C/P_W < a_{LC}/a_{LW}$. Because everyone will want to work in whichever industry offers the higher wage, the economy will specialize in the production of cheese if $P_C/P_W > a_{LC}/a_{LW}$; it will specialize in the production of wine if $P_C/P_W < a_{LC}/a_{LW}$. Only when P_C/P_W is equal to a_{LC}/a_{LW} will both goods be produced.

What is the significance of the number a_{LC}/a_{LW}? We saw in the previous section that it is the opportunity cost of cheese in terms of wine. We have therefore just derived a crucial proposition about the relationship between prices and production: *The economy will specialize in the production of cheese if the relative price of cheese exceeds its opportunity cost; it will specialize in the production of wine if the relative price of cheese is less than its opportunity cost.*

In the absence of international trade, Home would have to produce both goods for itself. But it will produce both goods only if the relative price of cheese is just equal to its opportunity cost. Since opportunity cost equals the ratio of unit labor requirements in cheese and wine, we can summarize the determination of prices in the absence of international trade with a simple labor theory of value: *In the absence of international trade, the relative prices of goods are equal to their relative unit labor requirements.*

TRADE IN A ONE-FACTOR WORLD

To describe the pattern and effects of trade between two countries when each country has only one factor of production is simple. Yet the implications of this analysis can be surprising. Indeed to those who have not thought about international trade many of these implications seem to conflict with common sense. Even this simplest of trade models can offer some important guidance on real-world issues, such as what constitutes fair international competition and fair international exchange.

Before we get to these issues, however, let us get the model stated. Suppose that there are two countries. One of them we again call Home and the other we call Foreign. Each of these countries has one factor of production (labor) and can produce two goods, wine and cheese. As before, we denote Home's labor force by L and Home's unit labor requirements in wine and cheese production by a_{LW} and a_{LC}, respectively. For Foreign we will use a convenient notation throughout this book: When we refer to some aspect of Foreign, we will use the same symbol that we use for Home, but with an asterisk. Thus Foreign's labor force will be denoted by L^*; Foreign's unit labor requirements in wine and cheese will be denoted by a_{LW}^* and a_{LC}^*, respectively, and so on.

In general the unit labor requirements can follow any pattern. For example, Home could be less productive than Foreign in wine but more productive in cheese, or vice versa. For the moment, we make only one arbitrary assumption: that

$$a_{LC}/a_{LW} < a_{LC}^*/a_{LW}^* \tag{2-2}$$

or, equivalently, that

$$a_{LC}/a_{LC}^* < a_{LW}/a_{LW}^*. \tag{2-3}$$

In words, we are assuming that the ratio of the labor required to produce a pound of cheese to that required to produce a gallon of wine is lower in Home than it is in Foreign. More briefly still, we are saying that Home's relative productivity in cheese is higher than it is in wine.

But remember that the ratio of unit labor requirements is equal to the opportunity cost of cheese in terms of wine; and remember also that we defined comparative advantage precisely in terms of such opportunity costs. So the assumption about relative productivities embodied in equations (2-2) and (2-3) amounts to saying that *Home has a comparative advantage in cheese*.

One point should be noted immediately: The condition under which Home has this comparative advantage involves all four unit labor requirements, not just two. You might think that to determine who will produce cheese, all you need to do is compare the two countries' unit labor requirements in cheese production, a_{LC} and a_{LC}^*. If $a_{LC} < a_{LC}^*$, Home labor is more efficient than Foreign in producing cheese. When one country can produce a unit of a good with less labor than another country, we say that the first country has an **absolute advantage** in producing that good. In our example, Home has an absolute advantage in producing cheese.

What we will see in a moment, however, is that we cannot determine the pattern of trade from absolute advantage alone. One of the most important sources of error in discussing international trade is to confuse comparative advantage with absolute advantage.

Given the labor forces and the unit labor requirements in the two countries, we can draw the production possibility frontier for each country. We have already done this for Home, by drawing PF in Figure 2-1. The production possibility frontier for Foreign is shown as PF^* in Figure 2-2. Since the slope of the production possibility frontier equals the opportunity cost of cheese in terms of wine, Foreign's frontier is steeper than Home's.

In the absence of trade the relative prices of cheese and wine in each country would be determined by the relative unit labor requirements. Thus in Home the relative price of cheese would be a_{LC}/a_{LW}; in Foreign it would be a_{LC}^*/a_{LW}^*.

Once we allow for the possibility of international trade, however, prices will no longer be determined purely by domestic considerations. If the relative price of cheese is higher in Foreign than in Home, it will be profitable to ship cheese from Home to Foreign and to

FIGURE 2-2

Foreign's Production Possibility Frontier

Because Foreign's relative unit labor requirement in cheese is higher than Home's (it needs to give up many more units of wine to produce one more unit of cheese), its production possibility frontier is steeper.

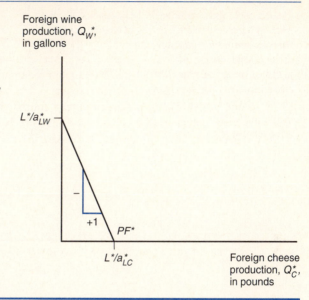

Foreign wine production, Q_W^*, in gallons

L^*/a_{LW}^*

−

+1

PF^*

L^*/a_{LC}^*

Foreign cheese production, Q_C^*, in pounds

ship wine from Foreign to Home. This cannot go on indefinitely, however. Eventually Home will export enough cheese and Foreign enough wine to equalize the relative price. But what determines the level at which that price settles?

DETERMINING THE RELATIVE PRICE AFTER TRADE

Prices of internationally traded goods, like other prices, are determined by supply and demand. In discussing comparative advantage, however, we must apply supply-and-demand analysis carefully. In some contexts, such as some of the trade policy analysis in Chapters 8 through 11, it is acceptable to focus only on supply and demand in a single market. In assessing the effects of U.S. import quotas on sugar, for example, it is reasonable to use **partial equilibrium analysis,** that is, to study a single market, the sugar market. When we study comparative advantage, however, it is crucial to keep track of the relationships between markets (in our example the markets for wine and cheese). Since Home exports cheese only in return for imports of wine, and Foreign exports wine in return for cheese, it can be misleading to look at the cheese and wine markets in isolation. What is needed is **general equilibrium analysis,** which takes account of the linkages between the two markets.

One useful way to keep track of two markets at once is to focus not just on the quantities of cheese and wine supplied and demanded but also on the *relative* supply and demand, that is, on the number of pounds of cheese supplied or demanded divided by the number of gallons of wine supplied or demanded.

Figure 2-3 shows world supply and demand for cheese relative to wine as functions of the price of cheese relative to that of wine. The **relative demand curve** is indicated by *RD;* the **relative supply curve** is indicated by *RS.* World general equilibrium requires that

FIGURE 2-3

World Relative Supply and Demand

The *RD* curve shows that the demand for cheese relative to wine is a decreasing function of the price of cheese relative to that of wine, while the *RS* curve shows that the supply of cheese relative to wine is an increasing function of the same relative price.

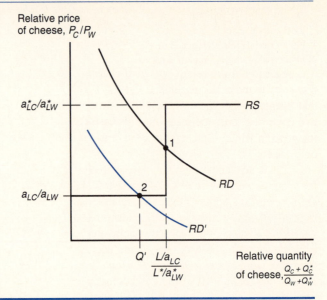

relative supply equal relative demand, and thus the world relative price is determined by the intersection of *RD* and *RS*.

The striking feature of Figure 2-3 is the funny shape of the relative supply curve *RS*: a "step" with flat sections linked by a vertical section. Once we understand the derivation of the *RS* curve, we will be almost home-free in understanding the whole model.

First, as drawn, the *RS* curve shows that there is no supply of cheese if the world price drops below a_{LC}/a_{LW}. To see why, recall that we showed that Home will specialize in the production of wine whenever $P_C/P_W < a_{LC}/a_{LW}$. Similarly, Foreign will specialize in wine production whenever $P_C/P_W < a_{LC}^*/a_{LW}^*$. At the start of our discussion of equation (2-2) we made the assumption that $a_{LC}/a_{LW} < a_{LC}^*/a_{LW}^*$. So at relative prices of cheese below a_{LC}/a_{LW}, there will be no world cheese production.

Next, when the relative price of cheese, P_C/P_W, is exactly a_{LC}/a_{LW}, we know that workers in Home can earn exactly the same amount making either cheese or wine. So Home will be willing to supply any relative amount of the two goods, producing a flat section to the supply curve.

We have already seen that if P_C/P_W is above a_{LC}/a_{LW}, Home will specialize in the production of cheese. As long as $P_C/P_W < a_{LC}^*/a_{LW}^*$, however, Foreign will continue to specialize in producing wine. When Home specializes in cheese production, it produces L/a_{LC} pounds. Similarly, when Foreign specializes in wine it produces L^*/a_{LW}^* gallons. So for any relative price of cheese between a_{LC}/a_{LW} and a_{LC}^*/a_{LW}^* the relative supply of cheese is

$$(L/a_{LC})/(L^*/a_{LW}^*). \tag{2-4}$$

At $P_C/P_W = a_{LC}^*/a_{LW}^*$, we know that Foreign workers are indifferent between producing cheese and wine. Thus here we again have a flat section of the supply curve.

Finally, for $P_C/P_W > a_{LC}^*/a_{LW}^*$, both Home and Foreign will specialize in cheese production. There will be no wine production, so that the relative supply of cheese will become infinite.

The relative demand curve RD does not require such exhaustive analysis. The downward slope of RD reflects substitution effects. As the relative price of cheese rises, consumers will tend to purchase less cheese and more wine, so the relative demand for cheese falls.

The equilibrium relative price of cheese is determined by the intersection of the relative supply and relative demand curves. Figure 2-3 shows a relative demand curve RD that intersects the RS curve at point 1, where the relative price of cheese is between the two countries' pretrade prices. In this case each country specializes in the production of the good in which it has a comparative advantage: Home produces only cheese, Foreign only wine.

This is not, however, the only possible outcome. If the relevant RD curve were RD′, for example, relative supply and relative demand would intersect on one of the horizontal sections of RS. At point 2 the world relative price of cheese after trade is a_{LC}/a_{LW}, the same as the opportunity cost of cheese in terms of wine in Home.

What is the significance of this outcome? If the relative price of cheese is equal to its opportunity cost in Home, the Home economy need not specialize in producing either cheese or wine. In fact, at point 2 Home must be producing both some wine and some cheese; we can infer this from the fact that the relative supply of cheese (point Q′ on horizontal axis) is less than it would be if Home were in fact completely specialized. Since P_C/P_W is below the opportunity cost of cheese in terms of wine in Foreign, however, Foreign does specialize completely in producing wine. It therefore remains true that if a country does specialize, it will do so in the good in which it has a comparative advantage.

Let us for the moment leave aside the possibility that one of the two countries does not completely specialize. Except in this case, the normal result of trade is that the price of a traded good (e.g., cheese) relative to that of another good (wine) ends up somewhere in between its pretrade levels in the two countries.

The effect of this convergence in relative prices is that each country specializes in the production of that good in which it has the relatively lower unit labor requirement. The rise in the relative price of cheese in Home will lead Home to specialize in the production of cheese, producing at point F in Figure 2-1. The fall in the relative price of cheese in Foreign will lead Foreign to specialize in the production of wine, producing at point F* in Figure 2-2.

THE GAINS FROM TRADE

We have now seen that countries whose relative labor productivities differ across industries will specialize in the production of different goods. We next show that both countries derive **gains from trade** from this specialization. This mutual gain can be demonstrated in two alternative ways.

The first way to show that specialization and trade are beneficial is to think of trade as an indirect method of production. Home could produce wine directly, but trade with Foreign allows it to "produce" wine by producing cheese and then trading the cheese for wine. This indirect method of "producing" a gallon of wine is a more efficient method than direct production. Consider two alternative ways of using an hour of labor. On one side, Home could use the hour directly to produce $1/a_{LW}$ gallons of wine. Alternatively, Home could use the hour to produce $1/a_{LC}$ pounds of cheese. This cheese could then be traded for wine, with each pound trading for P_C/P_W gallons, so our original hour of labor yields $(1/a_{LC})$ (P_C/P_W) gallons of wine. This will be more wine than the hour could have produced directly as long as

$$(1/a_{LC})(P_C/P_W) > 1/a_{LW}, \tag{2-5}$$

or

$$P_C/P_W > a_{LC}/a_{LW}.$$

But we just saw that in international equilibrium, if neither country produces both goods, we must have $P_C/P_W > a_{LC}/a_{LW}$. This shows that Home can "produce" wine more efficiently by making cheese and trading it than by producing wine directly for itself. Similarly, Foreign can "produce" cheese more efficiently by making wine and trading it. This is one way of seeing that both countries gain.

Another way to see the mutual gains from trade is to examine how trade affects each country's possibilities for consumption. In the absence of trade, consumption possibilities are the same as production possibilities (the solid lines PF and P^*F^* in Figure 2-4). Once trade is allowed, however, each economy can consume a different mix of cheese and wine from the mix it produces. Home's consumption possibilities are indicated by the colored line TF in Figure 2-4a, while Foreign's consumption possibilities are indicated by T^*F^* in Figure 2-4b. In each case trade has enlarged the range of choice, and therefore it must make residents of each country better off.

FIGURE 2-4

Trade Expands Consumption Possibilities

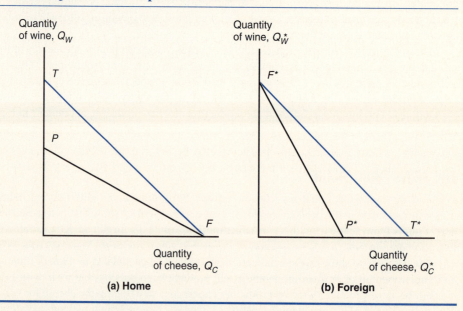

(a) Home

(b) Foreign

International trade allows Home and Foreign to consume anywhere within the colored lines, which lie outside the countries' production possibility frontiers.

A NUMERICAL EXAMPLE

In this section, we use a numerical example to solidify our understanding of two crucial points:

> When two countries specialize in producing the goods in which they have a comparative advantage, both countries gain from trade.
>
> *Comparative* advantage must not be confused with *absolute* advantage; it is comparative, not absolute advantage, that determines who will and should produce a good.

Suppose, then, that Home and Foreign have the unit labor requirements illustrated in Table 2-2.

A striking feature of this table is that Home has lower unit labor requirements, that is, has higher labor productivity, in both industries. Let us leave this observation for a moment, however, and focus on the pattern of trade.

The first thing we need to do is determine the relative price of cheese P_C/P_W. While the actual relative price depends on demand, we know that it must lie between the opportunity cost of cheese in the two countries. In Home, we have $a_{LC} = 1$, $a_{LW} = 2$; so the opportunity cost of cheese in terms of wine in Home is $a_{LC}/a_{LW} = \frac{1}{2}$. In Foreign, $a_{LC}^* = 6$, $a_{LW}^* = 3$; so the opportunity cost of cheese is 2. In world equilibrium, the relative price of cheese must lie between these values. In our example we assume that in world equilibrium a pound of cheese trades for a gallon of wine on world markets so that $P_C/P_W = 1$.

If a pound of cheese sells for the same price as a gallon of wine, both countries will specialize. It takes only half as many person-hours in Home to produce a pound of cheese as it takes to produce a gallon of wine (1 versus 2); so Home workers can earn more by producing cheese, and Home will specialize in cheese production. Conversely, it takes twice as many Foreign person-hours to produce a pound of cheese as it takes to produce a gallon of wine (6 versus 3), so Foreign workers can earn more by producing wine, and Foreign will specialize in wine production.

Let us confirm that this pattern of specialization produces gains from trade. First, we want to show that Home can "produce" wine more efficiently by making cheese and trading it for wine than by direct production. In direct production, an hour of Home labor produces only $\frac{1}{2}$ gallon of wine. The same hour could be used to produce 1 pound of cheese, which can then be traded for 1 gallon of wine. Clearly, Home does gain from trade. Similarly, Foreign could use 1 hour of labor to produce $\frac{1}{6}$ pound of cheese; if, however, it uses the hour to produce $\frac{1}{3}$ gallon of wine it could then trade the $\frac{1}{3}$ gallon of wine for $\frac{1}{3}$ pound of cheese. This is twice as much as the $\frac{1}{6}$ pound of cheese it gets using the hour to produce the cheese directly. In this example, each country can use labor twice as efficiently to trade for what it needs instead of producing its imports for itself.

TABLE 2-2		
Unit Labor Requirements		
	Cheese	**Wine**
Home	$a_{LC} = 1$ hour per pound	$a_{LW} = 2$ hours per gallon
Foreign	$a_{LC}^* = 6$ hours per pound	$a_{LW}^* = 3$ hours per gallon

RELATIVE WAGES

Political discussions of international trade often focus on comparisons of wage rates in different countries. For example, opponents of trade between the United States and Mexico often emphasize the point that workers in Mexico are paid only about $2 per hour, compared with more than $15 per hour for the typical worker in the United States. Our discussion of international trade up to this point has not explicitly compared wages in the two countries, but it is possible in the context of this numerical example to determine how the wage rates in the two countries compare.

In this example, once the countries have specialized, all Home workers are employed producing cheese. Since it takes 1 hour of labor to produce 1 pound of cheese, workers in Home earn the value of 1 pound of cheese per hour of their labor. Similarly, Foreign workers produce only wine; since it takes 3 hours for them to produce each gallon, they earn the value of $1/3$ of a gallon of wine per hour.

To convert these numbers into dollar figures, we need to know the prices of cheese and wine. Suppose that a pound of cheese and a gallon of wine both sell for $12; then Home workers will earn $12 per hour, while Foreign workers will earn $4 per hour. The **relative wage** of a country's workers is the amount they are paid per hour, compared with the amount workers in another country are paid per hour. The relative wage of Home workers will therefore be 3.

Clearly, this relative wage does not depend on whether the price of a pound of cheese is $12 or $20, as long as a gallon of wine sells for the same price. As long as the relative price of cheese—the price of a pound of cheese divided by the price of a gallon of wine—is 1, the wage of Home workers will be three times that of Foreign workers.

Notice that this wage rate lies between the ratios of the two countries' productivities in the two industries. Home is six times as productive as Foreign in cheese, but only one-and-a-half times as productive in wine, and it ends up with a wage rate three times as high as Foreign's. It is precisely because the relative wage is between the relative productivities that each country ends up with a *cost* advantage in one good. Because of its lower wage rate, Foreign has a cost advantage in wine, even though it has lower productivity. Home has a cost advantage in cheese, despite its higher wage rate, because the higher wage is more than offset by its higher productivity.

We have now developed the simplest of all models of international trade. Even though the Ricardian one-factor model is far too simple to be a complete analysis of either the causes or the effects of international trade, a focus on relative labor productivities can be a very useful tool for thinking about international trade. In particular, the simple one-factor model is a good way to deal with several common misconceptions about the meaning of comparative advantage and the nature of the gains from free trade. These misconceptions appear so frequently in public debate about international economic policy, and even in statements by those who regard themselves as experts, that in the next section we take time out to discuss some of the most common misunderstandings about comparative advantage in light of our model.

MISCONCEPTIONS ABOUT COMPARATIVE ADVANTAGE

There is no shortage of muddled ideas in economics. Politicians, business leaders, and even economists frequently make statements that do not stand up to careful economic analysis. For some reason this seems to be especially true in international economics.

Open the business section of any Sunday newspaper or weekly news magazine and you will probably find at least one article that makes foolish statements about international trade. Three misconceptions in particular have proved highly persistent, and our simple model of comparative advantage can be used to see why they are incorrect.

PRODUCTIVITY AND COMPETITIVENESS

Myth 1: Free trade is beneficial only if your country is strong enough to stand up to foreign competition. This argument seems extremely plausible to many people. For example, a well-known historian recently criticized the case for free trade by asserting that it may fail to hold in reality: "What if there is nothing you can produce more cheaply or efficiently than anywhere else, except by constantly cutting labor costs?" he worried.[2]

The problem with this commentator's view is that he failed to understand the essential point of Ricardo's model, that gains from trade depend on *comparative* rather than *absolute* advantage. He is concerned that your country may turn out not to have anything it produces more efficiently than anyone else—that is, that you may not have an absolute advantage in anything. Yet why is that such a terrible thing? In our simple numerical example of trade, Home has lower unit labor requirements and hence higher productivity in both the cheese and wine sectors. Yet, as we saw, both countries gain from trade.

It is always tempting to suppose that the ability to export a good depends on your country having an absolute advantage in productivity. But an absolute productivity advantage over other countries in producing a good is neither a necessary nor a sufficient condition for having a *comparative* advantage in that good. In our one-factor model the reason why absolute productivity advantage in an industry is neither necessary nor sufficient to yield competitive advantage is clear: *The competitive advantage of an industry depends not only on its productivity relative to the foreign industry, but also on the domestic wage rate relative to the foreign wage rate.* A country's wage rate, in turn, depends on relative productivity in its other industries. In our numerical example, Foreign is less efficient than Home in the manufacture of wine, but at even a greater relative productivity disadvantage in cheese. Because of its overall lower productivity, Foreign must pay lower wages than Home, sufficiently lower that it ends up with lower costs in wine production. Similarly, in the real world, Portugal has low productivity in producing, say, clothing as compared with the United States, but because Portugal's productivity disadvantage is even greater in other industries it pays low enough wages to have a comparative advantage in clothing all the same.

But isn't a competitive advantage based on low wages somehow unfair? Many people think so; their beliefs are summarized by our second misconception.

THE PAUPER LABOR ARGUMENT

Myth 2: Foreign competition is unfair and hurts other countries when it is based on low wages. This argument, sometimes referred to as the **pauper labor argument,** is a particular favorite of labor unions seeking protection from foreign competition. People who adhere to this belief argue that industries should not have to cope with foreign industries that

[2]Paul Kennedy, "The Threat of Modernization," *New Perspectives Quarterly* (Winter 1995), pp. 31–33.

are less efficient but pay lower wages. This view is widespread and has acquired considerable political influence. In 1993 Ross Perot, a self-made billionaire and former presidential candidate, warned that free trade between the United States and Mexico, with its much lower wages, would lead to a "great sucking sound" as U.S. industry moved south. In the same year Sir James Goldsmith, another self-made billionaire who was an influential member of the European Parliament, offered similar if less picturesquely expressed views in his book *The Trap* which became a best-seller in France.

Again, our simple example reveals the fallacy of this argument. In the example, Home is more productive than Foreign in both industries, and Foreign's lower cost of wine production is entirely due to its much lower wage rate. Foreign's lower wage rate is, however, irrelevant to the question of whether Home gains from trade. Whether the lower cost of wine produced in Foreign is due to high productivity or low wages does not matter. All that matters to Home is that it is cheaper *in terms of its own labor* for Home to produce cheese and trade it for wine than to produce wine for itself.

This is fine for Home, but what about Foreign? Isn't there something wrong with basing one's exports on low wages? Certainly it is not an attractive position to be in, but the idea that trade is good only if you receive high wages is our final fallacy.

EXPLOITATION

Myth 3: Trade exploits a country and makes it worse off if its workers receive much lower wages than workers in other nations. This argument is often expressed in emotional terms. For example, one columnist contrasted the $2 million income of the chief executive officer of the clothing chain The Gap with the $0.56 per hour paid to the Central American workers who produce some of its merchandise.[3] It can seem hard-hearted to try to justify the terrifyingly low wages paid to many of the world's workers.

If one is asking about the desirability of free trade, however, the point is not to ask whether low-wage workers deserve to be paid more but to ask whether they and their country are worse off exporting goods based on low wages than they would be if they refused to enter into such demeaning trade. And in asking this question one must also ask, *what is the alternative?*

Abstract though it is, our numerical example makes the point that one cannot declare that a low wage represents exploitation unless one knows what the alternative is. In that example, Foreign workers are paid much less than Home workers, and one could easily imagine a columnist writing angrily about their exploitation. Yet if Foreign refused to let itself be "exploited" by refusing to trade with Home (or by insisting on much higher wages in its export sector, which would have the same effect), real wages would be even lower: The purchasing power of a worker's hourly wage would fall from $1/3$ to $1/6$ pound of cheese.

The columnist who pointed out the contrast in incomes between the executive at The Gap and the workers who make its clothes was angry at the poverty of Central American workers. But to deny them the opportunity to export and trade might well be to condemn them to even deeper poverty.

---

[3]Bob Herbert, "Sweatshop Beneficiaries: How to Get Rich on 56 Cents an Hour," *New York Times* (July 24, 1995), p. A13.

COMPARATIVE ADVANTAGE WITH MANY GOODS

In our discussion so far we have relied on a model in which only two goods are produced and consumed. This simplified analysis allows us to capture many essential points about comparative advantage and trade and, as we saw in the last section, gives us a surprising amount of mileage as a tool for discussing policy issues. To move closer to reality, however, it is necessary to understand how comparative advantage functions in a model with a larger number of goods.

SETTING UP THE MODEL

Again, imagine a world of two countries, Home and Foreign. As before, each country has only one factor of production, labor. Each of these countries will now, however, be assumed to consume and to be able to produce a large number of goods—say, N different goods altogether. We assign each of the goods a number from 1 to N.

The technology of each country can be described by its unit labor requirement for each good, that is, the number of hours of labor it takes to produce one unit of each. We label Home's unit labor requirement for a particular good as a_{Li}, where i is the number we have assigned to that good. If cheese is now good number 7, a_{L7} will mean the unit labor requirement in cheese production. Following our usual rule, we label the corresponding Foreign unit labor requirements a_{Li}^*.

To analyze trade, we next pull one more trick. For any good we can calculate a_{Li}/a_{Li}^*, the ratio of Home's unit labor requirement to Foreign's. The trick is to relabel the goods so that the lower the number, the lower this ratio. That is, we reshuffle the order in which we number goods in such a way that

$$a_{L1}/a_{L1}^* < a_{L2}/a_{L2}^* < a_{L3}/a_{L3}^* < \ldots < a_{LN}/a_{LN}^*. \tag{2-6}$$

RELATIVE WAGES AND SPECIALIZATION

We are now prepared to look at the pattern of trade. This pattern depends on only one thing: the ratio of Home to Foreign wages. Once we know this ratio, we can determine who produces what.

Let w be the wage rate per hour in Home and w^* be the wage rate in Foreign. The ratio of wage rates is then w/w^*. The rule for allocating world production, then, is simply this: Goods will always be produced where it is cheapest to make them. The cost of making some good, say good i, is the unit labor requirement times the wage rate. To produce good i in Home will cost wa_{Li}. To produce the same good in Foreign will cost $w^*a_{Li}^*$. It will be cheaper to produce the good in Home if

$$wa_{Li} < w^*a_{Li}^*,$$

which can be rearranged to yield

$$a_{Li}^*/a_{Li} > w/w^*.$$

On the other hand, it will be cheaper to produce the good in Foreign if

$$wa_{Li} > w^*a_{Li}^*,$$

which can be rearranged to yield

$$a_{Li}^*/a_{Li} < w/w^*.$$

Thus we can restate the allocation rule: Any good for which $a_{Li}^*/a_{Li} > w/w^*$ will be produced in Home, while any good for which $a_{Li}^*/a_{Li} < w/w^*$ will be produced in Foreign.

We have already lined up the goods in increasing order of a_{Li}/a_{Li}^* (equation (2-6)). This criterion for specialization tells us that what happens is a "cut" in that lineup, determined by the ratio of the two countries' wage rates, w^*/w. All the goods to the left of the cut end up being produced in Home; all the goods to the right end up being produced in Foreign. (It is possible, as we will see in a moment, that the ratio of wage rates is exactly equal to the ratio of unit labor requirements for one good. In that case this borderline good may be produced in both countries.)

Table 2-3 offers a numerical example in which Home and Foreign both consume and are able to produce *five* goods: apples, bananas, caviar, dates, and enchiladas.

The first two columns of this table are self-explanatory. The third column is the ratio of the Foreign unit labor requirement to the Home unit labor requirement for each good— or, stated differently, the relative Home productivity advantage in each good. We have labeled the goods in order of Home productivity advantage, with the Home advantage greatest for apples and least for enchiladas.

Which country produces which goods depends on the ratio of Home and Foreign wage rates. Home will have a cost advantage in any good for which its relative productivity is higher than its relative wage, and Foreign will have the advantage in the others. If, for example, the Home wage rate is five times that of Foreign (a ratio of Home wage to Foreign wage of five to one), apples and bananas will be produced in Home and caviar, dates, and enchiladas in Foreign. If the Home wage rate is only three times that of Foreign, Home will produce apples, bananas, and caviar, while Foreign will produce only dates and enchiladas.

Is such a pattern of specialization beneficial to both countries? We can see that it is by using the same method we used earlier: comparing the labor cost of producing a good directly in a country with that of indirectly "producing" it by producing another good and trading for the desired good. If the Home wage rate is three times the Foreign wage (put another way, foreign's wage rate is one-third that of Home), Home will import dates and enchiladas. A unit of dates requires 12 units of Foreign labor to produce, but its cost in terms of Home labor, given the three-to-one wage ratio, is only 4 person-hours ($12 \div 3$). This cost of 4 person-hours is less than the 6 person-hours it would take to produce the unit

TABLE 2-3

Home and Foreign Unit Labor Requirements

Good	Home unit labor requirement (a_{Li})	Foreign unit labor requirement (a_{Li}^*)	Relative home productivity advantage (a_{Li}^*/a_{Li})
Apples	1	10	10
Bananas	5	40	8
Caviar	3	12	4
Dates	6	12	2
Enchiladas	12	9	0.75

of dates in Home. For enchiladas, Foreign actually has higher productivity along with lower wages; it will cost Home only 3 person-hours to acquire a unit of enchiladas through trade, compared with the 12 person-hours it would take to produce it domestically. A similar calculation will show that Foreign also gains; for each of the goods Foreign imports it turns out to be cheaper in terms of domestic labor to trade for the good rather than produce the good domestically. For example, it would take 10 hours of Foreign labor to produce a unit of apples; even with a wage rate only one-third that of Home workers, it will require only 3 hours of labor to earn enough to buy that unit of apples from Home.

In making these calculations, however, we have simply assumed that the relative wage rate is 3. How does this relative wage rate actually get determined?

DETERMINING THE RELATIVE WAGE IN THE MULTIGOOD MODEL

In the two-good model we determined relative wages by first calculating Home wages in terms of cheese and Foreign wages in terms of wine, then using the price of cheese relative to that of wine to deduce the ratio of the two countries' wage rates. We could do this because we knew that Home would produce cheese and Foreign wine. In the many-good case, who produces what can be determined only after we know the relative wage rate, so this procedure is unworkable. To determine relative wages in a multigood economy we must look behind the relative demand for goods to the implied relative demand for labor. This is not a direct demand on the part of consumers; rather, it is a **derived demand** that results from the demand for goods produced with each country's labor.

The relative derived demand for Home labor will fall when the ratio of Home to Foreign wages rises, for two reasons. First, as Home labor becomes more expensive relative to Foreign labor, goods produced in Home also become relatively more expensive, and world demand for these goods falls. Second, as Home wages rise, fewer goods will be produced in Home and more in Foreign, further reducing the demand for Home labor.

We can illustrate these two effects using our numerical example. Suppose we start with the following situation: The Home wage is initially 3.5 times the Foreign wage. At that level, Home would produce apples, bananas, and caviar while Foreign would produce dates and enchiladas. If the relative Home wage were to increase from 3.5 to just under 4, say 3.99, the pattern of specialization would not change, but as the goods produced in Home became relatively more expensive, the relative demand for these goods would decline and the relative demand for Home labor would decline with it.

Suppose now that the relative wage were to increase slightly from 3.99 to 4.01. This small further increase in the relative Home wage would bring about a shift in the pattern of specialization. Because it is now cheaper to produce caviar in Foreign than in Home, the production of caviar shifts from Home to Foreign. What does this imply for the relative demand for Home labor? Clearly it implies that as the relative wage rises from a little less than 4 to a little more than 4 there is an abrupt drop-off in the relative demand, as Home production of caviar falls to zero and Foreign acquires a new industry. If the relative wage continues to rise, relative demand for Home labor will gradually decline, then drop off abruptly at a relative wage of 8, at which wage production of bananas shifts to Foreign.

We can illustrate the determination of relative wages with a diagram like Figure 2-5. Unlike Figure 2-3, this diagram does not have relative quantities of goods or relative prices of goods on its axes. Instead it shows the relative quantity of labor and the relative wage rate. The world demand for Home labor relative to its demand for Foreign labor is shown by the curve *RD*. The world supply of Home labor relative to Foreign labor is shown by the line *RS*.

FIGURE 2-5

Determination of Relative Wages

In a many-good Ricardian model, relative wages are determined by the intersection of the derived relative demand curve for labor *RD* with the relative supply *RS*.

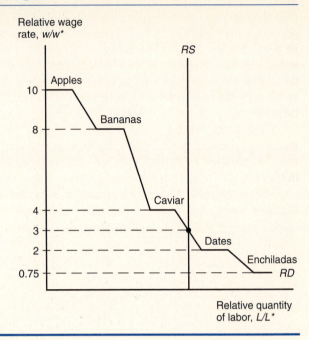

The relative supply of labor is determined by the relative size of Home and Foreign labor forces. Assuming that the number of person-hours available does not vary with the wage, the relative wage has no effect on relative labor supply and *RS* is a vertical line.

Our discussion of the relative demand for labor explains the "stepped" shape of *RD*. Whenever we increase the wage rate of Home workers relative to Foreign workers, the relative demand for goods produced in Home will decline and the demand for Home labor will decline with it. In addition, the relative demand for Home labor will drop off abruptly whenever an increase in the relative Home wage makes a good cheaper to produce in Foreign. So the curve alternates between smoothly downward sloping sections where the pattern of specialization does not change and "flats" where the relative demand shifts abruptly because of shifts in the pattern of specialization. As shown in the figure, these "flats" correspond to relative wages that equal the ratio of Home to Foreign productivity for each of the five goods.

The equilibrium relative wage is determined by the intersection of *RD* and *RS*. As drawn, the equilibrium relative wage is 3. At this wage, Home produces apples, bananas, and caviar while Foreign produces dates and enchiladas. The outcome depends on the relative size of the countries (which determines the position of *RS*) and the relative demand for the goods (which determines the shape and position of *RD*).

If the intersection of *RD* and *RS* happens to lie on one of the flats, both countries produce the good to which the flat applies.

ADDING TRANSPORT COSTS AND NONTRADED GOODS

We now extend our model another step closer to reality by considering the effects of transport costs. Transportation costs do not change the fundamental principles of comparative advantage or the gains from trade. Because transport costs pose obstacles to the movement of goods and services, however, they have important implications for the way a trading world economy is affected by a variety of factors such as foreign aid, international investment, and balance of payments problems. While we will not deal with the effects of these factors yet, the multigood one-factor model is a good place to introduce the effects of transport costs.

First, notice that the world economy described by the model of the last section is marked by very extreme international specialization. At most there is one good that both countries produce; all other goods are produced either in Home or in Foreign, not in both.

There are three main reasons why specialization in the real international economy is not this extreme.

1. The existence of more than one factor of production reduces the tendency toward specialization (as we see in the next two chapters).
2. Countries sometimes protect industries from foreign competition (discussed at length in Chapters 8 through 11).
3. It is costly to transport goods and services, and in some cases the cost of transportation is enough to lead countries into self-sufficiency in certain sectors.

In the multigood example of the last section we found that at a relative Home wage of 3, Home could produce apples, bananas, and caviar more cheaply than Foreign, while Foreign could produce dates and enchiladas more cheaply than Home. *In the absence of transport costs,* then, Home will export the first three goods and import the last two.

Now suppose there is a cost to transporting goods, and that this transport cost is a uniform fraction of production cost, say 100 percent. This transportation cost will discourage trade. Consider, for example, dates. One unit of this good requires 6 hours of Home labor or 12 hours of Foreign labor to produce. At a relative wage of 3, 12 hours of Foreign labor cost only as much as 4 hours of Home labor; so in the absence of transport costs Home imports dates. With a 100 percent transport cost, however, importing dates would cost the equivalent of 8 hours of Home labor, so Home will produce the good for itself instead.

A similar cost comparison shows that Foreign will find it cheaper to produce its own caviar than import it. A unit of caviar requires 3 hours of Home labor to produce. Even at a relative Home wage of 3, which makes this the equivalent of 9 hours of Foreign labor, this is cheaper than the 12 hours Foreign would need to produce caviar for itself. In the absence of transport costs, then, Foreign would find it cheaper to import caviar than to make it domestically. With a 100 percent cost of transportation, however, imported caviar would cost the equivalent of 18 hours of Foreign labor and would therefore be produced locally instead.

The result of introducing transport costs in this example, then, is that while Home still exports apples and bananas and imports enchiladas, caviar and dates become **nontraded goods,** which each country produces for itself.

In this example we have assumed that transport costs are the same fraction of production cost in all sectors. In practice there is a wide range of transportation costs. In some

means that we do not get a chance to see what countries do badly! In the world economy of the 1990s, countries often do not produce goods for which they are at a comparative disadvantage, so there is no way to measure their productivity in those sectors. For example, most countries do not produce airplanes, so there are no data on what their unit labor requirements would be if they did. Nonetheless, there are several pieces of evidence suggesting that differences in labor productivity continue to play an important role in determining world trade patterns.

Perhaps the most important point is that there continue to be both large differences in labor productivity between countries and considerable variation in those productivity differences across industries. For example, one study found that the average productivity of labor in Japanese manufacturing in 1990 was 20 percent lower than labor productivity in the United States. But in the automobile and auto parts industries Japanese productivity was 16 to 24 percent *higher* than American productivity.[5] It is not hard to believe that this disparity explained much of Japan's ability to export millions of automobiles to the United States.

In the case of automobiles, one might argue that the pattern of trade simply reflected absolute advantage: Japan had the highest productivity and was also the world's largest exporter. The principle of *comparative* advantage may be illustrated by the case of world trade in clothing. By any measure, advanced countries like the United States have higher labor productivity in the manufacture of clothing than newly industrializing countries like Mexico or China. But because the technology of clothing manufacture is relatively simple, the productivity advantage of advanced nations in the clothing industry is less than their advantage in many other industries. For example, in 1992 the average U.S. manufacturing worker was probably about five times as productive as the average Mexican worker; but in the clothing industry the productivity advantage was only about 50 percent. The result is that clothing is a major export from low-wage to high-wage nations.

In sum, while few economists believe that the Ricardian model is a fully adequate description of the causes and consequences of world trade, its two principal implications—that productivity differences play an important role in international trade and that it is comparative rather than absolute advantage that matters—do seem to be supported by the evidence.

Summary

1. We examined the *Ricardian model*, the simplest model that shows how differences between countries give rise to trade and gains from trade. In this model labor is the only factor of production and countries differ only in the productivity of labor in different industries.

2. In the Ricardian model, countries will export goods that their labor produces relatively efficiently and import goods that their labor produces relatively inefficiently. In other words, a country's production pattern is determined by *comparative advantage*.

3. That trade benefits a country can be shown in either of two ways. First, we can think of trade as an indirect method of production. Instead of producing a good for itself, a country can produce another good and trade it for the desired good. The simple model shows that whenever a good is imported it must be true that

---

[5]McKinsey Global Institute, *Manufacturing Productivity*, Washington, D.C., 1993.

this indirect "production" requires less labor than direct production. Second, we can show that trade enlarges a country's consumption possibilities, implying *gains from trade*.

4. The distribution of the gains from trade depends on the relative prices of the goods countries produce. To determine these relative prices it is necessary to look at the *relative world supply and demand* for goods. The relative price implies a *relative wage rate* as well.

5. The proposition that trade is beneficial is unqualified. That is, there is no requirement that a country be "competitive" or that the trade be "fair." In particular, we can show that three commonly held beliefs about trade are wrong. First, a country gains from trade even if it has lower productivity than its trading partner in all industries. Second, trade is beneficial even if foreign industries are competitive only because of low wages. Third, trade is beneficial even if a country's exports embody more labor than its imports.

6. Extending the one-factor, two-good model to a world of many commodities does not alter these conclusions. The only difference is that it becomes necessary to focus directly on the relative demand for labor to determine relative wages rather than to work via relative demand for goods. Also, a many-commodity model can be used to illustrate the important point that transportation costs can give rise to a situation in which some nontraded goods exist.

7. While some of the predictions of the Ricardian model are clearly unrealistic, its basic prediction—that countries will tend to export goods in which they have relatively high productivity—has been confirmed by a number of studies.

Key Terms

absolute advantage, p. 18

comparative advantage, p. 14

derived demand, p. 29

gains from trade, p. 21

general equilibrium analysis, p. 19

nontraded goods, p. 31

opportunity cost, p. 14

partial equilibrium analysis, p. 19

pauper labor argument, p. 25

production possibility frontier, p. 16

relative demand curve, p. 19

relative supply curve, p. 19

relative wage, p. 24

Ricardian model, p. 15

unit labor requirement, p. 15

Problems

1. Home has 1200 units of labor available. It can produce two goods, apples and bananas. The unit labor requirement in apple production is 3, while in banana production it is 2.
   a. Graph Home's production possibility frontier.
   b. What is the opportunity cost of apples in terms of bananas?
   c. In the absence of trade, what would the price of apples in terms of bananas be? Why?

2. Home is as described in problem 1. There is now also another country, Foreign, with a labor force of 800. Foreign's unit labor requirement in apple production is 5, while in banana production it is 1.
   a. Graph Foreign's production possibility frontier.
   b. Construct the world relative supply curve.

3. Now suppose world relative demand takes the following form:
   Demand for apples/demand for bananas = price of bananas/price of apples
   a. Graph the relative demand curve along with the relative supply curve.
   b. What is the equilibrium relative price of apples?
   c. Describe the pattern of trade.
   d. Show that both Home and Foreign gain from trade.

4. Suppose that instead of 1200 workers, Home had 2400. Find the equilibrium relative price. What can you say about the efficiency of world production and the division of the gains from trade between Home and Foreign in this case?

5. Suppose that Home has 2400 workers, but they are only half as productive in both industries as we have been assuming. Construct the world relative supply curve and determine the equilibrium relative price. How do the gains from trade compare with those in the case described in problem 4?

6. "Korean workers earn only $2.50 an hour; if we allow Korea to export as much as it likes to the United States, our workers will be forced down to the same level. You can't import a $5 shirt without importing the $2.50 wage that goes with it." Discuss.

7. Japanese labor productivity is roughly the same as that of the United States in the manufacturing sector (higher in some industries, lower in others), while the United States is still considerably more productive in the service sector. But most services are nontraded. Some analysts have argued that this poses a problem for the United States, because our comparative advantage lies in things we cannot sell on world markets. What is wrong with this argument?

8. Anyone who has visited Japan knows it is an incredibly expensive place; although Japanese workers earn about the same as their U.S. counterparts, the purchasing power of their incomes is about one-third less. Extend your discussion from question 7 to explain this observation. (Hint: Think about wages and the implied prices of nontraded goods.)

9. How does the fact that many goods are nontraded affect the extent of possible gains from trade?

10. We have focused on the case of trade involving only two countries. Suppose that there are many countries capable of producing two goods, and that each country has only one factor of production, labor. What could we say about the pattern of production and trade in this case? (Hint: Try constructing the world relative supply curve.)

Further Reading

Donald Davis. "Intraindustry Trade: A Heckscher-Ohlin-Ricardo Approach" (working paper, Harvard University). A recent revival of the Ricardian approach to explain trade between countries with similar resources.

Rudiger Dornbusch, Stanley Fischer, and Paul Samuelson. "Comparative Advantage, Trade and Payments in a Ricardian Model with a Continuum of Goods." *American Economic Review* 67 (December 1977), pp. 823–839. More recent theoretical modeling in the Ricardian mode, developing the idea of simplifying the many-good Ricardian model by assuming that the number of goods is so large as to form a smooth continuum.

Giovanni Dosi, Keith Pavitt, and Luc Soete. *The Economics of Technical Change and International Trade.* Brighton: Wheatsheaf, 1988. An empirical examination that suggests that international trade in manufactured goods is largely driven by differences in national technological competences.

G. D. A. MacDougall. "British and American Exports: A Study Suggested by the Theory of Comparative Costs." *Economic Journal* 61 (December 1951), pp. 697–724; 62 (September 1952), pp. 487–521. In this famous study, MacDougall used comparative data on U.S. and U.K. productivity to test the predictions of the Ricardian model.

John Stuart Mill. *Principles of Political Economy.* London: Longmans, Green, 1917. Mill's 1848 treatise extended Ricardo's work into a full-fledged model of international trade.

David Ricardo. *The Principles of Political Economy and Taxation.* Homewood, IL: Irwin, 1963. The basic source for the Ricardian model is Ricardo himself in this book, first published in 1817.

3

Specific Factors and Income Distribution

As we saw in Chapter 2, international trade can be mutually beneficial to the nations engaged in it. Yet throughout history, governments have protected sectors of the economy from import competition. For example, despite its commitment in principle to free trade, the United States limits imports of textiles, sugar, and other commodities. If trade is such a good thing for the economy, why is there opposition to its effects? To understand the politics of trade, it is necessary to look at the effects of trade, not just on a country as a whole but on the distribution of income within that country.

The Ricardian model of international trade developed in Chapter 2 illustrates the potential benefits from trade. In that model trade leads to international specialization, with each country shifting its labor force from industries in which that labor is relatively inefficient to industries in which it is relatively more efficient. Because labor is the only factor of production in the model, and it is assumed to be able to move freely from one industry to another, there is no possibility that individuals will be hurt by trade. The Ricardian model thus suggests not only that all countries gain from trade, but that every *individual* is made better off as a result of international trade, because trade does not affect the distribution of income. In the real world, however, trade has substantial effects on the income distribution within each trading nation, so that in practice the benefits of trade are often distributed very unevenly.

There are two main reasons why international trade has strong effects on the distribution of income. First, resources cannot move immediately or costlessly from one industry to another. Second, industries differ in the factors of production they demand: A shift in the mix of goods that a country produces will ordinarily reduce the demand for some factors of production, while raising the demand for others. For both of these reasons, international trade is not as unambiguously beneficial as it appeared to be in Chapter 2. While trade may benefit a nation as a whole, it often hurts significant groups within the country, at least in the short run.

Consider the effects of Japan's rice policy. Japan allows very little rice to be imported, even though the scarcity of land means that rice is much more expensive to produce in Japan than in other countries (including the United States). There is little question that Japan as a whole would have a higher standard of living if free imports of rice were allowed. Japanese rice farmers, however, would be hurt by free trade. While the farmers displaced by imports could probably find jobs in manufacturing or services in Japan's full employment economy, they would find changing employment costly and inconvenient. Furthermore, the value of the land that the farmers own would fall along with the price of rice. Not surprisingly, Japanese rice farmers are vehemently opposed to free trade in rice, and their organized political opposition has counted for more than the potential gains from trade for the nation as a whole.

A realistic analysis of trade must go beyond the Ricardian model to models in which trade can affect income distribution. This chapter concentrates on a particular model, known as the specific factors model, that brings income distribution into the story in a particularly clear way.

THE SPECIFIC FACTORS MODEL

The **specific factors model** was developed by Paul Samuelson and Ronald Jones.[1] Like the simple Ricardian model, it assumes an economy that produces two goods and that can allocate its labor supply between the two sectors. Unlike the Ricardian model, however, the specific factors model allows for the existence of factors of production besides labor. Whereas labor is a **mobile factor** that can move between sectors, these other factors are assumed to be **specific.** That is, they can be used only in the production of particular goods.

ASSUMPTIONS OF THE MODEL

Imagine an economy that can produce two goods, manufactures and food. Instead of one factor of production, however, the country has *three:* labor (L), capital (K), and land (T for *terrain*). Manufacturers are produced using capital and labor (but not land), while food is produced using land and labor (but not capital). Labor is therefore a *mobile* factor that can be used in either sector, while land and capital are both *specific* factors that can be used only in the production of one good.

How much of each good does the economy produce? The economy's output of manufactures depends on how much capital and labor are used in that sector. This relationship is summarized by a **production function** that tells us the quantity of manufactures that can be produced given any input of capital and labor. The production function for manufacturers can be summarized algebraically as

$$Q_M = Q_M(K, L_M),$$ (3-1)

where Q_M is the economy's output of manufactures, K is the economy's capital stock, and L_M is the labor force employed in manufactures. Similarly, for food we can write the production function

[1]Paul Samuelson, "Ohlin Was Right," *Swedish Journal of Economics* 73 (1971), pp. 365–384; and Ronald W. Jones, "A Three-Factor Model in Theory, Trade, and History," in Jagdish Bhagwati et al., eds., *Trade, Balance of Payments, and Growth* (Amsterdam: North-Holland, 1971), pp. 3–21.

WHAT IS A SPECIFIC FACTOR?

In the model developed in this chapter, we assume that there are two factors of production, land and capital, which are permanently tied to particular sectors of the economy. In advanced economies, however, agricultural land receives only a small part of national income. When economists apply the specific factors model to economies like that of the United States or France, they typically think of factor specificity not as a permanent condition but as a matter of time. For example, the vats used to brew beer and the stamping presses used to build auto bodies cannot be substituted for each other, and so these different kinds of equipment are industry-specific. Given time, however, it is possible to redirect investment from auto factories to breweries or vice versa, and so in a long-term sense both vats and stamping presses can be considered to be two manifestations of a single, mobile factor called *capital.*

In practice, then, the distinction between specific and mobile factors is not a sharp line. It is a question of the speed of adjustment, with factors more specific the longer it takes to redeploy them between industries. So how specific are the factors of production in the real economy?

Workers who have fairly general skills, as opposed to highly specific training, seem to be quite mobile, if not quite as mobile as labor in the model. One useful clue comes from the time it takes labor to move between geographic locations. One influential study finds that when a U.S. state hits economic difficulties, workers quickly begin leaving for other states; within six years the unemployment rate falls back to the national average.* This compares with a lifetime of 15 or 20 years for a typical specialized machine, and perhaps 50 years for a shopping mall or office building. So labor is certainly a less specific factor than most kinds of capital. On the other hand, highly trained workers are pretty much stuck with their craft: A brain surgeon might have made a pretty good violinist, but she cannot switch careers in mid-life.

*Olivier Blanchard and Lawrence Katz, "Regional Evolutions," *Brookings Papers on Economic Activity,* 1991.

$$Q_F = Q_F(T, L_F), \tag{3-2}$$

where Q_F is the economy's output of food, T is the economy's supply of land, and L_F is the labor force devoted to food production. For the economy as a whole, the labor employed must equal the total labor supply L:

$$L_M + L_F = L. \tag{3-3}$$

PRODUCTION POSSIBILITIES

The specific factors model assumes that each of the specific factors capital and land can be used in only one sector, manufactures and food, respectively. Only labor can be used in either sector. Thus to analyze the economy's production possibilities, we need only to ask how the economy's mix of output changes as labor is shifted from one sector to the other. This can be done graphically, first by representing the production functions (3-1) and (3-2), then by putting them together to derive the production possibility frontier.

Figure 3-1 illustrates the relationship between labor input and output of manufactures. The larger the input of labor, for a given capital supply, the larger will be output. In Figure 3-1, the slope of $Q_M(K, L_M)$ represents the **marginal product of labor,** that is, the addition to output generated by adding one more person-hour. However, if labor input is increased

FIGURE 3-1

The Production Function for Manufactures

The more labor that is employed in the production of manufactures, the larger the output. As a result of diminishing returns, however, each successive person-hour increases output by less than the previous one; this is shown by the fact that the curve relating labor input to output gets flatter at higher levels of employment.

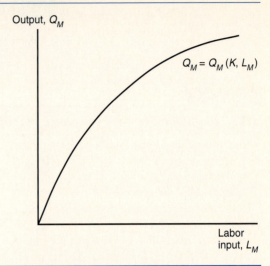

Output, Q_M

$Q_M = Q_M(K, L_M)$

Labor input, L_M

without increasing capital as well, there will normally be **diminishing returns:** Because adding a worker means that each worker has less capital to work with, each successive increment of labor will add less to production than the last. Diminishing returns are reflected in the shape of the production function: $Q_M(K,L_M)$ gets flatter as we move to the right, indicating that the marginal product of labor declines as more labor is used. Figure 3-2 shows

FIGURE 3-2

The Marginal Product of Labor

The marginal product of labor in the manufactures sector, equal to the slope of the production function shown in Figure 3-1, is lower the more labor the sector employs.

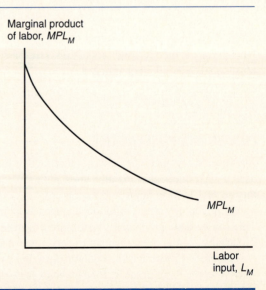

Marginal product of labor, MPL_M

MPL_M

Labor input, L_M

the same information a different way. In this figure we directly plot the marginal product of labor as a function of the labor employed. (In the appendix to this chapter we show that the area under the marginal product curve represents the total output of manufactures.)

A similar pair of diagrams can represent the production function for food. These diagrams can then be combined to derive the production possibility frontier for the economy, as illustrated in Figure 3-3. As we saw in Chapter 2, the **production possibility frontier**

FIGURE 3-3

The Production Possibility Frontier in the Specific Factors Model

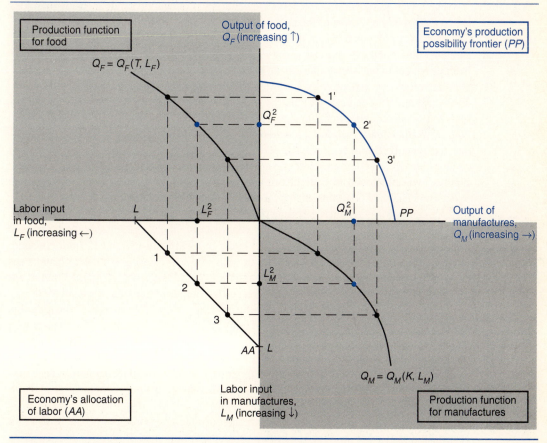

Production of manufactures and food is determined by the allocation of labor. In the lower left quadrant, the allocation of labor between sectors can be illustrated by a point on the line *AA,* which represents all combinations of labor input to manufactures and food that sum up to the total labor supply *L.* Corresponding to any particular point on *AA,* such as point 2, is a labor input to manufactures (L_M^2) and a labor input to food (L_F^2). The curves in the lower-right and upper-left quadrants represent the production functions for manufactures and food respectively; these allow determination of output (Q_M^2, Q_F^2) given labor input. Then in the upper-right quadrant the curve *PP* shows how the output of the two goods varies as the allocation of labor is shifted from food to manufactures, with the output points 1′, 2′, 3′ corresponding to the labor allocations 1, 2, 3. Because of diminishing returns, *PP* is a bowed-out curve instead of a straight line.

shows what the economy is capable of producing; in this case it shows how much food it can produce for any given output of manufactures and vice versa.

Figure 3-3 is a four-quadrant diagram. In the lower right quadrant we show the production function for manufactures illustrated in Figure 3-1. This time, however, we turn the figure on its side: A movement downward along the vertical axis represents an increase in the labor input to the manufactures sector, while a movement to the right along the horizontal axis represents an increase in the output of manufactures. In the upper left quadrant we show the corresponding production function for food; this part of the figure is also flipped around, so that a movement to the left along the horizontal axis indicates an increase in labor input to the food sector, while an upward movement along the vertical axis indicates an increase in food output.

The lower left quadrant represents the economy's allocation of labor. Both quantities are measured in the reverse of the usual direction. A downward movement along the vertical axis indicates an increase in the labor employed in manufactures; a leftward movement along the horizontal axis indicates an increase in labor employed in food. Since an increase in employment in one sector must mean that less labor is available for the other, the possible allocations are indicated by a downward sloping line. This line, labeled *AA,* slopes downward at a 45-degree angle, that is, it has a slope of -1. To see why this line represents the possible labor allocations, notice that if all labor were employed in food production, L_F would equal L, while L_M would equal 0. If one were then to move labor gradually into the manufacturing sector, each person-hour moved would increase L_M by one unit while reducing L_F by one unit, tracing a line with a slope of -1, until all the entire labor supply L was employed in manufactures. Any particular allocation of labor between the two sectors can then be represented by a point on *AA,* such as point 2.

We can now see how to determine production given any particular allocation of labor between the two sectors. Suppose that the allocation of labor were represented by point 2 in the lower left quadrant, that is, with L_M^2 hours in manufacturing and L_F^2 hours in food. Then we can use the production function for each sector to determine output: Q_M^2 units are produced in manufacturing, Q_F^2 in food. Using these coordinates Q_M^2, Q_F^2, point 2' in the upper right quadrant of Figure 3-3 shows the resulting output of manufactures and food.

To trace the whole production possibility frontier, we simply imagine repeating this exercise for many alternative allocations of labor. We might start with most of the labor allocated to food production, as at point 1 in the lower left quadrant, then gradually increase the amount of labor used in manufactures until very few workers are employed in food, as at point 3; the corresponding points in the upper right quadrant will trace out the curve running from 1' to 3'. Thus *PP* in the upper right quadrant shows the economy's production possibilities for given supplies of land, labor, and capital.

In the Ricardian model, where labor is the only factor of production, the production possibility frontier is a straight line because the opportunity cost of manufactures in terms of food is constant. In the specific factors model, however, the addition of other factors of production changes the shape of the production possibility frontier *PP* to a curve. The curvature of *PP* reflects diminishing returns to labor in each sector; these diminishing returns are the crucial difference between the specific factors and the Ricardian models.

Notice that when tracing *PP* we shift labor from the food to the manufacturing sector. If we shift one person-hour of labor from food to manufactures, however, this extra input will increase output in that sector by the marginal product of labor in manufactures, MPL_M. To increase manufactures output by one unit, then, we must increase labor input by $1/MPL_M$ hours. Meanwhile, each unit of labor input shifted out of food production will lower output in that sector by the marginal product of labor in food, MPL_F. To increase output of manufactures by one unit, then, the economy must reduce output of food by MPL_F/MPL_M units. The slope of PP, which measures the opportunity cost of manufactures in terms of food—that is, the number of units of food output that must be sacrificed to increase manufactures output by one unit—is therefore

$$\text{Slope of production possibilities curve} = -MPL_F/MPL_M.$$

We can now see why PP has the bowed shape it does. As we move from $1'$ to $3'$, L_M rises and L_F falls. We saw in Figure 3-2, however, that as L_M rises, the marginal product of labor in manufactures falls; correspondingly, as L_F falls, the marginal product of labor in food rises. So PP gets steeper as we move down it to the right.

We have now shown how output is determined, given the allocation of labor. The next step is to ask how a market economy determines the allocation of labor.

PRICES, WAGES, AND LABOR ALLOCATION

How much labor will be employed in each sector? To answer this we need to look at supply and demand in the labor market. The demand for labor in each sector depends on the price of output and the wage rate. In turn, the wage rate depends on the combined demand for labor by food and manufactures. Given the prices of manufactures and food together with the wage rate, we can determine each sector's employment and output.

First, let us focus on the demand for labor. In each sector, profit-maximizing employers will demand labor up to the point where the value produced by an additional person-hour equals the cost of employing that hour. In the manufacturing sector, for example, the value of an additional person-hour is the marginal product of labor in manufacturing multiplied by the price of one unit of manufactures: $MPL_M \times P_M$. If w is the wage rate of labor, employers will therefore hire workers up to the point where

$$MPL_M \times P_M = w. \tag{3-4}$$

But the marginal product of labor in manufacturing, already illustrated in Figure 3-2, slopes downward because of diminishing returns. So for any given price of manufactures P_M, the value of that marginal product, $MPL_M \times P_M$, will also slope down. We can therefore think of equation (3-4) as defining the demand curve for labor in manufactures: If the wage rate falls, other things equal, employers in the manufacturing sector will want to hire more workers.

Similarly, the value of an additional person-hour in food is $MPL_F \times P_F$. The demand curve for labor in the food sector may therefore be written

$$MPL_F \times P_F = w. \tag{3-5}$$

The wage rate w must be the same in both sectors, because of the assumption that labor is freely mobile between sectors. That is, because labor is a mobile factor, it will move from the low-wage sector to the high-wage sector until wages are equalized. The wage rate, in turn, is determined by the requirement that total labor demand (total employment) equal total labor supply:

$$L_M + L_F = L. \tag{3-6}$$

FIGURE 3-4

The Allocation of Labor

Labor is allocated so that the value of its marginal product ($P \times MPL$) is the same in manufactures and food. In equilibrium, the wage rate is equal to the value of labor's marginal product.

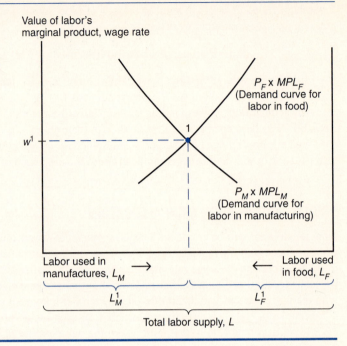

Value of labor's marginal product, wage rate

$P_F \times MPL_F$
(Demand curve for labor in food)

1

w^1

$P_M \times MPL_M$
(Demand curve for labor in manufacturing)

Labor used in manufactures, L_M →

← Labor used in food, L_F

L_M^1 L_F^1

Total labor supply, L

By representing these three equations in a diagram (Figure 3-4), we can see how the wage rate and employment in each sector are determined given the prices of food and manufactures. Along the horizontal axis of Figure 3-4 we show the total labor supply L. Measuring from the left of the diagram, we show the value of the marginal product of labor in manufactures, which is simply the MPL_M curve from Figure 3-2 multiplied by P_M. This is the demand curve for labor in the manufacturing sector. Measuring from the right, we show the value of the marginal product of labor in food, which is the demand for labor in food. The equilibrium wage rate and allocation of labor between the two sectors is represented by point 1. At the wage rate w^1 the sum of labor demanded by manufactures (L_M^1) and food (L_F^1) just equals the total labor supply L.

There is a useful relationship between relative prices and output that emerges clearly from this analysis of labor allocation; this relationship applies to more general situations than that described by the specific factors model. Equations (3-4) and (3-5) imply that

$$MPL_M \times P_M = MPL_F \times P_F = w$$

or, rearranging, that

$$-MPL_F/MPL_M = -P_M/P_F. \tag{3-7}$$

The left side of equation (3-7) is the slope of the production possibility frontier at the actual production point; the right side is minus the relative price of manufactures. This result tells us that *at the production point the production possibility frontier must be tangent to a line whose slope is minus the price of manufactures divided by that of food.* The result

FIGURE 3-5

Production in the Specific Factors Model

The economy produces at the point on its production possibility frontier (*PP*) where the slope of that frontier equals minus the relative price of manufactures.

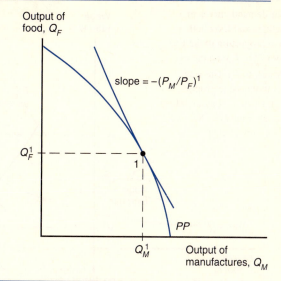

is illustrated in Figure 3-5: If the relative price of manufactures is $(P_M/P_F)^1$ the economy produces at point 1.

What happens to the allocation of labor and the distribution of income when the prices of food and manufactures change? Notice that any price change can be broken into two parts: an equal proportional change in both P_M and P_F, and a change in only one price. For example, suppose that the price of manufactures rises 17 percent and the price of food rises 10 percent. We can analyze the effects of this by first asking what happens if manufactures and food prices both rise by 10 percent, then by finding out what happens if manufactures prices rise by 7 percent. This allows us to separate the effect of changes in the overall price level from the effect of changes in relative prices.

An Equal Proportional Change in Prices. Figure 3-6 shows the effect of an equal proportional increase in P_M and P_F. P_M rises from P_M^1 to P_M^2; P_F rises from P_F^1 to P_F^2. If both goods prices increase by 10 percent, the labor demand curves will both shift up by 10 percent as well. As you can see from the diagram, these shifts lead to a 10 percent increase in the wage rate from w^1 (point 1) to w^2 (point 2). The allocation of labor between the sectors and the outputs of the two goods do not change.

In fact, when P_M and P_F change in the same proportion, no real changes occur. The wage rate rises in the same proportion as the prices, so *real* wage rates, the ratios of the wage rate to the prices of goods, are unaffected. With the same amount of labor employed in each sector, receiving the same real wage rate, the real incomes of capital owners and landowners also remain the same. So everyone is in exactly the same position as before. This illustrates a general principle: Changes in the overall price level have no real effects, that is, do not change any physical quantities in the economy. Only changes in relative prices—which in this case means the price of manufactures relative to food, P_M/P_F—affect welfare or the allocation of resources.

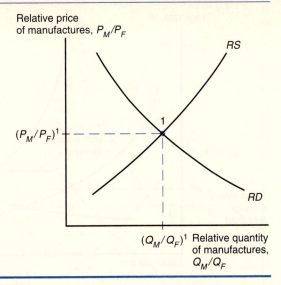

FIGURE 3-9

Determination of Relative Prices

In the specific factors model a higher relative price of manufactures will lead to an increase in the output of manufactures relative to that of food. Thus the relative supply curve RS is upward sloping. Equilibrium relative quantities and prices are determined by the intersection of RS with the relative demand curve RD.

P_M/P_F. This relative supply curve is shown as RS in Figure 3-9. As we showed in Chapter 2, we can also draw a relative demand curve, which is illustrated by the downward-sloping line RD. The equilibrium relative price $(P_M/P_F)^1$ and output $(Q_M/Q_F)^1$ are determined by the intersection of RS and RD.

RELATIVE PRICES AND THE DISTRIBUTION OF INCOME

So far we have examined the following aspects of the specific factors model: (1) the determination of production possibilities given an economy's resources and technology and (2) the determination of resource allocation, production, and relative prices in a market economy. Before turning to the effects of international trade we must consider the effect of changes in relative prices on the distribution of income.

Look again at Figure 3-7, which shows the effect of a rise in the price of manufactures. We have already noted that the demand curve for labor in the manufacturing sector will shift upward in proportion to the rise in P_M, so that if P_M rises by 10 percent, the curve defined by $P_M \times MPL_M$ also rises by 10 percent. We have also seen that unless the price of food also rises by at least 10 percent, w will rise by *less* than P_M. Thus if manufacturing prices rise by 10 percent, we would expect the wage rate to rise by only, say, 5 percent.

Let's look at what this outcome implies for the incomes of three groups: workers, owners of capital, and owners of land. Workers find that their wage rate has risen, but less than in proportion to the rise in P_M. Thus their real wage in terms of manufactures, w/P_M, falls, while their real wage in terms of food, w/P_F, rises. Given this information, we cannot say whether workers are better or worse off; this depends on the relative importance of manufactures and food in workers' consumption, a question that we will not pursue further.

Owners of capital, however, are definitely better off. The real wage rate in terms of manufactures has fallen, so that the profits of capital owners in terms of what they produce rises. That is, the income of capital owners will rise more than proportionately with the rise in P_M. Since P_M in turn has risen relative to P_F, the income of capitalists has clearly gone up in terms of both goods.

Conversely, landowners are definitely worse off. They lose for two reasons: The real wage in terms of food rises, squeezing their income, and the rise in manufactures prices reduces the purchasing power of any given income.

INTERNATIONAL TRADE IN THE SPECIFIC FACTORS MODEL

Now that we know how the specific factors model works for a single economy, we can turn to an analysis of international trade. Imagine that two countries, Japan and America, trade with each other; let's examine the effects of this trade on their welfare.

For trade to take place, the two countries must differ in the relative price of manufactures that would prevail in the absence of trade. In Figure 3-9 we saw how P_M/P_F is determined in a single economy in the absence of trade. Japan and America could have different relative prices of manufactures either because they differ in their relative demand or because they differ in their relative supply. We will assume away demand differences: that is, we assume that at any given P_M/P_F, relative demand is the same in the two countries. If both countries face the same relative price of manufactures, they will consume food and manufactures in the same proportions. Thus both countries will have the same relative demand curve. We will therefore focus on differences in relative supply as the source of international trade.

Why might relative supply differ? The countries could have different technologies, as in the Ricardian model. Now that our model has more than one factor of production, however, the countries could also differ in their resources. It is worth examining how differences in resources can affect relative supply.

RESOURCES AND RELATIVE SUPPLY

The basic relationship between resources and relative supply is straightforward: A country with a lot of capital and not much land will tend to produce a high ratio of manufactures to food at any given prices, while a country with a lot of land and not much capital will do the reverse. Consider what would happen if one of the countries experienced an increase in the supply of some resource. Suppose, for example, that Japan were to increase its capital stock. The effects of such an increase are shown in Figure 3-10.

Other things equal, an increase in the quantity of capital would raise the marginal productivity of labor in the manufacturing sector. Thus the demand curve for labor in manufacturing would shift to the right, from $P_M \times MPL_M^1$ to $P_M \times MPL_M^2$. At any given prices of manufactures and food, this increase in demand for manufacturing labor would shift the equilibrium from point 1 to point 2. More workers would be drawn into the manufacturing sector out of the food sector. Manufacturing output would rise, for two reasons: There would be more workers in the sector and they would have more capital to work with. Food output would fall because of reduced labor input. So at any given relative price of manufactures, the relative output of manufactures would rise. We therefore conclude that an increase in the supply of capital would shift the relative supply curve to the right.

Correspondingly, an increase in the supply of land would increase food output and reduce manufacturing output; the relative supply curve would shift left.

FIGURE 3-10

Changing the Capital Stock

An increase in the capital stock raises the marginal product of labor in manufactures for any given level of employment. This raises the demand for labor in the manufacturing sector, which drives up the overall wage rate. Because labor is pulled out of the food sector, output of manufactures rises, while output of food falls.

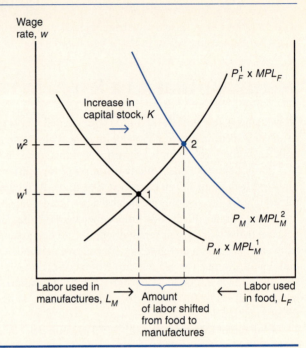

What about the effect of an increase in the labor force? This is a less clear-cut case. To induce employers to hire the additional workers, the wage rate must fall. This will lead to increased employment and output of *both* manufactures and food; the effect on relative output is ambiguous.

Suppose, however, that America and Japan have the same labor force, but that Japan has a larger supply of capital than America, while America has a larger supply of land than Japan. Then the situation will look like that in Figure 3-11. Japan's relative supply curve RS_J lies to the right of America's curve RS_A, because Japan's abundance of capital and scarcity of land leads it to produce a large quantity of manufactures and relatively little food at any given relative price of manufactures, whereas the reverse is true for America.

TRADE AND RELATIVE PRICES

In this model, as always, international trade leads to a convergence of relative prices, illustrated in Figure 3-11. Since relative demand is the same in Japan and America, RD_{WORLD} is both each country's relative demand curve and the world relative demand curve when the two countries trade. RS_J and RS_A represent the relative supply curves of Japan and America, respectively. Japan is assumed to be relatively well-endowed with capital and poorly endowed with land, while America is the reverse, so RS_J lies to the right of RS_A. The pretrade relative price of manufactures in Japan, $(P_M/P_F)_J$, is lower than the pretrade relative price in America, $(P_M/P_F)_A$.

FIGURE 3-11

Trade and Relative Prices

In the figure, Japan is assumed to have more capital per worker than America, while America has more land per worker than Japan. As a result, Japan's relative supply curve lies to the right of America's. When the two economies trade, the *world* relative supply curve RS_{WORLD} lies between the two national curves, and the equilibrium world relative price of manufactures—determined by the intersection of RS_{WORLD} with the relative demand curve RS_{WORLD}—lies between the levels of P_M/P_F that would have prevailed in the two countries in the absence of trade.

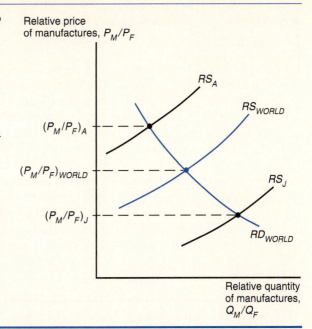

When the two countries open trade, they create an integrated world economy whose production of manufactures and food is the sum of the national outputs of the two goods. The world relative supply of manufactures (RS_{WORLD}) lies between the relative supplies in the two countries. The world relative price of manufactures, $(P_M/P_F)_{WORLD}$, therefore lies between the national pretrade prices. Trade has increased the relative price of manufactures in Japan and has lowered it in America.

THE PATTERN OF TRADE

If trade occurs initially because of differences in relative prices of manufactures, how does the convergence of P_M/P_F translate into a pattern of international trade? To answer this question, we need to state some basic relationships among prices, production, and consumption.

In a country that cannot trade, the output of a good must equal its consumption. If D_M is consumption of manufactures and D_F consumption of food, then in a closed economy $D_M = Q_M$ and $D_F = Q_F$. International trade makes it possible for the mix of manufactures and food consumed to differ from the mix produced. While the amounts of each good that a country consumes and produces may differ, however, a country cannot spend more than it earns: The *value* of consumption must be equal to the value of production. That is,

$$P_M \times D_M + P_F \times D_F = P_M \times Q_M + P_F \times Q_F. \qquad (3\text{-}8)$$

Equation (3-8) can be rearranged to yield the following:

$$D_F - Q_F = (P_M/P_F) \times (Q_M - D_M). \qquad (3\text{-}9)$$

$D_F - Q_F$ is the economy's food *imports*, the amount by which its consumption of food exceeds its production. The right-hand side of the equation is the product of the relative price of manufactures and the amount by which production of manufactures exceeds consumption, that is, the economy's *exports* of manufactures. The equation, then, states that imports of food equal exports of manufactures times the relative price of manufactures. While it does not tell us how much the economy will import or export, the equation does show that the amount the economy can afford to import is limited, or constrained, by the amount it exports. Equation (3-9) is therefore known as a **budget constraint.**[2]

Figure 3-12 illustrates two important features of the budget constraint for a trading economy. First, the slope of the budget constraint is minus P_M/P_F, the relative price of manufactures. The reason is that consuming one less unit of manufactures saves the economy P_M; this is enough to purchase P_M/P_F extra units of food. Second, the budget constraint is tangent to the production possibility frontier at the point that represents the economy's choice of production given the relative price of manufactures, shown in the figure as point 1. That is, the economy can always afford to consume what it produces.

We can now use the budget constraints of Japan and America to construct a picture of the trading equilibrium. In Figure 3-13, we show the outputs, budget constraints, and con-

---

FIGURE 3-12

The Budget Constraint for a Trading Economy

Point 1 represents the economy's production. The economy's consumption must lie along a line that passes through point 1 and has a slope equal to minus the relative price of manufactures.

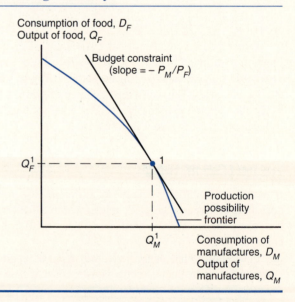

---

[2]The constraint that the value of consumption equals that of production (or, equivalently, that imports equal exports in value) may not hold when countries can borrow from other countries or lend to them. For now we assume that these possibilities are not available and that the budget constraint (equation (3–9)) therefore holds. International borrowing and lending are examined in Chapter 7, which shows that an economy's consumption *over time* is still constrained by the necessity of paying its debts to foreign lenders.

FIGURE 3-13

Trading Equilibrium

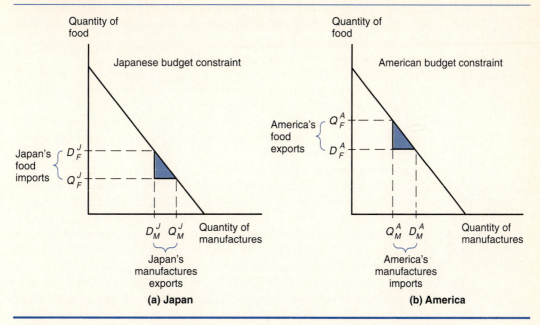

(a) Japan   **(b) America**

Japan's imports of food are exactly equal to America's exports, and America's imports of manufactures are exactly equal to Japan's exports.

sumption choices of Japan and America at equilibrium prices. In Japan, the rise in the relative price of manufactures leads to a rise in the consumption of food relative to manufactures and a fall in the relative output of food. Japan produces Q_F^J of food but consumes D_F^J; it therefore becomes a manufactures exporter and a food importer. In America, the post-trade fall in the relative price of manufactures leads to a rise in the consumption of manufactures relative to food and a fall in the relative output of manufactures; America therefore becomes a manufactures importer and a food exporter. In equilibrium Japan's exports of manufactures must exactly equal America's imports and Japan's imports of food exactly equal America's exports. These equalities are shown by the equality of the two colored triangles in Figure 3-13.

INCOME DISTRIBUTION AND THE GAINS FROM TRADE

We have seen how production possibilities are determined by resources and technology; how the choice of what to produce is determined by the relative price of manufactures; how changes in the relative price of manufactures affect the real incomes of different factors of production; and how trade affects both relative prices and the economy's budget constraint. Now we can ask the crucial question: Who gains and who loses from international trade? We begin by asking how the welfare of particular groups is affected, and then how trade affects the welfare of the country as a whole.

To assess the effects of trade on particular groups, the key point is that international trade shifts the relative price of manufactures and food. Consider first what happens in Japan. We are assuming that in the absence of trade Japan would have had a lower relative price of manufactures than the rest of the world. If this is the case, trade, which leads to a convergence of relative prices, will mean a rise in P_M/P_F. In Japan, then (as we saw in the previous section), the result of a rise in P_M/P_F is that owners of capital are better off, workers experience an ambiguous shift in their position, and landowners are worse off.

In America, the effect of trade on relative prices is just the reverse: The relative price of manufactures falls. So in America landowners are better off and capital owners worse off, and the effect on workers is once again ambiguous.

The general outcome, then, is simple: *Trade benefits the factor that is specific to the export sector of each country but hurts the factor specific to the import-competing sectors, with ambiguous effects on mobile factors.*

Do the gains from trade outweigh the losses? One way you might try to answer this question would be to sum up the gains of the winners and the losses of the losers and compare them. The problem with this procedure is that we are comparing welfare, an inherently subjective thing. Suppose that capitalists are dull people who get hardly any satisfaction out of increased consumption, while landowners are bons vivants who get immense pleasure out of it. Then one might well imagine that trade reduces the total amount of pleasure in Japan. But the reverse could equally be true. More to the point, it is outside the province of what we normally think of as economic analysis to try to figure out how much enjoyment individuals get out of their lives.

A better way to assess the overall gains from trade is to ask a different question: Could those who gain from trade compensate those who lose, and still be better off themselves? If so, then trade is *potentially* a source of gain to everyone.

To illustrate that trade is a source of potential gain for everyone, we proceed in three steps.

1. First, we notice that in the absence of trade the economy would have to produce what it consumed, and vice versa. Thus the *consumption* of the economy in the absence of trade would have to be a point on the *production* possibility frontier. In Figure 3-14, a typical pretrade consumption point is shown as point 2.

2. Next, we notice that it is possible for a trading economy to consume more of *both* goods than it would have in the absence of trade. The budget constraint in Figure 3-14 represents all the possible combinations of food and manufactures that the country could consume given the world relative price of manufactures. Part of that budget constraint—the part in the colored region—represents situations in which the economy consumes more of both manufactures and food than it could in the absence of trade. Notice that this result does not depend on the assumption that pretrade production and consumption was at point 2; unless pretrade production was at point 1, so that trade has no effect on production at all, there is always a part of the budget constraint that allows consumption of more of both goods.

3. Finally, observe that if the economy as a whole consumes more of both goods, then it is possible in principle to give each *individual* more of both goods. This would make everyone better off. This shows, then, that it is possible to ensure that everyone is better off as a result of trade. Of course, everyone might be still better off if they had less of one good and more of the other, but this only reinforces the conclusion that everyone can potentially gain from trade.

FIGURE 3-14

Trade Expands the Economy's Consumption Possibilities

Before trade, the economy's production and consumption were at point 2 on its production possibilities frontier (*PP*). After trade, the economy can consume at any point on its budget constraint. The portion of the budget constraint in the colored region consists of feasible posttrade consumption choices with consumption of both goods higher than at the pretrade point 2.

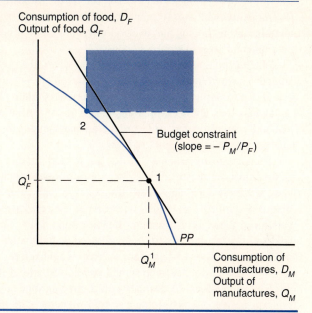

Consumption of food, D_F
Output of food, Q_F

2

Budget constraint
(slope = $-P_M/P_F$)

Q_F^1 ─ ─ ─ ─ ─ 1

PP

Q_M^1

Consumption of
manufactures, D_M
Output of
manufactures, Q_M

The fundamental reason why trade potentially benefits a country is that it *expands the economy's choices.* This expansion of choice means that it is always possible to redistribute income in such a way that everyone gains from trade.[3]

That everyone *could* gain from trade unfortunately does not mean that everyone actually does. In the real world, the presence of losers as well as winners from trade is one of the most important reasons why trade is not free.

THE POLITICAL ECONOMY OF TRADE: A PRELIMINARY VIEW

Trade often produces losers as well as winners. This insight is crucial to understanding the considerations that actually determine trade policy in the modern world economy. Trade policy is examined in detail in Chapters 8 through 11; it is possible, however, to take a preliminary view at this point.

There are two ways to look at trade policy (or any government policy): (1) Given its objectives, what *should* the government do? What is its *optimal* trade policy? (2) What are governments likely to do in practice? The income distribution effects of trade are important to the first way of looking at the issue and are crucial to the second.

---

[3]The argument that trade is beneficial because it enlarges an economy's choices is much more general than this picture. For a thorough discussion see Paul Samuelson, "The Gains from International Trade Once Again," *Economic Journal* 72 (1962), pp. 820–829.

OPTIMAL TRADE POLICY

Suppose a government wants to maximize the welfare of its population. If everyone were exactly the same in tastes and in income there would be a straightforward solution: The government would choose policies that make the representative individual as well off as possible. In this homogeneous economy, free international trade would clearly serve the government's objective.

When people are not exactly alike, however, the government's problem is less well-defined. The government must somehow weigh one person's gain against another person's loss. If, for example, the Japanese government is relatively more concerned about hurting landowners than about helping capitalists, then international trade, which in our analysis benefited capital owners and hurt landowners in Japan, might be a bad thing from the Japanese government's point of view.

There are many reasons why one group might matter more than another, but one of the most compelling reasons is that some groups need special treatment because they are already relatively poor. There is widespread sympathy in the United States for restrictions on imports of garments and shoes, even though the restrictions raise consumer prices, because workers in these industries are already poorly paid. The gains that affluent consumers would realize if more imports were allowed do not matter as much to the U.S. public as the losses low-paid shoe and garment workers would suffer.

Does this mean that trade should be allowed only if it doesn't hurt lower-income people? Few international economists would agree. In spite of the real importance of income distribution, most economists remain strongly in favor of more or less free trade. There are three main reasons why economists do *not* generally stress the income distribution effects of trade.

1. Income distribution effects are not specific to international trade. Every change in a nation's economy, including technological progress, shifting consumer preferences, exhaustion of old resources and discovery of new ones, and so on, affects income distribution. If every change in the economy were allowed only after it had been examined for its distributional effects, economic progress could easily end up snarled in red tape.

2. It is always better to allow trade and compensate those who are hurt by it than to prohibit the trade. (This applies to other forms of economic change as well.) All modern industrial countries provide some sort of "safety net" of income support programs (such as unemployment benefits and subsidized retaining and relocation programs) that can cushion the losses of groups hurt by trade. Economists would argue that if this cushion is felt to be inadequate, more support rather than less trade is the right answer.

3. Those who stand to lose from increased trade are typically better organized than those who stand to gain. This imbalance creates a bias in the political process that requires a counterweight. It is the traditional role of economists to strongly support free trade, pointing to the overall gains; those who are hurt usually have little trouble making their complaints heard.

Most economists, then, while acknowledging the effects of international trade on income distribution, believe that it is more important to stress the potential gains from trade than the possible losses to some groups in a country. Economists do not, however, often have the deciding voice in economic policy, especially when conflicting interests are at stake. Any realistic understanding of how trade policy is determined must look at the actual motivations of policy.

SPECIFIC FACTORS AND THE BEGINNINGS OF TRADE THEORY

The modern theory of international trade began with the demonstration by David Ricardo, writing in 1817, that trade is mutually beneficial to countries. We studied Ricardo's model in Chapter 2. Ricardo used his model to argue for free trade, in particular for an end to the tariffs that restricted England's imports of food. Yet almost surely the British economy of 1817 was better described by a specific factors model than by the one-factor model Ricardo presented.

To understand the situation, recall that from the beginning of the French Revolution in 1789 until the defeat of Napoleon at Waterloo in 1815, Britain was almost continuously at war with France. This war interfered with Britain's trade: Privateers (pirates licensed by foreign governments) raided shipping and the French attempted to impose a blockade on British goods. Since Britain was an exporter of manufactures and an importer of agricultural products, this limitation of trade raised the relative price of food in Britain. The profits of manufacturers suffered, but landowners actually prospered during the long war.

After the war, food prices in Britain fell. To avoid the consequences, the politically in-fluential landowners were able to get legislation, the so-called Corn Laws, that imposed fees to discourage importation of grain. It was against these Corn Laws that Ricardo was arguing.

Ricardo knew that repeal of the Corn Laws would make capitalists better off but landowners worse off. From his point of view this was all to the good; a London business-man himself, he preferred hard-working capitalists to idle landed aristocrats. But he chose to present his argument in the form of a model that assumed away issues of internal income distribution.

Why did he do this? Almost surely the answer is political: While Ricardo was in reality to some extent representing the interest of a single group, he emphasized the gains to the nation as a whole. This was a clever and thoroughly modern strategy, one that pioneered the use of economic theory as a political instrument. Then as now, politics and intellectual progress are not incompatible: The Corn Laws were repealed nearly a century and a half ago, yet Ricardo's model of trade remains one of the great insights in economics.

INCOME DISTRIBUTION AND TRADE POLITICS

It is easy to see why groups that lose from trade lobby their governments to restrict trade and protect their incomes. You might expect that those who gain from trade would lobby as strongly as those who lose from it, but this is rarely the case. In the United States and in most countries, those who want trade limited are more effective politically than those who want it extended. Typically, those who gain from trade in any particular product are a much less concentrated, informed, and organized group than those who lose.

A good example of this contrast between the two sides is the U.S. sugar industry. The United States has limited imports of sugar for many years; at the time of writing the price of sugar in the U.S. market was about twice its price in the world market. Most estimates put the cost of U.S. consumers of this import limitation at about $2 billion a year—that is, about $8 a year for every man, woman, and child. The gains to producers are much smaller, probably less than half as large.

If producers and consumers were equally able to get their interests represented, this policy would never have been enacted. In absolute terms, however, each consumer suffers very little. Eight dollars a year is not much; furthermore, most of the cost is hidden, because most sugar is consumed as an ingredient in other foods rather than purchased directly. Thus most consumers are unaware that the import quota even exists, let alone that it reduces their standard of living. Even if they were aware, $8 is not a large enough sum to provoke people into organizing protests and writing letters to their congressional representatives.

The sugar producers' situation is quite different. The average sugar producer gains thousands of dollars a year from the import quota. Furthermore, sugar producers are organized into trade associations and cooperatives that actively pursue their members' political interests. So the complaints of sugar producers about the effects of imports are loudly and effectively expressed.

As we will see in Chapters 8 through 11, the politics of import restriction in the sugar industry are an extreme example of a kind of political process that is common in international trade. That world trade in general became steadily freer from 1945 to 1980 depended, as we will see in Chapter 9, on a special set of circumstances that controlled what is probably an inherent political bias against international trade.

Summary

1. International trade often has strong effects on the distribution of income within countries, so that it often produces losers as well as winners. Income distribution effects arise for two reasons: Factors of production cannot move instantaneously and costlessly from one industry to another, and changes in an economy's output mix have differential effects on the demand for different factors of production.

2. A useful model of income distribution effects of international trade is the *specific factors model,* which allows for a distinction between general-purpose factors that can move between sectors and factors that are specific to particular uses. In this model, differences in resources can cause countries to have different relative supply curves, and thus cause international trade.

3. In the specific factors model, factors specific to export sectors in each country gain from trade, while factors specific to import-competing sectors lose. Mobile factors that can work in either sector may either gain or lose.

4. Trade nonetheless produces overall gains in the limited sense that those who gain could in principle compensate those who lose while still remaining better off than before.

5. Most economists do not regard the effects of international trade on income distribution as a good reason to limit this trade. In its distributional effects, trade is no different from many other forms of economic change, which are not normally regulated. Furthermore, economists would prefer to address the problem of income distribution directly, rather than by interfering with trade flows.

6. Nonetheless, in the actual politics of trade policy income distribution is of crucial importance. This is true in particular because those who lose from trade are usually a much more informed, cohesive, and organized group than those who gain.

Key Terms

budget constraint, p. 54

diminishing returns, p. 42

marginal product of labor, p. 41

mobile factor, p. 40

production function, p. 40

production possibilities frontier, p. 43

specific factor, p. 40

specific factors model, p. 40

Problems

1. In 1986, the price of oil on world markets dropped sharply. Since the United States is an oil-importing country, this was widely regarded as good for the U.S. economy. Yet in Texas and Louisiana 1986 was a year of economic decline. Why?

2. An economy can produce good 1 using labor and capital and good 2 using labor and land. The total supply of labor is 100 units. Given the supply of capital, the outputs of the two goods depends on labor input as follows:

Labor input to good 1	Output of good 1	Labor input to good 2	Output of good 2
0	0.0	0	0.0
10	25.1	10	39.8
20	38.1	20	52.5
30	48.6	30	61.8
40	57.7	40	69.3
50	66.0	50	75.8
60	73.6	60	81.5
70	80.7	70	86.7
80	87.4	80	91.4
90	93.9	90	95.9
100	100	100	100

   a. Graph the production functions for good 1 and good 2.
   b. Graph the production possibility frontier. Why is it curved?

3. The marginal product of labor curves corresponding to the production functions in problem 2 are as follows:

Workers employed	MPL in sector 1	MPL in sector 2
10	1.51	1.59
20	1.14	1.05
30	0.97	0.82
40	0.87	0.69
50	0.79	0.61
60	0.74	0.54
70	0.69	0.50
80	0.66	0.46
90	0.63	0.43
100	0.60	0.40

a. Suppose that the price of good 2 relative to that of good 1 is 2. Determine graphically the wage rate and the allocation of labor between the two sectors.

b. Using the graph drawn for problem 2, determine the output of each sector. Then confirm graphically that the slope of the production possibility frontier at that point equals the relative price.

c. Suppose that the relative price of good 2 falls to 1. Repeat (a) and (b).

d. Calculate the effects of the price change on the income of the specific factors in sectors 1 and 2.

4. In the text we examined the impacts of increases in the supply of capital and land. But what if the mobile factor, labor, increases in supply?

a. Analyze the qualitative effects of an increase in the supply of labor in the specific factors model, holding the prices of both goods constant.

b. Graph the effect on the equilibrium for the numerical example in problems 2 and 3, given a relative price of 1, when the labor force expands from 100 to 140.

Further Reading

Avinash Dixit and Victor Norman. *Theory of International Trade.* Cambridge: Cambridge University Press, 1980. The problem of establishing gains from trade when some people may be made worse off has been the subject of a long debate. Dixit and Norman show it is always possible in principle for a country's government to use taxes and subsidies to redistribute income in such a way that everyone is better off with free trade than with no trade.

Michael Mussa. "Tariffs and the Distribution of Income: The Importance of Factor Specificity, Substitutability, and Intensity in the Short and Long Run." *Journal of Political Economy* 82 (1974), pp. 1191–1204. An extension of the specific factors model that relates it to the factor proportions model of Chapter 4.

J. Peter Neary. "Short-Run Capital Specificity and the Pure Theory of International Trade." *Economic Journal* 88 (1978), pp. 488–510. A further treatment of the specific factors model that stresses how differing assumptions about mobility of factors between sectors affect the model's conclusions.

Mancur Olson. *The Logic of Collective Action.* Cambridge: Harvard University Press, 1965. A highly influential book that argues the proposition that in practice government policies favor small, concentrated groups over large ones.

David Ricardo. *The Principles of Political Economy and Taxation.* Homewood, IL: Irwin, 1963. While Ricardo's *Principles* emphasizes the national gains from trade at one point, elsewhere in his book the conflict of interest between landowners and capitalists is a central issue.

Appendix to Chapter 3

Further Details on Specific Factors

The specific factors model developed in this chapter is such a convenient tool of analysis that we take the time here to spell out some of its details more fully. We give a fuller treatment of two related issues: (1) the relationship between marginal and total product within each sector; (2) the income distribution effects of relative price changes.

MARGINAL AND TOTAL PRODUCT

In the text we illustrated the production function in manufacturing two different ways. In Figure 3-1 we showed total output as a function of labor input, holding capital constant. We then observed that the slope of that curve is the marginal product of labor and illustrated that marginal product in Figure 3-2. We now want to demonstrate that the total output is measured by the area under the marginal product curve. (Students who are familiar with calculus will find this obvious: Marginal product is the derivative of total, so total is the integral of marginal. Even for these students, however, an intuitive approach can be helpful.)

In Figure 3A-1 we show once again the marginal product curve in manufacturing. Suppose that we employ L_M person-hours. How can we show the total output of manufactures? Let's approximate this using the marginal product curve. First, let's ask what would happen if we used slightly fewer person-hours, say dL_M fewer. Then output would be less. The fall in output would be approximately

$$dL_M \times MPL_M,$$

that is, the reduction in the work force times the marginal product of labor at the initial level of employment. This reduction in output is represented by the area of the colored rectangle in Figure 3A-1. Now subtract another few person-hours; the output loss will be another rectangle. This time the rectangle will be taller, because the marginal product of labor rises as the quantity of labor falls. If we continue this process until all the labor is gone, our approximation of the total output loss will be the sum of all the rectangles shown in the figure. When no labor is employed, however, output will fall to zero. So we can approximate the total output of the manufacturing sector by the sum of the areas of all the rectangles under the marginal product curve.

This is, however, only an approximation, because we used the marginal product of only the first person-hour in each batch of labor removed. We can get a better approximation if we take smaller groups—the smaller the better. As the groups of labor removed get infinitesimally small, however, the rectangles get thinner and thinner, and we approximate ever more closely the total area under the marginal product curve. In the end, then, we find that the total output of manufactures produced with labor L_M is equal to the area under the marginal product of labor curve MPL_M up to L_M.

FIGURE 3A-1

Showing that Output Is Equal to the Area Under the Marginal Product Curve

By approximating the marginal product curve with a series of thin rectangles, one can show that the total output of manufactures is equal to the area under the curve.

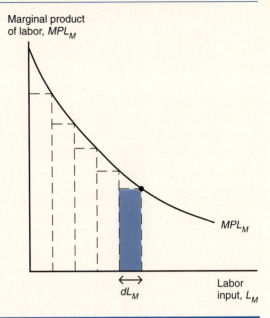

RELATIVE PRICES AND THE DISTRIBUTION OF INCOME

Figure 3A-2 uses the result we just found to show the distribution of income within the manufacturing sector for a given real wage. We know that employers will hire labor up to the point where the real wage in terms of manufactures, w/P_M, equals the marginal product. We can immediately read off the graph the total output to manufactures as the area under the marginal product curve. We can also read off the graph the part of manufacturing output that is paid out as wages, which is equal to the real wage times employment, and thus to the area of the rectangle shown. The part of the output that is kept by owners of capital, then, is the remainder. We can determine the distribution of food production between labor and landowners in the same way.

Suppose the relative price of manufactures now rises. We saw in Figure 3-7 that a rise in P_M/P_F lowers the real wage in terms of manufactures while raising it in terms of food. The effects of this on the income of capitalists and landowners can be seen in Figures 3A-3 and 3A-4. In the manufactures sector, the real wage is shown as falling from $(w/P_M)^1$ to $(w/P_M)^2$; as a result capitalists receive increased income. In the food sector, the real wage rises from $(w/P_F)^1$ to $(w/P_F)^2$, and landowners receive less income.

This effect on incomes is reinforced by the change in P_M/P_F itself. Owners of capital receive more income *in terms of manufactures;* their purchasing power is further increased by the rise in the price of manufactures relative to food. Landowners receive less income *in terms of food;* they are made still worse off because of the rise in the relative price of manufactures.

FIGURE 3A-2

The Distribution of Income Within the Manufacturing Sector

Labor income is equal to the real wage times employment. The rest of output accrues as income to the owners of capital.

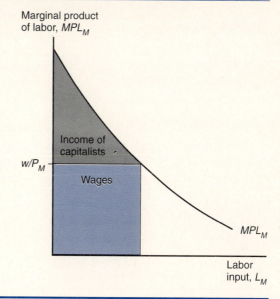

FIGURE 3A-3

A Rise in P_M Benefits the Owners of Capital

The real wage in terms of manufactures falls, leading to a rise in the income of capital owners.

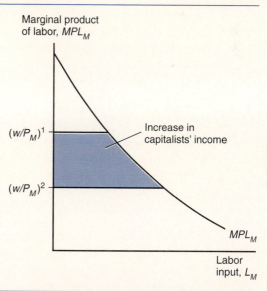

A Rise in P_M Hurts Landowners

The real wage in terms of food rises, reducing the income of land.

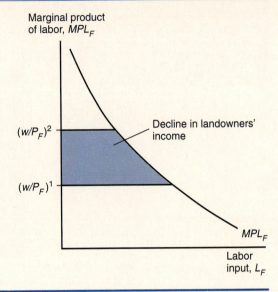

4 Resources and Trade: The Heckscher-Ohlin Model

If labor were the only factor of production, as the Ricardian model assumes, comparative advantage could arise only because of international differences in labor productivity. In the real world, however, while trade is partly explained by differences in labor productivity, it also reflects differences in countries' *resources*. Canada exports forest products to the United States not because its lumberjacks are more productive relative to their U.S. counterparts than other Canadians but because sparsely populated Canada has more forested land per capita than the United States. A realistic view of trade must allow for the importance not just of labor, but of other factors of production such as land, capital, and mineral resources.

To explain the role of resource differences in trade, this chapter examines a model in which resource differences are the *only* source of trade. This model shows that comparative advantage is influenced by the interaction between nations' resources (the relative **abundance** of factors of production) and the technology of production (which influences the relative **intensity** with which different factors of production are used in the production of different goods). The same idea was present in the specific factors model of Chapter 3, but the model we study in this chapter puts the interaction between abundance and intensity in sharper relief.

That international trade is largely driven by differences in countries' resources is one of the most influential theories in international economics. Developed by two Swedish economists, Eli Heckscher and Bertil Ohlin (Ohlin received the Nobel Prize in economics in 1977), the theory is often referred to as the **Heckscher-Ohlin theory.** Because the theory emphasizes the interplay between the proportions in which different factors of production are available in different countries and the proportions in which they are used in producing different goods, it is also referred to as the **factor-proportions theory.**

To develop the factor-proportions theory we begin by describing an economy that does not trade, then ask what happens when two such economies trade with each other. Since the factor-proportions theory is both an important theory and a controversial one, the chapter concludes with a discussion of the empirical evidence for and against the theory.

A MODEL OF A TWO-FACTOR ECONOMY

The simplest factor-proportions model is in many ways very similar to the specific factors model developed in Chapter 3. As in that model, it is assumed that each economy is able to produce two goods and that production of each good requires the use of two factors of production. In this case, however, we no longer assume that one of the factors used in each industry is specific to that industry. Instead, the *same* two factors are used in both sectors. This leads to a somewhat more difficult model, but also to some important new insights.

ASSUMPTIONS OF THE MODEL

The economy we are analyzing can produce two goods: cloth (measured in yards) and food (measured in calories). Production of these goods requires two inputs that are in limited supply: labor, which we measure in hours, and land, which we measure in acres. Let us define the following expressions:

$$a_{TC} = \text{acres of land used to produce one yard of cloth}$$

$$a_{LC} = \text{hours of labor used to produce one yard of cloth}$$

$$a_{TF} = \text{acres of land used to produce one calorie of food}$$

$$a_{LF} = \text{hours of labor used to produce one calorie of food}$$

$$L = \text{economy's supply of labor}$$

$$T = \text{economy's supply of land}$$

Notice that we speak in these definitions of the quantity of land or labor *used* to produce a given amount of food or cloth, rather than the amount *required* to produce that amount. The reason for this change from the Ricardian model is that in a two-factor economy there may be some room for choice in the use of inputs. A farmer, for example, may be able to grow more food per acre if he or she is willing to use more labor input to prepare the soil, weed, and so on. Thus the farmer may be able to choose to use less land and more labor per unit of output. In each sector, then, producers will face not fixed input requirements (as in the Ricardian model) but trade-offs like the one illustrated by curve *II* in Figure 4-1, which shows alternative input combinations that can be used to produce one calorie of food.

What input choice will producers actually make? It depends on the relative cost of land and labor. If land rents are high and wages low, farmers will choose to produce using relatively little land and a lot of labor; if rents are low and wages high, they will save on labor and use a lot of land. If w is the wage rate per hour of labor and r the cost of one acre

FIGURE 4-1

Input Possibilities in Food Production

A farmer can produce a calorie of food with less land if he or she uses more labor, and vice versa.

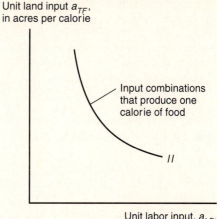

Unit land input a_{TF}, in acres per calorie

Input combinations that produce one calorie of food

II

Unit labor input, a_{LF}, in hours per calorie

of land, then the input choice will depend on the ratio of these two **factor prices,** *w/r*.[1] The relationship between factor prices and the ratio of land to labor use in production of food is shown in Figure 4-2 as the curve *FF*.

There is a corresponding relationship between *w/r* and the land-labor ratio in cloth production. This relationship is shown in Figure 4-2 as the curve *CC*. As drawn, *CC* lies to the left of *FF* indicating that at any given factor prices production of food will always use a higher ratio of land to labor than production of cloth. When this is true, we say that production of food is *land-intensive,* while production of cloth is *labor-intensive.* Notice that the definition of intensity depends on the ratio of land to labor used in production, not the ratio of land or labor to output. Thus a good cannot be both land- and labor-intensive.

FACTOR PRICES AND GOODS PRICES

Suppose for a moment that the economy produces both cloth and food. (This need not be the case if the economy engages in international trade, because it might specialize completely in producing one good or the other; but let us temporarily ignore this possibility.) Then competition among producers in each sector will ensure that the price of each good equals its cost of production. The cost of producing a good depends on factor prices: If the rental rate on land is higher, then other things equal the price of any good whose production involves land input will also have to be higher.

The importance of a particular factor price to the cost of producing a good depends, however, on how much of that factor the good's production involves. If cloth production makes use of very little land, then a rise in the price of land will not have much effect on

---

[1]The optimal choice of the land-labor ratio is explored at greater length in the appendix to this chapter.

FIGURE 4-2

Factor Prices and Input Choices

In each sector, the ratio of land to labor used in production depends on the cost of labor relative to the cost of land, *w/r*. The curve *FF* shows the land-labor ratio choices in food production, the curve *CC* the corresponding choices in cloth production. At any given wage-rental ratio, food production uses a higher land-labor ratio; when this is the case, we say that food production is *land-intensive* and that cloth production is *labor-intensive*.

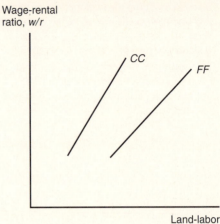

the price of cloth; whereas if food production uses a great deal of land, a rise in land prices will have a large effect on its price. We can therefore conclude that there is a one-to-one relationship between the ratio of the wage rate to the rental rate, *w/r*, and the ratio of the price of cloth to that of food, P_C/P_F. This relationship is illustrated by the upward-sloping curve *SS* in Figure 4-3.[2]

It is possible to put Figures 4-2 and 4-3 together. In Figure 4-4, the left panel is Figure 4-3 (of the *SS* curve) turned on its side, while the right panel reproduces Figure 4-2. By putting these two diagrams together, we see what may seem at first to be a surprising linkage of the prices of goods to the ratio of land to labor used in the production of each good. Suppose that the relative price of cloth is $(P_C/P_F)^1$ (left panel of Figure 4-4); if the economy produces both goods, the ratio of the wage rate to the rental rate on land must equal $(w/r)^1$. This ratio then implies that the ratios of land to labor employed in the production of cloth and food must be $(T_C/L_C)^1$ and $(T_F/L_F)^1$, respectively (right panel). If the relative price of cloth were to rise to the level indicated by $(P_C/P_F)^2$, the ratio of the wage rate to the rental rate on land would rise to $(w/r)^2$. Because land is now relatively cheaper the ratios of land to labor employed in the production of cloth and food would therefore rise to $(T_C/L_C)^2$ and $(T_F/L_F)^2$.

We can learn one more important lesson from this diagram. The left panel already tells us that an increase in the price of cloth relative to that of food will raise the income of workers relative to that of landowners. But it is possible to make a stronger statement:

---

[2]The relationship between goods prices and factor prices was clarified in a classic paper by Wolfgang Stolper and Paul Samuelson, "Protection and Real Wages," *Review of Economic Studies* 9 (1941), pp. 58–73, and is therefore known as the *Stolper-Samuelson effect.*

FIGURE 4-3

Factor Prices and Goods Prices

Because cloth production is labor-intensive while food production is land-intensive, there is a one-to-one relationship between the factor price ratio w/r and the relative price of cloth P_C/P_F; the higher the relative cost of labor, the higher must be the relative price of the labor-intensive good. This relationship is illustrated by the curve SS.

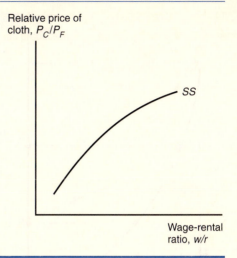

Relative price of cloth, P_C/P_F

SS

Wage-rental ratio, w/r

Such a change in relative prices will unambiguously raise the purchasing power of workers and lower the purchasing power of landowners, by raising real wages and lowering real rents in terms of *both* goods.

How do we know this? When P_C/P_F increases, the ratio of land to labor rises in both cloth and food production. But as we saw in Chapter 3, in a competitive economy factors of production are paid their marginal product—the real wage of workers in terms of cloth is equal to the marginal productivity of labor in cloth production, and so on. When the ratio of land to labor rises in producing either good, the marginal product of labor in terms of that good increases—so workers find their real wage higher in terms of both goods. On the other hand, the marginal product of land falls in both industries, so landowners find their real income lower in terms of both goods.

In this model, then, as in the specific factors model, changes in relative prices have strong effects on income distribution. Not only does a change in goods prices change the distribution of income; it always changes it so much that owners of one factor of production gain while owners of the other are made worse off.

RESOURCES AND OUTPUT

We can now complete the description of a two-factor economy by describing the relationship between goods prices, factor supplies, and output.

Suppose that we take the relative price of cloth as given. We know from Figure 4-4 that this determines the wage-rental ratio w/r, and thus the ratio of land to labor used in the production of both cloth and food. But the economy must fully employ its supplies of labor and land. It is this last condition that determines the allocation of resources between the two industries and, therefore, the economy's output.

be relatively better at producing food than an economy with a low ratio of land to labor. *Generally, an economy will tend to be relatively effective at producing goods that are intensive in the factors with which the country is relatively well-endowed.*

EFFECTS OF INTERNATIONAL TRADE BETWEEN TWO-FACTOR ECONOMIES

Having outlined the production structure of a two-factor economy, we can now look at what happens when two such economies, Home and Foreign, trade. As always, Home and Foreign are similar along many dimensions. They have the same tastes and therefore have identical relative demands for food and cloth when faced with the same relative price of the two goods. They also have the same technology: A given amount of land and labor yields the same output of either cloth or food in the two countries. The only difference between the countries is in their resources: Home has a higher ratio of labor to land than Foreign does.

RELATIVE PRICES AND THE PATTERN OF TRADE

Since Home has a higher ratio of labor to land than Foreign, Home is *labor-abundant* and Foreign is *land-abundant*. Note that abundance is defined in terms of a ratio and not in absolute quantities. If America has 80 million workers and 200 million acres (a labor-to-land ratio of one-to-two-and-a-half), while Britain has 20 million workers and 20 million acres (a labor-to-land ratio of one-to-one) we consider Britain to be labor-abundant even though it has less total labor than America. "Abundance" is always defined in relative terms, by comparing the ratio of labor to land in the two countries, so that no country is abundant in everything.

Since cloth is the labor-intensive good, Home's production possibility frontier relative to Foreign's is shifted out more in the direction of cloth than in the direction of food. Thus, other things equal, Home tends to produce a higher ratio of cloth to food.

Because trade leads to a convergence of relative prices, one of the other things that will be equal is the price of cloth relative to food. Because the countries differ in their factor abundances, however, for any given ratio of the price of cloth to that of food Home will produce a higher ratio of cloth to food than Foreign will: Home will have a larger *relative supply* of cloth. Home's relative supply curve, then, lies to the right of Foreign's.

The relative supply schedules of Home (*RS*) and Foreign (*RS**) are illustrated in Figure 4-8. The relative demand curve, which we have assumed to be the same for both countries, is shown as *RD*. If there were no international trade, the equilibrium for Home would be at point 1, the equilibrium for Foreign at point 3. That is, in the absence of trade the relative price of cloth would be lower in Home than in Foreign.

When Home and Foreign trade with each other, their relative prices converge. The relative price of cloth rises in Home and declines in Foreign, and a new world relative price of cloth is established at a point somewhere between the pretrade relative prices, say at point 2. In Home, the rise in the relative price of cloth leads to a rise in the production of cloth and a decline in relative consumption, so Home becomes an exporter of cloth and an importer of food. Conversely, the decline in the relative price of cloth in Foreign leads it to become an importer of cloth and an exporter of food.

To sum up what we have learned about the pattern of trade: Home has a higher ratio of labor to land than Foreign; that is, Home is abundant in labor and Foreign is abundant in

FIGURE 4-8

Trade Leads to a Convergence of Relative Prices

In the absence of trade, Home's equilibrium would be at point 1, where domestic relative supply *RS* intersects the relative demand curve *RD*. Similarly, Foreign's equilibrium would be at point 3. Trade leads to a world relative price that lies between the pretrade prices, e.g., at point 2.

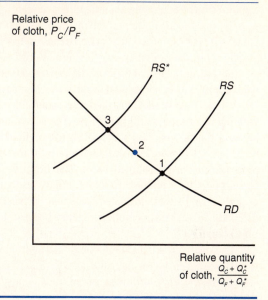

Relative price of cloth, P_C/P_F

Relative quantity of cloth, $\dfrac{Q_C + Q_C^*}{Q_F + Q_F^*}$

land. Cloth production uses a higher ratio of labor to land in its production than food; that is, cloth is labor-intensive and food is land-intensive. Home, the labor-abundant country, exports cloth, the labor-intensive good; Foreign, the land-abundant country, exports food, the land-intensive good. The general statement of the result is: *Countries tend to export goods whose production is intensive in factors with which they are abundantly endowed.*

TRADE AND THE DISTRIBUTION OF INCOME

Trade produces a convergence of relative prices. Changes in relative prices, in turn, have strong effects on the relative earnings of labor and land. A rise in the price of cloth raises the purchasing power of labor in terms of both goods while lowering the purchasing power of land in terms of both goods. A rise in the price of food has the reverse effect. Thus international trade has a powerful effect on income distribution. In Home, where the relative price of cloth rises, people who get their income from labor gain from trade but those who derive their income from land are made worse off. In Foreign, where the relative price of cloth falls, the opposite happens: Laborers are made worse off and landowners are made better off.

The resource of which a country has a relatively large supply (labor in Home, land in Foreign) is the **abundant factor** in that country, and the resource of which it has a relatively small supply (land in Home, labor in Foreign) is the **scarce factor.** The general conclusion about the income distribution effects of international trade is: *Owners of a country's abundant factors gain from trade, but owners of a country's scarce factors lose.*

This conclusion is similar to the one reached in our analysis of the case of specific factors. There we found that factors of production that are "stuck" in an import-competing industry lose from the opening of trade. Here we find that factors of production that are used intensively by the import-competing industry are hurt by the opening of trade. As a practical matter, however, there is an important difference between these two views. The specificity of factors to particular industries is often only a temporary problem: Garment makers cannot become computer manufacturers overnight, but given time the U.S. economy can shift its manufacturing employment from declining sectors to expanding ones. Thus income distribution effects that arise because labor and other factors of production are immobile represent a temporary, transitional problem (which is not to say that such effects are not painful to those who lose). In contrast, effects of trade on the distribution of income among land, labor, and capital are more or less permanent.

We will see shortly that the trade pattern of the United States suggests that compared with the rest of the world the United States is abundantly endowed with highly skilled labor and that low-skilled labor is correspondingly scarce. This means that international trade tends to make low-skilled workers in the United States worse off—not just temporarily, but on a sustained basis. The negative effect of trade on low-skilled workers poses a persistent political problem. Industries that use low-skilled labor intensively, such as apparel and shoes, consistently demand protection from foreign competition, and their demands attract considerable sympathy because low-skilled workers are relatively badly off to begin with.

The distinction between income distribution effects due to immobility and those due to differences in factor intensity also reveals that there is frequently a conflict between short-term and long-term interests in trade. Consider a highly skilled U.S. worker who is employed in an industry that is intensive in low-skilled labor. Her short-term interest is to restrict international trade, because she cannot instantly shift jobs. Over the long term, however, she would be better off with free trade, which will raise the income of skilled workers generally.

FACTOR PRICE EQUALIZATION

In the absence of trade, labor would earn less in Home than in Foreign, and land would earn more. Without trade, labor-abundant Home would have a lower relative price of cloth than land-abundant Foreign, and the difference in relative prices of *goods* implies an even larger difference in the relative prices of *factors*.

When Home and Foreign trade, the relative prices of goods converge. This convergence, in turn, causes convergence of the relative prices of land and labor. Thus there is clearly a tendency toward **equalization of factor prices.** How far does this tendency go?

The surprising answer is that in the model the tendency goes all the way. International trade leads to complete equalization of factor prices. Although Home has a higher ratio of labor to land than Foreign, once they trade with each other the wage rate and the rent on land are the same in both countries. To see this, refer back to Figure 4-3, which shows that given the prices of cloth and food we can determine the wage rate and the rental rate without reference to the supplies of land and labor. If Home and Foreign face the same relative prices of cloth and food, they will also have the same factor prices.

To understand how this equalization occurs, we have to realize that when Home and Foreign trade with each other more is happening than a simple exchange of goods. In an indirect way the two countries are in effect trading factors of production. Home lets Foreign have the use of some of its abundant labor, not by selling the labor directly but by trading goods produced with a high ratio of labor to land for goods produced with a low labor-land ratio. The goods that Home sells require more labor to produce than the goods it receives in return; that is, more labor is *embodied* in Home's exports than in its imports. Thus Home exports its labor, embodied in its labor-intensive exports. Conversely, Foreign's exports embody more land than its imports, thus Foreign is indirectly exporting its land. When viewed this way, it is not surprising that trade leads to equalization of the two countries' factor prices.

Although this view of trade is simple and appealing, there is a major problem: In the real world factor prices are *not* equalized. For example, there is an extremely wide range of wage rates across countries (Table 4-1). While some of these differences may reflect differences in the quality of labor, they are too wide to be explained away on this basis alone.

To understand why the model doesn't give us an accurate prediction, we need to look at its assumptions. Three assumptions crucial to the prediction of factor price equalization are in reality certainly untrue. These are the assumptions that (1) both countries produce both goods; (2) technologies are the same; and (3) trade actually equalizes the prices of goods in the two countries.

     1. To derive the wage and rental rates from the prices of cloth and food in Figure 4-3, we assumed that the country produced both goods. This need not, however, be the case. A country with a very high ratio of labor to land might produce only cloth, while a country with a very high ratio of land to labor might produce only food. This implies that factor price equalization occurs only if the countries involved are sufficiently similar in their relative factor endowments. (A more thorough discussion of this point is given in the appendix to this chapter.) Thus, factor prices need not be equalized between countries with radically different ratios of capital to labor or of skilled to unskilled labor.

     2. The proposition that trade equalizes factor prices will not hold if countries have different technologies of production. For example, a country with superior technology might have both a higher wage rate and a higher rental rate than a country with an inferior technology. As described later in this chapter, recent work suggests that it is essential to allow for such differences in technology to reconcile the factor proportions model with actual data on world trade.

     3. Finally, the proposition of complete factor price equalization depends on complete convergence of the prices of goods. In the real world, prices of goods are not

TABLE 4-1	

Comparative International Wage Rates (United States = 100)

Country	Hourly wage rate in 1992
United States	100
Germany	160
Japan	100
Spain	83
Greece	44
Hong Kong	24
Taiwan	32
Korea	30
Mexico	15

Source: Statistical Abstract of the United States, 1994.

fully equalized by international trade. This lack of convergence is due to both natural barriers (such as transportation costs) and barriers to trade such as tariffs, import quotas, and other restrictions.

CASE STUDY

NORTH-SOUTH TRADE AND INCOME INEQUALITY

Between the late 1970s and the early 1990s there was a sharp increase in the inequality of wages in the United States. For example, while the real wage of male workers at the 90th percentile (i.e., those earning more than the bottom 90 percent but less than the top 10 percent) rose 15 percent between 1970 and 1989, that of workers at the 10th percentile fell by 25 percent over the same period. The growing inequality of wages in the United States has arguably worsened the country's social problems: Falling wages at the bottom have made it more difficult for families to climb out of poverty, while the contrast between stagnating incomes for many families and rapidly rising incomes at the top may have contributed to a general social and political malaise.

Why has wage inequality increased? Many observers attribute the change to the growth of world trade and in particular to the growing exports of manufactured goods from newly industrializing economies (NIEs), such as South Korea and China. Until the 1970s trade between advanced industrial nations and less-developed economies—often referred to as "North-South" trade because most advanced nations are still in the temperate zone of the Northern Hemisphere—consisted overwhelmingly of an exchange of Northern manufactures for Southern raw materials and agricultural goods, such as oil and coffee. From 1970 onward, however, former raw material exporters increasingly began to sell manufactured goods to high-wage countries like the United States. As Table 4-2 shows, manufactured exports from newly industrializing countries rose from insignificance in 1970 to almost 2 percent of the incomes of advanced nations by the early 1990s. While NIEs also provided a rapidly growing market for exports from the high-wage nations, the exports of the newly industrializing economies obviously differed greatly in factor intensity from their imports. Overwhelmingly, NIE exports to advanced nations consisted of clothing, shoes, and other relatively unsophisti-

TABLE 4-2

Exports of Manufactured Goods from Developing Countries (Percent of Income in Destination)

	All industrial economies	European Union	United States
1970	0.24	0.22	0.28
1990	1.61	1.30	1.91

Source: Exports from UNCTAD, *Handbook of Trade and Development Statistics;* GDP from OECD *National Accounts Statistics.*

cated products whose production is intensive in unskilled labor, while advanced-country exports to the NIEs consisted of capital- or skill-intensive goods such as chemicals and aircraft.

To many observers the conclusion seemed straightforward: What was happening was a move toward factor price equalization. Trade between advanced countries that are abundant in capital and skill and NIEs with their abundant supply of unskilled labor was raising the wages of highly skilled workers and lowering the wages of less-skilled workers in the skill- and capital-abundant countries, just as the factor proportions model predicts.

This is an argument with much more than purely academic significance. If one regards the growing inequality of income in advanced nations as a serious problem, as many people do, and if one also believes that growing world trade is the main cause of that problem, it becomes difficult to maintain the traditional support of economists for free trade. (As we pointed out in Chapter 3, in principle taxes and government payments can offset the effect of trade on income distribution, but one may argue that this is unlikely to happen in practice.) Some influential commentators have argued that advanced nations will have to restrict their trade with low-wage countries if they want to remain basically middle-class societies.

While some economists believe that growing trade with low-wage countries has been the main cause of growing inequality of income in the United States, however, most empirical workers believed at the time of writing that international trade has been at most a contributing factor to that growth, and that the main causes lie elsewhere.[5] This skepticism rested on four main observations.

First, although advanced countries were exporting capital-intensive goods and importing labor-intensive goods, as of the early 1990s there had been virtually no change in the distribution of income between capital and labor; the share of compensation (wages plus benefits) in U.S. national income was the same (73 percent) in 1993 as it had been in 1973. So at most the trade story could apply to a shift in the distribution of income between skilled and unskilled workers, rather than between workers and capital.

Second, the factor proportions model says that international trade affects the income distribution via a change in relative goods prices. So if international trade was the main driving force behind growing income inequality, there ought to be clear evidence of a rise in the price of skill-intensive products compared with those of unskilled-labor-intensive goods. Studies of international price data, however, failed to find clear evidence of such a change in relative prices.

Third, the model predicts that relative factor prices should converge: If wages of skilled workers are rising and those of unskilled workers falling in the skill-abundant country, the reverse should be happening in the labor-abundant

[5]Among the important entries in the discussion of the impact of trade on income distribution have been Robert Lawrence and Matthew Slaughter, "Trade and U.S. Wages: Giant Sucking Sound or Small Hiccup?" *Brookings Papers on Economic Activity* 1:1993; Jeffrey Sachs and Howard Shatz, "Trade and Jobs in U.S. Manufacturing," *Brookings Papers on Economic Activity* 1:1994; and Adrian Wood, *North-South Trade, Employment, and Income Inequality,* Oxford: Clarendon, 1994. For a survey of this debate and related issues, see Robert Lawrence, *Single World, Divided Nations: Globalization and OECD Labor Markets,* Paris: OECD, 1995.

country. While data on wages and income distribution in the NIEs are poor, casual observation suggested that in many countries, notably in China, the reverse was true: Income inequality was increasing at least as rapidly in the NIEs as in the advanced countries, and skilled workers were doing very well.

Fourth, although trade between advanced countries and NIEs has grown rapidly, it still constitutes only a small percentage of total spending in the advanced nations. As a result, estimates of the "factor content" of this trade—the skilled labor exported, in effect, by advanced countries embodied in skill-intensive exports, and the unskilled labor, in effect, imported in labor-intensive exports—are still only a small fraction of the total supplies of skilled and unskilled labor. This suggests that these trade flows cannot have had a very large impact on income distribution.

What, then, *is* responsible for the growing gap between skilled and unskilled workers in the United States? The view of the majority is that the villain is not trade but technology, which has devalued less-skilled work. The view that trade is in fact the main explanation still has a number of adherents, however.

EMPIRICAL EVIDENCE ON THE HECKSCHER-OHLIN MODEL

Since the factor-proportions theory of trade is one of the most influential ideas in international economics, it has been the subject of extensive empirical testing.

TESTING THE HECKSCHER-OHLIN MODEL

Tests on U.S. Data.   Until recently, and to some extent even now, the United States has been a special case among countries. The United States was until a few years ago much wealthier than other countries, and U.S. workers visibly worked with more capital per person than their counterparts in other countries. Even now, although some Western European countries and Japan have caught up, the United States continues to be high on the scale of countries as ranked by capital-labor ratios.

One would expect, then, that the United States would be an exporter of capital-intensive goods and an importer of labor-intensive goods. Surprisingly, however, this was not the case in the 25 years after World War II. In a famous study published in 1953, the economist Wassily Leontief (winner of the Nobel Prize in 1973) found that U.S. exports were less capital-intensive than U.S. imports.[6] This result is known as the **Leontief paradox.** It is the single biggest piece of evidence against the factor-proportions theory.

Table 4-3 illustrates the Leontief paradox as well as other information about U.S. trade patterns. We compare the factors of production used to produce $1 million worth of 1962 U.S. exports with those used to produce the same value of 1962 U.S. imports. As the first two lines in the table show, Leontief's paradox was still present in that year: U.S. ex-

---

[6]See Leontief, "Domestic Production and Foreign Trade: The American Capital Position Re-Examined," *Proceedings of the American Philosophical Society* 97 (1953), pp. 331–349.

Factor Content of U.S. Exports and Imports for 1962

	Imports	Exports
Capital per million dollars	$2,132,000	$1,876,000
Labor (person-years) per million dollars	119	131
Capital-labor ratio (dollars per worker)	$17,916	$14,321
Average years of education per worker	9.9	10.1
Proportion of engineers and scientists in work force	0.0189	0.0255

Source: Robert Baldwin, "Determinants of the Commodity Structure of U.S. Trade," *American Economic Review* 61 (March 1971), pp. 126–145.

ports were produced with a lower ratio of capital to labor than U.S. imports. As the rest of the table shows, however, other comparisons of imports and exports are more in line with what one might expect. The U.S. exported products that were more *skilled* labor-intensive than its imports as measured by average years of education. We also tended to export products that were "technology-intensive," requiring more scientists and engineers per unit of sales. These observations are consistent with the position of the United States as a high-skill country, with a comparative advantage in sophisticated products.

Why, then, do we observe the Leontief paradox? No one is quite sure. A plausible explanation, however, might be the following: The United States has a special advantage in producing new products or goods made with innovative technologies such as aircraft and sophisticated computer chips. Such products may well be *less* capital-intensive than products whose technology has had time to mature and become suitable for mass production techniques. Thus the United States may be exporting goods that heavily use skilled labor and innovative entrepreneurship, while importing heavy manufactures (such as automobiles) that use large amounts of capital.[7]

Tests on Global Data.   More recently, economists have attempted to test the Heckscher-Ohlin model using data for a large number of countries. An important study by Harry P. Bowen, Edward E. Leamer, and Leo Sveikauskas[8] is based on the idea, described earlier, that trading goods is actually an indirect way of trading factors of production. Thus if we were to calculate the factors of production embodied in a country's exports and imports, we should find that a country is a net exporter of the factors of production with which it is relatively abundantly endowed, a net importer of those with which it is relatively poorly endowed.

Table 4-4 shows one of Bowen et al.'s key tests. For a sample of 27 countries and 12 factors of production, the authors calculated the ratio of each country's endowment of each factor to the world supply. They then compared these ratios with each country's share of world income. If the factor-proportions theory was right, a country would always export

---

[7]Recent studies point to the disappearance of the Leontief paradox by the early 1970s. For example, see Robert M. Stern and Keith E. Maskus, "Determinants of the Structure of U.S. Foreign Trade, 1958–76," *Journal of International Economics* 11 (May 1981), pp. 207–224. These studies show, however, the continuing importance of *human* capital in explaining U.S. exports.

[8]See Bowen, Leamer, and Sveikauskas, "Multicountry, Multifactor Tests of the Factor Abundance Theory," *American Economic Review* 77 (December 1987), pp. 791–809.

TABLE 4-4

Testing the Heckscher-Ohlin Model

Factor of production	Predictive success*
Capital	0.52
Labor	0.67
Professional workers	0.78
Managerial workers	0.22
Clerical workers	0.59
Sales workers	0.67
Service workers	0.67
Agricultural workers	0.63
Production workers	0.70
Arable land	0.70
Pasture land	0.52
Forest	0.70

*Fraction of countries for which net exports of factor runs in predicted direction.
Source: Harry P. Bowen, Edward E. Leamer, and Leo Sveikauskas, "Multicountry, Multifactor Tests of the Factor Abundance Theory," *American Economic Review* 77 (December 1987), pp. 791–809.

factors for which the factor share exceeded the income share, import factors for which it was less. In fact, for two-thirds of the factors of production, trade ran in the predicted direction less than 70 percent of the time. This result confirms the Leontief paradox on a broader level: Trade often does not run in the direction that the Heckscher-Ohlin theory predicts.

Tests on North-South Trade.   Although the overall pattern of international trade does not seem to be very well accounted for by a pure Heckscher-Ohlin model, North-South trade in manufactures seems to fit the theory much better (as our case study on North-South trade and income distribution already suggested). Consider, for example, Table 4-5, which shows some elements of the trade between the United States and South Korea.

TABLE 4-5

Trade Between the United States and South Korea, 1992 (million dollars)

Type of product	U.S. exports to South Korea	U.S. imports from South Korea
Chemicals, plastics, pharmaceuticals	1340	105
Power-generating equipment	705	93
Professional and scientific instruments	512	96
Transport equipment other than road vehicles (mainly aircraft)	1531	78
Clothing and shoes	11	4203

Source: Statistical Abstract of the United States, 1994.

Clearly the goods that the United States exports to South Korea are very different from those it imports in return! And it is also clear that the U.S. exports tend to be sophisticated, skill-intensive products like scientific instruments, while South Korean exports are still largely simple products like shoes. One would therefore expect that the predictions of the Heckscher-Ohlin model might look considerably better when applied to North-South trade than they do for overall international trade. And this turns out to be true in most studies.[9] These findings do not, however, contradict the observation that overall the Heckscher-Ohlin model does not seem to work very well, because North-South trade in manufactures accounts for only about 10 percent of total world trade.

IMPLICATIONS OF THE TESTS

The mixed results of tests of the factor-proportions theory place international economists in a difficult position. We saw in Chapter 2 that empirical evidence broadly supports the Ricardian model's prediction that countries will export goods in which their labor is especially productive. Most international economists, however, regard the Ricardian model as too limited to serve as their basic model of international trade. By contrast, the Heckscher-Ohlin model has long occupied a central place in trade theory, because it allows a simultaneous treatment of issues of income distribution and the pattern of trade. So the model that predicts trade best is too limiting for other purposes, while there is by now strong evidence against the pure Heckscher-Ohlin model.

Most trade theorists now believe that to explain both the pattern of international trade and the large differences in wage rates among nations it is necessary to drop the Heckscher-Ohlin assumption that countries share the same technologies. Instead, one must allow for the possibility that, say, the United States simply can produce more than Bangladesh from any given set of inputs.

Recent work suggests that one goes a long way toward resolving the difficulties with the Heckscher-Ohlin model by supposing that technological differences take the form of "factor augmentation"—that because of differences in technology, one U.S. worker is the equivalent of one-and-a-half British workers, five Portuguese workers, and so on.[10] The way such calculations work is as follows. First, one supposes that factor prices really are equalized—that the fact that Mexican workers receive only 15 percent of the wage of U.S. workers means that a Mexican worker is the equivalent of only 0.15 U.S. workers. One then uses this assumption to adjust estimated factor supplies. For example, Mexico has about 30 million workers, but using the 15 percent number we would estimate that Mexico has only 4.5 million "worker-equivalents," using U.S. workers as a standard. One makes similar adjustments for capital, land, and other factors. Finally, one uses these adjusted factor supplies to carry out the kind of tests described in Table 4-4. Preliminary work suggests that this adjusted model works much better than a model that assumes no technological differences among countries. The problem with this adjustment to the model is that these international differences in the productivity of resources are left unexplained.

---

[9]See Adrian Wood, "Give Heckscher and Ohlin a Chance!" *Weltwirtschaftliches Archiv* 130 (January 1994), pp. 20–49.

[10]See Daniel Trefler, "International Factor Price Differences: Leontief Was Right!" *Journal of Political Economy* 101 (December 1993), pp. 961–987.

While the Heckscher-Ohlin model has been less successful at explaining the actual patterns of international trade than one might hope, it remains vital for understanding the *effects* of trade, especially its effects on the distribution of income. Indeed, the growth of North-South trade in manufactures—a trade in which the factor intensity of the North's imports is very different from that of its exports—has brought the factor proportions approach into the center of practical debates over international trade policy.

Summary

1. To understand the role of resources in trade we develop a model in which two goods are produced using two factors of production. The two goods differ in their *factor intensity,* that is, at any given wage-rental ratio, production of one of the goods will use a higher ratio of land to labor than production of the other.

2. As long as a country produces both goods, there is a one-to-one relationship between the relative prices of *goods* and the relative prices of *factors* used to produce the goods. A rise in the relative price of the labor-intensive good will shift the distribution of income in favor of labor, and will do so very strongly: The real wage of labor will rise in terms of both goods, while the real income of landowners will fall in terms of both goods.

3. An increase in the supply of one factor of production expands production possibilities, but in a strongly *biased* way: At unchanged relative goods prices, the output of the good intensive in that factor rises while the output of the other good actually falls.

4. A country that has a large supply of one resource relative to its supply of other resources is *abundant* in that resource. A country will tend to produce relatively more of goods that use its abundant resources intensively. The result is the basic Heckscher-Ohlin theory of trade: Countries tend to export goods that are intensive in the factors with which they are abundantly supplied.

5. Because changes in relative prices of goods have very strong effects on the relative earnings of resources, and because trade changes relative prices, international trade has strong income distribution effects. The owners of a country's abundant factors gain from trade, but the owners of scarce factors lose.

6. In an idealized model international trade would actually lead to equalization of the prices of factors such as labor and capital between countries. In reality, complete *factor price equalization* is not observed because of wide differences in resources, barriers to trade, and international differences in technology.

7. Empirical evidence is mixed on the Heckscher-Ohlin model, but most researchers do not believe that differences in resources alone can explain the pattern of world trade or world factor prices. Instead, it seems to be necessary to allow for substantial international differences in technology. Nonetheless, the Heckscher-Ohlin model is extremely useful, especially as a way to analyze the effects of trade on income distribution.

Key Terms

abundant factor, p. 77

biased expansion of production
possibilities, p. 75

equalization of factor prices, p. 78

factor abundance, p. 67

factor intensity, p. 67

factor prices, p. 69

factor proportions theory, p. 68

Heckscher-Ohlin theory, p. 67

Leontief paradox, p. 82

scarce factor, p. 77

Problems

1. In the United States where land is cheap, the ratio of land to labor used in cattle rais-ing is higher than that of land used in wheat growing. But in more crowded coun-tries, where land is expensive and labor is cheap, it is common to raise cows by us-ing less land and more labor than Americans use to grow wheat. Can we still say that raising cattle is land intensive compared with farming wheat? Why or why not?

2. Suppose that at current factor prices cloth is produced using 20 hours of labor for each acre of land, and food is produced using only 5 hours of labor per acre of land.
   a. Suppose that the economy's total resources are 600 hours of labor and 60 acres of land. Using a diagram determine the allocation of resources.
   b. Now suppose that the labor supply increases first to 800, then 1000, then 1200 hours. Using a diagram like Figure 4-6, trace out the changing allocation of resources.
   c. What would happen if the labor supply were to increase even further?

3. "The world's poorest countries cannot find anything to export. There is no re-source that is abundant—certainly not capital nor land, and in small poor nations not even labor is abundant." Discuss.

4. The U.S. labor movement—which mostly represents blue-collar workers rather than professionals and highly educated workers—has traditionally favored limits on imports from less-affluent countries. Is this a shortsighted policy or a rational one in view of the interests of union members? How does the answer depend on the model of trade?

5. There is substantial inequality of wage levels between regions within the United States. For example, wages of manufacturing workers in equivalent jobs are about 20 percent lower in the Southeast than they are in the Far West. Which of the explanations of failure of factor price equalization might account for this? How is this case different from the divergence of wages between the United States and Mexico (which is geographically closer to both the U.S. Southeast and the Far West than the Southeast and Far West are to each other)?

6. Explain why the Leontief paradox and the more recent Bowen, Leamer, and Sveikauskas results reported in the text contradict the factor-proportions theory.

7. In the discussion of empirical results on the Heckscher-Ohlin model, we noted that recent work suggests that the efficiency of factors of production seems to differ in-ternationally. Explain how this would affect the concept of factor price equalization.

Finally, now, consider the effects of a rise in the price of cloth on the wage-rental ratio. If the price of cloth rises, it is necessary to produce fewer yards of cloth in order to have one dollar's worth. Thus the isoquant corresponding to a dollar's worth of cloth shift inward. In Figure 4A-4, the original isoquant is shown as CC^1, the new isoquant as CC^2.

Once again we must draw a line that is just tangent to both isoquants; the slope of that line is minus the wage-rental ratio. It is immediately apparent from the increased steepness of the isocost line (slope $= -(w/r)^2$) that the new w/r is higher than the previous one: A higher relative price of cloth implies a higher wage-rental ratio.

FIGURE 4A-4

A Rise in the Price of Cloth

If the price of cloth rises, a smaller output is now worth one dollar; so CC^1 is replaced by CC^2. The implied wage-rental ratio must therefore rise from $(w/r)^1$ to $(w/r)^2$.

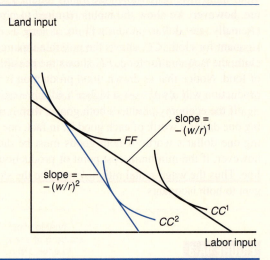

The Standard Trade Model

Previous chapters developed three different models of international trade, each of which makes different assumptions about the determinants of production possibilities. To bring out important points, each of these models leaves out aspects of reality that the other stress. These models are:

- *The Ricardian model.* Production possibilities are determined by the allocation of a single resource, labor, between sectors. This model conveys the essential idea of comparative advantage but does not allow us to talk about the distribution of income.
- *The specific factors model.* While labor can move freely between sectors, there are other factors specific to particular industries. This model is ideal for understanding income distribution but awkward for discussing the pattern of trade.
- *The Heckscher-Ohlin model.* Multiple factors of production can move between sectors. This is a harder model to work with than the first two but conveys a deeper understanding of how resources may drive trade patterns.

When we analyze real problems, we want to base our insights on a mixture of the models. For example, in the 1990s one of the central changes in world trade was the rapid growth in exports from newly industrializing economies. These countries experienced rapid productivity growth; to discuss the implications of this productivity growth we may want to apply the Ricardian model of Chapter 2. The changing pattern of trade has differential effects on different groups in the United States; to understand the effects of increased Pacific trade for U.S. income distribution, we may want to apply the specific factors model of Chapter 3. Finally, over time the resources of the newly industrializing nations have changed, as they accumulate capital and their labor grows more educated, while unskilled labor becomes scarcer. To understand the implications of this shift, we may wish to turn to the Heckscher-Ohlin model of Chapter 4.

In spite of the differences in their details, our models share a number of features.

1. The productive capacity of an economy can be summarized by its production possibility frontier, and differences in these frontiers give rise to trade.
2. Production possibilities determine a country's relative supply schedule.
3. World equilibrium is determined by world relative demand and a *world* relative supply schedule that lies between the national relative supply schedules.

Because of these common features, the models we have studied may be viewed as special cases of a more general model of a trading world economy. There are many important issues in international economics whose analysis can be conducted in terms of this general model, with only the details depending on which special model you choose. These issues include the effects of shifts in world supply resulting from economic growth; shifts in world demand resulting from foreign aid, war reparations, and other international transfers of income; and simultaneous shifts in supply and demand resulting from tariffs and export subsidies.

This chapter stresses those insights from international trade theory that are not strongly dependent on the details of the economy's supply side. We develop a standard model of a trading world economy of which the models of Chapters 2, 3, and 4 can be regarded as special cases and use this model to ask how a variety of changes in underlying parameters affect the world economy.

A STANDARD MODEL OF A TRADING ECONOMY

The **standard trade model** is built on four key relationships: (1) the relationship between the production possibility frontier and the relative supply curve; (2) the relationship between relative prices and relative demand; (3) the determination of world equilibrium by world relative supply and world relative demand; and (4) the effect of the **terms of trade**—the price of a country's exports divided by the price of its imports—on a nation's welfare.

PRODUCTION POSSIBILITIES AND RELATIVE SUPPLY

For the purposes of our standard model we assume that each country produces two goods, food (F) and cloth (C), and that each country's production possibility frontier is a smooth curve like that illustrated by TT in Figure 5-1.[1]

The point on its production possibility frontier at which an economy actually produces depends on the price of cloth relative to food, P_C/P_F. It is a basic proposition of microeconomics that a market economy that is not distorted by monopoly or other market failures is

---

[1]We have seen that when there is only one factor of production, as in Chapter 2, the production possibility frontier is a straight line. For most models, however, it will be a smooth curve, and the Ricardian result can be viewed as an extreme case.

FIGURE 5-1

Relative Prices Determine the Economy's Output

An economy whose production possibility frontier is TT will produce at Q, which is on the highest possible isovalue line.

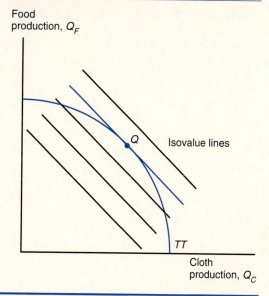

Food production, Q_F

Q

Isovalue lines

TT

Cloth production, Q_C

efficient in production, that is, maximizes the value of output at given market prices, $P_C Q_C + P_F Q_F$.

We can indicate the market value of output by drawing a number of **isovalue lines**—that is, lines along which the value of output is constant. Each of these lines is defined by an equation of the form $P_C Q_C + P_F Q_F = V$, or by rearranging, $Q_F = V/P_F - (P_C/P_F)Q_C$, where V is the value of output. The higher V is, the farther out an isovalue line lies; thus isovalue lines farther from the origin correspond to higher values of output. The slope of an isovalue line is minus the relative price of cloth. The economy will produce the highest value of output it can, which can be achieved by producing at point Q, where TT is just tangent to an isovalue line.[2]

Now suppose that P_C/P_F were to rise. Then the isovalue lines would be steeper than before. In Figure 5-2 the highest isovalue line the economy could reach before the change in P_C/P_F is shown as VV^1; the highest line after the price change is VV^2, the point at which the economy produces shifts from Q^1 to Q^2. Thus, as we might expect, a rise in the relative price of cloth leads the economy to produce more cloth and less food. The relative supply of cloth will therefore rise when the relative price of cloth rises.

---

[2]In our analysis of the specific factors model in Chapter 3 we showed explicitly that the economy always produces at a point on its production possibility curve where the slope of that curve equals the ratio of the two goods prices—that is, where the price line is tangent to the production possibility curve. Students may want to refer back to p. 47 in Chapter 3 to refresh their intuition.

FIGURE 5-2

How an Increase in the Relative Price of Cloth Affects Relative Supply

The isovalue lines become steeper when the relative price of cloth rises from $(P_C/P_F)^1$ to $(P_C/P_F)^2$ (shown by the rotation from VV^1 to VV^2). As a result, the economy produces more cloth and less food and the equilibrium output shifts from Q^1 to Q^2.

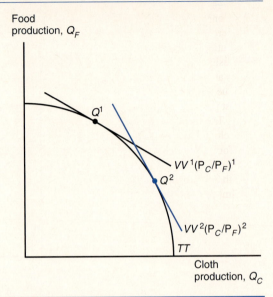

RELATIVE PRICES AND DEMAND

Figure 5-3 shows the relationship among production, consumption, and trade in the standard model. As we pointed out in Chapter 3, the value of an economy's consumption equals the value of its production:

$$P_C Q_C + P_F Q_F = P_C D_C + P_F D_F = V,$$

where D_C and D_F are the consumption of cloth and food, respectively. The equation above says that production and consumption must lie on the same isovalue line.

The economy's choice of a point on the isovalue line depends on the tastes of its consumers. For our standard model, we make the useful simplifying assumption that the economy's consumption decisions may be represented as if they were based on the tastes of a single representative individual.[3]

The tastes of an individual can be represented graphically by a series of **indifference curves.** An indifference curve traces a set of combinations of cloth (C) and food (F) consumption that leave the individual equally well off. Indifference curves have three properties:

---

[3]There are several sets of circumstances that can justify this assumption. One is that all individuals have the same tastes and the same share of all resources. Another is that the government redistributes income so as to maximize its view of overall social welfare. Essentially, the assumption requires that effects of changing income distribution on demand not be too important.

Grow

1
sector
direct
2
Chapt
tion—
produ
of eit
tensiv
give i

The b
able to pr
of food ac
Although
that is mo
rise in the
ward food

RELATIV

Suppose i
put of clo
for the wo
the world
shift resu
of Home'
Notic
of the gro
ative sup
hand, eit
shift of t
$(P_C/P_F)^1$ t
of Foreig
Grov
rection o
Similarly
Our anal
worsen a
biased g
world's e

INTERN

Using th
tional ef

FIGURE

World

The high
supply c
the lowe
relative
tive pric
by the in
supply a

then, is th
terms of t

DETERMI

Let's now
Home (wl
measured
cloth and
To de
relative de
cause an i
world rela
both count
tion of the
Now
fare are de
tant issues

ECONOM

The effects
cern and
growth in
or less valu
In asse
made on ei

FIGURE 5-3

Production, Consumption, and Trade in the Standard Model

The economy produces at point Q, where the production possibility frontier is tangent to the highest possible isovalue line. It consumes at point D, where that isovalue line is tangent to the highest possible indifference curve. The economy produces more cloth than it consumes and therefore exports cloth; correspondingly, it consumes more food than it produces and therefore imports food.

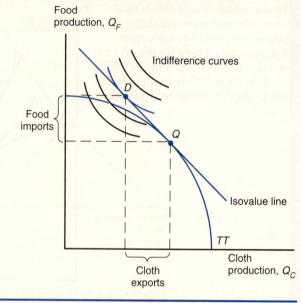

1. They are downward sloping: If an individual is offered less F, then to be made equally well off she must be given more C.

2. The farther up and to the right an indifference curve lies, the higher the level of welfare to which it corresponds: An individual will prefer more of both goods to less.

3. Each indifference curve gets flatter as we move to the right: The more C and the less F an individual consumes, the more valuable a unit of F is at the margin compared with a unit of C, so more C will have to be provided to compensate for any further reduction in F.

In Figure 5-3 we show a set of indifference curves for the economy that have these three properties. The economy will choose the point on the isovalue line that yields the three properties. The economy will choose to consume at the point on the isovalue line that yields the highest possible welfare. This point is where the isovalue line is tangent to the highest reachable indifference curve, shown here as point D. Notice that at this point the economy exports cloth (the quantity of cloth produced exceeds the quantity of cloth consumed) and imports food. (If this is not obvious, refer back to our discussion of the pattern of trade in Chapter 3.)

Now consider what happens when P_C/P_F is increased. In Figure 5-4 we show the effects. First, the economy produces more C and less F, shifting production from Q^1 to Q^2. This shifts the isovalue line on which consumption must lie, from VV^1 to VV^2. The economy's consumption choice therefore also shifts, from D^1 to D^2.

The move from D^1 to D^2 reflects two effects of the rise in P_C/P_F. First, the economy has moved to a higher indifference curve: It is better off. The reason is that this economy is an

Consider the following example. Suppose that there are not two but *three* goods: cloth, food, and haircuts. Only Home produces cloth; only Foreign produces food. Haircuts, however, are a nontraded good that each country produces for itself. Each country spends one-third of its income on each good. Even though these countries have the same tastes, each of them spends two-thirds of its income domestically and only one-third on imports.

Nontraded goods can give rise to what looks like a national preference for all goods produced domestically. But to analyze the effects of a transfer on the terms of trade we need to know what happens to the supply and demand for *exports*. Here the crucial point is that a country's nontraded goods compete with exports for resources. A transfer of income from the United States to the rest of the world lowers the demand for nontraded goods in the United States, releasing resources that can be used to produce U.S. exports. As a result, the supply of U.S. exports rises. At the same time, the transfer of income from the United States to the rest of the world increases the rest of the world's demand for nontraded goods because some of that income is spent on haircuts and other nontradables. The increase in the demand for nontraded goods in the rest of the world draws foreign resources away from exports and reduces the supply of foreign exports (which are U.S. imports). The result is that a transfer by the United States to other countries may lower the price of U.S. exports relative to foreign, worsening U.S. terms of trade.

Demand shifts also cause resources to move between the nontraded and import-competing sectors. As a practical matter, however, most international economists believe that the effect of barriers to trade *is* to validate the presumption that an international transfer of income worsens the donor's terms of trade. Thus, Keynes was right in practice.

CASE STUDY

THE TRANSFER PROBLEM AND THE DEBT CRISIS

During the 1980s, many low-income countries were caught up in the so-called "debt crisis." These countries had borrowed large sums of money from advanced nations during the 1970s and very early 1980s; then, for a variety of reasons, banks became unwilling to make further loans and demanded repayment as old loans came due. (The debt crisis is discussed in Chapter 22.) There was thus a sudden shift from net inflows of money to debtor countries in the form of new loans, to net outflows to pay interest and to repay loans coming due. It was as if low-income countries had suddenly shifted from being the recipients of large transfers from other countries, to being forced to make large transfer payments abroad instead.

If Keynes's presumption about the transfer problem were right, we would expect this change of fortune to be reflected in a deterioration of the terms of trade of the debtor countries. And this was, in fact, what happened. The table shows the terms of trade of developing countries other than oil exporters between 1980 and 1985. The initial deterioration from 1980 to 1982 could be attributed to a recession in the advanced countries, which reduced demand for developing country exports. After 1982, however, the advanced countries recovered, but the terms of trade of the developing countries did not. While there is still dispute among economists about why this happened, it is likely that the transfer problem created by the debt crisis played an important role.

If the debt crisis really did create a transfer problem, the burden of the debt was greater than the size of the payments alone, just as Keynes warned would happen if Germany were forced to pay large war reparations.

Terms of Trade of Non–Oil Developing Countries (1980 = 100)

1980	100.0
1981	95.0
1982	94.4
1983	93.5
1984	95.1
1985	92.8

Source: International Monetary Fund, *International Financial Statistics Yearbook,* 1994.

TARIFFS AND EXPORT SUBSIDIES: SIMULTANEOUS SHIFTS IN *RS* AND *RD*

Import tariffs (taxes levied on imports) and **export subsidies** (payments given to domestic producers who sell a good abroad) are not usually put in place to affect a country's terms of trade. These government interventions in trade usually take place for income distribution, for the promotion of industries thought to be crucial to the economy, or for balance of payments (these motivations are examined in Chapters 9, 10, and 11). Whatever the motive for tariffs and subsidies, however, they *do* have terms of trade effects that can be understood by using the standard trade model.

The distinctive feature of tariffs and export subsidies is that they create a difference between prices at which goods are traded on the world market and their prices within a country. The direct effect of a tariff is to make imported goods more expensive inside a country than they are outside. An export subsidy gives producers an incentive to export. It will therefore be more profitable to sell abroad than at home unless the price at home is higher, so such a subsidy raises the price of exported goods inside a country.

The price changes caused by tariffs and subsidies change both relative supply and relative demand. The result is a shift in the terms of trade of the country imposing the policy change and in the terms of trade of the rest of the world.

RELATIVE DEMAND AND SUPPLY EFFECTS OF A TARIFF

Tariffs and subsidies drive a wedge between the prices at which goods are traded internationally (**external prices**) and the prices at which they are traded within a country (**internal prices**). This means that we have to be careful in defining the terms of trade. The terms of trade are intended to measure the ratio at which countries exchange goods; for example, how many units of food can Home import for each unit of cloth that it exports? The terms of trade therefore correspond to external, not internal, prices. When analyzing the effects of a tariff or export subsidy, we want to know how it affects relative supply and demand *as a function of external prices.*

If Home imposes a 20 percent tariff on the value of food imports, the internal price of food relative to cloth faced by Home producers and consumers will be 20 percent higher than the external relative price of food on the world market. Equivalently, the internal relative price of cloth on which Home residents base their decisions will be lower than the relative price on the external market.

At any given world relative price of cloth, then, Home producers will face a lower relative cloth price and therefore will produce less cloth and more food. At the same time, Home consumers will shift their consumption toward cloth and away from food. From the point of view of the world as a whole, the relative supply of cloth will fall (from RS^1 to RS^2 in Figure 5-10) while the relative demand for cloth will rise (from RD^1 to RD^2). Clearly, the world relative price of cloth rises from $(P_C/P_F)^1$ to $(P_C/P_F)^2$, and thus Home's terms of trade improve at Foreign's expense.

The extent of this terms of trade effect depends on how large the country imposing the tariff is relative to the rest of the world—if the country is only a small part of the world, it cannot have much effect on world relative supply and demand and therefore cannot have much effect on relative prices. If the United States, a very large country, were to impose a 20 percent tariff, some estimates suggest that the U.S. terms of trade might rise by 15 percent. That is, the price of U.S. imports relative to exports might fall by 15 percent on the world market, while the relative price of imports would rise only 5 percent inside the United States. On the other hand, if Luxembourg or Paraguay were to impose a 20 percent tariff, the terms of trade effect would probably be too small to measure.

FIGURE 5-10

Effects of a Tariff on the Terms of Trade

An import tariff imposed by Home both reduces the relative supply of cloth (from RS^1 to RS^2) and increases the relative demand (from RD^1 to RD^2). As a result, the relative price of cloth must rise.

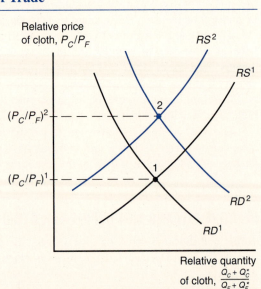

EFFECTS OF AN EXPORT SUBSIDY

Tariffs and export subsidies are often treated as similar policies, since they both seem to support domestic producers, but they have opposite effects on the terms of trade. Suppose that Home offers a 20 percent subsidy on the value of any cloth exported. For any given world prices this subsidy will raise Home's internal price of cloth relative to food by 20 percent. The rise in the relative price of cloth will lead Home producers to produce more cloth and less food, while leading Home consumers to substitute food for cloth. As illustrated in Figure 5-11, the subsidy will increase the world relative supply of cloth (from RS^1 to RS^2) and decrease the world relative demand for cloth (from RD^1 to RD^2), shifting equilibrium from point 1 to point 2. A Home export subsidy worsens Home's terms of trade and improves Foreign's.

IMPLICATIONS OF TERMS OF TRADE EFFECTS: WHO GAINS AND WHO LOSES?

The question of who gains and who loses from tariffs and export subsidies has two dimensions. First is the issue of the *international* distribution of income; second is the issue of the distribution of income *within* each of the countries.

The International Distribution of Income. If Home imposes a tariff, it improves its terms of trade at Foreign's expense. Thus tariffs hurt the rest of the world.

The effect on Home's welfare is not quite as clear-cut. The terms of trade improvement benefits Home; however, a tariff also imposes costs by distorting production and consumption incentives within Home's economy (see Chapter 8). The terms of trade gains

---

FIGURE 5-11

Effects of a Subsidy on the Terms of Trade

An export subsidy's effects are the reverse of those of a tariff. Relative supply of cloth rises, while relative demand falls. Home's terms of trade decline as the relative price of cloth falls from $(P_C/P_F)^1$ to $(P_C/P_F)^2$.

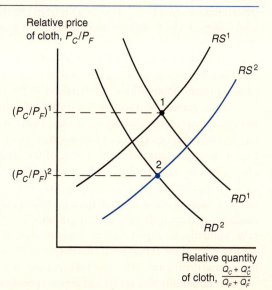

FIGURE 5A-2

Home's Offer Curve

The offer curve is generated by tracing out how Home's offer varies as the relative price of cloth is changed.

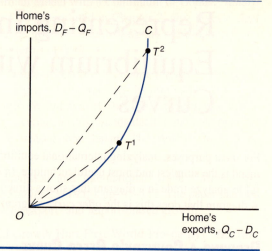

---

the slope of the line from the origin of Figure 5A-1 to T is equal to P_C/P_F. T is Home's offer at the assumed relative price: At that price, Home residents are willing to trade ($Q_C - D_C$) units of cloth for ($D_F - Q_F$) units of food.

By calculating Home's offer at different relative prices, we trace out Home's *offer curve* (Figure 5A-2). We saw in Figure 5-4 that as P_C/P_F rises, Q_C rises, Q_F falls, D_F rises, and D_C may rise or fall. Desired ($Q_C - D_C$) and ($D_F - Q_F$), however, both normally rise if income effects are not too strong. In Figure 5A-2, T^1 is the offer corresponding to Q^1, D^1 in Figure 5-4; T^2 the offer corresponding to Q^2, D^2. By finding Home's offer at many prices, we trace out the Home offer curve OC.

Foreign's offer curve OF may be traced out in the same way (Figure 5A-3). On the vertical axis we plot ($Q_F^* - D_F^*$), Foreign's desired exports of food, while on the horizontal axis we plot ($D_C^* - Q_C^*$), desired imports of cloth. The lower P_C/P_F is, the more food Foreign will want to export and the more cloth it will want to import.

INTERNATIONAL EQUILIBRIUM

In equilibrium it must be true that ($Q_C - D_C$) = ($D_C^* - Q_C^*$), and also that ($D_F - Q_F$) = ($Q_F^* - D_F^*$). That is, world supply and demand must be equal for both cloth and food. Given these equivalences, we can plot the Home and Foreign offer curves on the same diagram (Figure 5A-4). Equilibrium is at the point where the Home and Foreign offer curves cross. At the equilibrium point E the relative price of cloth is equal to the slope of OE. Home's exports of cloth, which equal Foreign's imports, are OX. Foreign's exports of food, which equal Home's imports, are OY.

This representation of international equilibrium helps us see that equilibrium is in fact *general* equilibrium, in which supply and demand are equalized in both markets at the same time.

FIGURE 5A-3

Foreign's Offer Curve

Foreign's offer curve shows how that country's desired imports of cloth and exports of food vary with the relative price.

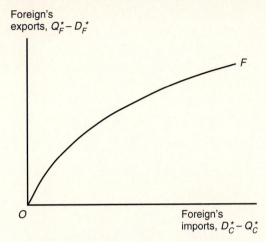

FIGURE 5A-4

Offer Curve Equilibrium

World equilibrium is where the Home and Foreign offer curves intersect.

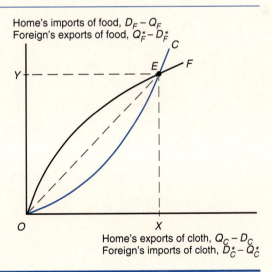

6

Economies of Scale, Imperfect Competition, and International Trade

In Chapter 2 we pointed out that there are two reasons why countries specialize and trade. First, countries differ either in their resources or in technology and specialize in the things they do relatively well; second, economies of scale (or increasing returns) make it advantageous for each country to specialize in the production of only a limited range of goods and services. The past four chapters considered models in which all trade is based on comparative advantage; that is, differences between countries are the only reason for trade. This chapter introduces the role of economies of scale.

The analysis of trade based on economies of scale presents certain problems that we have so far avoided. Up to now we have assumed that markets are perfectly competitive, so that all monopoly profits are always competed away. When there are increasing returns, however, large firms usually have an advantage over small, so that markets tend to be dominated by one firm (monopoly) or, more often, by a few firms (oligopoly). When increasing returns enter the trade picture, then, markets usually become imperfectly competitive.

This chapter begins with an overview of the concept of economies of scale and the economics of imperfect competition. We then turn to two models of international trade in which economies of scale and imperfect competition play a crucial role: the monopolistic competition model and the dumping model. The rest of the chapter addresses the role of a different kind of increasing returns, external economies, in determining trade patterns.

ECONOMIES OF SCALE AND INTERNATIONAL TRADE: AN OVERVIEW

The models of comparative advantage already presented were based on the assumption of constant returns to scale. That is, we assumed that if inputs to an industry were doubled, industry output would double as well. In practice, however, many industries are characterized by economies of scale (also referred to as increasing returns), so that production is more efficient the larger the scale at which it takes place. Where there are economies of scale, doubling the inputs to an industry will more than double the industry's production.

A simple example can help convey the significance of economies of scale for international trade. Table 6-1 shows the relationship between inputs and output of a hypothetical industry. Widgets are produced using only one input, labor; the table shows how the amount of labor required depends on the number of widgets produced. To produce 10 widgets, for example, requires 15 hours of labor, while to produce 25 widgets requires 30 hours. The presence of economies of scale may be seen from the fact that doubling the input of labor from 15 to 30 more than doubles the industry's output—in fact, output increases by a factor of 2.5. Equivalently, the existence of economies of scale may be seen by looking at the average amount of labor used to produce each unit of output: If output is only 5 widgets the average labor input per widget is 2 hours, while if output is 25 units the average labor input falls to 1.2 hours.

We can use this example to see why economies of scale provide an incentive for international trade. Imagine a world consisting of two countries, America and Britain, both of whom have the same technology for producing widgets, and suppose that initially each country produces 10 widgets. According to the table this requires 15 hours of labor in each country, so in the world as a whole 30 hours of labor produce 20 widgets. But now suppose that we concentrate world production of widgets in one country, say America, and let America employ 30 hours of labor in the widget industry. In a single country these 30 hours of labor can produce 25 widgets. So by concentrating production of widgets in America, the world economy can use the same amount of labor to produce 25 percent more widgets.

But where does America find the extra labor to produce widgets, and what happens to the labor that was employed in the British widget industry? To get the labor to expand its production of some goods, America must decrease or abandon the production of others; these goods will then be produced in Britain instead, using the labor formerly employed in the industries whose production has expanded in America. Imagine that there are many goods subject to economies of scale in production, and give them numbers: 1, 2, 3, ... To

---

TABLE 6-1

Relationship of Input to Output for a Hypothetical Industry

Output	Total labor input	Average labor input
5	10	2
10	15	1.5
15	20	1.333333
20	25	1.25
25	30	1.2
30	35	1.166667

take advantage of economies of scale, each of the countries must concentrate on producing only a limited number of goods. Thus, for example, America might produce goods 1, 3, 5, and so on while Britain produces 2, 4, 6, and so on. If each country produces only some of the goods, then each good can be produced at a larger scale than would be the case if each country tried to produce everything, and the world economy can therefore produce more of each good.

How does international trade enter the story? Consumers in each country will still want to consume a variety of goods. Suppose that industry 1 ends up in America and industry 2 in Britain; then American consumers of good 2 will have to buy goods imported from Britain, while British consumers of good 1 will have to import it from America. International trade plays a crucial role: It makes it possible for each country to produce a restricted range of goods and to take advantage of economies of scale without sacrificing variety in consumption. Indeed, as we will see below, international trade typically leads to an increase in the variety of goods available.

Our example, then, suggests how mutually beneficial trade can arise as a result of economies of scale. Each country specializes in producing a limited range of products, which enables it to produce these goods more efficiently than if it tried to produce everything for itself; these specialized economies then trade with each other to be able to consume the full range of goods.

Unfortunately, to go from this suggestive story to an explicit model of trade based on economies of scale is not that simple. The reason is that economies of scale typically lead to a market structure other than that of perfect competition, and it is necessary to be careful about analyzing this market structure.

ECONOMIES OF SCALE AND MARKET STRUCTURE

In the example in Table 6-1, we represented economies of scale by assuming that the labor input per unit of production is smaller the more units produced. We did not say how this production increase was achieved—whether existing firms simply produced more, or whether there was instead an increase in the number of firms. To analyze the effects of economies of scale on market structure, however, one must be clear about what kind of production increase is necessary to reduce average cost. **External economies of scale** occur when the cost per unit depends on the size of the industry but not necessarily on the size of any one firm. **Internal economies of scale** occur when the cost per unit depends on the size of an individual firm but not necessarily on that of the industry.

The distinction between external and internal economies can be illustrated with a hypothetical example. Imagine an industry that initially consists of ten firms, each producing 100 widgets, for a total industry production of 1000 widgets. Now consider two cases. First, suppose the industry were to double in size, so that it now consists of 20 firms, each one still producing 100 widgets. It is possible that the costs of each firm will fall as a result of the increased size of the industry; for example, a bigger industry may allow more efficient provision of specialized services or machinery. If this is the case, the industry exhibits external economies of scale. That is, the efficiency of firms is increased by having a larger industry, even though each firm is the same size as before.

Second, suppose the industry's output were held constant at 1000 widgets, but that the number of firms is cut in half, so that each of the remaining five firms produces 200 widgets. If the costs of production fall in this case, then there are internal economies of scale: A firm is more efficient if its output is larger.

External and internal economies of scale have different implications for the structure of industries. An industry where economies of scale are purely external (that is, where there are no advantages to large firms) will typically consist of many small firms and be perfectly competitive. Internal economies of scale, by contrast, give large firms a cost advantage over small and lead to an imperfectly competitive market structure.

Both external and internal economies of scale are important causes of international trade. Because they have different implications for market structure, however, it is difficult to discuss both types of scale economy–based trade in the same model. We will therefore deal with them one at a time.

We begin with a model based on internal economies of scale. As we have just argued, however, internal economies of scale lead to a breakdown of perfect competition. This outcome forces us to take time out to review the economics of imperfect competition before we can turn to the analysis of the role of internal economies of scale in international trade.

THE THEORY OF IMPERFECT COMPETITION

In a perfectly competitive market—a market in which there are many buyers and sellers, none of whom represents a large part of the market—firms are *price takers*. That is, sellers of products believe that they can sell as much as they like at the current price and cannot influence the price they receive for their product. For example, a wheat farmer can sell as much wheat as she likes without worrying that if she tries to sell more wheat she will depress the market price. The reason she need not worry about the effect of her sales on prices is that any individual wheat grower represents only a tiny fraction of the world market.

When only a few firms produce a good, however, matters are different. To take perhaps the most dramatic example, the aircraft manufacturing giant Boeing shares the market for large jet aircraft with only two rivals, Airbus and McDonnell-Douglas. Boeing therefore knows that if it produces more aircraft it will have a significant effect on the total supply of planes in the world and will therefore significantly drive down the price of airplanes. Or to put it the other way around, Boeing knows that if it wants to sell more airplanes, it can do so only by significantly reducing its price. In **imperfect competition,** then, firms are aware that they can influence the prices of their products and that they can sell more only by reducing their price. Imperfect competition is characteristic both of industries in which there are only a few major producers and of industries in which each producer's product is seen by consumers as strongly differentiated from those of rival firms. Under these circumstances each firm views itself as a *price setter,* choosing the price of its product, rather than a price taker.

When firms are not price takers, it is necessary to develop additional tools to describe how prices and outputs are determined. The simplest imperfectly competitive market structure to examine is that of a **pure monopoly,** a market in which a firm faces no competition; the tools we develop can then be used to examine more complex market structures.

MONOPOLY: A BRIEF REVIEW

Figure 6-1 shows the position of a single, monopolistic firm. The firm faces a downward-sloping demand curve, shown in the figure as *D*. The downward slope of *D* indicates that

FIGURE 6-1

Monopolistic Pricing and Production Decisions

A monopolistic firm chooses an output at which marginal revenue, the increase in revenue from selling an additional unit, equals marginal cost, the cost of producing an additional unit. This profit-maximizing output is shown as Q_M; the price at which this output is demanded is P_M. The marginal revenue curve MR lies below the demand curve D, because, for a monopoly, marginal revenue is always less than the price. The monopoly's profits are equal to the area of the shaded rectangle, the difference between price and average cost times Q_M.

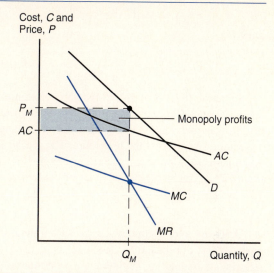

the firm can sell more units of output only if the price of the output falls. As you may recall from basic microeconomics, a **marginal revenue** curve corresponds to the demand curve. Marginal revenue is the extra or marginal revenue the firm gains from selling an additional unit. Marginal revenue for a monopolist is always less than the price because to sell an additional unit the firm must lower the price of *all* units (not just the marginal one). Thus for a monopolist the marginal revenue curve, *MR*, always lies below the demand curve.

Marginal Revenue and Price.   For our analysis of the monopolistic competition model later in this section it is important to determine the relationship between the price the monopolist receives per unit and marginal revenue. Marginal revenue is always less than the price—but how much less? The relationship between marginal revenue and price depends on two things. First, it depends on how much output the firm is already selling: A firm that is not selling very many units will not lose much by cutting the price it receives on those units. Second, the gap between price and marginal revenue depends on the slope of the demand curve, which tells us how much the monopolist has to cut his price to sell one more unit of output. If the curve is very flat, then the monopolist can sell an additional unit with only a small price cut and will therefore not have to lower the price on units he would have sold otherwise by very much, so marginal revenue will be close to the price per unit. On the other hand, if the demand curve is very steep, selling an additional unit will require a large price cut, implying marginal revenue much less than price.

We can be more specific about the relationship between price and marginal revenue if we assume that the demand curve the firm faces is a straight line. When this is so, the dependence of the monopolist's total sales on the price it charges can be represented by an equation of the form

$$Q = A - B \times P, \tag{6-1}$$

where Q is the number of units the firm sells, P the price it charges per unit, and A and B are constants. We show in the appendix to this chapter that in this case marginal revenue is

$$\text{Marginal revenue} = MR = P - Q/B, \tag{6-2}$$

implying

$$P - MR = Q/B.$$

Equation (6-2) reveals that the gap between price and marginal revenue depends on the initial sales Q of the firm and the slope parameter B of its demand curve. If sales quantity, Q, is higher, marginal revenue is lower, because the decrease in price required to sell a greater quantity costs the firm more. The greater is B, that is, the more sales fall for any given increase in price and the closer marginal revenue is to the price of the good. Equation (6-2) is crucial for our analysis of the monopolistic competition model of trade (pp. 124–142).

Average and Marginal Costs.   Returning to Figure 6-1, AC represents the firm's **average cost** of production, that is, its total cost divided by its output. Its downward slope reflects our assumption that there are economies of scale, so that the larger the firm's output is the lower are its costs per unit. MC represents the firm's **marginal cost** (the amount it costs the firm to produce one extra unit). We know from basic economics that when average costs are a decreasing function of output, marginal cost is always less than average cost. Thus MC lies below AC.

Equation (6-2) related price and marginal revenue. There is a corresponding formula relating average and marginal cost. Suppose the costs of a firm, C, take the form

$$C = F + c \times Q, \tag{6-3}$$

where F is a fixed cost that is independent of the firm's output, c is the firm's marginal cost, and Q is once again the firm's output. (This is called a linear cost function.) *The fixed cost in a linear cost function gives rise to economies of scale, because the larger the firm's output, the less is the fixed cost per unit.* Specifically, the firm's average cost (total cost divided by output) is

$$\text{Average cost} = AC = C/Q = F/Q + c. \tag{6-4}$$

This average cost declines as Q increases because the fixed cost is spread over a larger output.

If, for example, $F = 5$ and $c = 1$ the average cost of producing 10 units is $5/10 + 1 = 1.5$ and the average cost of producing 25 units is $5/25 + 1 = 1.2$. These numbers may look familiar, because they were used to construct Table 6-1. The relationship between output, average costs, and marginal costs given in Table 6-1 is shown graphically in Figure 6-2. Average cost approaches infinity at zero output and approaches marginal cost at very large output.

The profit-maximizing output of a monopolist is that at which marginal revenue (the revenue gained from selling an extra unit) equals marginal cost (the cost of producing an extra unit), that is, at the intersection of the MC and MR curves. In Figure 6-1 we can see

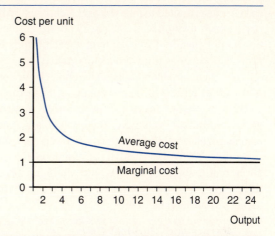

FIGURE 6-2

Average Versus Marginal Cost

This figure illustrates the average and marginal costs corresponding to the total cost function $C = 5 + x$. Marginal cost is always 1; average cost declines as output rises.

that the price at which the profit-maximizing output Q_M is demanded is P_M, which is greater than average cost. When $P > AC$, the monopolist is earning some monopoly profits.[1]

MONOPOLISTIC COMPETITION

Monopoly profits rarely go uncontested. A firm making high profits normally attracts competitors. Thus situations of pure monopoly are rare in practice. Instead, the usual market structure in industries characterized by internal economies of scale is one of **oligopoly:** several firms, each of them large enough to affect prices, but none with an uncontested monopoly.

The general analysis of oligopoly is a complex and controversial subject because in oligopolies the pricing policies of firms are *interdependent*. Each firm in an oligopoly will, in setting its price, consider not only the responses of consumers but also the expected responses of competitors. These responses, however, depend in turn on the competitors' expectations about the firm's behavior—and we are therefore in a complex game in which firms are trying to second-guess each others' strategies. We will briefly discuss the general problems of modeling oligopoly below. However, there is a special case of oligopoly, known as monopolistic competition, which is relatively easy to analyze. In recent years monopolistic competition models have been widely applied to international trade.

In **monopolistic competition** models two key assumptions are made to get around the problem of interdependence. First, each firm is assumed to be able to *differentiate its product* from that of its rivals. That is, because they want to buy this firm's particular product,

---

[1]The economic definition of *profits* is not the same as that used in conventional accounting, where any revenue over and above labor and material costs is called a profit. A firm that earns a rate of return on its capital less than what that capital could have earned in other industries is not making profits; from an economic point of view the normal rate of return on capital represents part of the firm's costs, and only returns over and above that normal rate of return represent profits.

the firm's customers will not rush to buy other firms' products because of a slight price difference. Product differentiation assures that each firm has a monopoly in its particular product within an industry and is therefore somewhat insulated from competition. Second, each firm is assumed to take the prices charged by its rivals as given—that is, it ignores the impact of its own price on the prices of other firms. As a result, the monopolistic competition model assumes that even though each firm is in reality facing competition from other firms, it behaves as if it were a monopolist—hence the model's name.

Are there any monopolistically competitive industries in the real world? Some industries may be reasonable approximations. For example, the automobile industry in Europe, where a number of major producers (Ford, General Motors, Volkswagon, Renault, Peugeot, Fiat, Volvo—and more recently Nissan) offer substantially different yet nonetheless competing automobiles, may be fairly well described by monopolistically competitive assumptions. The main appeal of the monopolistic competition model is not, however, its realism, but its simplicity. As we will see in the next section of this chapter, the monopolistic competition model gives us a very clear view of how economies of scale can give rise to mutually beneficial trade.

Before we can examine trade, however, we need to develop a basic model of monopolistic competition. Let us therefore imagine an industry consisting of a number of firms. These firms produce differentiated products, that is, goods that are not exactly the same but that are substitutes for one another. Each firm is therefore a monopolist in the sense that it is the only firm producing its particular good, but the demand for its good depends on the number of other similar products available and on the prices of other firms in the industry.

Assumptions of the Model.   We begin by describing the demand facing a typical monopolistically competitive firm. In general, we would expect a firm to sell more the larger the total demand for its industry's product and the higher the prices charged by its rivals. On the other hand, we expect the firm to sell less the greater the number of firms in the industry and the higher its own price. A particular equation for the demand facing a firm that has these properties is[2]

$$Q = S \times [1/n - b \times (P - \overline{P})], \tag{6-5}$$

where Q is the firm's sales, S is the total sales of the industry, n the number of firms in the industry, b a constant term representing the responsiveness of a firm's sales to its price, P the price charged by the firm itself, and $\overline{P}$ the average price charged by its competitors. Equation (6-5) may be given the following intuitive justification: If all firms charge the same price, each will have a market share $1/n$. A firm charging more than the average of other firms will have a smaller market share, a firm charging less a larger share.[3]

It is helpful to assume that total industry sales S are unaffected by the average price $\overline{P}$ charged by firms in the industry. That is, we assume that firms can gain customers only at each others' expense. This is an unrealistic assumption, but it simplifies the analysis and

[2]Equation (6-5) can be derived from a model in which consumers have different preferences and firms produce varieties tailored to particular segments of the market. See Stephen Salop, "Monopolistic Competition with Outside Goods," *Bell Journal of Economics* 10 (1979), pp. 141–156 for a development of this approach.

[3]Equation (6-5) may be rewritten as $Q = S/n - S \times b \times (P - \overline{P})$. If $P = \overline{P}$, this reduces to $Q = S/n$. If $P > \overline{P}$, $Q < S/n$, while if $P < \overline{P}$, $Q > S/n$.

helps focus on the competition among firms. In particular, it means that S is a measure of the size of the market and that if all firms charge the same price, each sells S/n units.

Next we turn to the costs of a typical firm. Here we simply assume that total and average costs of a typical firm are described by equations (6-3) and (6-4).

Market Equilibrium.   To model the behavior of this monopolistically competitive industry, we will assume that all firms in this industry are *symmetric,* that is, the demand function and cost function are identical for all firms (even though they are producing and selling somewhat differentiated products). When the individual firms are symmetric, the state of the industry can be described without enumerating the features of all firms in detail: All we really need to know to describe the industry is how many firms there are and what price the typical firm charges. To analyze the industry, for example to assess the effects of international trade, we need to determine the number of firms n and the average price they charge $\overline{P}$. Once we have a method for determining n and $\overline{P}$, we can ask how they are affected by international trade.

Our method for determining n and $\overline{P}$ involves three steps. (1) First, we derive a relationship between the number of firms and the *average cost* of a typical firm. We show that this relationship is upward sloping; that is, the more firms there are, the lower the output of each firm, and thus the higher its cost per unit of output. (2) We next show the relationship between the number of firms and the price each firm charges, which must equal $\overline{P}$ in equilibrium. We show that this relationship is downward sloping: the more firms there are, the more intense is competition among firms, and as a result the lower the prices they charge. (3) Finally, we argue that when the price exceeds average cost additional firms will enter the industry, while when the price is less than average cost firms will exit. So in the long run the number of firms is determined by the intersection of the curve that relates average cost to n and the curve that relates price to n.

1. *The number of firms and average cost.* As a first step toward determining n and $\overline{P}$, we ask how the average cost of a typical firm depends on the number of firms in the industry. Since all firms are symmetric in this model, in equilibrium they will all charge the same price. But when all firms charge the same price, so that $P = \overline{P}$, equation (6-5) tells us that $Q = S/n$; that is, each firm's output Q, is a $1/n$ share of the total industry sales S. But we saw in equation (6-4) that average cost depends inversely on a firm's output. We therefore conclude that average cost depends on the size of the market and the number of firms in the industry:

$$AC = F/Q + c = n \times F/S + c. \tag{6-6}$$

Equation (6-6) tells us that other things equal, *the more firms there are in the industry the higher is average cost.* The reason is that the more firms there are, the less each firm produces. For example, imagine an industry with total sales of 1 million widgets annually. If there are five firms in the industry, each will sell 200,000 annually. If there are ten firms, each will sell only 100,000, and therefore each firm will have higher average cost. The upward-sloping relationship between n and average cost is shown as CC in Figure 6-3.

2. *The number of firms and the price.* Meanwhile, the price the typical firm charges also depends on the number of firms in the industry. In general, we would expect that the more firms there are, the more intense will be the competition among

FIGURE 6-3

Equilibrium in a Monopolistically Competitive Market

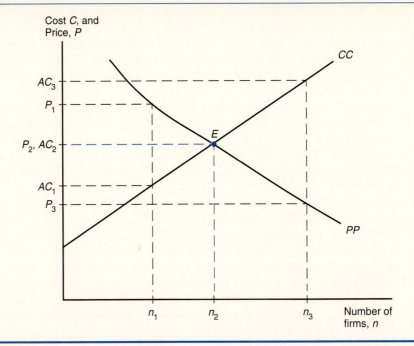

The number of firms in a monopolistically competitive market, and the prices they charge, are determined by two relationships. On one side, the more firms there are, the more intensely they compete, and hence the lower is the industry price. This relationship is represented by *PP*. On the other side, the more firms there are, the less each firm sells and therefore the higher is its average cost. This relationship is represented by *CC*. If price exceeds average cost (if the *PP* curve is above the *CC* curve), the industry will be making profits and additional firms will enter the industry; if price is less than average cost, the industry will be incurring losses and firms will leave the industry. The equilibrium price and number of firms occurs when price equals average cost, at the intersection of *PP* and *CC*.

them, and hence the lower the price. This turns out to be true in this model, but proving it takes a moment. The basic trick is to show that each firm faces a straight-line demand curve of the form we showed in equation (6-1), and then to use equation (6-2) to determine prices.

First recall that in the monopolistic competition model firms are assumed to take each others' prices as given; that is, each firm ignores the possibility that if it changes its price other firms will also change theirs. If each firm treats $\bar{P}$ as given, we can rewrite the demand curve (6-5) in the form

$$Q = (S/n + S \times b \times \bar{P}) - S \times b \times P, \qquad (6\text{-}7)$$

where *b* is the parameter in equation (6-5) that measured the sensitivity of each firm's market share to the price it charges. Now this is in the same form as (6-1), with $S/n + S \times b \times \bar{P}$ in place of the constant term *A* and $S \times b$ in place of the slope coefficient

B. If we plug these values back into the formula for marginal revenue (6-2), we have a marginal revenue for a typical firm of

$$MR = P - Q/(S \times b). \tag{6-8}$$

Profit-maximizing firms will set marginal revenue equal to their marginal cost *c,* so that

$$MR = P - Q/(S \times b) = c,$$

which can be rearranged to give the following equation for the price charged by a typical firm:

$$P = c + Q/(S \times b). \tag{6-9}$$

We have already noted, however, that if all firms charge the same price, each will sell an amount $Q = S/n$. Plugging this back into (6-9) gives us a relationship between the number of firms and the price each firm charges:

$$P = c + 1/(b \times n). \tag{6-10}$$

Equation (6-10) says algebraically that *the more firms there are in the industry, the lower the price each firm will charge.* Equation (6-10) is shown in Figure 6-3 as the downward-sloping curve *PP.*

3. *The equilibrium number of firms.* Let us now ask what Figure 6-3 means. We have summarized an industry by two curves. The downward-sloping curve *PP* shows that the more firms there are in the industry, the lower the price each firm will charge. This makes sense: The more firms there are, the more competition each firm faces. The upward-sloping curve *CC* tells us that the more firms there are in the industry, the higher the average cost of each firm. This also makes sense: If the number of firms increases, each firm will sell less, so firms will not be able to move as far down their average cost curve.

The two schedules intersect at point *E,* corresponding to the number of firms n_2. The significance of n_2 is that it is the *zero-profit* number of firms in the industry. When there are n_2 firms in the industry, their profit-maximizing price is P_2, which is exactly equal to their average cost AC_2.

What we will now argue is that in the long run the number of firms in the industry tends to move toward n_2, so that point *E* describes the industry's long-run equilibrium.

To see why, suppose that *n* were less than n_2, say n_1. Then the price charged by firms would be P_1, while their average cost would be only AC_1. Thus firms would be making monopoly profits. Conversely, suppose that *n* were greater than n_2, say n_3. Then firms would charge only the price P_3, while their average cost would be AC_3, firms would be suffering losses.

Over time, firms will enter an industry that is profitable, exit one in which they lose money. The number of firms will rise over time if it is less than n_2, fall if it is greater. This means that n_2 is the equilibrium number of firms in the industry and P_2 the equilibrium price.[4]

---

[4]This analysis slips past a slight problem: The number of firms in an industry must, of course, be a whole number like 5 or 8. What if n_2 turns out to equal 6.37? The answer is that there will be 6 firms in the industry, all making small monopoly profits, but not challenged by new entrants because everyone knows that a seven-firm industry would lose money. In most examples of monopolistic competition, this whole-number or "integer constraint" problem turns out not to be very important, and we ignore it here.

We have now developed a model of a monopolistically competitive industry in which we can determine the equilibrium number of firms and the average price that firms charge. We can use this model to derive some important conclusions about the role of economies of scale in international trade. But before we do, we should take a moment to note some limitations of the monopolistic competition model.

LIMITATIONS OF THE MONOPOLISTIC COMPETITION MODEL

The monopolistic competition model captures certain key elements of markets where there are economies of scale and thus imperfect competition. However, few industries are well described by monopolistic competition. Instead, the most common market structure is one of small-group oligopoly, where only a few firms are actively engaged in competition. In this situation the key assumption of the monopolistic competition model, which is that each firm will behave as if it were a true monopolist, is likely to break down. Instead, firms will be aware that their actions influence the actions of other firms and will take this interdependence into account.

Two kinds of behavior arise in the general oligopoly setting that are excluded by assumption from the monopolistic competition model. The first is *collusive* behavior. Each firm may keep its price higher than the apparent profit-maximizing level as part of an understanding that other firms will do the same; since each firm's profits are higher if its competitors charge high prices, such an understanding can raise the profits of all the firms (at the expense of consumers). Collusive price-setting behavior may be managed through explicit agreements (illegal in the United States) or through tacit coordination strategies, such as allowing one firm to act as a price leader for the industry.

Firms may also engage in *strategic* behavior; that is, they may do things that seem to lower profits, but that affect the behavior of competitors in a desirable way. For example a firm may build extra capacity not to use it but to deter potential rivals from entering its industry.

These possibilities for both collusive and strategic behavior make the analysis of oligopoly a complex matter. There is no one generally accepted model of oligopoly behavior, which makes modeling trade in oligopolistic industries problematic.

The monopolistic competition approach to trade is attractive because it avoids these complexities. Even though it may leave out some features of the real world, the monopolistic competition model is widely accepted as a way to provide at least a first cut at the role of economies of scale in international trade.

MONOPOLISTIC COMPETITION AND TRADE

Underlying the application of the monopolistic competition model to trade is the idea that trade increases market size. In industries where there are economies of scale, both the variety of goods that a country can produce and the scale of its production are constrained by the size of the market. By trading with each other, and therefore forming an integrated world market that is bigger than any individual national market, nations are able to loosen these constraints. Each country can specialize in producing a narrower range of products than it would in the absence of trade; yet by buying goods that it does not make from other countries, each nation can simultaneously increase the variety of goods available to its consumers. As a result, trade offers an opportunity for mutual gain even when countries do not differ in their resources or technology.

Suppose, for example, that there are two countries, each with an annual market for 1 million automobiles. By trading with each other, these countries can create a combined market of 2 million autos. In this combined market, more varieties of automobiles can be produced, at lower average costs, than in either market alone.

The monopolistic competition model can be used to show how trade improves the trade-off between scale and variety that individual nations face. We will begin by showing how a larger market leads, in the monopolistic competition model, to both a lower average price and the availability of a greater variety of goods. Applying this result to international trade, we observe that trade creates a world market larger than any of the national markets that comprise it. Integrating markets through international trade therefore has the same effects as growth of a market within a single country.

THE EFFECTS OF INCREASED MARKET SIZE

The number of firms in a monopolistically competitive industry and the prices they charge are affected by the size of the market. In larger markets there usually will be both more firms and more sales per firm; consumers in a large market will be offered both lower prices and a greater variety of products than consumers in small markets.

To see this in the context of our model, look again at the CC curve in Figure 6-3, which showed that average costs per firm are higher the more firms there are in the industry. The definition of the CC curve is given by equation (6-6):

$$AC = F/Q + c = n \times F/S + c.$$

Examining this equation, we see that an increase in total sales S will reduce average costs for any given number of firms n. The reason is that if the market grows while the number of firms is held constant, sales per firm will increase and the average cost of each firm will therefore decline. Thus if we compare two markets, one with higher S than the other, the CC curve in the larger market will be below that in the smaller one.

Meanwhile, the PP curve in Figure 6-3, which relates the price charged by firms to the number of firms, does not shift. The definition of that curve is given in equation (6-10):

$$P = c + 1/(b \times n).$$

The size of the market does not enter into this equation, so an increase in S does not shift the PP curve.

Figure 6-4 uses this information to show the effect of an increase in the size of the market on long-run equilibrium. Initially, equilibrium is at point 1, with a price P_1 and a number of firms n_1. An increase in the size of the market, measured by industry sales S, shifts the CC curve down from CC_1 to CC_2, while it has no effect on the PP curve. The new equilibrium is at point 2: The number of firms increases from n_1 to n_2, while the price falls from P_1 to P_2.

Clearly, consumers would prefer to be part of a large market rather than a small one. At point 2, a greater variety of products is available at a lower price than at point 1.

GAINS FROM AN INTEGRATED MARKET: A NUMERICAL EXAMPLE

International trade can create a larger market. We can illustrate the effects of trade on prices, scale, and the variety of goods available with a specific numerical example.

FIGURE 6-4

Effects of a Larger Market

An increase in the size of the market allows each firm, other things equal, to produce more and thus have lower average cost. This is represented by a downward shift from CC_1 to CC_2. The result is a simultaneous increase in the number of firms (and hence in the variety of goods available) and fall in the price of each

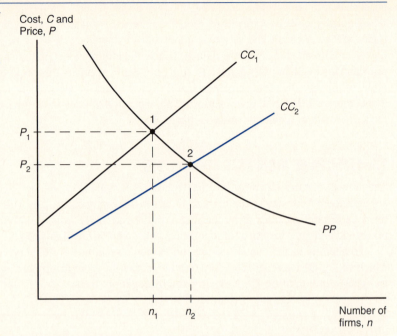

Imagine that automobiles are produced by a monopolistically competitive industry. The demand curve facing any given producer of automobiles is described by equation (6-5), with $b = 1/30,000$ (this value has no particular significance; it was chosen to make the example come out neatly). Thus the demand facing any one producer is given by

$$Q = S \times [1/n - (1/30,000) \times (P - \bar{P})],$$

where Q is the number of automobiles sold per firm, S the total sales of the industry, n the number of firms, P the price that a firm charges, and $\bar{P}$ the average price of other firms. We also assume that the cost function for producing automobiles is described by equation (6-3), with a fixed cost $F = \$750,000,000$ and a marginal cost $c = \$5000$ per automobile (again these values are chosen to give nice results). The total cost is

$$C = 750,000,000 + (5000 \times Q).$$

The average cost curve is therefore

$$AC = (750,000,000/Q) + 5000.$$

Now suppose there are two countries, Home and Foreign. Home has annual sales of 900,000 automobiles; Foreign has annual sales of 1.6 million. The two countries are assumed, for the moment, to have the same costs of production.

Figure 6-5a shows the PP and CC curves for the Home auto industry. We find that in the absence of trade, Home would have six automobile firms, selling at a price of \$10,000 each. (It is also possible to solve for n and P algebraically, as shown in the Mathematical

FIGURE 6-5

Equilibrium in the Automobile Market

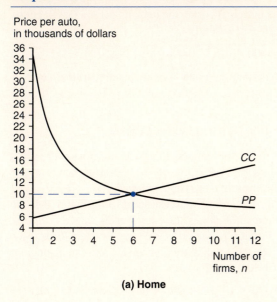

(a) Home

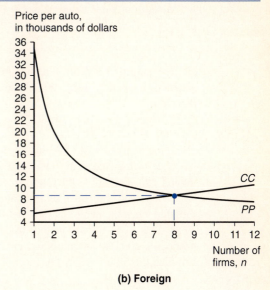

(b) Foreign

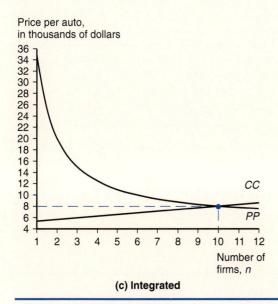

(c) Integrated

(a) The Home market: With a market size of 900,000 automobiles, Home's equilibrium, determined by the intersection of the *PP* and *CC* curves, occurs with six firms and an industry price of $10,000 per auto. (b) The Foreign market: With a market size of 1.6 million automobiles, Foreign's equilibrium occurs with eight firms and an industry price of $8750 per car. (c) The combined market: Integrating the two markets creates a market for 2.5 million autos. This market supports ten firms, and the price of an auto is only $8000.

Postscript to this chapter.) To confirm that this is the long-run equilibrium, we need to show both that the pricing equation (6-10) is satisfied and that the price equals average cost.

Substituting the actual values of the marginal cost c, the demand parameter b, and the number of Home firms n into equation (6-10), we find

$$P = \$10,000 = c + 1/(b \times n) = \$5000 + 1/[(1/30,000) \times 6] = \$5000 + \$5000,$$

so the condition for profit maximization—that marginal revenue equal marginal cost—is satisfied. Each firm sells 900,000 units/6 firms = 150,000 units/firm. Its average cost is therefore

$$AC = (\$750,000,000/150,000) + \$5000 = \$10,000.$$

Since the average cost of $10,000 per unit is the same as the price, all monopoly profits have been competed away. Thus six firms, selling at a price of $10,000, with each firm producing 150,000 cars, is the long-run equilibrium in the Home market.

What about Foreign? By drawing the PP and CC curves (panel (b) in Figure 6-5) we find that when the market is for 1.6 million automobiles, the curves intersect at $n = 8$, $P = 8750$. That is, in the absence of trade Foreign's market would support eight firms, each producing 200,000 automobiles, and selling them at a price of $8750. We can again confirm that this solution satisfies the equilibrium conditions:

$$P = \$8750 = c + 1/(b \times n) = \$5000 + 1/[(1/30,000) \times 8] = \$5000 + \$3750,$$

and

$$AC = (\$750,000,000/200,000) + \$5000 = \$8750.$$

Now suppose it is possible for Home and Foreign to trade automobiles costlessly with one another. This creates a new, integrated market (panel (c) in Figure 6-5) with total sales of 2.5 million. By drawing the PP and CC curves one more time, we find that this integrated market will support ten firms, each producing 250,000 cars and selling them at a price of $8000. The conditions for profit maximization and zero profits are again satisfied:

$$P = \$8000 = c + 1/(b \times n) = \$5000 + 1/[(1/30,000) \times 10] = \$5000 + \$3000,$$

and

$$AC = (\$750,000,000/250,000) + \$5000 = \$8000.$$

We summarize the results of creating an integrated market in Table 6-2. The table compares each market alone with the integrated market. The integrated market supports

TABLE 6-2

Hypothetical Example of Gains from Market Integration

	Home market, before trade	Foreign market, before trade	Integrated market, after trade
Total sales of autos	900,000	1,600,000	2,500,000
Number of firms	6	8	10
Sales per firm	150,000	200,000	250,000
Average cost	10.00	8.75	8.00
Price	10.00	8.75	8.00

more firms, each producing at a larger scale and selling at a lower price than either national market did on its own.

Clearly everyone is better off as a result of integration. In the larger market, consumers have a wider range of choice, yet each firm produces more and is therefore able to offer its product at a lower price.

To realize these gains from integration, the countries must engage in international trade. To achieve economies of scale, each firm must concentrate its production in one country—either Home or Foreign. Yet it must sell its output to customers in both markets. So each product will be produced in only one country and exported to the other.

ECONOMIES OF SCALE AND COMPARATIVE ADVANTAGE

Our example of a monopolistically competitive industry says little about the pattern of trade that results from economies of scale. The model assumes that the cost of production is the same in both countries and that trade is costless. These assumptions mean that although we know that the integrated market will support ten firms, we cannot say where they will be located. For example, four firms might be in Home and six in Foreign—but it is equally possible, as far as this example goes, that all ten will be in Foreign (or in Home).

To say more than that the market will support ten firms, it is necessary to go behind the partial equilibrium framework that we have considered so far and think about how economies of scale interact with comparative advantage to determine the pattern of international trade.

Let us therefore now imagine a world economy consisting, as usual, of our two countries Home and Foreign. Each of these countries has two factors of production, capital and labor. We assume that Home has a higher overall capital-labor ratio than Foreign, that is, that Home is the capital-abundant country. Let's also imagine that there are two industries, manufactures and food, with manufactures the more capital-intensive industry.

The difference between this model and the factor proportions model of Chapter 4 is that we now suppose that manufactures is not a perfectly competitive industry producing a homogeneous product. Instead, it is a monopolistically competitive industry in which a number of firms all produce differentiated products. *Because of economies of scale, neither country is able to produce the full range of manufactured products by itself; thus, although both countries may produce some manufactures, they will be producing different things.* The monopolistically competitive nature of the manufactures industry makes an important difference to the trade pattern, a difference that can best be seen by looking at what would happen if manufactures were *not* a monopolistically competitive sector.

If manufactures were *not* a differentiated product sector, we know from Chapter 4 what the trade pattern would look like. Because Home is capital-abundant and manufactures capital-intensive, Home would have a larger relative supply of manufactures and would therefore export manufactures and import food. Schematically, we can represent this trade pattern with a diagram like Figure 6-6. The length of the arrows indicates the value of trade in each direction; the figure shows that Home would export manufactures equal in value to the food it imports.

If we assume that manufactures is a monopolistically competitive sector (each firm's products are differentiated from other firms'), Home will still be a *net* exporter of manufactures and an importer of food. However, Foreign firms in the manufactures sector will

FIGURE 6-6

Trade in a World Without Increasing Returns

In a world without economies of scale, there would be a simple exchange of manufactures for food.

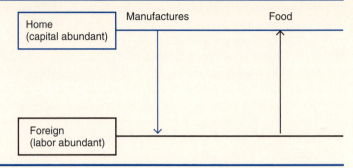

produce products different from those that Home firms produce. Because some Home consumers will prefer Foreign varieties, Home, although running a trade surplus in manufactures, will import as well as export within the manufacturing industry. With manufactures monopolistically competitive, then, the pattern of trade will look like Figure 6-7.

We can think of world trade in a monopolistic competition model as consisting of two parts. There will be two-way trade *within* the manufacturing sector. This exchange of manufactures for manufactures is called **intraindustry trade.** The remainder of trade is an exchange of manufactures for food called **interindustry trade.**

Notice these four points about this pattern of trade:

1. *Interindustry* (manufactures for food) trade reflects comparative advantage. The pattern of interindustry trade is that Home, the capital-abundant country, is a net exporter of capital-intensive manufactures and a net importer of labor-intensive food. So comparative advantage continues to be a major part of the trade story.

FIGURE 6-7

Trade with Increasing Returns and Monopolistic Competition

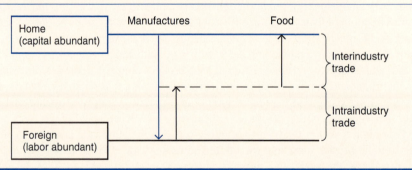

If manufactures is a monopolistically competitive industry, Home and Foreign will produce differentiated products. As a result, even if Home is a net exporter of manufactured goods, it will import as well as export manufactures, giving rise to intraindustry trade.

2. *Intraindustry* trade (manufactures for manufactures) does *not* reflect comparative advantage. Even if the countries had the same overall capital-labor ratio, their firms would continue to produce differentiated products and the demand of consumers for products made abroad would continue to generate intraindustry trade. It is economies of scale that keep each country from producing the full range of products for itself; thus economies of scale can be an independent source of international trade.

3. The pattern of intraindustry trade itself is unpredictable. We have not said anything about which country produces which goods within the manufactures sector because there is nothing in the model to tell us. All we know is that the countries will produce different products. Since history and accident determine the details of the trade pattern, an unpredictable component of the trade pattern is an inevitable feature of a world where economies of scale are important. Notice, however, that the unpredictability is not total. While the precise pattern of intraindustry trade within the manufactures sector is arbitrary, the pattern of interindustry trade between manufactures and food is determined by underlying differences between countries.

4. The relative importance of intraindustry and interindustry trade depends on how similar countries are. If Home and Foreign are similar in their capital-labor ratios, then there will be little interindustry trade, and intraindustry trade, based ultimately on economies of scale, will be dominant. On the other hand, if the capital-labor ratios are very different, so that, for example, Foreign specializes completely in food production, there will be no intraindustry trade based on economies of scale. All trade will be based on comparative advantage.

THE SIGNIFICANCE OF INTRAINDUSTRY TRADE

About one-fourth of world trade consists of intraindustry trade, that is, two-way exchanges of goods within standard industrial classifications. Intraindustry trade plays a particularly large role in the trade in manufactured goods among advanced industrial nations, which accounts for most of world trade. Over time, the industrial countries have become increasingly similar in their levels of technology and in the availability of capital and skilled labor. Since the major trading nations have become similar in technology and resources, there is often no clear comparative advantage within an industry, and much of international trade therefore takes the form of two-way exchanges within industries—probably driven in large part by economies of scale—rather than interindustry specialization driven by comparative advantage.

Table 63 shows measures of the importance of intraindustry trade for a number of U.S. manufacturing industries in 1993. The measure shown is intraindustry trade/total trade. The measure ranges from 0.99 for inorganic chemicals—an industry in which U.S. exports and imports are nearly equal—to 0.00 for footwear, an industry in which the United States has large imports but virtually no exports. The measure would be zero for an industry in which the United States was only an exporter or only an importer, not both; it would be one in an industry for which U.S. exports exactly equaled U.S. imports.

Table 6-3 shows that in many industries a large part of trade is intraindustry (closer to one) rather than interindustry (closer to zero). The industries are ranked by the relative importance of intraindustry trade, those with higher intraindustry trade first. Industries with high levels of intraindustry trade tend to be sophisticated manufactured goods, such as chemicals, pharmaceuticals, and power-generating equipment. These goods are exported principally by advanced nations and are probably subject to important economies of scale

TABLE 6-3	
Indexes of Intraindustry Trade for U.S. Industries, 1993	
Inorganic chemicals	0.99
Power-generating machinery	0.97
Electrical machinery	0.96
Organic chemicals	0.91
Medical and pharmaceutical	0.86
Office machinery	0.81
Telecommunications equipment	0.69
Road vehicles	0.65
Iron and steel	0.43
Clothing and apparel	0.27
Footwear	0.20

in production. At the other end of the scale, the industries with very little intraindustry trade are typically labor-intensive products, such as footwear and apparel. These are goods that the United States imports primarily from less developed countries, where comparative advantage is clear-cut and is the primary determinant of U.S. trade with these countries.[5]

WHY INTRAINDUSTRY TRADE MATTERS

Table 6-3 shows that a sizeable part of international trade is intraindustry trade rather than the interindustry trade we studied in Chapters 2 through 5. But does the importance of intraindustry trade change any of our conclusions?

First, intraindustry trade produces extra gains from international trade, over and above those from comparative advantage, because intraindustry trade allows countries to benefit from larger markets. As we have seen, by engaging in intraindustry trade a country can simultaneously reduce the number of products it produces *and* increase the variety of goods available to domestic consumers. By producing fewer varieties, a country can produce each at larger scale, with higher productivity and lower costs. At the same time, consumers benefit from the increased range of choice. In our numerical example of the gains from integrating a market, Home consumers found that intraindustry trade expanded their range of choice from six automobile models to ten even as it reduced the price of autos from $10,000 to $8000. As the case study of the North American auto industry indicates (p. 141), the advantages of creating an integrated industry in two countries can be substantial in reality as well.

In our earlier analysis of the distribution of gains from trade (Chapters 3 and 4), we were pessimistic about the prospects that everyone will benefit from trade, even though in-

---

[5]The growing trade between low-wage and high-wage nations sometimes produces trade that is classified as intraindustry even though it is really driven by comparative advantage. Suppose, for example, a U.S. company produces some sophisticated computer chips in California, ships them to Asia where they are assembled into a computer, and then ships that computer back home. Both the exported components and the imported computer are likely to be classified as being "computers and related devices," so that the transactions will be counted as intraindustry trade. Nonetheless, what is really going on is that the United States is exporting skill-intensive products (chips) and importing a labor-intensive service (computer assembly). Such "pseudo-intraindustry" trade is particularly common in trade between the United States and Mexico.

ternational trade could potentially raise everyone's income. In the models discussed earlier, trade had all its effects through changes in relative prices, which in turn have very strong effects on the distribution of income.

Suppose, however, that intraindustry trade is the dominant source of gains from trade. This will happen (1) when countries are similar in their relative factor supplies, so that there is not much interindustry trade, and (2) when scale economies and product differentiation are important, so that the gains from larger scale and increased choice are large. In these circumstances the income distribution effects of trade will be small and there will be substantial extra gains from intraindustry trade. The result may well be that despite the effects of trade on income distribution, everyone gains from trade.

When will this be most likely to happen? Intraindustry trade tends to be prevalent between countries that are similar in their capital-labor ratios, skill levels, and so on. Thus, intraindustry trade will be dominant between countries at a similar level of economic development. Gains from this trade will be large when economies of scale are strong and products are highly differentiated. This is more characteristic of sophisticated manufactured goods than of raw materials or more traditional sectors (such as textiles or footwear). Trade without serious income distribution effects, then, is most likely to happen in manufactures trade between advanced industrial countries.

This conclusion is borne out by postwar experience, particularly in Western Europe. In 1957 the major countries of continental Europe established a free trade area in manufactured goods, the Common Market, or European Economic Community (EEC). (The United Kingdom entered the EEC later, in 1973.) The result was a rapid growth of trade: Trade within the EEC grew twice as fast as world trade as a whole during the 1960s. One might have expected this rapid growth in trade to produce substantial dislocations and political problems. The growth in trade, however, was almost entirely intraindustry rather than interindustry; drastic economic dislocation did not occur. Instead of, say, workers in France's electrical machinery industry being hurt while those in Germany's gained, workers in both sectors gained from the increased efficiency of the integrated European industry. The result was that the growth in trade within Europe presented far fewer social and political problems than anyone anticipated.

There is both a good and a bad side to this favorable view of intraindustry trade. The good side is that under some circumstances trade is relatively easy to live with and therefore relatively easy to support politically. The bad side is that trade between very different countries or where scale economies and product differentiation are not important remains politically problematic. In fact, the progressive liberalization of trade that characterized the 30-year period from 1950 to 1980 was primarily concentrated on trade in manufactures among the advanced nations, as we will see in Chapter 9. If progress on other kinds of trade is important, the past record does not give us much encouragement.

CASE STUDY

INTRAINDUSTRY TRADE IN ACTION: THE NORTH AMERICAN AUTO PACT OF 1964

An unusually clear-cut example of the role of economies of scale in generating beneficial international trade is provided by the growth in automotive trade between the United States and Canada during the second half of the 1960s. While the case does not fit our model exactly, it does show that the basic concepts we have developed are useful in the real world.

Before 1965, tariff protection by Canada and the United States produced a Canadian auto industry that was largely self-sufficient, neither importing nor exporting much. The Canadian industry was controlled by the same firms as the U.S. industry—a departure from our model, since we have not yet examined the role of multinational firms—but these firms found it cheaper to have largely separate production systems than to pay the tariffs. Thus the Canadian industry was in effect a miniature version of the U.S. industry, at about one-tenth the scale.

The Canadian subsidiaries of U.S. firms found that small scale was a substantial disadvantage. This was partly because Canadian plants had to be smaller than their U.S. counterparts. Perhaps more important, U.S. plants could often be "dedicated"— that is, devoted to producing a single model or component—while Canadian plants had to produce several different things, requiring the plants to shut down periodically to change over from producing one item to producing another, to hold larger inventories, to use less specialized machinery, and so on. The Canadian auto industry had a labor productivity about 30 percent lower than that of the United States.

In an effort to remove these problems, the United States and Canada agreed in 1964 to establish a free trade area in automobiles (subject to certain restrictions). This allowed the auto companies to reorganize their production. Canadian subsidiaries of the auto firms sharply cut the number of products made in Canada. For example, General Motors cut in half the number of models assembled in Canada. The overall level of Canadian production and employment was, however, maintained. This was achieved by importing from the United States products no longer made in Canada and exporting the products Canada continued to make. In 1962, Canada exported $16 million worth of automotive products to the United States while importing $519 million worth. By 1968 the numbers were $2.4 and $2.9 billion, respectively. In other words, both exports and imports increased sharply: intraindustry trade in action.

The gains seem to have been substantial. By the early 1970s the Canadian industry was comparable to the U.S. industry in productivity.

DUMPING

The monopolistic competition model helps us understand how increasing returns promote international trade. As we noted earlier, however, this model assumes away many of the issues that can arise when firms are imperfectly competitive. Although it recognizes that imperfect competition is a necessary consequence of economies of scale, the monopolistic competition analysis does not focus on the possible consequences of imperfect competition itself for international trade.

In reality, imperfect competition has some important consequences for international trade. The most striking of these is that firms do not necessarily charge the same price for goods that are exported and those that are sold to domestic buyers.

THE ECONOMICS OF DUMPING

In imperfectly competitive markets, firms sometimes charge one price for a good when that good is exported and a different price for the same good when it is sold domestically.

In general, the practice of charging different customers different prices is called **price discrimination.** The most common form of price discrimination in international trade is **dumping,** a pricing practice in which a firm charges a lower price for exported goods than it does for the same goods sold domestically. Dumping is a controversial issue in trade policy, where it is widely regarded as an "unfair" practice and is subject to special rules and penalties. We will discuss the policy dispute surrounding dumping in Chapter 9. For now, we present some basic economic analysis of the dumping phenomenon.

Dumping can occur only if two conditions are met. First, the industry must be imperfectly competitive, so that firms set prices rather than taking market prices as given. Second, markets must be *segmented,* so that domestic residents cannot easily purchase goods intended for export. Given these conditions, a monopolistic firm may find that it is profitable to engage in dumping.

An example may help to show how dumping can be a profit-maximizing strategy. Imagine a firm that currently sells 1000 units of a good at home and 100 units abroad. Currently selling the good at $20 per unit domestically, it gets only $15 per unit on export sales. One might imagine that the firm would conclude that additional domestic sales are much more profitable than additional exports.

Suppose, however, that to expand sales by one unit, in either market, would require reducing the price by $0.01. Reducing the domestic price by a penny, then, would increase sales by one unit—directly adding $19.99 in revenue, but reducing the receipts on the 1000 units that would have sold at the $20 price by $10. So the marginal revenue from the extra unit sold is only $9.99. On the other hand, reducing the price charged to foreign customers and thereby expanding exports by one unit would directly increase revenue by only $14.99. The indirect cost of reduced receipts on the 100 units that would have been sold at the original price, however, would be only $1, so that marginal revenue on export sales would be $13.99. It would therefore be more profitable in this case to expand exports rather than domestic sales, even though the price received on exports is lower.

This example could be reversed, with the incentive being to charge less on domestic than foreign sales. However, price discrimination in favor of exports is more common. Since international markets are imperfectly integrated due to both transportation costs and protectionist trade barriers, domestic firms usually have a larger share of home markets than they do of foreign markets. This in turn usually means that their foreign sales are more affected by their pricing than their domestic sales. A firm with a 20 percent market share need not cut its price as much to double its sales as a firm with an 80 percent share. So firms typically see themselves as having less monopoly power, and a greater incentive to keep their prices low, on exports than on domestic sales.

Figure 6-8 offers a diagrammatic example of dumping. It shows an industry in which there is a single monopolistic domestic firm. The firm sells in two markets: a domestic market, where it faces the demand curve D_{DOM}, and an export market. In the export market we take the assumption that sales are highly responsive to the price the firm charges to an extreme, assuming the firm can sell as much as it wants at the price P_{FOR}. The horizontal line P_{FOR} is thus the demand curve for sales in the foreign market. We assume the markets are segmented, so that the firm can charge a higher price for domestically sold goods than it does for exports. MC is the marginal cost curve for total output, which can be sold on either market.

To maximize profits, the firm must set marginal revenue equal to marginal cost in *each* market. Marginal revenue on domestic sales is defined by the curve MR_{DOM}, which lies below D_{DOM}. Export sales take place at a constant price P_{FOR}, so the marginal revenue for an additional unit exported is just P_{FOR}. To set marginal cost equal to marginal revenue

FIGURE 6-8

Dumping

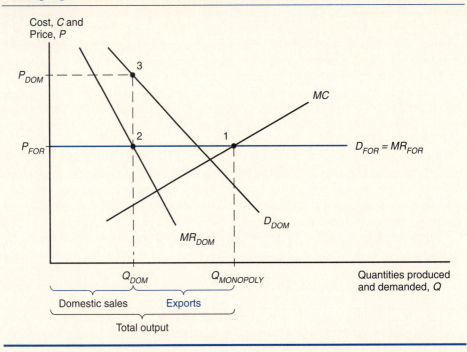

The figure shows a monopolist that faces a demand curve D_{DOM} for domestic sales, but which can also sell as much as it likes at the export price P_{FOR}. Since an additional unit can always be sold at P_{FOR}, the firm increases output until the marginal cost equals P_{FOR}; this profit-maximizing output is shown as $Q_{MONOPOLY}$. Since the firm's marginal cost at $Q_{MONOPOLY}$ is P_{FOR}, it sells output on the domestic market up to the point where marginal revenue equals P_{FOR}; this profit-maximizing level of domestic sales is shown as Q_{DOM}. The rest of its output, $Q_{MONOPOLY} - Q_{DOM}$ is exported.

The price at which domestic consumers demand Q_{DOM} is P_{DOM}. Since $P_{DOM} > P_{FOR}$, the firm sells exports at a lower price than it charges domestic consumers.

in both markets it is necessary to produce the quantity $Q_{MONOPOLY}$, to sell Q_{DOM} on the domestic market, and to export $Q_{MONOPOLY} - Q_{DOM}$.[6] The cost of producing an additional unit in this case is equal to P_{FOR}, the marginal revenue from exports, which in turn is equal to the marginal revenue for domestic sales.

The quantity Q_{DOM} will be demanded domestically at a price of P_{DOM}, which is above the export price P_{FOR}. Thus the firm is indeed dumping, selling more cheaply abroad than at home.

---

[6]It might seem that the monopolist should set domestic sales at the level where MC and MR_{DOM} intersect. But remember that the monopolist is producing a total output $Q_{MONOPOLY}$; this means that the cost of producing one more unit is equal to P_{FOR}, whether that unit is destined for the foreign or domestic market. And it is the actual cost of producing one more unit that must be set equal to marginal revenue. The intersection of MC and MR_{DOM} is where the firm would produce *if it did not have the option of exporting*—but that is irrelevant.

In both our numerical example and Figure 6-8, the reason the firm chooses to dump is the difference in the responsiveness of sales to price in the export and domestic markets. In Figure 6-8 we assume the firm can increase exports without cutting its price, so marginal revenue and price coincide on the export market. Domestically, by contrast, increased sales do lower the price. This is an extreme example of the general condition for price discrimination presented in microeconomics courses: Firms will price-discriminate when sales are more price-responsive in one market than in another.[7] (In this case we have assumed export demand is infinitely price-responsive.)

Dumping is widely regarded as an unfair practice in international trade. There is no good economic justification for regarding dumping as particularly harmful, but U.S. trade law prohibits foreign firms from dumping in our market and automatically imposes tariffs when such dumping is discovered.

The situation shown in Figure 6-8 is simply an extreme version of a wider class of situations in which firms have an incentive to sell exports for a lower price than the price they charge domestic customers.

ANTIDUMPING AS PROTECTIONISM

In the United States and a number of other countries, dumping is regarded as an unfair competitive practice. Firms that claim to have been injured by foreign firms who dump their products in the domestic market at low prices can appeal, through a quasi-judicial procedure, to the Commerce Department for relief. If their complaint is ruled valid—and from 1980 to 1989 54 percent of foreign companies accused of dumping were deemed guilty—an "antidumping duty" is imposed, equal to the calculated difference between the actual and "fair" price of imports.

Economists have never been very happy with the idea of singling dumping out as a prohibited practice. For one thing, price discrimination between markets may be a perfectly legitimate business strategy—like the discounts that airlines offer to students, senior citizens, and travelers who are willing to stay over a weekend. Also, the legal definition of dumping deviates substantially from the economic definition. Since it is often difficult to prove that foreign firms charge higher prices to domestic than export customers, the United States and other nations instead often try to calculate a supposed fair price based on estimates of foreign production costs. This "fair price" rule can interfere with perfectly normal business practices: A firm may well be willing to sell a product for a loss while it is lowering its costs through experience or breaking into a new market.

In spite of almost universal negative assessments from economists, however, formal complaints about dumping have been filed with growing frequency since

---

[7]The formal condition for price discrimination is that firms will charge lower prices in markets in which they face a higher *elasticity* of demand, where the elasticity is the percentage decrease in sales that results from a 1 percent increase in price. Firms will dump if they perceive a higher elasticity on export sales than on domestic sales.

about 1970. Is this just cynical abuse of the law, or does it reflect a real increase in the importance of dumping? The answer may be a little of both.

Why may dumping have increased? Because of the uneven pace at which countries have opened up their markets. Since 1970 trade liberalization and deregulation have opened up international competition in a number of previously sheltered industries. For example, it used to be taken for granted that telephone companies would buy their equipment from domestic manufacturers. With the breakup of AT&T in the United States and the privatization of phone companies in other countries, this is no longer the case everywhere. But in Japan and several European countries the old rules still apply. It is not surprising that the manufacturers of telephone equipment in these countries would continue to charge high prices at home while offering lower prices to customers in the United States—or at least that they would be accused of doing so.

At the time of writing, the United States had imposed antidumping duties on European steel exports, threatening to undermine trade negotiations already in progress. And Japan, usually the party accused of dumping, had turned accuser, imposing duties on allegedly dumped steel from China.

RECIPROCAL DUMPING

The analysis of dumping suggests that price discrimination can actually give rise to international trade. Suppose there are two monopolies, each producing the same good, one in Home and one in Foreign. To simplify the analysis, assume that these two firms have the same marginal cost. Suppose also that there are some costs of transportation between the two markets, so that if the firms charge the same price there will be no trade. In the absence of trade, each firm's monopoly would be uncontested.

If we introduce the possibility of dumping, however, trade may emerge. Each firm will limit the quantity it sells in its home market, recognizing that if it tries to sell more it will drive down the price on its existing domestic sales. If a firm can sell a little bit in the other market, however, it will add to its profits even if the price is lower than in the domestic market, because the negative effect on the price of existing sales will fall on the other firm, not on itself. So each firm has an incentive to "raid" the other market, selling a few units at a price that (net of transportation costs) is lower than the home market price but still above marginal cost.

If both firms do this, however, the result will be the emergence of trade even though there was (by assumption) no initial difference in the price of the good in the two markets, and even though there are some transportation costs. Even more peculiarly, there will be two-way trade in the same product. For example, a cement plant in country A might be shipping cement to country B while a cement plant in B is doing the reverse. The situation in which dumping leads to two-way trade in the same product is known as **reciprocal dumping**.[8]

This may seem like a strange case, and it is admittedly probably rare in international trade for exactly identical goods to be shipped in both directions at once. However, the re-

---

[8]The possibility of reciprocal dumping was first noted by James Brander, "Intraindustry Trade in Identical Commodities," *Journal of International Economics* 11 (1981), pp. 1–14.

ciprocal dumping effect probably tends to increase the volume of trade in goods that are not quite identical.

Is such peculiar and seemingly pointless trade socially desirable? The answer is ambiguous. It is obviously wasteful to ship the same good, or close substitutes, back and forth when transportation is costly. However, notice that the emergence of reciprocal dumping in our story eliminates what were initially pure monopolies, leading to some competition. The increased competition represents a benefit that may offset the waste of resources in transportation. The net effect of such peculiar trade on a nation's economic welfare is therefore uncertain.

THE THEORY OF EXTERNAL ECONOMIES

In the monopolistic competition model of trade it is presumed that the economies of scale that give rise to international trade occur at the level of the individual firm. That is, the larger any particular firm's output of a product, the lower its average cost. The inevitable result of such economies of scale at the level of the firm is imperfect competition, which in turn allows such practices as dumping.

As we pointed out early in this chapter, however, not all scale economies apply at the level of the individual firm. For a variety of reasons, it is often the case that concentrating production of an industry in one or a few locations reduces the industry's costs, even if the individual firms in the industry remain small. When economies of scale apply at the level of the industry rather than at the level of the individual firm, they are called *external economies*. The analysis of external economies goes back more than a century to the British economist Alfred Marshall, who was struck by the phenomenon of "industrial districts"—geographical concentrations of industry that could not be easily explained by natural resources. In Marshall's time the most famous examples included such concentrations of industry as the cluster of cutlery manufacturers in Sheffield and the cluster of hosiery firms in Northampton. Modern examples of industries where there seem to be powerful external economies include the semiconductor industry, concentrated in California's famous Silicon Valley; the investment banking industry, concentrated in New York; and the entertainment industry, concentrated in Hollywood.

Marshall argued that there were three main reasons why a cluster of firms may be more efficient than an individual firm in isolation: the ability of a cluster to support **specialized suppliers;** the way that a geographically concentrated industry allows **labor market pooling;** and the way that a geographically concentrated industry helps foster **knowledge spillovers.** These same factors continue to be valid today.

SPECIALIZED SUPPLIERS

In many industries, the production of goods and services—and to an even greater extent, the development of new products—requires the use of specialized equipment or support services; yet an individual company does not provide a large enough market for these services to keep the suppliers in business. A localized industrial cluster can solve this problem by bringing together many firms that collectively provide a large enough market to support a wide range of specialized suppliers. This phenomenon has been extensively documented in Silicon Valley: A recent study recounts how, as the local industry grew, "engineers left established semiconductor companies to start firms that manufactured capital goods such as diffusion ovens, step-and-repeat cameras, and testers, and materials and components such as photomasks, testing jigs, and specialized chemicals. . . . This independent equipment sector promoted the continuing formation of semiconductor firms by freeing individual producers from the expense of developing capital equipment internally and by spreading the costs of development. It also reinforced the tendency toward industrial localization, as most of these specialized inputs were not available elsewhere in the country."[9]

As the quote suggests, the availability of this dense network of specialized suppliers has given high-technology firms in Silicon Valley some considerable advantages over firms elsewhere. Key inputs are cheaper and more easily available because there are many firms competing to provide them, and firms can concentrate on what they do best, contracting out other aspects of their business. For example, some Silicon Valley firms that specialize in providing highly sophisticated computer chips for particular customers have chosen to become "fabless," that is, they do not have any factories in which chips can be fabricated. Instead, they concentrate on designing the chips, then hire another firm actually to fabricate them.

A company that tried to enter the industry in another location—for example, in a country that did not have a comparable industrial cluster—would be at an immediate disadvantage because it would lack easy access to Silicon Valley's suppliers and would either have to provide them for itself or be faced with the task of trying to deal with Silicon Valley–based suppliers at long distance.

LABOR MARKET POOLING

A second source of external economies is the way that a cluster of firms can create a pooled market for workers with highly specialized skills. Such a pooled market is to the advantage of both the producers and the workers as the producers are less likely to suffer from labor shortages, while the workers are less likely to become unemployed.

The point can best be made with a simplified example. Imagine that there are two companies that both use the same kind of specialized labor, say, two film studios that make use of experts in computer animation. Both employers are, however, uncertain about how many workers they will want to hire: If demand for its product is high, both companies will want to hire 150 workers, but if it is low, they will only want to hire 50. Suppose also that there are 200 workers with this special skill. Now compare two situations: one with both firms and all 200 workers in the same city, the other with the firms and 100 workers in two different cities. It is straightforward to show that both the workers and their employers are better off if everyone is in the same place.

First, consider the situation from the point of view of the companies. If they are in different locations, whenever one of the companies is doing well it will be confronted with a labor shortage; it will want to hire 150 workers, but only 100 will be available. If the firms are near each other, however, it is at least possible that one will be doing well when the other is doing badly, so that both firms may be able to hire as many workers as they want. So by locating near each other, the companies increase the likelihood that they will be able to take advantage of business opportunities.

From the workers' point of view, having the industry concentrated in one location is also an advantage. If the industry is divided between two cities, then whenever one of the firms has a low demand for workers the result will be unemployment; the firm will be will-

---

[9]See the book by Saxenian listed in Further Reading, p. 40.

ing to hire only 50 of the 100 workers who live nearby. But if the industry is concentrated in a single city, low labor demand from one firm will at least sometimes be offset by high demand from the other. As a result, workers will have a lower risk of unemployment.

Again, these advantages have been documented for Silicon Valley, where it is common both for companies to expand rapidly and for workers to change employers. The same study of Silicon Valley that was quoted previously notes that the concentration of firms in a single location makes it easy to switch employers, quoting one engineer as saying that "it wasn't that big a catastrophe to quit your job on Friday and have another job on Monday. . . . You didn't even necessarily have to tell your wife. You just drove off in another direction on Monday morning."[10] This flexibility makes Silicon Valley an attractive location both for highly skilled workers and for the companies that employ them.

KNOWLEDGE SPILLOVERS

It is by now a cliché that in the modern economy knowledge is at least as important an input as factors of production like labor, capital, and raw materials. This is especially true in highly innovative industries, where being only a few months behind the cutting edge in production techniques or product design can put a company at a major disadvantage.

But where does the specialized knowledge that is crucial to success in innovative industries come from? Companies can acquire technology through their own research and development efforts. They can also try to learn from competitors by studying their products and, in some cases, taking them apart to "reverse engineer" their design and manufacture. An important source of technical know-how, however, is the informal exchange of information and ideas that takes place at a personal level. And this kind of informal diffusion of knowledge often seems to take place most effectively when an industry is concentrated in a fairly small area, so that employees of different companies mix socially and talk freely about technical issues.

Marshall described this process memorably when he wrote that in a district with many firms in the same industry, "The mysteries of the trade become no mystery, but are as it were in the air. . . . Good work is rightly appreciated, inventions and improvements in machinery, in processes and the general organization of the business have their merits promptly discussed: if one man starts a new idea, it is taken up by others and combined with suggestions of their own; and thus it becomes the source of further new ideas."[11]

A journalist described how these knowledge spillovers worked during the rise of Silicon Valley (and also gave an excellent sense of the amount of specialized knowledge involved in the industry) as follows: "Every year there was some place, the Wagon Wheel, Chez Yvonne, Rickey's, the Roundhouse, where members of this esoteric fraternity, the young men and women of the semiconductor industry, would head after work to have a drink and gossip and trade war stories about phase jitters, phantom circuits, bubble memories, pulse trains, bounceless contacts, burst modes, leapfrog tests, p-n junctions, sleeping sickness modes, slow-death episodes, RAMs, NAKs, MOSes, PCMs, PROMs, PROM blowers, PROM blasters, and teramagnitudes. . . ."[12] This kind of informal information flow means that it is easier for companies in the Silicon Valley area to stay near the technological frontier than it is for companies elsewhere; indeed, many multinational firms

---

[10]Saxenian, p. 35.

[11]Alfred Marshall, *Principles of Economics,* London: MacMillan, 1920.

[12]Tom Wolfe, quoted in Saxenian, p. 33.

have established research centers and even factories in Silicon Valley simply in order to keep up with the latest technology.

EXTERNAL ECONOMIES AND INCREASING RETURNS

A geographically concentrated industry is able to support specialized suppliers, provide a pooled labor market, and facilitate knowledge spillovers in a way that a geographically dispersed industry cannot. But a country cannot have a large concentration of firms in an industry unless it possesses a large industry. Thus the theory of external economies indicates that when these external economies are important, a country with a large industry will, other things being equal, be more efficient in that industry than a country with a small industry. Or to put it differently, external economies can give rise to increasing returns to scale *at the level of the national industry.*

While the details of external economies in practice are often quite subtle and complex (as the example of Silicon Valley shows), it can be useful to abstract from the details and represent external economies simply by assuming that an industry's costs are lower, the larger the industry. If we ignore possible imperfections in competition, this means that the industry will have a **forward-falling supply curve:** The larger the industry's output, the lower the price at which firms are willing to sell their output.

EXTERNAL ECONOMIES AND INTERNATIONAL TRADE

External economies, like economies of scale that are internal to firms, play an important role in international trade, but they may be quite different in their effects. In particular, external economies can cause countries to get "locked in" to undesirable patterns of specialization and can even lead to losses from international trade.

EXTERNAL ECONOMIES AND THE PATTERN OF TRADE

When there are external economies of scale, a country that has large production in some industry will tend, other things equal, to have low costs of producing that good. This gives rise to an obvious circularity, since a country that can produce a good cheaply will also therefore tend to produce a lot of that good. Strong external economies tend to confirm existing patterns of interindustry trade, whatever their original sources: Countries that start out as large producers in certain industries, for whatever reason, tend to remain large producers. They may do so even if some other country could potentially produce the goods more cheaply.

Figure 6-9 illustrates this point. We show the cost of producing a watch as a function of the number of watches produced annually. Two countries are shown: "Switzerland" and "Thailand." The Swiss cost of producing a watch is shown as AC_{SWISS}; the Thai cost as $AC_{THAI}.$ D represents the world demand for watches, which we assume can be satisfied either by Switzerland or by Thailand.

Suppose that the economies of scale in watch production are entirely external to firms, and that since there are no economies of scale at the level of the firm the watch industry in each country consists of many small perfectly competitive firms. Competition therefore drives the price of watches down to its average cost.

External Economies and Specialization

The average cost curve for Thailand, AC_{THAI}, lies below the average cost curve for Switzerland, AC_{SWISS}. Thus Thailand could potentially supply the world market more cheaply than Switzerland. If the Swiss industry gets established first, however, it may be able to sell watches at the price P_1, which is below the cost C_0 that an individual Thai firm would face if it began production on its own. So a pattern of specialization established by historical accident may persist even when new producers could potentially have lower costs.

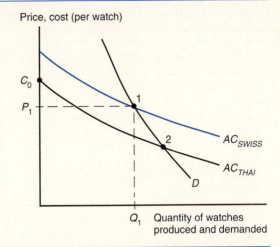

We assume that the Thai cost curve lies below the Swiss curve, say because Thai wages are lower than Swiss. This means that at any given level of production, Thailand could manufacture watches more cheaply than Switzerland. One might hope that this would always imply that Thailand will in fact supply the world market. Unfortunately, this need not be the case. Suppose that Switzerland, for historical reasons, establishes its watch industry first. Then initially world watch equilibrium will be established at point 1 in Figure 6-9, with Swiss production of Q_1 units per year and a price of P_1. Now introduce the possibility of Thai production. If Thailand could take over the world market, the equilibrium would move to point 2. However, if there is no initial Thai production ($Q = 0$), any individual Thai firm considering manufacture of watches will face a cost of production of C_0. As we have drawn it, this cost is above the price at which the established Swiss industry can produce watches. So although the Thai industry could potentially make watches more cheaply than Switzerland, Switzerland's head start enables it to hold onto the industry.

As this example shows, external economies potentially give a strong role to historical accident in determining who produces what, and may allow established patterns of specialization to persist even when they run counter to comparative advantage.

TRADE AND WELFARE WITH EXTERNAL ECONOMIES

Trade based on external economies has more ambiguous effects on national welfare than either trade based on comparative advantage or trade based on economies of scale at the level of the firm. There may be gains to the world economy from concentrating production in particular industries to realize external economies. On the other hand, there is no guarantee that the right country will produce a good subject to external economies, and it is possible that trade based on external economies may actually leave a country worse off than it would have been in the absence of trade.

FIGURE 6-10

External Economies and Losses from Trade

When there are external economies, trade can potentially leave a country worse off than it would be in the absence of trade. In this example, Thailand imports watches from Switzerland, which is able to supply the world market (D_{WORLD}) at a price (P_1) low enough to block entry by Thai producers who must initially produce the watches at cost C_0. Yet if Thailand were to block all trade in watches, it would be able to supply its domestic market (D_{THAI}) at the lower price P_2.

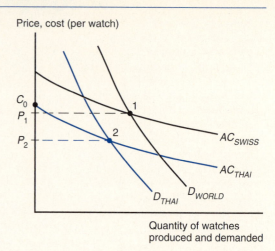

Quantity of watches
produced and demanded

An example of how a country can actually be worse off with trade than without is shown in Figure 6-10. In this example, as before, we imagine that Thailand and Switzerland could both manufacture watches, that Thailand could make them more cheaply, but that Switzerland has gotten there first. D_{WORLD} is the world demand for watches, and, given that Switzerland produces the watches, the equilibrium is at point 1. However, we now add to the figure the Thai demand for watches, D_{THAI}. If no trade in watches were allowed and Thailand were forced to be self-sufficient, then the Thai equilibrium would be at point 2. Because of its lower average cost curve, the price of Thai-made watches at point 2, P_2, is actually lower than the price of Swiss-made watches at point 1, P_1.

We have shown a situation in which the price of a good that Thailand imports would actually be lower if there were no trade and the country were forced to produce the good for itself. Clearly in this situation trade leaves the country worse off than it would be in the absence of trade.

There is an incentive in this case for Thailand to protect its potential watch industry from foreign competition. Before concluding that this justifies protectionism, however, we should note that in practice identifying cases like that in Figure 6-10 is far from easy. Indeed, as we will emphasize in Chapters 10 and 11, the difficulty of identifying external economies in practice is one of the main arguments against activist government policies toward trade.

It is also worth pointing out that while external economies can sometimes lead to disadvantageous patterns of specialization and trade, it is still to the benefit of the *world* economy to take advantage of the gains from concentrating industries. Canada might be better off if Silicon Valley were near Toronto instead of San Francisco; Germany might be better off if the City (London's financial district, which, along with Wall Street, dominates world financial markets) could be moved to Frankfurt. The world as a whole is, however, more efficient and thus richer because international trade allows nations to specialize in different industries and thus reap the gains from external economies as well as the gains from comparative advantage.

TINSELTOWN ECONOMICS

What is America's most important export sector? The answer depends to some extent on definitions; some people will tell you that it is agriculture, others that it is aircraft. By any measure, however, one of the biggest exporters in the United States is the entertainment sector, which earned more than $8 billion in overseas sales in 1994. American-made movies and television programs are shown almost everywhere on earth. The overseas market has also become crucial to Hollywood's finances: Action movies, in particular, often earn more outside the United States than they do at home.

Why is the United States the world's dominant exporter of entertainment? There are important advantages arising from the sheer size of the American market. A film aimed primarily at the French or Italian markets, which are far smaller than that of the United States, cannot justify the huge budgets of many American films. Thus films from these countries are typically dramas or comedies whose appeal fails to survive dubbing or subtitles. Meanwhile, American films can transcend the language barrier with lavish productions and spectacular special effects.

But an important part of the American dominance in the industry also comes from the external economies created by the immense concentration of entertainment firms in Hollywood. Hollywood clearly generates two of Marshall's types of external economies: specialized suppliers and labor market pooling. While the final product is provided by movie studios and television networks, these in turn draw on a complex web of independent producers, casting and talent agencies, legal firms, special effects experts, and so on. And the need for labor market pooling is obvious to anyone who has watched the credits at the end of a movie: Each production requires a huge but temporary army that includes not just cameramen and makeup artists but musicians, stunt men and women, and mysterious occupations like gaffers and grips (and—oh yes—actors and actresses). Whether it also generates the third kind of external economies—knowledge spillovers—is less certain. After all, as the author Nathaniel West once remarked, the key to understanding the movie business is to realize that "nobody knows anything." Still, if there is any knowledge to spill over, surely it does so better in the intense social environment of Hollywood than it could anywhere else.

An indication of the force of Hollywood's external economies has been its persistent ability to draw talent from outside the United States. From Garbo and von Sternberg to Arnold Schwarzenegger and Paul Verhoeven, "American" films have often been made by ambitious foreigners who moved to Hollywood—and in the end reached a larger audience even in their original nations than they could have if they had remained at home.

Is Hollywood unique? No, similar forces have led to the emergence of several other entertainment complexes. In India, whose film market has been protected from American domination partly by government policy and partly by cultural differences, a movie-making cluster known as "Bollywood" has emerged in Bombay. A substantial film industry catering to Chinese speakers has emerged in Hong Kong. And a specialty industry producing Spanish-language television programs for all of Latin America, focusing on so-called *telenovelas*, long-running soap operas, has emerged in Caracas, Venezuela. This last entertainment complex has discovered some unexpected export markets: Television viewers in Russia, it turns out, identify more readily with the characters in Latin American soaps than with those in U.S. productions.

DYNAMIC INCREASING RETURNS

Some of the most important external economies probably arise from the accumulation of knowledge. When an individual firm improves its products or production techniques through experience, other firms are likely to imitate the firm and benefit from its knowledge. This spillover of knowledge gives rise to a situation in which the production costs of individual firms fall as the industry as a whole accumulates experience.

Notice that external economies arising from the accumulation of knowledge differ somewhat from the external economies considered so far, in which industry costs depend on current output. In this alternative situation industry costs depend on experience, usually measured by the cumulative output of the industry to date. For example, the cost of producing a ton of steel might depend negatively on the total number of tons of steel produced by a country since the industry began. This kind of relationship is often summarized by a **learning curve** that relates unit cost to cumulative output. Such learning curves are illustrated in Figure 6-11. They are downward sloping because of the effect of the experience gained through production on costs. When costs fall with cumulative production over time, rather than with the current rate of production, this is referred to as a case of **dynamic increasing returns.**

Like ordinary external economies, dynamic external economies can lock in an initial advantage or head start in an industry. In Figure 6-11, the learning curve L is that of a country that pioneered an industry, while L^* is that of another country that has lower input costs—say, lower wages—but less production experience. Provided that the first country has a sufficiently large head start, the potentially lower costs of the second country may not allow it to enter the market. For example, suppose the first country has a cumulative output of Q_L units, giving it a unit cost of C_1, while the second country has never produced the good. Then the second country will have an initial start-up cost C_0^* that is higher than the current unit cost, C_1, of the established industry.

Dynamic scale economies, like external economies at a point in time, potentially justify protectionism. Suppose that a country could have low enough costs to produce a good

---

FIGURE 6-11

The Learning Curve

The learning curve shows that unit cost is lower, the greater the cumulative output of a country's industry to date. A country that has extensive experience in an industry (L) may have lower unit cost than another country with little or no experience, even if the second country's learning curve (L^*) is lower, for example, because of lower wages.

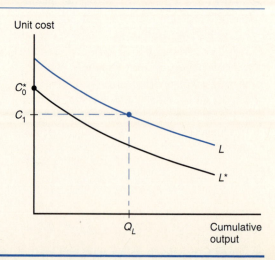

for export if it had more production experience, but that given the current lack of experience the good cannot be produced competitively. Such a country might increase its long-term welfare either by encouraging the production of the good by a subsidy or by protecting it from foreign competition until the industry could stand on its own feet. The argument for temporary protection of industries to enable them to gain experience is known as the **infant industry argument** and has played an important role in debates over the role of trade policy in economic development. We will discuss the infant industry argument at greater length in Chapter 10, but for now we simply note that situations like that illustrated in Figure 6-11 are just as hard to identify in practice in those involving nondynamic increasing returns.

Summary

1. Trade need not be the result of comparative advantage. Instead, it can result from increasing returns or economies of scale, that is, from a tendency of unit costs to be lower with larger output. Economies of scale give countries an incentive to specialize and trade even in the absence of differences between countries in their resources or technology. Economies of scale can be internal (depending on the size of the firm) or external (depending on the size of the industry).

2. Economies of scale normally lead to a breakdown of perfect competition, so that trade in the presence of economies of scale must be analyzed using models of imperfect competition. Two important models of this kind are the monopolistic competition model and the dumping model. A third model, that of external economies, is consistent with perfect competition.

3. In monopolistic competition, an industry contains a number of firms producing differentiated products. These firms act as individual monopolists, but additional firms enter a profitable industry until monopoly profits are competed away. Equilibrium is affected by the size of the market: A large market will support a larger number of firms, each producing at larger scale and thus lower average cost, than a small market.

4. International trade allows creation of an integrated market that is larger than any one country's market, and thus makes it possible simultaneously to offer consumers a greater variety of products and lower prices.

5. In the monopolistic competition model, trade may be divided into two kinds. Two-way trade in differentiated products within an industry is called intraindustry trade; trade that exchanges the products of one industry for the products of another is called interindustry trade. Intraindustry trade reflects economies of scale; interindustry trade reflects comparative advantage. Intraindustry trade does not generate the same strong effects on income distribution as interindustry trade.

6. Dumping occurs when a monopolistic firm charges a lower price on exports than it charges domestically. It is a profit-maximizing strategy when export sales are more price-responsive than domestic sales, and when firms can effectively segment markets, that is, prevent domestic customers from buying goods intended for export markets. Reciprocal dumping occurs when two monopolistic firms dump into each others' home markets; such reciprocal dumping can be a cause of international trade.

7. External economies are economies of scale that occur at the level of the industry instead of the firm. They give an important role to history and accident in determining the pattern of international trade. When external economies are important, a country starting with a large industry may retain that advantage even if another country could potentially produce the same goods more cheaply. When external economies are important, countries can conceivably lose from trade.

Key Terms

average cost, p. 126	labor market pooling, p. 147
dumping, p. 143	learning curve, p. 154
dynamic increasing returns, p. 154	marginal cost, p. 126
external economies of scale, p. 123	marginal revenue, p. 125
forward-falling supply curve, p. 150	monopolistic competition, p. 127
imperfect competition, p. 124	oligopoly, p. 127
infant industry argument, p. 155	price discrimination, p. 143
interindustry trade, p. 138	pure monopoly, p. 124
internal economies of scale, p. 123	reciprocal dumping, p. 146
intraindustry trade, p. 138	specialized suppliers, p. 147
knowledge spillovers, p. 147	

Problems

1. For each of the following examples, explain whether this is a case of external or internal economies of scale:
   a. Most musical wind instruments in the United States are produced by more than a dozen factories in Elkhart, Indiana.
   b. All Hondas sold in the United States are either imported or produced in Marysville, Ohio.
   c. All airframes for Airbus, Europe's only producer of large aircraft, are assembled in Toulouse, France.
   d. Hartford, Connecticut, is the insurance capital of the northeastern United States.

2. In perfect competition, firms set price equal to marginal cost. Why isn't this possible when there are internal economies of scale?

3. It is often argued that the existence of increasing returns is a source of conflict between countries, since each country is better off if it can increase its production in those industries characterized by economies of scale. Evaluate this view in terms of both the monopolistic competition and the external economy models.

4. Suppose the two countries we considered in the numerical example on pages 133–137 were to integrate their automobile market with a third country with an annual market for 3.75 million automobiles. Find the number of firms, the output per firm, and the price per automobile in the new integrated market after trade.

5. Evaluate the relative importance of economies of scale and comparative advantage in causing the following:
   a. Most of the world's aluminum is smelted in Norway or Canada.
   b. Half of the world's large jet aircraft are assembled in Seattle.

    c. Most semiconductors are manufactured in either the United States or Japan.

    d. Most Scotch whiskey comes from Scotland.

    e. Much of the world's best wine comes from France.

6. There are some shops in Japan that sell *Japanese* goods imported back from the United States at a discount over the prices charged by other Japanese shops. How is this possible?

7. Consider a situation similar to that in Figure 6-9, in which two countries that can produce a good are subject to forward-falling supply curves. In this case, however, suppose that the two countries have the same costs, so that their supply curves are identical.

    a. What would you expect to be the pattern of international specialization and trade? What would determine who produces the good?

    b. What are the *benefits* of international trade in this case? Do they accrue only to the country that gets the industry?

8. It is fairly common for an industrial cluster to break up and for production to move to locations with lower wages when the technology of the industry is no longer rapidly improving—when it is no longer essential to have the absolutely most modern machinery, when the need for highly skilled workers has declined, and when being at the cutting edge of innovation conveys only a small advantage. Explain this tendency of industrial clusters to break up in terms of the theory of external economies.

Further Reading

Frank Graham. "Some Aspects of Protection Further Considered." *Quarterly Journal of Economics* 37 (1923), pp. 199–227. An early warning that international trade may be harmful in the presence of external economies of scale.

Elhanan Helpman and Paul Krugman. *Market Structure and Foreign Trade.* Cambridge: MIT Press, 1985. A technical presentation of monopolistic competition and other models of trade with economies of scale.

Henryk Kierzkowski, ed. *Monopolistic Competition in International Trade.* Oxford: Clarendon Press, 1984. A collection of papers representing many of the leading researchers in imperfect competition and international trade.

Staffan Burenstam Linder. *An Essay on Trade and Transformation.* New York: John Wiley and Sons, 1961. An early and influential statement of the view that trade in manufactures among advanced countries mainly reflects forces other than comparative advantage.

Michael Porter. *The Competitive Advantage of Nations.* New York: Free Press, 1990. A best-selling book that explains national export success as the result of self-reinforcing industrial clusters, that is, external economies.

Annalee Saxenian. *Regional Advantage.* Cambridge: Harvard University Press, 1994. A fascinating comparison of two high-technology industrial districts, California's Silicon Valley and Boston's Route 128.

Appendix to Chapter 6

Determining Marginal Revenue

In our exposition of monopoly and monopolistic competition, we found it useful to have an algebraic statement of the marginal revenue faced by a firm given the demand curve it faced. Specifically, we asserted that if a firm faces the demand curve

$$Q = A - B \times P, \tag{6A-1}$$

its marginal revenue is

$$MR = P - (1/B) \times Q. \tag{6A-2}$$

In this appendix we demonstrate why this is true.

Notice first that the demand curve can be rearranged to state the price as a function of the firm's sales rather than the other way around. By rearranging (6A-1) we get

$$P = (A/B) - (1/B) \times Q. \tag{6A-3}$$

The revenue of a firm is simply the price it receives per unit multiplied by the number of units it sells. Letting R denote the firm's revenue, we have

$$R = P \times Q = [(A/B) - (1/B) \times Q] \times Q. \tag{6A-4}$$

Let us next ask how the revenue of a firm changes if it changes its sales. Suppose that the firm decides to increase its sales by a small amount dX, so that the new level of sales is $Q = Q + dQ$. Then the firm's revenue after the increase in sales, R', will be

$$R' = P' \times Q' = [(A/B) - (1/B) \times (Q + dQ)] \times (Q + dQ)$$
$$= [(A/B) - (1/B) \times Q] \times Q + [(A/B) - (1/B) \times Q] \times dQ$$
$$- (1/B) \times Q \times dQ - (1/B) \times (dQ)^2. \tag{6A-5}$$

Equation (6A-5) can be simplified by substitution in from (6A-1) and (6A-4) to get

$$R' = R + P \times dQ - (1/B) \times Q \times dQ - (1/B) \times (dQ)^2. \tag{6A-6}$$

When the change in sales dQ is small, however, its square $(dQ)^2$ is very small (e.g., the square of 1 is 1, but the square of 1/10 is 1/100). So for a small change in Q, the last term in (6A-6) can be ignored. This gives us the result that the *change* in revenue from a small change in sales is

$$R' - R = [P - (1/B) \times Q] \times dQ. \tag{6A-7}$$

So the increase in revenue *per unit of additional sales*—which is the definition of marginal revenue—is

$$MR = (R' - R)/dQ = P - (1/B) \times Q,$$

which is just what we asserted in equation (6A-2).

7

International Factor Movements

Up to this point we have concerned ourselves entirely with international *trade*. That is, we have focused on the causes and effects of international exchanges of goods and services. Movement of goods and services is not, however, the only form of international integration. This chapter is concerned with another form of integration, international movements of factors of production, or **factor movements.** Factor movements include labor migration, the transfer of capital via international borrowing and lending, and the subtle international linkages involved in the formation of multinational corporations.

The principles of international factor movement do not differ in their essentials from those underlying international trade in goods. Both international borrowing and lending and international labor migration can be thought of as analogous in their causes and effects to the movement of goods analyzed in Chapters 2 through 5. The role of the multinational corporation may be understood by extending some of the concepts developed in Chapter 6. So when we turn from trade in goods and services to factor movements we do not make a radical shift in emphasis.

Although there is a fundamental economic similarity between trade and factor movements, however, there are major differences in the political context. A labor-abundant country may under some circumstances import capital-intensive goods; under other circumstances it may acquire capital by borrowing abroad. A capital-abundant country may import labor-intensive goods or begin employing migrant workers. A country that is too small to support firms of efficient size may import goods where large firms have an advantage or allow those goods to be produced locally by subsidiaries of foreign firms. In each case the alternative strategies may be similar in their purely economic consequences but radically different in their political acceptability.

On the whole, international factor movement tends to raise even more political difficulties than international trade. Thus factor movements are subject to more restriction than trade in goods. Immigration restrictions are nearly universal. Until the 1980s several European countries, such as France, maintained controls on capital movements even though they had virtually free trade in goods with their neighbors. Investment by foreign-based multinational corporations is regarded with suspicion and tightly regulated through much of the world. The result is that factor movements are probably less important in practice than trade in goods, which is why we took an analysis of trade in the absence of factor movements as our starting point. Nonetheless, factor movements are very important, and it is valuable to spend a chapter on their analysis.

This chapter is in three parts. We begin with a simple model of international labor mobility. We then proceed to an analysis of international borrowing and lending, in which we show that this lending can be interpreted as trade *over time:* The lending country gives up resources now to receive repayment in the future, while the borrower does the reverse. Finally, the last section of the chapter analyzes multinational corporations.

INTERNATIONAL LABOR MOBILITY

We begin our discussion with an analysis of the effects of labor mobility. In the modern world, restrictions on the flow of labor are legion—just about every country imposes restrictions on immigration. Thus labor mobility is less prevalent in practice than capital mobility. It remains important, however; it is also simpler in some ways to analyze than capital movement, for reasons that will become apparent later in the chapter.

A ONE-GOOD MODEL WITHOUT FACTOR MOBILITY

As in the analysis of trade, the best way to understand factor mobility is to begin with a world that is not economically integrated, then examine what happens when international transactions are allowed. Let's assume that we have, as usual, a two-country world consisting of Home and Foreign, each with two factors of production, land and labor. We assume for the moment, however, that this world is even simpler than the one we examined in Chapter 4, in that the two countries produce only *one* good, which we will simply refer to as "output." Thus there is no scope for ordinary trade, the exchange of different goods, in this world. The only way for these economies to become integrated with each other is via movement of either land or labor. Land almost by definition cannot move, so this is a model of integration via international labor mobility.

Before we introduce factor movements, however, let us analyze the determinants of the level of output in each country. Land (T) and labor (L) are the only scarce resources. Thus the output of each country will depend, other things equal, on the quantity of these factors available. The relationship between the supplies of factors on one side and the output of the economy on the other is referred to as the economy's production function, which we denote by $Q(T, L)$.

We have already encountered the idea of a production function in Chapter 3. As we noted there, a useful way to look at the production function is to ask how output depends on the supply of one factor of production, holding the quantity of the other factor fixed.

FIGURE 7-1

An Economy's Production Function

This production function, $Q(T,L)$, shows how output varies with changes in the amount of labor employed, holding the amount of land, T, fixed. The larger the supply of labor, the larger is output; however, the marginal product of labor declines as more workers are employed.

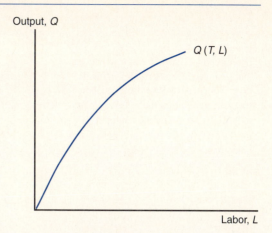

This is done in Figure 7-1, which shows how a country's output varies as its employment of labor is varied, holding fixed the supply of land; the figure is the same as Figure 3-1. The slope of the production function measures the increase in output that would be gained by using a little more labor and is thus referred to as the *marginal product of labor.* As the curve is drawn in Figure 7-1, the marginal product of labor is assumed to fall as the ratio of labor to land rises. This is the normal case: As a country seeks to employ more labor on a given amount of land, it must move to increasingly labor-intensive techniques of production, and this will normally become increasingly difficult the further the substitution of labor for land goes.

Figure 7-2, corresponding to Figure 3-2, contains the same information as Figure 7-1 but plots it in a different way. We now show directly how the marginal product of labor depends on the quantity of labor employed. We also indicate that the real wage earned by each unit of labor is equal to labor's marginal product. This will be true as long as the economy is perfectly competitive, which we assume to be the case.

What about the income earned by land? As we showed in the appendix to Chapter 3, the total output of the economy can be measured by the area under the marginal product curve. Of that total output, wages earned by workers equal the real wage rate times the employment of labor, and hence equal the indicated area on the figure. The remainder, also shown, equals rents earned by landowners.

Assume that Home and Foreign have the same technology but different overall land-labor ratios. If Home is the labor-abundant country, workers in Home will earn less than those in Foreign, while land in Home earns more than in Foreign. This obviously creates an incentive for factors of production to move. Home workers would like to move to Foreign; Foreign landowners would also like to move their land to Home, but we are supposing that this is impossible. Our next step is to allow workers to move and see what happens.

INTERNATIONAL LABOR MOVEMENT

Now suppose that workers are able to move between our two countries. Workers will move from Home to Foreign. This movement will reduce the Home labor force and thus

FIGURE 7-2

The Marginal Product of Labor

The marginal product of labor declines with employment. The area under the marginal product curve equals total output. Given the level of employment, the marginal product determines the real wage; thus the total payment to labor (the real wage times the number of employees) is shown by the rectangle in the figure. The rest of output consists of land rents.

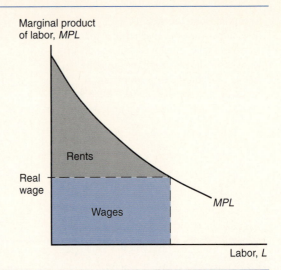

raise the real wage in Home, while increasing the labor force and reducing the real wage in Foreign. If there are no obstacles to labor movement, this process will continue until the marginal product of labor is the same in the two countries.

Figure 7-3 illustrates the causes and effects of international labor mobility. The horizontal axis represents the total world labor force. The workers employed in Home are measured from the left, the workers employed in Foreign from the right. The left vertical axis shows the marginal product of labor in Home; the right vertical axis shows the marginal product of labor in Foreign. Initially we assume that there are OL^1 workers in Home, L^1O^* workers in Foreign. Given this allocation, the real wage rate would be lower in Home (point C) than in Foreign (point B). If workers can move freely to whichever country offers the higher real wage, they will move from Home to Foreign until the real wage rates are equalized. The eventual distribution of the world's labor force will be one with OL^2 workers in Home, L^2O^* workers in Foreign (point A).

Three points should be noted about this redistribution of the world's labor force.

1. It leads to a convergence of real wage rates. Real wages rise in Home, fall in Foreign.
2. It increases the world's output as a whole. Foreign's output rises by the area under its marginal product curve from L^1 to L^2, while Home's falls by the corresponding area under its marginal product curve. We see from the figure that Foreign's gain is larger than Home's loss, by an amount equal to the colored area ABC in the figure.
3. Despite this gain, some people are hurt by the change. Those who would originally have worked in Home receive higher real wages, but those who would originally have worked in Foreign receive lower real wages. Landowners in Foreign benefit from the larger labor supply, but landowners in Home are made worse off. As in the case of the gains from international trade, then, international labor mobility, while allowing everyone to be made better off in principle, leaves some groups worse off in practice.

FIGURE 7-3

Causes and Effects of International Labor Mobility

Initially OL^1 workers are employed in Home, while L^1O* workers are employed in Foreign. Labor migrates from Home to Foreign until OL^2 workers are employed in Home, L^2O* in Foreign, and wages are equalized.

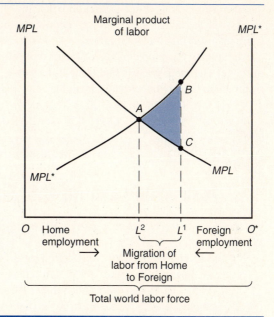

EXTENDING THE ANALYSIS

We have just seen that a very simple model tells us quite a lot about both why international factor movements occur and what effects they have. Labor mobility in our simple model, like trade in the model of Chapter 4, is driven by international differences in resources; also like trade, it is beneficial in the sense that it increases world production yet is associated with strong income distribution effects that make those gains problematic.

Let us consider briefly how the analysis is modified when we add some of the complications we have assumed away.

We need to remove the assumption that the two countries produce only one good. Suppose, then, that the countries produce two goods, one more labor intensive than the other. We already know from our discussion of the factor proportions model in Chapter 4 that in this case trade offers an alternative to factor mobility. Home can in a sense export labor and import land by exporting the labor-intensive good and importing the land-intensive good. It is possible in principle for such trade to lead to a complete equalization of factor prices without any need for factor mobility. If this happened, it would of course remove any incentive for labor to move from Home to Foreign.

In practice, while trade is indeed a substitute for international factor movement, it is not a perfect substitute. The reasons are those already summarized in Chapter 4. Complete factor price equalization is not observed in the real world because countries are sometimes too different in their resources to remain unspecialized; there are barriers to trade, both natural and artificial; and there are differences in technology as well as resources between countries.

We might wonder on the other side whether factor movements do not remove the incentive for international trade. Again the answer is that while in a simple model movement of factors of production can make international trade in goods unnecessary, in practice there are substantial barriers to free movement of labor, capital, and other potentially mobile resources. And some resources cannot be brought together—Canadian forests and Caribbean sunshine cannot migrate.

Extending the simple model of factor mobility, then, does not change its fundamental message. The main point is that trade in factors is, in purely economic terms, very much like trade in goods; it occurs for much the same reasons and produces similar results.

IMMIGRATION AND THE U.S. ECONOMY

During the twentieth century, the United States has experienced two great waves of immigration. The first, which began in the late nineteenth century, was brought to an end by restrictive legislation introduced in 1924. A new surge of immigration began in the mid-1960s, spurred in part by a major revision of the law in 1965. The table shows the number of legal immigrants that have entered the United States in each decade since 1880. There are also a rising number of illegal immigrants; the U.S. government estimates their number at 200,000 to 300,000 persons per year.

During the period of relatively low immigration between 1924 and 1965, immigrants probably had little effect on the U.S. economy in part because they were not very numerous. Their impact was also limited because the immigration laws allocated visas based on the 1920 ethnic composition of the U.S. population; as a result, immigrants came primarily from Canada and Europe, which meant that in terms of the skills they brought the immigrants were fairly similar to the work force already here. After 1965, however, immigration began to come primarily from Latin America and Asia, whose workers, on average, were substantially less educated than the average American worker.

One would expect the large-scale arrival of less educated workers to depress the wages of low-skill labor. And during the 1970s and 1980s, there was indeed—as we already pointed out in Chapter 4—a substantial widening in the wage differential between highly educated and less educated employees. In particular, the wages of workers who had not finished high school fell 10 percent compared with the average wage of workers with more education. Other factors surely contributed to this trend, but some estimates suggest that about a third of the relative wage decline could be attributed to immigration.[1]

Most public discussion of immigration did not, however, focus on this income distribution effect. Instead, politicians and voters were concerned about the impact

---

[1]George J. Borjas, Richard Freeman, and Lawrence Katz, "On the Labor Market Effects of Immigration and Trade," in Borjas and Freeman, eds., *Immigration and the Work Force: Economic Consequences for the United States and Source Areas* (Chicago: University of Chicago Press, 1992).

of immigrants on taxes and government spending. Immigrants have an ambiguous effect on the government budget. On one side, they pay taxes (and they increase the return to other factors of production, which also pay taxes). On the other hand, immigrants (like any residents of a country) increase the demand for public services, from education and highways to welfare and police. (As the Swiss author Max Frisch wrote about migrant workers in his own country, "We asked for workers, but human beings came.") Because recent immigrants to the United States have on average earned relatively low wages (which means that they do not pay much in taxes) and have been relatively likely to be on welfare or unemployed, it has been widely argued that they are a net drain on government budgets. It is by no means certain, however, that this is the case; different economists have reached different conclusions, essentially because such calculations depend on largely arbitrary assumptions about how much it costs to provide services to an additional resident. One thing that all estimates agree on, however, is that the net effect of immigration on the total income of the original residents (as opposed to the distribution of that income) is small, no more than a fraction of 1 percent either way.

Despite these fairly modest estimates, in the mid-1990s there was a strong political backlash against immigration. In the fall of 1994 California voters passed Proposition 187, a measure that imposed strict rules designed to prevent illegal immigrants from taking advantage of public services, including education for their children. The U.S. Congress also considered legislation that would deny many services to immigrants who were legally in the United States but had not become citizens, setting off a wave of applications for citizenship. At the time of writing, however, none of these measures had been implemented. Proposition 187, in particular, seemed likely to be tied up in legal challenges for years to come.

Immigration into the United States (1000 persons)

1881–1890	5247
1891–1900	3688
1901–1910	8796
1911–1920	5736
1921–1930	4107
1931–1940	528
1941–1950	1035
1951–1960	2516
1961–1970	3322
1971–1980	4493
1981–1990	7338

Source: George J. Borjas, "The Economics of Immigration," *Journal of Economic Literature* 32 (1994), pp. 1667–1717.

INTERNATIONAL BORROWING AND LENDING

International movements of capital are a prominent feature of the international economic landscape. It is tempting to analyze these movements in a way parallel to our analysis of labor mobility, and this is sometimes a useful exercise. There are some important differences, however. When we speak of international labor mobility, it is clear that workers are physically moving from one country to another. International capital movements are not so simple. When we speak of capital flows from the United States to Mexico, we do not mean that U.S. machines are literally being unbolted and shipped south. We are instead talking of a *financial* transaction. A U.S. bank lends to a Mexican firm, or U.S. residents buy stock in Mexico, or a U.S. firm invests through its Mexican subsidiary. We focus for now on the first type of transaction, in which U.S. residents make loans to Mexicans—that is, the U.S. residents grant Mexicans the right to spend more than they earn today in return for a promise to repay in the future.

The analysis of financial aspects of the international economy is the subject of the second half of this book. It is important to realize, however, that financial transactions do not exist simply on paper. They have real consequences. International borrowing and lending, in particular, can be interpreted as a kind of international trade. The trade is not of one good for another at a point in time but of goods today for goods in the future. This kind of trade is known as **intertemporal trade;** we will have much more to say about it later in this text, but for present purposes a simple model will be sufficient to make our point.[2]

INTERTEMPORAL PRODUCTION POSSIBILITIES AND TRADE

Even in the absence of international capital movements, any economy faces a trade-off between consumption now and consumption in the future. Economies usually do not consume all of their current output; some of their output takes the form of investment in machines, buildings, and other forms of productive capital. The more investment an economy undertakes now, the more it will be able to produce and consume in the future. To invest more, however, an economy must release resources by consuming less (unless there are unemployed resources, a possibility we temporarily disregard). Thus there is a trade-off between current and future consumption.

Let's imagine an economy that consumes only one good and will exist for only two periods, which we will call present and future. Then there will be a trade-off between present and future production of the consumption good, which we can summarize by drawing an **intertemporal production possibility frontier.** Such a frontier is illustrated in Figure 7-4. It looks just like the production possibility frontiers we have been drawing between two goods at a point in time.

The shape of the intertemporal production possibility frontier will differ among countries. Some countries will have production possibilities that are biased toward present output, while others are biased toward future output. We will ask what real differences these biases correspond to in a moment, but first let's simply suppose that there are two countries, Home and Foreign, with different intertemporal production possibilities. Home's possibilities are biased toward current consumption, while Foreign's are biased toward future consumption.

Reasoning by analogy, we already know what to expect. In the absence of international borrowing and lending, we would expect the relative price of future consumption to be higher in Home than in Foreign, and thus if we open the possibility of trade over time, we would expect Home to export present consumption and import future consumption.

This may, however, seem a little puzzling. What is the relative price of future consumption, and how does one trade over time?

---

[2]The appendix to this chapter contains a more detailed examination of the model developed in this section.

FIGURE 7-4

The Intertemporal Production Possibility Frontier

A country can trade current consumption for future consumption in the same way that it can produce more of one good by producing less of another.

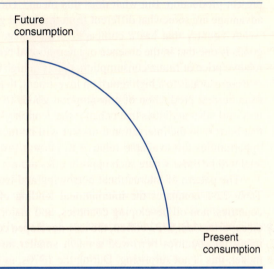

THE REAL INTEREST RATE

How does a country trade over time? Like an individual, a country can trade over time by borrowing or lending. Consider what happens when an individual borrows: She is initially able to spend more than her income or, in other words, to consume more than her production. Later, however, she must repay the loan with interest, and therefore in the future she consumes *less* than she produces. By borrowing, then, she has in effect traded future consumption for current consumption. The same is true of a borrowing country.

Clearly the price of future consumption in terms of present consumption has something to do with the interest rate. As we will see in the second half of this book, in the real world the interpretation of interest rates is complicated by the possibility of changes in the overall price level. For now, we bypass that problem by supposing that loan contracts are specified in "real" terms: When a country borrows, it gets the right to purchase some quantity of consumption at present in return for repayment of some larger quantity in the future. Specifically, the quantity of repayment in future will be $(1 + r)$ times the quantity borrowed in present, where r is the **real interest rate** on borrowing. Since the trade-off is one unit of consumption in present for $(1 + r)$ units in future, the relative price of future consumption is $1/(1 + r)$.

The parallel with our standard trade model is now complete. If borrowing and lending are allowed, the relative price of future consumption, and thus the world real interest rate, will be determined by the world relative supply and demand for future consumption. Home, whose intertemporal production possibilities are biased toward present consumption, will export present consumption and import future consumption. That is, Home will lend to Foreign in the first period and receive repayment in the second.

two countries eliminates the incentive for labor to migrate. Then, using the analysis in Chapter 5, show that a tariff by one country will create an incentive for labor migration.

3. Explain the analogy between international borrowing and lending and ordinary international trade.

4. Which of the following countries would you expect to have intertemporal production possibilities biased toward current consumption goods, and which biased toward future consumption goods?
   a. A country, like Argentina or Canada in the last century, that has only recently been opened for large-scale settlement and is receiving large inflows of immigrants.
   b. A country, like the United Kingdom in the late nineteenth century or the United States today, that leads the world technologically but is seeing that lead eroded as other countries catch up.
   c. A country that has discovered large oil reserves that can be exploited with little new investment (like Saudi Arabia).
   d. A country that has discovered large oil reserves that can be exploited only with massive investment (like Norway, whose oil lies under the North Sea).
   e. A country like South Korea that has discovered the knack of producing industrial goods and is rapidly gaining on advanced countries.

5. Which of the following is a direct foreign investment, and which is not?
   a. A Saudi businessman buys $10 million of IBM stock.
   b. The same businessman buys a New York apartment building.
   c. A French company merges with an American company; stockholders in the U.S. company exchange their stock for shares in the French firm.
   d. An Italian firm builds a plant in Russia and manages the plant as a contractor to the Russian government.

6. The Karma Computer Company has decided to open a Brazilian subsidiary. Brazilian import restrictions have prevented the firm from selling into that market, while the firm has been unwilling to sell or lease its patents to Brazilian firms because it fears this will eventually hurt its technological advantage in the U.S. market. Analyze Karma's decision in terms of the theory of multinational enterprise.

Further Reading

Richard A. Brecher and Robert C. Feenstra. "International Trade and Capital Mobility Between Diversified Economies." *Journal of International Economics* 14 (May 1983), pp. 321–339. A synthesis of the theories of trade and international factor movements.

Richard E. Caves. *Multinational Enterprises and Economic Analysis.* Cambridge: Harvard University Press, 1982. A view of multinational firms' activities.

Wilfred J. Ethier. "The Multinational Firm." *Quarterly Journal of Economics* 101 (November 1986), pp. 805–833. Models the internalization motive of multinationals.

Irving Fisher. *The Theory of Interest.* New York: Macmillan, 1930. The "intertemporal" approach described in this chapter owes its origin to Fisher.

Edward M. Graham and Paul R. Krugman. *Foreign Direct Investment in the United States.* Washington, D.C.: Institute for International Economics, 1989. A survey of the surge of foreign investment in the United States, with an emphasis on policy issues.

Charles P. Kindleberger. *American Business Abroad.* New Haven: Yale University Press, 1969. A good discussion of the nature and effects of multinational firms, written at a time when such firms were primarily United States-based.

Charles P. Kindleberger. *Europe's Postwar Growth: The Role of Labor Supply.* Cambridge: Harvard University Press, 1967. A good account of the role of labor migration during its height in Europe.

G. D. A. MacDougall. "The Benefits and Costs of Private Investment from Abroad: A Theoretical Approach." *Economic Record* 36 (1960), pp. 13–35. A clear analysis of the costs and benefits of factor movement.

Robert A. Mundell. "International Trade and Factor Mobility." *American Economic Review* 47 (1957), pp. 321–335. The paper that first laid out the argument that trade and factor movement can substitute for each other.

Jeffrey Sachs. "The Current Account and Macroeconomic Adjustment in the 1970s." *Brookings Papers on Economic Activity,* 1981. A study of international capital flows that takes the approach of viewing such flows as intertemporal trade.

Appendix to Chapter 7

More on Intertemporal Trade

This appendix contains a more detailed examination of the two-period intertemporal trade model described in the chapter. The concepts used are the same as those used in Chapter 5 to analyze international exchanges of different consumption goods at a *single* point in time. In the present setting, however, the trade model explains international patterns of investment and borrowing and the determination of the *intertemporal* terms of trade (that is, the real interest rate).

First consider Home, whose intertemporal production possibility frontier is shown in Figure 7A-1. Recall that the quantities of present and future consumption goods produced at Home depend on the amount of present consumption goods invested to produce future goods. As currently available resources are diverted from present consumption to investment, production of present consumption, Q_P, falls and production of future consumption, Q_F, rises. Increased investment therefore shifts the economy up and to the left along the intertemporal production possibility frontier.

The chapter showed that the price of future consumption in terms of present consumption is $1/(1 + r)$, where r is the real interest rate. Measured in terms of present con-

---

FIGURE 7A-1

Determining Home's Intertemporal Production Pattern

At a world real interest rate of r, Home's investment level maximizes the value of production over the two periods that the economy exists.

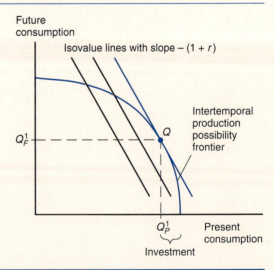

---

sumption, the value of the economy's total production over the two periods of its existence is therefore

$$V = Q_P + Q_F/(1 + r).$$

Figure 7A-1 shows the isovalue lines corresponding to the relative price $1/(1 + r)$ for different values of V. These are straight lines with slope $-(1 + r)$ (because future consumption is on the vertical axis). As in the standard trade model, firms' decisions lead to a production pattern that maximizes the value of production at market prices, $Q_P + Q_F/(1 + r)$. Production therefore occurs at point Q. The economy invests the amount shown, leaving Q_P^1 available for present consumption and producing an amount Q_F^1 of future consumption when the first-period investment pays off.

Notice that at point Q, the extra future consumption that would result from investing an additional unit of present consumption just equals $(1 + r)$. It would be inefficient to push investment beyond point Q because the economy could do better by lending additional present consumption to foreigners instead. Figure 7A-1 implies that a rise in the world real interest rate r, which steepens the isovalue lines, causes investment to fall.

Figure 7A-2 shows how Home's consumption pattern is determined for a given world interest rate. Let D_P and D_F represent the demands for present and future consumption goods, respectively. Since production is at point Q, the economy's consumption possibilities over the two periods are limited by the *intertemporal budget constraint:*

$$D_P + D_F/(1 + r) = Q_P^1 + Q_F^1/(1 + r).$$

FIGURE 7A-2

Determining Home's Intertemporal Consumption Pattern

Home's consumption places it on the highest indifference curve touching its intertemporal budget constraint. The economy exports $Q_P^1 - D_P^1$ units of present consumption and imports $D_F^1 - Q_F^1 = (1 + r) \times (Q_P^1 - D_P^1)$ units of future consumption.

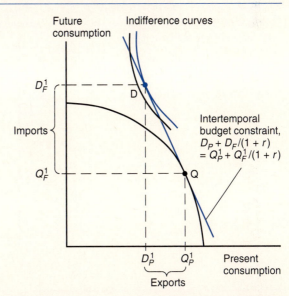

This constraint states that the value of Home's consumption over the two periods (measured in terms of present consumption) equals the value of consumption goods produced in the two periods (also measured in present consumption units). Put another way, production and consumption must lie on the same isovalue line.

Point D, where Home's budget constraint touches the highest attainable indifference curve, shows the present and future consumption levels chosen by the economy. Home's demand for present consumption, D_P^1, is smaller than its production of present consumption, Q_P^1, so it exports (that is, lends) $Q_P^1 - D_P^1$ units of present consumption to Foreigners. Correspondingly, Home imports $D_F^1 - Q_F^1$ units of future consumption from abroad when its first-period loans are repaid to it with interest. The intertemporal budget constraint implies that $D_F^1 - Q_F^1 = (1 + r) \times (Q_P^1 - D_P^1)$, so that trade is *intertemporally* balanced.

Figure 7A-3 shows how investment and consumption are determined in Foreign. Foreign is assumed to have a comparative advantage in producing *future* consumption goods. The diagram shows that at a real interest rate of r, Foreign borrows consumption goods in the first period and repays this loan using consumption goods produced in the second period. Because of its relatively rich domestic investment opportunities and its relative preference for present consumption, Foreign is an importer of present consumption and an exporter of future consumption.

As in Chapter 5 (appendix), international equilibrium can be portrayed by an offer curve diagram. Recall that a country's offer curve is the result of plotting its desired exports against its desired imports. Now, however, the exchanges plotted involve present and future consumption. Figure 7A-4 shows that the equilibrium real interest rate is determined by the

FIGURE 7A-3

Determining Foreign's Intertemporal Production and Consumption Patterns

Foreign produces at point Q^* and consumes at point D^*, importing $D_P^{*1} - Q_P^{*1}$ units of present consumption and exporting $Q_F^{*1} - D_F^{*1} = (1 + r) \times (D_P^{*1} - Q_P^{*1})$ units of future consumption.

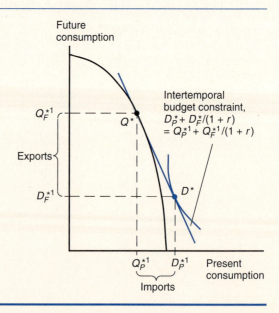

FIGURE 7A.4

International Intertemporal Equilibrium in Terms of Offer Curves

Equilibrium is at point E (with interest rate r^1) because desired Home exports of present consumption equal desired Foreign imports and desired Foreign exports of future consumption equal desired Home imports.

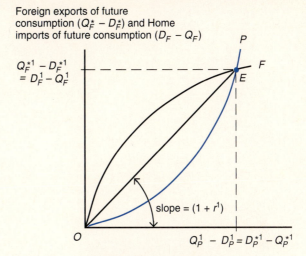

Foreign exports of future consumption $(Q_F^* - D_F^*)$ and Home imports of future consumption $(D_F - Q_F)$

$$Q_F^{*1} - D_F^{*1} = D_F^1 - Q_F^1$$

slope $= (1 + r^1)$

$Q_P^1 - D_P^1 = D_P^{*1} - Q_P^{*1}$

Home exports of present consumption $(Q_P - D_P)$ and Foreign imports of future consumption $(D_P^* - Q_P^*)$

intersection of the Home and Foreign offer curves OP and OF at point E. The ray OE has slope $(1 + r^1)$, where r^1 is the equilibrium world interest rate. At point E, Home's desired export of present consumption equals Foreign's desired import of present consumption. Put another way, at point E, Home's desired first-period lending equals Foreign's desired first-period borrowing. Supply and demand are therefore equal in both periods.

International Trade Policy

8

The Instruments of Trade Policy

Previous chapters have answered the question, "Why do nations trade?" by *describing* the causes and effects of international trade and the functioning of a trading world economy. While this question is interesting in itself, its answer is much more interesting if it helps answer the question, "What should a nation's trade policy be?" Should the United States use a tariff or an import quota to protect its automobile industry against competition from Japan and South Korea? Who will benefit and who will lose from an import quota? Will the benefits outweigh the costs?

This chapter examines the policies that governments adopt toward international trade, policies that involve a number of different actions. These actions include taxes on some international transactions, subsidies for other transactions, legal limits on the value or volume of particular imports, and many other measures. The chapter provides a framework for understanding the effects of the most important instruments of trade policy.

BASIC TARIFF ANALYSIS

A tariff, the simplest of trade policies, is a tax levied when a good is imported. **Specific tariffs** are levied as a fixed charge for each unit of goods imported (for example, $3 per barrel of oil). **Ad valorem tariffs** are taxes that are levied as a fraction of the value of the imported goods (for example, a 25 percent U.S. tariff on imported trucks). In either case the effect of the tariff is to raise the cost of shipping goods to a country.

Tariffs are the oldest form of trade policy and have traditionally been used as a source of government income. Until the introduction of the income tax, for instance, the U.S. government raised most of its revenue from tariffs. Their true purpose, however, has usually been not only to provide revenue but to protect particular domestic sectors. In the early nineteenth century the United Kingdom used tariffs (the famous Corn Laws) to protect its agriculture from import competition. In the late nineteenth century both Germany and the United States protected their new industrial sectors by imposing tariffs on imports of manufactured goods. The importance of tariffs has declined in modern times, because modern governments usually prefer to protect domestic industries through a variety of **nontariff barriers,** such as **import quotas** (limitations on the quantity of imports) and **export restraints** (limitations on the quantity of exports—usually imposed by the exporting country at the importing country's request). Nonetheless, an understanding of the effects of a tariff remains a vital basis for understanding other trade policies.

In developing the theory of trade in Chapters 2 through 7 we adopted a *general equilibrium* perspective. That is, we were keenly aware that events in one part of the economy have repercussions elsewhere. However, in many (though not all) cases trade policies toward one sector can be reasonably well understood without going into detail about the repercussions of that policy in the rest of the economy. For the most part, then, trade policy can be examined in a *partial equilibrium* framework. When the effects on the economy as a whole become crucial, we will refer back to general equilibrium analysis.

SUPPLY, DEMAND, AND TRADE IN A SINGLE INDUSTRY

Let's suppose there are two countries, Home and Foreign, both of which consume and produce wheat, which can be costlessly transported between the countries. In each country wheat is a simple competitive industry in which the supply and demand curves are functions of the market price. Normally Home supply and demand will depend on the price in terms of Home currency, and Foreign supply and demand will depend on the price in terms of Foreign currency, but we assume that the exchange rate between the currencies is not affected by whatever trade policy is undertaken in this market. Thus we quote prices in both markets in terms of Home currency.

Trade will arise in such a market if prices are different in the absence of trade. Suppose that in the absence of trade the price of wheat is higher in Home than it is in Foreign. Now allow foreign trade. Since the price of wheat in Home exceeds the price in Foreign, shippers begin to move wheat from Foreign to Home. The export of wheat raises its price in Foreign and lowers its price in Home until the difference in prices has been eliminated.

To determine the world price and the quantity traded, it is helpful to define two new curves: the Home **import demand curve** and the Foreign **export supply curve,** which are derived from the underlying domestic supply and demand curves. Home import demand is the excess of what Home consumers demand over what Home producers supply; Foreign export supply is the excess of what Foreign producers supply over what Foreign consumers demand.

Figure 8-1 shows how the Home import demand curve is derived. At the price P^1 Home consumers demand D^1, while Home producers supply only S^1, so Home import demand is $D^1 - S^1$. If we raise the price to P^2, Home consumers demand only D^2, while Home producers raise the amount they supply to S^2, so import demand falls to $D^2 - S^2$. These price-quantity combinations are plotted as points 1 and 2 in the right-hand panel of Figure 8-1. The import demand curve MD is downward sloping because as price increases, the quantity of imports demanded declines. At P_A, Home supply and demand are equal in

FIGURE 8-1

Deriving Home's Import Demand Curve

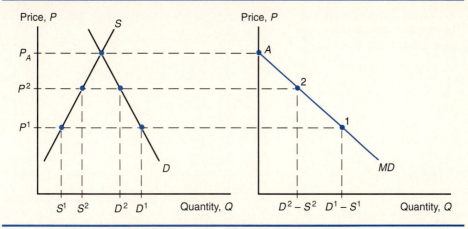

As the price of the good increases, Home consumers demand less, while Home producers supply more, so that the demand for imports declines.

the absence of trade, so the Home import demand curve intercepts the price axis at P_A (import demand = zero at P_A).

Figure 8-2 shows how the Foreign export supply curve XS is derived. At P^1 Foreign producers supply S^{*1}, while Foreign consumers demand only D^{*1}, so the amount of the total supply available for export is $S^{*1} - D^{*1}$. At P^2 Foreign producers raise the quantity they supply to S^{*2} and Foreign consumers lower the amount they demand to D^{*2}, so the quantity of the total supply available to export rises to $S^{*2} - D^{*2}$. Because the supply of

FIGURE 8-2

Deriving Foreign's Export Supply Curve

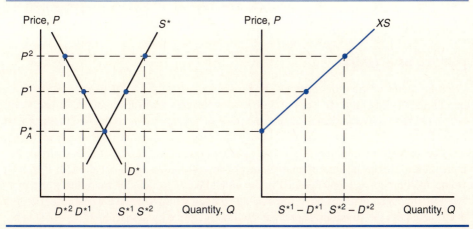

As the price of the good rises, Foreign producers supply more while Foreign consumers demand less, so that the supply available for export rises.

FIGURE 8-3

World Equilibrium

The equilibrium world price is where Home import demand (*MD* curve) equals Foreign export supply (*XS* curve).

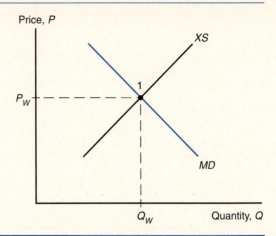

goods available for export rises as the price rises, the Foreign export supply curve is upward sloping. At P^{*A}, supply and demand would be equal in the absence of trade, so the Foreign export supply curve intercepts the price axis at P^{*A} (export supply = zero at P^{*A}).

World equilibrium occurs when Home import demand equals Foreign export supply (Figure 8-3). At the price P_w, where the two curves cross, world supply equals world demand. At the equilibrium point 1 in Figure 8-3,

Home demand − Home supply = Foreign supply − Foreign demand.

By adding and subtracting from both sides, this equation can be rearranged to say that

Home demand + Foreign demand = Home supply + Foreign supply

or, in other words,

World demand = World supply.

EFFECTS OF A TARIFF

From the point of view of someone shipping goods, a tariff is just like a cost of transportation. If Home imposes a tax of $2 on every bushel of wheat imported, shippers will be unwilling to move the wheat unless the price difference between the two markets is at least $2.

Figure 8-4 illustrates the effects of a specific tariff of t per unit of wheat (shown as t in the figure). In the absence of a tariff, the price of wheat would be equalized at P_w in both Home and Foreign as seen at point 1 in the middle panel, which illustrates the world market. With the tariff in place, however, shippers are not willing to move wheat from Foreign to Home unless the Home price exceeds the Foreign price by at least t. If no wheat is being shipped, however, there will be an excess demand for wheat in Home and an excess supply in Foreign. Thus the price in Home will rise and that in Foreign will fall until the price difference is t.

FIGURE 8-4

Effects of a Tariff

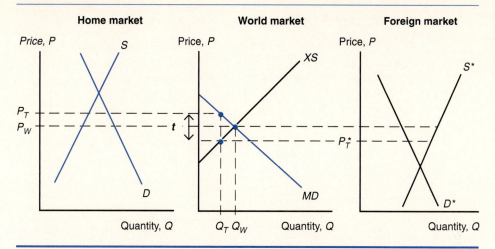

A tariff raises the price in Home while lowering the price in Foreign. The volume traded declines.

Introducing a tariff, then, drives a wedge between the prices in the two markets. The tariff raises the price in Home to P_T and lowers the price in Foreign to $P_T^* = P_T - t$. In Home producers supply more at the higher price, while consumers demand less, so that fewer imports are demanded (as you can see in the move from point 1 to point 2 on the MD curve). In Foreign the lower price leads to reduced supply and increased demand, and thus a smaller export supply (as seen in the move from point 1 to point 3 on the XS curve). Thus the volume of wheat traded declines from Q_W, the free trade volume, to Q_T, the volume with a tariff. At the trade volume Q_T, Home import demand equals Foreign export supply when $P_T - P_T^* = t$.

The increase in the price in Home, from P_W to P_T, is less than the amount of the tariff, because part of the tariff is reflected in a decline in Foreign's export price and thus is not passed on to Home consumers. This is the normal result of a tariff and of any trade policy that limits imports. The size of this effect on the exporters' price, however, is often in practice very small. When a small country imposes a tariff, its share of the world market for the goods it imports is usually minor to begin with, so that its import reduction has very little effect on the world (foreign export) price.

The effects of a tariff in the "small country" case where a country cannot affect foreign export prices are illustrated in Figure 8-5. In this case a tariff raises the price of the imported good in the country imposing the tariff by the full amount of the tariff, from P_W to $P_w + t$. Production of the imported good rises from S^1 to S^2, while consumption of the good falls from D^1 to D^2. As a result of the tariff, then, imports fall in the country imposing the tariff.

MEASURING THE AMOUNT OF PROTECTION

A tariff on an imported good raises the price received by domestic producers of that good. This effect is often the tariff's principal objective—to *protect* domestic producers from the

---

FIGURE 8-5

A Tariff in a Small Country

When a country is small, a tariff it imposes cannot lower the foreign price of the good it imports. As a result, the price of the import rises from P_w to $P_w + t$ and the quantity of imports demanded falls from $S^1 - D^1$ to $S^2 - D^2$.

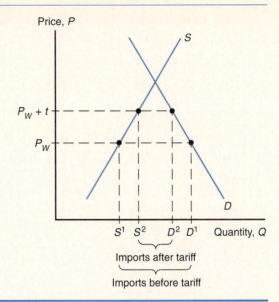

low prices that would result from import competition. In analyzing trade policy in practice, it is important to ask how much protection a tariff or other trade policy actually provides. The answer is usually expressed as a percentage of the price that would prevail under free trade. An import quota on sugar could, for example, raise the price received by U.S. sugar producers by 45 percent.

Measuring protection would seem to be straightforward in the case of a tariff: If the tariff is an ad valorem tax proportional to the value of the imports, the tariff rate itself should measure the amount of protection; if the tariff is specific, dividing the tariff by the price net of the tariff gives us the ad valorem equivalent.

There are two problems in trying to calculate the rate of protection this simply. First, if the small country assumption is not a good approximation, part of the effect of a tariff will be to lower foreign export prices rather than to raise domestic prices. This effect of trade policies on foreign export prices is sometimes significant.[1]

The second problem is that tariffs may have very different effects on different stages of production of a good. A simple example illustrates this point.

Suppose that an automobile sells on the world market for $8000 and that the parts out of which that automobile is made sell for $6000. Let's compare two countries: one that wants to develop an auto assembly industry and one that already has an assembly industry and wants to develop a parts industry.

To encourage a domestic auto industry, the first country places a 25 percent tariff on imported autos, allowing domestic assemblers to charge $10,000 instead of $8000. In this

---

[1]In theory (though rarely in practice) a tariff could actually lower the price received by domestic producers (the Metzler paradox discussed in Chapter 5).

case it would be wrong to say that the assemblers receive only 25 percent protection. Before the tariff, domestic assembly would take place only if it could be done for $2000 (the difference between the $8000 price of a completed automobile and the $6000 cost of parts) or less; now it will take place even if it costs as much as $4000 (the difference between the $10,000 price and the cost of parts). That is, the 25 percent tariff rate provides assemblers with an **effective rate of protection** of 100 percent.

Now suppose the second country, to encourage domestic production of parts, imposes a 10 percent tariff on imported parts, raising the cost of parts to domestic assemblers from $6000 to $6600. Even though there is no change in the tariff on assembled automobiles, this policy makes it less advantageous to assemble domestically. Before the tariff it would have been worth assembling a car locally if it could be done for $2000 ($8000 − $6000); after the tariff local assembly takes place only if it can be done for $1400 ($8000 − $6600). The tariff on parts, then, while providing positive protection to parts manufacturers, provides negative effective protection to assembly at the rate of −30 percent (−600/2000).

Reasoning similar to that seen in this example has led economists to make elaborate calculations to measure the degree of effective protection actually provided to particular industries by tariffs and other trade policies. Trade policies aimed at promoting economic development, for example (Chapter 10), often lead to rates of effective protection much higher than the tariff rates themselves.[2]

COSTS AND BENEFITS OF A TARIFF

A tariff raises the price of a good in the importing country and lowers it in the exporting country. As a result of these price changes, consumers lose in the importing country and gain in the exporting country. Producers gain in the importing country and lose in the exporting country. In addition, the government imposing the tariff gains revenue. To compare these costs and benefits, it is necessary to quantify them. The method for measuring costs and benefits of a tariff depends on two concepts common to much microeconomic analysis: consumer and producer surplus.

CONSUMER AND PRODUCER SURPLUS

Consumer surplus measures the amount a consumer gains from a purchase by the difference between the price he actually pays and the price he would have been willing to pay. If, for example, a consumer would have been willing to pay $8 for a bushel of wheat but the price is only $3, the consumer surplus gained by the purchase is $5.

---

[2]The effective rate of protection for a sector is formally defined as $(V_T − V_W)/V_W$, where V_W is value added in the sector at world prices and V_T value added in the presence of trade policies. In terms of our example, let P_A be the world price of an assembled automobile, P_C the world price of its components, t_A the ad valorem tariff rate on imported autos, and t_C the ad valorem tariff rate on components. You can check that if the tariffs don't affect world prices, they provide assemblers with an effective protection rate of

$$\frac{V_T − V_W}{V_W} = t_A + P_C \left(\frac{t_A − t_C}{P_A − P_C} \right).$$

FIGURE 8-6

Deriving Consumer Surplus from the Demand Curve

Consumer surplus on each unit sold is the difference between the actual price and what consumers would have been willing to pay.

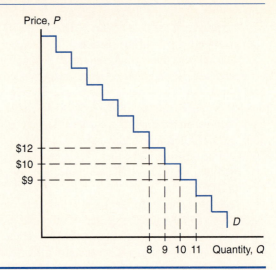

Consumer surplus can be derived from the market demand curve (Figure 8-6). For example, suppose the maximum price at which consumers will buy 10 units of a good is $10. Then the tenth unit of the good purchased must be worth $10 to consumers. If it were worth less, they would not purchase it; if it were worth more, they would have been willing to purchase it even if the price were higher. Now suppose that to get consumers to buy 11 units the price must be cut to $9. Then the eleventh unit must be worth only $9 to consumers.

Suppose that the price is $9. Then consumers are just willing to purchase the eleventh unit of the good and thus receive no consumer surplus from their purchase of that unit. They would have been willing to pay $10 for the tenth unit, however, and thus receive $1 in consumer surplus from that unit. They would have been willing to pay $12 for the ninth unit; if so, they receive $3 of consumer surplus on that unit, and so on.

Generalizing from this example, if P is the price of a good and Q the quantity demanded at that price, then consumer surplus is calculated by subtracting P times Q from the area under the demand curve up to Q (Figure 8-7). If the price is P^1, the quantity demanded is Q^1 and the consumer surplus is measured by the area labeled a. If the price falls to P^2, the quantity demanded rises to Q^2 and consumer surplus rises to equal a plus the additional area b.

Producer surplus is an analogous concept. A producer willing to sell a good for $2 but receiving a price of $5 gains a producer surplus of $3. The same procedure used to derive consumer surplus from the demand curve can be used to derive producer surplus from the supply curve. If P is the price and Q the quantity supplied at that price, then producer surplus is P times Q from the area under the supply curve up to Q (Figure 8-8). If the price is P^1, the quantity supplied will be Q^1, and producer surplus is measured by the area c. If the price rises to P^2, the quantity supplied rises to Q^2, and producer surplus rises to equal c plus the additional area d.

Some of the difficulties related to the concepts of consumer and producer surplus are technical issues of calculation that we can safely disregard. More important is the question

FIGURE 8-7

Geometry of Consumer Surplus

Consumer surplus is equal to the area under the demand curve and above the price.

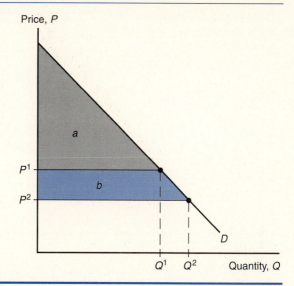

of whether the direct gains to producers and consumers in a given market accurately measure the *social* gains. Additional benefits and costs not captured by consumer and producer surplus are at the core of the case for trade policy activism discussed in Chapter 9. For now, however, we will focus on costs and benefits as measured by consumer and producer surplus.

MEASURING THE COSTS AND BENEFITS

Figure 8-9 illustrates the costs and benefits of a tariff for the importing country.

The tariff raises the domestic price from P_W to P_T but lowers the foreign export price from P_W to P_T^* (refer back to Figure 8-4). Domestic production rises from S^1 to S^2, while domestic consumption falls from D^1 to D^2. The costs and benefits to different groups can be expressed as sums of the areas of five regions, labeled a, b, c, d, e.

Consider first the gain to domestic producers. They receive a higher price and therefore have higher producer surplus. As we saw in Figure 8-8, producer surplus is equal to the area below the price but above the supply curve. Before the tariff, producer surplus was equal to the area below P_W but above the supply curve; with the price rising to P_T, this surplus rises by the area labeled a. That is, producers gain from the tariff.

Domestic consumers also face a higher price, which makes them worse off. As we saw in Figure 8-7, consumer surplus is equal to the area above the price but below the demand curve. Since the price consumers face rises from P_W to P_T, the consumer surplus falls by the area indicated by $a + b + c + d$. So consumers are hurt by the tariff.

There is a third player here as well: the government. The government gains by collecting tariff revenue. This is equal to the tariff rate t times the volume of imports $Q_T = D^2 - S^2$. Since $t = P_T - P_T^*$, the government's revenue is equal to the sum of the two areas c and e.

Since these gains and losses accrue to different people, the overall cost-benefit evaluation of a tariff depends on how much we value a dollar's worth of benefit to each group.

FIGURE 8-8

Geometry of Producer Surplus

Producer surplus is equal to the area above the supply curve and below the price.

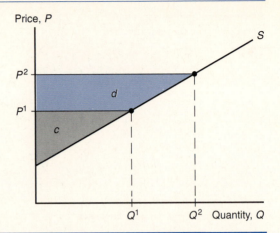

If, for example, the producer gain accrues mostly to wealthy owners of resources, while the consumers are poorer than average, the tariff will be viewed differently than if the good is a luxury bought by the affluent but produced by low-wage workers. Further ambiguity is introduced by the role of the government: Will it use its revenue to finance vitally needed public services or waste it on $1000 toilet seats? Despite these problems, it is common for analysts of trade policy to attempt to compute the net effect of a tariff on national welfare by assuming that at the margin a dollar's worth of gain or loss to each group is of the same social worth.

Let's look, then, at the net effect of a tariff on welfare. The net cost of a tariff is

$$\text{Consumer loss} - \text{producer gain} - \text{government revenue,} \qquad (8\text{-}1)$$

or, replacing these concepts by the areas in Figure 8-9,

$$(a + b + c + d) - a - (c + e) = b + d - e. \qquad (8\text{-}2)$$

That is, there are two "triangles" whose area measures loss to the nation as a whole and a "rectangle" whose area measures an offsetting gain. A useful way to interpret these gains and losses is the following: The loss triangles represent the **efficiency loss** that arises because a tariff distorts incentives to consume and produce, while the rectangle represents the **terms of trade gain** that arise because a tariff lowers foreign export prices.

The gain depends on the ability of the tariff-imposing country to drive down foreign export prices. If the country cannot affect world prices (the "small country" case illustrated in Figure 8-5), region e, which represents the terms of trade gain, disappears, and it is clear that the tariff reduces welfare. It distorts the incentives of both producers and consumers by inducing them to act as if imports were more expensive than they actually are. The cost of an additional unit of consumption to the economy is the price of an additional unit of imports, yet because the tariff raises the domestic price above the world price, consumers reduce their consumption to the point where that marginal unit yields them welfare equal to the tariff-inclusive domestic price. The value of an additional unit of production to the economy is the price of the unit of imports it saves, yet domestic producers expand production to the point where the marginal cost is equal to the tariff-inclusive price. Thus the

FIGURE 8-9

Costs and Benefits of a Tariff for the Importing Country

The costs and benefits to different groups can be represented as sums of the five areas a, b, c, d, and e.

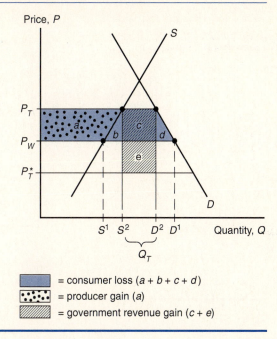

= consumer loss ($a + b + c + d$)
= producer gain (a)
= government revenue gain ($c + e$)

economy produces at home additional units of the good that it could purchase more cheaply abroad.

The net welfare effects of a tariff, then, are summarized in Figure 8-10. The negative effects consist of the two triangles b and d. The first triangle is a **production distortion loss,** resulting from the fact that the tariff leads domestic producers to produce too much of this good. The second triangle is a domestic **consumption distortion loss,** resulting from the fact that a tariff leads consumers to consume too little of the good. Against these losses must be set the terms of trade gain measured by the rectangle e, which results from the decline in the foreign export price caused by a tariff. In the important case of a small country that cannot significantly affect foreign prices, this last effect drops out, so that the costs of a tariff unambiguously exceed its benefits.

OTHER INSTRUMENTS OF TRADE POLICY

Tariffs are the simplest trade policies, but in the modern world most government intervention in international trade takes other forms, such as export subsidies, import quotas, voluntary export restraints, and local content requirements. Fortunately, once we understand tariffs it is not too difficult to understand these other trade instruments.

EXPORT SUBSIDIES: THEORY

An **export subsidy** is a payment to a firm or individual that ships a good abroad. Like a tariff, an export subsidy can be either specific (a fixed sum per unit) or ad valorem (a proportion of the value exported). When the government offers an export subsidy, shippers

FIGURE 8-10

Net Welfare Effects of a Tariff

The colored triangles represent efficiency losses, while the rectangle represents a terms of trade gain.

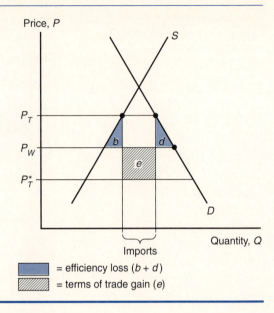

= efficiency loss ($b + d$)

= terms of trade gain (e)

will export the good up to the point where the domestic price exceeds the foreign price by the amount of the subsidy.

The effects of an export subsidy on prices are exactly the reverse of those of a tariff (Figure 8-11). The price in the exporting country rises from P_W to P_S, but because the price in the importing country falls from P_W to P_S^*, the price rise is less than the subsidy. In the exporting country, consumers are hurt, producers gain, and the government loses because it must expend money on the subsidy. The consumer loss is the area $a + b$; the producer gain is the area $a + b + c$; the government subsidy (the amount of exports times the amount of the subsidy) is the area $b + c + d + e + f + g$. The net welfare loss is therefore the sum of the areas $b + d + e + f + g$. Of these, b and d represent consumption and production distortion losses of the same kind that a tariff produces. In addition, and in contrast to a tariff, the export subsidy *worsens* the terms of trade by lowering the price of the export in the foreign market from P_W to P_S^*. This leads to the additional terms of trade loss $e + f + g$, equal to $P_W - P_S^*$ times the quantity exported with the subsidy. So an export subsidy unambiguously leads to costs that exceed its benefits.

CASE STUDY

EUROPE'S COMMON AGRICULTURAL POLICY

Since 1957, six Western European nations—Germany, France, Italy, Belgium, the Netherlands, and Luxembourg—have been members of the European Economic Community; they were later joined by the United Kingdom, Ireland, Den-

FIGURE 8-11

Effects of an Export Subsidy

An export subsidy raises prices in the exporting country while lowering them in the importing country.

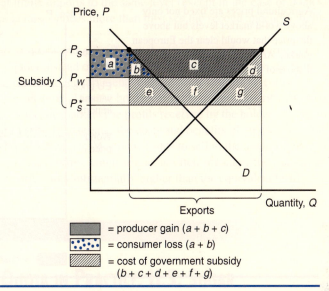

= producer gain ($a + b + c$)

= consumer loss ($a + b$)

= cost of government subsidy
($b + c + d + e + f + g$)

mark, Greece, and, most recently, Spain and Portugal. Now called the European Union (EU) its two biggest effects are on trade policy. First, the members of the European Union have removed all tariffs with respect to each other, creating a customs union (discussed in the next chapter). Second, the agricultural policy of the European Union has developed into a massive export subsidy program.

The European Union's Common Agricultural Policy (CAP) began not as an export subsidy, but as an effort to guarantee high prices to European farmers by having the European Union buy agricultural products whenever the prices fell below specified support levels. To prevent this policy from drawing in large quantities of imports, it was initially backed by tariffs that offset the difference between European and world agricultural prices.

Since the 1970s, however, the support prices set by the European Union have turned out to be so high that Europe, which would under free trade be an importer of most agricultural products, was producing more than consumers were willing to buy. The result was that the European Union found itself obliged to buy and store huge quantities of food. At the end of 1985, European nations had stored 780,000 tons of beef, 1.2 million tons of butter, and 12 million tons of wheat. To avoid unlimited growth in these stockpiles, the European Union turned to a policy of subsidizing exports to dispose of surplus production.

Figure 8-12 shows how the CAP works. It is, of course, exactly like the export subsidy shown in Figure 8-11, except that Europe would actually be an importer under free trade. The support price is set not only above the world price that would prevail in its absence but also above the price that would equate demand and supply even without imports. To export the resulting surplus, an export subsidy is paid that offsets the difference between European and world prices. The subsidized exports themselves tend to depress the world price, increasing the

In 1979, however, sharp oil price increases and temporary gasoline shortages caused the U.S. market to shift abruptly toward smaller cars. Japanese producers, whose costs had been falling relative to their U.S. competitors in any case, moved in to fill the new demand. As the Japanese market share soared and U.S. output fell, strong political forces in the United States demanded protection for the U.S. industry. Rather than act unilaterally and risk creating a trade war, the U.S. government asked the Japanese government to limit its exports. The Japanese, fearing unilateral U.S. protectionist measures if they did not do so, agreed to limit their sales. The first agreement, in 1981, limited Japanese exports to the United States to 1.68 million automobiles. A revision raised that total to 1.85 million in 1984 to 1985. In 1985, the agreement was allowed to lapse.

The effects of this voluntary export restraint were complicated by several factors. First, Japanese and U.S. cars were clearly not perfect substitutes. Second, the Japanese industry to some extent responded to the quota by upgrading its quality, selling larger autos with more features. Third, the auto industry is clearly not perfectly competitive. Nonetheless, the basic results were what the discussion of voluntary export restraints earlier would have predicted: The price of Japanese cars in the United States rose, with the rent captured by Japanese firms. The U.S. government estimates the total costs to the United States at $3.2 billion in 1984, primarily in transfers to Japan rather than efficiency losses.

LOCAL CONTENT REQUIREMENTS

A **local content requirement** is a regulation that requires that some specified fraction of a final good be produced domestically. In some cases this fraction is specified in physical units, like the U.S. oil import quota in the 1960s. In other cases the requirement is stated in value terms, by requiring that some minimum share of the price of a good represent domestic value added. Local content laws have been widely used by developing countries trying to shift their manufacturing base from assembly back into intermediate goods. In the United States, a local content bill for automobiles was proposed in 1982 but was never acted on.

From the point of view of the domestic producers of parts, a local content regulation provides protection in the same way an import quota does. From the point of view of the firms that must buy locally, however, the effects are somewhat different. Local content does not place a strict limit on imports. It allows firms to import more, provided that they also buy more domestically. This means that the effective price of inputs to the firm is an average of the price of imported and domestically produced inputs.

Consider, for example, the earlier automobile example in which the cost of imported parts is $6000. Suppose that to purchase the same parts domestically would cost $10,000 but that assembly firms are required to use 50 percent domestic parts. Then they will face an average cost of parts of $8000 (0.5 × $6000 + 0.5 × $10,000), which will be reflected in the final price of the car.

The important point is that a local content requirement does not produce either government revenue or quota rents. Instead, the difference between the prices of imports and domestic goods in effect gets averaged in the final price and is passed on to consumers.

An interesting innovation in local content regulations has been to allow firms to satisfy their local content requirement by exporting instead of using parts domestically.

AMERICAN BUSES, MADE IN HUNGARY

In 1995, sleek new buses began rolling on the streets of Miami and Baltimore. Probably very few riders were aware that these buses were made in, of all places, Hungary.

Why Hungary? Well, before the fall of communism in Eastern Europe Hungary had in fact manufactured buses for export to other Eastern bloc nations. These buses were, however, poorly designed and badly made; few people thought the industry could start exporting to Western countries anytime soon.

What changed the situation was the realization by some clever Hungarian investors that there is a loophole in a little-known but important U.S. law, the Buy American Act, originally passed in 1933. This law in effect imposes local content requirements on a significant range of products.

The Buy American Act affects *procurement*: purchases by government agencies, including state and local governments. It requires that American firms be given preference in all such purchases. A bid by a foreign company can only be accepted if it is a specified percentage below the lowest bid by a domestic firm. In the case of buses and other transportation equipment, the foreign bid must be at least 25 percent below the domestic bid, effectively shutting out foreign producers in most cases. Nor can an American company simply act as a sales agent for foreigners: While "American" products can contain some foreign parts, 51 percent of the materials must be domestic.

What the Hungarians realized was that they could set up an operation that just barely met this criterion. They set up two operations: One in Hungary, producing the shells of buses (the bodies, without anything else), and an assembly operation in Georgia. American axles and tires were shipped to Hungary, where they were put onto the bus shells; these were then shipped back to the United States, where American-made engines and transmissions were installed. The whole product was slightly more than 51 percent American, and thus these were legally "American" buses which city transit authorities were allowed to buy. The advantage of the whole scheme was the opportunity to use inexpensive Hungarian labor: Although Hungarian workers take about 1500 hours to assemble a bus compared with less than 900 hours in the United States, their $4 per hour wage rate made all the transshipment worthwhile.

This has become important in several cases: For example, U.S. auto firms operating in Mexico have chosen to export some components from Mexico to the United States, even though those components could be produced in the United States more cheaply, because this allows them to use less Mexican content in producing cars in Mexico for Mexico's market.

OTHER TRADE POLICY INSTRUMENTS

There are many other ways in which governments influence trade. We list some of them briefly.

   1. *Export credit subsidies.* This is like an export subsidy except that it takes the form of a subsidized loan to the buyer. The United States, like most countries, has a

government institution, the Export-Import Bank, that is devoted to providing at least slightly subsidized loans to aid exports.

2. *National procurement.* Purchases by the government or strongly regulated firms can be directed toward domestically produced goods even when these goods are more expensive than imports. The classic example is the European telecommunications industry. The nations of the European Union in principle have free trade with each other. The main purchasers of telecommunications equipment, however, are phone companies—and in Europe these companies have until recently all been government-owned. These government-owned telephone companies buy from domestic suppliers even when the suppliers charge higher prices than suppliers in other countries. The result is that there is very little trade in telecommunications equipment within Europe.

3. *Red-tape barriers.* Sometimes a government wants to restrict imports without doing so formally. Fortunately or unfortunately, it is easy to twist normal health, safety, and customs procedures so as to place substantial obstacles in the way of trade. The classic example is the French decree in 1982 that all Japanese videocassette recorders must pass through the tiny customs house at Poitiers—effectively limiting the actual imports to a handful.

THE EFFECTS OF TRADE POLICY: A SUMMARY

The effects of the major instruments of trade policy can be usefully summarized by Table 8-1, which compares the effect of four major kinds of trade policy on the welfare of consumers, producers, the government, and the nation as a whole.

This table does not look like an advertisement for interventionist trade policy. All four trade policies benefit producers and hurt consumers. The effects of the policies on economic welfare are at best ambiguous; two of the policies definitely hurt the nation as a whole, while tariffs and import quotas are potentially beneficial only for large countries that can drive down world prices.

TABLE 8-1

Effects of Alternative Trade Policies

	Tariff	Export subsidy	Import quota	Voluntary export restraint
Producer surplus	Increases	Increases	Increases	Increases
Consumer surplus	Falls	Falls	Falls	Falls
Government revenue	Increases	Falls (government spending rises)	No change (rents to license holders)	No change (rents to foreigners)
Overall national welfare	Ambiguous (falls for small country)	Falls	Ambiguous (falls for small country)	Falls

6.   Why, then, do governments so often act to limit imports or promote exports? We turn to this question in Chapter 9.

Summary

7.

1. In contrast to our earlier analysis, which stressed the general equilibrium interaction of markets, for analysis of trade policy it is usually sufficient to use a partial equilibrium approach.

2. A tariff drives a wedge between foreign and domestic prices, raising the domestic price but by less than the tariff rate. An important and relevant special case, however, is that of a "small" country that cannot have any substantial influence on foreign prices. In the small country case a tariff is fully reflected in domestic prices.

3. The costs and benefits of a tariff or other trade policy may be measured using the concepts of consumer surplus and producer surplus. Using these concepts, we can show that the domestic producers of a good gain, because a tariff raises the price they receive; the domestic consumers lose, for the same reason. There is also a gain in government revenue.

Furthe

Jag

4. If we add together the gains and losses from a tariff, we find that the net effect on national welfare can be separated into two parts. There is an efficiency loss, which results from the distortion in the incentives facing domestic producers and consumers. On the other hand, there is a terms of trade gain, reflecting the tendency of a tariff to drive down foreign export prices. In the case of a small country that cannot affect foreign prices, the second effect is zero, so that there is an unambiguous loss.

W.

Rol

5. The analysis of a tariff can be readily adapted to other trade policy measures, such as export subsidies, import quotas, and voluntary export restraints. An export subsidy causes efficiency losses similar to a tariff but compounds these losses by causing a deterioration of the terms of trade. Import quotas and voluntary export restraints differ from tariffs in that the government gets no revenue. Instead, what would have been government revenue accrues as rents to the recipients of import licenses in the case of a quota and to foreigners in the case of a voluntary export restraint.

Ga

Kal

Key Terms

D. I

ad valorem tariff, p. 187	import quota, p. 188
consumer surplus, p. 193	local content requirement, p. 204
consumption distortion loss, p. 197	nontariff barriers, p. 188
effective rate of protection, p. 193	producer surplus, p. 194
efficiency loss, p. 196	production distortion loss, p. 197
export restraint, p. 188	quota rent, p. 201
export subsidy, p. 197	specific tariff, p. 187
export supply curve, p. 188	terms of trade gain, p. 196
import demand curve, p. 188	voluntary export restraint (VER), p. 203

FIGURE 8AI-2

A Tariff in a Small Country

The country produces less of its export good and more of its imported good. Consumption is also distorted. The result is a reduction in both welfare and the volume of the country's trade.

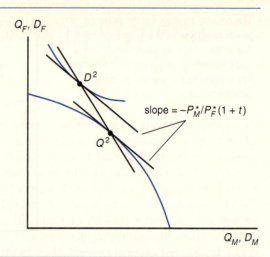

2. The reduction in welfare comes from two effects. (a) The economy no longer produces at a point that maximizes the value of income at world prices. The budget constraint that passes through Q^2 lies inside the constraint passing through Q^1. (b) Consumers do not choose the welfare-maximizing point on the budget constraint; they do not move up to an indifference curve that is tangent to the economy's true budget constraint. Both (a) and (b) result from the fact that domestic consumers and producers face prices that are different from world prices. The loss in welfare due to inefficient production (a) is the general equilibrium counterpart of the production distortion loss we described in the partial equilibrium approach in this chapter, and the loss in welfare due to inefficient consumption (b) is the counterpart of the consumption distortion loss.

3. Trade is reduced by the tariff. Exports and imports are both less after the tariff is imposed than before.

These are the effects of a tariff imposed by a small country. We next turn to the effects of a tariff imposed by a large country.

A TARIFF IN A LARGE COUNTRY

To address the large country case, we use the offer curve technique developed in the appendix to Chapter 5. We consider two countries: Home, which exports manufactures and imports food, and its trading partner Foreign. In Figure 8AI-3, Foreign's offer curve is represented by OF. Home's offer curve in the absence of a tariff is represented by OM^1. The free trade equilibrium is determined by the intersection of OF and OM^1, at point 1, with a relative price of manufactures on the world market $(P_M^*/P_F^*)^1$.

Now suppose that Home imposes a tariff. We first ask, how would its trade change if there were no change in its terms of trade? We already know the answer from the small country analysis: For a given world price, a tariff reduces both exports and imports. Thus

FIGURE 8AI-3

Effect of a Tariff on the Terms of Trade

The tariff causes the country to trade less at any *given* terms of trade; thus its offer curve shifts in. This implies, however, that the terms of trade must improve. The gain from improved terms of trade may offset the losses from the distortion of production and consumption, which reduce welfare at any given terms of trade.

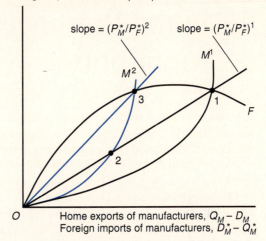

Home imports of food, $D_F - Q_F$
Foreign exports of food, $Q_F^* - D_F^*$

slope = $(P_M^*/P_F^*)^2$ slope = $(P_M^*/P_F^*)^1$

M^1

M^2

3

1

F

2

O

Home exports of manufacturers, $Q_M - D_M$
Foreign imports of manufacturers, $D_M^* - Q_M^*$

if the world relative price of manufactures remained at $(P_M^*/P_F^*)^1$, Home's offer would shift in from point 1 to point 2. More generally, if Home imposes a tariff its overall offer curve will shrink in to a curve like OM^2, passing through point 2.

But this shift in Home's offer curve will change the equilibrium terms of trade. In Figure 8AI-3, the new equilibrium is at point 3, with a relative price of manufactures $(P_M^*/P_F^*)^2 > (P_M^*/P_F^*)^1$. That is, the tariff improves Home's terms of trade.

The effects of the tariff on Home's welfare are ambiguous. On one side, if the terms of trade did not improve, we have just seen from the small country analysis that the tariff would reduce welfare. On the other side, the improvement in Home's terms of trade tends to increase welfare. So the welfare effect can go either way, just as in the partial equilibrium analysis.

Appendix II to Chapter 8

Tariffs and Import Quotas in the Presence of Monopoly

The trade policy analysis in this chapter assumed that markets are perfectly competitive, so that all firms take prices as given. As we argued in Chapter 6, however, many markets for internationally traded goods are imperfectly competitive. The effects of international trade policies can be affected by the nature of the competition in a market.

When we analyze the effects of trade policy in imperfectly competitive markets, a new consideration appears: International trade limits monopoly power, and policies that limit trade may therefore increase monopoly power. Even if a firm is the only producer of a good in a country, it will have little ability to raise prices if there are many foreign suppliers and free trade. If imports are limited by a quota, however, the same firm will be free to raise prices without fear of competition.

The link between trade policy and monopoly power may be understood by examining a model in which a country imports a good and its import-competing production is controlled by only *one* firm. The country is small on world markets, so that the price of the import is unaffected by its trade policy. For this model, we examine and compare the effects of free trade, a tariff, and an import quota.

THE MODEL WITH FREE TRADE

Figure 8AII-1 shows free trade in a market where a domestic monopolist faces competition from imports. D is the domestic demand curve: demand for the product by domestic residents. P_W is the world price of the good; imports are available in unlimited quantities at that price. The domestic industry is assumed to consist of only a single firm, whose marginal cost curve is MC.

If there were no trade in this market, the domestic firm would behave as an ordinary profit-maximizing monopolist. Corresponding to D is a marginal revenue curve MR, and the firm would choose the monopoly profit-maximizing level of output Q_M and price P_M.

With free trade, however, this monopoly behavior is not possible. If the firm tried to charge P_M, or indeed any price above P_W, nobody would buy its product, because cheaper imports would be available. Thus international trade puts a lid on the monopolist's price at P_W.

Given this limit on its price, the best the monopolist can do is produce up to the point where marginal cost is equal to the world price, at Q_f. At the price P_W, domestic consumers will demand D_f units of the good, so imports will be $D_f - Q_f$. This outcome, however, is exactly what would have happened if the domestic industry had been perfectly competitive. With free trade, then, the fact that the domestic industry is a monopoly does not make any difference to the outcome.

FIGURE 8AII-1

A Monopolist Under Free Trade

The threat of import competition forces the monopolist to behave like a perfectly competitive industry.

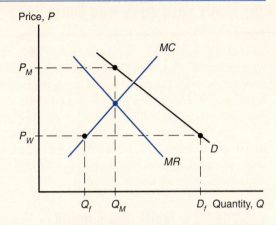

THE MODEL WITH A TARIFF

The effect of a tariff is to raise the maximum price the domestic industry can charge. If a specific tariff t is charged on imports, the domestic industry can now charge $P_w + t$ (Figure 8AII-2). The industry still is not free to raise its price all the way to the monopoly price, however, because consumers will still turn to imports if the price rises above the world price plus the tariff. Thus the best the monopolist can do is to set price equal to marginal cost, at Q_t. The tariff raises the domestic price as well as the output of the domestic indus-

FIGURE 8AII-2

A Monopolist Protected by a Tariff

The tariff allows the monopolist to raise its price, but the price is still limited by the threat of imports.

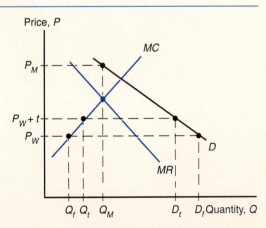

try, while demand falls to D_t and thus imports fall. However, the domestic industry still produces the same quantity as if it were perfectly competitive.[1]

THE MODEL WITH AN IMPORT QUOTA

Suppose the government imposes a limit on imports, restricting their quantity to a fixed level $\bar{Q}$. Then the monopolist knows that when it charges a price above P_w, it will not lose all its sales. Instead, it will sell whatever domestic demand is at that price, minus the allowed imports $\bar{Q}$. Thus the demand facing the monopolist will be domestic demand less allowed imports. We define the postquota demand curve as D_q; it is parallel to the domestic demand curve D but shifted $\bar{Q}$ units to the left (Figure 8AII-3).

Corresponding to D_q is a new marginal revenue curve MR_q. The firm protected by an import quota maximizes profit by setting marginal cost equal to this new marginal revenue, producing Q_q and charging the price P_q. (The license to import one unit of the good will therefore yield a rent of $P_q - P_w$.)

COMPARING A TARIFF AND A QUOTA

We now ask how the effects of a tariff and a quota compare. To do this, we compare a tariff and a quota that lead to *the same level of imports* (Figure 8AII-4). The tariff level t leads to a level of imports $\bar{Q}$; we therefore ask what would happen if instead of a tariff the government simply limited imports to $\bar{Q}$.

FIGURE 8AII-3

A Monopolist Protected by an Import Quota

The monopolist is now free to raise prices, knowing that the domestic price of imports will rise too.

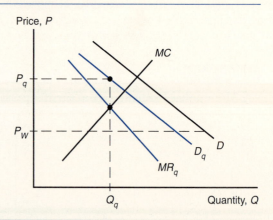

---

[1]There is one case in which a tariff will have different effects on a monopolistic industry than on a perfectly competitive one. This is the case where a tariff is so high that imports are completely eliminated (a prohibitive tariff). For a competitive industry, once imports have been eliminated, any further increase in the tariff has no effect. A monopolist, however, will be forced to limit its price by the *threat* of imports even if actual imports are zero. Thus an increase in a prohibitive tariff will allow a monopolist to raise its price closer to the profit-maximizing price P_M.

FIGURE 8AII-4

Comparing a Tariff and a Quota

A quota leads to lower domestic output and a higher price than a tariff that yields the same level of imports.

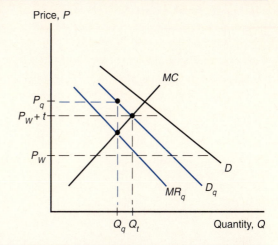

We see from the figure that the results are not the same. The tariff leads to domestic production of Q_t and a domestic price of $P_W + t$. The quota leads to a lower level of domestic production, Q_q, and a higher price, P_q. When protected by a tariff the monopolistic domestic industry behaves as if it were perfectly competitive; when protected by a quota it clearly does not.

The reason for this difference is that an import quota creates more monopoly power than a tariff. When monopolistic industries are protected by tariffs, domestic firms know that if they raise their prices too high they will still be undercut by imports. An import quota, on the other hand, provides absolute protection: No matter how high the domestic price, imports cannot exceed the quota level.

This comparison seems to say that if governments are concerned about domestic monopoly power, they should prefer tariffs to quotas as instruments of trade policy. In fact, however, protection has increasingly drifted away from tariffs toward nontariff barriers, including import quotas. To explain this, we need to look at considerations other than economic efficiency that motivate governments.

9

The Political Economy of Trade Policy

In 1981 the United States asked Japan to limit its exports of autos to the United States. This raised the prices of imported cars and forced U.S. consumers to buy domestic autos they clearly did not like as much. While Japan was willing to accommodate the U.S. government on this point, it was unwilling to do so on another—a request that Japan eliminate import quotas on beef and citrus products—quotas that forced Japanese consumers to buy incredibly expensive domestic products instead of cheap imports from the United States. The governments of both countries were thus determined to pursue policies that, according to the cost-benefit analysis developed in Chapter 8, produced more costs than benefits. Clearly, government policies reflect objectives that go beyond simple measures of cost and benefit.

In this chapter we examine some of the reasons governments either should not or, at any rate, do not base their policy on economists' cost-benefit calculations. The examination of the forces motivating trade policy in practice continues in Chapters 10 and 11, which discuss the characteristic trade policy issues facing developing and advanced countries, respectively.

The first step toward understanding actual trade policies is to ask what reasons there are for governments *not* to interfere with trade—that is, what is the case for free trade? With this question answered, arguments for intervention can be examined as challenges to the assumptions underlying the case for free trade.

THE CASE FOR FREE TRADE

Few countries have anything approaching completely free trade. The city-state of Hong Kong may be the only modern economy with no tariffs or import quotas, and this may change in 1997 when the government reverts to China, which is fairly protectionist. Nonetheless, since the time of Adam Smith economists have advocated free trade as an ideal toward which trade policy should strive. The reasons for this advocacy are not quite as simple as the idea itself. At one level, theoretical models suggest that free trade will avoid the efficiency losses associated with protection. Many economists believe that free trade produces additional gains beyond the elimination of production and consumption distortions. Finally, even among economists who believe free trade is a less than perfect policy, many believe free trade is usually better than any other policy a government is likely to follow.

FREE TRADE AND EFFICIENCY

The **efficiency case for free trade** is simply the reverse of the cost-benefit analysis of a tariff. Figure 9-1 shows the basic point once again for the case of a small country that cannot influence foreign export prices. A tariff causes a net loss to the economy measured by the area of the two triangles; it does so by distorting the economic incentives of both producers and consumers. Conversely, a move to free trade eliminates these distortions and increases national welfare.

A number of efforts have been made to add the total costs of distortions due to tariffs and import quotas in particular economies. Table 9-1 presents some representative estimates. It is noteworthy that the costs of protection to the United States are measured as quite small relative to national income. This situation reflects two facts: (1) the United States is relatively less dependent on trade than other countries, and (2) with some major exceptions, U.S. trade is fairly free. By contrast, some smaller countries that impose very restrictive tariffs and quotas are estimated to lose as much as 10 percent of their potential national income to distortions caused by their trade policies.

ADDITIONAL GAINS FROM FREE TRADE[1]

There is a widespread belief among economists that calculations of the kind reported in Table 9-1, even though they report substantial gains from free trade in some cases, do not represent the whole story. In small countries in general and developing countries in particular, many economists would argue that there are important gains from free trade not accounted for in conventional cost-benefit analysis.

One kind of additional gain involves economies of scale. Protected markets not only fragment production internationally, but by reducing competition and raising profits, they also lead too many firms to enter the protected industry. With a proliferation of firms in narrow domestic markets, the scale of production of each firm becomes inefficient. A good example of how protection leads to inefficient scale is the case of the Argentine automobile industry, which emerged because of import restrictions. An efficient scale assembly plant

---

[1]The additional gains from free trade that are discussed here are sometimes referred to as "dynamic" gains, because increased competition and innovation may need more time to take effect than the elimination of production and consumption distortions.

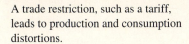

FIGURE 9-1

The Efficiency Case for Free Trade

A trade restriction, such as a tariff, leads to production and consumption distortions.

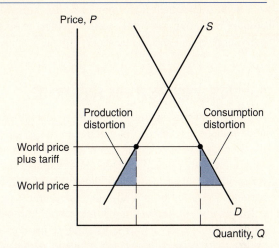

should make from 80,000 to 200,000 automobiles per year, yet in 1964 the Argentine industry, which produced only 166,000 cars, had no less than 13 firms! Some economists argue that the need to deter excessive entry and the resulting inefficient scale of production is a reason for free trade that goes beyond the standard cost-benefit calculations.

Another argument for free trade is that by providing entrepreneurs with an incentive to seek new ways to export or compete with imports, free trade offers more opportunities for learning and innovation than are provided by a system of "managed" trade, where the government largely dictates the pattern of imports and exports. Chapter 10 discusses the experiences of less-developed countries that discovered unexpected export opportunities when they shifted from systems of import quotas and tariffs to more open trade policies.

These additional arguments for free trade are for the most part not quantified. In 1985, however, Canadian economists Richard Harris and David Cox attempted to quantify the gains for Canada of free trade with the United States, taking into account the gains from a

TABLE 9-1

Estimated Cost of Protection, as a Percentage of National Income

Brazil (1966)	9.5
Turkey (1978)	5.4
Philippines (1978)	5.2
United States (1983)	0.26

Sources: Brazil: Bela Balassa, *The Structure of Protection in Developing Countries* (Baltimore: The Johns Hopkins Press, 1971); Turkey and Philippines, World Bank, *The World Development Report 1987* (Washington: World Bank, 1987); United States: David G. Tarr and Morris E. Morkre, *Aggregate Costs to the United States of Tariffs and Quotas on Imports* (Washington D.C.: Federal Trade Commission, 1984).

more efficient scale of production within Canada. They estimated that Canada's real income would rise by 8.6 percent—an increase about three times as large as the one typically estimated by economists who do not take into account the gains from economies of scale.[2]

If the additional gains from free trade are as large as some economists believe, the costs of distorting trade with tariffs, quotas, export subsidies, and so on are correspondingly larger than the conventional cost-benefit analysis measures.

POLITICAL ARGUMENT FOR FREE TRADE

A **political argument for free trade** reflects the fact that a political commitment to free trade may be a good idea in practice even though there may be better policies in principle. Economists often argue that trade policies in practice are dominated by special-interest politics rather than consideration of national costs and benefits. Economists can sometimes show that in theory a selective set of tariffs and export subsidies could increase national welfare, but in reality any government agency attempting to pursue a sophisticated program of intervention in trade would probably be captured by interest groups and converted into a device for redistributing income to politically influential sectors. If this argument is correct, it may be better to advocate free trade without exceptions, even though on purely economic grounds free trade may not always be the best conceivable policy.

The three arguments outlined in the previous section probably represent the standard view of most international economists, at least in the United States:

1. The conventionally measured costs of deviating from free trade are large.
2. There are other benefits from free trade that add to the costs of protectionist policies.
3. Any attempt to pursue sophisticated deviations from free trade will be subverted by the political process.

Nonetheless, there are intellectually respectable arguments for deviating from free trade, and these arguments deserve a fair hearing.

NATIONAL WELFARE ARGUMENTS AGAINST FREE TRADE

Most tariffs, import quotas, and other trade policy measures are undertaken primarily to protect the income of particular interest groups. Politicians often claim, however, that the policies are being undertaken in the interest of the nation as a whole, and sometimes they are even telling the truth. Although economists often argue that deviations from free trade reduce national welfare, there are, in fact, some theoretical grounds for believing that activist trade policies can sometimes increase the welfare of the nation as a whole.

---

[2]See Harris and Cox, *Trade, Industrial Policy, and Canadian Manufacturing* (Toronto: Ontario Economic Council, 1984); and, by the same authors, "Trade Liberalization and Industrial Organization: Some Estimates for Canada," *Journal of Political Economy* 93 (February 1985), pp. 115–145.

CASE STUDY

THE GAINS FROM 1992

In 1987 the nations of the European Community (now known as the European Union) agreed on what formally was called the Single European Act, with the intention to create a truly unified European market. Because the act was supposed to go into effect within five years, the measures it embodied came to be known generally as "1992."

The unusual thing about 1992 was that the European Community was already a customs union, that is, there were no tariffs or import quotas on intra-European trade. So what was left to liberalize? The advocates of 1992 argued that there were still substantial barriers to international trade within Europe. Some of these barriers involved the costs of crossing borders; for example, the mere fact that trucks carrying goods between France and Germany had to stop for legal formalities often meant long waits that were costly in time and fuel. Similar costs were imposed on business travelers, who might fly from London to Paris in an hour, then spend another hour waiting to clear immigration and customs. Differences in regulations also had the effect of limiting the integration of markets. For example, because health regulations on food differed among the European nations, one could not simply fill a truck with British goods and take them to France, or vice versa.

Eliminating these subtle obstacles to trade was a very difficult political process. Suppose France is going to allow goods from Germany to enter the country without any checks. What is to prevent the French people from being supplied with manufactured goods that do not meet French safety standards, foods that do not meet French health standards, or medicines that have not been approved by French doctors? The only way that countries can have truly open borders is if they are able to agree on common standards, so that a good that meets French requirements is acceptable in Germany and vice versa. The main task of the 1992 negotiations was therefore one of harmonization of regulations in hundreds of areas, negotiations that were often acrimonious because of differences in national cultures.

The most emotional examples involved food. All advanced countries regulate things such as artificial coloring, to ensure that consumers are not unknowingly fed chemicals that are carcinogens or otherwise harmful. The initially proposed regulations on artificial coloring would, however, have destroyed the appearance of several traditional British foods: pink bangers (breakfast sausages) would have become white, golden kippers gray, and mushy peas a drab rather than a brilliant green. Continental consumers did not mind; indeed they could not understand how the British could eat such things in the first place. But in Britain the issue became tied up with fear over the loss of national identity, and loosening the proposed regulations became a top priority for the government. Britain succeeded in getting the necessary exemptions. On the other hand, Germany was forced to accept imports of beer that did not meet its centuries-old purity laws, and Italy to accept pasta made from—horrors!—the wrong kind of wheat.

But why engage in all this difficult negotiating? What were the potential gains from 1992? Attempts to estimate the direct gains have always suggested that they are fairly modest. Costs associated with crossing borders amount to no more than a few percent of the value of the goods shipped; removing these costs could add at best a fraction of a percent to the real income of Europe as a whole. Yet economists at the European Commission (the administrative arm of the European Community) argued that the true gains would be much larger.

Their reasoning relied to a large extent on the view that the unification of the European market would lead to greater competition among firms and to a more efficient scale of production. Much was made of the comparison with the United States, a country whose purchasing power and population are similar to those of the European Union, but which is a borderless, fully integrated market. Commission economists pointed out that in a number of industries Europe seemed to have markets that were segmented: Instead of treating the whole continent as a single market, firms seemed to have carved it into local zones served by relatively small-scale national producers. They argued that with all barriers to trade removed, there would be a consolidation of these producers, with substantial gains in productivity. These putative gains raised the overall estimated benefits from 1992 to several percent of the initial income of European nations. The Commission economists argued further that there would be indirect benefits, because the improved efficiency of the European economy would improve the trade-off between inflation and unemployment. At the end of a series of calculations, the Commission estimated a gain from 1992 of 7 percent of European income.[3]

While nobody involved in this discussion regarded 7 percent as a particularly reliable number, many economists shared the conviction of the Commission that the gains would be large. There were, however, skeptics, who suggested that the segmentation of markets had more to do with culture than trade policy. For example, Italian consumers wanted washing machines that were quite different from those preferred in Germany. Italians tend to buy relatively few clothes, but those they buy are stylish and expensive, so they prefer slow, gentle washing machines that conserve their clothing investment.

It is too soon to pronounce a conclusive judgment on 1992, but initial observations suggest that both the supporters and the skeptics had a valid point. In some cases there have been notable consolidations of industry. For example, Hoover closed its vacuum cleaner plant in France and concentrated all its production in an efficient plant in Britain. In some cases old market segmentations have clearly broken down, and sometimes in surprising ways, like the emergence of British sliced bread as a popular item in France. But in other cases markets have shown little sign of merging. The Germans have shown little taste for imported beer, and the Italians none for pasta made with soft wheat.

---

[3]See *The Economics of 1992* (Brussels: Commission of the European Communities, 1988).

THE TERMS OF TRADE ARGUMENT FOR A TARIFF

One argument for deviating from free trade comes directly out of cost-benefit analysis: For a large country that is able to affect the prices of foreign exporters, a tariff lowers the price of imports and thus generates a terms of trade benefit. This benefit must be set against the costs of the tariff, which arise because the tariff distorts production and consumption incentives. It is possible, however, that in some cases the terms of trade benefits of a tariff outweigh its costs, so there is a **terms of trade argument for a tariff.**

The appendix to this chapter shows that for a sufficiently small tariff the terms of trade benefits must outweigh the costs. Thus at small tariff rates a large country's welfare is higher than with free trade (Figure 9-2). As the tariff rate is increased, however, the costs eventually begin to grow more rapidly than the benefits and the curve relating national welfare to the tariff rate turns down. A tariff rate that completely prohibits trade (t_p in Figure 9-2) leaves the country worse off than with free trade; further increases in the tariff rate beyond t_p have no effect, so the curve flattens out.

At point 1 on the curve in Figure 9-2, corresponding to the tariff rate t_o, national welfare is maximized. The tariff rate t_O that maximizes national welfare is the **optimum tariff.** (By convention the phrase *optimum tariff* is usually used to refer to the tariff justified by a terms of trade argument rather than to the best tariff given all possible considerations.) The optimum tariff rate is always positive but less than the prohibitive rate (t_p) that would eliminate all imports.

What policy would the terms of trade argument dictate for *export* sectors? Since an export subsidy *worsens* the terms of trade, and therefore unambiguously reduces national welfare, the optimal policy in export sectors must be a negative subsidy, that is, a *tax* on exports that raises the price of exports to foreigners. Like the optimum tariff, the optimum export tax is always positive but less than the prohibitive tax that would eliminate exports completely.

FIGURE 9-2

The Optimum Tariff

For a large country, there is an optimum tariff t_O at which the marginal gain from improved terms of trade just equals the marginal efficiency loss from production and consumption distortion.

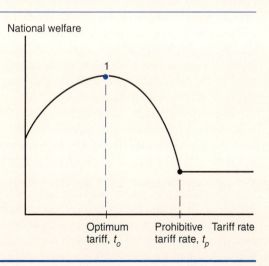

The policy of Saudi Arabia and other oil exporters has been to tax their exports of oil, raising the price to the rest of the world. Although oil prices fell in the mid-1980s, it is hard to argue that Saudi Arabia would have been better off under free trade.

The terms of trade argument against free trade has some important limitations, however. Most small countries have very little ability to affect the world prices of either their imports or other exports, so that the terms of trade argument is of little practical importance. For big countries like the United States, the problem is that the terms of trade argument amounts to an argument for using national monopoly power to extract gains at other countries' expense. The United States could surely do this to some extent, but such a predatory policy would probably bring retaliation from other large countries. A cycle of retaliatory trade moves would, in turn, undermine the attempts at international trade policy coordination described later in this chapter.

The terms of trade argument against free trade, then, is intellectually impeccable but of doubtful usefulness. In practice, it is emphasized more by economists as a theoretical proposition than it is used by governments as a justification for trade policy.

THE DOMESTIC MARKET FAILURE ARGUMENT AGAINST FREE TRADE

Leaving aside the issue of the terms of trade, the basic theoretical case for free trade rested on cost-benefit analysis using the concepts of consumer and producer surplus. Many economists have made a case against free trade based on the counterargument that these concepts, producer surplus in particular, do not properly measure costs and benefits.

Why might producer surplus not properly measure the benefits of producing a good? We consider a variety of reasons in the next two chapters: These include the possibility that the labor used in a sector would otherwise be unemployed or underemployed, the existence of defects in the capital or labor markets that prevent resources from being transferred as rapidly as they should be to sectors that yield high returns, and the possibility of technological spillovers from industries that are new or particularly innovative. These can all be classified under the general heading of **domestic market failures.** That is, each of these examples is one in which some market in the country is not doing its job right—the labor market is not clearing, the capital market is not allocating resources efficiently, and so on.

Suppose, for example, that the production of some good yields experience that will improve the technology of the economy as a whole but that the firms in the sector cannot appropriate this benefit and therefore do not take it into account in deciding how much to produce. Then there is a **marginal social benefit** to additional production that is not captured by the producer surplus measure. This marginal social benefit can serve as a justification for tariffs or other trade policies.

Figure 9-3 illustrates the domestic market failure argument against free trade. Figure 9-3a shows the conventional cost-benefit analysis of a tariff for a small country (which rules out terms of trade effects). Figure 9-3b shows the marginal benefit from production that is not taken account of by the producer surplus measure. The figure shows the effects of a tariff that raises the domestic price from P_W to $P_W + t$. Production rises from S^1 to S^2, with a resulting production distortion indicated by the area labeled a. Consumption falls from D^1 to D^2, with a resulting consumption distortion indicated by the area b. If we considered only consumer and producer surplus, we would find that the costs of the tariff exceed its benefits. Figure 9-3b shows, however, that this calculation overlooks an additional benefit that may make the tariff preferable to free trade. The increase in production yields a social benefit that may be measured by the area under the marginal social benefit curve

FIGURE 9-3

The Domestic Market Failure Argument for a Tariff

If production of a good yields extra social benefits (measured in panel (b) by
area c) not captured as producer surplus
(area b in panel (a)), a tariff can increase welfare.

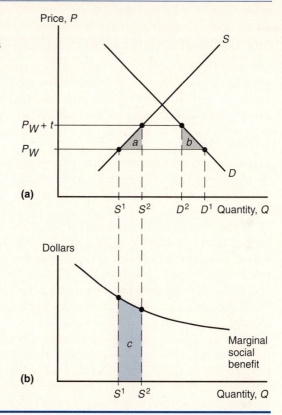

from S^1 to S^2, indicated by c. In fact, by an argument similar to that in the terms of trade
case, we can show that if the tariff is small enough the area c must always exceed the area
$a + b$ and that there is some welfare-maximizing tariff that yields a level of social welfare
higher than that of free trade.

The domestic market failure argument against free trade is a particular case of a more
general concept known in economics as the **theory of the second best.** This theory states
that a hands-off policy is desirable in any one market only if all other markets are working
properly. If they are not, a government intervention that appears to distort incentives in one
market may actually increase welfare by offsetting the consequences of market failures
elsewhere. For example, if the labor market is malfunctioning and fails to deliver full employment, a policy of subsidizing labor-intensive industries, which would be undesirable
in a full-employment economy, might turn out to be a good idea. It would be better to fix
the labor market, for example, by making wages more flexible, but if for some reason this
cannot be done, intervening in other markets may be a "second-best" way of alleviating the
problem.

When economists apply the theory of the second best to trade policy, they argue that imperfections in the *internal* functioning of an economy may justify interfering in its external economic relations. This argument accepts that international trade is not the source of the problem but suggests nonetheless that trade policy can provide at least a partial solution.

HOW CONVINCING IS THE MARKET FAILURE ARGUMENT?

When they were first proposed, market failure arguments for protection seemed to undermine much of the case for free trade. After all, who would want to argue that the real economies we live in are free from market failures? In poorer nations, in particular, market imperfections seem to be legion. For example, unemployment and massive differences between rural and urban wage rates are present in many less-developed countries (Chapter 10). The evidence that markets work badly is less glaring in advanced countries, but it is easy to develop hypotheses suggesting major market failures there as well—for example, the inability of innovative firms to reap the full rewards of their innovations. How can we defend free trade given the likelihood that there are interventions that could raise national welfare?

There are two lines of defense for free trade: The first argues that domestic market failures should be corrected by domestic policies aimed directly at the problems' sources; the second argues that economists cannot diagnose market failure well enough to prescribe policy.

The point that domestic market failure calls for domestic policy changes, not international trade policies, can be made by cost-benefit analysis, modified to account for any unmeasured marginal social benefits. Figure 9-3 showed that a tariff might raise welfare, despite the production and consumption distortion it causes, because it leads to additional production that yields social benefits. If the same production increase were achieved via a production subsidy rather than a tariff, however, the price to consumers would not increase and the consumption loss *b* would be avoided. In other words, by targeting directly the particular activity we want to encourage, a production subsidy would avoid some of the side costs associated with a tariff.

This example illustrates a general principle when dealing with market failures: It is always preferable to deal with market failures as directly as possible, because indirect policy responses lead to unintended distortions of incentives elsewhere in the economy. Thus, trade policies justified by domestic market failure are never the most efficient response; they are always "second-best" rather than "first-best" policies.

This insight has important implications for trade policymakers: Any proposed trade policy should always be compared with a purely domestic policy aimed at correcting the same problem. If the domestic policy appears too costly or has undesirable side effects, the trade policy is almost surely even less desirable—even though the costs are less apparent.

In the United States, for example, an import quota on automobiles has been supported on the grounds that it is necessary to save the jobs of autoworkers. The advocates of an import quota argue that U.S. labor markets are too inflexible for autoworkers to remain employed either by cutting their wages or by finding jobs in other sectors. Now consider a purely domestic policy aimed at the same problem: a subsidy to firms that employ autoworkers. Such a policy would encounter massive political opposition. For one thing, to preserve current levels of employment without protection would require large subsidy payments, which would either increase the federal government budget deficit or require a tax increase. Furthermore, autoworkers are among the highest-paid workers in the manufacturing sector; the general public would surely object to subsidizing them. It is hard to

MARKET FAILURES CUT BOTH WAYS: THE CASE OF CALIFORNIA

Critics of free trade sometimes seem to argue that market failures create a general presumption in favor of protection. In fact, the domestic market failure argument cuts both ways. It is just as likely that an industry will have hidden marginal social costs as that it will have hidden marginal social benefits, and thus it is just as possible that a tariff or import quota will produce extra costs over and above the conventional measures as that it will turn out to be beneficial.

An interesting case in which domestic market failure reinforces the case for free trade was noticed by some economists studying the likely effects of free trade between the United States and Mexico.

One of the important effects of the North American Free Trade Agreement (NAFTA) is that it opens the U.S. market to increased imports of fruits and vegetables from Mexico. These increased imports surely lead to some reduction in U.S. production, especially in southern California.

The interesting point that these economists noticed is that southern California's agriculture is overwhelmingly dependent on irrigation and that, for complex political and historical reasons, the farmers get their water at extremely subsidized prices. Southern California is an arid region; its water must be brought in from all over the western United States at a heavy cost in terms of the building and maintenance of dams, aqueducts, and so on. There are also significant if hard-to-measure costs in terms of environmental impact. And when California experiences a drought, as it sometimes does, it must impose water rationing, at considerable economic cost. Yet farmers pay very low prices for their water, only about one-seventh of the price paid by urban consumers, and (in the view of many economists) an even smaller fraction of the true economic cost.

What the economists studying NAFTA realized was that the increased importing of fruits and vegetables, causing southern California agriculture to contract, would free up water from a use in which it had a very low marginal social product precisely because it has been made available at such a low price. Potential benefits are that urban consumers would be less likely to face water shortages; governments would not need to invest as much in dams and aqueducts; and the burden on the environment would decrease. These indirect benefits of fruit and vegetable imports might be surprisingly large: The study estimated an annual benefit to the United States of more than $100 million.

The "first-best" answer to the problem of water use in California would, of course, be to induce conservation of water by requiring that everyone who uses it pay a price corresponding to its true marginal social cost. But the provision of cheap water for irrigation, like the import quota on sugar discussed in Chapter 8, is a classic example of a policy that provides large benefits to a few people, imposes much larger but diffuse costs on a large number of people, and yet seems to be politically untouchable.

believe an employment subsidy for autoworkers could pass Congress. Yet an import quota *would be even more expensive,* because while bringing about the same increase in employment, it would also distort consumer choice. The only difference is that the costs would be less visible, taking the form of higher automobile prices rather than direct government outlays.

Critics of the domestic market failure justification for protection argue that this case is typical: Most deviations from free trade are adopted not because their benefits exceed their costs but because the public fails to understand their true costs. Comparing the costs of trade policy with alternative domestic policies is a useful way to focus attention on how large these costs are.

The second defense of free trade is that because market failures are typically hard to identify precisely, it is difficult to be sure about the appropriate policy response. For example, suppose there is urban unemployment in a less-developed country; what is the appropriate policy? One hypothesis (examined more closely in Chapter 10) says that a tariff to protect urban industrial sectors will draw the unemployed into productive work and thus generate social benefits that more than compensate for its costs. Another hypothesis says, however, that this policy will encourage so much migration to urban areas that unemployment will, in fact, increase. It is difficult to say which of these hypotheses is right. While economic theory says much about the working of markets that function properly, it provides much less guidance on those that don't; there are many ways in which markets can malfunction, and the choice of a second-best policy depends on the details of the market failure.

The difficulty of ascertaining the right second-best trade policy to follow reinforces the political argument for free trade mentioned earlier. If trade policy experts are highly uncertain about how policy should deviate from free trade and disagree among themselves, it is all too easy for trade policy to ignore national welfare altogether and become dominated by special-interest politics. If the market failures are not too bad to start with, a commitment to free trade might in the end be a better policy than opening the Pandora's box of a more flexible approach.

This is, however, a judgment about politics rather than economics. We need to realize that economic theory does *not* provide a dogmatic defense of free trade, something that it is often accused of doing.

INCOME DISTRIBUTION AND TRADE POLICY

The discussion so far has focused on national welfare arguments for and against tariff policy. It is appropriate to start there, both because a distinction between national welfare and the welfare of particular groups helps to clarify the issues and because the advocates of trade policies usually claim they will benefit the nation as a whole. When looking at the actual politics of trade policy, however, it becomes necessary to deal with the reality that there is no such thing as national welfare; there are only the desires of individuals, which get more or less imperfectly reflected in the objectives of government.

How do the preferences of individuals get added up to produce the trade policy we actually see? There is no single, generally accepted answer, but there has been a growing body of economic analysis that explores models in which governments are assumed to be trying to maximize political success rather than an abstract measure of national welfare.

ELECTORAL COMPETITION

Political scientists have long used a simple model of competition among political parties to show how the preferences of voters might be reflected in actual policies.[4] The model runs

---

[4]See Anthony Downs, *An Economic Theory of Democracy* (Washington: Brookings, 1957).

as follows: Suppose that there are two competing parties, each of which is willing to promise whatever will enable it to win the next election. Suppose that policy can be described along a single dimension, say, the level of the tariff rate. And finally, suppose that voters differ in the policies they prefer. For example, imagine that a country exports skill-intensive goods and imports labor-intensive goods. Then voters with high skill levels will favor low tariff rates, but voters with low skills will be better off if the country imposes a high tariff (because of the Stolper-Samuelson effect discussed in Chapter 4). We can therefore think of lining up all the voters in the order of the tariff rate they prefer, with the voters who favor the lowest rate on the left and those who favor the highest rate on the right.

What policies will the two parties then promise to follow? The answer is that they will try to find the middle ground—specifically, both will tend to converge on the tariff rate preferred by the **median voter,** the voter who is exactly halfway up the lineup. To see why, consider Figure 9-4. In the figure, voters are lined up by their preferred tariff rate, which is shown by the hypothetical upward-sloping curve; t_M is the median voter's preferred rate. Now suppose that one of the parties has proposed the tariff rate t_A, which is considerably above that preferred by the median voter. Then the other party could propose the slightly lower rate t_B, and its program would be preferred by almost all voters who wanted a lower tariff, that is, by a majority. In other words, it would always be in the political interest of a party to undercut any tariff proposal that is higher than what the median voter wants.

But similar reasoning shows that self-interested politicians will always want to promise a higher tariff if their opponents propose one that is lower than the tariff the median voter prefers. So both parties end up proposing a tariff close to the one the median voter wants.

Political scientists have modified this simple model in a number of ways. For example, some analysts stress the importance of party activists to getting out the vote; since these activists are often ideologically motivated, the need for their support may prevent parties from being quite as cynical, or adopting platforms quite as indistinguishable, as this

---

FIGURE 9-4

Political Competition

Voters are lined up in order of the tariff rate they prefer. If one party proposes a high tariff of t_A, the other party can win over most of the voters by offering a somewhat lower tariff, t_B. This political competition drives both parties to propose tariffs close to t_P, the tariff preferred by the median voter.

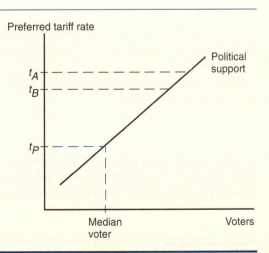

directly (as opposed to imposing more or less hidden costs on consumers) has limited the size of these subsidies. As a result of the government's reluctance, much of the protection in the United States is concentrated on the other major protected sector: the clothing industry.

Clothing.   The clothing industry consists of two parts: textiles (spinning and weaving of cloth) and apparel (assembly of that cloth into clothing). Both industries, but especially the apparel industry, have been heavily protected both through tariffs and through import quotas; they are currently subject to the Multi-Fiber Arrangement, which sets both export and import quotas for a large number of countries.

Apparel production has two key features. It is labor-intensive: A worker needs relatively little capital, in some cases no more than a sewing machine, and can do the job without extensive formal education. And the technology is relatively simple: There is no great difficulty in transferring the technology even to very poor countries. As a result, the apparel industry is one in which low-wage nations have a strong comparative advantage and high-wage countries have a strong comparative disadvantage. It is also traditionally a well-organized sector in advanced countries; for example, many American apparel workers have long been represented by the International Ladies' Garment Worker's Union.

Most estimates suggest that at this point the apparel industry alone accounts for most of the consumer costs from protection in the United States. For example, a recent estimate by the International Trade Commission puts the welfare cost of all U.S. trade restrictions at $15 billion per year, of which textiles and apparel account for more than $10 billion.

INTERNATIONAL NEGOTIATIONS AND TRADE POLICY

Our discussion of the politics of trade policy has not been very encouraging. We have argued that it is difficult to devise trade policies that raise national welfare and that trade policy is often dominated by interest group politics. "Horror stories" of trade policies that produce costs that greatly exceed any conceivable benefits abound; it is easy to be highly cynical about the practical side of trade theory.

Yet, in fact, from the mid-1930s until about 1980 the United States and other advanced countries gradually removed tariffs and some other barriers to trade, and by so doing aided a rapid increase in international integration. Figure 9-5 shows the average U.S. tariff rate on dutiable imports from 1920 to 1991; after rising sharply in the early 1930s, the rate has steadily declined.[7] Most economists believe this progressive trade liberalization was highly beneficial. Given what we have said about the politics of trade policy, however, how was this removal of tariffs politically possible?

At least part of the answer is that the great postwar liberalization of trade was achieved through **international negotiation.** That is, governments agreed to engage in

---

[7]Measures of changes in the average rate of protection can be problematic, because the composition of imports changes—partly because of tariff rates themselves. Imagine, for example, a country that imposes a tariff on some goods that is so high that it shuts off all imports of these goods. Then the average tariff rate on goods actually imported will be zero! To try to correct for this, the measure we use in Figure 9-4 shows the rate only on "dutiable" imports; that is, it excludes imports that for some reason were exempt from tariff. At their peak, U.S. tariff rates were so high that goods subject to tariffs accounted for only one-third of imports; by 1975 that share had risen to two-thirds. As a result, the average tariff rate on all goods fell much less than the rate on dutiable goods. The numbers shown in Figure 9-4, however, give a more accurate picture of the major liberalization of trade actually experienced by the United States.

FIGURE 9-5

The U.S. Tariff Rate

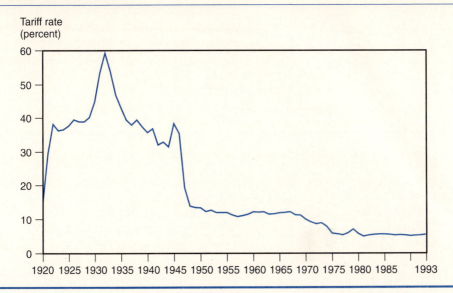

After rising sharply at the beginning of the 1930s, the average tariff rate of the United States has steadily declined.

mutual tariff reduction. These agreements linked reduced protection for each country's import-competing industries to reduced protection by other countries against that country's export industries. Such a linkage, as we will now argue, helps to offset some of the political difficulties that would otherwise prevent countries from adopting good trade policies.

THE ADVANTAGES OF NEGOTIATION

There are at least two reasons why it is easier to lower tariffs as part of a mutual agreement than to do so as a unilateral policy. First, a mutual agreement helps mobilize support for freer trade. Second, negotiated agreements on trade can help governments avoid getting caught in destructive trade wars.

The effect of international negotiations on support for freer trade is straightforward. We have noted that import-competing producers are usually better informed and organized than consumers. International negotiations can bring in domestic exporters as a counterweight. The United States and Japan, for example, could reach an agreement in which the United States refrains from imposing import quotas to protect some of its manufacturers from Japanese competition in return for removal of Japanese barriers to U.S. exports of agricultural or high-technology products to Japan. U.S. consumers might not be effective politically in opposing such import quotas on foreign goods, even though these quotas may be costly to them, but exporters who want access to foreign markets may, through their lobbying for mutual elimination of import quotas, protect consumer interests.

International negotiation can also help to avoid a **trade war.** The concept of a trade war can best be illustrated with a stylized example.

TABLE 9-2

The Problem of Trade Warfare

U.S. \ Japan	Free trade		Protection	
Free trade		10		20
	10		−10	
Protection		−10		−5
	20		−5	

Imagine that there are only two countries in the world, the United States and Japan, and that these countries have only two policy choices, free trade or protection. Suppose that these are unusually clear-headed governments that can assign definite numerical values to their satisfaction with any particular policy outcome (Table 9-2).

The particular values of the payoffs given in the table represent two assumptions. First we assume that each country's government would choose protection if it could take the other country's policy as given. That is, whichever policy Japan chooses, the U.S. government is better off with protection. This assumption is by no means necessarily true; many economists would argue that free trade is the best policy for the nation, regardless of what other governments do. Governments, however, must act not only in the public interest but in their own political interest. For the reasons discussed in the previous section, governments often find it politically difficult to avoid giving protection to some industries.

The second assumption built into Table 9-2 is that even though each government acting individually would be better off with protection, they would both be better off if both chose free trade. That is, the U.S. government has more to gain from an opening of Japanese markets than it has to lose from opening its own markets, and the same is true for Japan. We can justify this assumption simply by appealing to the gains from trade.

To those who have studied game theory, this situation is known as a **Prisoner's dilemma.** Each government, making the best decision for itself, will choose to protect. These choices lead to the outcome in the lower right box of the table. Yet both governments are better off if neither protects: The upper left box of the table yields a payoff that is higher for both countries. By acting unilaterally in what appear to be their best interests, the governments fail to achieve the best outcome possible. If the countries act unilaterally to protect, there is a trade war that leaves both worse off. Trade wars are not as serious as shooting wars, but avoiding them is similar to the problem of avoiding armed conflict or arms races.

Obviously, Japan and the United States need to establish an agreement (such as a treaty) to refrain from protection. Each government will be better off if it limits its own freedom of action, provided the other country limits its freedom of action as well. A treaty can make everyone better off.

This is a highly simplified example. In the real world there are both many countries and many gradations of trade policy between free trade and complete protection against imports. Nonetheless, the example suggests both that there is a need to coordinate trade policies through international agreements and that such agreements can actually make a difference. Indeed, the current system of international trade is built around a series of international agreements.

INTERNATIONAL TRADE AGREEMENTS: A BRIEF HISTORY

Internationally coordinated tariff reduction as a trade policy dates back to the 1930s. In 1930, the United States passed a remarkably irresponsible tariff law, the Smoot-Hawley Act. Under this act, tariff rates rose steeply and U.S. trade fell sharply; some economists argue that the Smoot-Hawley Act helped deepen the Great Depression. Within a few years after the act's passage, the U.S. administration concluded that tariffs needed to be reduced, but this posed serious problems of political coalition building. Any tariff reduction would be opposed by those members of Congress whose districts contained firms producing competing goods, while the benefits would be so widely diffused that few in Congress could be mobilized on the other side. To reduce tariff rates, tariff reduction needed to be linked to some concrete benefits for exporters. The initial solution to this political problem was bilateral tariff negotiations. The United States would approach some country that was a major exporter of some good—say, a sugar exporter—and offer to lower tariffs on sugar if that country would lower its tariffs on some U.S. exports. The attractiveness of the deal to U.S. exporters would help counter the political weight of the sugar interest. In the foreign country, the attractiveness of the deal to foreign sugar exporters would balance the political influence of import-competing interests. Such bilateral negotiations helped reduce the average duty on U.S. imports from 59 percent in 1932 to 25 percent shortly after World War II.

Bilateral negotiations, however, do not take full advantage of international coordination. For one thing, benefits from a bilateral negotiation may "spill over" to countries that have not made any concessions. For example, if the United States reduces tariffs on coffee as a result of a deal with Brazil, Colombia will also gain from a higher world coffee price. Furthermore, some advantageous deals may inherently involve more than two countries: The United States sells more to Europe, Europe sells more to Saudi Arabia, Saudi Arabia sells more to Japan, and Japan sells more to the United States. Thus the next step in international trade liberalization was to proceed to multilateral negotiations involving a number of countries.

Since 1945, there have been eight major multilateral trade agreements. The first five of these took the form of "parallel" bilateral negotiations, where each country negotiates pairwise with a number of countries at once. For example, if Germany were to offer a tariff reduction that would benefit both France and Italy, it could ask both of them for reciprocal concessions. The ability to make more extensive deals, together with the worldwide economic recovery from the war, helped to permit substantial tariff reductions.

The sixth multilateral trade agreement, known as the Kennedy Round, was completed in 1967. This agreement involved an across-the-board 50 percent reduction in tariffs by the major industrial countries, except for specified industries whose tariffs were left unchanged. The negotiations were over which industries to exempt rather than over the size of the cut for industries not given special treatment. Overall, the Kennedy Round reduced average tariffs by about 35 percent.

The so-called Tokyo Round of trade negotiations (completed in 1979) reduced tariffs by a formula more complex than that of the Kennedy Round. In addition, new codes were established in an effort to control the proliferation of nontariff barriers, such as voluntary export restraints and orderly marketing agreements. Finally, in 1994 an eighth round of negotiations, the so-called Uruguay Round, was completed. The provisions of that round were approved by the U.S. Congress after acrimonious debate; we describe the results of these negotiations in the next section.

The multilateral tariff reductions since World War II have taken place under the umbrella framework of the **General Agreement on Tariffs and Trade (GATT),** established

ENVIRONMENTALISM OR PROTECTIONISM?

As we mentioned in Chapter 8, "red tape"—bureaucratic measures applied at the border—can limit international trade even when tariffs are low. But when are red tape barriers allowed under international law?

There are some cases in which countries have a clear right to limit the international flow of goods for health and safety reasons. For example, the United States requires fumigation of imported produce to ensure that destructive pests are not introduced to U.S. farms. This procedure does not constitute unwarranted interference with trade, since there is a clear economic justification. The United States even allows individual states such as California to impose similar requirements on shipments of fruits and vegetables from other states, even though the Constitution prohibits restrictions of interstate trade.

Conversely, there are other red tape barriers that are clearly spurious—such as the Japanese refusal in the early 1980s to permit importation of U.S. aluminum baseball bats on the grounds that they were unsuited to Japanese conditions.

There is, however, an extensive gray area, involving regulations that serve laudable goals through questionable means.

In 1990 the United States tested this gray area when, in response to environmentalist concerns, it banned the import of tuna caught by methods that kill large numbers of dolphins. (In some areas of the Pacific, herds of these intelligent marine mammals on the surface are a sign of schools of tuna below. Encircling the dolphins with large nets is an effective way to catch tuna cheaply, but it kills many dolphins, too.) Mexico, which exports tuna to the United States, appealed to the GATT. An international tribunal ruled in Mexico's favor: The United States has no right to use trade policy to impose its environmental standards on other countries.

The legal reasoning behind this decision was clear, yet it left U.S. environmentalists understandably upset. (We might note that the moral and even economic case for the U.S. action on tuna seems, even in retrospect, a lot better than the case for antidumping duties, yet such duties are an accepted part of international trade law.) It seems likely that there will be future trade policy challenges over a variety of environmental issues, some of them even more compelling—for example, can we refuse to import goods whose production endangers the ozone layer? Many experts expect that so-called "trade and environment" issues will be at the top of the agenda in any future world trade negotiations.

---

in 1947. The GATT embodies a set of rules of conduct for international trade policy that are monitored by a bureaucracy headquartered in Geneva. As with any law, the provisions of the GATT are complex in detail, but the main constraints it places on trade policy are:

1. *Export subsidies.* Signatories to the GATT may not use export subsidies, except for agricultural products (an exception originally insisted on by the United States but now primarily exploited by the European Union).
2. *Import quotas.* Signatories to the GATT may not impose unilateral quotas on imports, except when imports threaten "market disruption" (an undefined phrase usually interpreted to mean surges of imports that threaten to put a domestic sector suddenly out of business).

3. *Tariffs.* Any new tariff or increase in a tariff must be offset by reductions in other tariffs to compensate the affected exporting countries.

Not all countries are members of the GATT. In particular, developing countries are by and large outside these rules. Nearly all advanced countries are members, however, and the trade policies they adopt are to some extent conditioned by the need to remain "GATT-legal."

THE URUGUAY ROUND

Major international trade negotiations invariably open with a ceremony in one exotic locale and conclude with a ceremonial signing in another. The eighth round of global trade negotiations carried out under the GATT began in 1986, with a meeting at the coastal resort of Punta del Este, Uruguay (hence the name Uruguay Round). The participants then repaired to Geneva, where they engaged in seven years of offers and counteroffers, threats and counterthreats, and, above all, tens of thousands of hours of meetings so boring that even the most experienced diplomat had difficulty staying awake. The round was scheduled for completion by 1990 but ran into serious political difficulties. In late 1993 the negotiators finally produced a basic document consisting of 400 pages of agreements, together with supplementary documents detailing the specific commitments of member nations with regard to particular markets and products—about 22,000 pages in all. The agreement was signed in Marrakesh, Morocco, in April 1994, and ratified by the major nations—after bitter political controversy in some cases, including the United States—by the end of that year.

As the length of the document suggests, the end results of the Uruguay Round are not that easy to summarize. The most important results may, however, be grouped under two headings, trade liberalization and administrative reforms.

TRADE LIBERALIZATION

The Uruguay Round, like previous GATT negotiations, cut tariff rates around the world. The numbers can sound impressive: The average tariff imposed by advanced countries will fall almost 40 percent as a result of the round. However, tariff rates were already quite low. In fact, the average tariff rate will fall only from 6.3 to 3.9 percent, enough to produce only a small increase in world trade.

More important than this overall tariff reduction are the moves to liberalize trade in two important sectors, agriculture and clothing.

World trade in agricultural products has been highly distorted. Japan is notorious for import restrictions that lead to internal prices of rice, beef, and other foods several times as high as world market prices; Europe's massive export subsidies under the Common Agricultural Program were described in Chapter 8. At the beginning of the Uruguay Round the United States had an ambitious goal: free trade in agricultural products by the year 2000. The actual achievement was far more modest but still significant. The agreement required agricultural exporters to reduce the value of subsidies by 36 percent, and the volume of subsidized exports by 21 percent, over a six-year period. Countries that protect their farmers with import quotas, like Japan, were required to replace quotas with tariffs, which may not be increased in the future.

World trade in textiles and clothing has also been highly distorted by the Multi-Fiber Arrangement also described in Chapter 8. The Uruguay Round will phase out the MFA over a ten-year period, eliminating all quantitative restrictions on trade in textiles and clothing. (Some high tariffs will, however, remain in place.) This is a fairly dramatic liberalization—remember that most estimates suggest that protection of clothing imposes a larger cost on U.S. consumers than all other protectionist measures combined. It is worth noting, however, that the formula to be used in phasing out the MFA is heavily "backloaded": Much of the liberalization will be postponed until late in the transition period, that is, around 2003 or 2004. Some trade experts are worried about the credibility of such long-range commitments, wondering whether a treaty signed in 1994 can really force politicians to take a politically difficult action ten years later.

A final important trade action under the Uruguay Round is a new set of rules concerning government procurement, purchases made not by private firms or consumers, but by government agencies. Such procurement has long provided protected markets for many kinds of goods, from construction equipment to vehicles. (Recall the box on Hungarian buses in Chapter 8.) The Uruguay Round set new rules that should open up a wide range of government contracts to imported products.

ADMINISTRATIVE REFORMS

Much of the publicity surrounding the Uruguay Round focused on its creation of a new institution, the impressively named World Trade Organization (WTO), to replace the so-called secretariat that administered the GATT until 1994. Indeed, among fringe political groups in the United States, the WTO has become a symbol of a supposed conspiracy to undermine U.S. sovereignty and place its citizens under the rule of a world government.

The reality of the new organization is, however, actually quite modest. No large new bureaucracy will be created; for the most part, the WTO will simply carry out old functions under a new name. The main difference from previous practice is that the charter of the WTO will include a new, accelerated process for resolving disputes between member countries. One major complaint about the GATT has always been that while the agreement did contain provisions for panels to adjudicate complaints by one nation against another—for example, cases in which the United States alleged that Japanese government practices in effect constituted illegal protection—such complaints could take as long as a decade to resolve, by which time whole industries might disappear. And when the GATT did rule against a country, there was no effective way to enforce that ruling. The WTO has a new "dispute settlement understanding" (yes, DSU), which is designed to reach judgments in a much shorter time. The DSU also contains provisions that in effect license countries to retaliate against what the WTO has deemed to be illegal practices, which should make such judgments carry more weight.

Finally, as part of the new agreement the signatories established a subagreement known as the General Agreement on Trade in Services (GATS). World trade in services—that is, in intangible things like insurance, consulting, and banking—has never been subject to any agreed-upon set of rules. As a result, many countries impose regulations that openly or de facto discriminate against foreign suppliers. This is a major omission, since services now account for at least 60 percent of the value of output in advanced economies. Many services are still effectively nontradeable (it is hard to get a haircut or help in finding an item in a store from someone in another country), but trade in commercial services has been a growing share of world trade and is currently more than 20 percent of the total.

The GATS did not directly remove any important barriers to trade in services. It did, however, set up a legal framework under which future negotiations to liberalize service trade could proceed and required the members of the WTO to begin negotiations on service trade by the year 2000.

BENEFITS AND COSTS

The economic impact of the Uruguay Round is difficult to estimate. If nothing else, think about the logistics: To do an estimate, one must translate an immense document from one impenetrable jargon (legalese) into another (economese), assign numbers to the translation, then feed the whole thing into a computer model of the world economy. The matter is made worse by the fact that major parts of the round were still up in the air right up to the very end, so that at the time this textbook was written the economic modelers were still scrambling to revise their estimates to match the final provisions of the agreement.

The most widely cited estimates are those of the GATT itself and of the Organization for Economic Cooperation and Development, another international organization (this one consisting only of rich countries, and based in Paris). Both estimates suggest a gain to the world economy as a whole of more than $200 billion annually once the agreement is fully in force; this would raise world real income by about 1 percent. As always, there are dissenting estimates on both sides. Some economists claim that the estimated gains are exaggerated, particularly because they assume that exports and imports will respond strongly to the new liberalizing moves. A probably larger minority of critics argues that these estimates are considerably too low, for the "dynamic" reasons discussed earlier in this chapter.

In any case, it is clear that the usual logic of trade liberalization will apply: The costs of the Uruguay Round will be felt by concentrated, often well-organized groups, while much of the benefit will accrue to broad, diffuse populations. The progress on agriculture will directly hurt the small but influential populations of farmers in Europe, Japan, and other countries where agricultural prices are far above world levels. These losses should be much more than offset by gains to consumers and taxpayers in those countries, but because these benefits will be very widely spread they may be little noticed. Similarly, the liberalization of trade in textiles and clothing will produce some concentrated pain for workers and companies in those industries, offset by considerably larger but far less visible consumer gains.

Given these strong distributional impacts of the Uruguay Round, it is actually remarkable that an agreement was reached at all. Indeed, after the failure to achieve anything close to agreement by the 1990 target, many commentators began to pronounce the whole trade negotiation process to be dead. That in the end agreement was achieved, if on a more modest scale than originally hoped, may be attributed to an interlocking set of political calculations. In the United States, the gains to agricultural exporters and the prospective gains to service exporters if the GATS opens the door to substantial liberalization helped offset the complaints of the clothing industry. Many developing countries supported the round because of the new opportunities it would offer to their own textile and clothing exports. Also, some of the "concessions" negotiated under the agreement were an excuse to make policy changes that would eventually have happened anyway. For example, the sheer expense of Europe's Common Agricultural Program in a time of budget deficits made it ripe for cutting in any case.

An important factor in the final success of the round, however, was fear of what would happen if it failed. By 1993, protectionist currents were evidently running strong in the United States and elsewhere. Trade negotiators in countries that might otherwise have refused to go along with the agreement—such as France, Japan, or South Korea, in all of which powerful farm lobbies angrily opposed trade liberalization—therefore feared that failure to agree would be dangerous. That is, they feared that a failed round would not mean mere lack of progress but substantial backsliding on the progress made toward free trade over the previous four decades.

PREFERENTIAL TRADING AGREEMENTS

The international trade agreements that we have described so far all involved a "nondiscriminatory" reduction in tariff rates. For example, when the United States agrees with Germany to lower its tariff on imported machinery, the new tariff rate applies to machinery from any nation rather than just imports from Germany. Such nondiscrimination is normal in most tariffs. Indeed, the United States grants many countries a status known formally as that of "most favored nation" (MFN), a guarantee that their exporters will pay tariffs no higher than that of the nation that pays the lowest. All countries granted MFN status pay the same rates. Tariff reductions under GATT always—with one important exception—are made on an MFN basis.

There are some important cases, however, in which nations establish **preferential trading agreements** under which the tariffs they apply to each others' products are lower than the rates on the same goods coming from other countries. The GATT in general prohibits such agreements but makes a rather strange exception: It is against the rules for country A to have lower tariffs on imports from country B than on those from country C, but it is acceptable if countries B and C agree to have zero tariffs on each others' products. That is, the GATT forbids preferential trading agreements in general, as a violation of the MFN principle, but allows them if they lead to free trade between the agreeing countries.[8]

In general, two or more countries agreeing to establish free trade can do so in one of two ways. They can establish a **free trade area,** in which each country's goods can be shipped to the other without tariffs, but in which the countries set tariffs against the outside world independently. Or they can establish a **customs union,** in which the countries must agree on tariff rates. The North American Free Trade Agreement, which establishes free trade among Canada, the United States, and Mexico, creates a free trade area: There is no requirement in the agreement that, for example, Canada and Mexico have the same tariff rate on textiles from China. The European Union, on the other hand, is a full customs union. All of the countries must agree to charge the same tariff rate on each imported good. Each system has both advantages and disadvantages; these are discussed in the accompanying box.

Subject to the qualifications mentioned earlier in this chapter, tariff reduction is a good thing that raises economic efficiency. At first it might seem that preferential tariff reductions are also good, if not as good as reducing tariffs all around. After all, isn't half a loaf better than none?

---

[8]The logic here seems to be legal rather than economic. Nations are allowed to have free trade within their boundaries: Nobody insists that California wine pay the same tariff as French wine when it is shipped to New York. That is, the MFN principle does not apply within political units. But what is a political unit? The GATT sidesteps that potentially thorny question by allowing any group of economies to do what countries do, and establish free trade within some defined boundary.

FREE TRADE AREA VERSUS CUSTOMS UNION

The difference between a free trade area and a customs union is, in brief, that the first is politically straightforward but an administrative headache, while the second is just the opposite.

Consider first the case of a customs union. Once such a union is established, tariff administration is relatively easy: Goods must pay tariffs when they cross the border of the union, but from then on can be shipped freely between countries. A cargo that is unloaded at Marseilles or Rotterdam must pay duties there, but will not face any additional charges if it then goes by truck to Munich. To make this simple system work, however, the countries must agree on tariff rates: The duty must be the same whether the cargo is unloaded at Marseilles, Rotterdam, or for that matter Hamburg, because otherwise importers would choose the point of entry that minimized their fees. So a customs union requires that Germany, France, the Netherlands, and all the other countries agree to charge the same tariffs. This is not easily done: Countries are, in effect, ceding part of their sovereignty to a supranational entity, the European Union.

This has been possible in Europe for a variety of reasons, including the belief that economic unity would help cement the postwar political alliance between European democracies. (One of the founders of the European Union once joked that it should erect a statue of Joseph Stalin, without whose menace the Union might never have been created.) But elsewhere these conditions are lacking. The three nations that formed NAFTA would find it very difficult to cede control over tariffs to any supranational body; if nothing else, it would be hard to devise any arrangement that would give due weight to U.S. interests without effectively allowing the United States to dictate trade policy to Canada and Mexico. NAFTA, therefore, while it permits Mexican goods to enter the United States without tariffs and vice versa, does not require that Mexico and the United States adopt a common external tariff on goods they import from other countries.

This, however, raises a different problem. Under NAFTA, a shirt made by Mexican workers can be brought into the United States freely. But suppose that the United States wants to maintain high tariffs on shirts imported from other countries, while Mexico does not impose similar tariffs. What is to prevent someone from shipping a shirt from, say, Bangladesh to Mexico, then putting it on a truck bound for Chicago?

The answer is that even though the United States and Mexico may have free trade, goods shipped from Mexico to the United States must still pass through a customs inspection. And they can enter the United States without duty only if they have documents proving that they are in fact Mexican goods, not transshipped imports from third countries.

But what is a Mexican shirt? If a shirt comes from Bangladesh, but Mexicans sew on the buttons, does that make it Mexican? Probably not. But if everything except the buttons were made in Mexico, it probably should be considered Mexican. The point is that administering a free trade area that is not a customs union requires not only that the countries continue to check goods at the border, but that they specify an elaborate set of "rules of origin" that determine whether a good is eligible to cross the border without paying a tariff.

As a result, free trade agreements like NAFTA impose a large burden of paperwork, which may be a significant obstacle to trade even when such trade is in principle free.

Perhaps surprisingly, this conclusion is too optimistic. It is possible for a country to make itself worse off by joining a customs union. The reason may be illustrated by a hypothetical example, using Britain, France, and the United States. The United States is a low-cost producer of wheat ($4 per bushel), France a medium-cost producer ($6 per bushel), and Britain a high-cost producer ($8 per bushel). Both Britain and France maintain tariffs against all wheat imports. If Britain forms a customs union with France, the tariff against French, but not U.S., wheat will be abolished. Is this good or bad for Britain? To answer this, consider two cases.

First, suppose that Britain's initial tariff was high enough to exclude wheat imports from either France or the United States. For example, with a tariff of $5 per bushel it would cost $9 to import U.S. wheat and $11 to import French wheat, so British consumers would buy $8 British wheat instead. When the tariff on French wheat is eliminated, imports from France will replace British production. From Britain's point of view this is a gain, because

DO TRADE PREFERENCES HAVE APPEAL?

Over the last few years the European Union has slipped repeatedly into bunches of trouble over the question of trade preferences for bananas.

Most of the world's banana exports come from several small Central American nations—the original "banana republics." Several European nations have, however, traditionally bought their bananas instead from their past or present West Indian colonies in the Caribbean. To protect the island producers, France and the United Kingdom impose import quotas against the "dollar bananas" of Central America, which are typically about 40 percent cheaper than the West Indian product. Germany, however, which has never had West Indian colonies, allows free entry to dollar bananas.

Since the integration of European markets after 1992, the existing banana regime has become impossible to maintain, because it is easy to import the cheaper dollar bananas into Germany and then ship them elsewhere in Europe. To prevent this outcome, the European Commission announced plans in 1993 to impose a new common European import quota against dollar bananas. Germany an-

grily protested the move and even denied its legality: The Germans pointed out that the Treaty of Rome, which established the European Community, contains an explicit guarantee (the "banana protocol") that Germany would be able to import bananas freely.

Why did the Germans go ape about bananas? During the years of communist rule in East Germany, bananas were a rare luxury. The sudden availability of inexpensive bananas after the fall of the Berlin Wall made them a symbol of freedom. So the German government was very unwilling to introduce a policy that would sharply increase banana prices.

In the end the Germans grudgingly went along with a new, unified system of European trade preferences on bananas. But that did not end the controversy: In 1995 the United States entered the fray, claiming that by monkeying around with the existing system of preferences the Europeans were hurting the interests not only of Central American nations but those of a powerful U.S. corporation, the Chiquita Banana Company.

At the time of writing efforts to resolve this latest banana split had still proved fruitless.

it costs $8 to produce a bushel of wheat domestically, while Britain needs to produce only $6 worth of export goods to pay for a bushel of French wheat.

On the other hand, suppose the tariff was lower, for example, $3 per bushel, so that before joining the customs union Britain bought its wheat from the United States (at a cost to consumers of $7 per bushel) rather than producing its own wheat. When the customs union is formed, consumers will buy French wheat at $6 rather than U.S. wheat at $7. So imports of wheat from the United States will cease. However, U.S. wheat is really cheaper than French wheat; the $3 tax that British consumers must pay on U.S. wheat returns to Britain in the form of government revenue and is therefore not a net cost to the British economy. Britain will have to devote more resources to exports to pay for its wheat imports and will be worse off rather than better off.

This possibility of a loss is another example of the theory of the second best. Think of Britain as initially having two policies that distort incentives: a tariff against U.S. wheat and a tariff against French wheat. Although the tariff against French wheat may seem to distort incentives, it may help to offset the distortion of incentives resulting from the tariff against the United States, by encouraging consumption of the cheaper U.S. wheat. Thus, removing the tariff on French wheat can actually reduce welfare.

Returning to our two cases, notice that Britain gains if the formation of a customs union leads to new trade—French wheat replacing domestic production—while it loses if the trade within the customs union simply replaces trade with countries outside the union. In the analysis of preferential trading arrangements, the first case is referred to as **trade creation,** while the second is **trade diversion.** Whether a customs union is desirable or undesirable depends on whether it largely leads to trade creation or trade diversion.

Summary

1. Although few countries practice free trade, most economists continue to hold up free trade as a desirable policy. This advocacy rests on three lines of argument. First is a formal case for the efficiency gains from free trade that is simply the cost-benefit analysis of trade policy read in reverse. Second, many economists believe that free trade produces additional gains that go beyond this formal analysis. Finally, given the difficulty of translating complex economic analysis into real policies, even those who do not see free trade as the best imaginable policy see it as a useful rule of thumb.

2. There is an intellectually respectable case for deviating from free trade. One argument that is clearly valid in principle is that countries can improve their *terms of trade* through optimal tariffs and export taxes. This argument is not too important in practice, however. Small countries cannot have much influence on their import or export prices, so they cannot use tariffs or other policies to raise their terms of trade. Large countries, on the other hand, *can* influence their terms of trade, but in imposing tariffs they run the risk of disrupting trade agreements and provoking retaliation.

3. The other argument for deviating from free trade rests on *domestic market failures.* If some domestic market, such as the labor market, fails to function properly, deviating from free trade can sometimes help reduce the consequences of this malfunctioning. The *theory of the second best* states that if one market fails to

work properly it is no longer optimal for the government to abstain from intervention in other markets. A tariff may raise welfare if there is a *marginal social benefit* to production of a good that is not captured by producer surplus measures.

4. Although market failures are probably common, the domestic market failure argument should not be applied too freely. First, it is an argument for domestic policies rather than trade policies; tariffs are always an inferior, "second-best" way to offset domestic market failure, which is always best treated at its source. Furthermore, market failure is difficult to analyze well enough to be sure of the appropriate policy recommendation.

5. In practice, trade policy is dominated by considerations of income distribution. No single way of modeling the politics of trade policy exists, but several useful ideas have been proposed. Political scientists often argue that policies are determined by competition among political parties that try to attract as many votes as possible. In the simplest case, this leads to the adoption of policies that serve the interests of the *median voter*. While useful for thinking about many issues, however, this approach seems to yield unrealistic predictions for trade policies, which typically favor the interest of small, concentrated groups over the general public. Economists and political scientists generally explain this by appealing to the problem of *collective action*. Because individuals may have little incentive to act politically on behalf of groups to which they belong, those groups which are well organized—typically small groups with a lot at stake—are often able to get policies that serve their interests at the expense of the majority.

6. If trade policy were made on a purely domestic basis, progress toward freer trade would be very difficult to achieve. In fact, however, industrial countries have achieved substantial reductions in tariffs through a process of *international negotiation*. International negotiation helps the cause of tariff reduction in two ways: It helps broaden the constituency for freer trade by giving exporters a direct stake, and it helps governments avoid the mutually disadvantageous *trade wars* that internationally uncoordinated policies could bring.

7. Although some progress was made in the 1930s toward trade liberalization via bilateral agreements, since World War II international coordination has taken place primarily via multilateral agreements under the auspices of the *General Agreement on Tariffs and Trade*. The GATT, which comprises both a bureaucracy and a set of rules of conduct, is the central institution of the international trading system. The most recent worldwide GATT agreement also sets up a new organization, the World Trade Organization (WTO), to monitor and enforce the agreement.

8. In addition to the overall reductions in tariffs that have taken place through multilateral negotiation, some groups of countries have negotiated *preferential trading agreements* under which they lower tariffs with respect to each other but not the rest of the world. Two kinds of preferential trading agreements are allowed under the GATT: *customs unions*, in which the members of the agreement set up common external tariffs, and *free trade areas*, in which they do not charge tariffs on each others' products but set their own tariff rates against the outside world. Either kind of agreement has ambiguous effects on economic welfare. If joining

such an agreement leads to replacement of high-cost domestic production by imports from other members of the agreement—the case of *trade creation*—a country gains. But if joining leads to the replacement of low-cost imports from outside the zone with higher-cost goods from member nations—the case of *trade diversion*—a country loses.

Key Terms

collective action, p. 232

customs union, p. 242

domestic market failure, p. 226

efficiency case for free trade, p. 220

free trade area, p. 242

General Agreement on Tariffs and Trade (GATT), p. 237

international negotiation, p. 234

marginal social benefit, p. 226

median voter, p. 231

optimum tariff, p. 225

political argument for free trade, p. 222

preferential trading agreement, p. 242

Prisoner's dilemma, p. 236

terms of trade argument for a tariff, p. 225

theory of the second best, p. 227

trade creation, p. 245

trade diversion, p. 245

trade war, p. 235

Problems

1. "For a small country like the Philippines, a move to free trade would have huge advantages. It would let consumers and producers make their choices based on the real costs of goods, not artificial prices determined by government policy; it would allow escape from the confines of a narrow domestic market; it would open new horizons for entrepreneurship; and, most important, it would help to clean up domestic politics." Separate out and identify the arguments for free trade in this statement.

2. Which of the following are potentially valid arguments for tariffs or export subsidies, and which are not (explain your answers)?
   a. "The more oil the United States imports, the higher the price of oil will go in the next world shortage."
   b. "The growing exports of off-season fruit from Chile, which now accounts for 80 percent of the U.S. supply of such produce as winter grapes, are contributing to sharply falling prices of these former luxury goods."
   c. "U.S. farm exports don't just mean higher incomes for farmers—they mean higher income for everyone who sells goods and services to the U.S. farm sector."
   d. "Semiconductors are the crude oil to technology; if we don't produce our own chips, the flow of information that is crucial to every industry that uses microelectronics will be impaired."
   e. "The real price of timber has fallen 40 percent, and thousands of timber workers have been forced to look for other jobs."

3. A small country can import a good at a world price of 10 per unit. The domestic supply curve of the good is

$$S = 50 + 5P.$$

The demand curve is

$$D = 400 - 10P.$$

In addition, each unit of production yields a marginal social benefit of 10.

  a. Calculate the total effect on welfare of a tariff of 5 per unit levied on imports.
  b. Calculate the total effect of a production subsidy of 5 per unit.
  c. Why does the production subsidy produce a greater gain in welfare than the tariff?
  d. What would the *optimal* production subsidy be?

4. Suppose that demand and supply are exactly as described in problem 3 but there is no marginal social benefit to production. However, for political reasons the government counts a dollar's worth of gain to producers as being worth $2 of either consumer gain or government revenue. Calculate the effects *on the government's objective* of a tariff of 5 per unit.

5. "There is no point in the United States complaining about trade policies in Japan and Europe. Each country has a right to do whatever is in its own best interest. Instead of complaining about foreign trade policies, the United States should let other countries go their own way, and give up our own prejudices about free trade and follow suit." Discuss both the economics and the political economy of this viewpoint.

6. Which of the following actions would be legal under GATT, and which would not?

  a. A U.S. tariff of 20 percent against any country that exports more than twice as much to the United States as it imports in return.
  b. A subsidy to U.S. wheat exports, aimed at recapturing some of the markets lost to the European Union.
  c. A U.S. tariff on Canadian lumber exports, not matched by equivalent reductions on other tariffs.
  d. A Canadian tax on lumber *exports,* agreed to at the demand of the United States to placate U.S. lumber producers.
  e. A program of subsidized research and development in areas related to high-technology goods such as electronics and semiconductors.
  f. Special government assistance for workers who lose their jobs because of import competition.

7. As a result of political and economic liberalization in Eastern Europe, there has been widespread speculation that Eastern European nations such as Poland and Hungary may join the European Union. Discuss the potential economic *costs* of such an expansion of the European Union, from the point of view of (1) Western Europe; (2) Eastern Europe; and (3) other nations.

Further Reading

Robert E. Baldwin. *The Political Economy of U.S. Import Policy.* Cambridge: MIT Press, 1985. A basic reference on how and why trade policies are made in the United States.

Robert E. Baldwin. "Trade Policies in Developed Countries," in Ronald W. Jones and Peter B. Kenen, eds. *Handbook of International Economics.* Vol. 1. Amsterdam:

North-Holland, 1984. A comprehensive survey of theory and evidence on a broad range of trade-related policies.

Jagdish Bhagwati, ed. *Import Competition and Response.* Chicago: University of Chicago Press, 1982. Analytical papers on the economic and political issues raised when imports compete with domestic production.

Jagdish Bhagwati. *Protectionism.* Cambridge: MIT Press, 1988. A cogent summary of the arguments for and against protectionism, ending with a set of proposals for strengthening free trade.

W. Max Corden. *Trade Policy and Economic Welfare.* Oxford: Clarendon Press, 1974. A careful survey of economic arguments for and against protection.

Harry Flam. "Product Markets and 1992: Full Integration, Large Gains?" *The Journal of Economic Perspectives* (Fall 1992), pp. 7–30. A careful review of the possible economic effects of "1992," the effort to integrate European markets. Notable for the way it tries to test the common belief that there will be large "dynamic" gains from removing trade barriers, even though the measured costs of those barriers appear small.

John H. Jackson. *The World Trading System.* Cambridge: MIT Press, 1989. A comprehensive view of the legal framework of international trade, with emphasis on the role of the GATT.

Dominick Salvatore, ed. *The New Protectionist Threat to World Welfare.* Amsterdam: North-Holland, 1987. A collection of essays on the causes and consequences of increasing protectionist pressure in the 1980s.

Jeffrey Schott. *The Uruguay Round: An Assessment.* Washington, D.C.: Institute for International Economics, 1994. A mercifully brief and readable survey of the issues and accomplishments of the most recent GATT round, together with a survey of much of the relevant research.

Robert M. Stern, ed. *U.S. Trade Policies in a Changing World Economy.* Cambridge: MIT Press, 1987. More essays on current trade policy issues.

to be used to finance investment in new sectors (such as manufacturing), then growth of new industries will be restricted by the ability of firms in these industries to earn current profits. Thus low initial profits will be an obstacle to investment even if the long-term returns on this investment are high. The first-best policy is to create a better capital market, but protection of new industries, which would raise profits and thus allow more rapid growth, can be justified as a second-best policy option.

The *appropriability argument* for infant industry protection can take many forms, but all have in common the idea that firms in a new industry generate social benefits for which they are not compensated. For example, the firms that first enter an industry may have to incur "start-up" costs of adapting technology to local circumstances or of opening new markets. If other firms are able to follow their lead without incurring these start-up costs, the pioneers will be prevented from reaping any returns from these outlays. Thus, pioneering firms may, in addition to producing physical output, create intangible benefits (such as knowledge or new markets) in which they are unable to establish property rights. In some cases the social benefits from creation of a new industry will exceed its costs, yet because of the problem of appropriability no private entrepreneurs will be willing to enter. The first-best answer is to compensate firms for their intangible contributions. When this is not possible, however, there is a second-best case for encouraging entry into a new industry by using tariffs or other trade policies.

Both the imperfect capital markets argument and the appropriability case for infant industry protection are clearly special cases of the *market failures* justification for interfering with free trade. The difference is that in this case the arguments apply specifically to new industries rather than to any industry. The general problems with the market failure approach remain, however. In practice it is difficult to evaluate which industries really warrant special treatment, and there are risks that a policy intended to promote development will end up being captured by special interests. There are many stories of infant industries that have never grown up and remain dependent on protection.

PROMOTING MANUFACTURING THROUGH PROTECTION

Although there are doubts about the infant industry argument, many developing countries have seen this argument as a compelling reason to provide special support for the development of manufacturing industries. In principle such support could be provided in a variety of ways. For example, countries could provide subsidies to manufacturing production in general, or they could focus their efforts on subsidies for the export of some manufactured goods in which they believe they can develop a comparative advantage. In most developing countries, however, the basic strategy for industrialization has been to develop industries oriented toward the domestic market by using trade restrictions such as tariffs and quotas to encourage the replacement of imported manufactures by domestic products. The strategy of encouraging domestic industry by limiting imports of manufactured goods is known as the strategy of **import-substituting industrialization.**

One might ask why a choice needs to be made. Why not encourage both import substitution and exports? The answer goes back to the general equilibrium analysis of tariffs in Chapter 5: A tariff that reduces imports also necessarily reduces exports. By protecting import-substituting industries, countries draw resources away from actual or potential export sectors. So a country's choice to seek to substitute for imports is also a choice to discourage export growth.

The reasons why import substitution rather than export growth has usually been chosen as an industrialization strategy are a mixture of economics and politics. First, until the 1970s many developing countries were skeptical about the possibility of exporting manufactured goods (although this skepticism also calls into question the infant industry argument for manufacturing protection). They believed that industrialization was necessarily based on a substitution of domestic industry for imports rather than on a growth of manufactured exports. Second, in many cases import-substituting industrialization policies dovetailed naturally with existing political biases. We have already noted the case of Latin American nations that were compelled to develop substitutes for imports during the 1930s because of the Great Depression and during the first half of the 1940s because of the wartime disruption of trade (Chapter 9). In these countries import substitution directly benefited powerful, established interest groups, while export promotion had no natural constituency.

It is also worth pointing out that some advocates of a policy of import substitution believed that the world economy was rigged against new entrants, that the advantages of established industrial nations were simply too great to be overcome by newly industrializing economies. Extreme proponents of this view called for a general policy of delinking developing countries from advanced nations; but even among milder advocates of protectionist development strategies the view that the international economic system systematically works against the interests of developing countries remained common until the 1980s.

The 1950s and 1960s saw the high tide of import-substituting industrialization. Developing countries typically began by protecting final stages of industry, such as food processing and automobile assembly. In the larger developing countries, domestic products almost completely replaced imported consumer goods (although the manufacturing was often carried out by foreign multinational firms). Once the possibilities for replacing consumer goods imports had been exhausted, these countries turned to protection of intermediate goods, such as automobile bodies, steel, and petrochemicals.

In most developing economies, the import-substitution drive stopped short of its logical limit: Sophisticated manufactured goods such as computers, precision machine tools, and so on continued to be imported. Nonetheless, the larger countries pursuing import-substituting industrialization reduced their imports to remarkably low levels. Usually, the smaller a country's economic size (as measured, for example, by the value of its total output) the larger will be the share of imports and exports in national income. Yet as Table 10-2 shows, India, with a domestic market less than 5 percent that of the United States, exported a smaller fraction of its output than the United States did in 1990. Brazil is the most extreme case: In 1990, exports were only 7 percent of output, a share less than that of the United States and far less than that of large industrial countries such as Germany.

As a strategy for encouraging growth of manufacturing, import-substituting industrialization has clearly worked. Latin American economies now generate almost as large a

TABLE 10-2

Exports as a Percentage of National Income, 1990

Brazil	7
India	8
United States	10
Japan	11
West Germany	32
South Korea	32
Hong Kong	137
Singapore	190

Source: World Bank, *World Development Report* (Washington, D.C.: World Bank), 1992.

share of their output from manufacturing as advanced nations. (India generates less, but only because its poorer population continues to spend a high proportion of its income on food.) For these countries, however, the encouragement of manufacturing was not a goal in itself; it was a means to the end goal of economic development. Has import-substituting industrialization promoted economic development? Here serious doubts have appeared. Although many economists approved of import-substitution measures in the 1950s and early 1960s, since the 1960s import-substituting industrialization has come under increasingly harsh criticism. Indeed, much of the focus of economic analysts and of policymakers has shifted from trying to encourage import substitution to trying to correct the damage done by bad import-substitution policies.

 **CASE STUDY**

THE END OF IMPORT SUBSTITUTION IN CHILE

Chile was one of the first countries to abandon the strategy of import-substituting industrialization. Until the early 1970s Chile, a relatively affluent developing country with an unusually strong democratic tradition, had followed policies similar to those of other Latin American nations. A manufacturing base was developed behind elaborate import restrictions, while the country's exports continued to consist largely of traditional products, particularly copper. In the early 1970s, however, the election of an avowedly communist government led to political turmoil and finally to a seizure of power by the country's military, which brutally and bloodily suppressed its opponents.

The new government brought with it what was at the time an unusual faith in free market policies. Import restrictions were removed, replaced with low tariff rates. Whether because of these policies or in spite of them (a drastic fall in world copper prices contributed to the Chile's woes), the economy passed through a very difficult period in the mid-1970s. A recovery in the late 1970s and early 1980s was followed by a second severe slump, as Chile was caught up in the world debt crisis (see Chapter 22).

By the second half of the 1980s, however, Chilean economic performance was beginning to look quite impressive. New exports, including off-season fruits shipped to Northern Hemisphere markets in winter, increasingly high-quality wine, and manufactured goods such as furniture, had weaned the country from its previous dependence on copper. The Chilean economy began growing faster than it ever had before, outpacing other Latin American nations and nearly matching the performance of Asian countries. As a result, free-trade policies—originally very unpopular, and identified with the harsh rule of the Chilean military—began to command wide political support.

In 1990 the military withdrew from Chilean politics, although it remains at the time of writing a sort of state within the state, unwilling to take orders from civilian politicians. By this time, however, the economic policies of the past 17 years were widely credited with leading the way to Chilean prosperity. As a result, the thrust of economic policy under the freely elected government remained unchanged. And Chile's economic success story continued: In 1990–1994 the economy achieved a growth rate of 6.9 percent, far higher than that of the rest of Latin America.

RESULTS OF FAVORING MANUFACTURING: PROBLEMS OF IMPORT-SUBSTITUTING INDUSTRIALIZATION

The attack on import-substituting industrialization starts from the fact that many countries that have pursued import substitution have not shown any signs of catching up with the advanced countries. In some cases, the development of a domestic manufacturing base seems to have led to a stagnation of per capita income instead of an economic takeoff. This is true of India, which, after 20 years of ambitious economic plans between the early 1950s and the early 1970s, found itself with per capita income only a few percent higher than before. It is also true of Argentina, once considered a wealthy country, whose economy has grown at a snail's pace for decades. Other countries, such as Mexico, have achieved economic growth but have not narrowed the gap between themselves and advanced countries. Only a few developing countries really seem to have moved dramatically upward on the income scale—and these countries either have never pursued import substitution or have moved sharply away from it.

Why didn't import-substituting industrialization work the way it was supposed to? The most important reason seems to be that the infant industry argument was not as universally valid as many people assumed. A period of protection will not create a competitive manufacturing sector if there are fundamental reasons why a country lacks a comparative advantage in manufacturing. Experience has shown that the reasons for failure to develop often run deeper than a simple lack of experience with manufacturing. Poor countries lack skilled labor, entrepreneurs, and managerial competence and have problems of social organization that make it difficult to maintain reliable supplies of everything from spare parts to electricity. These problems may not be beyond the reach of economic policy, but they cannot be solved by *trade* policy: An import quota can allow an inefficient manufacturing sector to survive, but it cannot directly make that sector more efficient. The infant industry argument is that, given the temporary shelter of tariffs or quotas, the manufacturing industries of less-developed nations will learn to be efficient. In practice, this is not always, or even usually, true.

With import substitution failing to deliver the promised benefits, attention has turned to the costs of the policies used to promote industry. On this issue, a growing body of evidence shows that the protectionist policies of many less-developed countries have badly distorted incentives. Part of the problem has been that many countries have used excessively complex methods to promote their infant industries. That is, they have used elaborate and often overlapping import quotas, exchange controls, and domestic content rules instead of simple tariffs. It is often difficult to determine how much protection an administrative regulation is actually providing, and studies show that the degree of protection is often both higher and more variable across industries than the government intended. As Table 10-3 shows, some industries in Latin America and South Asia have been protected by regulations that are the equivalent of tariff rates of 200 percent or more. These high rates of effective protection have allowed industries to exist even when their cost of production is three or four times the price of the imports they replace. Even the most enthusiastic advocates of market failure arguments for protection find rates of effective protection that high difficult to defend.

A further cost that has received considerable attention is the tendency of import restrictions to promote production at an inefficiently small scale. The domestic markets of

TABLE 10-3

Effective Protection of Manufacturing in Some Developing Countries (percent)

Mexico (1960)	26
Philippines (1965)	61
Brazil (1966)	113
Chile (1961)	182
Pakistan (1963)	271

Source: Bela Balassa. *The Structure of Protection in Developing Countries* (Baltimore: Johns Hopkins Press, 1971).

even the largest developing countries are only a small fraction of the size of that of the United States or the European Union. Often, the whole domestic market is not large enough to allow an efficient-scale production facility. Yet when this small market is protected, say, by an import quota, if only a single firm were to enter the market it could earn monopoly profits. The competition for these profits typically leads several firms to enter a market that does not really even have room enough for one, and production is carried out at highly inefficient scale. The answer for small countries to the problem of scale is, as noted in Chapter 6, to specialize in the production and export of a limited range of products and to import other goods. Import-substituting industrialization eliminates this option by focusing industrial production on the domestic market.

Those who criticize import-substituting industrialization also argue that it has aggravated other problems, such as income inequality and unemployment (discussed later in this chapter under Problems of the Dual Economy).

By the late 1980s, the critique of import-substituting industrialization had been widely accepted, not only by economists but by international organizations like the World Bank and even by policymakers in the developing countries themselves. Statistical evidence appeared to suggest that developing countries that followed relatively free trade policies had on average grown more rapidly than those that followed protectionist policies (although this statistical evidence has been challenged by some economists).[2] This intellectual sea change led to a considerable shift in actual policies, as many developing countries removed import quotas and lowered tariff rates.

PROBLEMS OF THE DUAL ECONOMY

While the trade policy of less-developed countries is partly a response to their relative backwardness as compared with advanced nations, it is also a response to uneven development *within* the country. Often a relatively modern, capital-intensive, high-wage industrial sector exists in the same country as a very poor traditional agricultural sector. The division of a single economy into two sectors that appear to be at very different levels of development is referred to as **economic dualism,** and an economy that looks like this is referred to as a **dual economy.**

[2]See Sebastian Edwards, "Openness, Trade Liberalization, and Growth in Developing Countries," *Journal of Economic Literature* (September 1993) for a survey of this evidence.

Why does dualism have anything to do with trade policy? One answer is that dualism is probably a sign of markets working poorly: In an efficient economy, for example, workers would not earn hugely different wages in different sectors. Whenever markets are working badly, there may be a market failure case for deviating from free trade. The presence of economic dualism is often used to justify tariffs that protect the apparently more efficient manufacturing sector.

A second reason for linking dualism to trade policy is that trade policy may itself have a great deal to do with dualism. As import-substituting industrialization has come under attack, some economists have argued that import-substitution policies have actually helped to create the dual economy or at least aggravate some of its symptoms.

THE SYMPTOMS OF DUALISM

There is no precise definition of a dual economy, but in general a dual economy is one in which there is a "modern" sector (typically producing manufactured goods that are protected from import competition) that contrasts sharply with the rest of the economy in a number of ways:

1. The value of output per worker is much higher in the modern sector than in the rest of the economy. In most developing countries, the goods produced by a worker in the manufacturing sector carry a price several times that of the goods produced by an agricultural worker. Sometimes this difference runs as high as 15 to 1.

2. Accompanying the high value of output per worker is a higher wage rate. Industrial workers may earn ten times what agricultural laborers make (although their wages still seem low in comparison with North America, Western Europe, or Japan).

3. Although wages are high in the manufacturing sector, however, returns on capital are not necessarily higher. In fact, it often seems to be the case that capital earns *lower* returns in the industrial sector.

4. The high value of output per worker in the modern sector is at least partly due to a higher capital intensity of production. Manufacturing in less-developed countries typically has much higher capital intensity than agriculture (this is *not* true of advanced countries, where agriculture is quite capital-intensive). In the developing world, agricultural workers often work with primitive tools, while industrial facilities are not much different from those in advanced nations.

5. Many less-developed countries have a persistent unemployment problem. Especially in urban areas, there are large numbers of people either without jobs or with only occasional, extremely low-wage employment. These urban unemployed coexist with the relatively well-paid urban industrial workers.

CASE STUDY

ECONOMIC DUALISM IN INDIA

The economy of India presents a classic case of economic dualism. In a country of more than 700 million people, only 6 million are employed in the manufacturing sector. These manufacturing workers, however, produce 15 percent of the gross national product and receive wages more than six times as high as agricultural wages. Manufacturing is far more capital-intensive than agriculture; indeed, for the past 30 years investment on capital equipment for the tiny manufacturing labor force has consistently been larger than total investment in agriculture.

This sharp distinction between manufacturing and agriculture has actually grown over time. Since 1960, for example, the real wages of manufacturing workers have risen by about 80 percent, while those of farm workers have risen only about 5 percent.

Why is the gap between sectors so large? It seems likely that government policies play a key role. In India, government subsidies and protectionist policies have encouraged investment in manufacturing, and in the most capital-intensive sectors in particular. At the same time, labor laws designed to protect workers' interests have probably helped the bargaining position of unions, enabling organized workers to win large wage increases even though there are millions of workers who would be willing to take their jobs at lower wages.

In the heady early days of independence, India's economic planners hoped that the manufacturing sector would eventually grow and absorb the traditional economy. But from 1960 to 1980, manufacturing employment in India grew at an annual rate of only 3 percent, not much faster than the nation's population.

In the early 1990s India began limited moves toward economic reform, removing some barriers to trade and foreign investment. It was unclear, however, whether there was a political consensus for a radical change of policy. Nationalist opposition to foreign investment, in particular, remained strong. During 1995, in particular, local governments in several parts of India acted against foreign corporations in ways that seemed to undermine the central government's attempts to encourage their investment. One Indian state abruptly cancelled a power development contract with an American firm, Enron, and at the time of writing was refusing to pay the large sums already owed under the contract. Another local government closed Kentucky Fried Chicken franchises on what almost all observers said were spurious complaints about hygiene.

DUAL LABOR MARKETS AND TRADE POLICY

The symptoms of dualism are present in many countries and are clear signs of an economy that is not working well, especially in its labor markets. The trade policy implications of these symptoms have been a subject of great dispute among students of economic development.

In the 1950s many economists argued that wage differences between manufacturing and agriculture provided another justification, beyond the infant industry argument, for encouraging manufacturing at agriculture's expense. This argument, known as the **wage differentials argument,** can be stated in market failure terms. Suppose that, for some reason, an equivalent worker would receive a higher wage in manufacturing than he would in agriculture. Whenever a manufacturing firm decides to hire an additional worker, then, it generates a marginal social benefit for which it receives no reward, because a worker gains a wage increase when he moves from agriculture to manufacturing. This is in contrast to what would happen without a wage difference, where the marginal worker would be indifferent between manufacturing and agricultural employment and there would be no marginal social benefit of hiring a worker other than the profits earned by the hiring firm.

The effects of a wage differential on the economy's allocation of labor can be illustrated using the *specific factors model* presented in Chapter 3. Assume that an economy produces only two goods, manufactures and food. Manufactures are produced using labor and capital; food is produced using labor and land. Then the allocation of resources can be represented with a diagram like Figure 10-1. The vertical axis represents wage rates and marginal products; the horizontal axis represents employment. Employment in manufactures is measured from the left origin O_M, while employment in food is measured from the right origin O_F. MPL_M is the marginal product of labor in manufactures, MPL_F the marginal product in food; P_M is the price of manufactures, P_F the price of food. Thus the two curves in the figure represent the *value* of the marginal product of an additional worker in each sector.

When there is a wage differential, workers in manufactures must be paid a higher wage than workers in food; in the figure the manufactures wage is assumed to be W_M, the food wage W_F. Employers in each sector will hire workers up to the point where the value of a worker's marginal product equals his wage; thus employment in manufactures is $O_M L^1$ (point *B*), employment in food is $L^1 O_F$ (point *C*).

Suppose the economy were now able to shift one worker from food to manufactures. Manufactures output would rise; food output would fall. The value of the additional manufactures output, however, would be the wage rate in manufactures, W_M, while the value of the reduction in food output would be the lower wage rate in food, W_F. The total value of the economy's output, then, would rise by $W_M - W_F$. The fact that the value of output can

---

FIGURE 10-1

The Effect of a Wage Differential

If manufactures must pay a higher wage than food, the economy will employ too few workers in manufactures and too many in food, resulting in an output shortfall equal to the area of triangle *ABC*.

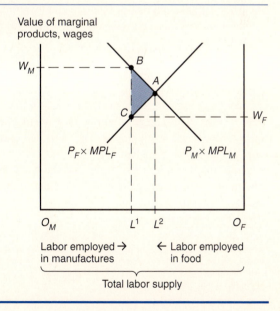

be increased by shifting labor from food to manufactures shows that the economy is allocating too little labor to manufactures. An efficient economy would set the marginal product of labor equal in both sectors, which would be achieved if $O_M L^2$ workers were employed in manufactures, $L^2 O_F$ in food (point A). (The increase in output achieved by moving to this efficient allocation of labor would be equal to the colored area ABC in the figure.)

If there is a wage differential, then, markets will misallocate labor; firms in the industrial sector will hire too few workers. A government policy that induces them to hire more can raise national welfare.

As usual, trade policy is not the first-best policy to expand manufacturing employment. Ideally, government policy should target employment directly, either by eliminating the wage differential or by subsidizing firms to hire more workers. A subsidy to manufacturing production is not as good, because it encourages capital as well as labor to move into manufacturing[3]—and capital does not receive an especially high return in manufacturing. A tariff or import quota is still worse, because it also distorts demand. Nonetheless, as a second-best alternative (or more strictly third-best), a tariff on manufactures could be justified by the wage differentials argument.

In the 1950s and 1960s this seemed to be a fairly convincing argument. In a famous paper published in 1970, however, the economists John Harris and Michael Todaro offered a devastating reinterpretation of the labor markets of less-developed countries.[4] They pointed out a link between rural-urban migration and unemployment that undermines the case for favoring manufacturing employment, even though manufacturing does offer higher wages.

Harris and Todaro began from the observation that countries with highly dualistic economies also seem to have a great deal of urban unemployment. Although one might suppose that this unemployment strengthens the case for creating more urban jobs in manufacturing, Harris and Todaro pointed out that despite this unemployment, migration from rural to urban areas continues. They concluded that rural workers were willing to come to the cities and take the risk of being unemployed in return for the chance of getting high-paying industrial jobs. The chance of getting a job depends, of course, on how many jobs are available.

According to the Harris-Todaro model, an increase in the number of manufacturing jobs will lead to a rural-urban migration so large that urban unemployment actually rises. When an additional worker is hired by the manufacturing sector, two or three more workers may leave agriculture to swell the ranks of the urban unemployed. Although the lucky worker gains, his wage gain will be largely (maybe even completely) offset by the wage losses of the newly unemployed. The supposed social benefit of additional manufacturing employment is therefore lost.

Like the infant industry argument, the wage differentials argument for protection is now in disfavor with economists. This is partly because of arguments like that of Harris

---

[3]This cannot be seen in the specific factors model, because that model assumes that capital cannot be used in the agricultural sector. In the factor proportions model, however, the superiority of a wage subsidy to a production subsidy can be demonstrated. See Harry G. Johnson, "Optimal Trade Intervention in the Presence of Domestic Distortions," in Robert E. Baldwin et al., *Trade, Growth, and the Balance of Payments* (Chicago: Rand McNally, 1965), pp. 3–34.

[4]John R. Harris and Michael P. Todaro, "Migration, Unemployment, and Development: A Two-Sector Analysis," *American Economic Review* 60 (1970), pp. 126–142.

and Todaro and partly because of the general backlash against import-substitution policies. In fact, trade policies adopted as a response to economic dualism are now often accused of actually making that dualism worse.

TRADE POLICY AS A CAUSE OF ECONOMIC DUALISM

Trade policy has been accused both of widening the wage differential between manufacturing and agriculture and of fostering excessive capital intensity.

The reasons for huge wage differentials between agriculture and industry are not well understood. Some economists believe these differentials are a natural market response. Firms, so the argument goes, offer high wages to ensure low turnover and high work effort in countries not used to the discipline of industrial work. Other economists argue, however, that the wage differentials also reflect the monopoly power of unions whose industries are sheltered by import quotas from foreign competition. With freer trade, they argue, industrial wages would be lower and agricultural wages higher. If so, dualism—and unemployment—may be worsened by import restrictions, especially those undertaken in the name of import substitution.

The excessive capital intensity of manufacturing is partly due to relatively high wages, which give firms an incentive to substitute capital for labor. To the extent that trade restrictions are responsible for these high wages, they are to blame. Also, in some countries a controlled banking system in effect provides subsidized credit to industrial firms, making capital-labor substitution cheap. The most direct channel, however, has been through selective import control. In many cases, imports of capital goods enter without tariff or other restriction, and sometimes with de facto import subsidies. This policy further encourages the use of capital-intensive techniques.

EXPORT-ORIENTED INDUSTRIALIZATION: THE EAST ASIAN MIRACLE

As pointed out previously, in the 1950s and 1960s it was widely believed that developing countries could create industrial bases only by substituting domestic manufactured goods for imports. From the mid-1960s onward, however, it became increasingly apparent that there was another possible path to industrialization: via *exports* of manufactured goods, primarily to advanced nations. Moreover, the countries that have developed in this manner—a group that the World Bank now refers to as the **high performance Asian economies** (**HPAEs**)[5]—have achieved spectacular economic growth, in some cases at more than 10 percent per year.

While the achievement of the HPAEs is not in doubt, and while there is also no question that their success refutes the previous conventional wisdom that industrial development must take place via import substitution, there remain major controversies about the implications of the "East Asian miracle." In particular, different observers place very different interpretations on the role of government policies, including trade policy, in fostering economic growth. To some observers the success of Asian economies

[5]For an extremely useful survey of the growth of the HPAEs, see World Bank, *The East Asian Miracle: Economic Growth and Public Policy* (Oxford: Oxford University Press, 1993).

demonstrates the virtues of relatively free trade and a hands-off government policy; to others it demonstrates the effectiveness of sophisticated government intervention; and there are some economists who believe that trade and industrial policy made little difference either way.

THE FACTS OF ASIAN GROWTH

The World Bank's definition of HPAEs contains three groups of countries, whose "miracles" began at different times. First is Japan, which began rapid economic growth soon after World War II and now has per capita income comparable to the United States and Western Europe; we will leave the discussion of Japanese experience to Chapter 11, which discusses trade and industrial policy in advanced countries. In the 1960s rapid economic growth began in four smaller Asian economies, often known as the four "tigers": Hong Kong, Taiwan, South Korea, and Singapore.[6] Finally, in the late 1970s and the 1980s rapid growth began in Malaysia, Thailand, Indonesia, and, most spectacularly, in China.

Each group has achieved very high growth rates. Real gross domestic product in the "tiger" economies has grown at an average of 8–9 percent since the mid-1960s, compared with 2–3 percent in the United States and Western Europe. Recent growth rates in the other Asian economies have been comparable, and China has reported growth rates of more than 10 percent (although there are some questions about the accuracy of Chinese statistics).

In addition to their very high growth rates, the HPAEs have another distinguishing feature: They are very open to international trade, and have become more so over time. In fact, the rapidly growing Asian economies are much more export oriented than other developing countries, particularly in Latin America and South Asia. Table 10-2 shows exports as a share of gross domestic product for several of the HPAEs; the numbers are remarkably high, in the case of both Singapore and Hong Kong exceeding 100 percent of GDP. How is it possible for a country's exports to exceed its total output? Gross domestic product represents the value *added* by an economy, not the total sales. For example, when a clothing factory in Hong Kong assembles cloth woven elsewhere into a suit, the addition to GDP is only the difference between the cost of the cloth and the value of the suit, not the whole price of the suit. But if the suit is exported, its full price counts as part of the export total. Because modern manufacturing often consists of adding a relatively small amount of value to imported inputs, exports can easily exceed total national output.

The undisputed facts, then, are that a group of Asian economies has achieved high rates of economic growth and that they have done so via a process that involves rapid growth of exports rather than substitution of domestic production for imports. But what does their experience say about economic policy?

TRADE POLICY IN THE HPAEs

Some economists have tried to tell a simple story that attributes the success of East Asian economies to an "outward-oriented" trade policy. In this view, the high ratios of exports

---

[6]The political status of two of the tigers is confusing. Hong Kong was a British colony during its takeoff, but reverts to Chinese control in 1997. The treaty returning Hong Kong to China states that the city will retain its social and economic institutions, i.e., remain a free-market economy, but many observers are skeptical. Taiwan is a de facto independent nation claimed by China, which has avoided explicitly claiming independence in order to avoid provoking its powerful neighbor. The World Bank tiptoes around the issue by referring pedantically to "Taiwan, China."

and imports to GDP in Asian nations are the consequences of trade policies that, while they might not correspond precisely to free trade, nonetheless leave trade much freer than in developing countries that have tried to develop through import substitution. And high growth rates are the payoff to this relatively open trade regime.

Unfortunately, the evidence for this story is not as strong as its advocates would like. In the first place, it is unclear to what extent the high trade ratios in the HPAEs can really be attributed to free trade policies. With the exception of Hong Kong, the HPAEs have in fact not had anything very close to free trade: All of them continue to have fairly substantial tariffs, import quotas, export subsidies, and other policies that manage their trade. Are the HPAEs following policies that are closer to free trade than those of other developing countries? Probably, although the complexity of the trade policies followed by developing countries in general makes comparisons difficult.[7] Table 10-4 shows data assembled by the World Bank, comparing average rates of protection (tariffs plus the tariff equivalent of import quotas) for several groups of developing countries: The data do suggest that the HPAEs have been less protectionist than other, less successful developing countries, although they have by no means followed a policy of complete free trade.

While trade policy has thus contributed to the openness of the HPAEs, however, most economists who have studied these economies believe that their high trade ratios are as much an effect as a cause of their economic success. For example, both the exports and the imports of Thailand have soared in recent years. Why? Because the country has become a favorite production site for multinational companies. These companies directly generate most of the new exports, and their imports of raw material also account for much of the surge in imports; the rest is accounted for by the rising income of the Thai population. So Thailand has large imports and exports because it is doing well, not the other way around.

This conclusion means that while there is a *correlation* between rapid growth in exports and rapid overall economic growth, the correlation does not necessarily demonstrate that free trade policies have been the main reason for the high growth. Instead, most economists who have studied the issue now believe that while the relatively low rates of protection in the HPAEs helped them to grow, they are only a partial explanation of the "miracle."

TABLE 10-4

Average Rates of Protection, 1985 (percent)

High-performance Asian economies	24
Other Asia	42
South America	46
Sub-Saharan Africa	34

Source: World Bank, *The East Asian Miracle: Economic Growth and Public Policy* (Oxford: Oxford University Press, 1993), p. 300.

---

[7]See World Bank, *The East Asian Miracle,* Chapter 6 for some attempts at international comparisons of protection.

CHINA'S BOOM

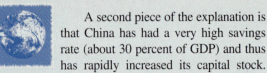

Although China, with 1.2 billion citizens, is by far the world's most populous country, until recently it played little role in the world economy. From 1949 to 1978 the country's communist regime largely sealed the country off from international trade. In any case, political factors stunted the economy's growth. Not only was private enterprise forbidden, but individual success of any kind was suspect; for example, during the so-called Cultural Revolution from 1966 to 1972 many managers, civil servants, teachers, and so on were forced from their jobs and sent to hard labor in the countryside.

In 1978, however, Chinese policy took a surprising turn. Declaring that "to grow rich is glorious," the Communist party opened the doors both to internal private enterprise and to external trade. The results were astonishing. Since 1978 the Chinese economy has reported growth rates averaging nearly 10 percent per year. By some estimates China has already become the world's second-largest economy after the United States. Although China is still far poorer than Japan, the second-biggest advanced country, it has ten times the population, and may well have more than one-tenth of Japan's per capita income.

How has China achieved this growth? Recent research is beginning to offer a provisional set of answers. Part of the explanation of Chinese growth is that it never happened, that is, that some of the growth is a statistical illusion. There is evidence that Chinese statistics understate inflation and overstate real growth; the actual growth rates have been at least 2 percentage points below the official numbers. But this still leaves a very impressive growth of 7 percent or more per year.

A second piece of the explanation is that China has had a very high savings rate (about 30 percent of GDP) and thus has rapidly increased its capital stock. This is consistent with the experience of other HPAEs, which have grown rapidly in large part simply through rapid accumulation of inputs.

Finally, researchers believe that China can be seen as an economy in the process of correcting a very serious problem of dualism. China's pre-1978 policies discouraged workers from moving to urban, industrial jobs, and at the same time prevented the agricultural sector from shedding unproductive labor. As a result, the marginal product of workers in the farm sector was very low compared with that in the cities. With the liberalization of the economy, there has been a massive shift of workers out of agriculture. This has had little effect on farm output, because the farm sector had large amounts of surplus labor in any case, but has helped make the spectacular expansion of manufacturing possible.

Can China continue to grow this fast? Probably not: The farm sector is starting to run out of surplus labor, and the high investment rates will probably start to run into diminishing returns. There are also some potentially serious problems looming on the horizon, notably the continuing inefficiency of a large state-owned sector and massive corruption among government officials.

Nonetheless, given China's huge population it does not need to be as productive as the current advanced nations to become one of the world's most important economies. Indeed, it is sobering to realize that China need only achieve one-fifth of America's per capita income to become the world's largest economy.

INDUSTRIAL POLICY IN THE HPAEs

Some commentators believe that the success of the HPAEs, far from demonstrating the effectiveness of free trade policies, actually represents a payoff to sophisticated interventionism.[8] It is in fact the case that several of the highly successful economies have pursued policies that favor particular industries over others; such *industrial policies* included not only tariffs, import restrictions, and export subsidies, but also more complex policies such as low-interest loans and government support for research and development.

The assessment of industrial policies is, in general, quite difficult; we will discuss this issue at some length in Chapter 11. Here, we just need to note that most economists studying this issue have been skeptical about the importance of such policies, for at least three reasons.

First, HPAEs have followed a wide variety of policies, ranging from detailed government direction of the economy in Singapore to virtual laissez-faire in Hong Kong. South Korea deliberately promoted the formation of very large industrial firms; Taiwan's economy remains dominated by small, family-run companies. Yet all of these economies have achieved similarly high growth rates.

Second, despite considerable publicity given to industrial policies, the actual impact on industrial structure may not have been large. The World Bank, in its study of the Asian miracle, found surprisingly little evidence that countries with explicit industrial policies have moved into the targeted industries any faster than those which have not.

Finally, there have been some notable failures of industrial policy even in otherwise highly successful economies. For example, from 1973 to 1979 South Korea followed a policy of promoting "heavy and chemical" industries, chemicals, steel, automobiles, and so on. This policy proved extremely costly, and was eventually judged to be premature and was abandoned.

While it is probably fair to say that the mainstream position is that industrial policy was not a key driving force behind Asian success, this is by no means a settled debate, and the attempt to assess the impact of industrial policies remains a major area of research.

OTHER FACTORS IN GROWTH

In the last few years several researchers have suggested that the whole focus on trade and industrial policy in Asian growth may have been misplaced. After all, international trade and trade policy are only part of the story for any economy, even one with a high ratio of exports to national income. Other aspects of the economy may well have been more important determinants of success.

And in fact, the fast-growing Asian economies are distinctive in ways other than their high trade shares. Almost all of these economies, it turns out, have very high savings rates,

---

[8]For the most part, commentators who believe that rapid growth in the HPAEs is due to aggressive government intervention are not trained economists; indeed, the whole debate over the sources of Asian growth is tied up with a broader and quite acrimonious debate over the usefulness of economic theory in general. For an influential example both of the claim that Asian growth was fostered by interventionist policies, and of hostility to economists, see James Fallows, *Looking at the Sun: The Rise of the New East Asian Economic and Political System* (New York: Pantheon, 1994).

which means that they are able to finance very high rates of investment. Almost all of them have also made great strides in public education. Several recent estimates suggest that the combination of high investment rates and rapidly improving educational levels explains a large fraction, perhaps almost all, of the rapid growth in East Asia.[9] If this is true, the whole focus on trade and industrial policy is largely misplaced. Perhaps one can argue that the Asian economies have had trade policy that is good in the sense that it has *permitted* rapid growth, but it is greatly overstating the importance of that policy to say that it *caused* growth.

Like almost everything that concerns Asian growth, this interpretation is highly controversial. Nonetheless, it has helped shake the certainties of all sides in the ongoing debate.

One thing is, however, certain about the East Asian experience. Whatever else one may say about it, it definitely refutes some assumptions about economic development that used to be widely accepted. First, the presumption that industrialization and development must be based on an inward-looking strategy of import substitution is clearly false. On the contrary, the success stories of development have all involved an outward-looking industrialization based on exports of manufactured goods. Second, the pessimistic view that the world market is rigged against new entrants, preventing poor countries from becoming rich, has turned out to be spectacularly wrong: Never in human history have so many people seen their standard of living rise so rapidly.

Summary

1. Trade policy in less-developed countries can be analyzed using the same analytical tools used to discuss advanced countries. The particular issues characteristic of *developing countries* are, however, different. In particular, trade policy in developing countries is concerned with two objectives: promoting industrialization and coping with the uneven development of the domestic economy.

2. Government policy to promote industrialization has often been justified by the infant industry argument, which says that new industries need a temporary period of protection from competition from established competitors in other countries. The infant industry argument is valid only if it can be cast as a market failure argument for intervention. Two usual justifications are the existence of *imperfect capital markets* and the problem of *appropriability* of knowledge generated by pioneering firms.

3. Using the infant industry argument as justification, many less-developed countries have pursued policies of *import-substituting industrialization* in which domestic industries are created under the protection of tariffs or import quotas. Although these policies have succeeded in promoting manufacturing, by and large they have not delivered the expected gains in economic growth and living standards. Many economists are now harshly critical of the results of import substitution, arguing that it has fostered high-cost, inefficient production.

4. Most developing countries are characterized by economic *dualism:* A high-wage, capital-intensive industrial sector coexists with a low-wage traditional sector. Dual economies also often have a serious problem of urban unemployment.

[9]For a summary of this research and its implications, see P. Krugman, "The Myth of Asia's Miracle," *Foreign Affairs* (November 1994).

5. The difference in wages between the modern and traditional sectors has sometimes been used as a case for tariff protection of the industrial sector. This is the *wage differentials* case for protection. This view no longer receives much credence among economists, however. More recent analyses suggest that protection will lead to more rural-urban migration, which worsens the urban unemployment problem and may worsen the symptoms of dualism.

6. The view that economic development must take place via import substitution—and the pessimism about economic development that spread as import substituting industrialization seemed to fail—have been confounded by the rapid economic growth of a number of Asian economies. These high performance Asian economies (HPAEs) have industrialized not via import substitution but via exports of manufactured goods. They are characterized both by very high ratios of trade to national income and by extremely high growth rates. The reasons for the success of the HPAEs are highly disputed. Some observers point to the fact that, while they do not practice free trade, they do have lower rates of protection than other developing countries. Others assign a key role to the interventionist *industrial policies* pursued by some of the HPAEs. Recent research suggests, however, that the roots of success may lie largely in domestic causes, especially high savings rates and rapid improvements in education.

Key Terms

appropriability, p. 255

developing countries, p. 253

dual economy, p. 260

economic dualism, p. 260

high performance Asian economies
(HPAEs), p. 265

imperfect capital markets, p. 255

import-substituting industrialization, p. 256

wage differentials argument, p. 262

Problems

1. "Japan's experience makes the infant industry case for protection better than any theory. In the early 1950s Japan was a poor nation that survived by exporting textiles and toys. The Japanese government protected what at first were inefficient, high-cost steel and automobile industries, and those industries came to dominate world markets." Discuss critically.

2. A country currently imports automobiles at $8000 each. Its government believes domestic producers could manufacture autos for only $6000 given time but that there would be an initial shakedown period during which autos would cost $10,000 to produce domestically.
   a. Suppose that each firm that tries to produce autos must go through the shakedown period of high costs on its own. Under what circumstances would the existence of the initial high costs justify infant industry protection?
   b. Now suppose, on the contrary, that once one firm has borne the costs of learning to produce autos at $6000 each, other firms can imitate it and do the same. Explain how this can prevent development of a domestic industry, and how infant industry protection can help.

it is a potentially valid application of the idea that deviations from free trade may be beneficial if the economy suffers from domestic distortions. It is also subject to the same questions as the wage differentials argument in other contexts: Why does this wage differential persist? Might an effort to promote high-wage sectors have other adverse consequences?

This is not a purely theoretical discussion. The specific idea that deindustrialization has been a major source of U.S. economic difficulties has been the subject of a number of empirical analyses. On the face of it, the hypothesis seems plausible. Workers in U.S. manufacturing do, in fact, earn higher average wages than workers in the service sector. Meanwhile, the share of the U.S. work force employed in manufacturing has steadily declined: It was 27 percent in 1970 but only 16 percent in 1995. Might this shift not have been a major drag on wages and hence on overall national income?

In fact, however, attempts to quantify the effect of deindustrialization on wages have yielded rather small estimates. There are two main reasons for these low estimates. First, most of the decline in the share of the work force employed in manufacturing does not seem to be due to international trade. Of the 11 percentage point decline in the manufacturing share since 1970, not much more than 1 percentage point can be attributed to international trade.[3] The rest is due to domestic forces that are turning all advanced countries increasingly into service economies. In particular, technological advance has been more rapid in goods-producing sectors like manufacturing than in service-producing sectors like retail trade. (It takes less than half as many workers to produce a ton of steel now than it did in 1970, but it takes just as many people to give a haircut or serve a meal.) Meanwhile, consumer demand has risen at about the same rate for goods and services; this means that a growing share of the work force ends up being employed in service industries.

Second, while manufacturing jobs do on average pay higher wages than service jobs, the popular image, which contrasts $20 per hour steelworkers with $4 per hour fast food workers, overstates the difference. Most manufacturing jobs do not pay the wages that powerful unions were once able to extract in a few high-profile industries and many service sector jobs pay quite well. Typical estimates of the true wage differential are not much more than 10 percent.

Given the limited impact of international trade on manufacturing employment and the limited wage differential, the consequences of deindustrialization for the U.S. economy appear to be far smaller than are often claimed. A typical estimate for the mid-1990s would be that U.S. trade deficits in manufacturing have shifted approximately 1 million workers from the manufacturing to the service sector, where they earn on average perhaps $4000 less annually. This implies a net loss of $4 billion, which sounds like a lot, but is less than 0.1 percent of U.S. national income.

Concerns about competition for high-wage jobs, then, are conceptually reasonable. The issue appears, however, to be far less important quantitatively than the rhetoric of competitiveness would suggest.

COMPETING FOR HIGH-TECHNOLOGY SECTORS

While much of the discussion of competitiveness has focused on the rivalry for industries with high value added or high-wage rates, there is also much emphasis on a third kind of rivalry: competition in **high-technology** industries.

---

[3]See P. Krugman and R. Lawrence, "Trade, Jobs, and Wages," *Scientific American* (April 1994); and J. Sachs and H. Shatz, "Trade and Jobs in U.S. Manufacturing," *Brookings Papers on Economic Activity*, 1:1994. It is important, by the way, to have a sense of the scale of the economy. A shift of 1 percent of the labor force from manufacturing to services is small in terms of its impact on wages, but it represents well over a million jobs.

A high-technology industry is, loosely speaking, an industry in which the success of companies depends largely on their ability to keep up with rapid innovations in products, production processes, or both. Statistical classifications of high-technology industries typically rely on indicators like the ratio of expenditures on research and development to sales, or the share of scientists and engineers in the work force. In *Head to Head,* Thurow listed seven high-technology sectors that he regarded as crucial: microelectronics, biotechnology, the new materials-science industries, telecommunications, civilian aviation, robotics plus machine tools, and computers plus software. He went on to assert: "Not everyone will get those seven key industries. Some will win; some will lose."

Why is it important to "win" these industries? Some writers lump high-technology, high value added, and high-wages together: High-technology sectors are supposedly crucial because they are the high-value, high-wage sectors. As we have just seen, however, these are poor arguments. In fact, high value added is not a good criterion for promoting an industry, and in any case high-technology sectors do not necessarily have particularly high value added per worker. The high-wage criterion does a little better: It is true that high-technology sectors on average pay workers somewhat more than other sectors, even when an adjustment is made for the unusual fraction of highly educated employees. But estimates of the potential impact of international trade on these "rents" earned by workers in high-wage sectors suggests that it is quite small—that if this is what is at stake, it cannot matter very much to a country's economic welfare whether a country wins the competition for the seven key industries or not.[4]

There is, however, an argument that is harder to dismiss, namely, that a strong position in these or other high-technology industries is crucial to the rate of technological progress in the economy as a whole. That is, the claim is that these industries generate important **technological spillovers.** This argument, like the wage differentials argument, in effect justifies a strategic trade policy on the grounds that there is a domestic market failure. It may not be immediately obvious why technological spillovers constitute a market failure. But rather than explain why here, let us examine the role of technological spillovers in the context of a more general discussion of sophisticated arguments for strategic trade policy.

SOPHISTICATED ARGUMENTS FOR STRATEGIC TRADE POLICY

Nothing in the analytical framework developed in Chapters 8 and 9 rules out the desirability of industrial policy. That framework *does* show that activist government policy needs a specific kind of justification; namely, it must offset some preexisting domestic market failure. The problem with many arguments for strategic trade policy is precisely that they do not link the case for government intervention to any particular failure of the assumptions on which the case for laissez-faire rests.

The problem with market failure arguments for intervention is how to know a market failure when you see one. Economists studying industrial countries have identified two kinds of market failure that seem to be present and relevant to the trade policies of advanced countries. One of these is the inability of firms in high-technology industries to capture the benefits of that part of their contribution to knowledge that spills over to other

---

[4]See William Dickens, "Do Labor Rents Justify Strategic Trade and Industrial Policy?" National Bureau of Economics Research Paper 5137 (May 1995).

firms. The other is the presence of monopoly profits in highly concentrated oligopolistic industries.

TECHNOLOGY AND EXTERNALITIES

The discussion of the infant industry argument in Chapter 10 noted that there is a potential market failure arising from difficulties of appropriating knowledge. If firms in an industry generate knowledge that other firms can also use without paying for it, the industry is in effect producing some extra output—the marginal social benefit of the knowledge—that is not reflected in the incentives of firms. Where such **externalities** (benefits that accrue to parties other than the firms that produce them) can be shown to be important, there is a good case for subsidizing the industry.

At an abstract level this argument is the same for the infant industries of less-developed countries as it is for the established industries of the advanced countries. In advanced countries, however, the argument has a special edge because in those countries there are important high-technology industries in which the generation of knowledge is in many ways the central aspect of the enterprise. In high-technology industries, firms devote a great deal of their resources to improving technology, either by explicit spending on research and development or by being willing to take initial losses on new products and processes to gain experience. Such activities take place in nearly all industries, of course, so that there is no sharp line between high-tech and the rest of the economy. There are clear differences in degree, however, and it makes sense to talk of a high-technology sector in which investment in knowledge is the key part of the business.

The point for strategic trade policy is that while firms can appropriate some of the benefits of their own investment in knowledge (otherwise they would not be investing!), they usually cannot appropriate them fully. Some of the benefits accrue to other firms that can imitate the ideas and techniques of the leaders. In electronics, for example, it is not uncommon for firms to "reverse engineer" their rivals' designs, taking their products apart to figure out how they work and how they were made. Because patent laws provide only weak protection for innovators, there is a reasonable presumption that under laissez-faire high-technology firms do not receive as strong an incentive to innovate as they should.

The Case for Government Support of High-Technology Industries.   Should the U.S. government subsidize high-technology industries? While there is a pretty good case for such a subsidy, we need to exercise some caution. Two questions in particular arise: first, the ability of government policy to target the right thing; second, the quantitative importance of the argument.

Although high-technology industries probably produce extra social benefits because of the knowledge they generate, much of what goes on even in a high-technology industry has nothing to do with generating knowledge. There is no reason to subsidize the employment of capital or nontechnical workers in high-technology industries; on the other hand, innovation and technological spillovers happen to some extent even in industries that are mostly not at all high-tech. A general principle is that trade and industrial policy should be targeted specifically on the activity in which the market failure occurs. Thus policy should seek to subsidize the generation of knowledge that firms cannot appropriate. A general subsidy for a set of industries in which this kind of knowledge generation is believed to go on is a pretty blunt instrument for the purpose.

Perhaps, instead, government should subsidize research and development wherever it occurs. The problem here is one of definition. How do we know when a firm is engaged in creating knowledge? A loose definition could lend itself to abuse: Who is to say whether paper clips and company cars were really supporting the development of knowledge or were placed in the research department's budget to inflate the subsidy? A strict definition, on the other hand, would risk favoring large, bureaucratic forms of research where the allocation of funds can be strictly documented over the smaller, informal organizations that are widely believed to be the key to the most original thinking.

The United States *does* in effect subsidize research and development (R&D), at least as compared with other kinds of investment. Research and development can be claimed by firms as a current expense and thus counts as an immediate deduction against the corporate profit tax. By contrast, investment in plant and equipment cannot be claimed as an immediate expense and can be written off only through gradual depreciation. This effective favorable treatment for knowledge is an accident of tax history rather than an explicit policy, but we should note it before concluding that the United States spends too little on R&D or that the high-technology sector needs further encouragement. To reach such a conclusion we would need to know how much subsidy is justified.

How Important Are Externalities?   The question of the appropriate level of subsidy for high technology depends on the answer to a difficult empirical problem: How important, quantitatively, is the technological spillover argument for targeting high-technology industries? Is the optimal subsidy 10, 20, or 100 percent? The honest answer is that no one has a good idea. It is in the nature of externalities, benefits that do not carry a market price, that they are hard to measure.

Further, even if the externalities generated by high-technology industries could be shown to be large, there may be only a limited incentive for any one country to support these industries. The reason is that many of the benefits of knowledge created in one country may in fact accrue to firms in other countries. Thus if, say, a Belgian firm develops a new technique for making steel, most of the firms that can imitate this technique will be in other European countries, the United States, and Japan rather than in Belgium. A world government might find it worthwhile to subsidize this innovation; the Belgian government might not. Such problems of appropriability at the level of the *nation* (as opposed to the firm) are less severe but still important even for a nation as large as the United States.

Despite the criticism, the technological spillover argument is probably the best case one can make intellectually for an active industrial policy. In contrast to many simplistic criteria for choosing "desirable" industries, which can be strongly rejected, the case for or against targeting "knowledge-intensive" industries is a judgment call.

IMPERFECT COMPETITION AND STRATEGIC TRADE POLICY

During the 1980s a new argument for industrial targeting received substantial theoretical attention. Originally proposed by the economists Barbara Spencer and James Brander of the University of British Columbia, this argument locates the market failure that justifies government intervention in the lack of perfect competition. In some industries, they point out, there are only a few firms in effective competition. Because of the small number of firms, the assumptions of perfect competition do not apply. In particular, there will typically be **excess returns;** that is, firms will make profits above what equally risky investments elsewhere in the economy can earn. There will be an international competition over who gets these profits.

Spencer and Brander noticed that, in this case, it is possible in principle for a government to alter the rules of the game to shift these excess returns from foreign to domestic firms. In the simplest case, a subsidy to domestic firms, by deterring investment and production by foreign competitors, can raise the profits of domestic firms by more than the amount of the subsidy. Setting aside the effects on consumers—for example, when the firms are selling only in foreign markets—this capture of profits from foreign competitors would mean the subsidy raises national income at other countries' expense.

The Brander-Spencer Analysis: An Example.   The **Brander-Spencer analysis** can be illustrated with a simple example in which there are only two firms competing, each from a different country. Bearing in mind that any resemblance to actual events may be coincidental, let's call the firms Boeing and Airbus, and the countries the United States and Europe. Suppose there is a new product, 150-seat aircraft, that both firms are capable of making. For simplicity, assume each firm can make only a yes/no decision: either to produce 150-seat aircraft or not.

Table 11-2 illustrates how the profits earned by the two firms might depend on their decisions. (The setup is similar to the one we used to examine the interaction of different countries' trade policies in Chapter 9.) Each row corresponds to a particular decision by Boeing, each column to a decision by Airbus. In each box are two entries: The entry on the lower left represents the profits of Boeing, while that on the upper right represents the profits of Airbus.

As set up, the table reflects the following assumption: Either firm alone could earn profits making 150-seat aircraft, but if both firms try to produce them, both will make losses. Which firm will actually get the profits? This depends on who gets there first. Suppose Boeing is able to get a small head start and commits itself to produce 150-seat aircraft before Airbus can get going. Airbus will find that it has no incentive to enter. The outcome will be in the upper right of the table, with Boeing earning profits.

Now comes the Brander-Spencer point: The European government can reverse this situation. Suppose the European government commits itself to pay its firm a subsidy of 25 if it enters. The result will be to change the table of payoffs to that represented in Table 11-3. It is now profitable for Airbus to produce 150-seat aircraft whatever Boeing does.

TABLE 11-2

Two-Firm Competition

Boeing \ Airbus	Produce	Don't produce
Produce	−5 (Airbus) / −5 (Boeing)	0 (Airbus) / 100 (Boeing)
Don't produce	100 (Airbus) / 0 (Boeing)	0 (Airbus) / 0 (Boeing)

TABLE 11-3

Effects of a Subsidy to Airbus

Boeing \ Airbus	Produce		Don't produce	
		20		0
Produce	−5		100	
		125		0
Don't produce	0		0	

Let's work through the implications of this shift. Boeing now knows that whatever it does, it will have to compete with Airbus and will therefore lose money if it chooses to produce. So now it is Boeing that will be deterred from entering. In effect, the government subsidy has removed the advantage of a head start that we assumed was Boeing's and has conferred it on Airbus instead.

The end result is that the equilibrium shifts from the upper right of Table 11-2 to the lower left of Table 11-3. Airbus ends up with profits of 125 instead of 0, profits that arise because of a government subsidy of only 25. That is, the subsidy raises profits by more than the amount of the subsidy itself, because of its deterrent effect on foreign competition. The subsidy has this effect because it creates an advantage for Airbus comparable with the *strategic* advantage it would have had if it, not Boeing, had had a head start in the industry.

Problems with the Brander-Spencer Analysis.   This hypothetical example might seem to indicate that this strategic trade policy argument provides a compelling case for government activism. A subsidy by the European government sharply raises profits of a European firm at the expense of its foreign rivals. Leaving aside the interest of consumers, this seems clearly to raise European welfare (and reduce U.S. welfare). Shouldn't the U.S. government put this argument into practice?

In fact, this strategic justification for trade policy, while it has attracted much interest, has also received much criticism. Critics argue that to make practical use of the theory would require more information than is likely to be available, that such policies would risk foreign retaliation, and that in any case the domestic politics of trade and industrial policy would prevent use of such subtle analytical tools.

The problem of insufficient information has two aspects. The first is that even when looking at an industry in isolation, it may be difficult to fill in the entries in a table like Table 11-2 with any confidence. And if the government gets it wrong, a subsidy policy may turn out to be a costly misjudgment. To see this, suppose that instead of Table 11-2 the reality is represented by the seemingly similar payoffs in Table 11-4. The numbers are not much different, but the difference is crucial. In Table 11-4, Boeing is assumed to have some underlying advantage—maybe a better technology—so that even if Airbus enters, Boeing will still find it profitable to produce. Airbus, however, cannot produce profitably if Boeing enters.

In the absence of a subsidy, the outcome in Table 11-4 will be in the upper right corner; Boeing produces and Airbus does not. Now suppose that, as in the previous case, the

During the 1950s and 1960s, the ministries used this power to follow a growth strategy similar to what the advocates of the "popular" criteria we discussed earlier might have suggested. The government channeled funds into heavy industries with high value added per worker and away from traditional labor-intensive industries such as textiles. They tried to encourage those industries that they believed reflected Japan's future comparative advantage rather than its current trade pattern. Intermediate goods industries such as steel were special favorites.

The result is history: Japan's economy grew extremely rapidly. Indeed, it is Japan's success that helps lend plausibility to the popular arguments we discussed.

The crucial question is whether Japan's strategic trade policy was really the key to the rapid growth. Might the economy have grown just as rapidly without the policy? There are at least two reasons to be cautious about attributing success primarily to the strategic trade policy.

First, we are not sure whether the activities of Japan's government were actually pushing Japan into heavy industry faster than they would have gone under laissez-faire. Japan's trade strategy was not applied to an otherwise unregulated economy. Instead, the government first disconnected the normal channels of allocation, by rationing foreign exchange and credit, then made up for the lack of a market by allocating these resources directly. Some economists have argued that in the end Japan arrived at the same outcome as if the government had stayed out of the picture. To put it another way, the government may have been making sensible investment decisions, but the market might have made similar decisions if left to itself. There is some evidence supporting this view in Japan's pattern of trade in the 1970s, which was not very different from what would have been predicted from its resources and level of economic development, even without its industrial policy.

Second, there is the possibility that the dynamism of Japanese industry had its roots in factors other than strategic trade policy and that Japan would have done well in any case. Reasons for Japan's success are many: Japan had the highest savings rate in the world, an effective educational system, good labor-management relations, and a business-oriented culture in which the most ambitious and talented channeled their energy into corporate management. It is possible that trade strategy may have been a minor positive factor or even a drag on economic growth. Some of Japan's most successful industries, notably automobiles and consumer electronics, were not among those that received high priority.

The Japanese policy of the 1950s and 1960s remains the picture of Japan that many retain. The country is seen as "Japan, Inc.," a society in which the allocation of resources is under the central control of MITI. Such a picture has become increasingly out of date, however. Since 1970, the traditional levers of Japanese trade strategy have lost much of their force. Foreign exchange and credit are no longer scarce and rationed, while the use of trade restrictions has become constrained by the demand of other countries that Japan open its markets. Trade strategy since 1975 or so has taken a different and more subtle form.

Current Japanese Policy.   Japan's policy since the mid-1970s has aimed at encouraging a new set of industries, the "knowledge-intensive," or high-technology, industries. The tools of strategic policy have been a combination of modest subsidies for research and development and encouragement of joint government-industry research projects aimed at developing promising new technologies. The whole enterprise has been on a much smaller scale relative to the total economy than the old strategic trade policy.

The justification for targeting high technology is not especially clear. The Japanese themselves do not seem to be clear whether they are targeting high technology because it is the growth sector of the future or because it is a generator of technological spillovers. The new Japanese policy is, however, easier to justify in terms of a market failure argument than the old one.

How much effect do the new policies have? The industries targeted since 1975 remain a small part of Japan's economy. Neither automobiles nor consumer electronics (televisions, stereos, VCRs, and so on) are part of the high-technology area that has been the focus of research joint ventures. So the Japanese consumer products that have made Japan's export success so visible do not reflect the new technology policy. Japan has, however, become a significant producer of some products in which recent strategic trade policy has played a key role. Most famous and most important of these is semiconductor chips, a case we will examine shortly.

This brief history gives some perspective on the reality of Japan's policy. Japan is often seen as an almost militarily organized society, centrally commanded to achieve economic objectives. This view exaggerated the role of the Japanese government even during its period of greatest influence and exaggerates it still more today.

STRATEGIC TRADE POLICY IN OTHER COUNTRIES

Other countries have pursued strategic trade policies to some degree in the postwar period, though none with the degree of government control, or success, that Japan did. France has pursued strategic trade policies with varying degrees of vigor. Also, the United States, though without an explicit trade strategy, does have policies—notably its support of agriculture and military procurement—that look to some observers like strategic trade policies.

French Industrial Policy.   France has long had a policy of promoting particular industries. The aspect of French strategic trade policy that has attracted the most attention has been the efforts of the government to bolster French firms in technological competition with foreign firms. Since the 1960s, the French government has worried that world technology will become dominated by large U.S. or, more recently, Japanese companies. To prevent this domination, the government has attempted to ensure that there are French firms, called national champions, that can compete on world markets. To create national champions, the French government has encouraged mergers of smaller firms into large units. It has also used its influence over demand to provide privileged markets, for example, by requiring the state-run phone company to buy its telecommunications and computer equipment from French firms. And in a few cases, notably aircraft, extensive government subsidies have been used to promote industries that are regarded as key.

How has France's industrial policy worked? The French economy performed quite well until the late 1970s, achieving rates of growth slightly higher than Germany's and much higher than Britain's. Since then France has had severe unemployment, but this is a problem shared by almost all of Europe. Notable about France, however, is that while the economy as a whole has done well, the sectors most coveted by the government have not. France's computer industry remains dependent on protected markets, and efforts to develop an aircraft industry have achieved technological success only at the cost of heavy monetary losses. For this reason few would regard France's strategic trade policy as the key to its economic growth.

U.S. Strategic Trade Policy.   The United States has a commitment to free market ideology that would preclude any explicit government direction of the economy such as

THE HDTV DEBATE

In 1988 and 1989 concerns over lagging U.S. technology came to focus on one issue in particular: the apparent decision on the part of U.S. electronics firms not to compete in the emerging market for high-definition television (HDTV).

High-definition television will represent in effect a cross between a television and a computer. It will receive a digitized signal, process it, and produce a picture with about twice the resolution and substantially higher quality than current television screens. Enthusiasts argue that the new technology will transform both consumer electronics and business applications. For example, while HDTV would have only a modest effect on the viewability of current-sized television sets, it would make a large difference on bigger sets; if new technologies for large, flat-screen televisions become economically practical, they would both require and encourage use of HDTV technology. Similarly, HDTV could be important for business workstations and other computer applications where image quality is crucial.

As of 1989, while both Japanese and European firms were investing substantial sums in the development of HDTV, no U.S. firms were doing so. This led to widespread concern that the United States was once again about to lose a technological race and to calls for a government-subsidized program to keep the United States competitive in HDTV.

The HDTV case illustrates quite clearly, however, the difficulty of making strategic trade policy. At first sight HDTV had all the characteristics of an industry suitable for targeting. It was undeniably a high-technology industry, which might be expected to generate externalities both through the technology it develops and by providing a domestic market for other high-technology products, such as semiconductors. It was also likely to be a fairly concentrated industry, so that a strategic trade policy argument could also be made on HDTV's behalf. To many members of Congress the case for subsidizing the development of a U.S. HDTV industry seemed overwhelming.

Yet there were serious doubts. Skeptics—notably the Congressional Budget Office—pointed out that there was considerable uncertainty about the size of the eventual market for HDTV, suggesting that hype about its prospects could easily lead to worldwide overcapacity. Moreover, they argued that even if the HDTV market turned out to be as large as, say, the market for ordinary television sets, it will still represent only a small part of the market for the high-technology items, mainly semiconductors, for which its development was allegedly crucial. Advocates of an HDTV program countered that HDTV would be much more important for certain specialized applications, which they alleged would then generate important externalities to more broadly defined technologies.

One peculiar aspect of the debate was the question of what constitutes an American product. In the absence of a U.S. government program to support HDTV, it seemed likely that Japanese and European firms would dominate the industry. However, it also seemed likely that much of the *production* of these firms would take place in the United States. Although most of the color televisions sold in the United States are manufactured by foreign firms, most of them are made in this country—with the major exception being the sets made by the U.S. firm Zenith, which are made in Mexico. Both advocates and opponents of an HDTV program agreed that most HDTV manufacturing for the U.S. market would take place in the United States, whoever won the technology race. Thus the HDTV debate was really as much a debate about foreign direct investment as about industrial policy.

The great irony of the HDTV debate, however, is that it turned out to be beside the point, because surprise technological developments made the HDTV systems that Japanese and European firms were working on obsolete before they were introduced. New techniques for compressing data completely changed the nature of the game. Suppose a network is transmitting a television show in which the actors spend several minutes in front of a background that includes a large area of blue sky. The old technique would send several thousand instructions each fraction of a second, repeatedly telling the television to color each "pixel" (small area of the screen) blue. The new methods would, in effect, inform the "intelligent" television that "the whole top left part of the screen should be colored blue until further notice." It turns out that data compression will allow HDTV to be introduced much more cheaply and with much less change in current methods of broadcasting than the techniques previously contemplated.

Two further ironies: At the time of writing, U.S. firms are well ahead in developing techniques of data compression, which have found widespread applications in multimedia, videoconferencing, and on the Internet. Meanwhile, broadcasters are reconsidering the whole idea of HDTV: Viewers, they now suspect, might prefer to retain the current level of definition but be offered a wider choice of programs instead.

that of Japan during the early phase. There are some areas, however, in which the U.S. government has had a major role in promoting industries.

The most notable of these areas is agriculture. Here the U.S. government has come closest to the kind of strategic policy that we might recommend on the basis of the sophisticated criteria discussed earlier. Recall that the problem of appropriating knowledge can be a reason for intervening in an industry. In agriculture, which remains mostly a matter of family farms, this problem is especially acute: A farmer who makes a major innovation can be imitated by thousands of others, who derive the benefits without sharing the risks. To alleviate this problem, the U.S. government has long engaged both in research into agricultural techniques and in the dissemination of improved techniques through the Agricultural Extension Service. Also, the government has taken a leading role in large-scale projects, such as irrigation facilities, that require collective action. These interventions fit nicely into a market failure framework and are commended even by economists who are skeptical about most government intervention.

Another major role for the U.S. government is in defense. Both because it has a larger national income than other industrial countries and because it spends relatively more on defense, the U.S. government is far and away the world's largest market for military hardware. Not surprisingly, the United States dominates the production of military goods such as fighter aircraft that involve large economies of scale. In some cases it is likely that U.S. spending on military goods has helped give U.S. firms an advantage in civilian markets as well. For example, one of the most successful civilian aircraft produced by Boeing, the Boeing 707 (introduced in 1960), owed a great deal to a previously developed military plane (the B-52 bomber). The military market surely sometimes helps U.S. firms gain economies of scale that help them in civilian markets—the Boeing 707 continues to be manufactured, long after its civilian sales are over, as the

AWACS reconnaissance plane. Military research and development sometimes gives U.S. firms knowledge that they can apply elsewhere. As usual in strategic trade policy issues, however, the quantitative importance of these effects is a matter of dispute. European commentators, who sometimes feel they are losing a race with the United States and Japan, have suggested that in practice the United States has as effective a strategic trade policy as Japan.

CASE STUDIES OF STRATEGIC TRADE POLICIES

How effective is strategic trade policy? These policies have been applied in a wide variety of industries. To see the difficulties involved in evaluation, we examine three examples: Japan's targeting of steel in the 1960s and early 1970s, European support of aircraft production, and Japan's targeting of semiconductors in the late 1970s and early 1980s.

CASE STUDY

JAPANESE TARGETING OF STEEL (1960–EARLY 1970S)

Beginning in the 1950s the Japanese government designated steel as a sector that should receive priority in growth. Japanese steel production tripled from 1963 to 1970, not only meeting the rapidly growing demands of the domestic economy but also making Japan the world's largest exporter. This development was especially remarkable given that virtually all the raw materials for steel making have to be imported into resource-poor Japan from other countries. When a world steel glut developed after the energy crisis in 1973, Japan's industry had the most modern plants with the lowest operating costs and was thus able to continue to operate in an environment in which the steel industries of other industrial countries were either contracting sharply (as in the United States) or being supported by government subsidy (as in Europe).

This experience raises two major questions. Was government policy the cause of steel's rapid growth? Was this policy good for Japan's economy?

Given the previous description of Japan's trade strategy, we must ask whether the government's targeting of steel only moved the economy in the same direction market forces would have moved it anyway. Japan would probably have developed a comparative advantage in steel even with laissez-faire. On one side, Japan's high savings rate gave it a growing comparative advantage in capital-intensive industries like steel. On the other side, falling transport costs and the emergence of new sources of iron ore and coal made it less necessary for steel industries in general to locate near coal fields or iron deposits. Thus Japan might well have had a growing steel industry even without government intervention. Nonetheless, it is a good guess that the Japanese government encouraged steel to grow even faster than it would have in a free market economy. This is supported by the observation that Japan's steel industry grew rapidly despite a profit rate substantially *below* the average for Japanese manufacturing.

The more important question, however, is whether the policy accelerated Japanese economic growth. In answering this question, it is important to be careful. The policy was successful in making the steel industry grow—but that is not the question. The question is whether it made the Japanese economy *as a whole* grow faster. This amounts to asking whether the resources used in steel yielded a higher payoff to society than they would have elsewhere.

As noted above, the return directly earned by the resources used in steel was actually not as high as the return the same resources were earning elsewhere. Capital invested in steel earned a rate of return only a little more than half the average rate of return in Japanese manufacturing even during the prosperous 1960s and earned an even lower return during the 1970s.[6] Japan's promotion of steel can be justified only if there were marginal social benefits not included in the market return.

Economists who have studied the issue have not identified important marginal social benefits. Steel is not a "high-technology" industry that could be expected to yield important technological externalities. Nor are there high returns to be snatched from foreign rivals by strategic trade policy. Creation of jobs did not represent an extra benefit in Japan, because the economy was already running at full employment. Unless a plausible source of marginal social benefits can be identified, we must conclude that the targeting of steel—despite the industry's growth—was a mistake. It diverted resources to areas where their return was lower than elsewhere and thus acted as a drag on Japan's growth.

The case of Japanese steel is instructive. It is a reminder that the economic success of a strategic trade policy cannot be measured simply by looking at the growth or market share of the targeted industry.

CASE STUDY

EUROPEAN SUPPORT OF AIRCRAFT

The continued U.S. dominance in the manufacture of aircraft is a potent symbol of U.S. technological prowess. It is a symbol especially visible to policymakers, who spend much of their time flying between meetings. It is not surprising, then, that there is a long history of attempts by European governments to develop aircraft industries that can compete with the U.S. firms. In the 1950s and 1960s,

---

[6]See Paul R. Krugman, "Targeted Industrial Policies: Theory and Evidence," in Dominick Salvatore, ed., *The New Protectionist Threat to World Welfare* (Amsterdam: North-Holland, 1987).

these efforts were undertaken at a national level, with little success. Since the late 1960s, however, there have been two major cooperative efforts at government-sponsored aircraft development in Europe.

One of these was the joint development by Britain and France of a supersonic aircraft, the Concorde. Construction of a supersonic passenger plane became technologically feasible in the late 1960s, but private airplane manufactures were unconvinced that it would be profitable to develop. A political campaign to have the U.S. government finance development of such a plane failed. In Europe, however, France and Britain agreed to foot the bill for development. The logic behind this agreement was complex. To some extent there was hope of large technological spillovers. More important, however, was the prestige appeal of the project and the usefulness of the Concorde as a symbol of European cooperation.

In commercial terms the results have been disastrous. Concordes are extremely expensive to run, and the saving of a few hours in travel time has not been enough to counteract this difference in expense. Only a few Concordes have been sold, and those were bought by the state-owned airlines of Britain and France (British Airways and Air France). The best that can be said of the Concorde is that the experience of its development may have yielded technological spillovers to the next European attempt at aircraft production, the Airbus.

Airbus is a consortium of European governments that produces large passenger airplanes that compete directly with the main U.S. strength. The costs of capital and some of the other costs have been subsidized by the member governments. While the size of government support is a subject of considerable dispute—European governments claim that it is much smaller than U.S. estimates—few would question that Airbus is the world's largest example of strategic trade policy. It may be larger than all other such programs put together. It is also a project that has achieved some important successes. Unlike the Concorde project, Airbus has succeeded in producing planes that are commercially viable; although Airbus has no counterpart to Boeing's giant 747s, in smaller size classes Airbus passenger jets are comparable in performance and operating costs with U.S. planes, and have taken a substantial share of the market. Profitability is another matter. Airbus's accounting is deliberately opaque, but it seems clear that at least until very recently it has depended on a continuing flow of government subsidies to remain aloft, and very little of the capital advanced by European governments has been repaid.

Has Airbus been a successful program? If one tries to justify the program strictly in terms of the Brander-Spencer analysis, it clearly has not: The company has not succeeded in earning excess returns, and in fact has earned less than the market return to capital. Nor is it easy to make a case that there are strong technological spillovers to other sectors: The technology used in the aircraft industry seems, at least on casual observation, to be rather special and not very applicable elsewhere. Nonetheless, some analysts have argued that Airbus has been a net plus to the European economy, for two reasons. First, the existence of Airbus means a more competitive market for aircraft, that is, the existence of Airbus limits what would otherwise be monopoly power on the part of Boeing. Second, workers in aircraft are paid high wages, so the wage differential argument works in the industry's favor. Even on favorable estimates, however, the gains from the Airbus program have been tiny compared with the size of the European economy.

One final point: the interest in Airbus, and the seeming simplicity of the basic situation—two major producers, manufacturing only a limited range of products—has led to a number of attempts to produce workable theoretical models of the aircraft industry. By common consensus, these models have been highly unsatisfactory in explaining major features of the industry such as pricing policies and investment decisions. The whole episode has served as a reminder of how hard it can be to have a real understanding of an industry; you may know a lot about the technology and the market, but that does not necessarily translate into the ability to do useful policy analysis.

 **CASE STUDY**

JAPANESE TARGETING OF SEMICONDUCTORS (SINCE THE MID-1970s)

As we noted earlier, since the mid-1970s Japanese industrial policy has shifted to a focus on high-technology industries. The best-known and most controversial case has been semiconductors. Semiconductor chips, complex electronic circuits etched at microscopic scale onto chips of silicon, are key components of many new products. Until the mid-1970s, the technology for making such chips was largely a U.S. monopoly. Japan made a deliberate effort to break into this industry, with the government sponsoring joint research projects and at least initially providing a protected domestic market. In the late 1970s and early 1980s Japanese producers shocked their U.S. competitors by taking a dominant share of the market for one kind of chip, random access memories.

That Japan targeted semiconductors, and that the industry achieved a large market share, is fact. What is hotly disputed is how much support the Japanese industry actually received, how decisive that support was, and whether the policy helped Japan and/or hurt the United States.

We know that not much government money was provided; the subsidy component of the targeting was actually quite small. We also know that explicit home market protection, by tariffs and quotas, was mostly removed after the mid-1970s. Some would argue that, in fact, the Japanese semiconductor industry succeeded with little government help.

Others argue that more subtle government help was crucial. The proponents of this view argue that the joint research projects, which would have been blocked in the United States by antitrust laws, were a highly effective way of improving the technology. They also argue that the Japanese market was effectively closed through a tacit "buy Japanese" policy discreetly encouraged by the government. As evidence they note that U.S. firms had a much smaller market share in Japan than in the United States or Europe.

Economists do not know which of these views is correct. (It may be that the Japanese don't know either.) If we assume for the sake of argument that government policy was, in fact, crucial, was it a good idea?

As in the case of steel, the direct returns on Japan's investment in semiconductors have been quite low. Exact figures are not available, but it is generally believed that Japanese firms have earned a low rate of return on semiconductors since the late 1970s.

Nonetheless, by about 1990 it was widely believed that Japan had scored a major success through its targeting of semiconductors. This belief rested on two expectations. First, Japan's dominance of the market for memory chips was expected to be highly persistent. This segment of the semiconductor market has been one in which the economies of scale have been steadily rising relative to the size of the market, and in which the number of competitors has been falling in each successive technological generation. So most observers expected that the Japanese firms that dominated the market by 1990 would continue to do so in the future. Second, it was widely believed that manufacture of memories, which are the chips produced in the greatest volume, would be crucial to a country's ability to stay at the cutting edge of production technology—in other words, that Japan's success in memories would soon translate into a dominance of the whole semiconductor industry.

To almost everyone's surprise, however, Japan's market share in semiconductors began dropping again during the first half of the 1990s. On one side, it turned out that memories, relatively simple, mass-produced chips, could be manufactured in developing countries. South Korean firms, in particular, took a substantial share of the market away from the Japanese. On the other hand, the importance of memory production for success in other kinds of semiconductor manufacture turned out to be less than had been assumed; U.S. firms with no memory production, such as Intel, continued to maintain and even extend their technological advantage in other products such as microprocessors (the brains of personal computers) and a variety of so-called ASICs (application-specific integrated circuits).

The semiconductor case has turned out to be an object lesson in the virtues of humility. In 1990 the Japanese industry was widely viewed as a compelling example of successful strategic trade policy. But that assessment was based on fairly casual assumptions, especially about technological spillovers, which seem to have been falsified by experience.

This brief survey of strategic trade policies in practice is not comprehensive. Each example does, however, illustrate an important point: Strategic trade policy cannot be judged by asking whether the targeted industries grew. All three cases are of industries that did eventually grow and achieve substantial market share, but this does not mean that policies accelerated economic growth, because an interventionist policy will not accelerate overall growth unless it corrects a market failure. In the case of steel, it is hard to identify a market failure, so the Japanese government's promotion of steel probably retarded economic growth by channeling resources into an area of low return. In the case of aircraft, European subsidies may in principle have helped Airbus gain a strategic advantage, but it is questionable whether any advantage was gained in fact. In the case of semiconductors, the justification for the Japanese targeting rested on presumed external economies that have not turned out to be as important as most people expected.

Some extravagant claims have been made about the effectiveness of strategic trade policy. We cannot show that such policies never work, but we can show that they have not always worked and that assessing them requires a more careful analysis of the data than most observers have carried out.

Summary

1. *Strategic trade policies* are policies that attempt to improve economic performance by promoting particular exports or discouraging particular imports. Such policies have been extensively practiced by some successful economies, such as Japan and South Korea.

2. Advocates of strategic trade policies often base their case for intervention on the view that nations are engaged in a competitive, win-lose struggle for world markets, in which the prizes are certain, especially desirable industries. Popular criteria that supposedly make an industry desirable include *high value added per worker, high wages,* and the use of *high technology.* However, high value added turns out to be an economically flawed criterion. Concerns over the loss of high-wage jobs, usually tied to fears of *deindustrialization,* have also been found by economic researchers to be largely unwarranted. High-technology industries may be more likely than other sectors to yield valuable *technological spillovers,* but this is simply a particular case of the market failures argument for government intervention advanced in earlier chapters.

3. There are two sophisticated arguments for strategic trade policies that have attracted considerable attention from international economists. One is the argument that governments should promote industries that yield *technological externalities.* The other is the *Brander-Spencer analysis,* which shows how activist government policies can in principle help national firms increase their profits at the expense of foreign rivals. These arguments are theoretically persuasive; however, many economists worry that they are too subtle and require too much information to be useful in practice.

4. Strategic trade policy in practice is much more varied and uncertain in effect than popular descriptions might indicate. Japan's policy has shifted from extensive government control over the economy in the 1950s and 1960s to a much lighter government hand today. Other countries have had less consistent policies; even the United States has, in effect, had a widely approved strategic policy in agriculture, and some foreigners allege that the U.S. defense budget acts like a strategic trade policy for the high-technology industries.

5. Assessing the effect of those policies is not easy. Looking at market shares or the growth of the industry is not enough. Instead, one must do a cost-benefit analysis. An examination of some major examples of strategic trade policy is not very encouraging about the track record of governments in their targeting.

our study of international macroeconomics, we will learn how the interactions of national economies influence the worldwide pattern of macroeconomic activity.

Macroeconomic analysis emphasizes four aspects of economic life that we have usually kept in the background until now to simplify our discussion of international economics:

1. *Unemployment.* We know that in the real world workers may be unemployed and factories may be idle. Macroeconomics studies the factors that cause unemployment and the steps governments can take to prevent it. A main concern of international macroeconomics is the problem of ensuring full employment in economies open to international trade.

2. *Saving.* In earlier chapters we usually assumed that every country consumes an amount exactly equal to its income—no more and no less. In reality, though, households can put aside part of their income to provide for the future, or they can borrow temporarily to spend more than they earn. A country's saving or borrowing behavior affects domestic employment and future levels of national wealth. From the standpoint of the international economy as a whole, the world saving rate determines how quickly the world stock of productive capital can grow.

3. *Trade imbalances.* As we saw in earlier chapters, the value of a country's imports equals the value of its exports when spending equals income. This state of balanced trade is seldom attained by actual economies, however. Trade imbalances play a large role in the following chapters because they redistribute wealth among countries and are a main channel through which one country's macroeconomic policies affect its trading partners. It should be no surprise, therefore, that trade imbalances, particularly when they are large and persistent, quickly can become a source of international discord.

4. *Money and the price level.* The trade theory you have studied so far is a barter theory, one in which goods are exchanged directly for other goods on the basis of their relative prices. In practice it is more convenient to use money, a widely acceptable medium of exchange, in transactions, and to quote prices in terms of money. Because money changes hands in virtually every transaction that takes place in a modern economy, fluctuations in the supply of money or the demand for it can affect both output and employment. International macroeconomics takes into account that every country uses a currency and that a monetary change in one country (for example, a change in money supply) can have effects that spill across its borders to other countries. Stability in money price levels is an important goal of international macroeconomic policy.

This chapter takes the first step in our study of international macroeconomics by explaining the accounting concepts economists use to describe a country's level of production and its international transactions. To get a complete picture of the macroeconomic linkages among economies that engage in international trade, we have to master two related and essential tools. The first of these tools, **national income accounting,** records all the expenditures that contribute to a country's income and output. The second tool, **balance of payments accounting,** helps us keep track of both changes in a country's indebtedness to foreigners and the fortunes of its export- and import-competing industries. The balance of payments accounts also show the connection between foreign transactions and national money supplies.

THE NATIONAL INCOME ACCOUNTS

Of central concern to macroeconomic analysis is a country's **gross national product (GNP),** the value of all final goods and services produced by its factors of production and sold on the market in a given time period. GNP, which is the basic measure of a country's output studied by macroeconomists, is calculated by adding up the market value of all expenditures on final output. GNP therefore includes the value of goods like bread sold in a supermarket and textbooks sold in a bookstore, as well as the value of services provided by supermarket checkers and baggers and by university professors. Because output cannot be produced without the aid of factor inputs, the expenditures that make up GNP are closely linked to the employment of labor, capital, and other factors of production.

To distinguish among the different types of expenditure that make up a country's GNP, government economists and statisticians who compile national income accounts divide GNP among the four possible uses for which a country's output is purchased: *consumption* (the amount consumed by private domestic residents), *investment* (the amount put aside by private firms to build new plant and equipment for future production), *government purchases* (the amount used by the government), and the *current account balance* (the amount of net exports of goods and services to foreigners). The term *national income accounts,* rather than *national output accounts,* is used to describe this fourfold classification because a country's income in fact equals its output. Thus, the national income accounts can be thought of as classifying each transaction that contributes to national income according to the type of expenditure that gives rise to it. Figure 12-1 shows how U.S. GNP was divided among its four components in 1994.[1]

Why is it useful to divide GNP into consumption, investment, government purchases, and the current account? One major reason is that we cannot hope to understand the cause of a particular recession or boom without knowing how the main categories of spending have changed. And without such an understanding, we cannot recommend a sound policy response. In addition, the national income accounts provide information essential for studying why some countries are rich—that is, have a high level of GNP relative to population size—while some are poor.

NATIONAL PRODUCT AND NATIONAL INCOME

Our first task in understanding how economists analyze GNP is to explain in greater detail why the GNP a country generates over some time period must equal its **national income,** the income earned in that period by its factors of production.

The reason for this equality is that every dollar used to purchase goods or services automatically ends up in somebody's pocket. A visit to the doctor provides a simple example of how an increase in national output raises national income by the same amount. The $75 you pay the doctor represents the market value of the services he or she provides for you,

---

[1]Our definition of the current account is not strictly accurate when a country is a net donor or recipient of foreign gifts. This possibility, along with some others, also complicates our identification of GNP with national income. We describe later in this chapter how the definitions of national income and the current account must be changed in such cases.

FIGURE 12-1

U.S. GNP and Its Components, 1994

America's $6.7 trillion 1994 gross national product can be broken down into the four components shown.

Source: U.S. Department of Commerce, *Survey of Current Business*, April 1995.

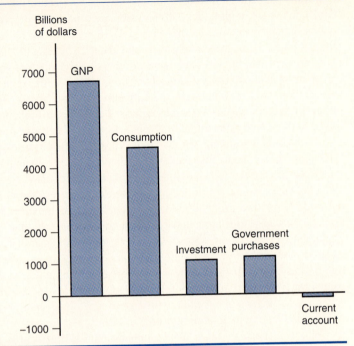

so your visit raises GNP by $75. But the $75 you pay the doctor also raises his or her income. So national income rises by $75.

The principle that output and income are the same also applies to goods, even goods that are produced with the help of many factors of production. Consider the example of an economics textbook. When you purchase a new book from the publisher, the value of your purchase enters GNP. But your payment enters the income of the productive factors that have cooperated in producing the book, because the publisher must pay for their services with the proceeds of sales. First, there are the authors, editors, artists, and typesetters who provide the labor inputs necessary for the book's production. Second, there are the publishing company's shareholders, who receive dividends for having financed acquisition of the capital used in production. Finally, there are the suppliers of paper and ink, who provide the intermediate materials used in producing the book.

The paper and ink purchased by the publishing house to produce the book are *not* counted separately in GNP because their contribution to the value of national output is already included in the book's price. It is to avoid such double counting that we allow only the sale of *final* goods and services to enter into the definition of GNP: Sales of intermediate goods, such as paper and ink purchased by a publisher, are not counted. Notice also that the sale of a used textbook does not enter GNP. Our definition counts only final goods and services that are *produced,* and a used textbook does not qualify: It was counted in GNP at the time it was first sold. Equivalently, the sale of a used textbook does not generate income for any factor of production.

CAPITAL DEPRECIATION, INTERNATIONAL TRANSFERS, AND INDIRECT BUSINESS TAXES

Because we have defined GNP and national income so that they are necessarily equal, their equality is really an identity. Some adjustments to the definition of GNP must be made, however, before the identification of GNP and national income is entirely correct in practice.

     1. GNP does not take into account the economic loss due to the tendency of machinery and structures to wear out as they are used. This loss, called *depreciation,* reduces the income of capital owners. To calculate national income over a given period, we must therefore subtract from GNP the depreciation of capital over the period. GNP less depreciation is called *net national product (NNP).*

     2. A country's income may include gifts from residents of foreign countries, called *unilateral transfers.* Examples of unilateral transfers are pension payments to retired citizens living abroad, reparation payments, and foreign aid such as relief funds donated to drought-stricken nations. For the United States in 1994, the balance of such payments amounted to around $34 billion, representing a 0.5 percent of GNP net transfer to foreigners. Net unilateral transfers are part of a country's income but are not part of its product, and they must be added to NNP in calculations of national income.

     3. National income depends on the prices producers *receive* for their goods, GNP on the prices purchasers *pay.* These two sets of prices need not, however, be identical. For example, sales taxes make buyers pay more than sellers receive, leading GNP to overestimate national income. The amount of this tax wedge, called *indirect business taxes,* must therefore be subtracted from GNP in calculating true national income.

National income equals GNP *less* depreciation, *plus* net unilateral transfers, *less* indirect business taxes. The difference between GNP and national income is by no means an insignificant amount, but macroeconomics has little to say about it, and it is of little importance for macroeconomic analysis. Therefore, for the purposes of this text we usually use the terms *GNP* and *national income* interchangeably, emphasizing the distinction between the two only when it is essential.

GROSS DOMESTIC PRODUCT

Most countries other than the United States have long reported **gross domestic product (GDP)** rather than GNP as their primary measure of national economic activity. In 1991 the United States began to follow this practice as well. GDP is supposed to measure the volume of production within a country's borders. GNP equals GDP *plus* net receipts of factor income from the rest of the world. These net receipts are the income domestic residents earn on wealth they hold in other countries less the payments domestic residents make to foreign owners of wealth located at home.

     GDP does not correct, as GNP does, for the portion of countries' production carried out using services provided by foreign-owned capital. Consider an example. The earnings of a Spanish factory with British owners are counted in Spain's GDP but are part of Britain's GNP. The services British capital provides in Spain are a service export from Britain, therefore they are added to British GDP in calculating British GNP. At the same time, to figure Spain's GNP we must subtract from its GDP the corresponding service import from Britain.

As a practical matter, movements in GDP and GNP usually do not differ greatly. We will focus on GNP in this book, however, because GNP tracks national income more closely than GDP, and national welfare depends more directly on national income than on domestic product.

NATIONAL INCOME ACCOUNTING FOR AN OPEN ECONOMY

In this section we extend to the case of an open economy the closed-economy national income accounting framework you may have seen in earlier economics courses. We begin with a discussion of the national income accounts because they highlight the key role of international trade in open-economy macroeconomic theory. Since a closed economy's residents cannot purchase foreign output or sell their own to foreigners, all of national income must be generated by domestic consumption, investment, or government purchases. In an economy open to international trade, however, the closed-economy version of national income accounting must be modified because some domestic output is exported to foreigners while some domestic income is spent on imported foreign products.

The main lesson of this section concerns the relation among national saving, investment, and trade imbalances. We will see that in open economies, saving and investment are not necessarily equal as they are in a closed economy. This is because countries can save by exporting more than they import, and they can *dissave*—that is, reduce their wealth—by exporting less than they import.

CONSUMPTION

The portion of GNP purchased by the private sector to fulfill current wants is called **consumption.** Purchases of movie tickets, food, dental work, and washing machines all fall into this category. Consumption expenditure is the largest component of GNP in most economies. In the United States, for example, the fraction of GNP devoted to consumption has fluctuated in a range of about 62 to 69 percent since the Korean War.

INVESTMENT

The part of output used by private firms to produce future output is called **investment.** Investment spending may be viewed as the portion of GNP used to increase the nation's stock of capital. Steel and bricks used to build a factory are part of investment spending, as are services provided by a technician who helps build business computers. Firms' purchases of inventories are also counted in investment spending because carrying inventories is just another way for firms to transfer output from current use to future use. Investment is usually more variable than consumption. In the United States, (gross) investment has fluctuated between 12 and 19 percent of GNP in recent years. While we often use the word *investment* to describe individual households' purchases of stocks, bonds, or real estate, you should be careful not to confuse this everyday meaning of the word with the economic definition of investment as a component of GNP. When you buy a share of Microsoft stock, you are buying neither a good nor a service, so your purchase does not show up in GNP.

GOVERNMENT PURCHASES

Any goods and services purchased by federal, state, or local governments are classified as **government purchases** in the national income accounts. Included in government purchases are federal military spending, government support of cancer research, and government funds spent on highway repair and education. Government transfer payments like social security and unemployment benefits do not require the recipient to give the government any goods or services in return. Thus, transfer payments are not included in government purchases.

Government purchases currently take up about 18 percent of U.S. GNP, and this share has not changed much since the late 1950s. (The corresponding figure for 1959, for example, was around 20 percent.) In 1929, however, government purchases accounted for only 8.5 percent of U.S. GNP.

THE NATIONAL INCOME IDENTITY FOR AN OPEN ECONOMY

In a closed economy any final good or service that is not purchased by households or the government must be used by firms to produce new plant, equipment, and inventories. If consumption goods are not sold immediately to consumers or the government, firms (perhaps reluctantly) add them to existing inventories, thus increasing investment.

This information leads to a fundamental identity for closed economies. Let Y stand for GNP, C for consumption, I for investment, and G for government purchases. Since all of a closed economy's output must be consumed, invested, or bought by the government, we can write

$$Y = C + I + G.$$

We derived the national income identity for a closed economy by assuming that all output was consumed or invested by the country's citizens or purchased by its government. When foreign trade is possible, however, some output is purchased by foreigners while some domestic spending goes to purchase goods and services produced abroad. The GNP identity for open economies shows how the national income a country earns by selling its goods and services is divided between sales to domestic residents and sales to foreign residents.

Since residents of an open economy may spend some of their income on imports, that is, goods and services purchased from abroad, only the portion of their spending that is not devoted to imports is part of domestic GNP. The value of imports, denoted by IM, must be substracted from total domestic spending, $C + I + G$, to find the portion of domestic spending that generates domestic national income. Imports from abroad add to foreign countries' GNPs but do not add directly to domestic GNP.

Similarly, the goods and services sold to foreigners make up a country's exports. Exports, denoted by EX, are the amount foreign residents' purchases add to the national income of the domestic economy.

The national income of an open economy is therefore the sum of domestic and foreign expenditure on the goods and services produced by domestic factors of production. Thus, the national income identity for an open economy is

$$Y = C + I + G + EX - IM. \tag{12-1}$$

AN IMAGINARY OPEN ECONOMY

To make identity (12-1) concrete, let's consider an imaginary closed economy, Agraria, whose only output is wheat. Each citizen of Agraria is a consumer of wheat, but each is also a farmer and therefore can be viewed as a firm. Farmers invest by putting aside a portion of each year's crop as seed for the following year's planting. There is also a government that appropriates part of the crop to feed the Agrarian army. Agraria's total annual crop is 100 bushels of wheat. Agraria can import milk from the rest of the world in exchange for exports of wheat. We cannot draw up the Agrarian national income accounts without knowing the price of milk in terms of wheat because all the components in the GNP identity (12-1) must be measured in the same units. If we assume the price of milk is 0.5 bushel of wheat per gallon, and that at this price Agrarians want to consume 40 gallons of milk, then Agraria's imports are equal in value to 20 bushels of wheat.

In Table 12-1 we see that Agraria's total output is 100 bushels of wheat. Consumption is divided between wheat and milk, with 55 bushels of wheat and 40 gallons of milk (equal in value to 20 bushels of wheat) consumed over the year. The value of consumption in terms of wheat is $55 + (0.5 \times 40) = 55 + 20 = 75$.

The 100 bushels of wheat produced by Agraria are used as follows: 55 are consumed by domestic residents, 25 are invested, 10 are purchased by the government, and 10 are exported abroad. National income ($Y = 100$) equals domestic spending ($C + I + G = 110$) plus exports ($EX = 10$) less imports ($IM = 20$).

THE CURRENT ACCOUNT AND FOREIGN INDEBTEDNESS

In reality a country's foreign trade is exactly balanced only rarely. The difference between exports of goods and services and imports of goods and services is known as the **current account balance** (or current account). If we denote the current account by *CA*, we can express this definition in symbols as

$$CA = EX - IM.$$

When a country's imports exceed its exports, we say the country has a *current account deficit*. A country has a *current account surplus* when its exports exceed its imports.[2]

The GNP identity, equation (12-1), shows one reason why the current account is important in international macroeconomics. Since the right-hand side of (12-1) is total expenditure on domestic output, changes in the current account can be associated with changes in output and, thus, employment.

The current account is also important because it measures the size and direction of international borrowing. When a country imports more than it exports, it is buying more from foreigners than it sells to them and must somehow finance this current account deficit. How does it pay for additional imports once it has spent its export earnings? Since the country as a whole can import more than it exports only if it can borrow the difference

---

[2]In addition to net exports of goods and services, the current account balance includes net unilateral transfers, which we discussed briefly above. Following our earlier assumption, we continue to ignore transfers for now to simplify the discussion. We will see how transfers enter the current account later in this chapter when we analyze the U.S. balance of payments in detail.

TABLE 12-1

National Income Accounts for Agraria, an Open Economy (bushels of wheat)

GNP (total output)	=	Consumption	+	Investment	+	Government purchases	+	Exports	−	Imports
100	=	75[a]	+	25	+	10	+	10	−	20[b]

[a] 55 bushels of wheat + (0.5 bushel per gallon) × (40 gallons of milk).
[b] 0.5 bushel per gallon × 40 gallons of milk.

from foreigners, a country with a current account deficit must be increasing its net foreign debts by the amount of the deficit.[3]

Similarly, a country with a current account surplus is earning more from its exports than it spends on imports. This country finances the current account deficit of its trading partners by lending to them. The foreign wealth of a surplus country rises because foreigners pay for any imports not covered by their exports by issuing IOUs that they will eventually have to redeem. The preceding reasoning shows that *a country's current account balance equals the change in its net foreign wealth.*

We have defined the current account as the difference between exports and imports. Equation (12-1) says that the current account is also equal to the difference between national income Y and domestic residents' spending $C + I + G$:

$$Y - (C + I + G) = CA.$$

It is only by borrowing abroad that a country can have a current account deficit and use more output than it is currently producing. If it uses less than its output, it has a current account surplus and is lending the surplus to foreigners.[4] International borrowing and lending were identified with *intertemporal trade* in Chapter 7. A country with a current account deficit is importing present consumption and exporting future consumption. A country with a current account surplus is exporting present consumption and importing future consumption.

As an example, consider again the imaginary economy of Agraria described in Table 12-1. The total value of its consumption, investment, and government purchases, at 110 bushels of wheat, is greater than its output of 100 bushels. This inequality would be impossible in a closed economy; it *is* possible in this open economy because Agraria now imports 40 gallons of milk, worth 20 bushels of wheat, but exports only 10 bushels of wheat. The current account deficit of 10 bushels is the value of Agraria's borrowing from foreigners, which the country will have to repay in the future.

---

[3] Alternatively, a country could finance a current account deficit by using previously accumulated foreign wealth to pay for imports. This country would be running down its net foreign wealth, which is the same as running up its net foreign debts.

[4] The sum $C + I + G$ is often called domestic *absorption* in the literature on international macroeconomics. Using this terminology, we can describe the current account surplus as the difference between income and absorption.

FIGURE 12-2

The U.S. Current Account and Net Foreign Wealth Position, 1977–1993

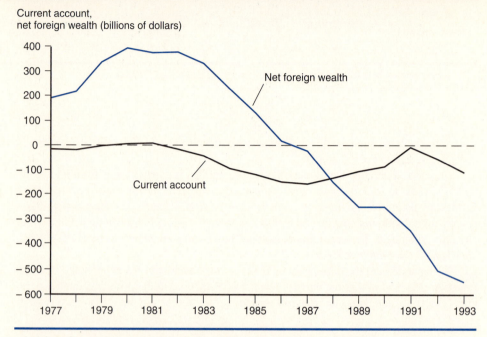

A string of current account deficits in the 1980s reduced America's net foreign wealth until, by the decade's end, the country had accumulated a substantial net foreign debt.

Source: U.S. Department of Commerce, *Survey of Current Business,* June 1994.

Figure 12-2 gives a vivid illustration of how a string of current account deficits can add up to a large foreign debt. The figure plots the U.S. current account balance since the late 1970s along with a measure of the nation's stock of net foreign wealth. As you can see, the United States had accumulated substantial foreign wealth by the early 1980s, when a sustained current account deficit of proportions unprecedented in the twentieth century opened up. In 1987 the country became a net debtor to foreigners for the first time since World War I.

As the Case Study on p. 323 shows, it is surprisingly hard to measure accurately a country's net foreign wealth. Some economic analysts therefore question the data in Figure 12-2 and disagree over when the United States became a debtor country and how large its foreign debt really is. But there is no question that a large decrease in U.S. foreign assets did occur over the 1980s.

SAVING AND THE CURRENT ACCOUNT

Simple as it is, the GNP identity has many illuminating implications. To explain the most important of these implications, we define the concept of **national saving,** that is, the portion of output, Y, that is not devoted to household consumption, C, or government purchases, G.[5] *In a closed economy, national saving always equals investment.* This tells us that the economy as a whole can increase its wealth only by accumulating new capital.

Let S stand for national saving. Our definition of S tells us that

$$S = Y - C - G.$$

Since the closed-economy GNP identity, $Y = C + I + G$, may also be written as $I = Y - C - G$, then

$$S = I,$$

and national saving must equal investment in a closed economy. While in a closed economy saving and investment must always be equal, in an open economy they can differ. Remembering that national saving, S, equals $Y - C - G$ and that $CA = EX - IM$, we can rewrite the GNP identity (12-1) as

$$S = I + CA.$$

The equation highlights an important difference between open and closed economies: *An open economy can save either by building up its capital stock or by acquiring foreign wealth, but a closed economy can save only by building up its capital stock.*

Unlike a closed economy, an open economy with profitable investment opportunities does not have to increase its saving in order to exploit them. The preceding expression shows that it is possible simultaneously to raise investment and foreign borrowing without changing saving. For example, if New Zealand decides to build a new hydroelectric plant, it can import the materials it needs from the United States and borrow American funds to pay for them. This transaction raises New Zealand's domestic investment because the imported materials contribute to expanding the country's capital stock. The transaction also raises New Zealand's current account deficit by an amount equal to the increase in investment. New Zealand's saving does not have to change, even though investment rises. For this to be possible, however, U.S. residents must be willing to save more so that the resources needed to build the plant are freed for New Zealand's use. The result is another example of intertemporal trade, in which New Zealand imports present consumption (when it borrows from the United States) and exports future consumption (when it pays off the loan).

Because one country's savings can be borrowed by a second country to increase the second country's stock of capital, a country's current account surplus is often referred to as its *net foreign investment.* Of course, when one country lends to another to finance investment, part of the income generated by the investment in future years must be used to pay back the lender. Domestic investment and foreign investment are two different ways in which a country can use current savings to increase its future income.

---

[5]The U.S. national income accounts assume that government purchases are not used to enlarge the nation's capital stock. We follow this convention here by subtracting *all* government purchases from output to calculate national saving. Most other countries' national accounts distinguish between government consumption and government investment (for example, investment by publicly owned enterprises) and include the latter as part of national saving. Often, however, government investment figures include purchases of military equipment.

PRIVATE AND GOVERNMENT SAVING

So far our discussion of saving has not stressed the distinction between saving decisions made by the private sector and saving decisions made by the government. Unlike private saving decisions, however, government saving decisions are often made with an eye toward their effect on output and employment. The national income identity can help us to analyze the channels through which government saving decisions influence macroeconomic conditions. To use the national income identity in this way, we first have to divide national saving into its private and government components.

Private saving is defined as the part of disposable income that is saved rather than consumed. Disposable income is national income, Y, less the net taxes collected from households and firms by the government, T.[6] Private saving, denoted S^p, can therefore be expressed as

$$S^p = Y - T - C.$$

Government saving is defined similarly to private saving. The government's "income" is its net tax revenue, T, while its "consumption" is government purchases, G. If we let S^g stand for government saving, then

$$S^g = T - G.$$

The two types of saving we have defined, private and government, add up to national saving. To see why, recall the definition of national saving, S, as $Y - C - G$. Then

$$S = Y - C - G = (Y - T - C) + (T - G) = S^p + S^g.$$

We can use the definitions of private and government saving to rewrite the national income identity in a form that is useful for analyzing the effects of government saving decisions on open economies. Because $S = S^p + S^g = I + CA$,

$$S^p = I + CA - S^g = I + CA - (T - G) = I + CA + (G - T). \qquad (12\text{-}2)$$

Equation (12-2) relates private saving to domestic investment, the current account surplus, and government saving. To interpret equation (12-2), we define the **government budget deficit** as $G - T$, that is, as government saving preceded by a minus sign. The government budget deficit measures the extent to which the government is borrowing to finance its expenditures. Equation (12-2) then states that a country's private saving can take three forms: investment in domestic capital (I), purchases of wealth from foreigners (CA), and purchases of the domestic government's newly issued debt ($G - T$).[7] The usefulness of equation (12-2) is illustrated by the following Case Study.

---

[6]Net taxes are taxes less government transfer payments. The term *government* refers to the federal, state, and local governments considered as a single unit.

[7]In a closed economy the current account is always zero, so equation (12-2) is simply $S^p = I + (G - T)$.

CASE STUDY

Do Government Budget Deficits Worsen the Current Account?

Unusually large imbalances in the current accounts of the United States and Japan developed in the 1980s, with America's current account moving to a record deficit and Japan's to a record surplus. Because much of Japan's export surplus went to the United States and Japan imported little from the United States in return, that country became a leading target for the resentment of those hurt by foreign imports. By 1995 trade tensions between the United States and Japan had soured their relations in other areas and pushed them to the brink of a trade war.

Some international policymakers blamed the origin of the current account imbalances on growing government budget deficits in the United States and shrinking government deficits in Japan. The administration of President Ronald Reagan, which had unleashed the American government deficits by cutting taxes and increasing government purchases, tried at first to deflect blame for the worsening of the U.S. current account. Administration officials pointed to buoyant domestic investment as the cause, citing investment incentives that had accompanied the tax-cut legislation.

Identity (12-2), which can be written as

$$CA = S^p - I - (G - T),$$

provides a framework for analyzing the current accounts of the United States and Japan in the 1980s. Because private saving, investment, the current account, and the government deficit are jointly determined variables, we cannot fully determine the cause of a current account change by using the identity above alone. Nonetheless, the identity can give us some useful clues.

The table below presents data on the four variables linked by identity (12-2) for the United States. (The variables are expressed as percentages of GNP so that their values in different years can be compared more easily; they don't add up exactly as required by (12-2) because of errors in data collection.) We examine gross saving and investment rates, rather than net, because the depreciation data used to calculate the net flows are very unreliable.

United States (percentage of GNP)

Year	CA	S^p	I	$G - T$
1981	0.3	19.1	18.2	1.0
1982	−0.1	19.4	15.8	3.4
1983	−1.0	18.7	15.9	4.1
1984	−2.5	19.5	18.9	2.9
1985	−2.9	18.1	17.6	3.1
1986	−3.3	16.9	16.8	3.4

(continued)

Year	CA	S^p	I	$G - T$
1987	−3.4	16.1	16.5	2.5
1988	−2.4	16.3	16.2	2.0
1989	−1.7	15.6	15.8	1.5
1990	−1.4	15.5	14.5	2.5
1991	0.1	16.3	13.0	3.2
1992	−0.9	16.3	13.1	4.3
1993	−1.5	15.8	13.9	3.4
1994	−2.1	15.7	15.4	2.0

Source: Economic Report of the President, February 1995, and U.S. Department of Commerce, *Survey of Current Business,* April 1995.

Identity (12-2) tells us that, other things being equal, a rise in private saving must increase the current account surplus; a rise in investment or the government budget deficit must lower it. The U.S. data above show that between 1981 and 1983, the current account moved from a small surplus of 0.3 percent of GNP to a deficit of 1.0 percent of GNP as the government budget deficit rose sharply from 1 to 4.1 percent of GNP. A large fall in investment (from 18.2 to 15.8 percent of GNP) accompanied the U.S. economy's slide into a severe recession in 1981–1982.

The American economy grew quickly in 1984 and investment recovered sharply in that year, rising to 18.9 percent of GNP. Private saving rose compared with 1983, and with government tax revenues increasing automatically as the economy grew the government deficit declined from 4.1 to 2.9 percent of GNP. But the investment surge of 1984 was so large that the current account deficit (measured as a fraction of GNP) widened to 2.5 percent of GNP, a level unmatched since the nineteenth century.

The events of 1984 do not, however, prove the Reagan administration's case that high investment caused the U.S. current account deficit to widen. If we compare 1985–1986, when the recovery from recession had leveled off, with 1981, we see that the gap between private saving and investment is a bit smaller in the later years but that both of the "twin deficits" are much higher. Higher government budget deficits would have resulted in much higher current account deficits in 1982 and 1983 had investment not plummeted in the recession. This fall in investment temporarily masked the effect on the current account of the higher government deficits, but that effect was apparent by 1985, once investment had returned closer to normal levels.

Between 1987 and 1989 public-sector belt-tightening reduced the government's deficit; at the same time the current account deficit finally fell below 2 percent of GNP. As the United States slipped into a new recession in 1990, tax revenues fell and the government deficit again ballooned. Despite an accompanying fall in private saving, however, the external deficit continued to drop, with the United States reaching approximate current account balance in 1991. The reason: a dizzying fall in investment to a level not seen even during the 1981–1982 recession. As private saving fell and investment rose in the economic recovery that followed, the current account deficit for 1994 edged back above 2 percent of GNP—a level virtually identical to the government deficit.

Let's look next at comparable figures for Japan so that we can analyze its current account surplus:

Japan (percentage of GNP)

Year	CA	S^p	I	$G - T$
1981	0.4	27.6	23.4	3.8
1982	0.6	26.7	22.5	3.6
1983	1.8	24.9	19.6	3.6
1984	2.8	24.8	20.0	2.1
1985	3.6	25.1	20.6	0.8
1986	4.3	25.8	20.6	0.9
1987	3.6	24.6	21.6	−0.5
1988	2.7	24.3	23.1	−1.5
1989	2.0	24.1	24.6	−2.5
1990	1.2	24.1	25.8	−2.9
1991	2.2	24.6	25.4	−3.0
1992	3.2	25.1	23.7	−1.8

Source: Current account and general government deficit ratios from International Monetary Fund, *World Economic Outlook,* October 1994. Investment ratio (excluding public investment) calculated from GNP and investment data reported in OECD Economic Survey of Japan, 1993–1994. Private saving ratio calculated as a residual.

Japan's current account surplus swelled after 1981 despite a declining private saving rate. (Japan's gross private saving rate remained, however, much higher than that of the United States!) The growing current account surplus reflected both a declining investment rate and a shrinking government budget deficit.

Only after 1986 did Japan's current account surplus appear to decline as a share of GNP, a steadily rising government surplus notwithstanding. Accompanying this change were a fall in private saving and a substantial rise in investment, part of which was due to higher public investment. As the Japanese economy slid into a prolonged downturn in the early 1990s, however, rising saving and falling investment pushed the current account to a large surplus once again.

As in the U.S. case, we see that changes in the Japanese government budget deficit have been an important factor behind the country's current account performance. The data confirm a tendency for increases in the government budget deficit to lower the current account surplus while decreases in the government budget deficit raise it. But the data also show that this relationship is not a simple one.

THE BALANCE OF PAYMENTS ACCOUNTS

In the previous section, we examined the components of the national income accounts: consumption, investment, government purchases, and the current account (the measure of a country's net foreign investment or, equivalently, of the difference between its exports and imports). In addition to national income accounts, government economists and statisticians also keep balance of payments accounts, a detailed record of the composition of the current account balance and of the many transactions that finance it. Balance of payments figures are of great interest to the general public, as indicated by the attention that various

ings and import expenditures must be matched by a promise to repay the difference, usually with interest, in the future.

8. International asset transactions carried out by *central banks* are included in the capital account. Any central bank transaction in private markets for foreign currency assets is called *official foreign exchange intervention.* One reason intervention is important is that central banks use it as a way of altering the amount of money in circulation. A country has a deficit in its *balance of payments* when it is running down its *official international reserves* or borrowing from foreign central banks; it has a surplus in the opposite case.

Key Terms

asset, p. 316

balance of payments accounting, p. 302

capital account, p. 316

capital inflow, p. 319

capital outflow, p. 319

central bank, p. 320

consumption, p. 306

current account balance, p. 308

government budget deficit, p. 312

government purchases, p. 307

gross domestic product (GDP), p. 305

gross national product (GNP), p. 303

investment, p. 306

macroeconomics, p. 301

microeconomics, p. 301

national income, p. 303

national income accounting, p. 302

national saving, p. 310

official foreign exchange intervention, p. 321

official international reserves, p. 320

official settlements balance (or balance of payments), p. 323

private saving, p. 312

Problems

1. We stated in this chapter that GNP accounts avoid double counting by including only the value of *final* goods and services sold on the market. Should the measure of imports used in the GNP accounts therefore be defined to include only imports of final goods and services from abroad? What about exports?

2. Equation (12-2) tells us that to reduce a current account deficit, a country must increase its private saving, reduce domestic investment, or cut its government budget deficit. Yet, as we saw in the Case Study of the American and Japanese current accounts in the 1980s, many people recommended restrictions on imports from Japan (and other countries) to reduce the American current account deficit. How would higher U.S. barriers to imports affect its private saving, domestic investment, and government deficit? Do you agree that import restrictions would necessarily reduce a U.S. current account deficit?

3. Explain how each of the following transactions generates two entries—a credit and a debit—in the American balance of payments accounts, and describe how each entry would be classified:
   a. An American buys a share of German stock, paying by writing a check on an account with a Swiss bank.
   b. An American buys a share of German stock, paying the seller with a check on an American bank.

c. The French government carries out an official foreign exchange intervention in which it uses dollars held in an American bank to buy French currency from its citizens.

d. A tourist from Detroit buys a meal at an expensive restaurant in Lyons, France, paying with a traveler's check.

e. A California winegrower contributes a case of cabernet sauvignon for a London wine tasting.

f. A U.S.-owned factory in Britain uses local earnings to buy additional machinery.

4. A New Yorker travels to New Jersey to buy a $100 telephone answering machine. The New Jersey company that sells the machine then deposits the $100 check in its account at a New York bank. How would these transactions show up in the balance of payments accounts of New York and New Jersey? What if the New Yorker pays cash for the machine?

5. The nation of Pecunia had a current account deficit of $1 billion and a nonreserve capital account surplus of $500 million in 1998.

a. What was the balance of payments of Pecunia in that year? What happened to the country's net foreign assets?

b. Assume that foreign central banks neither buy nor sell Pecunian assets. How did the Pecunian central bank's foreign reserves change in 1998? How would this official intervention show up in the balance of payments accounts of Pecunia?

c. How would your answer to (b) change if you learned that foreign central banks had purchased $600 million of Pecunian assets in 1998? How would these official purchases enter foreign balance of payments accounts?

d. Draw up the Pecunian balance of payments accounts for 1998 under the assumption that the event described in (c) occurred in that year.

6. Can you think of reasons why a government might be concerned about a large current account deficit or surplus? Why might a government be concerned about its official settlements balance (that is, its balance of payments)?

7. Do data on the U.S. official settlements balance give an accurate picture of the extent to which foreign central banks buy and sell dollars in currency markets?

8. Is it possible for a country to have a current account deficit at the same time it has a surplus in its balance of payments? Explain your answer, using hypothetical figures for the current and nonreserve capital accounts. Be sure to discuss the possible implications for official international reserve flows.

Further Reading

Peter Hooper and J. David Richardson, eds. *International Economic Transactions.* Chicago: University of Chicago Press, 1991. Useful papers on international economic measurement.

David H. Howard. "Implications of the U.S. Current Account Deficit." *Journal of Economic Perspectives* 3 (Fall 1989), pp. 153–165. Examines how recent U.S. current account deficits may affect American welfare and net foreign wealth.

International Monetary Fund. *Final Report of the Working Party on the Statistical Discrepancy in World Current Account Balances.* Washington, D.C.: International Monetary Fund, September 1987. Discusses the statistical discrepancy in the world current account balance, its implications for policy analysis, and recommendations for more accurate measurement.

Robert E. Lipsey. "Changing Patterns of International Investment in and by the United States," in Martin S. Feldstein, ed. *The United States in the World Economy.* Chicago: University of Chicago Press, 1988, pp. 475–545. Historical perspective on capital flows to and from the United States.

Rita M. Maldonado. "Recording and Classifying Transactions in the Balance of Payments." *International Journal of Accounting* 15 (Fall 1979), pp. 105–133. Provides detailed examples of how various international transactions enter the balance of payments accounts.

James E. Meade. *The Balance of Payments,* Chapters 1–3. London: Oxford University Press, 1952. A classic analytical discussion of balance of payments concepts.

Lois Stekler. "Adequacy of International Transactions and Position Data for Policy Coordination," in William H. Branson, Jacob A. Frenkel, and Morris Goldstein, eds. *International Policy Coordination and Exchange Rate Fluctuations.* Chicago: University of Chicago Press, 1990, pp. 347–371. A critical look at the interpretation of official data on current accounts and external indebtedness.

Robert M. Stern, Charles F. Schwartz, Robert Triffin, Edward M. Bernstein, and Walther Lederer. *The Presentation of the Balance of Payments: A Symposium,* Princeton Essays in International Finance 123. International Finance Section, Department of Economics, Princeton University, August 1977. A discussion of changes in the presentation of the U.S. balance of payments accounts.

U.S. Bureau of the Budget, Review Committee for Balance of Payments Statistics. *The Balance of Payments Statistics of the United States: A Review and Appraisal.* Washington, D.C.: Government Printing Office, 1965. A major official reappraisal of U.S. balance of payments accounting procedures. Chapter 9 focuses on conceptual difficulties in defining surpluses and deficits in the balance of payments.

13 Exchange Rates and the Foreign Exchange Market: An Asset Approach

In 1985 American students flocked to Europe in record numbers to enjoy the castles of the Loire valley, the cuisine of Tuscany, and the London theater. By the 1990s, however, their younger brothers and sisters were finding that a summer vacation in Europe had become an expensive luxury. What economic forces had raised the price of foreign travel? One major factor was a sharp rise in the dollar prices of foreign currencies, a development that made foreign food, lodging, and transport more expensive for Americans.

The price of one currency in terms of another is called an **exchange rate.** At 3 P.M. New York time on June 19, 1995, you would have needed 71.56 cents to buy one unit of the German currency, the Deutschemark (DM), so the dollar's exchange rate against the DM was $0.7156 per DM. Because of their strong influence on the current account and other macroeconomic variables, exchange rates are among the most important prices in an open economy.

Because an exchange rate, as the price of one country's money in terms of another's, is also an asset price, the principles governing the behavior of other asset prices also govern the behavior of exchange rates. As you will recall from Chapter 12, the defining characteristic of an asset is that it is a form of wealth, a way of transferring purchasing power from the present into the future. The price that an asset commands today is therefore directly related to the purchasing power over goods and services that buyers expect it to yield in the future. Similarly, *today's* dollar/DM exchange rate is closely tied to people's expectations about the *future* level of that rate. Just as the price of Microsoft stock rises immediately upon favorable news about Microsoft's future prospects, so do exchange rates respond immediately to any news concerning future currency values.

20 percent. The real rate of return offered by the wine is 15 percent (= 25 percent − 10 percent) while that offered by the bond is only 10 percent (= 20 percent − 10 percent). Notice that the difference between the dollar returns of the two assets (25 percent − 20 percent) must equal the difference between their real returns (15 percent − 10 percent). The reason for this equality is that, given the two assets' dollar returns, a change in the rate at which the dollar prices of goods are rising changes both assets' real returns by the same amount.

The distinction between real rates of return and dollar rates of return illustrates an important concept in studying how savers evaluate different assets: The returns on two assets cannot be compared unless they are measured in the *same* units. For example, it makes no sense to compare directly the real return on the bottle of wine (15 percent in our example) with the dollar return on the bond (20 percent) or to compare the dollar return on old paintings with the DM return on gold. Only after the returns are expressed in terms of a common unit of measure—for example, all in terms of dollars—can we tell which asset offers the highest expected real rate of return.

RISK AND LIQUIDITY

All else equal, individuals prefer to hold those assets offering the highest expected real rate of return. Our later discussions of particular assets will show, however, that "all else" often is not equal. Some assets may be valued by savers for attributes other than the expected real rate of return they offer. Savers care about two main characteristics of an asset other than its return: its **risk,** the variability it contributes to savers' wealth, and its **liquidity,** the ease with which the asset can be sold or exchanged for goods.

   1. *Risk.* An asset's real return is usually unpredictable and may turn out to be quite different from what savers expect when they purchase the asset. In our last example, savers found the expected real rate of return on an investment in bonds (10 percent) by subtracting from the expected rate of increase in the investment's dollar value (20 percent) the expected rate of increase in dollar prices (10 percent). But if expectations are wrong and the bonds' dollar value stays constant instead of rising by 20 percent, the saver ends up with a real return of *negative* 10 percent (= 0 percent − 10 percent). Savers dislike uncertainty and are reluctant to hold assets that make their wealth highly variable. An asset with a high expected rate of return may appear undesirable to savers if its realized rate of return fluctuates widely.

   2. *Liquidity.* Assets also differ according to the cost and speed at which savers can dispose of them. A house, for example, is not very liquid because its sale usually requires time and the services of brokers, inspectors, and lawyers. In contrast, cash is the most liquid of assets: It is always acceptable at face value as payment for goods or other assets. Savers prefer to hold some liquid assets as a precaution against unexpected expenses that might force them to sell less liquid assets at a loss. They will therefore consider an asset's liquidity as well as its expected return and risk in deciding how much of it to hold.

INTEREST RATES

As in other asset markets, participants in the foreign exchange market base their demands for deposits of different currencies on a comparison of these assets' expected rates of return. To compare returns on different deposits, market participants need two pieces of information. First, they need to know how the money values of the deposits will change. Second, they need to know how exchange rates will change so that they can translate rates of return measured in different currencies into comparable terms.

The first piece of information needed to compute the rate of return on a deposit of a particular currency is the currency's **interest rate,** the amount of that currency an individual can earn by lending a unit of the currency for a year. At a dollar interest rate of 0.10 (quoted as 10 percent per year), the lender of $1 receives $1.10 at the end of the year, $1 of which is principal and 10 cents of which is interest. Looked at from the other side of the transaction, the interest rate on dollars is also the amount that must be paid to borrow $1 for a year. When you buy a U.S. Treasury bill, you earn the interest rate on dollars because you are lending dollars to the U.S. government.

Interest rates play an important role in the foreign exchange market because the large deposits traded there pay interest, each at a rate reflecting its currency of denomination. For example, when the interest rate on dollars is 10 percent per year, a $100,000 deposit is worth $110,000 after a year; when the interest rate on DM is 5 percent per year, a DM 100,000 deposit is worth DM 105,000 after a year. Deposits pay interest because they are really loans from the depositor to the bank. When a corporation or a financial institution deposits a currency in a bank, it is lending that currency to the bank rather than using it for some current expenditure. In other words, the depositor is acquiring an asset denominated in the currency it deposits.

The dollar interest rate is simply the dollar rate of return on dollar deposits. You "buy" the deposit by lending a bank $100,000, and when you are paid back with 10 percent interest at the end of the year your asset is worth $110,000. This gives a rate of return of $(110,000 - 100,000)/100,000 = 0.10$, or 10 percent per year. Similarly, a foreign currency's interest rate measures the foreign currency return on deposits of that currency. Figure 13-2 shows the behavior of monthly interest rates on dollars and DM since mid-1973. These interest rates are not measured in comparable terms, so there is no reason for them to be close to each other or to move in similar ways over time.[5]

EXCHANGE RATES AND ASSET RETURNS

The interest rates offered by a dollar and a DM deposit tell us how their dollar and DM values will change over a year. The other piece of information we need to compare the rates of return offered by dollar and DM deposits is the expected change in the dollar/DM exchange rate over the year. To see which deposits, DM or dollar, offers a higher expected rate of return, you must ask the question: If I use dollars to buy a DM deposit, how many dollars will I get back after a year? When you answer this question, you are calculating the *dollar* rate of return on a DM deposit because you are comparing its *dollar* price today with its *dollar* value a year from today.

To see how to approach this type of calculation, let's look at the following situation: Suppose that today's exchange rate (quoted in American terms) is $0.700 per DM, but that you expect the rate to be $0.760 per DM in a year (perhaps because you expect unfavor-

---

[5]Chapter 7 discussed *real* interest rates, which are simply real rates of return on loans, that is, interest rates expressed in terms of a consumption basket. Interest rates expressed in terms of currencies are called *nominal* interest rates. The connection between real and nominal interest rates is discussed in detail in Chapter 15.

FIGURE 13-2

Interest Rates on Dollar and Deutschemark Deposits, 1973–1995

Interest rates (percent per year)

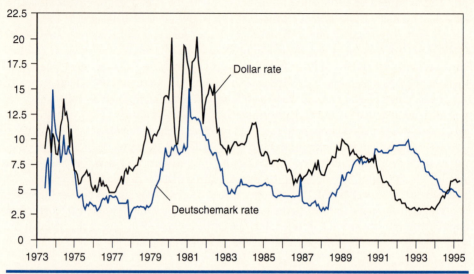

Since dollar and DM interest rates are not measured in comparable terms, they can move quite differently over time.

Source: Morgan Guaranty Trust Company of New York, *World Financial Markets*. Rates shown are one-month Euro-deposit rates, at end of month.

able developments in the U.S. economy). Suppose also that the dollar interest rate is 10 percent per year while the DM interest rate is 5 percent per year. This means a deposit of $1.00 pays $1.10 after a year while a deposit of DM 1 pays DM 1.05 after a year. Which of these deposits offers the higher return?

The answer can be found in five steps.

Step 1.   Use today's dollar/DM exchange rate to figure out the dollar price of a DM deposit of, say, DM 1. If the exchange rate today is $0.700 per DM, the dollar price of a DM 1 deposit is just $0.700.

Step 2.   Use the DM interest rate to find the amount of DM you will have a year from now if you purchase a DM 1 deposit today. You know that the interest rate on DM deposits is 5 percent per year. So at the end of a year, your DM 1 deposit will be worth DM 1.05.

Step 3.   Use the exchange rate you expect to prevail a year from today to calculate the expected dollar value of the DM amount determined in Step 2. Since you expect the dollar to depreciate against the DM over the coming year so that the exchange rate 12 months from today is $0.760 per DM, then you expect the dollar value of your DM deposit after a year to be $0.760 per DM × DM 1.05 = $0.798.

Step 4.   Now that you know the dollar price of a DM 1 deposit today ($0.700) and can forecast its value in a year ($0.798), you can calculate the expected *dollar* rate of return on a DM deposit as (0.798 − 0.700)/0.700 = 0.14, or 14 percent per year.

Step 5.   Since the dollar rate of return on dollar deposits (the dollar interest rate) is only 10 percent per year, you expect to do better by holding your wealth in the form of DM deposits. Despite the fact that the dollar interest rate exceeds the DM interest rate by 5 percent per year, the DM's expected appreciation against the dollar gives DM holders a prospective capital gain that is large enough to make DM deposits the higher-yield asset.

A SIMPLE RULE

There is a simple rule that shortens this calculation. First, define the **rate of depreciation** of the dollar against the DM as the percentage increase in the dollar/DM exchange rate over a year. In the last example, the dollar's expected depreciation rate is $(0.760 - 0.700)/0.700 = 0.086$, or roughly 9 percent per year. Once you have calculated the rate of depreciation of the dollar against the DM, our rule is this: *The dollar rate of return on DM deposits is approximately the DM interest rate plus the rate of depreciation of the dollar against the DM.* In other words, to translate the DM return on DM deposits into dollar terms, you need to add the rate at which the DM's dollar price rises over a year to the DM interest rate.

In our example, the sum of the DM interest rate (5 percent) and the expected depreciation rate of the dollar (roughly 9 percent) is about 14 percent, which is what we found to be the expected dollar return on DM deposits in our first calculation.

We summarize our discussion by introducing some notation:

R_{DM} = today's interest rate on one-year DM deposits,
$E_{\$/DM}$ = today's dollar/DM exchange rate (number of dollars per DM),
$E_{\$/DM}^e$ = dollar/DM exchange rate (number of dollars per DM) expected to prevail a year from today.

(The superscript ^{e} attached to this last exchange rate indicates that it is a forecast of the future exchange rate based on what people know today.)

Using these symbols, we write the expected rate of return on a DM deposit, measured in terms of dollars, as the sum of (1) the DM interest rate and (2) the expected rate of dollar depreciation against the DM,

$$R_{DM} + (E_{\$/DM}^e - E_{\$/DM})/E_{\$/DM}.$$

This expected return is what must be compared with the interest rate on one-year dollar deposits, $R_\$$, in deciding whether dollar or DM deposits offer the higher expected rate of return.[6] The expected rate of return difference between dollar and DM deposits is therefore equal to $R_\$$ less the above expression,

---

[6]If you compute the expected dollar return on DM deposits using the exact five-step method we described before introducing the simple rule, you'll find that it actually equals

$$(1 + R_{DM})(E_{\$/DM}^e/E_{\$/DM}) - 1.$$

This exact formula can be rewritten, however, as

$$R_{DM} + (E_{\$/DM}^e - E_{\$/DM})/E_{\$/DM} + R_{DM} \times (E_{\$/DM}^e - E_{\$/DM})/E_{\$/DM}.$$

The expression above is very close to the formula derived from the simple rule when, as is usually the case, the product $R_{DM} \times (E_{\$/DM}^e - E_{\$/DM})/E_{\$/DM}$ is a small number.

TABLE 13-3

Comparing Dollar Rates of Return on Dollar and DM Deposits

Case	Dollar interest rate $R_\$$	DM interest rate R_{DM}	Expected rate of dollar depreciation against DM $\dfrac{E^e_{\$/DM} - E_{\$/DM}}{E_{\$/DM}}$	Rate of return difference between dollar and DM deposits $R_\$ - R_{DM} - \dfrac{(E^e_{\$/DM} - E_{\$/DM})}{E_{\$/DM}}$
1	0.10	0.06	0.00	0.04
2	0.10	0.06	0.04	0.00
3	0.10	0.06	0.08	−0.04
4	0.10	0.12	−0.04	0.02

$$R_\$ - [R_{DM} + (E^e_{\$/DM} - E_{\$/DM})/E_{\$/DM}]$$
$$= R_\$ - R_{DM} - (E^e_{\$/DM} - E_{\$/DM})/E_{\$/DM}. \qquad (13\text{-}1)$$

When the difference above is positive, dollar deposits yield the higher expected rate of return; when it is negative, DM deposits yield the higher expected rate of return.

Table 13-3 carries out some illustrative comparisons. In case 1, the interest difference in favor of dollar deposits is 4 percent per year ($R_\$ - R_{DM} = 0.10 - 0.06 = 0.04$), and no change in the exchange rate is expected [$(E^e_{\$/DM} - E_{\$/DM})/E_{\$/DM} = 0.00$]. This means that the expected annual real rate of return on dollar deposits is 4 percent higher than that on DM, so that, other things equal, you would prefer to hold your wealth as dollar rather than DM deposits.

In case 2 the interest difference is the same (4 percent), but it is just offset by an expected depreciation rate of the dollar of 4 percent. The two assets therefore have the same expected rate of return.

Case 3 is similar to the one discussed earlier: A 4 percent interest difference in favor of dollar deposits is more than offset by an 8 percent expected depreciation of the dollar, so DM deposits are preferred by market participants.

In case 4, there is a 2 percent interest difference in favor of DM deposits, but the dollar is expected to *appreciate* against the DM by 4 percent over the year. The expected rate of return on dollar deposits is therefore 2 percent per year higher than that on DM.

So far we have been translating all returns into dollar terms. But the rate of return differentials we calculated would have been the same had we chosen to express returns in terms of DM or in terms of some third currency. Suppose, for example, we wanted to measure the return on dollar deposits in terms of DM. Following our simple rule, we would add to the dollar interest rate $R_\$$ the expected rate of depreciation of the DM against the dollar. But the expected rate of depreciation of the DM against the dollar is approximately the expected **rate of appreciation** of the dollar against the DM, that is, the expected rate of depreciation of the dollar against the DM with a minus sign in front of it. This means that in terms of DM, the return on a dollar deposit is

$$R_\$ - (E^e_{\$/DM} - E_{\$/DM})/E_{\$/DM}.$$

The difference between the expression above and R_{DM} is identical to equation (13-1). Thus, it makes no difference to our comparison whether we measure returns in terms of dollars or DM, as long as we measure in terms of a single currency.

RETURN, RISK, AND LIQUIDITY IN THE FOREIGN EXCHANGE MARKET

We observed earlier that a saver deciding which assets to hold may care about assets' riskiness and liquidity in addition to their expected real rates of return. Similarly, the demand for foreign currency assets depends not only on returns but on risk and liquidity. Even if the expected dollar return on DM deposits is higher than that on dollar deposits, for example, people may be reluctant to hold DM deposits if the payoff to holding them varies erratically.

There is no consensus among economists about the importance of risk in the foreign exchange market. Even the definition of "foreign exchange risk" is a topic of debate. For now we will avoid the complex questions involved by assuming that the real returns on all deposits have equal riskiness, regardless of the currency of denomination. In other words, we are assuming that risk differences do not influence the demand for foreign currency assets. We discuss the role of foreign exchange risk in greater detail, however, in Chapters 17 and 21.[7]

Some market participants may be influenced by liquidity factors in deciding which currencies to hold. Most of these participants are firms and individuals involved in international trade. An American importer of French goods, for example, may find it convenient to hold French francs for routine payments even if the expected rate of return on francs is lower than that on dollars. Because payments connected with international trade make up a very small fraction of total foreign exchange transactions, we ignore the liquidity motive for holding foreign currencies.

We are therefore assuming for now that participants in the foreign exchange market base their demands for foreign currency assets exclusively on a comparison of those assets' expected rates of return. The main reason for making this assumption is that it simplifies our analysis of how exchange rates are determined in the foreign exchange market. In addition, the risk and liquidity motives for holding foreign currencies appear to be of secondary importance for many of the international macroeconomic issues discussed in the next few chapters.

EQUILIBRIUM IN THE FOREIGN EXCHANGE MARKET

We now use what we have learned about the demand for foreign currency assets to describe how exchange rates are determined. We will show that the exchange rate at which the market settles is the one that makes market participants content to hold existing supplies of de-

---

[7]In discussing spot and forward foreign exchange transactions, some textbooks make a distinction between foreign exchange "speculators"—market participants who allegedly care only about expected returns—and "hedgers"—market participants whose concern is to avoid risk. We depart from this textbook tradition because it can mislead the unwary: While the speculative and hedging motives are both potentially important in exchange rate determination, the same person can be both a speculator and a hedger if she cares about both return and risk. Our assumption that risk is unimportant in determining the demand for foreign currency assets means, in terms of the traditional language, that the speculative motive for holding foreign currencies is far more important than the hedging motive.

posits of all currencies. When market participants willingly hold the existing supplies of deposits of all currencies, we say that the foreign exchange market is in equilibrium.

The description of exchange rate determination given in this section is only a first step: A full explanation of the exchange rate's current level can be given only after we examine how participants in the foreign exchange market form their expectations about exchange rates they expect to prevail in the future. The next two chapters look at the factors that influence expectations of future exchange rates. For now, however, we will take expected future exchange rates as given.

INTEREST PARITY: THE BASIC EQUILIBRIUM CONDITION

The foreign exchange market is in equilibrium when deposits of all currencies offer the same expected rate of return. The condition that the expected returns on deposits of any two currencies are equal when measured in the same currency is called the **interest parity condition.** It implies that potential holders of foreign currency deposits view them all as equally desirable assets.

Let's see why the foreign exchange market is in equilibrium only when the interest parity condition holds. Suppose the dollar interest rate is 10 percent and the DM interest rate is 6 percent, but that the dollar is expected to depreciate against the DM at an 8 percent rate over a year. (This is case 3 in Table 13-3.) In the circumstances described, the rate of return on DM deposits would be 4 percent per year higher than that on dollar deposits. We assumed at the end of the last section that individuals always prefer to hold deposits of currencies offering the highest expected return. This means that if the expected return on DM deposits is 4 percent greater than that on dollar deposits, no one will be willing to continue holding dollar deposits, and holders of dollar deposits will be trying to sell them for DM deposits. There will therefore be an excess supply of dollar deposits and an excess demand for DM deposits in the foreign exchange market.

As a contrasting example, suppose that dollar deposits again offer a 10 percent interest rate but DM deposits offer a 12 percent rate and the dollar is expected to *appreciate* against the DM by 4 percent over the coming year. (This is case 4 in Table 13-3.) Now the return on dollar deposits is 2 percent higher. In this case no one would demand DM deposits, so they would be in excess supply and dollar deposits would be in excess demand.

When, however, the dollar interest rate is 10 percent, the DM interest rate is 6 percent, and the dollar's expected depreciation rate against the DM is 4 percent, dollar and DM deposits offer the same rate of return and participants in the foreign exchange market are willing to hold either. (This is case 2 in Table 13-3.)

Only when all expected rates of return are equal—that is, when the interest parity condition holds—is there no excess supply of some type of deposit and no excess demand for another. The foreign exchange market is in equilibrium when no type of deposit is in excess demand or excess supply. We can therefore say that the foreign exchange market is in equilibrium when the interest parity condition holds.

To represent interest parity between dollar and DM deposits symbolically, we use expression (13-1), which shows the difference between the two assets' expected rates of return measured in dollars. The expected rates of return are equal when

$$R_\$ = R_{DM} + (E^e_{\$/DM} - E_{\$/DM})/E_{\$/DM}. \tag{13-2}$$

You probably suspect that when dollar deposits offer a higher return than DM deposits, the dollar will appreciate against the DM as investors all try to shift their funds into dollars. Conversely, the dollar should depreciate against the DM when it is DM deposits that initially offer the higher return. This intuition is exactly correct. To understand the mechanism at work, however, we must take a careful look at how exchange rate changes like these help to maintain equilibrium in the foreign exchange market.

HOW CHANGES IN THE CURRENT EXCHANGE RATE AFFECT EXPECTED RETURNS

As a first step in understanding how the foreign exchange market finds its equilibrium, we examine how changes in today's exchange rate affect the expected return on a foreign currency deposit when interest rates and expectations about the future exchange rate do not change. Our analysis will show that, other things equal, depreciation of a country's currency today *lowers* the expected domestic currency return on foreign currency deposits. Conversely, appreciation of the domestic currency today, all else equal, *raises* the domestic currency return expected of foreign currency deposits.

It is easiest to see why these relationships hold by looking at an example: How does a change in today's dollar/DM exchange rate, all else held constant, change the expected return, measured in terms of dollars, on DM deposits? Suppose that today's dollar/DM rate is $0.712 per DM and the exchange rate you expect for this day next year is $0.747 per DM. Then the expected rate of dollar depreciation against the DM is (0.747 − 0.712)/0.712 = 0.05, or 5 percent per year. This means that when you buy a DM deposit, you not only earn the interest R_{DM} but also get a 5 percent "bonus" in terms of dollars. Now suppose that today's exchange rate suddenly jumps up to $0.722 per DM (a depreciation of the dollar and an appreciation of the DM) but the expected future rate is *still* $0.747 per DM. What has happened to the "bonus" you expected to get from the DM's increase in value in terms of dollars? The expected rate of dollar depreciation is now only (0.747 − 0.722)/0.722 = 0.035, or 3.5 percent instead of 5 percent. Since R_{DM} has not changed, the dollar return on DM deposits, which is the sum of R_{DM} and the expected rate of dollar depreciation, has *fallen* by 1.5 percent per year (5 percent − 3.5 percent).

In Table 13-4 we work out the dollar return on DM deposits for various levels of today's dollar/DM exchange rate $E_{S/DM}$, always assuming the expected *future* exchange rate remains fixed at $0.747 per DM and the DM interest rate is 5 percent per year. As you can see, a rise in today's dollar/DM exchange rate (a depreciation of the dollar against the DM) always *lowers* the expected dollar return on DM deposits (as in our example), while a fall in today's dollar/DM rate (an appreciation of the dollar against the DM) always *raises* this return.

It may run counter to your intuition that a depreciation of the dollar against the DM makes DM deposits less attractive relative to dollar deposits (by lowering the expected dollar return on DM deposits) while an appreciation of the dollar makes DM deposits more attractive. This result will seem less surprising if you remember we have assumed that the expected future dollar/DM rate and interest rates do not change. A dollar depreciation today, for example, means the dollar now needs to depreciate by a *smaller* amount to reach any given expected future level. If the expected future dollar/DM exchange rate does not change when the dollar depreciates today, the dollar's expected future depreciation against the DM therefore falls, or, alternatively, the dollar's expected future appreciation rises. Since interest rates also are unchanged, today's dollar depreciation thus makes DM deposits less attractive compared with dollar deposits.

Put another way, a current dollar depreciation that affects neither exchange rate expectations nor interest rates leaves the expected future dollar payoff of a DM deposit the

TABLE 13-4

Today's Dollar/DM Exchange Rate and the Expected Dollar Return on DM Deposits When $E^e_{\$/DM} = \$0.747$ per DM

Today's dollar/DM exchange rate $E_{\$/DM}$	Interest rate on DM deposits R_{DM}	Expected dollar depreciation rate against DM $\dfrac{0.747 - E_{\$/DM}}{E_{\$/DM}}$	Expected dollar return on DM deposits $R_{DM} + \dfrac{0.747 - E_{\$/DM}}{E_{\$/DM}}$
0.771	0.05	−0.03	0.02
0.747	0.05	0.00	0.05
0.732	0.05	0.02	0.07
0.722	0.05	0.035	0.085
0.712	0.05	0.05	0.10

same but raises the deposit's current dollar cost. This change naturally makes DM deposits less attractive relative to dollars.

It may also run counter to your intuition that *today's* exchange rate can change while the exchange rate expected for the *future* does not. We will indeed study cases later in this book when both of these rates do change at once. We nonetheless hold the expected future exchange rate constant in the present discussion because that is the clearest way to illustrate the effect of today's exchange rate on expected returns. If it helps, you can imagine we are looking at the impact of a *temporary* change so brief that it has no effect on the exchange rate expected for next year.

Figure 13-3 shows the calculations in Table 13-4 in a graphic form that will be helpful in our analysis of exchange rate determination. The vertical axis in the figure measures today's dollar/DM exchange rate and the horizontal axis measures the expected dollar return on DM deposits. For *fixed* values of the expected future dollar/DM exchange rate and the DM interest rate, the relation between today's dollar/DM exchange rate and the expected dollar return on DM deposits defines a downward-sloping schedule.

THE EQUILIBRIUM EXCHANGE RATE

Now that we understand why the interest parity condition must hold if the foreign exchange market is in equilibrium and how today's exchange rate affects the expected return on foreign currency deposits, we can see how equilibrium exchange rates are determined. Our main conclusion will be that exchange rates always adjust to maintain interest parity. We continue to assume that the dollar interest rate $R_\$$, the DM interest rate R_{DM}, and the expected future dollar/DM exchange rate $E^e_{\$/DM}$, are all *given*.

Figure 13-4 illustrates how the equilibrium dollar/DM exchange rate is determined under this assumption. The vertical schedule in the graph indicates the given level of $R_\$$, the return on dollar deposits measured in terms of dollars. The downward-sloping schedule shows how the expected return on DM deposits measured in terms of dollars depends on the current dollar/DM exchange rate. This second schedule is derived in the same way as the one shown in Figure 13-3.

FIGURE 13-3

The Relation Between the Current Dollar/DM Exchange Rate and the Expected Dollar Return on DM Deposits

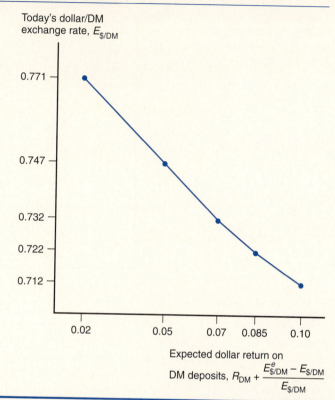

Given $E^e_{\$/DM} = 0.747$ and $R_{DM} = 0.05$, an appreciation of the dollar against the DM raises the expected return on DM deposits, measured in terms of dollars.

Today's dollar/DM exchange rate, $E_{\$/DM}$

Expected dollar return on DM deposits, $R_{DM} + \dfrac{E^e_{\$/DM} - E_{\$/DM}}{E_{\$/DM}}$

The equilibrium dollar/DM rate is the one indicated by the intersection of the two schedules at point 1, $E^1_{\$/DM}$. At this exchange rate, the returns on dollar and DM deposits are equal, so that the interest parity condition (13-2),

$$R_\$ = R_{DM} + (E^e_{\$/DM} - E^1_{\$/DM})/E^1_{\$/DM},$$

is satisfied.

Let's see why the exchange rate will tend to settle at point 1 in Figure 13-4 if it is initially at a point such as 2 or 3. Suppose first that we are at point 2, with the exchange rate equal to $E^2_{\$/DM}$. The downward-sloping schedule measuring the expected dollar return on DM deposits tell us that at the exchange rate $E^2_{\$/DM}$, the rate of return on DM deposits is less than the rate of return on dollar deposits, $R_\$$. In this situation anyone holding DM deposits wishes to sell them for the more lucrative dollar deposits: The foreign exchange market is out of equilibrium because participants are *unwilling* to hold DM deposits.

How does the exchange rate adjust? The unhappy owners of DM deposits attempt to sell them for dollar deposits, but because the return on dollar deposits is higher than that on DM deposits at the exchange rate $E^2_{\$/DM}$, no holder of a dollar deposit is willing to sell it for DM at that rate. As DM holders try to entice dollar holders to trade by offering them a bet-

FIGURE 13-4

Determination of the Equilibrium Dollar/DM Exchange Rate

Equilibrium in the foreign exchange market is at point 1, where the expected dollar returns on dollar and DM deposits are equal.

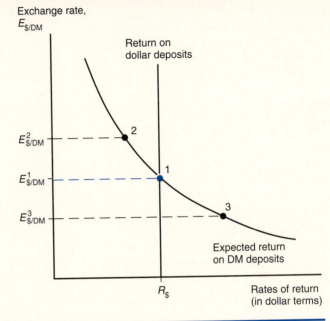

ter price for dollars, the dollar/DM exchange rate falls toward $E^1_{\$/DM}$; that is, DM become cheaper in terms of dollars. Once the exchange rate reaches $E^1_{\$/DM}$, DM and dollar deposits offer equal returns and holders of DM deposits no longer have an incentive to try to sell them for dollars. The foreign exchange market is therefore in equilibrium. In falling from $E^2_{\$/DM}$ to $E^1_{\$/DM}$, the exchange rate equalizes the expected returns on the types of deposit by increasing the rate at which the dollar is expected to depreciate in the future, thereby making DM deposits more attractive.

The same process works in reverse if we are initially at point 3 with an exchange rate of $E^3_{\$/DM}$. At point 3, the return on DM deposits exceeds that on dollar deposits, so there is now an excess supply of the latter. As unwilling holders of dollar deposits bid for the more attractive DM deposits, the price of DM in terms of dollars tend to rise; that is, the dollar tends to depreciate against the DM. When the exchange rate has moved to $E^1_{\$/DM}$, rates of return are equalized across currencies and the market is in equilibrium. The depreciation of the dollar from $E^3_{\$/DM}$ to $E^1_{\$/DM}$ makes DM deposits less attractive relative to dollar deposits by reducing the rate at which the dollar is expected to depreciate in the future.[8]

---

[8]We could have developed our diagram from the perspective of Germany, with the DM/dollar exchange rate $E_{DM/\$}$ ($= 1/E_{\$/DM}$) on the vertical axis, a schedule vertical at R_{DM} to indicate the DM return on DM deposits, and a downward-sloping schedule showing how the DM return on dollar deposits varies with $E_{DM/\$}$. An exercise at the end of the chapter asks you to show that this alternative way of looking at equilibrium in the foreign exchange market gives the same answers as the method used in the text.

INTEREST RATES, EXPECTATIONS, AND EQUILIBRIUM

Having seen how exchange rates are determined by interest parity, we now take a look at how current exchange rates are affected by changes in interest rates and in expectations about the future, the two factors we held constant in our previous discussions. We will see that the exchange rate (which is the relative price of two assets) responds to factors that alter the expected rates of return on those two assets.

THE EFFECT OF CHANGING INTEREST RATES ON THE CURRENT EXCHANGE RATE

We often read in the newspaper that the dollar is strong because U.S. interest rates are high or that it is falling because U.S. interest rates are falling. Can these statements be explained using our analysis of the foreign exchange market?

To answer this question we again turn to a diagram. Figure 13-5 shows a rise in the interest rate on dollars, from $R_\$^1$ to $R_\$^2$, as a rightward shift of the vertical dollar deposits schedule. At the initial exchange rate $E_{\$/DM}^1$, the expected return on dollar deposits is now higher than that on DM deposits by an amount equal to the distance between points 1 and 1'. As we have seen, this difference causes the dollar to appreciate to $E_{\$/DM}^2$ (point 2). Because there has been no change in the DM interest rate or in the expected future exchange

---

FIGURE 13-5

Effect of a Rise in the Dollar Interest Rate

A rise in the interest rate offered by dollar deposits from $R_\$^1$ to $R_\$^2$ causes the dollar to appreciate from $E_{\$/DM}^1$ (point 1) to $E_{\$/DM}^2$ (point 2).

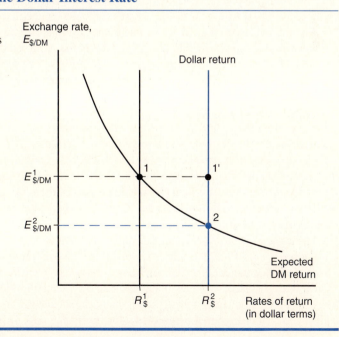

FIGURE 13-6

Effect of a Rise in the DM Interest Rate

A rise in the interest rate paid by DM deposits causes the dollar to depreciate from $E^1_{\$/DM}$ (point 1) to $E^2_{\$/DM}$ (point 2). (This figure also describes the effect of a rise in the expected future \$/DM exchange rate.)

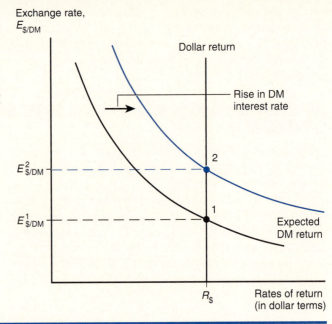

rate, the dollar's appreciation today raises the expected dollar return on DM deposits by increasing the rate at which the dollar is expected to depreciate in the future.

Figure 13-6 shows the effect of a rise in the DM interest rate R_{DM}. This change causes the downward-sloping schedule (which measures the expected dollar return on DM deposits) to shift rightward. (To see why, ask yourself how a rise in the DM interest rate alters the dollar return on DM deposits, given the current exchange rate and the expected future rate.)

At the initial exchange rate $E^1_{\$/DM}$ the expected depreciation rate of the dollar is the same as before the rise in R_{DM}, so the expected return on DM deposits now exceeds that on dollar deposits. The dollar/DM exchange rate rises (from $E^1_{\$/DM}$ to $E^2_{\$/DM}$) to eliminate the excess supply of dollar assets at point 1. As before, the dollar's depreciation against the DM eliminates the excess supply of dollar assets by lowering the expected dollar rate of return on DM deposits. A rise in German interest rates therefore leads to a depreciation of the dollar against the DM or, looked at from the German perspective, an appreciation of the DM against the dollar.

Our discussion shows that, all else equal, *an increase in the interest paid on deposits of a currency causes that currency to appreciate against foreign currencies.*

Before we conclude that the newspaper account of the effect of interest rates on exchange rates is correct, we must remember that our assumption of a *constant* expected future exchange rate often is unrealistic. In many cases a change in interest rates will be accompanied by a change in the expected future exchange rate. This change in the expected

THE PERILS OF FORECASTING EXCHANGE RATES

If exchange rates are asset prices that respond immediately to changes in expectations and interest rates, they should have properties similar to those of other asset prices, for example, stock prices. Like stock prices, exchange rates should respond strongly to "news," that is, unexpected economic and political events; and, like stock prices, they therefore should be very hard to forecast.

Despite the notorious difficulty of forecasting stock prices, there is no shortage of newsletters and television programs devoted to stock market prediction. Similarly, numerous firms sell exchange rate forecasts to individual investors, international corporations, and others with financial interests in the foreign exchange market. In a well-known study, Richard M. Levich of New York University surveyed the track record of a dozen exchange rate forecasting companies through 1982.*

The results were depressing for would-be exchange rate oracles but encouraging for the asset approach to exchange rates. Levich

found little evidence over his sample period that professional forecasters do systematically better than an individual who, for example, uses the three-month forward exchange rate as a forecast of the spot rate that will materialize in three months.† This finding does not mean that forward rates are accurate predictors; on the contrary, the evidence suggests that forward rates usually contain little information useful in predicting future spot rates (as we shall see in Chapter 21). What Levich's results do show is that inherently unpredictable "news" plays such a dominant role in determining exchange rates that exchange rate movements, like movements in stock prices, are almost completely impossible to forecast.

*See "Evaluating the Performance of the Forecasters," in Donald R. Lessard, ed., *International Financial Management: Theory and Application*, 2nd ed. (New York: John Wiley and Sons, 1985), pp. 218–233.

†This chapter's appendix suggests one reason for thinking that forward exchange rates might be closely related to expected future spot rates.

future exchange rate will depend, in turn, on the economic causes of the interest rate change. We compare different possible relationships between interest rates and expected future exchange rates in Chapter 15. Keep in mind for now that in the real world, we cannot predict how a given interest rate change will alter exchange rates unless we know *why* the interest rate is changing.

THE EFFECT OF CHANGING EXPECTATIONS ON THE CURRENT EXCHANGE RATE

Figure 13-6 may also be used to study the effect on today's exchange rate of a rise in the expected future dollar/DM exchange rate, $E^e_{\$/DM}$.

Given today's exchange rate, a rise in the expected future price of DM in terms of dollars raises the dollar's expected depreciation rate. For example, if today's exchange rate is \$0.712 per DM and the rate expected to prevail in a year is \$0.747 per DM, the expected depreciation rate of the dollar against the DM is $(0.747 - 0.712)/0.712 = 0.05$; if the expected future exchange rate now rises to \$0.755 per DM, the expected depreciation rate also rises, to $(0.755 - 0.712)/0.712 = 0.06$.

Because a rise in the expected depreciation rate of the dollar raises the expected dollar return on DM deposits, the downward-sloping schedule shifts to the right, as in Figure 13-6. At the initial exchange rate $E^1_{S/DM}$ there is now an excess supply of dollar deposits: DM deposits offer a higher expected rate of return (measured in dollar terms) than do dollar deposits. The dollar therefore depreciates against the DM until equilibrium is reached at point 2.

We conclude that, all else equal, *a rise in the expected future exchange rate causes a rise in the current exchange rate. Similarly, a fall in the expected future exchange rate causes a fall in the current exchange rate.*

Summary

1. An *exchange rate* is the price of one country's currency in terms of another country's currency. Exchange rates play a role in spending decisions because they enable us to translate different countries' prices into comparable terms. All else equal, a *depreciation* of a country's currency against foreign currencies (a rise in the home currency prices of foreign currencies) makes its exports cheaper and its imports more expensive. An *appreciation* of its currency (a fall in the home currency prices of foreign currencies) makes its exports more expensive and its imports cheaper.

2. Exchange rates are determined in the *foreign exchange market.* The major participants in that market are commercial banks, international corporations, nonbank financial institutions, and national central banks. Commercial banks play a pivotal role in the market because they facilitate the exchanges of interest-bearing bank deposits that make up the bulk of foreign exchange trading. Even though foreign exchange trading takes place in many financial centers around the world, modern telecommunication technology links those centers together into a single market that is open 24 hours a day. An important category of foreign exchange trading is *forward* trading, in which parties agree to exchange currencies on some future date at a prenegotiated exchange rate. In contrast, *spot* trades are (for practical purposes) settled immediately.

3. Because the exchange rate is the relative price of two assets, it is most appropriately thought of as being an asset price itself. The basic principle of asset pricing is that an asset's current value depends on its expected future purchasing power. In evaluating an asset, savers look at the expected *rate of return* it offers, that is, the rate at which the value of an investment in the asset is expected to rise over time. It is possible to measure an asset's expected rate of return in different ways, each depending on the units in which the asset's value is measured. Savers care about an asset's expected *real rate of return,* the rate at which its value expressed in terms of a representative output basket is expected to rise.

4. When relative asset returns are relevant, as in the foreign exchange market, it is appropriate to compare expected changes in assets' currency values, provided those values are expressed in the same currency. If *risk* and *liquidity* factors do not strongly influence the demands for foreign currency assets, participants in the

foreign exchange market always prefer to hold those assets yielding the highest expected rate of return.

5. The returns on deposits traded in the foreign exchange market depend on *interest rates* and expected exchange rate changes. To compare the expected rates of return offered by dollar and DM deposits, for example, the return on DM deposits must be expressed in dollar terms by adding to the DM interest rate the expected *rate of depreciation* of the dollar against the DM (or *rate of appreciation* of the DM against the dollar) over the deposit's holding period.

6. Equilibrium in the foreign exchange market requires *interest parity;* that is, deposits of all currencies must offer the same expected rate of return when returns are measured in comparable terms.

7. For given interest rates and a given expectation of the future exchange rate, the interest parity condition tells us the current equilibrium exchange rate. When the expected dollar return on DM deposits exceeds that on dollar deposits, for example, the dollar immediately depreciates against the DM. Other things equal, a dollar depreciation today reduces the expected dollar return on DM deposits by reducing the depreciation rate of the dollar against the DM expected for the future. Similarly, when the expected return on DM deposits is below that on dollar deposits, the dollar must immediately appreciate against the DM. Other things equal, a current appreciation of the dollar makes DM deposits more attractive by increasing the dollar's expected future depreciation against the German currency.

8. All else equal, a rise in dollar interest rates causes the dollar to appreciate against the DM while a rise in DM interest rates causes the dollar to depreciate against the DM. Today's exchange rate is also altered by changes in its expected future level. If there is a rise in the expected future level of the dollar/DM rate, for example, then at unchanged interest rates today's dollar/DM rate will also rise.

Key Terms

appreciation, p. 333

arbitrage, p. 338

depreciation, p. 333

exchange rate, p. 331

foreign exchange market, p. 335

forward exchange rate, p. 339

interbank trading, p. 335

interest parity condition, p. 350

interest rate, p. 345

liquidity, p. 344

rate of appreciation, p. 348

rate of depreciation, p. 347

rate of return, p. 341

real rate of return, p. 343

risk, p. 344

spot exchange rate, p. 339

vehicle currency, p. 338

Problems

1. In Munich a bratwurst costs 2 DM; a hot dog costs $1 at Boston's Fenway Park. At an exchange rate of $0.5 per DM, what is the price of a bratwurst in terms of hot dogs? All else equal, how does this relative price change if the dollar appreci-

ates to \$0.4 per DM? Compared with the initial situation, has a hot dog become more or less expensive relative to a bratwurst?

2. A U.S. dollar costs 5 French francs, but the same dollar can be purchased for 1.25 Swiss francs. What is the French franc/Swiss franc exchange rate?

3. Calculate the dollar rates of return on the following assets:
   a. A painting whose price rises from \$200,000 to \$250,000 in a year.
   b. A bottle of a rare Burgundy, Domaine de la Romanée-Conti 1978, whose price rises from \$180 to \$216 between 1999 and 2000.
   c. A £10,000 deposit in a London bank in a year when the interest rate on pounds is 10 percent and the \$/£ exchange rate moves from \$1.50 per pound to \$1.38 per pound.

4. What would be the real rates of return on the assets in the preceding question if the price changes described were accompanied by a simultaneous 10 percent increase in all dollar prices?

5. Suppose the dollar interest rate and the pound sterling interest rate are the same, 5 percent per year. What is the relation between the current equilibrium \$/£ exchange rate and its expected future level? Suppose the expected future \$/£ exchange rate, \$1.52 per pound, remains constant as Britain's interest rate rises to 10 percent per year. If the U.S. interest rate also remains constant, what is the new equilibrium \$/£ exchange rate?

6. Traders in asset markets suddenly learn that the interest rate on dollars will decline in the near future. Use the diagrammatic analysis of the chapter to determine the effect on the *current* dollar/DM exchange rate, assuming current interest rates on dollar and DM deposits do not change.

7. We noted that we could have developed our diagrammatic analysis of foreign exchange market equilibrium from the perspective of Germany, with the DM/dollar exchange rate $E_{DM/\$}(= 1/E_{\$/DM})$ on the vertical axis, a schedule vertical at R_{DM} to indicate the DM return on DM deposits, and a downward-sloping schedule showing how the DM return on dollar deposits varies with $E_{DM/\$}$. Derive this alternative picture of equilibrium and use it to examine the effect of changes in interest rates and the expected future exchange rate. Do your answers agree with those we found earlier?

8. The following report appeared in the *New York Times* on August 7, 1989 ("Dollar's Strength a Surprise," p. D1):

> But now the sentiment is that the economy is heading for a "soft landing," with the economy slowing significantly and inflation subsiding, but without a recession.
>
> This outlook is good for the dollar for two reasons. A soft landing is not as disruptive as a recession, so the foreign investments that support the dollar are more likely to continue.
>
> Also, a soft landing would not force the Federal Reserve to push interest rates sharply lower to stimulate growth. Falling interest rates can put downward pressure on the dollar because they make investments in dollar-denominated securities less attractive to foreigners, prompting the selling of dollars. In addition, the optimism sparked by the expectation of a soft landing can even offset some of the pressure on the dollar from lower interest rates.

a. Show how you would interpret the third paragraph of this report using this chapter's model of exchange rate determination.

b. What additional factors in exchange rate determination might help you explain the second paragraph?

9. Suppose the dollar exchange rates of the DM and the pound sterling are equally variable. The DM, however, tends to depreciate unexpectedly against the dollar when the return on the rest of your wealth is unexpectedly high, while the pound tends to appreciate unexpectedly in the same circumstances. As a U.S. resident, which currency, the DM or the pound, would you consider riskier?

10. Does any of the discussion in this chapter lead you to believe that dollar deposits may have liquidity characteristics different from those of other currency deposits? If so, how would the differences affect the interest differential between, say, dollar and French franc deposits? Do you have any guesses about how the liquidity of DM, pound sterling, and yen deposits may be changing over time?

11. In October 1979, the U.S. central bank (the Federal Reserve System) announced it would play a less active role in limiting fluctuations in dollar interest rates. After this new policy was put into effect, the dollar's exchange rates against foreign currencies became more volatile. Does our analysis of the foreign exchange market suggest any connection between these two events?

12. Imagine that everyone in the world pays a tax of τ percent on interest earnings and on any capital gains due to exchange rate changes. How would such a tax alter the analysis of the interest parity condition? How does the answer change if the tax applies to interest earnings but *not* to capital gains, which are untaxed?

13. Suppose the one-year forward $/DM exchange rate is 0.73 per DM and the spot exchange rate is $0.695 per DM. What is the forward premium on DM (the forward discount on dollars)? What is the difference between the interest rate on one-year dollar deposits and that on one-year DM deposits (assuming no political risk)?

Further Reading

J. Orlin Grabbe. *International Financial Markets,* 3rd edition. Englewood Ciffs: Prentice-Hall, 1996. Chapters 4–7 are especially pertinent to topics discussed in this chapter.

Peter B. Kenen. *The Role of the Dollar as an International Currency.* Occasional Paper 13. New York: Group of Thirty, 1983. Evidence on the U.S. dollar's use in international trade and financial transactions.

John Maynard Keynes. *A Tract on Monetary Reform,* Chapter 3. London: MacMillan, 1923. Classic analysis of the forward exchange market and covered interest parity.

Paul R. Krugman. "The International Role of the Dollar: Theory and Prospect," in John F. O. Bilson and Richard C. Marston, eds. *Exchange Rate Theory and Practice.* Chicago: University of Chicago Press, 1984, pp. 261–278. Theoretical and empirical analysis of the dollar's position as an "international money."

Roger M. Kubarych. *Foreign Exchange Markets in the United States,* revised edition. New York: Federal Reserve Bank of New York, 1983. A detailed description of the structure and functions of the foreign exchange market.

Ronald I. McKinnon. *Money in International Exchange: The Convertible Currency System.* New York: Oxford University Press, 1979. Theoretical and institutional analysis of the place of the foreign exchange market in international monetary relations.

Michael Mussa. "Empirical Regularities in the Behavior of Exchange Rates and Theories of the Foreign Exchange Market," in Karl Brunner and Allan H. Meltzer, eds. *Policies for Employment, Prices and Exchange Rates,* Carnegie-Rochester Conference Series on Public Policy 11. Amsterdam: North-Holland, 1979, pp. 9–57. Examines the empirical basis of the asset price approach to exchange rate determination.

Julian Walmsley. *The Foreign Exchange and Money Markets Guide.* New York: John Wiley and Sons, 1992. A basic text on the terminology and institutions of the foreign exchange market.

Appendix to Chapter 13

Forward Exchange Rates and Covered Interest Parity

This appendix explains how forward exchange rates are determined. Under the assumption that the interest parity condition always holds, a forward exchange rate equals the spot exchange rate expected to prevail on the forward contract's value date.

As the first step in the discussion, we point out the close connection among the forward exchange rate between two currencies, their spot exchange rate, and the interest rates on deposits denominated in those currencies. The connection is described by the *covered interest parity* condition, which is similar to the (noncovered) interest parity condition defining foreign exchange market equilibrium but involves the forward exchange rate rather than the expected future spot exchange rate.

To be concrete, we again consider dollar and DM deposits. Suppose you want to buy a DM deposit with dollars but would like to be *certain* about the number of dollars it will be worth at the end of a year. You can avoid exchange rate risk by buying a DM deposit and, at the same time, selling the proceeds of your investment forward. When you buy a DM deposit with dollars and at the same time sell the principal and interest forward for dollars, we say you have "covered" yourself, that is, avoided the possibility of an unexpected depreciation of the DM.

The covered interest parity condition states that the rates of return on dollar deposits and "covered" foreign deposits must be the same. An example will clarify the meaning of the condition and illustrate why it must always hold. Let $F_{\$/DM}$ stand for the one-year forward price of DM in terms of dollars, and suppose $F_{\$/DM} = \$0.742$ per DM. Assume that at the same time, the spot exchange rate $E_{\$/DM} = \$0.700$ per DM, $R_\$ = 0.10$, and $R_{DM} = 0.05$. The (dollar) rate of return on a dollar deposit is clearly 0.10, or 10 percent per year. What is the rate of return on a covered DM deposit?

We answer this question as in the chapter. A DM 1 deposit costs $0.700 today, and it is worth DM 1.05 after a year. If you sell DM 1.05 forward today at the forward exchange rate of $0.742 per DM, the dollar value of your investment at the end of a year is ($0.742 per DM) $\times$ DM 1.05 = $0.779. The rate of return on a covered purchase of a DM deposit is therefore $(0.779 - 0.700)/0.700 = 0.113$. This 11.3 percent per year rate of return exceeds the 10 percent offered by dollar deposits, so covered interest parity does not hold. In this situation, no one would be willing to hold dollar deposits; everyone would prefer covered DM deposits.

More formally, we can express the covered return on a DM deposit as

$$\frac{F_{\$/DM}(1 + R_{DM}) - E_{\$/DM}}{E_{\$/DM}},$$

which is approximately equal to

$$R_{DM} + \frac{F_{\$/DM} - E_{\$/DM}}{E_{\$/DM}}$$

when the product $R_{DM} \times (F_{\$/DM} - E_{\$/DM})/E_{\$/DM}$ is a small number. The covered interest parity condition can therefore be written

$$R_\$ = R_{DM} + (F_{\$/DM} - E_{\$/DM})/E_{\$/DM}.$$

The quantity

$$(F_{\$/DM} - E_{\$/DM})/E_{\$/DM}$$

is called the *forward premium* on DM against dollars. (It is also called the *forward discount* on dollars against DM.) Using this terminology, we can state the covered interest parity condition as follows: *The interest rate on dollar deposits equals the interest rate on DM deposits plus the forward premium on DM against dollars (the forward discount on dollars against DM).*

There is strong empirical evidence that the covered interest parity condition holds for different foreign currency deposits issued within a single financial center. Indeed, currency traders often set the forward exchange rates they quote by looking at current interest rates and spot exchange rates and using the covered interest parity formula.[9] Deviations from covered interest parity can occur, however, if the deposits being compared are located in different countries. These deviations occur when asset holders fear that governments may impose regulations which prevent the free movement of foreign funds across national borders. Our derivation of the covered interest parity condition implicitly assumed there was no political risk of this kind.[10]

By comparing the (noncovered) interest parity condition,

$$R_\$ = R_{DM} + (E^e_{\$/DM} - E_{\$/DM})/E_{\$/DM},$$

with the *covered* interest parity condition, you will find that both conditions can be true at the same time only if the one-year forward $/DM rate quoted today equals the spot exchange rate people expect to materialize a year from today:

$$F_{\$/DM} = E^e_{\$/DM}.$$

This makes intuitive sense. When two parties agree to trade foreign exchange on a date in the future, the exchange rate they agree on is the spot rate they expect to prevail on that

---

[9]Empirical evidence supporting the covered interest parity condition is provided by Frank McCormick in "Covered Interest Arbitrage: Unexploited Profits? Comment," *Journal of Political Economy* 87 (April 1979), pp. 411–417, and by Kevin Clinton in "Transactions Costs and Covered Interest Arbitrage: Theory and Evidence," *Journal of Political Economy* 96 (April 1988), pp. 358–370.

[10]For a more detailed discussion of the role of political risk in the forward exchange market, see Robert Z. Aliber, "The Interest Parity Theorem: A Reinterpretation," *Journal of Political Economy* 81 (November/December 1973), pp. 1451–1459. Of course, actual restrictions on cross-border money movements can also cause covered interest parity deviations.

date. The important difference between covered and noncovered transactions should be kept in mind, however. Covered transactions do not involve exchange rate risk, noncovered transactions do.[11]

The theory of covered interest parity helps explain the close correlation between movements in spot and forward exchange rates shown in Figure 13-1, a correlation typical of all major currencies. The unexpected economic events that affect expected asset returns often have a relatively small effect on international interest rate differences between deposits with short maturities (for example, three months). To maintain covered interest parity, therefore, spot and forward rates for the corresponding maturities must change roughly in proportion to each other.

We conclude this appendix with one further application of the covered interest parity condition. To illustrate the role of forward exchange rates, the chapter used the example of an American importer of Japanese radios anxious about the $/¥ exchange rate he would face in 30 days when the time came to pay his supplier. In the example, the importer solved his problem by selling forward for yen enough dollars to cover the cost of the radios. But he could have solved his problem in a different, more complicated way. He could have (1) borrowed dollars from his bank; (2) sold those dollars immediately for yen at the spot exchange rate and placed the yen in a 30-day yen bank deposit; (3) then, after 30 days, used the proceeds of the maturing yen deposit to pay his Japanese supplier; and (4) used the realized proceeds of his U.S. radio sales, less his profits, to repay his original dollar loan.

Which course of action—the forward purchase of yen or the sequence of four transactions described in the preceding paragraph—is more profitable for the importer? We leave it to you, as an exercise, to show that the two strategies yield the same profit when the covered interest parity condition holds.

---

[11]We indicated in the text that the (noncovered) interest parity condition, while a useful simplification, may not always hold exactly if the riskiness of currencies influences demands in the foreign exchange market. Therefore, the forward rate may differ from the expected future spot rate by a risk factor even if *covered* interest parity holds true. As noted earlier, the role of risk in exchange rate determination is discussed more fully in Chapters 17 and 21.

14 Money, Interest Rates, and Exchange Rates

Chapter 13 showed how the exchange rate between currencies depends on two factors, the interest that can be earned on deposits of those currencies and the expected future exchange rate. To understand fully the determination of exchange rates, however, we have to learn how interest rates themselves are determined and how expectations of future exchange rates are formed. In the next three chapters we examine these topics by building an economic model that links exchange rates, interest rates, and other important macroeconomic variables such as the inflation rate and output.

The first step in building the model is to explain the effects of a country's money supply and of the demand for its money on its interest rate and exchange rate. Because exchange rates are the relative prices of national monies, factors that affect a country's money supply or demand are among the most powerful determinants of its currency's exchange rate against foreign currencies. It is therefore natural to begin a deeper study of exchange rate determination with a discussion of money supply and money demand.

Monetary developments influence the exchange rate *both* by changing interest rates *and* by changing people's expectations about future exchange rates. Expectations about future exchange rates are closely connected with expectations about the future money prices of countries' products; these price movements, in turn, depend on changes in money supply and demand. In examining monetary influences on the exchange rate, we therefore look at how monetary factors influence output prices along with interest rates. Expectations of future exchange rates depend on many factors other than money, however, and these nonmonetary factors are taken up in the next chapter.

Once the theories and determinants of money supply and demand are laid out, we use them to examine how equilibrium interest rates are determined by the equality of money supply and money demand. Then we combine our model of interest rate determination with the interest parity condition to study the effects of monetary shifts on the exchange rate, given the prices of goods and services, the level of output, and market expectations about the future. Finally, we take a first look at the long-term effects of monetary changes on output prices and expected future exchange rates.

Money Defined: A Brief Review

We are so accustomed to using money that we seldom notice the roles it plays in almost all of our everyday transactions. As with many other modern conveniences, we take money for granted until something goes wrong with it! In fact, the easiest way to appreciate the importance of money is to imagine what economic life would be like without it.

In this section we do just that. Our purpose in carrying out this "thought experiment" is to distinguish money from other assets and to describe the characteristics of money that lead people to hold it. These characteristics are central to an analysis of the demand for money.

Money as a Medium of Exchange

The most important function of money is to serve as a *medium of exchange,* a generally accepted means of payment. To see why a medium of exchange is necessary, imagine how time-consuming it would be for people to purchase goods and services in a world where the only type of trade possible was barter trade—the trade of goods or services for other goods or services.

Money eliminates the enormous search costs connected with a barter system because it is universally acceptable. It eliminates these search costs by enabling an individual to sell the goods and services she produces to people other than the producers of the goods and services she wishes to consume. A complex modern economy would cease functioning without some standardized and convenient means of payment.

Money as a Unit of Account

Money's second important role is as a *unit of account,* that is, as a widely recognized measure of value. It is in this role that we encountered money in Chapter 13: Prices of goods, services, and assets are typically expressed in terms of money. Exchange rates allow us to translate different countries' money prices into comparable terms.

The convention of quoting prices in money terms simplifies economic calculations by making it easy to compare the prices of different commodities. The international price comparisons in Chapter 13, which used exchange rates to compare the prices of different countries' outputs, are similar to the calculations you would have to do many times each day if different commodities' prices were not expressed in terms of a standardized unit of account. If the calculations in Chapter 13 gave you a headache, imagine what it would be like to have to calculate the relative prices of each good and service you consume in terms of several other goods and services. This thought experiment should give you a keener appreciation of using money as a unit of account.

MONEY AS A STORE OF VALUE

Because money can be used to transfer purchasing power from the present into the future, it is also an asset, or a *store of value*. This attribute is essential for any medium of exchange because no one would be willing to accept it in payment if its value in terms of goods and services evaporated immediately.

Money's usefulness as a medium of exchange, however, automatically makes it the most *liquid* of all assets. As you will recall from the last chapter, an asset is said to be liquid when it can be transformed into goods and services rapidly and without high transaction costs, such as brokers' fees. Since money is readily acceptable as a means of payment, money sets the standard against which the liquidity of other assets is judged.

WHAT IS MONEY?

Currency and bank deposits on which checks may be written certainly qualify as money. These are widely accepted means of payment that can be transferred between owners at low cost. Households and firms hold currency and checking deposits as a convenient way of financing routine transactions as they arise. Assets such as real estate do not qualify as money because, unlike currency and checking deposits, they lack the essential property of liquidity.

When we speak of the **money supply** in this book, we are referring to the monetary aggregate the Federal Reserve calls M1, that is, the total amount of currency and checking deposits held by households and firms. In the United States at the end of 1994, the total money supply amounted to $1.148 trillion, equal to 17.1 percent of that year's GNP.[1]

The large deposits traded by participants in the foreign exchange market are not considered part of the money supply. These deposits are less liquid than money and are not used to finance routine transactions.

HOW THE MONEY SUPPLY IS DETERMINED

An economy's money supply is controlled by its central bank. The central bank directly regulates the amount of currency in existence and also has indirect control over the amount of checking deposits issued by private banks. The procedures through which the central

---

[1]A broader Federal Reserve measure of money supply, M2, includes time deposits, but these are less liquid than the assets included in M1 because the funds in them typically cannot be withdrawn early without penalty. An even broader measure, known as M3, is also tracked by the Fed. A decision on where to draw the line between money and near-money must be somewhat arbitrary and therefore controversial. For further discussion of this question, see Frederic S. Mishkin, *The Economics of Money, Banking and Financial Markets,* 4th ed., Chapter 3 (New York: HarperCollins Publishers, 1995).

bank controls the money supply are complex, and we assume for now that the central bank simply sets the size of the money supply at the level it desires. We go into the money supply process in more detail, however, in Chapters 17 and 21.

THE DEMAND FOR MONEY BY INDIVIDUALS

Having discussed the functions of money and the definition of the money supply, we now examine the factors that determine the amount of money an individual desires to hold. The determinants of individual money demand can be derived from the theory of asset demand discussed in the last chapter.

We saw in the last chapter that individuals base their demand for an asset on three characteristics:

1. The expected return the asset offers compared with the returns offered by other assets.
2. The riskiness of the asset's expected return.
3. The asset's liquidity.

While liquidity plays no important role in determining the relative demands for assets traded in the foreign exchange market, households and firms hold money *only* because of its liquidity. To understand how the economy's households and firms decide the amount of money they wish to hold, we must look more closely at how the three considerations listed above influence money demand.

EXPECTED RETURN

Currency pays no interest. Checking deposits often do pay some interest, but they offer a rate of return that usually fails to keep pace with the higher return offered by less liquid forms of wealth. When you hold money, you therefore sacrifice the higher interest rate you could earn by holding your wealth in a government bond, a large time deposit, or some other relatively illiquid asset. It is this last rate of interest we have in mind when we refer to "the" interest rate. Since the interest paid on currency is zero while that paid on "checkable" deposits tends to be relatively constant, the difference in rates of return between money in general and less-liquid alternative assets is reflected by the market interest rate: The higher the interest rate, the more you sacrifice by holding wealth in the form of money.[2]

Suppose, for example, that the interest rate you could earn from a U.S. Treasury bill is 10 percent per year. If you use $10,000 of your wealth to buy a Treasury bill, you will be paid $11,000 by Uncle Sam at the end of a year, but if you choose instead to keep the $10,000 as cash in a safe-deposit box, you give up the $1000 interest you could have earned by buying the Treasury bill. You thus sacrifice a 10 percent rate of return by holding your $10,000 as money.

---

[2]Many of the illiquid assets that individuals can choose from do not pay their returns in the form of interest. Stocks, for example, pay returns in the form of dividends and capital gains. The family summer house on Cape Cod pays a return in the form of capital gains and the pleasure of vacations at the beach. The assumption behind our analysis of money demand is that once allowance is made for risk, all assets other than money offer an expected rate of return (measured in terms of money) equal to the interest rate. This assumption allows us to use the interest rate to summarize the return an individual forgoes by holding money rather than an illiquid asset.

The theory of asset demand developed in the last chapter shows how changes in the rate of interest affect the demand for money. The theory states that, other things equal, people prefer assets offering higher expected returns. Because an increase in the interest rate is a rise in the rate of return on less liquid assets relative to the rate of return on money, individuals will want to hold more of their wealth in nonmoney assets that pay the market interest rate and less of their wealth in the form of money if the interest rate rises. We conclude that *all else equal, a rise in the interest rate causes the demand for money to fall.*

We can also describe the influence of the interest rate on money demand in terms of the economic concept of *opportunity cost*—the amount you sacrifice by taking one course of action rather than another. The interest rate measures the opportunity cost of holding money rather than interest-bearing bonds. A rise in the interest rate therefore raises the cost of holding money and causes money demand to fall.

RISK

Risk is not an important factor in money demand. It is risky to hold money because an unexpected increase in the prices of goods and services could reduce the value of your money in terms of the commodities you consume. Since interest-paying assets such as government bonds have face values fixed in terms of money, however, the same unexpected increase in prices would reduce the real value of those assets by the same percentage. Because any change in the riskiness of money causes an equal change in the riskiness of bonds, changes in the risk of holding money need not cause individuals to reduce their demand for money and increase their demand for interest-paying assets.

LIQUIDITY

The main benefit of holding money comes from its liquidity. Households and firms hold money because it is the easiest way of financing their everyday purchases. Some large purchases can be financed through the sale of a substantial illiquid asset. An art collector, for example, could sell one of her Picassos to buy a house. To finance a continuing stream of smaller expenditures at various times and for various amounts, however, households and firms have to hold some money.

An individual's need for liquidity rises when the average daily value of his transactions rises. A student who takes the bus every day, for example, does not need to hold as much cash as a business executive who takes taxis during rush hour. We conclude that *a rise in the average value of transactions carried out by a household or firm causes its demand for money to rise.*

AGGREGATE MONEY DEMAND

Our discussion of how individual households and firms determine their demands for money can now be applied to derive the determinants of **aggregate money demand,** the total demand for money by all households and firms in the economy. Aggregate money demand is just the sum of all the economy's individual money demands.

Three main factors determine aggregate money demand:

1. *The interest rate.* A rise in the interest rate causes each individual in the economy to reduce her demand for money. All else equal, aggregate money demand therefore falls when the interest rate rises.

2. *The price level.* The economy's **price level** is the price of a broad reference basket of goods and services in terms of currency. If the price level rises, individual households and firms must spend more money than before to purchase their usual weekly baskets of goods and services. To maintain the same level of liquidity as before the price level increase, they will therefore have to hold more money.

3. *Real national income.* When real national income (GNP) rises, more goods and services are being sold in the economy. This increase in the real value of transactions raises the demand for money, given the price level.

If P is the price level, R is the interest rate, and Y is real GNP, the aggregate demand for money, M^d, can be expressed as

$$M^d = P \times L(R,Y), \tag{14-1}$$

where the value of $L(R,Y)$ falls when R rises, and rises when Y rises.[3] To see why we have specified that aggregate money demand is *proportional* to the price level, imagine that all prices doubled but the interest rate and everyone's *real* incomes remained unchanged. The money value of each individual's average daily transactions would then simply double, as would the amount of money each wished to hold.

We usually write the aggregate money demand relation (14-1) in the equivalent form

$$M^d/P = L(R,Y), \tag{14-2}$$

and call $L(R,Y)$ aggregate *real* money demand. This way of expressing money demand shows that the aggregate demand for liquidity, $L(R,Y)$, is not a demand for a certain number of currency units but is instead a demand to hold a certain amount of purchasing power in liquid form. The ratio M^d/P—that is, desired money holdings measured in terms of a typical reference basket of commodities—equals the amount of purchasing power people would like to hold in liquid form. For example, if people wished to hold $1000 in cash at a price level of $100 per commodity basket, their real money holdings would be equivalent to $1000/($100 per basket) = 10 baskets. If the price level doubled (to $200 per basket), the purchasing power of their $1000 in cash would be halved, since it would now be worth only 5 baskets.

Figure 14-1 shows how aggregate real money demand is affected by the interest rate for a fixed level of real income, Y. The aggregate real money demand schedule $L(R,Y)$ slopes downward because a fall in the interest rate raises the desired real money holdings of each household and firm in the economy.

For a given level of real GNP, changes in interest rates cause movements *along* the $L(R,Y)$ schedule. Changes in real GNP, however, cause the schedule itself to shift. Figure

---

[3]Naturally, $L(R,Y)$ rises when R falls, and falls when Y falls.

FIGURE 14-1

Aggregate Real Money Demand and the Interest Rate

The downward-sloping real money demand schedule shows that for a given real income level, Y, real money demand rises as the interest rate falls.

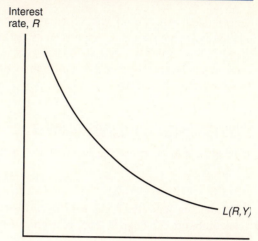

14-2 shows how a rise in real GNP from Y^1 to Y^2 affects the position of the aggregate real money demand schedule. Because a rise in real GNP raises aggregate real money demand for a given interest rate, the schedule $L(R, Y^2)$ lies to the right of $L(R, Y^1)$ when Y^2 is greater than Y^1.

FIGURE 14-2

Effect on the Aggregate Real Money Demand Schedule of a Rise in Real Income

An increase in real income from Y^1 to Y^2 raises the demand for real money balances at every level of the interest rate and causes the whole demand schedule to shift upward.

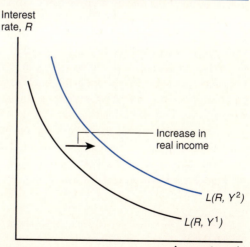

THE EQUILIBRIUM INTEREST RATE: THE INTERACTION OF MONEY SUPPLY AND DEMAND

As you might expect from other economics courses you've taken, the money market is in equilibrium when the money supply set by the central bank equals aggregate money demand. In this section we see how the interest rate is determined by money market equilibrium, given the price level and output, both of which are temporarily assumed to be unaffected by monetary changes.

EQUILIBRIUM IN THE MONEY MARKET

If M^s is the money supply, the condition for equilibrium in the money market is

$$M^s = M^d. \tag{14-3}$$

After dividing both sides of this equality by the price level, we can express the money market equilibrium condition in terms of aggregate real money demand as

$$M^s/P = L(R,Y). \tag{14-4}$$

Given the price level, P, and output, Y, the equilibrium interest rate is the one at which aggregate real money demand equals the real money supply.

In Figure 14-3, the aggregate real money demand schedule intersects the real money supply schedule at point 1 to give an equilibrium interest rate of R^1. The money supply schedule is vertical at M^s/P because M^s is set by the central bank while P is taken as given.

Let's see why the interest rate tends to settle at its equilibrium level by considering what happens if the market is initially at point 2, with an interest rate, R^2, that is above R^1.

At point 2 the demand for real money holdings falls short of the supply by $Q^1 - Q^2$, so there is an excess supply of money. If individuals are holding more money than they desire given the interest rate of R^2, they will attempt to reduce their liquidity by using some money to purchase interest-bearing assets. In other words, individuals will attempt to get rid of their excess money by lending it to others. Since there is an aggregate excess supply of money at R^2, however, not everyone can succeed in doing this: there are more people who would like to lend money to reduce their liquidity than there are people who would like to borrow it to increase theirs. Those who cannot unload their extra money try to tempt potential borrowers by lowering the interest rate they charge for loans below R^2. The downward pressure on the interest rate continues until the rate reaches R^1. At this interest rate, anyone wishing to lend money can do so because the aggregate excess supply of money has disappeared; that is, supply once again equals demand. Once the market reaches point 1, there is therefore no further tendency for the interest rate to drop.[4]

Similarly, if the interest rate is initially at a level R^3 below R^1, it will tend to rise. As Figure 14-3 shows, there is excess demand for money equal to $Q^3 - Q^1$ at point 3.

---

[4]Another way to view this process is as follows: We saw in the last chapter that an asset's rate of return falls when its current price rises relative to its future value. When there is an excess supply of money, the current money prices of illiquid assets that pay interest will be bid up as individuals attempt to reduce their money holdings. This rise in current asset prices lowers the rate of return on nonmoney assets, and since this rate of return is equal to the interest rate (after adjustment for risk), the interest rate also must fall.

ket, moving to a new trend line along which depreciation is more rapid than it was up to time t_0.[4]

Notice how different assumptions about the speed of price level adjustment lead to contrasting predictions about how exchange and interest rates interact. In the example of a fall in the money supply under sticky prices, an interest rate rise is needed to preserve money market equilibrium, given that the price level cannot do so by dropping immediately in response to the money supply reduction. In that sticky price case, an interest rate rise is associated with lower expected inflation and a long-run currency appreciation, so the currency appreciates immediately. In our monetary-approach example of a rise in money supply growth, however, an interest rate increase is associated with higher expected inflation and a currency that will be weaker on all future dates. An immediate currency *depreciation* is the result.[5]

These contrasting results of interest rate changes underlie our earlier warning that an explanation of exchange rates based on interest rates must carefully account for the factors that cause interest rates to move. These factors can simultaneously affect expected future exchange rates and can therefore have a decisive impact on the foreign exchange market's response to the interest rate change.

Figure 15-2 bears out the main long-run prediction of the Fisher effect. The figure plots inflation rates and interest rates for three countries that have had somewhat different inflationary experiences since 1970: Switzerland, the United States, and Italy. In each country interest rates tend to rise after inflation rises as prices adjust and as people learn to expect higher inflation in the future; reductions in inflation eventually lower interest rates for the same reason. Moreover, the average level of interest rates is lowest in Switzerland, which has the lowest average inflation rate, and highest in Italy, which has the highest average inflation rate.

The Fisher effect can be broadly correct even when PPP is not, so we can't take the evidence in Figure 15-2 as confirmation of the monetary approach. We now look at evidence bearing more directly on the validity of PPP itself.

EMPIRICAL EVIDENCE ON PPP AND THE LAW OF ONE PRICE

How well does the PPP theory explain actual data on exchange rates and national price levels? A brief answer is that all versions of the PPP theory do badly in explaining the facts. In particular, changes in national price levels often tell us little or nothing about exchange rate movements.

Do not conclude from this evidence, however, that the effort you've put into learning about PPP has been wasted. As we'll see later in this chapter, PPP is a key building block of exchange rate models more realistic than the monetary approach. Indeed, the empirical failures of PPP give us important clues about how more realistic models should be set up.

---

[4]In the general case in which Germany's inflation rate π_G is not zero, the dollar, rather than depreciating against the DM at rate π before t_0 and at rate $\pi + \Delta\pi$ afterward, depreciates at rate $\pi - \pi_G$ until t_0 and at rate $\pi + \Delta\pi - \pi_G$ thereafter.

[5]National money supplies typically trend upward over time, as in Figure 15-1a. Such trends lead to corresponding upward trends in price levels; if two countries' price level trends differ, PPP implies a trend in their exchange rate as well. From now on, when we refer to a change in the money supply, price level, or exchange rate, we will mean by this a change in the variable *relative to its previously expected trend rate of increase.* When instead we want to consider changes in trends themselves, we will say so explicitly.

Inflation and Interest Rates in Switzerland, the United States, and Italy, 1970–1994

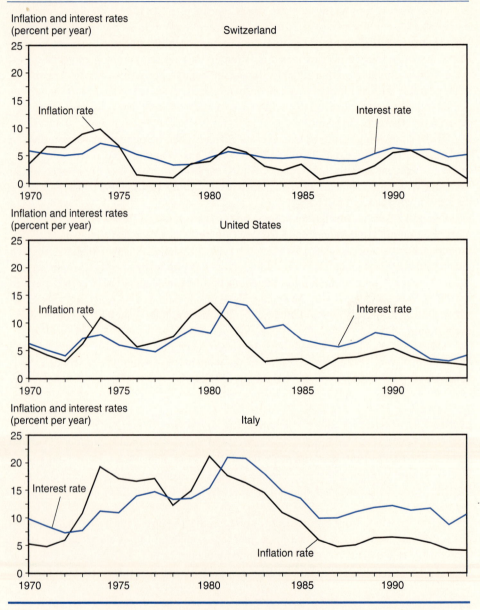

Inflation and interest rates show a long-run tendency to move together, as the Fisher effect suggests.

Source: OECD, *Main Economic Indicators.* Inflation rates are year-to-year percentage changes in consumer price indexes. Interest rates: Switzerland, yield of confederation bonds; United States, 3-month Treasury bill rate; Italy, bond yields of credit institutions; all measured at end of second quarter.

To test *absolute* PPP, economic researchers compare the international prices of a broad reference basket of commodities, making careful adjustments for intercountry quality differences among supposedly identical goods. These comparisons typically conclude that absolute PPP is way off the mark: The prices of identical commodity baskets, when converted to a single currency, differ substantially across countries. Even the law of one price does not fare well in some recent studies of price data broken down by commodity type. Manufactured goods that are very similar to each other have sold at widely different prices in various markets since the early 1970s. Because the argument leading to absolute PPP builds on the law of one price, it is not surprising that PPP does not stand up well to the data.[6]

Relative PPP is sometimes a reasonable approximation to the data, but it, too, usually performs poorly. Figure 15-3 illustrates relative PPP's weakness by plotting both the dollar/DM exchange rate, $E_{\$/DM}$, and the ratio of the U.S. and German price levels, P_{US}/P_G. Price levels are measured by indexes reported by the U.S. and German governments.[7] Relative PPP predicts that $E_{\$/DM}$ and P_{US}/P_G should move proportionally, and, as you can see in the figure, this was more or less so through 1970. But PPP broke down completely after 1970, with the dollar depreciating sharply between 1970 and 1973 even though U.S. prices *fell* slightly relative to German prices over those years. From 1973 through 1979, PPP is somewhat more successful: As U.S. prices rose relative to German prices, the dollar (in all but one of these years) depreciated against the DM. But the magnitude of the dollar's depreciation between 1973 and 1979 was far greater than relative PPP would predict.

A dramatic violation of relative PPP occurs in the years after 1979. In those years the dollar first sustained a massive appreciation against the DM even though the U.S. price level continued to rise relative to that of Germany; subsequently the dollar depreciated by far more than PPP would predict. Relative PPP does hold over the period 1964–1983 taken as a whole: Over those two decades, the percentage rise in the dollar/DM exchange rate is very close to the percentage increase in the U.S. price level relative to the German price level. In view of the wide departures from relative PPP over long subperiods of the 1964–1983 span and after 1983, however, PPP appears to be of limited use even as a long-run explanation of exchange rate movements.

Studies of other currencies largely confirm the results in Figure 15-3. Relative PPP has not held up well since the early 1970s, but in the 1960s it is a more reliable guide to the relationship among exchange rates and national price levels.[8] As you will learn later in this

---

[6]Some of the negative evidence on absolute PPP is discussed in the Case Study to follow. Regarding the law of one price, see, for example, Peter Isard, "How Far Can We Push the Law of One Price?" *American Economic Review* 67 (December 1977), pp. 942–948; Irving B. Kravis and Robert E. Lipsey, "Price Behavior in the Light of Balance of Payments Theories," *Journal of International Economics* 8 (May 1978), pp. 193–246; and the paper by Froot and Rogoff in Further Reading.

[7]The price level measures in Figure 15-3 are index numbers, not dollar amounts. For example, the U.S. consumer price index (CPI) was 100 in the base year 1967 and 298.4 in 1983, so the dollar price of a reference commodity basket of typical U.S. consumption purchases nearly tripled between 1967 and 1983. Base years for the U.S. and German price indexes were chosen so that their 1964 ratio would equal the 1964 exchange rate, but this imposed equality does *not* mean that absolute PPP held in 1964. Although Figure 15-3 uses CPIs, other price indexes lead to similar pictures.

[8]See, for example, Hans Genberg, "Purchasing Power Parity Under Fixed and Flexible Exchange Rates," *Journal of International Economics* 8 (May 1978), pp. 247–276; Jacob A. Frenkel, "The Collapse of Purchasing Power Parities During the 1970s," *European Economic Review* 16 (1981), pp. 145–165; and Robert E. Cumby and Maurice Obstfeld, "International Interest Rate and Price Level Linkages Under Flexible Exchange Rates: A Review of Recent Evidence," in John F. O. Bilson and Richard C. Marston, eds., *Exchange Rate Theory and Practice* (Chicago: University of Chicago Press, 1984), pp. 121–151.

FIGURE 15-3

The Dollar/DM Exchange Rate and Relative U.S./German Price Levels, 1964–1994

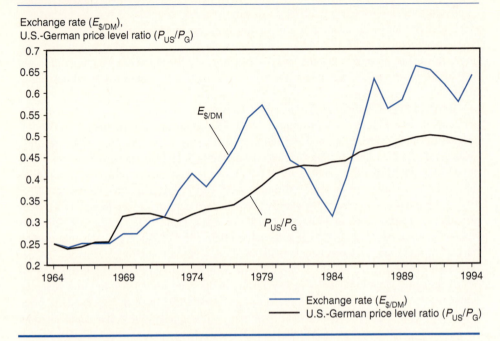

Exchange rate ($E_{\$/DM}$),
U.S.-German price level ratio (P_{US}/P_G)

— Exchange rate ($E_{\$/DM}$)
— U.S.-German price level ratio (P_{US}/P_G)

The graph shows that relative PPP does not explain the dollar/DM exchange rate after 1970.
Source: OECD, *Main Economic Indicators*. Exchange rates and price levels are end-of-year data.

book, between the end of World War II in 1945 and the early 1970s exchange rates were fixed within narrow internationally agreed margins through the intervention of central banks in the foreign exchange market. During the first half of the 1920s, when many exchange rates were market-determined as in the 1970s, 1980s, and 1990s, important deviations from relative PPP also occurred.[9]

EXPLAINING THE PROBLEMS WITH PPP

What explains the negative empirical results described in the previous section? There are several immediate problems with our rationale for the PPP theory of exchange rates, which was based on the law of one price:

1. Contrary to the assumption of the law of one price, transport costs and restrictions on trade certainly do exist. These trade barriers may be high enough to prevent some goods and services from being traded between countries.

[9]See Paul R. Krugman, "Purchasing Power Parity and Exchange Rates: Another Look at the Evidence," *Journal of International Economics* 8 (August 1978), pp. 397–407; and Paul De Grauwe, Marc Janssens, and Hilde Leliaert, *Real-Exchange-Rate Variability from 1920 to 1926 and 1973 to 1982,* Princeton Studies in International Finance 56 (International Finance Section, Department of Economics, Princeton University, September 1985).

SOME MEATY EVIDENCE ON THE LAW OF ONE PRICE

In the summer of 1986 the *Economist* magazine conducted an extensive survey on the prices of Big Mac hamburgers at McDonald's restaurants throughout the world. This apparently whimsical undertaking was not the result of an outbreak of editorial giddiness. The magazine wanted to poke fun at economists who confidently declare exchange rates to be "overvalued" or "undervalued" on the basis of PPP comparisons. Since Big Macs are "sold in 41 countries, with only the most trivial changes of recipe," the magazine argued, a comparison of hamburger prices should serve as a "medium-rare guide to whether currencies are trading at the right exchange rates."* Since 1986 the *Economist* has periodically updated its calculations.

One way of interpreting the *Economist* survey is as a test of the law of one price. Viewed in this way, the results of the initial test are quite startling. The dollar prices of Big Macs turned out to be wildly different in different countries. The price of a Big Mac in New York was 50 percent higher than in Australia and 64 percent higher than in Hong Kong. In contrast, a Parisian Big Mac cost 54 percent more than its New York counterpart; a Tokyo Big Mac cost 50 percent more. Only in Britain and Ireland were the dollar prices of the burgers close to New York levels.

How can this dramatic violation of the law of one price be explained? As the *Economist* noted, transport costs and government regulations are part of the explanation. Product differentiation is probably an important additional factor. Because relatively few close substitutes for Big Macs are available in some countries, product differentiation may give McDonald's some power to tailor prices to the local market. Finally, remember that the price of a Big Mac must cover not only the cost of ground meat and buns, but also the wages of serving people, rent, electricity, and so on.

The prices of these nonfood inputs can differ sharply in different countries.

What about the long run? Subsequent Big Mac surveys have shown no universal tendency toward a narrowing of the 1986 price differentials. The April 1989 survey showed the Big Mac selling for only 12 percent more in Paris than in Manhattan but selling for 153 percent more in Manhattan than in Hong Kong.† Significantly, the magazine also reported price differences among the four American cities of Atlanta, Chicago, New York, and San Francisco that were in many cases larger than the international disparities! This suggests that of the possible factors causing the law of one price to break down in this case, direct government restraint of international trade is not the most important.

We have reproduced the table that summarized the *Economist's* April 1995 survey report. Column 1 reports local-currency prices for Big Macs. Column 2 calculates local *dollar* prices by dividing column 1 by column 4, the local-currency price of a U.S. dollar. Column 3 is the local price of a Big Mac divided by its average dollar price in the four U.S. cities mentioned above, $2.32. This "implied PPP" is the exchange rate—quoted in indirect terms, as foreign currency units per dollar—that would prevail if the law of one price governed hamburger prices.

The last column gives the percentage by which the hamburger PPP rate in column 3 exceeds the actual price of a U.S. dollar in column 4. (It is often said that a currency is "overvalued" when its exchange rate makes domestic goods look expensive relative to similar goods sold abroad and "undervalued" in the opposite case.) Thus, the reported 66 percent overvaluation of the French franc relative to the dollar means that the dollar price of a Parisian Big Mac was one- and two-thirds

(continued)

The hamburger standard

	Big Mac prices		Implied PPP* of the dollar	Actual $ exchange rate 7/4/95	Local currency under(-)/over(+) valuation†, %
	In local currency	In dollars			
UNITED STATES§	**$2.32**	**2.32**	—	—	—
Argentina	Peso3.00	3.00	1.29	1.00	+29
Australia	A$2.45	1.82	1.06	1.35	-22
Austria	Sch39.0	4.01	16.8	9.72	+73
Belgium	BFr109	3.84	47.0	28.4	+66
Brazil	Real 2.42	2.69	1.04	0.90	+16
Britain	£ 1.74	2.80	1.33††	1.61††	+21
Canada	C$2.77	1.99	1.19	1.39	-14
Chile	Peso950	2.40	409	395	+4
China	Yuan9.00	1.05	3.88	8.54	-55
Czech Republic	CKr50.0	1.91	21.6	26.2	-18
Denmark	DKr26.75	4.92	11.5	5.43	+112
France	FFr18.5	3.85	7.97	4.80	+66
Germany	DM4.80	3.48	2.07	1.38	+50
Holland	Fl5.45	3.53	2.35	1.55	+52
Hong Kong	HK$9.50	1.23	4.09	7.73	-47
Hungary	Forint191	1.58	82.3	121	-32
Indonesia	Rupiah3,900	1.75	1,681	2,231	-25
Israel	Shekel8.90	3.01	3.84	2.95	+30
Italy	Lire4,500	2.64	1,940	1,702	+14
Japan	¥391	4.65	169	84.2	+100
Malaysia	M$3.76	1.51	1.62	2.49	-35
Mexico	Peso10.9	1.71	4.70	6.37	-26
New Zealand	NZ$2.95	1.96	1.27	1.51	-16
Poland	Zloty3.40	1.45	1.47	2.34	-37
Russia	Rouble8,100	1.62	3,491	4,985	-30
Singapore	S$2.95	2.10	1.27	1.40	-9
South Korea	Won2,300	2.99	991	769	+29
Spain	Ptas355	2.86	153	124	+23
Sweden	SKr26.0	3.54	11.2	7.34	+53
Switzerland	SFr5.90	5.20	2.54	1.13	+124
Taiwan	NT$65.0	2.53	28.0	25.7	+9
Thailand	Baht48.0	1.95	20.7	24.6	-16

*Purchasing-power parity: local price divided by price in the United States   †Against dollar
§Average of New York, Chicago, San Francisco and Atlanta   ††Dollars per pound
Source: McDonald's

times the price of a Big Mac in the United States. Similarly, the Tokyo price was double the U.S. price.

Notice that the world's cheapest Big Macs, by far, are sold in China. It is doubtful McDonald's is making much money in that market, despite the low wages Chinese workers earn. The operation has generated much favorable publicity for the company, however, and McDonald's Chinese beachhead gives it a strategic position that may prove profitable in the future as the country's living standards rise.

*"On the Hamburger Standard," *Economist,* September 6–12, 1986.

†"The Hamburger Standard," *Economist,* April 15, 1989.

2. Monopolistic or oligopolistic practices in goods markets may interact with transport costs and other trade barriers to weaken further the link between the prices of similar goods sold in different countries.

3. Because the inflation data reported in different countries are based on different commodity baskets, there is no reason for exchange rate changes to offset official measures of inflation differences, even when there are no barriers to trade and all products are tradable.

TRADE BARRIERS AND NONTRADABLES

Transport costs and trade restrictions make it expensive to move goods between markets located in different countries and therefore weaken the law of one price mechanism underlying PPP. Suppose once again that the same sweater sells for $45 in New York and for £30 in London, but that it costs $2 to ship a sweater between the two cities. At an exchange rate of $1.45 per pound, the dollar price of a London sweater is ($1.45 per pound) $\times$ (£30) = $43.50, but an American importer would have to pay $43.50 + $2 = $45.50 to purchase the sweater in London and get it to New York. At an exchange rate of $1.45 per pound, it therefore would not pay to ship sweaters from London to New York, even though their dollar price would be higher in the latter location. Similarly, at an exchange rate of $1.55 per pound, an American exporter would lose money by shipping sweaters from New York to London even though the New York price of $45 would then be below the dollar price of the sweater in London, $46.50.

The lesson of this example is that transport costs sever the close link between exchange rates and goods prices implied by the law of one price. The greater the transport costs, the greater the range over which the exchange rate can move, given goods prices in different countries. Official trade restrictions such as tariffs have a similar effect, because a fee paid to the customs inspector affects the importer's profit in the same way as an equivalent shipping fee. Either type of trade impediment weakens the basis of PPP by allowing the purchasing power of a given currency to differ more widely from country to country. For example, in the presence of trade impediments, a dollar need not go as far in Tokyo as in Chicago—and it doesn't, as anyone who has been to Tokyo has found out.

As you will recall from Chapter 2, transport costs may be so large relative to the cost of producing some goods and services that they can never be traded internationally at a profit. Such goods and services are called *nontradables*. The time-honored classroom example of a nontradable is the haircut. A Frenchman desiring an American haircut would have to transport himself to the United States or transport an American barber to France; in either case, the cost of transport is so large relative to the price of the service being purchased that (tourists excepted) French haircuts are consumed only by residents of France while American haircuts are consumed only by residents of the United States.

The existence in all countries of nontraded goods and services whose prices are not linked internationally allows systematic deviations even from relative PPP. Because the price of a nontradable is determined entirely by its *domestic* supply and demand curves, shifts in those curves may cause the domestic price of a broad commodity basket to change relative to the foreign price of the same basket. Other things equal, a rise in the price of a country's nontradables will raise its price level relative to foreign price levels (measuring all countries' price levels in terms of a single currency). Looked at another way, the purchasing power of any given currency will fall in countries where the prices of nontradables rise.

Each country's price level includes a wide variety of nontradables, including (along with haircuts) routine medical treatment, aerobic dance instruction, and housing, among others. Broadly speaking, we can identify traded goods with manufactured products, raw materials, and agricultural products. Nontradables are primarily services and the output of the construction industry. There are naturally exceptions to this rule. For example, financial services provided by banks and brokerage houses often can be traded internationally. In addition, trade restrictions, if sufficiently severe, can cause goods that would normally be traded to become nontraded. Thus, in most countries some manufacturers are nontraded.

FIGURE 15-6

Sectoral Productivity Growth Differences and the Change in the Relative Price of Nontraded Goods, 1970–1985

A higher traded–nontraded productivity growth difference is associated with a higher rate of increase in the relative price of nontradables.

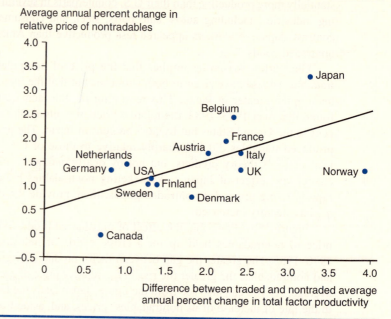

complex in practice than that simple formula suggests. Despite this complexity, economic policymakers who hope to influence exchange rates, as well as private individuals who wish to forecast them, cannot succeed without understanding the factors that cause countries' interest rates to differ.

In this section we therefore extend our earlier discussion of the Fisher effect to include real exchange rate movements. We do this by showing that in general, interest rate differences between countries depend not only on differences in expected inflation, as the monetary approach asserts, but also on expected changes in the real exchange rate.

We begin by recalling that the change in $q_{\$/DM}$, the real dollar/DM exchange rate, is the *deviation* from relative PPP; that is, the change in $q_{\$/DM}$ is the percentage change in the nominal dollar/DM exchange rate less the international difference in inflation rates between the United States and Germany. We thus arrive at the corresponding relationship between the *expected* change in the real exchange rate, the *expected* change in the nominal rate, and *expected* inflation,

$$(q^e_{\$/DM} - q_{\$/DM})/q_{\$/DM} = [(E^e_{\$/DM} - E_{\$/DM})/E_{\$/DM}] - (\pi^e_{US} - \pi^e_{G}), \qquad (15\text{-}8)$$

where $q^e_{\$/DM}$ (as per our usual notation) is the real exchange rate expected for a year from today.

Now return to the interest parity condition between dollar and DM deposits,

$$R_\$ - R_{DM} = (E^e_{\$/DM} - E_{\$/DM})/E_{\$/DM}.$$

An easy rearrangement of (15-8) shows that the expected rate of change in the *nominal* dollar/DM exchange rate is just the expected rate of change in the *real* dollar/DM exchange rate *plus* the U.S.-German expected inflation difference. Combining (15-8) with the above interest parity condition, we thus are led to the following breakdown of the international interest gap:

$$R_\$ - R_{DM} = [(q^e_{\$/DM} - q_{\$/DM})/q_{\$/DM}] + (\pi^e_{US} - \pi^e_G). \qquad (15\text{-}9)$$

Notice that when the market expects relative PPP to prevail, $q^e_{\$/DM} = q_{\$/DM}$ and the first term on the right side of this equation drops out. In this special case, (15-9) reduces to the simpler (15-5), which we derived by assuming relative PPP.

In general, however, the dollar-DM interest difference is the sum of *two* components: (1) the expected rate of real dollar depreciation against the DM and (2) the expected inflation difference between the United States and Germany. For example, if U.S. inflation will be 5 percent per year forever and German inflation zero, the long-run interest difference between dollar and DM deposits need not be the 5 percent that PPP (and interest parity) would suggest. If, in addition, everyone knows that output demand and supply trends will make the dollar decline against the DM in real terms at a rate of 1 percent per year, the international interest spread will actually be 6 percent.

REAL INTEREST PARITY

Economics makes an important distinction between **nominal interest rates,** which are rates of return measured in monetary terms, and **real interest rates,** which are rates of return measured in *real* terms, that is, in terms of a country's output. Because real rates of return often are uncertain, we usually will refer to *expected* real interest rates. The interest rates we discussed in connection with the interest parity condition and the determinants of money demand were nominal rates, for example, the dollar return on dollar deposits. But for many other purposes, economists need to analyze behavior in terms of real rates of return. No one who is thinking of investing money, for example, could make a decision knowing only that the nominal interest rate is 15 percent. The investment would be quite attractive at zero inflation, but disastrously unattractive if inflation were bounding along at 100 percent per year![22]

We conclude this chapter by showing that when the nominal interest parity condition equates nominal interest rate differences between currencies to expected changes in *nominal* exchange rates, a *real* interest parity condition equates expected real interest rate differences to expected changes in *real* exchange rates. Only when relative PPP is expected to hold (meaning no real exchange rate change is anticipated) are expected real interest rates in all countries identical.

The expected real interest rate, denoted r^e, is defined as the nominal interest rate, R, less the expected inflation rate, π^e:

$$r^e = R - \pi^e.$$

---

[22]We could get away with examining nominal return *differences* in the foreign exchange market because (as Chapter 13 showed) nominal return differences equal real return differences for any given investor. In the context of the money market, the *nominal* interest rate is the *real* rate of return you sacrifice by holding interest-barren currency.

In other words, the expected real interest rate in a country is just the real rate of return a domestic resident expects to earn on a loan of its currency. The definition of the expected real interest rate clarifies the generality of the forces behind the Fisher effect: Any increase in the expected inflation rate that does not alter the expected real interest rate must be reflected, one for one, in the nominal interest rate.

A useful consequence of the preceding definition is a formula for the difference in expected real interest rates between two countries such as the United States and Germany:

$$r_{US}^e - r_G^e = (R_\$ - \pi_{US}^e) - (R_{DM} - \pi_G^e).$$

If we rearrange equation (15-9) and combine it with the equation above, we get the desired *real interest parity condition:*

$$r_{US}^e - r_G^e = (q_{\$/DM}^e - q_{\$/DM})/q_{\$/DM}. \tag{15-10}$$

Equation (15-10) looks much like the nominal interest parity condition from which it is derived, but it explains differences in expected *real* interest rates between the United States and Germany by expected movements in the dollar/DM *real* exchange rate.

Expected real interest rates are the same in different countries when relative PPP is expected to hold (in which case (15-10) implies that $r_{US}^e = r_G^e$). More generally, however, expected real interest rates in different countries need not be equal, even in the long run, if continuing change in output markets is expected.[23] Suppose, for example, that productivity in the South Korean tradables sector is expected to rise during the next two decades while productivity stagnates in South Korean nontradables and in all U.S. industries. If the Balassa-Samuelson hypothesis is valid, people should expect the U.S. dollar to depreciate in real terms against South Korea's currency, the won, as the prices of South Korea's nontradables trend upward. Equation (15-10) thus implies that the expected real interest rate should be higher in the United States than in South Korea.

Do such real interest differences imply unnoticed profit opportunities for international investors? Not necessarily. A cross-border real interest difference does imply that residents of two countries perceive different real rates of return on wealth. Nominal interest parity tells us, however, that any *given* investor expects the same real return on domestic and foreign currency assets. Two investors residing in different countries need not calculate this single real rate of return in the same way if relative PPP does not link the prices of their consumption baskets, but there is no way either can profit from their disagreement by shifting funds between currencies.

Summary

1. The *purchasing power parity* theory, in its absolute form, asserts that the exchange rate between countries' currencies equals the ratio of their price levels, as measured by the money prices of a reference commodity basket. An equivalent statement of PPP is that the purchasing power of any currency is the same in any country. Absolute PPP implies a second version of the PPP theory, *relative PPP,*

---

[23]The two-period analysis of international borrowing and lending in Chapter 7 assumed that all countries face a single worldwide real interest rate. Relative PPP must hold in that analysis, however, because there is only one consumption good in each period.

which predicts that percentage changes in exchange rates equal differences in national inflation rates.

2. A building block of the PPP theory is the *law of one price,* which states that under free competition and in the absence of trade impediments, a good must sell for a single price regardless of where in the world it is sold. Proponents of the PPP theory often argue, however, that its validity does not require the law of one price to hold for every commodity.

3. The *monetary approach to the exchange rate* uses PPP to explain long-term exchange rate behavior exclusively in terms of money supply and demand. In that theory long-run international interest differentials result from different national rates of ongoing inflation, as the *Fisher effect* predicts. Sustained international differences in monetary growth rates are, in turn, behind different long-term rates of continuing inflation. The monetary approach thus finds that a rise in a country's interest rate will be associated with a depreciation of its currency. Relative PPP implies that international interest differences, which equal the expected percentage change in the exchange rate, also equal the international expected inflation gap.

4. The empirical support for PPP and the law of one price is weak in recent data. The failure of these propositions in the real world is related to trade barriers and departures from free competition. In addition, different definitions of price levels in different countries bedevil attempts to test PPP using the price indexes governments publish. For some products, including many services, international transport costs are so steep that these products become nontradable.

5. Deviations from relative PPP can be viewed as changes in a country's *real exchange rate,* the price of a typical foreign expenditure basket in terms of the typical domestic expenditure basket. All else equal, a country's currency undergoes a long-run *real appreciation* against foreign currencies when the world relative demand for its output rises. In this case the country's real exchange rate, as just defined, falls. The home currency undergoes a long-run *real depreciation* against foreign currencies when home output expands relative to foreign output. In this case the real exchange rate rises.

6. The long-run determination of *nominal exchange rates* can be analyzed by combining two theories: the theory of the long-run *real* exchange rate and the theory of how domestic monetary factors determine long-run price levels. A stepwise increase in a country's money stock ultimately leads to a proportional increase in its price level and a proportional fall in its currency's foreign exchange value, just as relative PPP predicts. Changes in monetary growth rates also have long-run effects consistent with PPP. Supply or demand changes in output markets, however, cause exchange rate movements that do not conform to PPP.

7. The interest parity condition equates international differences in *nominal interest rates* to the expected percentage change in the nominal exchange rate. If interest parity holds in this sense, a real interest parity condition equates international differences in expected *real interest rates* to the expected change in the real exchange rate. Real interest parity also implies that international differences in

nominal interest rates equal the difference in expected inflation *plus* the expected percentage change in the real exchange rate.

Key Terms

Fisher effect, p. 407

law of one price, p. 400

monetary approach to the exchange rate, p. 403

nominal exchange rate, p. 421

nominal interest rate, p. 431

purchasing power parity (PPP), p. 400

real appreciation, p. 423

real depreciation, p. 422

real exchange rate, p. 421

real interest rate, p. 431

relative PPP, p. 402

Problems

1. Suppose Brazil's inflation rate is 100 percent over one year but the inflation rate in Holland is only 5 percent. According to relative PPP, what should happen over the year to the Dutch guilder's exchange rate against the Brazilian cruzeiro?

2. Discuss why it is often asserted that exporters suffer when their home currencies appreciate in real terms against foreign currencies and prosper when their home currencies depreciate in real terms.

3. Other things equal, how would you expect the following shifts to affect a currency's real exchange rate against foreign currencies?
   a. The overall level of spending doesn't change, but domestic residents decide to spend more of their income on nontraded products and less on tradables.
   b. Foreign residents shift their demand away from their own goods and toward the home country's exports.

4. Large-scale wars typically bring a suspension of international trading and financial activities. Exchange rates lose much of their relevance under these conditions, but once the war is over governments wishing to fix exchange rates face the problem of deciding what the new rates should be. The PPP theory has often been applied to this problem of postwar exchange rate realignment. Imagine that you are a British Chancellor of the Exchequer and World War I has just ended. Explain how you would figure out the dollar/pound exchange rate implied by PPP. When might it be a bad idea to use the PPP theory in this way?

5. In the late 1970s Britain seemed to have struck it rich. Having developed its North Sea oil-producing fields in earlier years, Britain suddenly found its real income higher as a result of a dramatic increase in world oil prices in 1979–1980. In the early 1980s, however, oil prices receded as the world economy slid into a deep recession and world oil demand faltered.

   Below, we show index numbers for the average real exchange rate of the pound against several foreign currencies. (Such average index numbers are called real *effective* exchange rates.) A rise in one of these numbers indicates a real *appreci-*

ation of the pound, that is, an increase in Britain's price level relative to the average price level abroad measured in pounds. A fall is a real depreciation.

Real Effective Exchange Rate of the Pound Sterling 1976–1984 (1980 = 100)

1976	1977	1978	1979	1980	1981	1982	1983	1984
68.3	66.5	72.2	81.4	100.0	102.8	100.0	92.5	89.8

Source: International Monetary Fund, *International Financial Statistics.* The real exchange rate measures are based on indexes of net output prices called value-added deflators.

Use the clues we have given about the British economy to explain the rise and fall of the pound's real effective exchange rate between 1978 and 1984. Pay particular attention to the role of nontradables.

6. Every week the Federal Reserve announces how quickly the money supply grew in the week ending ten days previously. (There is a ten-day delay because it takes that long to assemble data on bank deposits.) Economists have noticed that when the announced increase in the money supply is greater than expected, nominal interest rates *rise* just after the announcement; they *fall* when the market learns the money supply grew more slowly than expected. Two competing explanations of this phenomenon are (1) unexpectedly high money growth raises expected inflation and thus raises nominal interest rates through the Fisher effect; and (2) unexpectedly high money growth leads the market to expect future Fed action to reduce the money supply, causing a decrease in the amount of deposits supplied to the public by banks but no increase in expected inflation. How would you use data from the foreign exchange market to decide between these two hypotheses? (For an answer, see the paper by Engel and Frankel in Further Reading.)

7. Explain how permanent shifts in national real money-demand functions affect real and nominal exchange rates in the long run.

8. In Chapter 5 we discussed the effect of transfers between countries, such as the indemnity imposed on Germany after World War I. Use the theory developed in this chapter to discuss the mechanisms through which a permanent transfer from Germany to France would affect the real French franc/DM exchange rate in the long run.

9. Continuing with the preceding problem, discuss how the transfer would affect the long-run *nominal* exchange rate between the two currencies.

10. A country imposes a tariff on imports from abroad. How does its action change the long-run real exchange rate between home and foreign currency? How is the long-run nominal exchange rate affected?

11. Imagine that two identical countries have restricted imports to identical levels, but one has done so using tariffs while the other has done so using quotas. After these policies are in place, both countries experience identical, balanced expansions of domestic spending. Where should the demand expansion cause a greater real currency appreciation, in the tariff-using country or in the quota-using country?

12. Explain how the nominal dollar/DM exchange rate would be affected (all else equal) by permanent changes in the expected rate of real depreciation of the dollar against the DM.

13. Can you suggest an event that would cause a country's nominal interest rate to rise and its currency to appreciate simultaneously, in a world of perfectly flexible prices?

14. Suppose that the expected real interest rate in the United States is 9 percent per year while that in Germany is 3 percent per year. What do you expect to happen to the real dollar/DM exchange rate over the next year?

15. In the short run of a model with sticky prices, a reduction in the money supply raises the nominal interest rate and appreciates the currency (see Chapter 14). What happens to the expected real interest rate? Explain why the subsequent path of the real exchange rate satisfies the real interest parity condition.

16. Discuss the following statement: "When a change in a country's nominal interest rate is caused by a rise in the expected real interest rate, the domestic currency appreciates. When the change is caused by a rise in expected inflation, the currency depreciates."

17. The difference between the nominal interest rate and the actual inflation rate is often called the ex post real interest rate (as opposed to the ex ante, or expected real interest rate). Figure 15-2 shows that between 1976 and 1980, the ex post real interest rate in Switzerland was usually positive while that in the United States was usually negative. Assume that people were able to forecast inflation accurately in both countries during these years. What would you guess about the dollar's strength against the Swiss franc in the foreign exchange market between 1976 and 1980? What do you think happened to the dollar/Swiss franc exchange rate in 1981–1982? Check your answer by looking up the history of the exchange rate. (See, for example, the International Monetary Fund's publication, *International Financial Statistics*.)

Further Reading

Gustav Cassel. *Post-War Monetary Stabilization.* New York: Columbia University Press, 1928. Applies the purchasing power parity theory of exchange rates in analyzing the monetary problems that followed World War I.

Robert E. Cumby and Frederic S. Mishkin. "The International Linkage of Real Interest Rates: The U.S.-European Connection." *Journal of International Money and Finance* 5 (March 1986), pp. 5–23. An econometric study of the relationship between real interest rates in the United States and Europe.

Rudiger Dornbusch. "Purchasing Power Parity," in *The New Palgrave Dictionary of Money & Finance,* Vol. 3. New York: Stockton Press, 1992, pp. 236–244. Examines the role of the purchasing power parity theory in international macroeconomics.

Rudiger Dornbusch. "The Theory of Flexible Exchange Rate Regimes and Macroeconomic Policy," in Jan Herin, Assar Lindbeck, and Johan Myhrman, eds. *Flexible Exchange Rates and Stabilization Policy.* Boulder, CO: Westview Press, 1977, pp. 123–143. Develops a long-run model of exchange rates incorporating traded and nontraded goods and services.

Charles Engel and Jeffrey Frankel. "Why Money Announcements Move Interest Rates: An Answer from the Foreign Exchange Market," in *Sixth West Coast Academic/Federal Reserve Economic Research Seminar* (Economic Review Conference Supplement). San Francisco: Federal Reserve Bank of San Francisco, 1983, pp. 1–26. Studies the link between Fed money announcements, interest rates, and the exchange rate.

Kenneth A. Froot and Kenneth Rogoff. "Perspectives on PPP and Long-Run Real Exchange Rates," in Gene M. Grossman and Kenneth Rogoff, eds. *Handbook of International Economics,* Vol. 3. Amsterdam: North-Holland Publishing Company, 1995. Up-to-date critical survey of theory and empirical work.

Irving B. Kravis. "Comparative Studies of National Incomes and Prices." *Journal of Economic Literature* 22 (March 1984), pp. 1–39. An account of the findings of a United Nations–sponsored research project that compared the real incomes and price levels of more than 100 countries.

Robin Marris. "Comparing the Incomes of Nations: A Critique of the International Comparison Project." *Journal of Economic Literature* 22 (March 1984), pp. 40–57. A critical appraisal of the research described in the previous reading by Kravis.

Lloyd A. Metzler. "Exchange Rates and the International Monetary Fund," in *International Monetary Policies.* Postwar Economic Studies 7. Washington, D.C.: Board of Governors of the Federal Reserve System, 1947, pp. 1–45. The author applies purchasing power parity with skill and skepticism to evaluate the fixed exchange rates established by the International Monetary Fund after World War II.

Frederic S. Mishkin. *The Economics of Money, Banking and Financial Markets,* 4th edition. New York: HarperCollins Publishers, 1995. Chapter 6 discusses inflation and the Fisher effect.

Lawrence Officer. *Purchasing Power Parity and Exchange Rates: Theory, Evidence and Relevance.* Greenwich, CT: JAI Press Inc., 1982. A comprehensive review of the history and validity of the purchasing power parity doctrine.

Alan C. Stockman. "The Equilibrium Approach to Exchange Rates." *Federal Reserve Bank of Richmond Economic Review* 73 (March/April 1987), pp. 12–30. Theory and evidence on an equilibrium exchange rate model similar to the long-run model of this chapter.

John Williamson, ed. *Estimating Equilibrium Exchange Rates.* Washington, D.C.: Institute for International Economics, 1994. Essays on alternative approaches to calculating long-run real exchange rates in practice.

16

Output and the Exchange Rate in the Short Run

As the 1990s began most European currencies appreciated against the American dollar, but while Germany experienced inflationary pressures, its European neighbors suffered from recession. This chapter will help us to understand the complicated factors that cause output, exchange rates, and inflation to change by completing the macroeconomic model built in the last two chapters.

Chapters 14 and 15 explained the connections among exchange rates, interest rates, and price levels but always assumed that output levels were determined outside of the model. Those chapters give us only a partial picture of how macroeconomic changes affect an open economy because events that change exchange rates, interest rates, and price levels may also affect output. Now we complete the picture by examining how output and the exchange rate are determined in the short run.

Our discussion combines what we have learned about asset markets and the long-run behavior of exchange rates with a new element, a theory of how the output market adjusts to demand changes when product prices in the economy are themselves slow to adjust. As we learned in Chapter 14, institutional factors like long-term nominal contracts can give rise to "sticky" or slowly adjusting output market prices. By putting a short-run model of the output market together with our models of the foreign exchange and money markets (the asset markets), we build a model that explains the short-run behavior of all the important macroeconomic variables in an open economy. The long-run exchange rate model of the preceding chapter provides the framework that participants in the asset markets use to form their expectations about future exchange rates.

Because output changes may push the economy away from full employment, the links among output and other macroeconomic variables such as the merchandise trade balance and the current account are of great concern to economic policymakers. In the last part of this chapter we use our short-run model to examine how macroeconomic policy tools affect output and the current account, and how those tools can be used to maintain full employment.

DETERMINANTS OF AGGREGATE DEMAND IN AN OPEN ECONOMY

To analyze how output is determined in the short run when product prices are sticky, we introduce the concept of **aggregate demand** for a country's output. Aggregate demand is the amount of a country's goods and services demanded by households and firms throughout the world. Just as the output of an individual good or service depends in part on the demand for it, a country's overall short-run output level depends on the aggregate demand for its products. The economy is at full employment in the long run (by definition) because wages and the price level eventually adjust to ensure full employment. In the long run, domestic output therefore depends only on the available domestic supplies of factors of production such as labor and capital. As we will see, however, these productive factors can be over- or underemployed in the short run as a result of shifts in aggregate demand that have not yet had their full long-run effects on prices.

In Chapter 12 we learned that an economy's output is the sum of four types of expenditure that generate national income: consumption, investment, government purchases, and the current account. Correspondingly, aggregate demand for an open economy's output is the sum of consumption demand (C), investment demand (I), government demand (G), and net export demand, that is, the current account (CA). Each of these components of aggregate demand depends on various factors. In this section we examine the factors that determine consumption demand and the current account. We discuss government demand later in this chapter when we examine the effects of fiscal policy; for now we assume that G is given. To avoid complicating our model, we also assume that investment demand is given. The determinants of investment demand are incorporated into the model in Appendix I to this chapter.

DETERMINANTS OF CONSUMPTION DEMAND

In this chapter we view the amount a country's residents wish to consume as depending on disposable income, Y^d (that is, national income less taxes, $Y - T$).[1] (C, Y, and T are all measured in terms of domestic output units.) With this assumption, a country's desired consumption level can be written as a function of disposable income:

$$C = C(Y^d).$$

Because each consumer naturally demands more goods and services as his or her real income rises, we expect consumption to increase as disposable income increases at the ag-

---

[1] A more complete model would allow other factors, such as real wealth and the real interest rate, to affect consumption plans. This chapter's Appendix II links the formulation here to the microeconomic theory of the consumer, which was the basis of the discussion in the appendix to Chapter 7.

gregate level, too. Thus, consumption demand and disposable income are positively related. When disposable income rises, however, consumption demand generally rises by *less* because part of the income increase is saved.

DETERMINANTS OF THE CURRENT ACCOUNT

The current account balance, viewed as the demand for a country's exports less that country's own demand for imports, is determined by two main factors: the domestic currency's real exchange rate against foreign currency (that is, the price of a typical foreign expenditure basket in terms of domestic expenditure baskets) and domestic disposable income. (In reality, a country's current account depends on many other factors, such as the level of foreign expenditure, but for now we regard these other factors as being held constant.)[2]

We express a country's current account balance as a function of its currency's real exchange rate, $q = EP^*/P$, and of domestic disposable income, Y^d:

$$CA = CA(EP^*/P, Y^d).$$

As a reminder of the last chapter's discussion, note that the domestic currency prices of representative foreign and domestic expenditure baskets are, respectively, EP^* and P, where E (the nominal exchange rate) is the price of foreign currency in terms of domestic, P^* is the foreign price level, and P is the home price level. The *real* exchange rate q, defined as the price of the foreign basket in terms of the domestic one, is therefore EP^*/P. If, for example, the representative basket of German goods and services costs DM 100 (P^*), the representative U.S. basket costs \$50 (P), and the dollar/DM exchange rate is \$0.40 per DM (E), then the price of the German basket in terms of U.S. baskets is

$$EP^*/P = \frac{(0.40\ \$/DM) \times (100\ DM/German\ basket)}{(50\ \$/U.S.\ basket)}$$
$$= 0.8\ U.S.\ basket/German\ basket.$$

Real exchange rate changes affect the current account because they reflect changes in the prices of domestic goods and services relative to foreign. Disposable income affects the current account through its effect on total spending by domestic consumers. To understand how these real exchange rate and disposable income effects work, it is helpful to look separately at the demand for a country's exports, EX, and the demand for imports by the country's residents, IM. As we saw in Chapter 12 the current account is related to exports and imports by the identity

$$CA = EX - IM$$

when CA, EX, and IM all are measured in terms of domestic output.

---

[2]In Chapter 19 we study a two-country framework that takes account of how events in the domestic economy affect foreign output and how these changes in foreign output, in turn, feed back to the domestic economy. As the previous footnote observed, we are ignoring a number of factors (such as wealth and interest rates) that affect consumption along with disposable income. Since some part of any consumption change goes into imports, these omitted determinants of consumption also help to determine the current account. Following the convention of Chapter 12, we are also ignoring unilateral transfers in analyzing the current account balance.

HOW REAL EXCHANGE RATE CHANGES AFFECT THE CURRENT ACCOUNT

You will recall that a representative domestic expenditure basket includes some imported products but places a relatively heavier weight on goods and services produced domestically. At the same time, the representative foreign basket is skewed toward goods and services produced in the foreign country. Thus a rise in the price of the foreign basket in terms of domestic baskets, say, will be associated with a rise in the relative price of foreign output in general relative to domestic.[3]

To determine how such a change in the relative price of national outputs affects the current account, other things equal, we must ask how it affects both EX and IM. If EP^*/P rises, for example, foreign products have become more expensive relative to domestic products: Each unit of domestic output now purchases fewer units of foreign output. Foreign consumers will respond to this price shift by demanding more of our exports. This response by foreigners will therefore raise EX and will tend to improve the domestic country's current account.

The effect of the same real exchange rate increase on IM is more complicated. Domestic consumers respond to the price shift by purchasing fewer units of the more expensive foreign products. Their response does not imply, however, that IM must fall. IM denotes the value of imports *measured in terms of domestic output*, and not the volume of foreign products imported: Because a rise in EP^*/P tends to raise the value of each unit of imports in terms of domestic output units, imports measured in domestic output units may rise as a result of a rise in EP^*/P even if imports decline when measured in foreign output units. IM can therefore rise or fall when EP^*/P rises, so the effect of a real exchange rate change on the current account CA is ambiguous.

Whether the current account improves or worsens depends on which effect of a real exchange rate change is dominant, the *volume effect* of consumer spending shifts on export and import quantities or the *value effect*, which changes the domestic output worth of a given volume of foreign imports. We assume for now that the volume effect of a real exchange rate change always outweighs the value effect, so that, other things equal, a real depreciation of the currency improves the current account and a real appreciation of the currency worsens the current account.[4]

HOW DISPOSABLE INCOME CHANGES AFFECT THE CURRENT ACCOUNT

The second factor influencing the current account is domestic disposable income. Since a rise in Y^d causes domestic consumers to increase their spending on *all* goods, including imports from abroad, an increase in disposable income worsens the current account, other things equal. (An increase in Y^d has no effect on export demand because we are holding foreign income constant and not allowing Y^d to affect it.)

---

[3]The real exchange rate is being used here essentially as a convenient summary measure of the relative prices of domestic against foreign products. A more exact (but much more complicated) analysis would work explicitly with separate demand and supply functions for each country's nontradables and tradables but would lead to conclusions very much like those we reach below.

[4]This assumption requires that import and export demands be relatively *elastic* with respect to the real exchange rate. Appendix III to this chapter describes a precise condition, called the Marshall-Lerner condition, under which the assumption in the text will be valid. The appendix also examines empirical evidence on the time horizon over which the Marshall-Lerner condition holds.

TABLE 16-1	

Factors Determining the Current Account

Change	Effect on current account, *CA*
Real exchange rate, $EP^*/P \uparrow$	$CA \uparrow$
Real exchange rate, $EP^*/P \downarrow$	$CA \downarrow$
Disposable income, $Y^d \uparrow$	$CA \downarrow$
Disposable income, $Y^d \downarrow$	$CA \uparrow$

Table 16-1 summarizes our discussion of how real exchange rate and disposable income changes influence the domestic current account.

THE EQUATION OF AGGREGATE DEMAND

We now combine the four components of aggregate demand to get an expression for total aggregate demand, denoted *D:*

$$D = C(Y - T) + I + G + CA(EP^*/P, Y - T),$$

where we have written disposable income Y^d as output, *Y,* less taxes, *T.* This equation shows that aggregate demand for home output can be written as a function of the real exchange rate, disposable income, investment demand, and government spending:

$$D = D(EP^*/P, Y - T, I, G).$$

We now want to see how aggregate demand depends on the real exchange rate and domestic GNP given the level of taxes, *T,* investment demand, *I,* and government purchases, *G.*

THE REAL EXCHANGE RATE AND AGGREGATE DEMAND

A rise in EP^*/P makes domestic goods and services cheaper relative to foreign goods and services and shifts both domestic and foreign spending from foreign goods to domestic goods. As a result, *CA* rises (as assumed in the previous section) and aggregate demand *D* therefore goes up. *A real depreciation of the home currency raises aggregate demand for home output, other things equal; a real appreciation lowers aggregate demand for home output.*

REAL INCOME AND AGGREGATE DEMAND

The effect of domestic real income on aggregate demand is slightly more complicated. If taxes are fixed at a given level, a rise in *Y* represents an equal rise in disposable income Y^d. While this rise in Y^d raises consumption, it worsens the current account by raising home spending on foreign imports. The first of these effects raises aggregate demand, but the second lowers it. Since the increase in consumption is divided between higher spending on home products and higher spending on foreign imports, however, the first effect (the effect of disposable income on total consumption) is greater than the second (the effect of disposable income on import spending alone). Therefore, *a rise in domestic real income*

FIGURE 16-1

Aggregate Demand as a Function of Output

Aggregate demand is a function of the real exchange rate (EP^*/P), disposable income ($Y - T$), investment demand (I), and government spending (G). If all other factors remain unchanged, a rise in output (real income), Y, increases aggregate demand. Because the increase in aggregate demand is less than the increase in output, the slope of the aggregate demand function is less than one (as indicated by its position within the 45-degree angle).

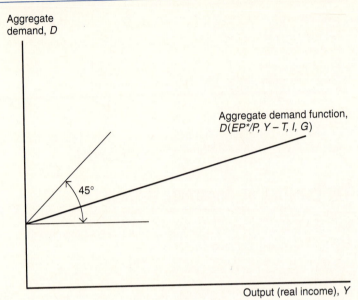

raises aggregate demand for home output, other things equal, and a fall in domestic real income lowers aggregate demand for home output.

Figure 16-1 shows the relation between aggregate demand and real income Y for fixed values of the real exchange rate, taxes, investment demand, and government spending. As Y rises, consumption rises by a fraction of the increase in income. Part of this increase in consumption, moreover, goes into import spending. The effect of an increase in Y on the aggregate demand for home output is therefore smaller than the accompanying rise in consumption demand, which is smaller, in turn, than the increase in Y. We show this in Figure 16-1 by drawing the aggregate demand schedule with a slope less than 1. (The schedule intersects the vertical axis above the origin because investment, government, and foreign demand would make aggregate demand greater than zero, even in the hypothetical case of zero domestic output.)

HOW OUTPUT IS DETERMINED IN THE SHORT RUN

Having discussed the factors that influence the demand for an open economy's output, we now study how output is determined in the short run. We show in this section that the output market is in equilibrium when real output, Y, equals the aggregate demand for domestic output:

$$Y = D(EP^*/P, Y - T, I, G). \tag{16-1}$$

The equality of aggregate supply and demand therefore determines the short-run equilibrium output level.[5]

Our analysis of real output determination applies to the short run because we assume that the money prices of goods and services are *temporarily fixed.* As we will see later in the chapter, the short-run real output changes that occur when prices are temporarily fixed eventually cause price level changes that move the economy to its long-run equilibrium. In long-run equilibrium, factors of production are fully employed, the level of real output is completely determined by factor supplies, and the real exchange rate has adjusted to equate long-run real output to aggregate demand.[6]

The determination of national output in the short run is illustrated in Figure 16-2, where we again graph aggregate demand as a function of output for fixed levels of the real exchange rate, taxes, investment demand, and government spending. The intersection (at point 1) of the aggregate demand schedule and a 45-degree line drawn from the origin (the

FIGURE 16-2

The Determination of Output in the Short Run

In the short run output settles at Y^1 (point 1), where aggregate demand, D^1, equals aggregate output, Y^1.

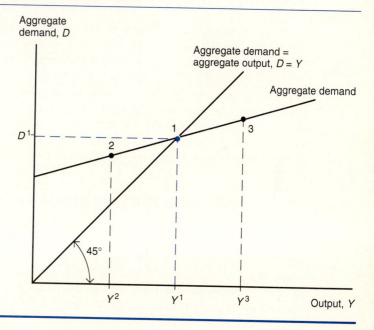

[5]Superficially, equation (16-1), which may be written as $Y = C(Y^d) + I + G + CA(EP^*/P, Y^d)$, looks like the GNP identity we discussed in Chapter 12, $Y = C + I + G + CA$. How do the two equations differ? They differ in that (16-1) is an equilibrium condition, not an identity. As you will recall from Chapter 12, the investment quantity I appearing in the GNP identity includes *undesired* or involuntary inventory accumulation by firms, so that the GNP identity always holds as a matter of definition. The investment demand appearing in equation (16-1), however, is *desired* or planned investment. Thus, the GNP identity always holds but equation (16-1) holds only if firms are not unwillingly building up or drawing down inventories of goods.

[6]Thus, equation (16-1) also holds in long-run equilibrium, but the equation determines the long-run real exchange rate when Y is at its long-run value.

equation $D = Y$) gives us the unique output level Y^1 at which aggregate demand equals output.

Let's use Figure 16-2 to see why output tends to settle at Y^1 in the short run. At an output level of Y^2, aggregate demand (point 2) is higher than output. Firms therefore increase their production to meet this excess demand. (If they did not, they would have to meet the excess demand out of inventories, reducing investment below the desired level I.) Thus, output expands until national income reaches Y^1.

At point 3 there is an excess supply of domestic output and firms find themselves involuntarily accumulating inventories (involuntarily raising their investment spending above its desired level). As inventories start to build up, firms cut back on production; only when output has fallen to Y^1 will firms be content with their level of production. Once again, output settles at point 1, the point at which output exactly equals aggregate demand. In this short-run equilibrium, consumers, firms, the government, and foreign buyers of domestic products are all able to realize their desired expenditures with no output left over.

OUTPUT MARKET EQUILIBRIUM IN THE SHORT RUN: THE *DD* SCHEDULE

Now that we understand how output is determined for a given real exchange rate EP^*/P, let's look at how the exchange rate and output are simultaneously determined in the short run. To understand this process, we need two elements. The first element, developed in this section, is the relationship between output and the exchange rate (the *DD* schedule) that must hold when the output market is in equilibrium. The second element, developed in the next section, is the relationship between output and the exchange rate that must hold when the home money market and the foreign exchange market (the asset markets) are in equilibrium. As we will see, both elements are necessary because the economy as a whole is in equilibrium only when both the output market and the asset markets are in equilibrium.

OUTPUT, THE EXCHANGE RATE, AND OUTPUT MARKET EQUILIBRIUM

Figure 16-3 illustrates the relationship between the exchange rate and output implied by output market equilibrium. Specifically, the figure illustrates the effect of a depreciation of the domestic currency against foreign currency (that is, a rise in E from E^1 to E^2) for fixed values of the domestic price level, P, and the foreign price level, P^*. With fixed price levels at home and abroad, the rise in the nominal exchange rate makes foreign goods and services more expensive relative to domestic goods and services. This relative price change shifts the aggregate demand schedule upward.

The fall in the relative price of domestic output shifts the aggregate demand schedule upward because at each level of domestic output, the demand for domestic products is now higher. Output expands from Y^1 to Y^2 as firms find themselves faced with excess demand at initial production levels.

Although we have considered the effect of a change in E with P and P^* held fixed, it is straightforward to analyze the effects of changes in P or P^* on output. *Any rise in the real exchange rate EP^*/P (whether due to a rise in E, a rise in P^*, or a fall in P) will cause an upward shift in the aggregate demand function and an expansion of output, all else equal.* (A rise in P^*, for example, has effects qualitatively identical to those of a rise in E.)

FIGURE 16-3

Output Effect of a Currency Depreciation with Fixed Output Prices

A rise in the exchange rate from E^1 to E^2 (a currency depreciation) raises aggregate demand to *aggregate demand* (E^2) and output to Y^2, all else equal.

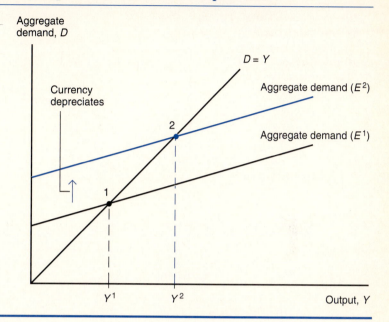

Similarly, any fall in EP*/P, regardless of its cause (a fall in E, a fall in P*, or a rise in P), will cause output to contract, all else equal. (A rise in P, with E and P* held fixed, for example, makes domestic products more expensive relative to foreign products, reduces aggregate demand for domestic output, and causes output to fall.)

DERIVING THE *DD* SCHEDULE

If we assume P and P^* are fixed in the short run, a depreciation of the domestic currency (a rise in E) is associated with a rise in domestic output, Y, while an appreciation (a fall in E) is associated with a fall in Y. This association provides us with one of the two relationships between E and Y needed to describe the short-run macroeconomic behavior of an open economy. We summarize this relationship by the **DD schedule,** which shows all combinations of output and the exchange rate for which the output market is in short-run equilibrium (aggregate demand = aggregate output).

Figure 16-4 shows how to derive the *DD* schedule, which relates E and Y when P and P^* are fixed. The upper part of the figure reproduces the result of Figure 16-3 (a depreciation of the domestic currency shifts the aggregate demand function upward, causing output to rise). The *DD* schedule in the lower part graphs the resulting relationship between the exchange rate and output (given that P and P^* are held constant). Point 1 on the *DD* schedule gives the output level Y^1 at which aggregate demand equals aggregate supply when the exchange rate is E^1. A depreciation of the currency to E^2 leads to the higher output level Y^2 according to the figure's upper part, and this information allows us to locate point 2 on *DD*.

FIGURE 16-4

Deriving the *DD* Schedule

The *DD* schedule (shown in the lower panel) slopes upward because a rise in the exchange rate from E^1 to E^2, all else equal, causes output to rise from Y^1 to Y^2.

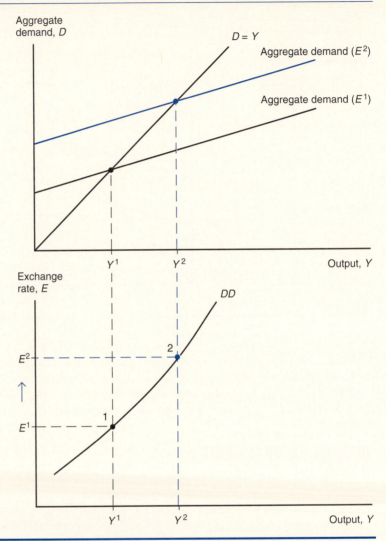

FACTORS THAT SHIFT THE *DD* SCHEDULE

A number of factors affect the position of the *DD* schedule: the levels of government demand, taxes, and investment; the domestic and foreign price levels; variations in domestic consumption behavior; and the foreign demand for home output. To understand the effects of shifts in each of these factors, we must study how the *DD* schedule shifts when it changes. In the following discussions we assume that all other factors remain fixed.

   1. *A change in G.* Figure 16-5 shows the effect on *DD* of a rise in government purchases from G^1 to G^2, given a fixed exchange rate of E^0. As shown in the upper

FIGURE 16-5

Government Demand and the Position of the *DD* Schedule

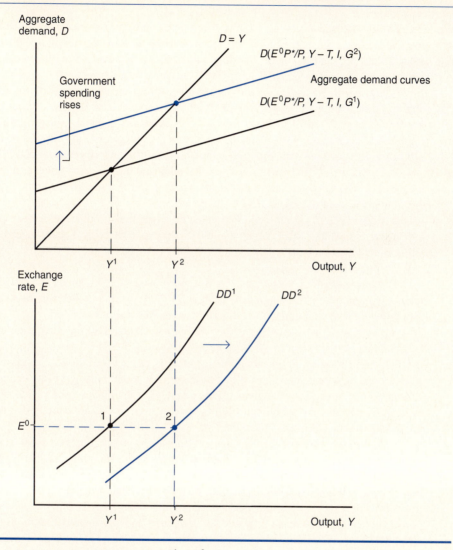

A rise in government demand from G^1 to G^2 raises output at every level of the exchange rate. The change therefore shifts *DD* to the right.

part of the figure, the exchange rate E^0 leads to an equilibrium output level Y^1 at the initial level of government demand; so point 1 is one point on DD^1.

An increase in G causes the aggregate demand schedule in the upper part of the figure to shift upward. Everything else remaining unchanged, output increases from Y^1 to Y^2. Point 2 in the bottom part shows the higher level of output Y^2 at which aggregate demand and supply are now equal, *given an unchanged exchange rate of E^0.* Point 2 is on a new *DD* curve, DD^2.

For any given exchange rate, the level of output equating aggregate demand and supply is higher after the increase in G. This implies that *an increase in G causes DD to shift to the right, as shown in Figure 16-5. Similarly, a decrease in G causes DD to shift to the left.*

The method and reasoning we have just used to study how an increase in G shifts the DD curve can be applied to all the cases that follow. Here we summarize the results. To test your understanding use diagrams similar to Figure 16-5 to illustrate how the economic factors listed below change the curves.

2. *A change in T.* Taxes, T, affect aggregate demand by changing disposable income, and thus consumption, for any level of Y. It follows that an increase in taxes causes the aggregate demand function of Figure 16-1 to shift *downward* given the exchange rate E. Since this effect is the opposite of that of an increase in G, an increase in T must cause the DD schedule to shift leftward. Similarly, a fall in T causes a rightward shift of DD.

3. *A change in I.* An increase in investment demand has the same effect as an increase in G: The aggregate demand schedule shifts upward and DD shifts to the right. A fall in investment demand shifts DD to the left.

4. *A change in P.* Given E and P*, an increase in P makes domestic output more expensive relative to foreign output and lowers net export demand. The DD schedule shifts to the left as aggregate demand falls. A fall in P makes domestic goods cheaper and causes a rightward shift of DD.

5. *A change in P*.* Given E and P, a rise in P* makes foreign goods and services relatively more expensive. Aggregate demand for domestic output therefore rises and DD shifts to the right. Similarly, a fall in P* causes DD to shift to the left.

6. *A change in the consumption function.* Suppose residents of the home economy suddenly decide they want to consume more and save less at each level of disposable income. If the increase in consumption spending is not devoted entirely to imports from abroad, aggregate demand for domestic output rises and the aggregate demand schedule shifts upward for any given exchange rate E. This implies a shift to the right of the DD schedule. An autonomous fall in consumption (if it is not entirely due to a fall in import demand) shifts DD to the left.

7. *A demand shift between foreign and domestic goods.* Suppose there is no change in the domestic consumption function but domestic and foreign residents suddenly decide to devote more of their spending to goods and services produced in the home country. If home disposable income and the real exchange rate remain the same, this shift in demand *improves* the current account by raising exports and lowering imports. The aggregate demand schedule shifts upward and DD therefore shifts to the right. The same reasoning shows that a shift in world demand away from domestic products and toward foreign products causes DD to shift to the left.

You may have noticed that a simple rule allows you to predict the effect on DD of any of the disturbances we have discussed: *Any disturbance that raises aggregate demand for domestic output shifts the DD schedule to the right; any disturbance that lowers aggregate demand for domestic output shifts the DD schedule to the left.*

Asset Market Equilibrium in the Short Run: The *AA* Schedule

We have now derived the first element in our account of short-run exchange rate and income determination, the relation between the exchange rate and output that is consistent with the equality of aggregate demand and supply. That relation is summarized by the DD schedule, which shows all exchange rate and output levels at which the output market is in short-run equilibrium. As we noted at the beginning of the preceding section, however, equilibrium in the economy as a whole requires equilibrium in the asset markets as well as in the output market, and there is no reason in general why points on the DD schedule should lead to asset market equilibrium.

To complete the story of short-run equilibrium, we therefore introduce a second element to ensure that the exchange rate and output level consistent with output market equilibrium are also consistent with asset market equilibrium. The schedule of exchange rate and output combinations that are consistent with equilibrium in the domestic money market and the foreign exchange market is called the *AA* **schedule.**

OUTPUT, THE EXCHANGE RATE, AND ASSET MARKET EQUILIBRIUM

In Chapter 13 we studied the interest parity condition, which states that the foreign exchange market is in equilibrium only when the expected rates of return on domestic and foreign currency deposits are equal. In Chapter 14 we learned how the interest rates that enter the interest parity relationship are determined by the equality of real money supply and real money demand in national money markets. Now we combine these asset market equilibrium conditions to see how the exchange rate and output must be related when all asset markets simultaneously clear. Because the focus for now is on the domestic economy, the foreign interest rate is taken as given.

For a given expected future exchange rate, E^e, the interest parity condition describing foreign exchange market equilibrium is equation (13-2),

$$R = R^* + (E^e - E)/E,$$

where R is the interest rate on domestic currency deposits and R^* is the interest rate on foreign currency deposits. In Chapter 14 we saw that the domestic interest rate satisfying the interest parity condition must also equate the real domestic money supply (M^s/P) to aggregate real money demand (see equation (14-4)):

$$M^s/P = L(R,Y).$$

You will recall that aggregate real money demand $L(R,Y)$ rises when the interest rate falls because a fall in R makes interest-bearing nonmoney assets less attractive to hold. (Conversely, a rise in the interest rate lowers real money demand.) A rise in real output, Y, increases real money demand by raising the volume of monetary transactions people must carry out (and a fall in real output reduces real money demand by reducing transactions needs).

We now use the diagrammatic tools developed in Chapter 14 to study the changes in the exchange rate that must accompany output changes so that asset markets remain in equilibrium. Figure 16-6 shows the equilibrium domestic interest rate and exchange rate associated with the output level Y^1 for a given nominal money supply, M^s, a given domestic price level, P, a given foreign interest rate, R^*, and a given value of the expected future exchange rate, E^e. In the lower part of the figure, we see that with real output at Y^1 and the real money supply at M^s/P, the interest rate R^1 clears the home money market (point 1) while the exchange rate E^1 clears the foreign exchange market (point 1'). The exchange rate E^1 clears the foreign exchange market because it equates the expected rate of return on foreign deposits, measured in terms of domestic currency, to R^1.

A rise in output from Y^1 to Y^2 raises aggregate real money demand from $L(R,Y^1)$ to $L(R,Y^2)$, shifting out the entire money demand schedule in the lower part of Figure 16-6.

FIGURE 16-6

Output and the Exchange Rate in Asset Market Equilibrium

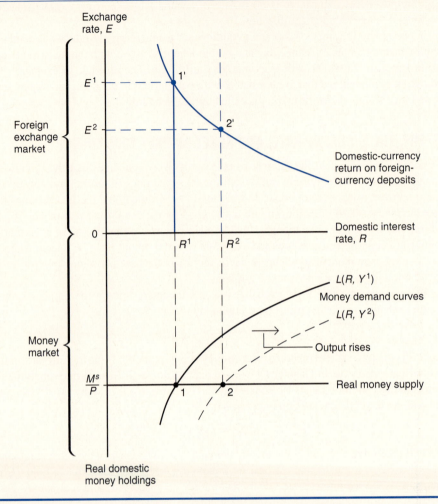

For the asset (foreign exchange and money) markets to remain in equilibrium, a rise in output must be accompanied by an appreciation of the currency, all else equal.

This shift, in turn, raises the equilibrium domestic interest rate to R^2 (point 2). With E^e and R^* fixed, the domestic currency must appreciate from E^1 to E^2 to bring the foreign exchange market back into equilibrium at point 2'. The domestic currency appreciates by just enough that the increase in the rate at which it is expected to *depreciate* in the future offsets the increased interest rate advantage of home currency deposits. *For asset markets to remain in equilibrium, a rise in domestic output must be accompanied by an appreciation of the domestic currency, all else equal, and a fall in domestic output must be accompanied by a depreciation.*

FIGURE 16-7

The *AA* Schedule

The asset market equilibrium schedule *AA* slopes downward because a rise in output from Y^1 to Y^2, all else equal, causes a rise in the home interest rate and a domestic currency appreciation from E^1 to E^2.

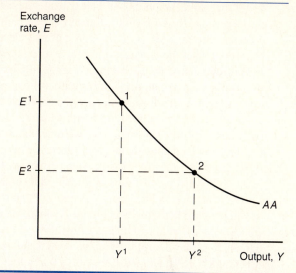

DERIVING THE *AA* SCHEDULE

While the *DD* schedule plots exchange rates and output levels at which the output market is in equilibrium, the *AA* schedule relates exchange rates and output levels that keep the money and foreign exchange markets in equilibrium. Figure 16-7 shows the *AA* schedule. From Figure 16-6 we see that for any output level, *Y*, there is a unique exchange rate, *E*, satisfying the interest parity condition (given the real money supply, the foreign interest rate, and the expected future exchange rate). Our previous reasoning tells us that other things equal, a rise in Y^1 to Y^2 will produce an appreciation of the domestic currency, that is, a fall in the exchange rate from E^1 to E^2. The *AA* schedule therefore has a negative slope, as shown.

FACTORS THAT SHIFT THE *AA* SCHEDULE

Five factors cause the *AA* schedule to shift: changes in the domestic money supply, M^s; changes in the domestic price level, *P;* changes in the expected future exchange rate, E^e; changes in the foreign interest rate, *R**; and shifts in the aggregate real money demand schedule.

     1. *A change in* M^s. For a fixed level of output, an increase in M^s causes the domestic currency to depreciate in the foreign exchange market, all else equal (that is, *E* rises). Since for each level of output the exchange rate *E* is higher after the rise in M^s, the rise in M^s causes *AA* to shift *upward*. Similarly, a fall in M^s causes *AA* to shift *downward*.

     2. *A change in P*. An increase in *P* reduces the *real* money supply and drives the interest rate upward. Other things (including *Y*) equal, this rise in the interest rate

causes E to fall. The effect of a rise in P is therefore a downward shift of AA. A fall in P results in an upward shift of AA.

3. *A change in E^e.* Suppose participants in the foreign exchange market suddenly revise their expectations about the exchange rate's future value so that E^e rises. Such a change shifts the curve in the top part of Figure 16-6 (which measures the expected domestic currency return on foreign currency deposits) to the right. The rise in E^e therefore causes the domestic currency to depreciate, other things equal. Because the exchange rate producing equilibrium in the foreign exchange market is higher after a rise in E^e, given output, AA shifts upward when a rise in the expected future exchange rate occurs. It shifts downward when the expected future exchange rate falls.

4. *A change in R^*.* A rise in R^* raises the expected return on foreign currency deposits and therefore shifts the downward-sloping schedule at the top of Figure 16-6 to the right. Given output, the domestic currency must depreciate to restore interest parity. A rise in R^* therefore has the same effect on AA as a rise in E^e: It causes an upward shift. A fall in R^* results in a downward shift of AA.

5. *A change in real money demand.* Suppose domestic residents decide they would prefer to hold lower real money balances at each output level and interest rate. (Such a change in asset-holding preferences is a *reduction in money demand*.) A reduction in money demand implies an inward shift of the aggregate real money demand function $L(R, Y)$ for any fixed level of Y, and it thus results in a lower interest rate and a rise in E. A reduction in money demand therefore has the same effect as an increase in the money supply, in that it shifts AA upward. The opposite disturbance of an increase in money demand would shift AA downward.

SHORT-RUN EQUILIBRIUM FOR AN OPEN ECONOMY: PUTTING THE *DD* AND *AA* SCHEDULES TOGETHER

By assuming that output prices are temporarily fixed, we have derived two separate schedules of exchange rate and output levels: the *DD* schedule, along which the output market is in equilibrium, and the *AA* schedule, along which the asset markets are in equilibrium. A short-run equilibrium for the economy as a whole must lie on *both* schedules because such a point must bring about equilibrium simultaneously in the output and asset markets. We can therefore find the economy's short-run equilibrium by finding the intersection of the *DD* and *AA* schedules. Once again, it is the assumption that output prices are temporarily fixed that makes this intersection a *short-run* equilibrium. The analysis in this section continues to assume that the foreign interest rate R^* and the expected future exchange rate E^e also are fixed.

Figure 16-8 combines the *DD* and *AA* schedules to locate short-run equilibrium. The intersection of *DD* and *AA* at point 1 is the only combination of exchange rate and output consistent with both the equality of aggregate demand and aggregate supply *and* asset market equilibrium. The short-run equilibrium levels of the exchange rate and output are therefore E^1 and Y^1.

To convince yourself that the economy will indeed settle at point 1, imagine that the economy is instead at a position like point 2 in Figure 16-9. At point 2, which lies above *AA* and *DD*, both the output and asset markets are out of equilibrium. Because E is so high relative to *AA*, the rate at which E is expected to fall in the future is also high relative to the

FIGURE 16-8

Short-Run Equilibrium: The Intersection of *DD* and *AA*

The short-run equilibrium of the economy occurs at point 1, where the output market (whose equilibrium points are summarized by the *DD* curve) and asset market (whose equilibrium points are summarized by the *AA* curve) simultaneously clear.

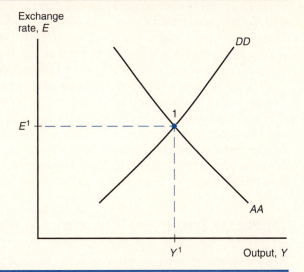

rate that would maintain interest parity. The high expected future appreciation rate of the domestic currency implies that the expected domestic currency return on foreign deposits is below that on domestic deposits, so there is an excess demand for the domestic currency in the foreign exchange market. The high level of E at point 2 also makes domestic goods cheap for foreign buyers (given the goods' domestic-currency prices), causing an excess demand for output at that point.

FIGURE 16-9

How the Economy Reaches its Short-Run Equilibrium

Because asset markets adjust very quickly, the exchange rate jumps immediately from point 2 to point 3 on *AA*. The economy then moves to point 1 along *AA* as output rises to meet aggregate demand.

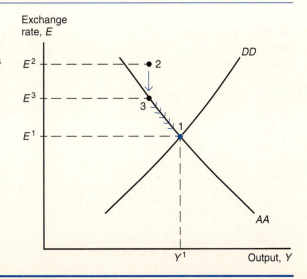

The excess demand for domestic currency leads to an immediate fall in the exchange rate from E^2 to E^3. This appreciation equalizes the expected returns on domestic and foreign deposits and places the economy at point 3 on the asset market equilibrium curve AA. But since point 3 is above the DD schedule, there is still excess demand for domestic output. As firms raise production to avoid depleting their inventories, the economy travels along AA to point 1, where aggregate demand and supply are equal. Because asset prices can jump immediately while changes in production plans take some time, the asset markets remain in continual equilibrium even while output is changing.

The exchange rate falls as the economy approaches point 1 along AA because rising national output causes money demand to rise, pushing the interest rate steadily upward. (The currency must appreciate steadily to lower the expected rate of future domestic currency appreciation and maintain interest parity.) Once the economy has reached point 1 on DD, aggregate demand equals output and producers no longer face involuntary inventory depletion. The economy therefore settles at point 1, the only point at which the output *and* asset markets clear.

Temporary Changes in Monetary and Fiscal Policy

Now that we have seen how the economy's short-run equilibrium is determined, we can study how shifts in government macroeconomic policies affect output and the exchange rate. Our interest in the effects of macroeconomic policies stems from their usefulness in counteracting economic disturbances that cause fluctuations in output, employment, and inflation. In this section we learn how government policies can be used to maintain full employment in open economies.

We concentrate on two types of government policy, **monetary policy,** which works through changes in the money supply, and **fiscal policy,** which works through changes in government spending or taxes.[7] To avoid the complications that would be introduced by ongoing inflation, however, we do not look at situations in which the money supply grows over time. Thus, the only type of monetary policies we will study explicitly are one-shot increases or decreases in money supplies.[8]

In this section we examine *temporary* policy shifts, shifts that the public expects to be reversed in the near future. The expected future exchange rate, E^e, is now assumed to equal the long-run exchange rate discussed in Chapter 15, that is, the exchange rate that prevails once full employment is reached and domestic prices have adjusted fully to past disturbances in the output and asset markets. In line with this interpretation, a temporary policy change does *not* affect the long-run expected exchange rate, E^e.

We assume throughout that events in the economy we are studying do not influence the foreign interest rate, R^*, or price level, P^*, and that the domestic price level, P, is fixed in the short run.

---

[7]Other policies, such as commercial policies (tariffs, quotas, etc.), have macroeconomic side effects. Such policies, however, are not used routinely for purposes of macroeconomic stabilization, so we do not discuss them in this chapter. (A problem at the end of this chapter does ask you to think about the macroeconomic effects of a tariff.)

[8]You can extend the results below to a setting with ongoing inflation by thinking of the exchange rate and price level changes we describe as departures from time paths along which E and P trend upward at constant rates.

FIGURE 16-10

Effects of a Temporary Increase in the Money Supply

By shifting AA^1 upward, a temporary increase in the money supply causes a currency depreciation and a rise in output.

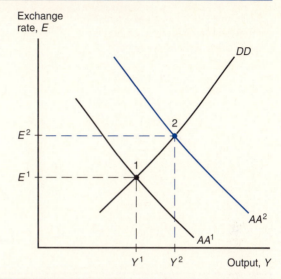

MONETARY POLICY

The short-run effect of a temporary increase in the domestic money supply is shown in Figure 16-10. An increased money supply shifts AA^1 upward to AA^2 but does not affect the position of DD. The upward shift of the asset market equilibrium schedule moves the economy from point 1, with exchange rate E^1 and output Y^1, to point 2, with exchange rate E^2 and output Y^2. An increase in the money supply causes a depreciation of the domestic currency, an expansion of output, and therefore an increase in employment.

We can understand the economic forces causing these results by recalling our earlier discussions of asset market equilibrium and output determination. At the initial output level Y^1 and given the fixed price level, an increase in money supply must push down the home interest rate, R. We have been assuming the monetary change is temporary and does not affect the expected future exchange rate, E^e, so to preserve interest parity in the face of a decline in R (given that the foreign interest rate, R^*, does not change), the exchange rate must depreciate immediately to create the expectation that the home currency will appreciate in the future at a faster rate than was expected before R fell. The immediate depreciation of the domestic currency, however, makes home products cheaper relative to foreign products. There is therefore an increase in aggregate demand, which must be matched by an increase in output.

FISCAL POLICY

As we saw earlier, expansionary fiscal policy can take the form of an increase in government spending, a cut in taxes, or some combination of the two that raises aggregate demand. A temporary fiscal expansion (which does not affect the expected future exchange rate) therefore shifts the DD schedule to the right but does not move AA.

FIGURE 16-11

Effects of a Temporary Fiscal Expansion

By shifting DD^1 to the right, a temporary fiscal expansion causes a currency
appreciation and a rise in output.

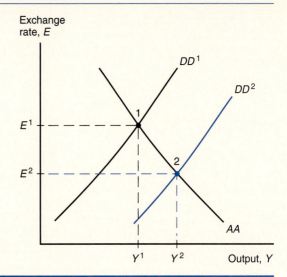

Figure 16-11 shows how expansionary fiscal policy affects the economy in the short run. Initially the economy is at point 1, with an exchange rate E^1 and output Y^1. Suppose the government decides to spend $5 billion to develop a new space shuttle. This one-time increase in government purchases moves the economy to point 2, causing the currency to appreciate to E^2 and output to expand to Y^2. The economy would respond in a similar way to a temporary cut in taxes.

What economic forces produce the movement from point 1 to point 2? The increase in output caused by the increase in government spending raises the transactions demand for real money holdings. Given the fixed price level, this increase in money demand pushes the interest rate, R, upward. Because the expected future exchange rate, E^e, and the foreign interest rate, R^*, have not changed, the domestic currency must appreciate to create the expectation of a subsequent depreciation just large enough to offset the higher international interest rate difference in favor of domestic currency deposits.

POLICIES TO MAINTAIN FULL EMPLOYMENT

The analysis of this section can be applied to the problem of maintaining full employment in open economies. Because temporary monetary expansion and temporary fiscal expansion both raise output and employment, they can be used to counteract the effects of temporary disturbances that lead to recession. Similarly, disturbances that lead to overemployment can be offset through contractionary macroeconomic policies.

Figure 16-12 illustrates this use of macroeconomic policy. Suppose the economy's initial equilibrium is at point 1, where output equals its full-employment level, denoted Y^f. Suddenly there is a temporary shift in consumer tastes away from domestic products. As we saw earlier in this chapter, such a shift is a decrease in aggregate demand for domestic

FIGURE 16-12

Maintaining Full Employment After a Temporary Fall in World Demand for Domestic Products

A temporary fall in world demand shifts DD^1 to DD^2 reducing output from Y^f to Y^2 and causing the currency to depreciate from E^1 to E^2 (point 2). Temporary fiscal expansion can restore full employment (point 1) by shifting the DD schedule back to its original position. Temporary monetary expansion can restore full employment (point 3) by shifting AA^1 to AA^2. The two policies differ in their exchange rate effects: The fiscal policy restores the currency to its previous value (E^1); the monetary policy causes the currency to depreciate further to E^3.

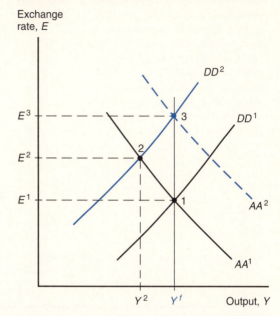

goods, and it causes the curve DD^1 to shift leftward, to DD^2. At point 2, the new short-run equilibrium, the currency has depreciated to E^2 and output, at Y^2, is below its full-employment level and the economy is in a recession. Because the shift in preferences is assumed to be temporary, it does not affect E^e, so there is no change in the position of AA^1.

To restore full employment, the government may use monetary or fiscal policy, or both. A temporary fiscal expansion shifts DD^2 back to its original position, restoring full employment and returning the exchange rate to E^1. A temporary money supply increase shifts the asset market equilibrium curve to AA^2 and places the economy at point 3, a move that restores full employment but causes the home currency to depreciate even further.

Another possible cause of recession is a temporary increase in the demand for money, illustrated in Figure 16-13. An increase in money demand pushes up the domestic interest rate and appreciates the currency, thereby making domestic goods more expensive and causing output to contract. Figure 16-13 shows this asset market disturbance as the downward shift of AA^1 to AA^2, which moves the economy from its initial full-employment equilibrium at point 1 to point 2.

Expansionary macroeconomic policies can again restore full employment. A temporary money supply increase shifts the AA curve back to AA^1 and moves the economy back to its initial position at point 1. This temporary increase in money supply completely offsets the increase in money demand by giving domestic residents the additional money they

FIGURE 16-13

Policies to Maintain Full Employment After a Money-Demand Increase

After a temporary money-demand increase (shown by the shift from AA^1 to AA^2) either an increase in the money supply or temporary fiscal ease can be used to maintain full employment. The two policies have different exchange rate effects: The monetary policy restores the exchange rate back to E^1, the fiscal policy leads to greater appreciation (E^3).

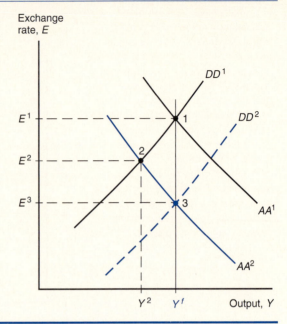

desire to hold. Temporary fiscal expansion shifts DD^1 to DD^2 and restores full employment at point 3. But the move to point 3 involves an even greater appreciation of the currency.

INFLATION BIAS AND OTHER PROBLEMS OF POLICY FORMULATION

The apparent ease with which full employment is maintained in our model is misleading, and you should not come away from our discussion of policy with the idea that it is easy to keep the macroeconomy on a steady course. Here are just a few of the many problems that can arise:

    1. Sticky nominal prices not only give governments the power to raise output when it is abnormally low, but also may tempt them to create a politically useful economic boom, say, just before a close election. This temptation causes problems when workers and firms anticipate it in advance, for they will raise wage demands and prices in the expectation of expansionary policies. The government will then find itself in the position of having to use expansionary policy tools merely to prevent the recession that higher domestic prices otherwise would cause! As a result, macroeconomic policy will display an **inflation bias,** leading to high inflation but no average gain in output. The inflation bias problem has led to a search for institutions, for example, central banks that operate independently of the government in power, that might convince market actors that government policies will not be used in a short-

sighted way, at the expense of long-term price stability. Chapters 20 and 22 will discuss some of these efforts.[9]

2. In practice it is sometimes hard to be sure whether a disturbance to the economy originates in the output or asset markets. Yet a government concerned about the exchange rate effect of its policy response needs to know this before it can choose between monetary and fiscal policy.

3. Real-world policy choices are frequently determined by bureaucratic necessities rather than by detailed consideration of whether shocks to the economy are real (that is, they originate in the output market) or monetary. Shifts in fiscal policy often can be made only after lengthy legislative deliberation, while monetary policy, in contrast, is usually exercised by the central bank. To avoid procedural delays, governments are likely to respond to disturbances by changing monetary policy even when a shift in fiscal policy would be more appropriate.

4. Another problem with fiscal policy is its impact on the government budget. A tax cut or spending increase may lead to a government budget deficit that must sooner or later be closed by a fiscal reversal. Unfortunately, there is no guarantee that the government will have the political will to synchronize these actions with the state of the business cycle. The state of the electoral cycle may be more important, as we have seen.

5. Policies that appear to act swiftly in our simple model operate in reality with lags of varying length. At the same time, the difficulty of evaluating the size and persistence of a given shock makes it hard to know precisely how much monetary or fiscal medicine to administer. These uncertainties force policymakers to base their actions on forecasts and hunches that may turn out to be quite wide of the mark.

PERMANENT SHIFTS IN MONETARY AND FISCAL POLICY

A permanent policy shift affects not only the current value of the government's policy instrument (the money supply, government spending, or taxes) but also the *long-run* exchange rate. This in turn affects expectations about future exchange rates. Because these changes in expectations have a major influence on the exchange rate prevailing in the short run, the effects of permanent policy shifts differ from those of temporary shifts. In this section we look at the effects of permanent changes in monetary and fiscal policy, in both the short and long run.[10]

To make it easier to grasp the long-run effects of policies, we assume that the economy is initially at a long-run equilibrium position and that the policy changes we examine

---

[9]For a clear and detailed discussion of the inflation bias problem, see Chapter 15 in Andrew B. Abel and Ben S. Bernanke, *Macroeconomics,* 2nd ed. (Reading, MA: Addison-Wesley, 1995). The inflation bias problem can arise even when the government's policies are not politically motivated, as Abel and Bernanke explain. The basic idea is that when factors like minimum wage laws keep output inefficiently low by lowering employment, monetary expansion that raises employment may move the economy toward a more efficient use of its total resources. The government might wish to reach a better resource allocation purely on the grounds that such a change potentially benefits everyone in the economy.

[10]You may be wondering whether a permanent change in fiscal policy is always possible. For example, if a government starts with a balanced budget, doesn't a fiscal expansion lead to a deficit, and thus require an eventual fiscal contraction? Problem 3 at the end of this chapter suggests an answer.

FIGURE 16-14

Short-Run Effects of a Permanent Increase in the Money Supply

A permanent increase in the money supply, which shifts AA^1 to AA^2 and moves the economy from point 1 to point 2, has stronger effects on the exchange rate and output than an equal temporary increase, which moves the economy only to point 3.

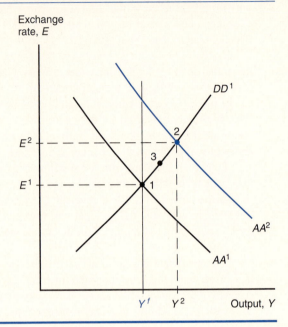

are the only economic changes that occur (our usual "other things equal" clause). These assumptions mean that the economy starts out at full employment with the exchange rate at its long-run level and with no change in the exchange rate expected. In particular, we know that the domestic interest rate must initially equal the foreign rate, R^*.

A PERMANENT INCREASE IN THE MONEY SUPPLY

Figure 16-14 shows the short-run effects of a permanent increase in the money supply on an economy initially at its full-employment output level Y^f (point 1). As we saw earlier, even a temporary increase in M^s causes the asset market equilibrium schedule to shift upward from AA^1 to AA^2. Because the increase in M^s is now permanent, however, it also affects the exchange rate expected for the future, E^e. Chapter 14 showed how a permanent increase in the money supply affects the long-run exchange rate: A permanent increase in M^s must ultimately lead to a proportional rise in E. Therefore, the rise in M^s causes E^e, the expected future exchange rate, to rise proportionally.

Because a rise in E^e accompanies a *permanent* increase in the money supply, the upward shift of AA^1 to AA^2 is greater than that caused by an equal, but transitory, increase. At point 2, the economy's new short-run equilibrium, Y and E are both higher than they would be were the change in the money supply temporary. (Point 3 shows the equilibrium that might result from a temporary increase in M^s.)

ADJUSTMENT TO A PERMANENT INCREASE IN THE MONEY SUPPLY

The increase in the money supply shown in Figure 16-14 is not reversed by the central bank, so it is natural to ask how the economy is affected *over time*. At the short-run equilibrium, shown as point 2 in Figure 16-14, output is above its full-employment level and labor and machines are working overtime. Upward pressure on the price level develops as workers demand higher wages and producers raise prices to cover their increasing production costs. Chapter 14 showed that while an increase in the money supply must eventually cause all money prices to rise in proportion, it has no lasting effect on output, relative prices, or interest rates. Over time, the inflationary pressure that follows a permanent money supply expansion pushes the price level to its new long-run value and returns the economy to full employment.

Figure 16-15 will help you visualize the adjustment back to full employment. Whenever output is greater than its full-employment level Y^f and productive factors are working overtime, the price level P is rising to keep up with rising production costs. Although the DD and AA schedules are drawn for a constant price level P, we have seen how increases in P cause them to shift. A rise in P makes domestic goods more expensive relative to foreign goods, discouraging exports and encouraging imports. A rising domestic price level therefore causes DD^1 to shift to the left over time. Because a rising price level steadily reduces the real money supply over time, AA^2 also travels to the left as prices rise.

The DD and AA schedules stop shifting only when they intersect at the full-employment output level Y^f; as long as output differs from Y^f, the price level will change and the

---

Long-Run Adjustment to a Permanent Increase in the Money Supply

After a permanent money-supply increase, a steadily increasing price level shifts the DD and AA schedules to the left until a new long-run equilibrium (point 3) is reached.

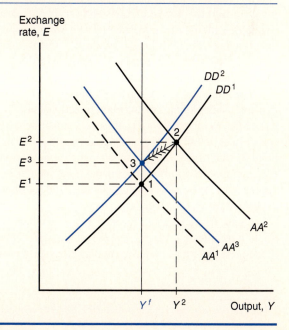

two schedules will continue to shift. The schedules' final positions are shown in Figure 16-15 as DD^2 and AA^3. At point 3, their intersection, the exchange rate, E, and the price level, P, have risen in proportion to the increase in the money supply, as required by the long-run neutrality of money. (AA^2 does not shift all the way back to its original position because E^e is permanently higher after a permanent increase in the money supply: It too has risen by the same percentage as M^s.)

Notice that along the adjustment path between the initial short-run equilibrium (point 2) and the long-run equilibrium (point 3), the domestic currency actually appreciates (from E^2 to E^3) following its initial sharp depreciation (from E^1 to E^2). This exchange rate behavior is an example of the *overshooting* phenomenon discussed in Chapter 14, in which the exchange rate's initial response to some change is greater than its long-run response.[11]

We can draw on our conclusions to describe the proper policy response to a permanent monetary disturbance. A permanent increase in money demand, for example, can be offset with a permanent increase in the money supply of equal magnitude. Such a policy maintains full employment, but because the price level would fall in the absence of the policy, the policy will not have inflationary consequences. Instead, monetary expansion can move the economy straight to its long-run, full-employment position. Keep in mind, however, that it is hard in practice to diagnose the origin or persistence of a particular shock to the economy.

A PERMANENT FISCAL EXPANSION

A permanent fiscal expansion not only has an immediate impact in the output market but also affects the asset markets through its impact on long-run exchange rate expectations. Figure 16-16 shows the short-run effects of a government decision to spend an extra $5 billion a year on its space travel program forever. As before, the direct effect of this rise in G on aggregate demand causes DD^1 to shift right to DD^2. But because the increase in government demand for domestic goods and services is permanent in this case, it causes a long-run appreciation of the currency, as we saw in Chapter 15. The resulting fall in E^e pushes the asset market equilibrium schedule AA^1 downward to AA^2. Point 2, where the new schedules DD^2 and AA^2 intersect, is the economy's short-run equilibrium, and at that point the currency has appreciated to E^2 from its initial level while output is unchanged at Y^f.

The important result illustrated in Figure 16-16 is that when a fiscal expansion is permanent, the additional currency appreciation caused by the shift in exchange rate expectations reduces the policy's expansionary effect on output. Without this additional expectations effect due to the permanence of the fiscal change, equilibrium would initially be at point 3, with higher output and a smaller appreciation. The greater the downward shift of the asset market equilibrium schedule, the greater the appreciation of the currency. This appreciation "crowds out" aggregate demand for domestic products by making them more expensive relative to foreign products.

Figure 16-16 is drawn to show a case in which fiscal expansion, contrary to what you might have guessed, has no net effect on output. This case is not, however, a special one; in fact, it is inevitable under the assumptions we have made. The argument that establishes

---

[11]While the exchange rate initially overshoots in the case shown in Figure 16-15, overshooting does not have to occur in all circumstances.

FIGURE 16-16

Effects of a Permanent Fiscal Expansion

Because a permanent fiscal expansion changes exchange-rate expectations, it shifts AA^1 leftward as it shifts DD^1 to the right. The effect on output (point 2) is nil if the economy starts in long-run equilibrium. A comparable *temporary* fiscal expansion, in contrast, would leave the economy at point 3.

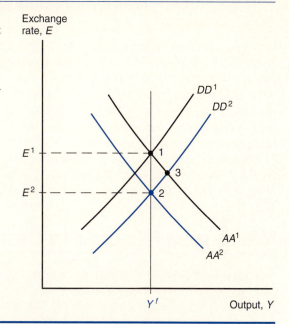

this point requires five steps; by taking the time to understand it you will solidify your understanding of the ground we have covered so far:

1. As a first step, convince yourself (perhaps by reviewing Chapter 14) that because the fiscal expansion does not affect the money supply, M^s, or the long-run values of the domestic interest rate (which equals the foreign interest rate) and output (Y^f), it can have no impact on the long-run price level.

2. Next, recall our assumption that the economy starts out in long-run equilibrium with the domestic interest rate, R, just equal to the foreign rate, R^*, and output equal to Y^f. Observe also that the fiscal expansion leaves the real money supply, M^s/P, unchanged in the short run (neither the numerator nor the denominator changes).

3. Now imagine, contrary to what Figure 16-16 shows, that output *did* rise above Y^f. Because M^s/P doesn't change in the short run (step 2), the domestic interest rate, R, would have to rise above its initial level of R^* to keep the money market in equilibrium. Since the foreign interest rate remains at R^*, however, a rise in Y to any level above Y^f implies an expected *depreciation* of the domestic currency (by interest parity).

4. Notice that there is something wrong with this conclusion: We already know (from step 1) that the long-run price level is not affected by the fiscal expansion, so people can expect a nominal domestic currency depreciation just after the policy change only if the currency depreciates in *real* terms as the economy returns to long-run equilibrium. Such a real depreciation, by making domestic products relatively cheap, would only worsen the initial situation of overemployment that we have imagined to exist, and thus would prevent output from ever actually returning to Y^f.

5. Finally, conclude that the apparent contradiction is resolved only if output does *not* rise at all after the fiscal policy move. The only logical possibility is that the currency appreciates right away to its new long-run value. This appreciation crowds out just enough net export demand to leave output at the full-employment level despite the higher level of *G*.

Notice that this exchange rate change, which allows the output market to clear at full employment, leaves the asset markets in equilibrium as well. Since the exchange rate has jumped to its new long-run value, *R* remains at *R**. With output also at Y^f, however, the long-run money market equilibrium condition $M^s/P = L(R^*, Y^f)$ still holds, as it did before the fiscal action. So our story hangs together: The currency appreciation that a permanent fiscal expansion provokes immediately brings the asset markets as well as the output market to positions of long-run equilibrium.

We conclude that *if the economy starts at long-run equilibrium, a permanent change in fiscal policy has no net effect on output. Instead, it causes an immediate and permanent exchange rate jump that offsets exactly the fiscal policy's direct effect on aggregate demand.*

MACROECONOMIC POLICIES AND THE CURRENT ACCOUNT

Policymakers are often concerned about the level of the current account. As we will discuss more fully in Chapter 18, an excessive imbalance in the current account—either a surplus or a deficit—may have undesirable long-run effects on national welfare. Large external imbalances may also generate political pressures for government restrictions on trade. It is therefore important to know how monetary and fiscal policies aimed at domestic objectives affect the current account.

Figure 16-17 shows how the *DD-AA* model can be extended to illustrate the effects of macroeconomic policies on the current account. In addition to the *DD* and *AA* curves, the figure contains a new curve, labeled *XX,* which shows combinations of the exchange rate and output at which the current account balance would be equal to some desired level, say $CA(EP^*/P, Y - T) = X$. The curve slopes upward because, other things equal, a rise in output encourages spending on imports and thus worsens the current account if it is not accompanied by a currency depreciation. Since the actual level of *CA* can differ from *X,* the economy's short-run equilibrium does *not* have to be on the *XX* curve.

The central feature of Figure 16-17 is that *XX* is *flatter* than *DD.* The reason is seen by asking how the current account changes as we move up along the *DD* curve from point 1, where all three curves intersect (so that, initially, *CA = X*). As we increase *Y* in moving up along *DD,* the *domestic* demand for domestic output rises by less than the rise in output itself (since some income is saved and some spending falls on imports). Along *DD,* however, *total aggregate demand has to equal supply.* To prevent an excess supply of home output, *E* therefore must rise sharply enough along *DD* to make export demand rise faster than imports. In other words, net foreign demand—the current account—must rise sufficiently along *DD* as output rises to take up the slack left by domestic saving. Thus to the right of point 1, *DD* is above the *XX* curve, where *CA > X;* similar reasoning shows that to the left of point 1 *DD* lies below the *XX* curve (where *CA < X*).

The current account effects of macroeconomic policies can now be examined. As shown earlier, an increase in the money supply, for example, shifts the economy to a position like point 2, expanding output and depreciating the currency. Since point 2 lies above

FIGURE 16-17

How Macroeconomic Policies Affect the Current Account

Along the curve *XX*, the current account is constant at the level *CA* = *X*. Monetary expansion moves the economy to point 2 and thus raises the current account balance. Temporary fiscal expansion moves the economy to point 3 while permanent fiscal expansion moves it to point 4; in either case the current account balance falls.

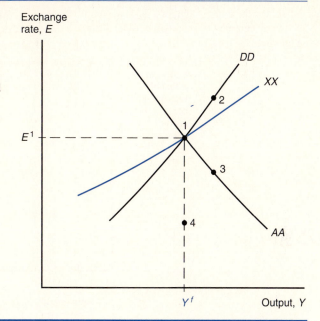

XX, the current account has improved as a result of the policy action. *Monetary expansion causes the current account balance to increase in the short run.*

Consider next a temporary fiscal expansion. This action shifts *DD* to the right and moves the economy to point 3 in the figure. Because the currency appreciates and income rises, there is a deterioration in the current account. A permanent fiscal expansion has the additional effect of shifting *AA* leftward, producing an equilibrium at point 4. Like point 3, point 4 is below *XX*, so once again the current account worsens. *Expansionary fiscal policy reduces the current account balance.*

GRADUAL TRADE FLOW ADJUSTMENT AND CURRENT ACCOUNT DYNAMICS

An important assumption underlying the *DD-AA* model is that other things equal, a real depreciation of the home currency immediately improves the current account while a real appreciation causes the current account immediately to worsen. In reality, however, the behavior underlying trade flows may be far more complex than we have so far suggested, involving dynamic elements—on the supply as well as the demand side—that lead the current account to adjust only gradually to exchange rate changes. In this section we discuss some dynamic factors that seem important in explaining actual patterns of current account adjustment and indicate how their presence might modify the predictions of our model.

FIGURE 16-18

The J-Curve

The J-curve describes the time lag with which a real currency depreciation improves the current account.

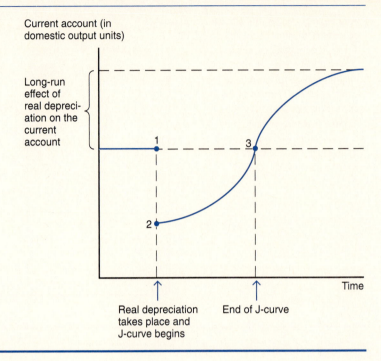

Current account (in domestic output units)

Long-run effect of real depreciation on the current account

Real depreciation takes place and J-curve begins

End of J-curve

Time

THE J-CURVE

It is sometimes observed that a country's current account *worsens* immediately after a real currency depreciation and begins to improve only some months later, contrary to the assumption we made in deriving the *DD* curve. If the current account initially worsens after a depreciation, its time path, shown in Figure 16-18, has an initial segment reminiscent of a J and therefore is called the **J-curve.**

The current account, measured in domestic output, can deteriorate sharply right after a real currency depreciation (the move from point 1 to point 2 in the figure) because most import and export orders are placed several months in advance. In the first few months after the depreciation, export and import volumes therefore may reflect buying decisions that were made on the basis of the old real exchange rate: The primary effect of the depreciation is to raise the value of the precontracted level of imports in terms of domestic products. Because exports measured in domestic output do not change while imports measured in domestic output rise, there is an initial fall in the current account, as shown.

Even after the old export and import contracts have been fulfilled, it still takes time for new shipments to adjust fully to the relative price change. On the production side, producers of exports may have to install additional plants and equipment and hire new workers. To the extent that imports consist of intermediate materials used in domestic manufacturing, import adjustment will also occur gradually as importers switch to new production techniques that economize on intermediate inputs. There are lags on the consumption side as well. To expand significantly foreign consumption of domestic exports, for example, it may be necessary to build new retailing outlets abroad, a time-consuming process.

The result of these lags in adjustment is the gradually improving current account shown in Figure 16-18 as the move from point 2 to point 3. Only after point 3 does the current account exceed its predepreciation level. Eventually, the increase in the current account tapers off as the adjustment to the real depreciation is completed.

Empirical evidence indicates for most industrial countries a J-curve lasting more than six months but less than a year. Thus, point 3 in the figure is typically reached within a year of the real depreciation and the current account continues to improve afterward.[12]

The existence of a significant J-curve effect forces us to modify some of our earlier conclusions, at least for the short run of a year or less. Monetary expansion, for example, can depress output initially by depreciating the home currency. In this case, it may take some time before an increase in the money supply results in an improved current account and therefore in higher aggregate demand.

If expansionary monetary policy actually depresses output in the short run, the domestic interest rate will need to fall further than it normally would to clear the home money market. Correspondingly, the exchange rate will overshoot more sharply to create the larger expected domestic currency appreciation required for foreign exchange market equilibrium. By introducing an additional source of overshooting, J-curve effects amplify the volatility of exchange rates.

EXCHANGE RATE PASS-THROUGH AND INFLATION

Our discussion of how the current account is determined in the *DD-AA* model has assumed that nominal exchange rate changes cause proportional changes in real exchange rates in the short run. Because the *DD-AA* model assumes that the nominal output prices P and P^* cannot suddenly jump, movements in the real exchange rate, $q = EP^*/P$, correspond perfectly in the short run to movements in the nominal rate, E. In reality, however, even the short-run correspondence between nominal and real exchange rate movements, while quite close, is less than perfect. To understand fully how *nominal* exchange rate movements affect the current account in the short run, we need to examine more closely the linkage between the nominal exchange rate and the prices of exports and imports.

The domestic currency price of foreign output is the product of the exchange rate and the foreign currency price, or EP^*. We have assumed until now that when E rises, for example, P^* remains fixed so that the domestic currency price of goods imported from abroad rises in proportion. The percentage by which import prices rise when the home currency depreciates by one percent is known as the degree of **pass-through** from the exchange rate to import prices. In the version of the *DD-AA* model we studied above, the degree of pass-through is 1; any exchange rate change is passed through completely to import prices.

---

[12]See the discussion of Table 16AIII-1 in Appendix III.

Contrary to this assumption, however, exchange rate pass-through can be incomplete. One possible reason for incomplete pass-through is international market segmentation, which allows imperfectly competitive firms to charge different prices for the same product in different countries. A large foreign firm supplying automobiles to the United States may be so worried about losing market share that it does not immediately raise its U.S. prices by 10 percent when the dollar depreciates by 10 percent, despite the fact that its revenue from American sales, measured in its own currency, will decline. Similarly, the firm may hesitate to lower its U.S. prices by 10 percent after a dollar appreciation of that size because it can thereby earn higher profits without investing resources immediately in expanding its shipments to the United States. In either case the firm may wait to find out if the currency movement reflects a definite trend before making price and production commitments that are costly to undo.

We thus see that while a permanent nominal exchange rate change may be fully reflected in import prices in the long run, the degree of pass-through may be far less than 1 in the short run. Incomplete pass-through will have complicated effects, however, on the timing of current account adjustment. On the one hand, the short-run J-curve effect of a nominal currency change will be dampened by a low responsiveness of import prices to the exchange rate. On the other hand, incomplete pass-through implies that currency movements have less-than-proportional effects on the relative prices determining trade volumes. The failure of relative prices to adjust quickly will in turn be accompanied by a slow adjustment of trade volumes.

Notice also how the link between nominal and real exchange rates may be further weakened by *domestic* price responses. In highly inflationary economies, for example, it is difficult to alter the real exchange rate EP^*/P simply by changing the nominal rate E, because the resulting increase in aggregate demand quickly sparks domestic inflation, which in turn raises P. To the extent that a country's export prices rise when its currency depreciates, any favorable effect on its competitive position in world markets will be dissipated. Such price increases, however, like partial pass-through, may weaken the J-curve.

MEXICO'S TRADE BALANCE AND THE PESO'S EXCHANGE RATE

When U.S. President Bill Clinton overcame fierce domestic opposition and persuaded Congress to approve the North American Free Trade Agreement (NAFTA) in November 1993, one of his strongest arguments was Mexico's buoyant demand for exports from north of its border. Slightly over a year later, in December 1994, Mexico's peso fell sharply against the dollar (we will see why in Chapters 17 and 22). As Mexican goods became cheaper relative to U.S. goods, Mexico's imports from the United States plummeted and U.S. imports from Mexico soared. Those in the United States who had opposed NAFTA renewed their criticism, and Republicans in Congress accused the Democratic administration of having covered up its knowledge of Mexico's problems.

The figure below shows monthly data on both the peso/dollar exchange rate and Mexico's merchandise trade surplus with the United States. As you can see, the peso's sharp depreciation against the dollar starting in December 1994 brought an immediate and dramatic improvement in its net exports.

Conspicuously absent are any of the complications suggested by our discussion of the J-curve. Four factors seem to be particularly important in explaining this. First, the peso's depreciation was massive—the peso price of dollars rose by more than 60 percent in the very short span of time between early December and February. Second, the financial crisis that accompanied the peso's fall could leave no doubt that the depreciation was permanent—a circumstance giving exporters and importers every incentive to adjust quickly. Third, the crisis was accompanied by a sharp contraction in Mexican domestic spending and output, which exerted a direct negative effect on the country's import demand. The final factor at work probably was NAFTA itself. The trade liberalization already undertaken made import and export volumes more sensitive to relative price changes than they would have been if higher trade barriers had been present.

Mexico's Trade Balance with the United States and the Peso/Dollar Exchange Rate, 1994–1995

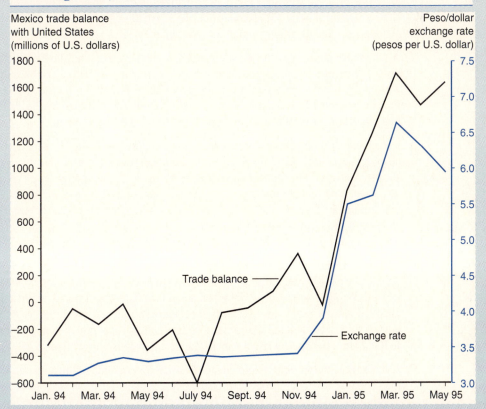

The peso's sharp depreciation against the dollar in December 1994, coupled with a precipitous fall in domestic income in Mexico, led to an immediate surge in Mexico's trade surplus with the United States.

Source: OECD, *Monthly Statistics of Foreign Trade*.

Summary

1. The *aggregate demand* for an open economy's output consists of four components, corresponding to the four components of GNP: consumption demand, investment demand, government demand, and the current account (net export demand). An important determinant of the current account is the real exchange rate, the ratio of the foreign price level (measured in domestic currency) to the domestic price level.

2. Output is determined in the short run by the equality of aggregate demand and aggregate supply. When aggregate demand is greater than output, firms increase production to avoid unintended inventory depletion. When aggregate demand is less than output, firms cut back production to avoid unintended accumulation of inventories.

3. The economy's short-run equilibrium occurs at the exchange rate and output level where—given the price level, the expected future exchange rate, and foreign economic conditions—aggregate demand equals aggregate supply and the asset markets are in equilibrium. In a diagram with the exchange rate and real output on its axes, the short-run equilibrium can be visualized as the intersection of an upward-sloping *DD* schedule, along which the output market clears, and a downward-sloping *AA* schedule, along which the asset markets clear.

4. A temporary increase in the money supply, which does not alter the long-run expected exchange rate, causes a depreciation of the currency and a rise in output. Temporary fiscal expansion also results in a rise in output, but it causes the currency to appreciate. *Monetary policy* and *fiscal policy* can be used by the government to offset the effects of disturbances to output and employment.

5. Permanent shifts in the money supply, which do alter the long-run expected exchange rate, cause sharper exchange rate movements and therefore have stronger short-run effects on output than transitory shifts. If the economy is at full employment, a permanent increase in the money supply leads to a rising price level that ultimately reverses the effect on the real exchange rate of the nominal exchange rate's initial depreciation. In the long run, output returns to its initial level and all money prices rise in proportion to the increase in the money supply.

6. Because permanent fiscal expansion changes the long-run expected exchange rate, it causes a sharper currency appreciation than an equal temporary expansion. If the economy starts out in long-run equilibrium, the additional appreciation makes domestic goods and services so expensive that the resulting "crowding out" of net export demand nullifies the policy's effect on output and employment. In this case, a permanent fiscal expansion has no expansionary effect at all.

7. A major practical problem is to ensure that the government's ability to stimulate the economy does not tempt it to gear policy to short-term political goals, thus creating an *inflation bias*. Other problems include the difficulty in identifying the sources or durations of economic changes and time lags in implementing policies.

8. If exports and imports adjust gradually to real exchange rate changes, the current account may follow a *J-curve* pattern after a real currency depreciation, first worsening and then improving. If such a J-curve exists, currency depreciation may have a contractionary initial effect on output, and exchange rate overshoot-

ing will be amplified. Limited exchange rate *pass-through,* along with domestic price increases, may reduce the effect of a nominal exchange rate change on the real exchange rate.

Key Terms

AA schedule, p. 451

aggregate demand, p. 440

DD schedule, p. 447

fiscal policy, p. 456

inflation bias, p. 460

J-curve, p. 468

monetary policy, p. 456

pass-through, p. 469

Problems

1. How does the *DD* schedule shift if there is a decline in investment demand?

2. Suppose the government imposes a tariff on all imports. Use the *DD-AA* model to analyze the effects this measure would have on the economy. Analyze both temporary and permanent tariffs.

3. Imagine that Congress passes a constitutional amendment requiring the U.S. government to maintain a balanced budget at all times. Thus, if the government wishes to change government spending, it must change taxes by the same amount, that is, $\Delta G = \Delta T$ always. Does the constitutional amendment imply that the government can no longer use fiscal policy to affect employment and output? (Hint: Analyze a "balanced-budget" increase in government spending, one that is accompanied by an equal tax hike.)

4. Suppose there is a permanent fall in private aggregate demand for a country's output (a downward shift of the entire aggregate demand schedule). What is the effect on output? What government policy response would you recommend?

5. How does a permanent cut in taxes affect the current account? What about a permanent increase in government spending? Reread the first Case Study in Chapter 12 and see if your answer accurately reflects the U.S. experience in the early 1980s.

6. If a government initially has a balanced budget but then cuts taxes, it is running a deficit that it must somehow finance. Suppose people think the government will finance its deficit by printing the extra money it now needs to cover its expenditures. Would you still expect the tax cut to cause a currency appreciation?

7. You observe that a country's currency depreciates but its current account worsens at the same time. What data might you look at to decide whether you are witnessing a J-curve effect? What other macroeconomic change might bring about a currency depreciation coupled with a deterioration of the current account, even if there is no J-curve?

8. A new government is elected and announces that once it is inaugurated, it will increase the money supply. Use the *DD-AA* model to study the economy's response to this announcement.

9. Many economists put part of the blame for the persistent U.S. current account deficit of the late 1980s on the apparently small size of the relative price change

between U.S. imports and exports. The first Case Study in Chapter 12, however, linked the slow current account adjustment to private and government saving behavior. Try to give a unified account of the current account data, reconciling both price and expenditure effects.

10. How would you draw the *DD-AA* diagram when the current account's response to exchange rate changes follows a J-curve? Use this modified diagram to examine the effects of temporary and permanent changes in monetary and fiscal policy.

11. What does the Marshall-Lerner condition look like if the country whose real exchange rate changes does *not* start out with a current account of zero? (The Marshall-Lerner condition is derived in Appendix III under the "standard" assumption of an initially balanced current account.)

12. Our model takes the price level *P* as given in the short run, but in reality the currency appreciation caused by a permanent fiscal expansion might cause *P* to fall a bit by lowering some import prices. If *P* can fall slightly as a result of a permanent fiscal expansion, is it still true that there are no output effects? (As above, assume an initial long-run equilibrium.)

13. Suppose that interest parity does not hold exactly, but that the true relationship is $R = R^* + (E^e - E)/E + \rho$ where ρ is a term measuring the differential riskiness of domestic versus foreign deposits. Suppose a permanent rise in domestic government spending, by creating the prospect of future government deficits, also raises ρ, that is, makes domestic currency deposits more risky. Evaluate the policy's output effects in this situation.

14. If an economy does *not* start out at full employment, is it still true that a permanent change in fiscal policy has no current effect on output?

15. See if you can retrace the steps in the five-step argument on pp. 465–466 to show that a permanent fiscal expansion cannot cause output to *fall*.

Further Reading

Victor Argy and Michael G. Porter. "The Forward Exchange Market and the Effects of Domestic and External Disturbances Under Alternative Exchange Rate Systems." *International Monetary Fund Staff Papers* 19 (November 1972), pp. 503–532. Advanced analysis of a macroeconomic model similar to the one in this chapter.

Victor Argy and Joanne K. Salop. "Price and Output Effects of Monetary and Fiscal Policies Under Flexible Exchange Rates." *International Monetary Fund Staff Papers* 26 (June 1979), pp. 224–256. The effects of macroeconomic policies under alternative institutional assumptions about wage indexation and the wage-price adjustment process in general.

C. Fred Bergsten. *International Adjustment and Financing: The Lessons of 1985–1991*. Washington, D.C.: Institute for International Economics, 1991. Analysis and debate on the behavior of industrial-economy current accounts.

Ralph C. Bryant et al., eds. *Empirical Macroeconomics for Interdependent Economies*. Washington, D.C.: Brookings Institution, 1988. This study compares what 12 leading econometric models predict about the domestic and foreign effects of individual countries' macroeconomic policies.

Rudiger Dornbusch. "Exchange Rate Expectations and Monetary Policy." *Journal of International Economics* 6 (August 1976), pp. 231–244. A formal examination of monetary policy and the exchange rate in a model with a J-curve.

Rudiger Dornbusch and Paul Krugman. "Flexible Exchange Rates in the Short Run." *Brookings Papers on Economic Activity* 3:1976, pp. 537–575. Theory and evidence on short-run macroeconomic adjustment under floating exchange rates.

Jacob A. Frenkel and Assaf Razin. "The Mundell-Fleming Model a Quarter Century Later: A Unified Exposition." *International Monetary Fund Staff Papers* 34 (December 1987), pp. 567–620. Further variations and background on models like the ones this chapter studies.

Peter Hooper and Jaime Marquez. "Exchange Rates, Prices, and External Adjustment in the United States and Japan," in Peter B. Kenen, ed. *Understanding Interdependence: The Macroeconomics of the Open Economy.* Princeton: Princeton University Press, 1995. Surveys empirical work on the macroeconomic determinants of trade balances.

Paul R. Krugman. "Pricing to Market When the Exchange Rate Changes," in Sven W. Arndt and J. David Richardson, eds. *Real-Financial Linkages Among Open Economies.* Cambridge: MIT Press, 1987, pp. 49–70. Theoretical discussion of interactions between exchange rates and import prices.

Robert Z. Lawrence. "U.S. Current Account Adjustment: An Appraisal." *Brookings Papers on Economic Activity* 2:1990, pp. 343–392. Thorough statistical analysis of U.S. current account behavior in the late 1980s.

Robert A. Mundell. *International Economics,* Chapter 17. New York: Macmillan, 1968. A classic account of macroeconomic policy effects under floating exchange rates.

Appendix I to Chapter 16

The *IS-LM* Model and the *DD-AA* Model

In this appendix we examine the relationship between the *DD-AA* model of the chapter and another model frequently used to answer questions in international macroeconomics, the *IS-LM* model. The *IS-LM* model generalizes the *DD-AA* model by allowing the real domestic interest rate to affect aggregate demand.

The diagram usually used to analyze the *IS-LM* model has the nominal interest rate and output, rather than the nominal exchange rate and output, on its axes. Like the *DD-AA* diagram, the *IS-LM* diagram determines the short-run equilibrium of the economy as the intersection of two individual market equilibrium curves, called *IS* and *LM*. The *IS* curve is the schedule of nominal interest rates and output levels at which the output and foreign exchange markets are in equilibrium, while the *LM* curve shows points at which the money market is in equilibrium.[13]

The *IS-LM* model assumes that investment, and some forms of consumer purchases (such as purchases of autos and other durable goods), are negatively related to the expected real interest rate. When the expected real interest rate is low, firms find it profitable to borrow and undertake investment plans. (The appendix to Chapter 7 presented a model of this link between investment and the real interest rate.) A low expected real interest rate also makes it more profitable to carry inventories rather than alternative assets. For both these reasons, we would expect investment to rise when the expected real interest rate falls. Similarly, because consumers find borrowing cheap and saving unattractive when the real interest rate is low, interest-responsive consumer purchases also rise when the real interest rate falls. As the next appendix shows, however, theoretical arguments as well as the evidence suggest the consumption response to the interest rate is weaker than the investment response.

In the *IS-LM* model, aggregate demand is therefore written as a function of the real exchange rate, disposable income, *and* the real interest rate,

$$D(EP^*/P, Y - T, R - \pi^e)$$
$$= C(Y - T, R - \pi^e) + I(R - \pi^e) + G + CA(EP^*/P, Y - T, R - \pi^e),$$

where π^e is the expected inflation rate and $R - \pi^e$ therefore the expected real interest rate. The model assumes that P, P^*, G, T, R^*, and E^e are all given. (To simplify the notation, we've left G out of the aggregate demand function D.)

---

[13]In a closed-economy context, the original exposition of the *IS-LM* model is in J. R. Hicks, "Mr. Keynes and the 'Classics': A Suggested Interpretation," *Econometrica* 5 (April 1937), pp. 147–159. Hicks's article still makes enjoyable and instructive reading today. The name *IS* comes from the fact that in a closed economy (but not necessarily in an open economy!) the output market is in equilibrium when investment (*I*) and saving (*S*) are equal. Along the *LM* schedule, real money demand (*L*) equals the real money supply (M^s/P in our notation).

To find the *IS* curve of *R* and *Y* combinations such that aggregate demand equals output,

$$Y = D(EP^*/P, Y - T, R - \pi^e),$$

we must first write this output market equilibrium condition so that it does not depend on *E*.

We solve for *E* using the interest parity condition, $R = R^* + (E^e - E)/E$. If we solve this equation for *E*, the result is

$$E = E^e/(1 + R - R^*).$$

Substitution of this expression into the aggregate demand function shows that we can express the condition for output market equilibrium as

$$Y = D[E^e P^*/P(1 + R - R^*), Y - T, R - \pi^e].$$

To get a complete picture of how output changes affect goods market equilibrium, we must remember that the inflation rate in the economy depends positively on the gap between actual output, *Y*, and full employment output, Y^f. We therefore write π^e as an increasing function of that gap:

$$\pi^e = \pi^e(Y - Y^f).$$

Under this assumption on expectations, the goods market is in equilibrium when

$$Y = D[E^e P^*/P(1 + R - R^*), Y - T, R - \pi^e(Y - Y^f)].$$

This condition shows that a fall in the nominal interest rate *R* raises aggregate demand through two channels: (1) Given the expected future exchange rate, a fall in *R* causes a domestic currency depreciation that improves the current account. (2) Given expected inflation, a fall in *R* directly encourages consumption and investment spending that falls only partly on imports. Only the second of these channels—the effect of the interest rate on spending—would be present in a closed-economy *IS-LM* model.

The *IS* curve is found by asking how output must respond to such a fall in the interest rate to maintain output market equilibrium. Since a fall in *R* raises aggregate demand, the output market will remain in equilibrium after *R* falls only if *Y* rises. The *IS* curve therefore slopes downward, as shown in Figure 16AI-1. Even though the *IS* and *DD* curves both reflect output market equilibrium, *IS* slopes downward while *DD* slopes upward. The reason for this difference is that the interest rate and the exchange rate are inversely related by the interest parity condition, given the expected future exchange rate.[14]

The slope of the *LM* (or money market equilibrium) curve is much easier to derive. Money market equilibrium holds when $M^s/P = L(R, Y)$. Because a rise in the interest rate reduces money demand, it results in an excess supply of money for a given output level. To

---

[14]In concluding that *IS* has a negative slope, we have argued that a rise in output reduces the excess demand for output caused by a fall in *R*. This reduction in excess demand occurs because while consumption demand rises with a rise in output, it rises by less. Notice, however, that a rise in output also raises expected inflation and thus stimulates demand. So it is conceivable that a fall in output, not a rise, eliminates excess demand in the output market. We assume this perverse possibility (which would give an upward sloping *IS* curve) does not arise.

FIGURE 16AI-1

Short-Run Equilibrium in the *IS-LM* Model

Equilibrium is at point 1, where the output and asset markets simultaneously clear.

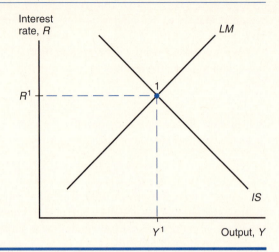

maintain equilibrium in the money market after R rises, Y must therefore rise also (because a rise in output stimulates the transactions demand for money). The *LM* curve thus has a positive slope, as shown in Figure 16AI-1. The intersection of the *IS* and *LM* curves at point 1 determines the short-run equilibrium values of output, Y^1, and the nominal interest rate, R^1. The equilibrium interest rate, in turn, determines a short-run equilibrium exchange rate through the interest parity condition.

The *IS-LM* model can be used to analyze the effects of monetary and fiscal policies. A temporary increase in the money supply, for example, shifts *LM* to the right, lowering the interest rate and expanding output. A *permanent* increase in the money supply, however, shifts *LM* to the right but also shifts *IS* to the right, since in an open economy that schedule depends on E^e, which now rises. The right-hand side of Figure 16AI-2 shows these shifts. At the new short-run equilibrium following a permanent increase in the money supply (point 2), output and the interest rate are higher than at the short-run equilibrium (point 3) following an equal temporary increase. The nominal interest rate can even be higher at point 2 than at point 1. This possibility provides another example of how the Fisher expected inflation effect of Chapter 15 can push the nominal interest rate upward after a monetary expansion.

The left-hand side of Figure 16AI-2 shows how the monetary changes affect the exchange rate. This is our usual picture of equilibrium in the foreign exchange market, but it has been rotated counterclockwise so that a movement to the left along the horizontal axis is an increase in E (a depreciation of the home currency). The interest rate R^2 following a permanent increase in the money supply implies foreign exchange market equilibrium at point 2', since the accompanying rise in E^e shifts the curve that measures the expected domestic currency return on foreign deposits. That curve does not shift if the money supply increase is temporary, so the equilibrium interest rate R^3 that results in this case leads to foreign exchange equilibrium at point 3'.

FIGURE 16AI-2

Effects of Permanent and Temporary Increases in the Money Supply in the *IS-LM* Model

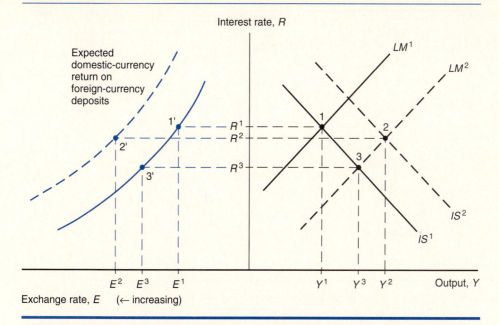

A temporary increase in the money supply shifts the *LM* curve alone to the right, but a permanent increase shifts both the *IS* and *LM* curves in that direction.

Fiscal policy is analyzed in Figure 16AI-3, which assumes a long-run equilibrium starting point. A temporary increase in government spending, for example, shifts IS^1 to the right but has no effect on *LM*. The new short-run equilibrium at point 2 shows a rise in output and a rise in the nominal interest rate, while the foreign exchange market equilibrium at point 2′ indicates a temporary currency appreciation. A permanent increase in government spending causes a fall in the long-run equilibrium exchange rate and thus a fall in E^e. The *IS* curve therefore does not shift out as much as in the case of a temporary policy. In fact, it does not shift at all: As in the *DD-AA* model, *a permanent fiscal expansion has no effect on output or the home interest rate.* The reason why permanent fiscal policy moves are weaker than transitory can be seen in the figure's left-hand side (point 3′). The accompanying change in exchange rate expectations generates a sharper currency appreciation and thus, through the response of net exports, a complete "crowding out" effect on aggregate demand.[15]

---

[15]One way the *IS-LM* model differs from the *DD-AA* model is that in the former, monetary expansion can cause a deterioration of the current account (even when there are no J-curve effects) by lowering the real interest rate and thus encouraging domestic spending. We leave it to the interested student to derive the *IS-LM* version of this chapter's *XX* curve.

FIGURE 16AI-3

Effects of Permanent and Temporary Fiscal Expansions in the *IS-LM* Model

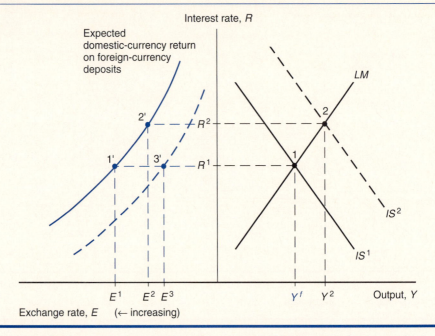

Temporary fiscal expansion has a positive effect on output while permanent fiscal expansion has none.

Appendix II to Chapter 16

Intertemporal Trade and Consumption Demand

We assume in the chapter that private consumption demand is a function of disposable income, $C = C(Y^d)$, with the property that when Y^d rises, consumption rises by less (so that saving, $Y - C(Y^d)$, goes up, too). This appendix interprets this assumption in the context of the intertemporal model of consumption behavior discussed in the appendix to Chapter 7.

The discussion in Chapter 7 assumed that consumers' welfare depends on present consumption demand D_P and future consumption demand D_F. If present income is Q_P and future income is Q_F, consumers can use borrowing or saving to allocate their consumption over time in any way consistent with the *intertemporal budget constraint*

$$D_P + D_F/(1 + r) = Q_P + Q_F/(1 + r),$$

where r is the real rate of interest.

Figure 16AII-1 reminds you of how consumption and saving were determined in Chapter 7. If present and future output are initially described by the point labeled 1 in the

---

FIGURE 16AII-1

Change in Output and Saving

A one-period increase in output raises saving.

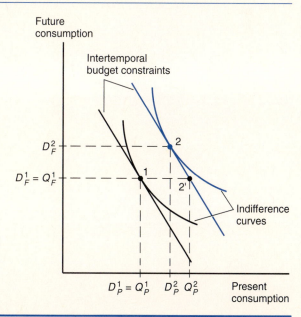

figure, the consumer's wish to pick the highest utility indifference curve consistent with their budget constraints leads to consumption at point 1 as well.

We have assumed zero saving at point 1 to show most clearly the effect of a rise in current output, which we turn to next. Suppose present output rises while future output doesn't, moving the income endowment to point 2′, which lies horizontally to the right of point 1. You can see that the consumer will wish to spread the increase in consumption this allows her over her *entire* lifetime. She can do this by saving some of the present income rise, $Q_P^2 - Q_P^1$, and moving up to the left along her budget line from her endowment point 2′ to point 2.

If we now reinterpret the notation so that present output, Q_P, corresponds to disposable income, Y^d, and present consumption demand corresponds to $C(Y^d)$, we see that while consumption certainly depends on factors other than current disposable income—notably, future income and the real interest rate—its behavior does imply that a rise in lifetime income that is concentrated in the present will indeed lead to a rise in current consumption that is less than the rise in current income. Since the output changes we have been considering in this chapter are all temporary changes that result from the short-run stickiness of domestic money prices, the consumption behavior we simply assumed in the chapter does capture the feature of intertemporal consumption behavior essential for the *DD-AA* model to work.

We could also use Figure 16AII-1 to look at the consumption effects of the real interest rate, which we introduced in Appendix I. If the economy is initially at point 1, a fall in the real interest rate r causes the budget line to rotate counterclockwise about point 1, causing a rise in present consumption. If initially the economy had been saving a positive amount, however, as at point 2, this effect would be ambiguous, a reflection of the contrary pulls of the income and substitution effects we introduced in Chapter 5. Empirical evidence indicates that the positive effect of a lower real interest rate on consumption probably is weak.

Use of the preceding framework to analyze the intertemporal aspects of fiscal policy would lead us too far afield, although this is one of the most fascinating topics in macroeconomics. We refer readers instead to any good intermediate macroeconomics text.[16]

---

[16]For example, see Abel and Bernanke, *Macroeconomics*, Chapter 16.

Appendix III to Chapter 16

The Marshall-Lerner Condition and Empirical Estimates of Trade Elasticities

The chapter assumed that a real depreciation of a country's currency improves its current account. As we noted, however, the validity of this assumption depends on the response of export and import volumes to real exchange rate changes. In this appendix we derive a condition on those responses for the assumption in the text to be valid. The condition, called the *Marshall-Lerner condition,* states that, all else equal, a real depreciation improves the current account if export and import volumes are sufficiently elastic with respect to the real exchange rate. (The condition is named after two of the economists who discovered it, Alfred Marshall and Abba Lerner.) After deriving the Marshall-Lerner condition, we look at empirical estimates of trade elasticities and analyze their implications for actual current account responses to real exchange rate changes.

To start, write the current account, measured in domestic output units, as the difference between exports and imports of goods and services similarly measured:

$$CA(EP^*/P, Y^d) = EX(EP^*/P) - IM(EP^*/P, Y^d).$$

Above, export demand is written as a function of EP^*/P alone because foreign income is being held constant.

Let q denote the real exchange rate EP^*/P and let EX^* denote domestic imports measured in terms of *foreign,* rather than domestic, output. The notation EX^* is used because domestic imports from abroad, measured in foreign output, equal the volume of foreign exports to the home country. If we identify q with the price of foreign products in terms of domestic products, then IM and EX^* are related by

$$IM = q \times EX^*,$$

that is, imports measured in domestic output = (domestic output units/foreign output unit) $\times$ (imports measured in foreign output units).[17]

---

[17]As we warned earlier in the chapter, the identification of the real exchange rate with relative output prices is not quite exact since, as we defined it, the real exchange rate is the relative price of expenditure baskets. For most practical purposes, however, the discrepancy is not qualitatively important. A more serious problem with our analysis is that national outputs consist in part of nontradables, and the real exchange rate covers their prices as well as those of tradables. To avoid the additional complexity that would result from a more detailed treatment of the composition of national outputs, we assume in deriving the Marshall-Lerner condition that the real exchange rate can be approximately identified with the relative price of imports in terms of exports.

The current account can therefore be expressed as

$$CA(q,Y^d) = EX(q) - q \times EX^*(q,Y^d).$$

Now let EX_q stand for the effect of a rise in q (a real depreciation) on export demand and let EX^*_q stand for the effect of a rise in q on import volume. Thus,

$$EX_q = \Delta EX/\Delta q, \; EX^*_q = \Delta EX^*/\Delta q.$$

As we saw in the chapter, EX_q is positive (a real depreciation makes home products relatively cheaper and stimulates exports) while EX^*_q is negative (a relative cheapening of home products reduces domestic import demand). Using these definitions, we can now ask how a rise in q affects the current account, all else equal.

If superscript ^{1} indicates the initial value of a variable while superscript ^{2} indicates its value after q has changed by $\Delta q = q^2 - q^1$, then the change in the current account caused by a real exchange rate change Δq is

$$\Delta CA = CA^2 - CA^1 = (EX^2 - q^2 \times EX^{*2}) - (EX^1 - q^1 \times EX^{*1})$$
$$= \Delta EX - (q^2 \times \Delta EX^*) - (\Delta q \times EX^{*1}).$$

Dividing through by Δq gives the current account's response to a change in q,

$$\Delta CA/\Delta q = EX_q - (q^2 \times EX^*_q) - EX^{*1}.$$

This equation summarizes the two current account effects of a real depreciation discussed in the text, the *volume* effect and the *value* effect. The terms involving EX_q and EX^*_q represent the volume effect, the effect of the change in q on the number of output units exported and imported. These terms are always positive because $EX_q > 0$ and $EX^*_q < 0$. The last term above, EX^{*1}, represents the value effect, and it is preceded by a minus sign. This last term tells us that a rise in q worsens the current account to the extent that it raises the domestic output value of the initial volume of imports.

We are interested in knowing when the right-hand side of the equation above is positive, so that a real depreciation causes the current account balance to increase. To answer this question, we first define the *elasticity of export demand* with respect to q,

$$\eta = (q^1/EX^1)EX_q,$$

and the *elasticity of import demand* with respect to q,

$$\eta^* = -(q^1/EX^{*1})EX^*_q.$$

(The definition of η^* involves a minus sign because $EX^*_q < 0$ and we are defining trade elasticities as positive numbers.) Returning to our equation for $\Delta CA/\Delta q$, we multiply its right-hand side by (q^1/EX^1) to express it in terms of trade elasticities. Then if the current account is initially zero (that is, $EX^1 = q^1 \times EX^{*1}$), this last step shows that $\Delta CA/\Delta q$ is positive when

$$\eta + (q^2/q^1)\eta^* - 1 > 0.$$

If the change in q is assumed to be small, so that $q^2 \approx q^1$, the condition for an increase in q to improve the current account is

$$\eta + \eta^* > 1.$$

This is the Marshall-Lerner condition. The condition states that if the current account is initially zero, a real currency depreciation causes a current account surplus if the sum of the relative price elasticities of export and import demand exceeds 1. (If the current account is not zero initially, the condition becomes substantially more complex.) In applying the Marshall-Lerner condition, remember that its derivation assumes that disposable income is held constant when q changes.

Now that we have the Marshall-Lerner condition, we can ask whether empirical estimates of trade equations imply price elasticities consistent with this chapter's assumption that a real exchange rate depreciation improves the current account. Table 16AIII-1 presents International Monetary Fund elasticity estimates for trade in manufactured goods. The table reports export and import price elasticities measured over three successively longer time horizons, and thus allows for the possibility that export and import demands adjust gradually to relative price changes, as in our discussion of the J-curve and beachhead effects. "Impact" elasticities measure the response of trade flows to relative price changes in the first six months after the change; "short-run" elasticities apply to a one-year adjustment period; and "long-run" elasticities measure the response of trade flows to the price changes over a hypothetical infinite adjustment period.

For most countries, the impact elasticities are so small that the sum of the impact export and import elasticities is less than 1. Since the impact elasticities usually fail to satisfy the Marshall-Lerner condition, the estimates support the existence of an initial J-curve effect that causes the real current account to deteriorate immediately following a real depreciation.

It is also true, however, that most countries represented in the table satisfy the Marshall-Lerner condition in the short run and that virtually all do so in the long run. The evidence is therefore consistent with the assumption made in the chapter: Except over short time periods, a real depreciation is likely to improve the current account while a real appreciation is likely to worsen it.

TABLE 16AIII-1

Estimated Price Elasticities for International Trade in Manufactured Goods

Country	η Impact	η Short-run	η Long-run	η^* Impact	η^* Short-run	η^* Long-run
Austria	0.39	0.71	1.37	0.03	0.36	0.80
Belgium	0.18	0.59	1.55	—	—	0.70
Britain	—	—	0.31	0.60	0.75	0.75
Canada	0.08	0.40	0.71	0.72	0.72	0.72
Denmark	0.82	1.13	1.13	0.55	0.93	1.14
France	0.20	0.48	1.25	—	0.49	0.60
Germany	—	—	1.41	0.57	0.77	0.77
Italy	—	0.56	0.64	0.94	0.94	0.94
Japan	0.59	1.01	1.61	0.16	0.72	0.97
Netherlands	0.24	0.49	0.89	0.71	1.22	1.22
Norway	0.40	0.74	1.49	—	0.01	0.71
Sweden	0.27	0.73	1.59	—	—	0.94
Switzerland	0.28	0.42	0.73	0.25	0.25	0.25
United States	0.18	0.48	1.67	—	1.06	1.06

Note: Estimates are taken from Jacques R. Artus and Malcolm D. Knight, *Issues in the Assessment of the Exchange Rates of Industrial Countries,* Occasional Paper 29. Washington, D.C.: International Monetary Fund, July 1984, Table 4. Unavailable estimates are indicated by dashes.

17

Fixed Exchange Rates and Foreign Exchange Intervention

In the past several chapters we have developed a model that helps us understand how a country's exchange rate and national income are determined by the interaction of asset and output markets. Using that model, we saw how monetary and fiscal policies can be used to maintain full employment and a stable price level.

To keep our discussion simple, we assumed that exchange rates are *completely* flexible, that is, that national monetary authorities themselves do not trade in the foreign exchange market to influence exchange rates. In reality, however, the assumption of complete exchange rate flexibility is rarely accurate. As we mentioned earlier, the world economy operated under a system of *fixed* dollar exchange rates between the end of World War II and 1973, with central banks routinely trading foreign exchange to hold their exchange rates at internationally agreed levels. Industrialized countries now operate under a hybrid system of **managed floating exchange rates**—a system in which governments may attempt to moderate exchange rate movements without keeping exchange rates rigidly fixed. Many developing countries have retained some form of government exchange rate fixing, for reasons that we discuss in Chapter 22.

In this chapter we study how central banks intervene in the foreign exchange market to fix exchange rates and how macroeconomic policies work when exchange rates are fixed. The chapter will help us understand the role of central bank foreign exchange intervention in the determination of exchange rates under a system of managed floating.

How does the central bank intervention hold the exchange rate fixed after the fiscal expansion? The process is the one we illustrated in Figure 17-1. Initially, there is an excess demand for money because the rise in output raises money demand. To prevent the excess money demand from pushing up the home interest rate and appreciating the currency, the central bank must buy foreign assets with money, thereby increasing the money supply. In terms of Figure 17-3, intervention holds the exchange rate at E^0 by shifting AA^1 rightward to AA^2. At the new equilibrium (point 3), output is higher than originally, the exchange rate is unchanged, and official international reserves (and the money supply) are higher.

Unlike monetary policy, fiscal policy can be used to affect output under a fixed exchange rate. Indeed, it is even more effective than under a floating rate! Under a floating rate, fiscal expansion is accompanied by an appreciation of the domestic currency that makes domestic goods and services more expensive and so tends to counteract the policy's positive direct effect on aggregate demand. To prevent this appreciation, a central bank that is fixing the exchange rate is forced to expand the money supply through foreign exchange purchases. The additional expansionary effect of this involuntary increase in the money supply explains why fiscal policy is more potent than under a floating rate.

CHANGES IN THE EXCHANGE RATE

A country that is fixing its exchange rate sometimes decides on a sudden change in the foreign currency value of the domestic currency. A **devaluation** occurs when the central bank raises the domestic currency price of foreign currency, E, and a **revaluation** occurs when the central bank lowers E. All the central bank has to do to devalue or revalue is announce its willingness to trade domestic against foreign currency, in unlimited amounts, at the new exchange rate.[6]

Figure 17-4 shows how a devaluation affects the economy. A rise in the level of the fixed exchange rate, from E^0 to E^1, makes domestic goods and services cheaper relative to foreign goods and services (given that P and P^* are fixed in the short run). Output therefore moves to the higher level Y^2 shown by point 2 on the DD schedule. Point 2, however, does not lie on the initial asset market equilibrium schedule AA^1: At point 2, there is initially an excess demand for money due to the rise in transactions accompanying the output increase. This excess money demand would push the home interest rate above the world interest rate if the central bank did not intervene in the foreign exchange market. To maintain the exchange rate at its new fixed level, E^1, the central bank must therefore buy foreign assets and expand the money supply until the asset market curve reaches AA^2 and passes through point 2. Devaluation therefore causes a rise in output, a rise in official reserves,

---

[6]We observe a subtle distinction between the terms *devaluation* and *depreciation* (and between *revaluation* and *appreciation*). Depreciation (appreciation) is a rise in E (a fall in E) when the exchange rate floats, while devaluation (revaluation) is a rise in E (a fall in E) when the exchange rate is fixed. Depreciation (appreciation) thus involves the active voice (as in "the currency appreciated"), while devaluation (revaluation) involves the passive voice (as in "the currency was devalued"). Put another way, devaluation (revaluation) reflects a deliberate government decision while depreciation (appreciation) is an outcome of government actions and market forces acting together.

FIGURE 17-4

Effect of a Currency Devaluation

When a currency is devalued from E^0 to E^1, the economy's equilibrium moves from point 1 to point 2 as both output and the money supply expand.

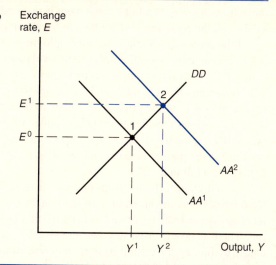

and an expansion of the money supply. A private capital inflow matches the central bank's reserve gain (an official outflow) in the balance of payments accounts.[7]

The effects of devaluation illustrate the three main reasons why governments sometimes choose to devalue their currencies. First, devaluation allows the government to fight domestic unemployment despite the lack of effective monetary policy. If government spending and budget deficits are politically unpopular, for example, or if the legislative process is slow, a government may opt for devaluation as the most convenient way of boosting aggregate demand. A second reason for devaluing is the resulting improvement in the current account, a development the government may believe to be desirable. The third motive behind devaluations is their effect on the central bank's foreign reserves. If the central bank is running low on reserves, a sudden, one-time devaluation can be used to draw in more.[8]

---

[7]After the home currency is devalued, market participants expect that the new higher exchange rate, rather than the old rate, will prevail in the future. The change in expectations alone shifts AA^1 to the right, but without central bank intervention this by itself is insufficient to move AA^1 all the way to AA^2. At point 2, as at point 1, $R = R^*$ if the foreign exchange market clears. Because output is higher at point 2 than at point 1, however, real money demand is also higher at the former point. With P fixed, an expansion of the money supply is therefore necessary to make point 2 a position of money market equilibrium, that is, a point on the new AA schedule. Central bank purchases of foreign assets are therefore a necessary part of the economy's shift to its new fixed exchange rate equilibrium.

[8]Because an unexpected devaluation lowers the foreign currency value of the government's domestic currency liabilities to the private sector, the initial reserve gain by the central bank is financed essentially by a surprise tax on holders of government bonds and money.

assumption and consistently show central banks to have practiced sterilized intervention throughout the twentieth century and earlier.[11]

In spite of widespread sterilized intervention, there is considerable disagreement among economists about its effects. In this section we study the role of sterilized intervention in exchange rate management.

PERFECT ASSET SUBSTITUTABILITY AND THE INEFFECTIVENESS OF STERILIZED INTERVENTION

When a central bank carries out a sterilized foreign exchange intervention, its transactions leave the domestic money supply unchanged. A rationale for such a policy is difficult to find using the model of exchange rate determination developed above, for the model predicts that without an accompanying change in the money supply, the central bank's intervention will not affect the domestic interest rate and therefore will not affect the exchange rate.

Our model also predicts that sterilization will be fruitless under a fixed exchange rate. The example of a fiscal expansion illustrates why a central bank might wish to sterilize under a fixed rate and why our model says the policy will fail. Recall that to hold the exchange rate constant when fiscal policy becomes more expansive, the central bank must buy foreign assets and expand the home money supply. The policy raises output but also causes inflation, which the central bank may try to avoid by sterilizing the increase in the money supply that its fiscal policy has induced. But as quickly as the central bank sells domestic assets to reduce the money supply, it will have to *buy* more foreign assets to keep the exchange rate fixed. The ineffectiveness of monetary policy under a fixed exchange rate implies that sterilization is a self-defeating policy.

The key feature of our model that leads to these results is the assumption that the foreign exchange market is in equilibrium only when the expected returns on domestic and foreign currency bonds are the same.[12] This assumption is often called **perfect asset substitutability.** Two assets are perfect substitutes when, as our model assumed, investors don't care how their portfolios are divided between them provided both yield the same expected rate of return. With perfect asset substitutability in the foreign exchange market, the exchange rate is therefore determined so that the interest parity condition holds. When this is the case there is nothing a central bank can do through foreign exchange intervention that it could not do as well through purely domestic open-market operations.

In contrast to perfect asset substitutability, **imperfect asset substitutability** exists when it is possible for assets' expected returns to differ in equilibrium. As we saw in Chap-

[11]Three empirical studies of recent experiences are Leroy O. Laney and Thomas D. Willett, "The International Liquidity Explosion and Worldwide Inflation: The Evidence from Sterilization Coefficient Estimates," *Journal of International Money and Finance* 1 (August 1982), pp. 141–152; Robert E. Cumby and Maurice Obstfeld, "Capital Mobility and the Scope for Sterilization: Mexico in the 1970s," in Pedro Aspe Armella, Rudiger Dornbusch, and Maurice Obstfeld, eds., *Financial Policies and the World Capital Market: The Problem of Latin American Countries* (Chicago: University of Chicago Press, 1983), pp. 245–269; and Cristina Mastropasqua, Stefano Micossi, and Roberto Rinaldi, "Interventions, Sterilization, and Monetary Policy in European Monetary System Countries, 1979–87," in Francesco Giavazzi, Stefano Micossi, and Marcus Miller, eds., *The European Monetary System* (Cambridge, U.K.: Cambridge University Press, 1988), pp. 252–287.

[12]We are assuming that all interest-bearing (nonmoney) assets denominated in *the same* currency, whether illiquid time deposits or government bonds, are perfect substitutes in portfolios. The single term *bonds* will generally be used to refer to all these assets.

ter 13, the main factor that may lead to imperfect asset substitutability in the foreign exchange market is *risk.* If bonds denominated in different currencies have different degrees of risk, investors may be willing to earn lower expected returns on bonds that are less risky. Correspondingly, they will hold a very risky asset only if the expected return it offers is relatively high.

In a world of perfect asset substitutability, participants in the foreign exchange market care only about expected rates of return; since these rates are determined by monetary policy, actions such as sterilized intervention that do not affect the money supply also do not affect the exchange rate. Under imperfect asset substitutability both risk *and* return matter, so central bank actions that alter the riskiness of domestic currency assets can move the exchange rate even when the money supply does not change. To understand how sterilized intervention can alter the riskiness of domestic currency assets, however, we must modify our model of equilibrium in the foreign exchange market.

FOREIGN EXCHANGE MARKET EQUILIBRIUM UNDER IMPERFECT ASSET SUBSTITUTABILITY

When domestic and foreign currency bonds are perfect substitutes, the foreign exchange market is in equilibrium only if the interest parity condition holds:

$$R = R^* + (E^e - E)/E. \tag{17-1}$$

When domestic and foreign currency bonds are *imperfect* substitutes, the condition above does not hold in general. Instead, equilibrium in the foreign exchange market requires that the domestic interest rate equal the expected domestic currency return on foreign bonds *plus* a **risk premium,** ρ, that reflects the difference between the riskiness of domestic and foreign bonds:

$$R = R^* + (E^e - E)/E + \rho. \tag{17-2}$$

Appendix I to this chapter develops a detailed model of foreign exchange market equilibrium with imperfect asset substitutability. The main conclusion of that model is that the risk premium on domestic assets rises when the stock of domestic government bonds available to be held by the public rises and falls when the central bank's domestic assets rise. It is not hard to grasp the economic reasoning behind this result. Private investors become more vulnerable to unexpected changes in the home currency's exchange rate as the stock of domestic government bonds they hold rises. Investors will be unwilling to assume the increased risk of holding more domestic government debt, however, unless they are compensated by a higher expected rate of return on domestic currency assets. An increased stock of domestic government debt will therefore raise the difference between the expected returns on domestic and foreign currency bonds. Similarly, when the central bank buys domestic assets, the market need no longer hold them; private vulnerability to home currency exchange rate risk is thus lower, and the risk premium on home currency assets falls.

This alternative model of foreign market equilibrium implies that the risk premium depends positively on the stock of domestic government debt, denoted by *B,* less the domestic assets of the central bank, denoted by *A:*

$$\rho = \rho(B - A). \tag{17-3}$$

The risk premium on domestic bonds therefore rises when $B - A$ rises. This relation between the risk premium and the central bank's domestic asset holdings allows the bank to

FIGURE 17-6

Effect of a Sterilized Central Bank Purchase of Foreign Assets Under Imperfect Asset Substitutability

A sterilized purchase of foreign assets leaves the money supply unchanged but raises the risk-adjusted return that domestic currency deposits must offer in equilibrium. As a result, the return curve in the upper panel shifts up and to the right. Other things equal, this depreciates the domestic currency from E^1 to E^2.

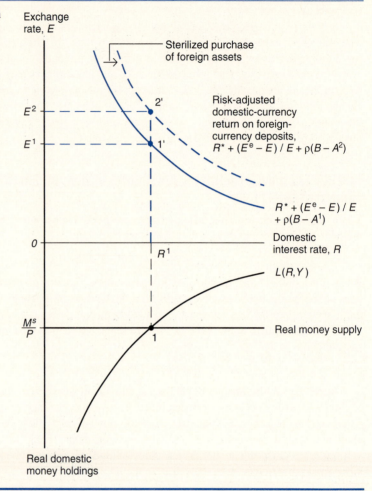

affect the exchange rate through sterilized foreign exchange intervention. It also implies that official operations in domestic and foreign assets may differ in their asset market impacts.[13]

THE EFFECTS OF STERILIZED INTERVENTION WITH IMPERFECT ASSET SUBSTITUTABILITY

Figure 17-6 modifies our earlier picture of asset market equilibrium by adding imperfect asset substitutability to illustrate how sterilized intervention can affect the exchange rate. The lower part of the figure, which shows the money market in equilibrium at point 1, does

---

[13]The stock of central bank domestic assets is often called domestic *credit*.

not change. The upper part of the figure is also much the same as before, except that the downward-sloping schedule now shows how the *sum* of the expected domestic currency return on foreign assets *and* the risk premium depends on the exchange rate. (The curve continues to slope downward because the risk premium itself is assumed not to depend on the exchange rate.) Equilibrium in the foreign exchange market is at point 1′, which corresponds to a domestic government debt of B and central bank domestic asset holdings of A^1. At that point, the domestic interest rate equals the risk-adjusted domestic currency return on foreign deposits (as in equation (17-2)).

Let's use the diagram to examine the effects of a sterilized purchase of foreign assets by the central bank. By matching its purchase of foreign assets with a sale of domestic assets, the central bank holds the money supply constant at M^s and avoids any change in the lower part of Figure 17-6. As a result of the domestic asset sale, however, the central bank's domestic assets are lower (they fall to A^2) and the stock of domestic assets that the market must hold, $B - A^2$, is therefore higher than the initial stock $B - A^1$. This increase pushes the risk premium ρ upward and shifts to the right the negatively sloped schedule in the upper part of the figure. The foreign exchange market now settles at point 2′, and the domestic currency depreciates to E^2.

With imperfect asset substitutability, even sterilized purchases of foreign exchange cause the home currency to depreciate. Similarly, sterilized sales of foreign exchange cause the home currency to appreciate. A slight modification of our analysis shows that the central bank can also use sterilized intervention to hold the exchange rate fixed as it varies the money supply to achieve domestic objectives such as full employment. In effect, the exchange rate and monetary policy can be managed independently of each other in the short run when sterilized intervention is effective.

EVIDENCE ON THE EFFECTS OF STERILIZED INTERVENTION

In the early 1980s European countries called on the United States to intervene systematically in the foreign exchange market and resist sharp movements in the dollar's exchange rate against other currencies. Leaders of the seven largest industrial economies discussed intervention at an economic summit meeting held at Versailles in June 1982.[14] As a result of the discussion, government economists in the summit countries were asked to prepare a study of the effects of alternative intervention practices.

The conclusions of the study were published in 1983 as the "Report of the Working Group on Exchange Market Intervention." The report asked in particular if sterilized intervention might allow central banks to manage exchange rates without corresponding adjustments in domestic monetary policies. Little evidence was found to support the idea that sterilized intervention had been a major independent factor influencing exchange rates.

This conclusion agrees with the one reached by most academic studies of sterilized intervention.[15] As we discuss at length in Chapter 21, however, there is also considerable evidence against the view that bonds denominated in different currencies are perfect substitutes. Some economists conclude from these conflicting results that while risk premiums

---

[14]The countries represented were Britain, Canada, France, Germany, Italy, Japan, and the United States.

[15]An article by Kenneth Rogoff analyzes Canadian data and surveys results for other countries. See Rogoff, "On the Effects of Sterilized Intervention: An Analysis of Weekly Data," *Journal of Monetary Economics* 14 (September 1984), pp. 133–150. The findings of the Federal Reserve participants in the Versailles project are summarized in the piece by Henderson and Sampson in Further Reading.

are important, they do not depend on central bank asset transactions in the simple way our model assumes.[16] Others contend that the tests that have been used to detect the effects of sterilized intervention are flawed.[17] Given the meager evidence that sterilized intervention has a reliable effect on exchange rates, however, a skeptical attitude is probably in order.

THE SIGNALING EFFECT OF INTERVENTION

A phenomenon sometimes referred to as the **signaling effect of foreign exchange intervention** is an important complicating factor in econometric efforts to study the effects of sterilization. Our discussion of sterilized intervention has assumed that it does not change the market's exchange rate expectations. If market participants are unsure about the future direction of macroeconomic policies, however, sterilized intervention may give an indication of where the central bank expects (or desires) the exchange rate to move. This signal, in turn, can alter the market's view of the future and cause an immediate exchange rate change even when bonds denominated in different currencies are perfect substitutes.

The signaling effect is most important when the government is unhappy with the exchange rate's level and declares in public that it will alter monetary or fiscal policies to bring about a change. By simultaneously intervening on a sterilized basis, the central bank sometimes lends credibility to this announcement. A sterilized purchase of foreign assets, for example, may convince the market that the central bank intends to bring about a home currency depreciation because the bank will lose money if an appreciation occurs instead. Even central banks must watch their budgets!

A government may be tempted to exploit the signaling effect for temporary benefits, however, even when it has no intention of changing monetary or fiscal policy to bring about a different long-run exchange rate. The result of crying "Wolf!" too often is the same in the foreign exchange market as elsewhere. If governments do not follow up on their exchange market signals with concrete policy moves, the signals soon become ineffective. Thus, intervention signaling cannot be viewed as a policy weapon to be wielded independently of monetary and fiscal policy.[18]

RESERVE CURRENCIES IN THE WORLD MONETARY SYSTEM

Until now, we have studied a single country that fixes its exchange rate in terms of a hypothetical single foreign currency by trading domestic for foreign assets when necessary. In the real world there are many currencies, and it is possible for a country to fix the exchange rates of its domestic currency against some foreign currencies while allowing them to float against others. This has been the case in the European Monetary System, whose members have held their mutual exchange rates fixed while allowing their currencies' dollar prices to fluctuate.

---

[16]For this view, see Robert J. Hodrick and Sanjay Srivastava, "An Investigation of Risk and Return in Forward Foreign Exchange," *Journal of International Money and Finance* 3 (April 1984), pp. 5–29.

[17]See, for example, Richard N. Cooper, "Comment," *Brookings Papers on Economic Activity* 2:1985, pp. 451–456.

[18]For discussion of the role played by the signaling effect in more recent exchange rate experience, see Owen F. Humpage, "Intervention and the Dollar's Decline," *Federal Reserve Bank of Cleveland Economic Review* 24 (Quarter 2, 1988), pp. 2–16; Maurice Obstfeld, "The Effectiveness of Foreign-Exchange Intervention: Recent Experience, 1985–1988" in William H. Branson, Jacob A. Frenkel, and Morris Goldstein, eds., *International Policy Coordination and Exchange Rate Fluctuations* (Chicago: University of Chicago Press, 1990), pp. 197–237; and Kathryn M. Dominguez and Jeffrey A. Frankel, *Does Foreign Exchange Intervention Work?* (Washington, D.C.: Institute for International Economics, 1993).

This section and the next adopt a global perspective and study the macroeconomic behavior of the world economy under two possible systems for fixing the exchange rates of *all* currencies against each other.

The first such fixed-rate system is very much like the one we have been studying. In it, one currency is singled out as a **reserve currency,** the currency central banks hold in their international reserves, and each nation's central bank fixes its currency's exchange rate against the reserve currency by standing ready to trade domestic money for reserve assets at that rate. Between the end of World War II and 1973, the U.S. dollar was the main reserve currency and almost every country pegged the dollar exchange rate of its currency.

The second fixed-rate system (studied in the next section) is a **gold standard.** Under a gold standard, central banks peg the prices of their currencies in terms of gold, and hold gold as official international reserves. The heyday of the international gold standard was between 1870 and 1914, although many countries attempted unsuccessfully to restore a permanent gold standard after the end of World War I in 1918.

Both reserve currency standards and the gold standard result in fixed exchange rates between *all* pairs of currencies in the world. But the two systems have very different implications about how countries share the burden of balance of payments financing and about the growth and control of national money supplies.

THE MECHANICS OF A RESERVE CURRENCY STANDARD

The workings of a reserve currency system are illustrated by the system based on the U.S. dollar set up at the end of World War II. Under that system, every central bank fixed the dollar exchange rate of its currency through foreign exchange market trades of domestic currency for dollar assets. The frequent need to intervene meant that each central bank had to have on hand sufficient dollar reserves to meet any excess supply of its currency that might arise. Central banks therefore held a large portion of their international reserves in the form of U.S. Treasury bills and short-term dollar deposits, which pay interest and can be turned into cash at relatively low cost.

Because each currency's dollar price was fixed by its central bank, the exchange rate between any two currencies was automatically fixed as well through arbitrage in the foreign exchange market. How did this process work? Let's suppose the French franc price of dollars was fixed at FFr 5 per dollar while the DM price of dollars was fixed at DM 4 per dollar. The exchange rate between the franc and the DM had to remain constant at DM 0.80 per franc = (DM 4 per dollar) ÷ (FFr 5 per dollar), even though no central bank was directly trading francs for DM to hold the relative price of those two currencies fixed. At a DM/FFr rate of DM 0.85 per franc, for example, you could have made a sure profit of $6.25 by selling $100 to the French central bank, the Bank of France, for ($100) × (FFr 5 per dollar) = FFr 500, selling your FFr 500 in the foreign exchange market for (FFr 500) × (DM 0.85 per franc) = DM 425, and then selling the DM to the German Bundesbank for (DM 425) ÷ (DM 4 per dollar) = $106.25. With everyone trying to exploit this profit opportunity by selling francs for DM in the foreign exchange market, however, the DM would have appreciated against the franc until the DM/FFr rate reached DM 0.80 per franc. Similarly, at a rate of DM 0.75 per franc, pressure in the foreign exchange market would have forced the DM to depreciate against the franc until the rate of DM 0.80 per franc was reached.

Even though each central bank tied its currency's exchange rate only to the dollar, market forces automatically held all other exchange rates—called cross rates—constant at

14. "When domestic and foreign bonds are perfect substitutes, a central bank should be indifferent about using domestic or foreign assets to implement monetary policy." Discuss.

15. United States foreign exchange intervention is sometimes done by an Exchange Stabilization Fund or ESF (a branch of the Treasury Department) that manages a portfolio of U.S. government and foreign currency bonds. An ESF intervention to support the yen, for example, would take the form of a portfolio shift out of dollar and into yen assets. Show that ESF interventions are automatically sterilized and thus do not alter money supplies. How do ESF operations affect the foreign exchange risk premium?

16. Use a diagram like Figure 17-6 to explain how a central bank can alter the domestic interest rate, while holding the exchange rate fixed, under imperfect asset substitutability.

Further Reading

Anatol Balbach. "The Mechanics of Intervention in Exchange Markets." *Federal Reserve Bank of St. Louis Review* 60 (February 1978), pp. 2–7. A detailed account of central bank intervention procedures.

William H. Branson. "Causes of Appreciation and Volatility of the Dollar," in *The U.S. Dollar—Recent Developments, Outlook, and Policy Options*. Kansas City: Federal Reserve Bank of Kansas City, 1985, pp. 33–52. Develops and applies a model of exchange rate determination with imperfect asset substitutability.

Dale W. Henderson and Stephanie Sampson. "Intervention in Foreign Exchange Markets: A Summary of Ten Staff Studies." *Federal Reserve Bulletin* 69 (November 1983), pp. 830–836. Presents the major findings of the Federal Reserve intervention study that followed the June 1982 Versailles economic summit meeting.

Owen F. Humpage. "Institutional Aspects of U.S. Intervention." *Federal Reserve Bank of Cleveland Economic Review* 30 (Quarter 1, 1994), pp. 2–19. How the U.S. Treasury and Federal Reserve coordinate foreign exchange intervention.

Ronald I. McKinnon. *A New Tripartite Monetary Agreement or a Limping Dollar Standard?* Princeton Essays in International Finance 106. International Finance Section, Department of Economics, Princeton University, October 1974. Critical analysis of intervention arrangements under the post-World War II fixed exchange rate system.

Robert A. Mundell. "Capital Mobility and Stabilization Policy Under Fixed and Flexible Exchange Rates." *Canadian Journal of Economics and Political Science* 29 (November 1963), pp. 475–485. Reprinted as Chapter 18 in Mundell's *International Economics*. New York: Macmillan, 1968. Classic account of the effects of monetary and fiscal policies under alternative exchange rate regimes.

Michael Mussa. "The Exchange Rate, the Balance of Payments and Monetary and Fiscal Policy Under a Regime of Controlled Floating," in Jan Herin, Assar Lindbeck, and Johan Myhrman, eds. *Flexible Exchange Rates and Stabilization Policy*. Boulder, CO: Westview Press, 1977, pp. 97–116. An exposition of the monetary approaches to the balance of payments and the exchange rate.

Michael Mussa. *The Role of Official Intervention.* Occasional Paper 6. New York: Group of Thirty, 1981. Discusses the theory and practice of central bank foreign exchange intervention under a dirty float.

Maurice Obstfeld. "Models of Currency Crises with Self-Fulfilling Features." *European Economic Review* 40 (April 1996), pp. 1037–1048. Discusses recent thinking on the nature of balance-of-payments crises.

Anna J. Schwartz. *Money in Historical Perspective.* Chicago: University of Chicago Press, 1987. Chapters 13–16 cover the gold standard and alternative exchange rate systems.

Warren E. Weber. "Do Sterilized Interventions Affect Exchange Rates?" *Federal Reserve Bank of Minneapolis Quarterly Review* 10 (Summer 1986), pp. 14–23. More evidence on whether sterilized intervention influences exchange rates.

Appendix I to Chapter 17

Equilibrium in the Foreign Exchange Market with Imperfect Asset Substitutability

This appendix develops a model of the foreign exchange market in which risk factors may make domestic currency and foreign currency assets imperfect substitutes. The model gives rise to a risk premium that can separate the expected rates of return on domestic and foreign assets.[24]

DEMAND

Because individuals dislike risky situations in which their wealth may vary greatly from day to day, they decide how to allocate wealth among different assets by looking at the riskiness of the resulting portfolio as well as at the expected return it offers. Someone who puts her wealth entirely into British pounds, for example, may expect a high return but can be wiped out if the pound unexpectedly depreciates. A more sensible strategy is to invest in several currencies, even if some have lower expected returns than the pound, and thus reduce the impact on wealth of bad luck with any one currency. By spreading risk in this way among several currencies, an individual can reduce the variability of her wealth.

Considerations of risk make it reasonable to assume that an individual's demand for interest-bearing domestic currency assets increases when the interest they offer (R) rises relative to the domestic currency return on foreign currency assets $[R^* + (E^e - E)/E]$. Put another way, an individual will be willing to increase the riskiness of her portfolio by investing more heavily in domestic currency assets only if she is compensated by an increase in the relative expected return on those assets.

We summarize this assumption by writing individual i's demand for domestic currency bonds, B_i^d as an increasing function of the rate-of-return difference between domestic and foreign bonds,

$$B_i^d = B_i^d[R - R^* - (E^e - E)/E].$$

Of course, B_i^d also depends on other factors specific to individual i, such as her wealth and income. The demand for domestic currency bonds can be negative or positive, and in the

---

[24]The Mathematical Postscript to Chapter 21 develops a microeconomic model of individual demand for risky assets.

former case individual i is a net borrower in the home currency, that is, a *supplier* of domestic currency bonds.

To find the *aggregate* private demand for domestic currency bonds, we need only add up individual demands B_i^d for all individuals i in the world. This summation gives the aggregate demand for domestic currency bonds, B^d, which is also an increasing function of the expected rate of return difference in favor of domestic currency assets. Therefore,

$$\text{Demand} = B^d[R - R^* - (E^e - E)/E]$$
$$= \text{sum for all } i \text{ of } B_i^d[R - R^* - (E^e - E)/E].$$

Since some private individuals may be borrowing, and therefore supplying bonds, B^d should be interpreted as the private sector's *net* demand for domestic currency bonds.

SUPPLY

Since we are interpreting B^d as the private sector's *net* demand for domestic currency bonds, the appropriate supply variable to define market equilibrium is the net supply of domestic currency bonds to the private sector, that is, the supply of bonds that are not the liability of any private individual. Net supply therefore equals the value of domestic currency *government* bonds held by the public, B, less the value of domestic currency assets held by the central bank, A:

$$\text{Supply} = B - A.$$

A must be subtracted from B to find the net supply of bonds because purchases of bonds by the central bank reduce the supply available to private investors. (More generally, we would also subtract from B domestic currency assets held by foreign central banks.)

EQUILIBRIUM

The risk premium, ρ, is determined by the interaction of supply and demand. The risk premium is defined as

$$\rho = R - R^* - (E^e - E)/E,$$

that is, as the expected return difference between domestic and foreign bonds. We can therefore write the private sector's net demand for domestic currency bonds as an increasing function of ρ. Figure 17AI-1 shows this relationship by drawing the demand curve for domestic currency bonds with a positive slope.

The bond supply curve is vertical at $B - A^1$ because the net supply of bonds to the market is determined by decisions of the government and central bank and is independent of the risk premium. Equilibrium occurs at point 1 (at a risk premium of ρ^1), where the private sector's net demand for domestic currency bonds equals the net supply. Notice that for given values of R, R^*, and E^e, the equilibrium shown in the diagram can also be viewed as determining the exchange rate, since $E = E^e/(1 + R - R^* - \rho)$.

Figure 17AI-1 shows the effect of a central bank sale of domestic assets that lowers its domestic asset holdings to $A^2 < A^1$. This sale raises the net supply of domestic currency

FIGURE 17AI-1

The Domestic Bond Supply and the Foreign Exchange Risk Premium Under Imperfect Asset Substitutability

An increase in the supply of domestic currency bonds that the private sector must hold raises the risk premium on domestic currency assets.

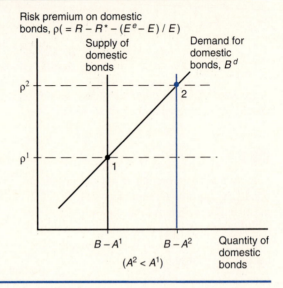

bonds to $B - A^2$ and shifts the supply curve to the right. The new equilibrium occurs at point 2, at a risk premium of $\rho^2 > \rho^1$. Similarly, an increase in the domestic currency government debt, B, would raise the risk premium.

The model therefore establishes that the risk premium is an increasing function of $B - A$, as we assumed in the discussion of sterilized intervention that led to equation (17-3).

Appendix II to Chapter 17

The Monetary Approach to the Balance of Payments

The close link discussed above between a country's balance of payments and its money supply suggests that fluctuations in central bank reserves can be thought of as the result of changes in the money market. This method of analyzing the balance of payments is called the *monetary approach to the balance of payments*. The monetary approach was developed in the 1950s and 1960s by the International Monetary Fund's research department under Jacques J. Polak, and by Harry G. Johnson, Robert A. Mundell, and their students at the University of Chicago.[25]

The monetary approach can be illustrated through a simple model linking the balance of payments to developments in the money market. To begin, recall that the money market is in equilibrium when the real money supply equals real money demand, that is, when

$$M^s/P = L(R,Y). \tag{17AII-1}$$

Now let F^* denote the central bank's foreign assets (measured in domestic currency) and A its domestic assets (domestic credit). If μ is the *money multiplier* that defines the relation between total central bank assets $(F^* + A)$ and the money supply, then

$$M^s = \mu(F^* + A). \tag{17AII-2}$$

The change in central bank foreign assets over any time period, ΔF^*, equals the balance of payments (for a nonreserve currency country). By combining (17AII-1) and (17AII-2), we can express the central bank's foreign assets as

$$F^* = (1/\mu)PL(R,Y) - A.$$

If we assume that μ is a constant, the balance of payments surplus is

$$\Delta F^* = (1/\mu)\Delta[PL(R,Y)] - \Delta A. \tag{17AII-3}$$

The last equation summarizes the monetary approach. The first term on its right-hand side reflects changes in nominal money demand and tells us that, all else equal, an increase in money demand will bring about a balance of payments surplus and an accompanying increase in the money supply that maintains money market equilibrium. The second term in the balance of payments equation reflects supply factors in the money market. An increase

---

[25]Many original articles using the monetary approach are collected in Jacob A. Frenkel and Harry G. Johnson, eds., *The Monetary Approach to the Balance of Payments* (London: George Allen and Unwin, 1976), and International Monetary Fund, *The Monetary Approach to the Balance of Payments* (Washington, D.C.: International Monetary Fund, 1977).

available in the rest of the world. In this case, paying back loans from foreigners poses no problem because a profitable investment will generate a return high enough to cover the interest and principal on those loans. Similarly, a current account surplus may pose no problem if domestic savings are being invested more profitably abroad than they would be at home.

More generally, we may think of current account imbalances as providing another example of how countries gain from trade. The trade involved is what we have called *intertemporal trade,* that is, the trade of consumption over time (Chapter 7). Just as countries with differing abilities to produce goods at a single point in time gain from concentrating their production on what they do best and trading, countries can gain from concentrating the world's investment in those economies best able to turn current output into future output. Countries with weak investment opportunities should invest little at home and channel their savings into more productive investment activity abroad. Put another way, countries where investment is relatively unproductive should be net exporters of currently available output (and thus have current account surpluses), while countries where investment is relatively productive should be net importers of current output (and have current account deficits). To pay off their foreign debts when the investments mature, the latter countries export output to the former countries and thereby complete the exchange of present output for future output.

Other considerations may also justify an unbalanced current account. A country where output drops temporarily (for example, because of an unusually bad crop failure) may wish to borrow from foreigners to avoid the sharp temporary fall in its consumption that would otherwise occur. In the absence of this borrowing, the price of present output in terms of future output would be higher in the low-output country than abroad, so the intertemporal trade that eliminates this price difference leads to mutual gains.

Insisting that all countries be in current account equilibrium makes no allowance for these important gains from trade over time. Thus, no realistic policymaker would want to adopt a balanced current account as a policy target appropriate in all circumstances.

At a given point, however, policymakers generally adopt *some* current account target as an objective, and this target defines their external balance goal. While the target level of the current account is generally not zero, governments usually try to avoid extremely large external surpluses or deficits unless they have clear evidence that large imbalances are justified by potential intertemporal trade gains. (After the sharp rise in oil prices in the early 1970s, for example, Norway's government allowed extensive foreign borrowing to fund the development of the country's North Sea oil reserves.) Governments are cautious because the exact current account balance that maximizes the gains from intertemporal trade is difficult if not impossible to figure out. In addition, this optimal current account balance can change unpredictably over time as conditions in the economy change. Current account balances that are very wide of the mark can, however, cause serious problems.

Problems with Excessive Current Account Deficits.   Why do governments prefer to avoid current account deficits that are too large? As noted, a current account deficit (which means that the economy is borrowing from abroad) may pose no problem if the borrowed funds are channeled into productive domestic investment projects that pay for themselves with the revenue they generate in the future. Sometimes, however, large current account deficits represent temporarily high consumption resulting from misguided government policies or some other malfunction in the economy. At other times, the investment projects that draw on foreign funds may be badly planned and based on overoptimistic expectations about future profitability. In such cases, the government might wish to reduce the current account deficit immediately rather than face problems in repaying debts to foreigners later. In particular, a large current account deficit caused by an expansionary fiscal policy that does not simultaneously make domestic investment opportunities more profitable may signal a need for the government to restore external balance by changing its economic course.

At times the external target is imposed from abroad rather than chosen by the domestic government. When countries begin to have trouble meeting their payments on past foreign loans, foreign creditors become reluctant to lend them new funds and may even demand immediate repayment of the earlier loans. After 1982, many developing economies (particularly those in Latin America) faced this problem of a limited ability to borrow abroad. In such cases, the home government may have to take severe action to reduce the country's desired borrowing from foreigners to feasible levels.

Problems with Excessive Current Account Surpluses.

An excessive current account surplus poses problems that are different from those posed by deficits. A surplus in the current account implies that a country is accumulating assets located abroad. Why are growing domestic claims to foreign wealth ever a problem? One potential reason stems from the fact that, for a given level of national saving, an increased current account surplus implies lower investment in domestic plant and equipment. (This follows from the national income identity, $S = CA + I$, which says that total domestic saving, S, is divided between foreign asset accumulation, CA, and domestic investment, I.) Several factors might lead policymakers to prefer that domestic saving be devoted to higher levels of domestic investment and lower levels of foreign investment. First, the returns on domestic capital may be easier to tax than those on assets abroad. Second, an addition to the home capital stock may reduce domestic unemployment and therefore lead to higher national income than an equal addition to foreign assets. Finally, domestic investment by one firm may have beneficial technological spillover effects on other domestic producers that the investing firm does not capture.

If a large home current account surplus reflects excessive external borrowing by foreigners, the home country may in the future find itself unable to collect the money it is owed. Put another way, the home country may lose part of its foreign wealth if foreigners find they have borrowed more than they can repay. In contrast, nonrepayment of a loan between domestic residents leads to a redistribution of national wealth within the home country but causes no change in the level of national wealth.

Excessive current account surpluses may also be inconvenient for political reasons. Countries with large surpluses can become targets for discriminatory protectionist measures by trading partners with external deficits. To avoid such damaging restrictions, surplus countries may try to keep their surpluses from becoming too large.

Although high surpluses, like deficits, can pose problems, governments whose economies are in deficit usually face much more intense pressures to restore external balance. This difference reflects a basic asymmetry. A borrowing country is dependent on its creditors, who may withdraw their credit at any time. In contrast, a lending country faces no such market-imposed limit on its surplus. Its government often can postpone external adjustment, if it chooses, for an indefinite period, even though the surplus may be detrimental to national welfare.

To summarize, the goal of external balance is a level of the current account that allows the most important gains from trade over time to be realized without risking the problems discussed above. Because governments do not know this current account level exactly, they usually try to avoid large deficits or surpluses unless there is clear evidence of large gains from intertemporal trade.

INTERNATIONAL MACROECONOMIC POLICY UNDER THE GOLD STANDARD, 1870–1914

The gold standard period between 1870 and 1914 was based on ideas about international macroeconomic policy very different from those that have formed the basis of international monetary arrangements in the second half of the twentieth century. Nevertheless, the period warrants attention because subsequent attempts to reform the international monetary system on the basis of fixed exchange rates can be viewed as attempts to build on the strengths of the gold standard while avoiding its weaknesses. (Some of these strengths and weaknesses were discussed in Chapter 17.) This section looks at how the gold standard functioned in practice before World War I and examines how well it enabled countries to attain goals of internal and external balance.

ORIGINS OF THE GOLD STANDARD

The gold standard had its origin in the use of gold coins as a medium of exchange, unit of account, and store of value. While gold has been used in this way since ancient times, the gold standard as a legal institution dates from 1819, when the British Parliament passed the Resumption Act. This law derived its name from its requirement that the Bank of England *resume* its practice—discontinued four years after the outbreak of the Napoleonic Wars (1793–1815)—of exchanging currency notes for gold on demand at a fixed rate. The Resumption Act marks the first adoption of a true gold standard because it simultaneously repealed long-standing restrictions on the export of gold coins and bullion from Britain.

Later in the nineteenth century, Germany, Japan, and other countries also adopted the gold standard. At the time, Britain was the world's leading economic power, and other nations hoped to achieve similar economic success by imitating British institutions. The United States effectively joined the gold standard in 1879 when it pegged to gold the paper "greenbacks" issued during the Civil War. The U.S. Gold Standard Act of 1900 institutionalized the dollar-gold link. Given Britain's preeminence in international trade and the advanced development of its financial institutions, London naturally became the center of the international monetary system built on the gold standard.

EXTERNAL BALANCE UNDER THE GOLD STANDARD

Under the gold standard, the primary responsibility of a central bank was to preserve the official parity between its currency and gold; to maintain this price, the central bank needed an adequate stock of gold reserves. Policymakers therefore viewed external balance not in terms of a current account target but as a situation in which the central bank was neither gaining gold from abroad nor (more important) losing gold to foreigners at too rapid a rate.

In the modern terminology of Chapter 12, central banks tried to avoid sharp fluctuations in the *balance of payments* (or official settlements balance), the sum of the current account balance and the nonreserve component of the capital account balance. Because international reserves took the form of gold during this period, the surplus or deficit in the balance of payments had to be financed by gold shipments between central banks.[2] To avoid large gold movements, central banks adopted policies that pushed the nonreserve component of the capital account surplus (or deficit) into line with the current account deficit (or surplus). A country is said to be in **balance of payments equilibrium** when the sum of its current and its nonreserve capital accounts equals zero, so that the current account balance is financed entirely by international lending without reserve movements.

Many governments took a laissez-faire attitude toward the current account. Britain's current account surplus between 1870 and World War I averaged 5.2 percent of its GNP, a figure that is remarkably high by post-1945 standards. (Today, a current account/GNP ratio half that size would be considered sizable.) Several borrowing countries, however, did experience difficulty at one time or another in paying their foreign debts. Perhaps because Britain was the world's leading exporter of international economic theory as well as of capital during these years, the economic writing of the gold standard era places little emphasis on problems of current account adjustment.[3]

THE PRICE-SPECIE-FLOW MECHANISM

The gold standard contains some powerful automatic mechanisms that contribute to the simultaneous achievement of balance of payments equilibrium by all countries. The most important of these, the **price-specie-flow mechanism,** was recognized by the eighteenth century (when precious metals were referred to as "specie"). David Hume, the Scottish philosopher, in 1752 described the price-specie-flow mechanism as follows:

> Suppose four-fifths of all the money in Great Britain to be annihilated in one night, and the nation reduced to the same condition, with regard to specie, as in the reigns of the Harrys and the Edwards, what would be the consequence? Must not the price of all labour and commodities sink in proportion, and everything be sold as cheap as they were in those ages? What nation could then dispute with us in any foreign market, or pretend to navigate or to sell manufactures at the same price, which to us would afford sufficient profit? In how little time, therefore, must this bring back the money which we had lost, and raise us to the level of all the neighbouring nations? Where, after we have arrived, we immediately lose the advantage of the cheapness of labour and commodities; and the farther flowing in of money is stopped by our fulness and repletion.
>
> Again, suppose that all the money in Great Britain were multiplied fivefold in a night, must not the contrary effect follow? Must not all labour and commodities rise to such an exorbitant height, that no neighbouring nations could afford to buy from us; while their commodities, on the other hand, became comparatively so cheap, that,

---

[2]In reality, central banks had begun to hold foreign currencies in their reserves even before 1914. (The pound sterling was the leading reserve currency.) It is still true, however, that the balance of payments was financed mainly by gold shipments during this period.

[3]While the economic consequences of the current account were often ignored (at least by surplus countries), governments sometimes restricted international lending by their residents to put political pressure on foreign governments. The political dimensions of international capital flows before World War I are examined in a famous study by Herbert Feis, *Europe, the World's Banker* (New Haven: Yale University Press, 1930).

in spite of all the laws which could be formed, they would run in upon us, and our money flow out; till we fall to a level with foreigners, and lose that great superiority of riches which had laid us under such disadvantages?[4]

It is easy to translate Hume's description of the price-specie-flow mechanism into more modern terms. Suppose that Britain's current account surplus is greater than its non-reserve capital account deficit. Because foreigners' net imports from Britain are not being financed entirely by British loans, the balance must be matched by flows of international reserves—that is, of gold—into Britain. These gold flows automatically reduce foreign money supplies and swell Britain's money supply, pushing foreign prices downward and British prices upward. (Notice that Hume fully understood the lesson of Chapter 14 (p. 384), that price levels and money supplies move proportionally in the long run.[5])

The simultaneous rise in British prices and fall in foreign prices—a real appreciation of the pound, given the fixed exchange rate—reduces foreign demand for British goods and services and at the same time increases British demand for foreign goods and services. These demand shifts work in the direction of reducing Britain's current account surplus and reducing the foreign current account deficit. Eventually, therefore, reserve movements stop and both countries reach balance of payments equilibrium. The same process also works in reverse, eliminating an initial situation of foreign surplus and British deficit.

THE GOLD STANDARD "RULES OF THE GAME": MYTH AND REALITY

The price-specie-flow mechanism could operate automatically under the gold standard to bring countries' current and capital accounts into line and eliminate international gold movements. But the reactions of central banks to gold flows across their borders furnished another potential mechanism to help restore balance of payments equilibrium. Central banks that were persistently losing gold faced the risk of becoming unable to meet their obligation to redeem currency notes. They were therefore motivated to contract their domestic asset holdings when gold was being lost, pushing domestic interest rates upward and attracting inflows of capital from abroad. Central banks gaining gold had much weaker incentives to eliminate their own imports of the metal. The main incentive was the greater profitability of interest-bearing domestic assets compared with "barren" gold. A central bank that was accumulating gold might be tempted to purchase domestic assets, thereby increasing capital outflows and driving gold abroad.

These domestic credit measures, if undertaken by central banks, reinforced the price-specie-flow mechanism in pushing all countries toward balance of payments equilibrium. After World War I, the practices of selling domestic assets in the face of a deficit and buying domestic assets in the face of a surplus came to be known as the gold standard "rules of the game"—a phrase reportedly coined by Keynes. Because such measures speeded the

---

[4]Hume, "Of the Balance of Trade," reprinted (in abridged form) in Barry Eichengreen, ed., *The Gold Standard in Theory and History* (London: Methuen, 1985), pp. 39–48.

[5]As mentioned in footnote 21 on p. 516, there are several ways in which the reduction in foreign money supplies, and the corresponding increase in Britain's money supply, might have occurred in Hume's day. Foreign residents could have melted gold coins into bars and used them to pay for imports. The British recipients of the gold bars could have then sold them to the Bank of England for British coins or paper currency. Alternatively, the foreign residents could have sold paper money to their central banks in return for gold and shipped this gold to Britain. Since gold coins were then part of the money supply, both transactions would have affected money supplies in the same way.

movement of all countries toward their external balance goals, they increased the efficiency of the automatic adjustment processes inherent in the gold standard.

Later research has shown that the supposed "rules of the game" of the gold standard were frequently violated before 1914. As noted, the incentives to obey the rules applied with greater force to deficit than to surplus countries, so in practice it was the deficit countries that bore the burden of bringing the payments balances of *all* countries into equilibrium. By not always taking actions to reduce gold inflows, the surplus countries worsened a problem of international policy coordination inherent in the system: Deficit countries competing for a limited supply of gold reserves might adopt overcontractionary monetary policies that harmed employment while doing little to improve their reserve positions.

In fact, countries often reversed the rules and *sterilized* gold flows, that is, sold domestic assets when foreign reserves were rising and bought domestic assets as foreign reserves fell. Government interference with private gold exports also undermined the system. The picture of smooth and automatic balance of payments adjustment before World War I therefore did not always match reality. Governments sometimes ignored both the "rules of the game" and the effects of their actions on other countries.[6]

INTERNAL BALANCE UNDER THE GOLD STANDARD

By fixing the prices of currencies in terms of gold, the gold standard aimed to limit monetary growth in the world economy and thus to ensure stability in world price levels. While price levels within gold standard countries did not rise as much between 1870 and 1914 as over the period after World War II, national price levels moved unpredictably over shorter horizons as periods of inflation and deflation followed each other. The gold standard's mixed record on price stability reflected a problem discussed in the last chapter, change in the relative prices of gold and other commodities.

In addition, the gold standard does not seem to have done much to ensure full employment. The U.S. unemployment rate, for example, averaged 6.8 percent between 1890 and 1913, but it averaged under 5.7 percent between 1946 and 1992.[7]

A fundamental cause of short-term internal instability under the pre-1914 gold standard was the subordination of economic policy to external objectives. Before World War I, governments had not assumed responsibility for maintaining internal balance as fully as they did after World War II. The importance of internal policy objectives increased after World War I as a result of the worldwide economic instability of the interwar years, 1918–1939. And the unpalatable internal consequences of attempts to restore the gold standard after 1918 helped mold the thinking of the architects of the fixed exchange rate system adopted after 1945. To understand how the post-World War II international monetary system tried to reconcile the goals of internal and external balance, we therefore must examine the economic events of the period between the two world wars.

---

[6]An influential modern study of central bank practices under the gold standard is Arthur I. Bloomfield, *Monetary Policy Under the International Gold Standard: 1880–1914* (New York: Federal Reserve Bank of New York, 1959).

[7]Data on price levels are given by Cooper (cited on p. 516 in Chapter 17) and data for U.S. unemployment are adapted from the same source. Caution should be used in comparing gold standard and post-World War II unemployment data because the methods used to assemble the earlier data were much cruder. A critical study of pre-1930 U.S. unemployment data is Christina Romer, "Spurious Volatility in Historical Unemployment Data," *Journal of Political Economy* 94 (February 1986), pp. 1–37.

HUME VERSUS THE MERCANTILISTS

David Hume's forceful account of the price-specie-flow mechanism is another example of the skillful use of economic theory to mold economic policy. An influential school of economic thinkers called *mercantilists* held that without severe restrictions on international trade and payments, Britain might find itself impoverished and without an adequate supply of circulating monetary gold as a result of balance of payments deficits. Hume refuted their arguments by demonstrating that the balance of payments would automatically regulate itself to ensure an adequate supply of money in every country.

Mercantilism, which originated in the seventeenth century, held that silver and gold were the mainstays of national wealth and essential to vigorous commerce. Mercantilists therefore viewed specie outflows with alarm and had as a main policy goal a continuing surplus in the balance of payments (that is, a continuing inflow of precious metals). As the mercantilist writer Thomas Mun put it around 1630: "The ordinary means therefore to increase our wealth and treasure is by foreign trade, wherein we must ever observe this rule: to sell more to strangers yearly than we consume of theirs in value."

Hume's reasoning showed that a perpetual surplus is impossible: Since specie inflows drive up domestic prices and restore equilibrium in the balance of payments, any surplus eventually eliminates itself. Similarly, a shortage of currency leads to low domestic prices and a foreign payments surplus that eventually brings into the country as much money as needed. Government interference with international transactions, Hume argued, would harm the economy without bringing about the ongoing increase in "wealth and treasure" that the mercantilists favored.

Hume pointed out that the mercantilists overemphasized a single and relatively minor component of national wealth, precious metals, while ignoring the nation's main source of wealth, its productive capacity. In making this observation Hume was putting forward a very modern view. Well into the twentieth century, however, policymakers concerned with external balance often focused on international gold flows at the expense of broader indicators of changes in national wealth. Since the mercantilists were discredited by the attacks of Hume and like-minded thinkers, this relative neglect of the current account and its relation to domestic investment and productivity is puzzling. Perhaps mercantilistic instincts survived in the hearts of central bankers.

THE INTERWAR YEARS, 1918–1939

Governments effectively suspended the gold standard during World War I and financed part of their massive military expenditures by printing money. Further, labor forces and productive capacity had been reduced sharply through war losses. As a result, price levels were higher everywhere at the war's conclusion in 1918.

Several countries experienced runaway inflation as their governments attempted to aid the reconstruction process through public expenditures. These governments financed their purchases simply by printing the money they needed, as they sometimes had during the war. The result was a sharp rise in money supplies and price levels.

THE GERMAN HYPERINFLATION

The most celebrated episode of interwar inflation is the German hyperinflation, during which Germany's price index rose from a level of 262 in January 1919 to a level of 126,160,000,000,000 in December 1923—a factor of 481.5 billion!

The Versailles Treaty ending World War I saddled Germany with a huge burden of reparations payments to the Allies. Rather than raising taxes to meet these payments, the German government ran its printing presses. The inflation accelerated most dramatically in January 1923 when France, citing lagging German compliance with the Versailles terms, sent its troops into Germany's industrial heartland, the Ruhr. German workers went on strike to protest the French occupation, and the German government supported their action by issuing even more money to pay them. Within the year, the price level rose by a factor of 452,998,200. Under these conditions, people were unwilling to hold the German currency, which became all but useless.

The hyperinflation was ended toward the end of 1923 as Germany instituted a currency reform, obtained some relief from its reparations burdens, and moved toward a balanced government budget.

THE FLEETING RETURN TO GOLD

The United States returned to gold in 1919. By the early 1920s, other countries yearned increasingly for the comparative financial stability of the gold standard era. In 1922, at a conference in Genoa, Italy, a group of countries including Britain, France, Italy, and Japan agreed on a program calling for a general return to the gold standard and cooperation among central banks in attaining external and internal objectives. Realizing that gold supplies might be inadequate to meet central banks' demands for international reserves (a problem of the gold standard noted in Chapter 17), the Genoa Conference sanctioned a partial gold *exchange* standard in which smaller countries could hold as reserves the currencies of several large countries whose own international reserves would consist entirely of gold.

In 1925 Britain returned to the gold standard by pegging the pound to gold at the prewar price. Chancellor of the Exchequer Winston Churchill, a champion of the return to the old parity, argued that any deviation from the prewar price would undermine world confidence in the stability of Britain's financial institutions, which had played the leading role in international finance during the gold standard era. Though Britain's price level had been falling since the war, in 1925 it was still higher than in the days of the prewar gold standard. To return the pound price of gold to its prewar level, the Bank of England was therefore forced to follow contractionary monetary policies that contributed to severe unemployment.

The depression in Britain that accompanied the return to gold had been predicted by Keynes and others, but it was not unprecedented. More than a century earlier, Britain's return to the gold standard at the parity prevailing before the Napoleonic Wars had also set off a sustained and deep depression. In both cases, the return to an exchange rate made obsolete by wartime price level increases amounted to a *revaluation* of the pound against foreign currencies, a move that shifted world demand away from British products.

British stagnation in the 1920s accelerated London's decline as the world's leading financial center. Britain's economic weakening proved problematic for the stability of the restored gold standard. In line with the recommendations of the Genoa Conference, many countries held international reserves in the form of pound deposits in London. Britain's gold reserves were limited, however, and the country's persistent stagnation did little to inspire confidence in its ability to meet its foreign obligations. The onset of the Great Depression in 1929 was shortly followed by bank failures throughout the world. Britain was forced off gold in 1931 when foreign holders of pounds (including several central banks) lost confidence in Britain's commitment to maintain its currency's value and began converting their pound holdings to gold.

INTERNATIONAL ECONOMIC DISINTEGRATION

As the depression continued, many countries renounced their gold standard obligations and allowed their currencies to float in the foreign exchange market. The United States left the gold standard in 1933 but returned to it in 1934, having raised the dollar price of gold from $20.67 to $35 per ounce. Countries that clung to the gold standard without devaluing their currencies suffered most during the Great Depression. Indeed, recent research places much of the blame for the depression's worldwide propagation on the gold standard itself (see the Case Study that follows).

Major economic harm was done by restrictions on international trade and payments, which proliferated as countries attempted to discourage imports and keep aggregate demand bottled up at home. The Smoot-Hawley tariff imposed by the United States in 1930 had a damaging effect on employment abroad. The foreign response involved retaliatory trade restrictions and preferential trading agreements among groups of countries. A measure that raises domestic welfare is called a *beggar-thy-neighbor policy* when it benefits the home country only because it worsens economic conditions abroad (Chapter 11). During the worldwide depression, tariffs and other beggar-thy-neighbor policies inevitably provoked foreign retaliation and often left all countries worse off in the end.

Uncertainty about government policies led to sharp reserve movements for countries with pegged exchange rates and sharp exchange rate movements for those with floating rates. Prohibitions on private capital account transactions were used by many countries to limit these effects of foreign exchange market developments. Some governments also used administrative methods or multiple exchange rates to allocate scarce foreign exchange reserves among competing uses. Trade barriers and deflation in the industrial economies of American and Europe led to widespread repudiations of international debts, particularly by Latin American countries, whose export markets were disappearing. In short, the world economy disintegrated into increasingly autarkic (that is, self-sufficient) national units in the early 1930s.

Considerable turbulence in world markets continued until the beginning of World War II in 1939, in spite of limited moves toward international economic cooperation in the late 1930s. In the face of the Great Depression, many countries had resolved the choice between external and internal balance by curtailing their trading links with the rest of the world and eliminating, by government decree, the possibility of any significant external imbalance. But this path, by reducing the gains from trade, imposed high costs on the world economy and contributed to the slow recovery from depression, which in many countries was still incomplete in 1939. All countries would have been better off in a world with freer international trade, provided international cooperation had helped each country preserve its external balance and financial stability without sacrificing internal policy goals. It was this realization that inspired the blueprint for the postwar international monetary system, the **Bretton Woods agreement.**

CASE STUDY

THE INTERNATIONAL GOLD STANDARD AND THE GREAT DEPRESSION

One of the most striking features of the decade-long Great Depression that started in 1929 was its global nature. Rather than being confined to the United States and its main trading partners, the downturn spread rapidly and forcefully to Europe, Latin America, and elsewhere. What explains the Great Depression's nearly universal scope? Recent scholarship shows that the international gold standard played a central role in starting, deepening, and spreading the twentieth century's greatest economic crisis.[8]

In 1929 most market economies were once again on the gold standard. At the time, however, the United States, attempting to slow its overheated economy through monetary contraction, and France, having just ended an inflationary period and returned to gold, faced large capital inflows. Through the resulting balance-of-payments surpluses, both countries were absorbing the world's monetary gold at a startling rate. (By 1932 the two countries alone held more than 70 percent of it!) Other countries on the gold standard had no choice but to engage in domestic asset sales if they wished to conserve their dwindling gold stocks. The resulting worldwide monetary contraction, combined with the shock waves from the October 1929 New York stock market crash, sent the world into deep recession.

Waves of bank failures, starting in the United States in 1930, only accelerated the world's downward economic spiral. The gold standard again was a key culprit. Many countries desired to safeguard their gold reserves in order to be able to remain on the gold standard. This desire often discouraged them from providing banks with the liquidity that might have allowed the banks to stay in business. After all, any cash provided to banks by their home governments would have increased potential private claims to the government's precious gold holdings.

Perhaps the clearest evidence of the gold standard's role is the contrasting behavior of output and the price level in countries that left the gold standard relatively early, such as the United Kingdom, and those that stubbornly hung on. Figure 18-1 plots 1935 industrial production levels relative to their 1929 values against 1935 wholesale price indexes relative to their 1929 values for a number of countries. Countries that abandoned the gold standard freed themselves to adopt expansionary monetary policies that limited (or prevented) both domestic deflation and output contraction. Thus, Figure 18-1 shows a strong positive relation-

---

[8]Important contributions to this research include Ehsan U. Choudhri and Levis A. Kochin, "The Exchange Rate and the International Transmission of Business Cycle Disturbances: Some Evidence from the Great Depression," *Journal of Money, Credit and Banking* 12 (1980), pp. 565–574, Peter Temin, *Lessons from the Great Depression* (Cambridge, MA: MIT Press, 1989), and Barry Eichengreen, *Golden Fetters: The Gold Standard and the Great Depression, 1919–1939* (New York: Oxford University Press, 1992). A concise and lucid summary is Ben S. Bernanke, "The World on a Cross of Gold: A Review of 'Golden Fetters: The Gold Standard and the Great Depression, 1919–1939,'" *Journal of Monetary Economics* 31 (April 1993), pp. 251–267.

FIGURE 18-1

Industrial Production and Wholesale Price Index Changes, 1929–1935

Countries such as Australia and the United Kingdom that left the gold standard early and adopted counter-deflationary monetary policies experienced milder declines in output during the Great Depression. Countries such as France and Switzerland that stuck with the gold standard had greater declines in output.

Source: Ben Bernanke and Kevin Carey, "Nominal Wage Stickiness and Aggregate Supply in the Great Depression," Working Paper, Princeton University, January 1994.

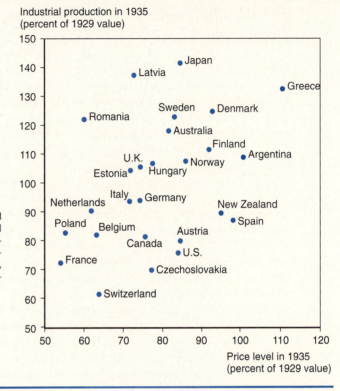

ship between price-level and output changes over 1929–1935. The countries with the biggest deflations and output contractions include France, Switzerland, Belgium, the Netherlands, and Poland, all of which stayed on the gold standard until 1936.

THE BRETTON WOODS SYSTEM AND THE INTERNATIONAL MONETARY FUND

In July 1944 representatives of 44 countries meeting in Bretton Woods, New Hampshire, drafted and signed the Articles of Agreement of the **International Monetary Fund (IMF).** Even as the war continued, statesmen in the Allied countries were looking ahead to the economic needs of the postwar world. Remembering the disastrous economic events of the interwar period, they hoped to design an international monetary system that would foster full employment and price stability while allowing individual countries to attain external balance without imposing restrictions on international trade.[9]

The system set up by the Bretton Woods agreement called for fixed exchange rates against the U.S. dollar and an unvarying dollar price of gold—$35 an ounce. Member countries held their official international reserves largely in the form of gold or dollar assets and had the right to sell dollars to the Federal Reserve for gold at the official price. The system was thus a gold exchange standard, with the dollar as its principal reserve currency. In the terminology of Chapter 17, the dollar was the "Nth currency" in terms of which the $N-1$ exchange rates of the system were defined. The United States itself intervened only rarely in the foreign exchange market. Usually, the $N-1$ foreign central banks intervened when necessary to fix the system's $N-1$ exchange rates, while the United States was responsible in theory for fixing the dollar price of gold.

GOALS AND STRUCTURE OF THE IMF

The IMF Articles of Agreement were heavily influenced by the interwar experience of financial and price level instability, unemployment, and international economic disintegration. The articles tried to avoid a repetition of those events through a mixture of discipline and flexibility.

The major discipline on monetary management was the requirement that exchange rates be fixed to the dollar, which, in turn, was tied to gold. If a central bank other than the Federal Reserve pursued excessive monetary expansion, it would lose international reserves and eventually become unable to maintain the fixed dollar exchange rate of its currency. Since high U.S. monetary growth would lead to dollar accumulation by foreign central banks, the Fed itself was constrained in its monetary policies by its obligation to redeem those dollars for gold. The official gold price of $35 an ounce served as a further brake on American monetary policy, since that price would be pushed upward if too many dollars were created. Fixed exchange rates were viewed as more than a device for imposing monetary discipline on the system, however. Rightly or wrongly, the interwar experience had convinced the Fund's architects that floating exchange rates were a cause of speculative instability and were harmful to international trade.

The interwar experience had shown also that national governments would not be willing to maintain both free trade and fixed exchange rates at the price of long-term domestic unemployment. After the experience of the Great Depression, governments were widely viewed as responsible for maintaining full employment. The IMF agreement therefore tried to incorporate sufficient flexibility to allow countries to attain external balance in an orderly fashion without sacrificing internal objectives or fixed exchange rates.

Two major features of the IMF Articles of Agreement helped promote this flexibility in external adjustment:

---

[9]The same conference set up a second institution, the World Bank, whose goals were to help the belligerents rebuild their shattered economies and to help the former colonial territories develop and modernize theirs. Only in 1947 was the General Agreement on Tariffs and Trade (GATT) inaugurated as a forum for the multilateral reduction of trade barriers. The GATT was meant as a prelude to the creation of an International Trade Organization (ITO) whose goals in the trade area would parallel those of the IMF in the financial area. Unfortunately, the ITO was doomed by the failures of Congress and Parliament to ratify its charter.

1. *IMF lending facilities.* The IMF stood ready to lend foreign currencies to members to tide them over periods during which their current accounts were in deficit but a tightening of monetary or fiscal policy would have an adverse effect on domestic employment. A pool of gold and currencies contributed by members provided the IMF with the resources to be used in these lending operations.

How did IMF lending work? On joining the Fund, a new member was assigned a *quota,* which determined both its contribution to the reserve pool and its right to draw on IMF resources. Each member contributed to the Fund an amount of gold equal in value to one-fourth of its quota. The remaining three-fourths of its quota took the form of a contribution of its own national currency. A member was entitled to use its own currency to purchase temporarily from the Fund gold or foreign currencies equal in value to its gold subscription. Further gold or foreign currencies (up to a limit) could be borrowed from the Fund, but only under increasingly stringent Fund supervision of the borrower's macroeconomic policies. **IMF conditionality** is the name for this surveillance over the policies of member countries who are heavy borrowers of Fund resources.

2. *Adjustable parities.* Although each country's exchange rate was fixed, it could be changed—devalued or revalued against the dollar—if the IMF agreed that the country's balance of payments was in a situation of "fundamental disequilibrium." The term *fundamental disequilibrium* was not defined in the Articles of Agreement, but the clause was meant to cover countries that suffered permanent adverse international shifts in the demand for their products. Without a devaluation, such a country would experience higher unemployment and a higher current account deficit until the domestic price level fell enough to restore internal and external balance. A devaluation, on the other hand, could simultaneously improve employment and the current account, thus sidestepping a long and painful adjustment process during which international reserves might in any case run out. Remembering Britain's experience with an overvalued currency after 1925, the IMF's founders built in the flexibility of (hopefully infrequent) exchange rate changes. This flexibility was not available, however, to the "Nth currency" of the Bretton Woods system, the U.S. dollar.

CONVERTIBILITY

Just as the general acceptability of national currency eliminates the costs of barter within a single economy, the use of national currencies in international trade makes the world economy function more efficiently. To promote efficient multilateral trade, the IMF Articles of Agreement urged members to make their national currencies convertible as soon as possible. A **convertible currency** is one that may be freely exchanged for foreign currencies. The U.S. and Canadian dollars became convertible in 1945. This meant, for example, that a Canadian resident who acquired U.S. dollars could use them to make purchases in the United States, could sell them in the foreign exchange market for Canadian dollars, or could sell them to the Bank of Canada, which then had the right to sell them to the Federal Reserve (at the fixed dollar/gold exchange rate) in return for gold. General *in*convertibility would make international trade extremely difficult. A French citizen might be unwilling to sell goods to a German in return for inconvertible DM because these DM would then be usable only subject to restrictions imposed by the German government. With no market in inconvertible francs, the German would be unable to obtain French currency to pay for the French goods. The only way of trading would therefore be through barter, the direct exchange of goods for goods.

The IMF articles called for convertibility on *current* account transactions only: Countries were explicitly allowed to restrict capital account transactions provided they permitted the free use of their currencies for transactions entering the current account. The experience of 1918–1939 had led policymakers to view private capital movements as a factor leading to economic instability, and they feared that speculative movements of "hot money" across national borders might sabotage their goal of free trade based on fixed exchange rates. By insisting on convertibility for current account transactions only, the designers of the Bretton Woods system hoped to facilitate free trade while avoiding the possibility that private capital flows might tighten the external constraints faced by policymakers.[10]

Most countries in Europe did not restore convertibility until the end of 1958, with Japan following in 1964. Germany also allowed substantial capital account convertibility, although this was not required by the IMF articles. Prior to that date, a European Payments Union had functioned as a clearinghouse for inconvertible European currencies, performing some of the functions of a foreign exchange market and thus facilitating intra-European trade. Britain had made an early "dash for convertibility" in 1947 but had retreated in the face of large foreign reserve losses.

The early convertibility of the U.S. dollar, together with its special position in the Bretton Woods system, made it the postwar world's key currency. Because dollars were freely convertible, much international trade tended to be invoiced in dollars and importers and exporters held dollar balances for transactions. In effect, the dollar became an international money—a universal medium of exchange, unit of account, and store of value. Also contributing to the dollar's dominance was the strength of the American economy relative to the devastated economies of Europe and Japan: Dollars were attractive because they could be used to purchase badly needed goods and services that only the United States was in a position to supply. Central banks naturally found it advantageous to hold their international reserves in the form of interest-bearing dollar assets.

INTERNAL AND EXTERNAL BALANCE UNDER THE BRETTON WOODS SYSTEM

How did the international monetary system created at Bretton Woods allow its members to reconcile their external commitments with the internal goals of full employment and price stability? As the world economy evolved in the years after World War II, the meaning of "external balance" changed and conflicts between internal and external goals increasingly threatened the fixed exchange rate system. The special external balance problem of the United States, the issuer of the principal reserve currency, was a major concern that led to proposals to reform the system.

THE CHANGING MEANING OF EXTERNAL BALANCE

In the first decade of the Bretton Woods system, many countries ran current account deficits as they reconstructed their war-torn economies. Since the main external problem of

---

[10]It was believed that official capital flows such as reserve movements and World Bank lending would allow countries to reap most gains from intertemporal trade.

these countries, taken as a group, was to acquire enough dollars to finance necessary purchases from the United States, these years are often called the period of "dollar shortage." The United States helped limit the severity of this shortage through the Marshall Plan, a program of dollar grants from the United States to European countries initiated in 1948.

Individually, each country's overall current account deficit was limited by the difficulty of borrowing any foreign currencies in an environment of heavily restricted capital account transactions. With virtually no private capital movements, current account imbalances had to be financed almost entirely through official reserve transactions and government loans. (The current account deficit equals the sum of the private and official capital account surpluses.) Without access to foreign credit, countries could therefore run current account deficits only if their central banks were willing to reduce their foreign exchange reserves. Central banks were unwilling to let reserves fall to low levels, in part because their ability to fix the exchange rate would be endangered.

The restoration of convertibility in 1958 gradually began to change the nature of policymakers' external constraints. As foreign exchange trading expanded, financial markets in different countries became more tightly integrated—an important step toward the creation of today's worldwide foreign exchange market. With growing opportunities to move funds across borders, national interest rates became more closely linked and the speed with which policy changes might cause a country to lose or gain international reserves increased. After 1958, and increasingly over the next 15 years, central banks had to be attentive to foreign financial conditions or take the risk that sudden reserve losses might leave them without the resources needed to peg exchange rates. Faced with a sudden rise in foreign interest rates, for example, a central bank would be forced to sell domestic assets and raise the domestic interest rate to hold its international reserves steady.

The restoration of convertibility did not result in immediate and complete international financial integration, as assumed in the model of fixed exchange rates set out in Chapter 17. On the contrary, most countries continued to maintain restrictions on capital account transactions, as noted above. But the opportunities for *disguised* capital flows increased dramatically. For example, importers within a country could effectively purchase foreign assets by accelerating payments to foreign suppliers relative to actual shipments of goods; they could effectively borrow from foreign suppliers by delaying payments. These trade practices—known, respectively, as "leads" and "lags"—provided two of many ways through which official barriers to private capital movements could be evaded. Even though the condition of international interest rate equality assumed in the last chapter did not hold exactly, the links among countries' interest rates tightened as the Bretton Woods system matured.

SPECULATIVE CAPITAL FLOWS AND CRISES

Current account deficits and surpluses took on added significance under the new conditions of increased private capital mobility. A country with a large and persistent current account deficit might be suspected of being in "fundamental disequilibrium" under the IMF Articles of Agreement, and thus ripe for a currency devaluation. Suspicion of an impending devaluation could, in turn, spark a balance of payments crisis (see Chapter 17).

Anyone holding pound deposits during a devaluation of the pound, for example, would suffer a loss, since the foreign currency value of pound assets would decrease suddenly by the amount of the exchange rate change. If Britain had a current account deficit, therefore, holders of pounds would become nervous and shift their wealth into other currencies. To hold the pound's exchange rate against the dollar pegged, the Bank of England would have to buy pounds and supply the foreign assets that market participants wished to hold. This loss of foreign reserves, if large enough, might force a devaluation by leaving the Bank of England without enough reserves to prop up the exchange rate.

Similarly, countries with large current account surpluses might be viewed by the market as candidates for revaluation. In this case their central banks would find themselves swamped with official reserves, the result of selling the home currency in the foreign exchange market to keep it from appreciating. A country in this position would face the problem of having its money supply grow uncontrollably, a development that could push the price level up and upset internal balance.

Balance of payments crises became increasingly frequent and violent throughout the 1960s and early 1970s. A record British trade balance deficit in early 1964 led to a period of intermittent speculation against the pound that complicated British policy-making until November 1967, when the pound was finally devalued. France devalued its franc and Germany revalued its DM in 1969 after similar speculative attacks. These crises became so massive by the early 1970s that they eventually brought down the Bretton Woods structure of fixed exchange rates. The events leading up to the system's collapse are covered later in this chapter.

The possibility of a balance of payments crisis therefore lent increased importance to the external goal of a current account target. Even current account imbalances justified by differing international investment opportunities or caused by purely temporary factors might fuel market suspicions of an impending parity change. In this environment, policymakers had additional incentives to avoid sharp current account changes.

ANALYZING POLICY OPTIONS UNDER THE BRETTON WOODS SYSTEM

To describe the problem an individual country (other than the United States) faced in pursuing internal and external balance under the Bretton Woods system of fixed exchange rates, let's return to the framework used in Chapter 17. Assume that domestic (R) and foreign (R^*) interest rates are always equal,

$$R = R^*.$$

As noted above, this equality does not fit the Bretton Woods facts exactly (particularly just after 1958), but it leads to a fairly accurate picture of the external constraints policymakers then faced in using their macroeconomic tools. The framework will show how a country's position with respect to its internal and external goals depends on the level of its fixed exchange rate, E, and its fiscal policy. Throughout, E is the domestic currency price of the dollar. The analysis applies to the short run because the home and foreign price levels (P and P^*, respectively) are assumed to be fixed.[11]

---

[11]By assumption there is no ongoing balance of payments crisis, that is, no expectation of a future exchange rate change. The point of this assumption is to highlight the difficult choices policymakers faced, even under favorable conditions.

MAINTAINING INTERNAL BALANCE

First consider internal balance. If both P^* and E are permanently fixed, domestic inflation depends primarily on the amount of aggregate demand pressure in the economy, not on expectations of future inflation. Internal balance therefore requires only full employment, that is, that aggregate demand equal the full-employment level of output, Y^f.[12]

Recall that aggregate demand for domestic output is the sum of consumption, C, investment, I, government purchases, G, and the current account, CA. Consumption is an increasing function of disposable income, $Y - T$, where T denotes net taxes. The current account surplus is a decreasing function of disposable income and an increasing function of the real exchange rate, EP^*/P (Chapter 16). Finally, investment is assumed constant. The condition of internal balance is therefore

$$Y^f = C(Y^f - T) + I + G + CA(EP^*/P, Y^f - T). \tag{18-1}$$

Equation (18-1) shows the policy tools that affect aggregate demand and therefore affect output in the short run. Fiscal expansion (a rise in G or a fall in T) stimulates aggregate demand and causes output to rise. Similarly, a devaluation of the currency (a rise in E) makes domestic goods and services cheaper relative to those sold abroad and also increases demand and output. The policymaker can hold output steady at its full employment level, Y^f, through fiscal policy or exchange rate changes.

Notice that monetary policy is not a policy tool under fixed exchange rates. This is because, as shown in Chapter 17, an attempt by the central bank to alter the money supply by buying or selling domestic assets will cause an offsetting change in foreign reserves, leaving the domestic money supply unchanged. Domestic asset transactions by the central bank can be used to alter the level of foreign reserves but not to affect the state of employment and output.

The II schedule in Figure 18-2 shows combinations of exchange rates and fiscal policy that hold output constant at Y^f and thus maintain internal balance. The schedule is downward-sloping because currency devaluation (a rise in E) and fiscal expansion (a rise in G or a fall in T) both tend to raise output. To hold output constant, a revaluation of the currency (which reduces aggregate demand) must therefore be matched by fiscal expansion (which increases aggregate demand). Schedule II shows precisely how the fiscal stance must change as E changes to maintain full employment. To the right of II fiscal policy is more expansionary than needed for full employment, so the economy's productive factors are overemployed. To the left of II fiscal policy is too restrictive, and there is unemployment.

MAINTAINING EXTERNAL BALANCE

We have seen how fiscal policy or exchange rate changes can be used to influence output and thus help the government achieve its internal goal of full employment. How do these

---

[12]If P^* is unstable because of foreign inflation, for example, full employment alone will not guarantee price stability under a fixed exchange rate. This complex problem is considered below when worldwide inflation under fixed exchange rates is examined.

FIGURE 18-2

Internal Balance (*II*), External Balance (*XX*), and the "Four Zones of Economic Discomfort"

The diagram shows what different levels of the exchange rate and fiscal ease imply for employment and the current account. Along *II*, output is at its full-employment level, Y^f. Along *XX*, the current account is at its target level, *X*.

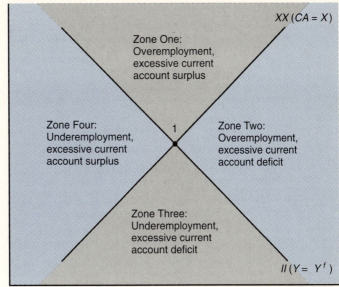

Exchange rate, *E*

$XX\,(CA = X)$

Zone One:
Overemployment,
excessive current
account surplus

Zone Four: 1   Zone Two:
Underemployment,   Overemployment,
excessive current   excessive current
account surplus   account deficit

Zone Three:
Underemployment,
excessive current
account deficit

$II\,(Y = Y^f)$

Fiscal ease
$(G\uparrow \text{ or } T\downarrow)$

policy tools affect the economy's external balance? To answer this question, assume the government has a target value, *X*, for the current account surplus. The goal of external balance requires the government to manage fiscal policy and the exchange rate so that the equation

$$CA(EP^*/P, Y - T) = X \tag{18-2}$$

is satisfied.

Given *P* and *P**, a rise in *E* makes domestic goods cheaper and improves the current account. Fiscal expansion, however, has the opposite effect on the current account. A fall in *T* raises output, *Y*; the resulting increase in disposable income raises home spending on foreign goods and worsens the current account. Similarly, a rise in *G* causes *CA* to fall by increasing *Y*.

To maintain its current account at *X* as it devalues the currency (that is, as it raises *E*), the government must expand its purchases or lower taxes. Figure 18-2 therefore shows that the *XX* schedule, along which external balance holds, is positively sloped. The *XX* schedule shows how much fiscal expansion is needed to hold the current account surplus at *X* as the currency is devalued by a given amount.[13] Since a rise in E raises net exports, the current account is in surplus, relative to its target level X, above XX. Similarly, below XX the current account is in deficit relative to its target level.[14]

EXPENDITURE-CHANGING AND EXPENDITURE-SWITCHING POLICIES

The II and XX schedules divide the diagram into four regions, sometimes called the "four zones of economic discomfort." Each of these zones represents the effects of different policy settings. In zone 1 the level of employment is too high and the current account surplus too great; in zone 2 the level of employment is too high but the current account deficit is too great; in zone 3 there is underemployment and an excessive deficit; and in zone 4 underemployment is coupled with a current account surplus greater than the target level. Used together, fiscal and exchange rate policy can place the economy at the intersection of II and XX (point 1), the point at which both internal and external balance hold. Point 1 shows the policy setting that places the economy in the position that the policymaker would prefer.

If the economy is initially away from point 1, appropriate adjustments in fiscal policy and the exchange rate are needed to bring about internal and external balance. The change in fiscal policy that moves the economy to point 1 is called an **expenditure-changing policy** because it alters the *level* of the economy's total demand for goods and services. The accompanying exchange rate adjustment is called an **expenditure-switching policy** because it changes the *direction* of demand, shifting it between domestic output and imports. In general, both expenditure changing and expenditure switching are needed to reach internal and external balance.

Under the Bretton Woods rules, exchange rate changes (expenditure-switching policy) were supposed to be infrequent. This left fiscal policy as the main tool for moving the economy toward internal and external balance. But as Figure 18-2 shows, one instrument, fiscal policy, is generally insufficient to attain the two goals of internal and external balance. Only if the economy had been displaced horizontally from point 1 would fiscal policy be able to do the job alone. In addition, fiscal policy is an unwieldy tool, since it often cannot be implemented without legislative approval. Another drawback is that a fiscal expansion, for example, might have to be reversed after some time if it leads to chronic government budget deficits.

---

[13]Can you see how to derive the XX schedule in Figure 18-2 from the different (but related) XX schedule shown in Figure 16-17 on p. 467? (Hint: Use the latter diagram to analyze the effects of fiscal expansion.)

[14]Since the central bank does not affect the economy when it raises its foreign reserves by an open-market sale of domestic assets, no separate reserve constraint is shown in Figure 18-2. In effect, the bank can borrow reserves freely from abroad by selling domestic assets to the public. (During a devaluation scare this tactic would not work because no one would want to sell the bank foreign assets for domestic money.) Our analysis, however, assumes perfect asset substitutability between domestic and foreign bonds (see Chapter 17). Under imperfect asset substitutability, central bank domestic asset sales to attract foreign reserves would drive up the domestic interest rate relative to the foreign rate. Thus, while imperfect asset substitutability would give the central bank an additional policy tool (monetary policy), it would also make the bank responsible for an additional policy target (the domestic interest rate). If the government is concerned about the domestic interest rate because it affects investment, for example, the additional policy tool would not necessarily increase the set of attractive policy options. Imperfect substitutability was exploited by central banks under Bretton Woods, but it did not get countries out of the policy dilemmas illustrated in the text.

One poss
of the dollar
and would ha
producing co
to expect furt
thus possibly

Triffin hi
tral banks wo
the IMF woul
same way a c
Triffin's plan

In 1967 I
an artificial r
used in transa
the functionin
cause by the l
that would so
tion of the Un

CAS

THE
SYS

The s
intern
becar
excha
the ta
tem's
ternal

The (

In 19
currer
currer
eign c
in that
1960
period
to gol

FIGURE 18-3

Policies to Bring About Internal and External Balance

Unless the currency is de-valued and the degree of fiscal ease increased, inter-nal and external balance (point 1) cannot be reached. Acting alone, fis-cal policy can attain *either* internal balance (point 3) or external balance (point 4), but only at the cost of increasing the economy's distance from the goal that is sacrificed.

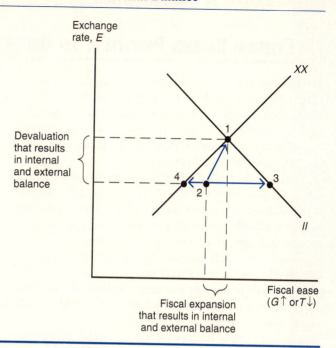

As a result of the exchange rate's inflexibility, policymakers sometimes found them-selves in dilemma situations. With the fiscal policy and exchange rate indicated by point 2 in Figure 18-3, there is underemployment and an excessive current account deficit. Only the combination of devaluation and fiscal expansion indicated in the figure moves the economy to internal and external balance (point 1). Expansionary fiscal policy, acting alone, can eliminate the unemployment by moving the economy to point 3, but the cost of reduced unemployment is a larger external deficit. While contractionary fiscal policy alone can bring about external balance (point 4), output falls as a result and the economy moves further from internal balance. It is no wonder that policy dilemmas such as the one at point 2 gave rise to suspicions that the currency was about to be devalued. Devaluation improves the current account and aggregate demand by raising the real exchange rate EP^*/P in one stroke; the alternative is a long and politically unpalatable period of unemployment to bring about an equal rise in the real exchange rate through a fall in P.[15]

In practice, countries did sometimes use changes in their exchange rates to move closer to internal and external balance, although the changes were typically accompanied by balance of payments crises. Many countries also tightened controls on capital account

---

[15]As an exercise to test understanding, show that a fall in P, all else equal, lowers both II and XX, moving point 1 vertically downward.

[18]Triffin's plan wa
1940s. Keynes's bl

On the whole, the period from 1961 to 1965 was a calm one for the United States, although some other countries, most notably Britain, faced external problems. The U.S. current account surplus widened and the threat of large-scale conversions of dollars into gold by foreign central banks receded. Continuing private capital outflows from the United States, which augmented the dollar component of foreign official reserves, were, however, a source of concern to the Kennedy and Johnson administrations. Starting in 1963, therefore, the United States moved to discourage capital outflows by taxes on purchases of foreign assets by Americans and other measures.

Early in this period, Germany faced a dilemma between internal and external balance that was to recur more dramatically toward the end of the decade. In 1960 Germany experienced an employment boom coupled with large inflows of international reserves. In terms of Figure 18-2, the German authorities found themselves in zone 1. Attempts to restrain the boom through contractionary monetary policy only succeeded in increasing the Bundesbank's international reserves more quickly as the central bank was forced to sell DM for dollars to keep the DM from appreciating. A small revaluation of the DM (by 5 percent) in March 1961 moved the economy closer to internal and external balance as output growth slowed and the current account surplus declined. Although the system successfully avoided a major crisis in this case, this was in part due to the foreign exchange market's perception that the DM revaluation reflected German macroeconomic problems rather than American problems. That perception was to change over the next decade.

The Vietnam Military Buildup and the Great Society: 1965–1968

Many economists view the U.S. macroeconomic policy package of 1965–1968 as a major blunder that helped unravel the system of fixed exchange rates. In 1965, government military purchases began rising as President Lyndon B. Johnson widened America's involvement in the Vietnam conflict. At the same time, other categories of government spending also rose dramatically as the president's "Great Society" programs (which included funds for public education and urban redevelopment) expanded. Figure 18-4a shows how the growth rate of nominal government purchases began to rise, slowly in 1965 and then quite sharply the next year. These increases in government expenditures were not matched by a prompt increase in taxes: 1966 was an election year, and President Johnson was reluctant to invite close congressional scrutiny of his spending by asking for a tax increase.

The result was a substantial fiscal expansion that helped set U.S. prices rising and caused a sharp fall in the U.S. current account surplus (Figures 18-4b and 18-4c). Although monetary policy (as measured by the growth rate of the money supply) initially turned contractionary as output expanded, the negative effect of the resulting high interest rates on the construction industry led the Federal Reserve to choose a much more expansionary monetary course in 1967 and 1968 (Figure 18-4d). As Figure 18-4b shows, this further push to the domestic price level left the United States with an inflation rate near 6 percent per year by the end of the decade.

FIGURE 18-4

U.S. Macroeconomic Data, 1964–1972

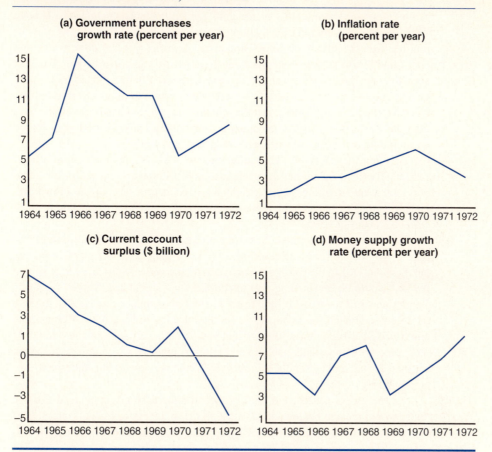

Source: *Economic Report of the President,* 1985. Money supply growth rate is the December to December percentage increase in M1. Inflation rate is the percentage increase in each year's average consumer price index over the average consumer price index for the previous year.

From the Gold Crisis to the Collapse: 1968–1973

Early signals of future problems came from the London gold market. In late 1967 and early 1968 private speculators began buying gold in anticipation of a rise in its dollar price. It was thought at the time that the speculation had been triggered by the British pound's devaluation in November 1967, but the sharp U.S. monetary expansion over 1967 and rising U.S. inflation probably influenced speculative sentiments as well. After massive gold sales by the Federal Reserve and European central banks, the Bank of England closed the gold market on March 15, 1968. Two days later the central banks announced the creation of a *two-tier* gold market, with one tier private and the other official. Private gold traders would continue to trade on the London gold market, but the gold price set there would be allowed to fluctuate. In contrast, central banks would continue to transact with each other in the official tier at the official gold price of $35 an ounce.

The creation of the two-tier market was a turning point for the Bretton Woods system. A prime goal of the gold exchange standard created at Bretton Woods was to prevent inflation by tying down gold's dollar price. By severing the link between the supply of dollars and a fixed *market* price of gold, the central banks had jettisoned the system's built-in safeguard against inflation. The new arrangements did not eliminate the external constraint on the United States altogether, because foreign central banks retained the right to purchase gold for dollars from the Federal Reserve. But the *official* price of gold had been reduced to a fictitious device for squaring accounts among central banks; it no longer placed an automatic constraint on worldwide monetary growth.

As Figure 18-4b shows, U.S. inflation rose in 1970 despite the onset of a recession. By then, inflationary expectations had become entrenched in the economy and were affecting wage settlements even in the face of the slowdown. Falling aggregate demand did, however, contribute to an improvement in the U.S. current account in 1970.

The improvement in the U.S. current account proved transitory. Adverse balance of payments figures released in early 1971 helped set off massive private purchases of DM in the foreign exchange market, motivated by expectations that the DM would be revalued against the dollar. On a single day, May 4, 1971, the Bundesbank had to buy $1 billion to hold its dollar exchange rate fixed in the face of the great demand for its currency. On the morning of May 5, the Bundesbank purchased $1 billion during the first hour of foreign exchange trading alone! At that point the Bundesbank gave up and allowed its currency to float, rather than see the German money supply balloon even further as a result of Bundesbank dollar purchases.

As the weeks passed, the markets became increasingly convinced that the dollar would have to be devalued against all the major European currencies. U.S. unemployment was still high in 1971 and the U.S. price level had risen substantially over the previous years. To restore full employment and a balanced current account, the United States somehow had to bring about a real depreciation of the dollar.

That real depreciation could be brought about in two ways. The first option was a fall in the U.S. price level in response to domestic unemployment, coupled with a rise in foreign price levels in response to continuing purchases of dollars by foreign central banks. The second option was a fall in the dollar's nominal value in terms of foreign currencies. The first route—unemployment in the United States and inflation abroad—seemed a painful one for policymakers to follow. The markets rightly guessed that a change in the dollar's value was inevitable. Their realization led to renewed sales of dollars in the foreign exchange market that reached a climax in August 1971.

Devaluation was no easy matter for the United States, however. Any other country could change its exchange rates against all currencies simply by fixing its *dollar* rate at a new level. But as the *N*th currency, the dollar could be devalued only if foreign governments agreed to peg their currencies against the dollar at new rates. In effect, all countries had to agree simultaneously to *revalue* their currencies against the dollar. Dollar devaluation could therefore be accomplished only through extensive multilateral negotiations. And some foreign countries were not anxious to revalue because revaluation would make their goods more expensive relative to U.S. goods and would therefore hurt their export- and import-competing industries.

President Richard M. Nixon forced the issue on August 15, 1971. First, he ended U.S. gold losses by announcing the United States would no longer automatically sell gold to foreign central banks for dollars. This action effectively cut the remaining link between the dollar and gold. Second, the president announced a 10 percent tax on all imports to the United States, to remain effective until America's trading partners agreed to revalue their currencies against the dollar.

An international agreement on exchange rate realignment was reached in December 1971 at the Smithsonian Institution in Washington, D.C. On average, the dollar was devalued against foreign currencies by about 8 percent, and the 10 percent import surcharge that the United States had imposed to force the realignment was removed. The official gold price was raised to $38 an ounce, but the move had no economic significance because the United States did not agree to resume sales of gold to foreign central banks. The Smithsonian agreement made clear that the last remnant of the gold standard had been abandoned.

The Smithsonian realignment, although hailed at the time by President Nixon as "the most significant monetary agreement in the history of the world," was in shambles less than 15 months later. A sharp deterioration of the U.S. current account in 1972, together with sharply higher U.S. monetary growth prior to that year's presidential election, convinced markets that the Smithsonian dollar devaluation had been insufficient. Throughout 1972 there were further speculative capital flows out of dollars and into other currencies, particularly the DM and the yen. Germany tightened controls on capital inflows to impede reserve movements that were bloating Germany's money supply.

Early in February 1973, another massive speculative attack on the dollar started and the foreign exchange market was closed while the United States and its main trading partners negotiated on dollar support measures. A further 10 percent devaluation of the dollar was announced on February 12, but speculation against the dollar resumed as soon as governments allowed the foreign exchange market to reopen. After European central banks purchased $3.6 billion on March 1 to prevent their currencies from appreciating, the foreign exchange market was closed down once again.

When the foreign exchange market reopened on March 19, the currencies of Japan and most European countries were floating against the dollar.[19] The floating of the industrialized countries' dollar exchange rates was viewed at the time as a temporary response to unmanageable speculative capital movements. But the interim arrangements adopted in March 1973 turned out to be permanent and marked the end of fixed exchange rates and the beginning of a turbulent new period in international monetary relations.

[19]Many developing countries continued to peg to the dollar, and a number of European countries were continuing to peg their mutual exchange rates as part of an informal arrangement called the "snake." As we see in Chapter 20, the snake ultimately evolved into the European Monetary System.

TABLE 18-2

Changes in Germany's Money Supply and International Reserves, 1968–1972 (percent per year)

Growth rate of	1968	1969	1970	1971	1972
Money supply	6.4	−6.3	8.9	12.3	14.7
Official international reserves	37.8	−43.6	215.7	36.1	35.8

Source: Organization for Economic Cooperation and Development. *Main Economic Indicators: Historical Statistics, 1964–1983.* Paris: OECD, 1984. Figures are percentage increases in each year's end-of-year money supply or international reserves over the level at the end of the previous year. Official reserves are measured net of gold holdings.

to individual economies also played a role. In Britain, for example, inflation speeds up markedly in 1968, the year following the pound's devaluation. Since (as seen in the last chapter) devaluation is neutral in the long run, it must raise the long-run domestic price level proportionally. The devaluation is probably part of the explanation for the rise in British inflation. Strikes in France in 1968 led to large wage increases, a French-German currency crisis, and a devaluation of the franc in 1969. These events partly explain the sharp increase in French inflation in 1968–1969. The role of imported inflation was greatest in Germany, where the painful earlier experience with hyperinflation had made policymakers determined to resist price level increases.

Evidence on money supplies confirms that European and Japanese monetary growth accelerated in the late 1960s, as our theory predicts. Table 18-2 shows the evolution of the international reserves and money supply of West Germany over the years 1968–1972. The table shows how monetary growth rose dramatically after 1969 as the Bundesbank's international reserves expanded.[20] This evidence is consistent with the view that American inflation was imported into Germany through the Bundesbank's purchases of dollars in the foreign exchange market.

The acceleration of German money growth probably cannot be explained entirely as a direct consequence of the acceleration in U.S. monetary growth, however. A comparison of Figure 18-4 and Table 18-2 shows that German monetary growth accelerated by much more than U.S. monetary growth after 1969. This difference suggests that much of the growth in Germany's international reserves reflected speculation on a possible dollar devaluation in the early 1970s and the resulting shift by market participants away from dollar assets and into DM assets.

U.S. monetary policy certainly contributed to inflation abroad by its direct effect on prices and money supplies. It helped wreck the fixed rate system by confronting foreign policymakers with a choice between fixed rates and imported inflation. But the U.S. fiscal policy that helped make a dollar devaluation necessary also contributed to foreign inflation by giving further encouragement to speculative capital flows out of dollars. U.S. fiscal policy in the later 1960s must be viewed as an additional cause of the Bretton Woods system's demise.

Thus, the collapse of the Bretton Woods system was due, in part, to the lopsided macroeconomic power of the United States. But it was also due to the fact that the key ex-

---

[20]The behavior of reserves in 1968 and 1969—a large increase followed by a large decrease—reflects speculation on a DM revaluation against the franc during the French-German currency crisis of those years.

penditure-switching tool needed for internal and external balance—discrete exchange rate adjustment—inspired speculative attacks that made both internal and external balance progressively more difficult to achieve. The architects of the Bretton Woods system had hoped its most powerful member would see beyond purely domestic goals and adopt policies geared to the welfare of the world economy as a whole. When the United States proved unwilling to shoulder this responsibility after the mid-1960s, the fixed exchange rate system came apart.

Summary

1. In an open economy, policymakers try to maintain *internal balance* (full employment and a stable price level) and *external balance* (a current account level that is neither so negative that the country may be unable to repay its foreign debts nor so positive that foreigners are put in that position). The definition of external balance depends on a number of factors, including the exchange rate regime and world economic conditions. Because each country's macroeconomic policies have repercussions abroad, a country's ability to reach internal and external balance depends on the policies other countries adopt.

2. The gold standard system contains a powerful automatic mechanism for assuring external balance, the *price-specie-flow mechanism*. The flows of gold accompanying deficits and surpluses cause price changes that reduce current account imbalances and therefore tend to return all countries to external balance. The system's performance in maintaining internal balance was mixed, however. With the eruption of World War I in 1914, the gold standard was suspended.

3. Attempts to return to the prewar gold standard after 1918 were unsuccessful. As the world economy moved into general depression after 1929, the restored gold standard fell apart and international economic integration weakened. In the turbulent economic conditions of the period, governments made internal balance their main concern and tried to avoid the external balance problem by partially shutting their economies off from the rest of the world. The result was a world economy in which all countries' situations could have been bettered through international cooperation.

4. The architects of the *International Monetary Fund (IMF)* hoped to design a fixed exchange rate system that would encourage growth in international trade while making the requirements of external balance sufficiently flexible that they could be met without sacrificing internal balance. To this end, the IMF charter provided financing facilities for deficit countries and allowed exchange rate adjustments in conditions of "fundamental disequilibrium." All countries pegged their currencies to the dollar. The United States pegged to gold and agreed to exchange gold for dollars with foreign central banks at a price of $35 an ounce.

5. After *currency convertibility* was restored in Europe in 1958, countries' financial markets became more closely integrated, monetary policy became less effective (except for the United States), and movements in international reserves became more volatile. These changes revealed a key weakness in the system. To reach internal and external balance at the same time, *expenditure-switching* as well as *expenditure-changing* policies were needed. But the possibility of expenditure-

switching policies (exchange rate changes) could give rise to speculative capital flows that undermined fixed exchange rates. As the main reserve currency country, the United States faced a unique external balance problem: the *confidence problem* that would arise as foreign official dollar holdings inevitably grew to exceed U.S. gold holdings.

6. U.S macroeconomic policies in the late 1960s helped cause the breakdown of the Bretton Woods system by early 1973. Overexpansionary U.S. fiscal policy contributed to the need for a devaluation of the dollar in the early 1970s, and fears that this would occur touched off speculative capital flows out of dollars that caused foreign money supplies to balloon. Higher U.S. money growth fueled inflation at home and abroad, making foreign governments increasingly reluctant to continue importing U.S. inflation through fixed exchange rates. A series of international crises beginning in the spring of 1971 led in stages to the abandonment of both the dollar's link to gold and fixed dollar exchange rates for the industrialized countries.

Key Terms

balance of payments equilibrium, p. 541

Bretton Woods agreement, p. 546

confidence problem, p. 558

convertible currency, p. 550

expenditure-changing policy, p. 556

expenditure-switching policy, p. 556

external balance, p. 536

IMF conditionality, p. 550

internal balance, p. 536

International Monetary Fund (IMF), p. 548

price-specie-flow mechanism, p. 541

Special Drawing Right (SDR), p. 559

Problems

1. If you were in charge of macroeconomic policies in a small open economy, what qualitative effect would each of the following events have on your target for external balance?
   a. Large deposits of uranium are discovered in the interior of your country.
   b. The world price of your main export good, copper, rises permanently.
   c. The world price of copper rises temporarily.
   d. There is a temporary rise in the world price of oil.

2. Under a gold standard of the kind analyzed by Hume, describe how balance of payments equilibrium between two countries, A and B, would be restored after a transfer of income from B to A.

3. In spite of the flaws of the pre-1914 gold standard, exchange rate changes were rare. In contrast, such changes became quite frequent in the interwar period. Can you think of reasons for this contrast?

4. Under a gold standard, countries may adopt excessively contractionary monetary policies as all scramble in vain for a larger share of the limited supply of world gold reserves. Can the same problem arise under a reserve currency standard when bonds denominated in different currencies are all perfect substitutes?

5. A central bank that adopts a fixed exchange rate may sacrifice its autonomy in setting domestic monetary policy. It is sometimes argued that when this is the

case, the central bank also gives up the ability to use monetary policy to combat the wage-price spiral. The argument goes like this: "Suppose workers demand higher wages and employers give in, but that the employers then raise output prices to cover their higher costs. Now the price level is higher and real balances are momentarily lower, so to prevent an interest rate rise that would appreciate the currency, the central bank must buy foreign exchange and expand the money supply. This action accommodates the initial wage demands with monetary growth and the economy moves permanently to a higher level of wages and prices. With a fixed exchange rate there is thus no way of keeping wages and prices down." What is wrong with this argument?

6. Economists have long debated whether the growth of dollar reserve holdings in the Bretton Woods years was "demand-determined" (that is, determined by central banks' desire to add to their international reserves) or "supply-determined" (that is, determined by the speed of U.S. monetary growth). What would your answer be? What are the consequences for analyzing the relationship between growth in the world stock of international reserves and worldwide inflation?

7. Suppose the central bank of a small country is faced by a rise in the world interest rate, R^*. What is the effect on its foreign reserve holdings? On its money supply? Can it offset either of these effects through domestic open-market operations?

8. How might restrictions on private capital account transactions alter the problem of attaining internal and external balance with a fixed exchange rate? What costs might such restrictions involve?

Further Reading

Michael D. Bordo and Barry Eichengreen, eds. *A Retrospective on the Bretton Woods System.* Chicago: University of Chicago Press, 1993. A collection of essays reevaluating the Bretton Woods experience.

W. Max Corden. "The Geometric Representation of Policies to Attain Internal and External Balance," in Richard N. Cooper, ed. *International Finance.* Harmondsworth, U.K.: Penguin Books, 1969, pp. 256–290. A classic diagrammatic analysis of expenditure-switching and expenditure-changing macroeconomic policies.

Barry Eichengreen, ed. *The Gold Standard in Theory and History.* London: Methuen, 1985. A valuable collection of readings on the performance of the gold standard in different historical periods.

Richard N. Gardner. *Sterling-Dollar Diplomacy in Current Perspective.* New York: Columbia University Press, 1980. Readable account of the negotiations that established the IMF, World Bank, and GATT.

Charles P. Kindleberger. *The World in Depression 1929–1939.* Revised edition. Berkeley and Los Angeles: University of California Press, 1986. A leading international economist examines the causes and effects of the Great Depression.

Lawrence B. Krause and Walter S. Salant, eds. *Worldwide Inflation: Theory and Recent Experience.* Washington, D.C.: Brookings Institution, 1977. A collection of analytical studies on global inflationary experience in the 1960s and early 1970s.

Ronald I. McKinnon. "The Rules of the Game: International Money in Historical Perspective." *Journal of Economic Literature* 31 (March 1993), pp. 1–44. An illuminating overview of the mechanics and implicit rules of alternative international monetary arrangements.

Robert A. Mundell. *Monetary Theory.* Pacific Palisades, CA: Goodyear, 1971. The book's second part discusses international monetary problems of the late Bretton Woods years.

Ragnar Nurkse. *International Currency Experience: Lessons of the Inter-War Period.* Geneva: League of Nations, 1944. Classic critique of the nationalistic macroeconomic policies many countries adopted between the world wars.

Maurice Obstfeld. "International Finance," in *The New Palgrave Dictionary of Money & Finance.* Vol. 2. New York: Stockton Press, 1992, pp. 457–466. Discusses changing conceptions of internal and external balance.

Robert Solomon. *The International Monetary System, 1945–1981.* New York: Harper & Row, 1982. Chapters 1–14 chronicle international monetary relations between World War II and the early 1970s. The author was chief of the Federal Reserve's international finance division during the period leading up to the breakdown of fixed exchange rates.

19 Macroeconomic Policy and Coordination Under Floating Exchange Rates

As the Bretton Woods system of fixed exchange rates began to show signs of strain in the late 1960s, many economists recommended that countries allow currency values to be determined freely in the foreign exchange market. When the governments of the industrialized countries adopted floating exchange rates early in 1973, they viewed their step as a temporary emergency measure and were not consciously following the advice of the economists then advocating a permanent floating-rate system. So far, however, it has proved impossible to put the fixed-rate system back together again: The dollar exchange rates of the industrialized countries have continued to float since 1973.

The advocates of floating saw it as a way out of the conflicts between internal and external balance that often arose under the rigid Bretton Woods exchange rates. By the mid-1980s, however, economists and policymakers had become more skeptical about the benefits of an international monetary system based on floating rates. Some critics describe the post-1973 currency arrangements as an international monetary "nonsystem," a free-for-all in which national macroeconomic policies are frequently at odds. Many observers now feel that the current exchange rate system is badly in need of reform.

Why has the performance of floating rates been so disappointing, and what direction should reform of the current system take? In this chapter our models of fixed and floating exchange rates are applied to examine the recent performance of floating rates and to compare the macroeconomic policy problems of different exchange rate regimes.

THE CASE FOR FLOATING EXCHANGE RATES

As international currency crises of increasing scope and frequency erupted in the late 1960s, most economists began advocating greater flexibility of exchange rates. Many argued that a system of floating exchange rates (one in which central banks did not intervene in the foreign exchange market to fix rates) would not only automatically ensure exchange rate flexibility but would also produce several other benefits for the world economy. The case for floating exchange rates rested on three major claims:

1. *Monetary policy autonomy.* If central banks were no longer obliged to intervene in currency markets to fix exchange rates, governments would be able to use monetary policy to reach internal and external balance. Further, no country would be forced to import inflation (or deflation) from abroad.

2. *Symmetry.* Under a system of floating rates the inherent asymmetries of Bretton Woods would disappear and the United States would no longer be able to set world monetary conditions all by itself. At the same time, the United States would have the same opportunity as other countries to influence its exchange rate against foreign currencies.

3. *Exchange rates as automatic stabilizers.* Even in the absence of an active monetary policy, the swift adjustment of market-determined exchange rates would help countries maintain internal and external balance in the face of changes in aggregate demand. The long and agonizing periods of speculation preceding exchange rate realignments under the Bretton Woods rules would not occur under floating.

MONETARY POLICY AUTONOMY

Under the Bretton Woods fixed-rate system, countries other than the United States had little scope to use monetary policy to attain internal and external balance. Monetary policy was weakened by the mechanism of offsetting capital flows (discussed in Chapter 17). A central bank purchase of domestic assets, for example, would put temporary downward pressure on the domestic interest rate and cause the domestic currency to weaken in the foreign exchange market. The exchange rate then had to be propped up through central bank sales of official foreign reserves. Pressure on the interest and exchange rates disappeared, however, only when official reserve losses had driven the domestic money supply back down to its original level. Thus, in the closing years of fixed exchange rates, central banks imposed increasingly stringent restrictions on international payments to keep control over their money supplies. These restrictions were only partially successful in strengthening monetary policy, and they had the damaging side effect of distorting international trade.

Advocates of floating rates pointed out that removal of the obligation to peg currency values would restore monetary control to central banks. If, for example, the central bank faced unemployment and wished to expand its money supply in response, there would no longer be any legal barrier to the currency depreciation this would cause. As in the analysis of Chapter 16, the currency depreciation would reduce unemployment by lowering the relative price of domestic products and increasing world demand for them. Similarly, the central bank of an overheated economy could cool down activity by contracting the money supply without worrying that undesired reserve inflows would undermine its stabilization effort. Enhanced control over monetary policy would allow countries to dismantle their distorting barriers to international payments.

Advocates of floating also argued that floating rates would allow each country to choose its own desired long-run inflation rate rather than passively importing the inflation rate established abroad. We saw in the last chapter that a country faced with a rise in the foreign price level will be thrown out of balance and ultimately will import the foreign inflation if it holds its exchange rate fixed: By the end of the 1960s many countries felt that they were importing inflation from the United States. By revaluing its currency—that is, by lowering the domestic currency price of foreign currency—a country can insulate itself completely from an inflationary increase in foreign prices, and so remain in internal and external balance. One of the most telling arguments in favor of floating rates was their ability, in theory, to bring about automatically exchange rate changes that insulate economies from ongoing foreign inflation.

The mechanism behind this insulation is purchasing power parity (Chapter 15). Recall that when all changes in the world economy are monetary, PPP holds true in the long run: Exchange rates eventually move to offset exactly national differences in inflation. If U.S. monetary growth leads to a long-run doubling of the U.S. price level, while Germany's price level remains constant, PPP predicts that the long-run DM price of the dollar will be halved. This nominal exchange rate change leaves the *real* exchange rate between the dollar and DM unchanged and thus maintains Germany's internal and external balance. In other words, the long-run exchange rate change predicted by PPP is exactly the change that insulates Germany from U.S. inflation.

A money-induced increase in U.S. prices also causes an *immediate* appreciation of foreign currencies against the dollar when the exchange rate floats. In the short run, the size of this appreciation can differ from what PPP predicts, but the foreign exchange speculators who might have mounted an attack on fixed dollar exchange rates speed the adjustment of floating rates. Since they know foreign currencies will appreciate according to PPP in the long run, they act on their expectations and push exchange rates in the direction of their long-run levels.

Countries operating under the Bretton Woods rules were forced to choose between matching U.S. inflation to hold their dollar exchange rates fixed or deliberately revaluing their currencies in proportion to the rise in U.S. prices. Under floating, however, the foreign exchange market automatically brings about the exchange rate changes that shield countries from U.S. inflation. Since this outcome does not require any government policy decisions, the revaluation crises that occurred under fixed exchange rates are avoided.[1]

SYMMETRY

The second argument put forward by the advocates of floating was that abandonment of the Bretton Woods system would remove the asymmetries that caused so much international disagreement in the 1960s and early 1970s. There were two main asymmetries, both the result of the dollar's central role in the international monetary system. First, because central banks pegged their currencies to the dollar and accumulated dollars as international reserves, the U.S. Federal Reserve played the leading role in determining the world money supply and central banks abroad had little scope to determine their own domestic money

---

[1]Countries can also avoid importing undesired *deflation* by floating, since the analysis above goes through, in reverse, for a fall in the foreign price level.

supplies. Second, any foreign country could devalue its currency against the dollar in conditions of "fundamental disequilibrium," but the system's rules did not give the United States the option of devaluing against foreign currencies. Thus, when the dollar was at last devalued in December 1971, it was only after a long and economically disruptive period of multilateral negotiation.

A system of floating exchange rates, its proponents argued, would do away with these asymmetries. Since countries would no longer peg dollar exchange rates or need to hold dollar reserves for this purpose, each would be in a position to guide monetary conditions at home. For the same reason, the United States would not face any special obstacle to altering its exchange rate through monetary or fiscal policies. All countries' exchange rates would be determined symmetrically by the foreign exchange market, not by government decisions.[2]

EXCHANGE RATES AS AUTOMATIC STABILIZERS

The third argument in favor of floating rates concerned their ability, theoretically, to promote swift and relatively painless adjustment to certain types of economic changes. One such change, discussed above, is foreign inflation. Figure 19-1, which uses the *DD-AA* model presented in Chapter 16, examines another type of change by comparing the economy's response under a fixed and a floating exchange rate to a temporary fall in foreign demand for its exports.

A fall in demand for the home country's exports reduces aggregate demand for every level of the exchange rate, E, and so shifts the DD schedule leftward from DD^1 to DD^2. (Recall that the DD schedule shows exchange rate and output pairs for which aggregate demand equals aggregate output.) Figure 19-1a shows how this shift affects the economy's equilibrium when the exchange rate floats. Because the demand shift is assumed to be temporary, it does not change the long-run expected exchange rate and so does not move the asset market equilibrium schedule AA^1. (Recall that the AA schedule shows exchange rate and output pairs at which the foreign exchange market and the domestic money market are in equilibrium.) The economy's short-run equilibrium is therefore at point 2; compared with the initial equilibrium at point 1, the currency depreciates (E rises) and output falls. Why does the exchange rate rise from E^1 to E^2? As demand and output fall, reducing the transactions demand for money, the home interest rate must also decline to keep the money market in equilibrium. This fall in the home interest rate causes the domestic currency to depreciate in the foreign exchange market, and the exchange rate therefore rises from E^1 to E^2.

The effect of the same export demand disturbance under a fixed exchange rate is shown in Figure 19-1b. Since the central bank must prevent the currency depreciation that occurs under a floating rate, it buys domestic money with foreign currency, an action that contracts the money supply and shifts AA^1 left to AA^2. The new short-run equilibrium of the economy under a fixed exchange rate is at point 3, where output equals Y^3.

---

[2]The symmetry argument is not an argument against fixed-rate systems in general, but an argument against the specific type of fixed-exchange rate system that broke down in the early 1970s. As we saw in Chapter 17, a fixed-rate system based on a gold standard can be completely symmetric. The creation of an artificial reserve asset, the SDR, in the late 1960s was an attempt to attain the symmetry of a gold standard without the other drawbacks of that system.

FIGURE 19-1

Effects of a Fall in Export Demand

The response to a fall in export demand (seen in the shift from DD^1 to DD^2) differs under floating and fixed exchange rates. (a) With a floating rate, output falls only to Y^2 as the currency's depreciation (from E^1 to E^2) shifts demand back toward domestic goods. (b) With the exchange rate fixed at E^1, output falls all the way to Y^3 as the central bank reduces the money supply (reflected in the shift from AA^1 to AA^2).

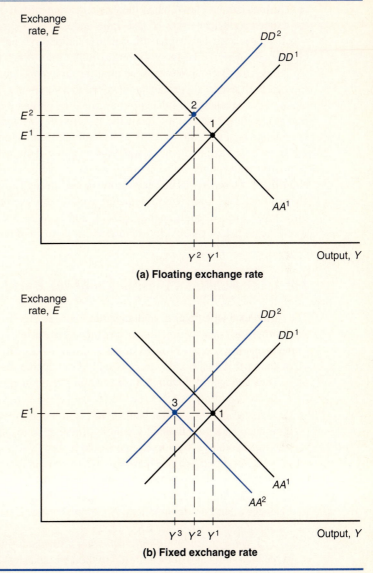

Figure 19-1 shows that output actually falls more under a fixed rate than under a floating rate, dropping all the way to Y^3 rather than Y^2. In other words, the movement of the floating exchange rate stabilizes the economy by reducing the shock's effect on employment relative to its effect under a fixed rate. Currency depreciation in the floating rate case makes domestic goods and services cheaper when the demand for them falls, partially offsetting the initial reduction in demand. In addition to reducing the departure from internal balance caused by the fall in export demand, the depreciation reduces the current account deficit that occurs under fixed rates by making domestic products more competitive in international markets.

We have considered the case of a transitory fall in export demand, but even stronger conclusions can be drawn when there is a *permanent* fall in export demand. In this case, the expected exchange rate E^e also rises and AA shifts upward as a result. A permanent shock causes a greater depreciation than a temporary one, and the movement of the exchange rate therefore cushions domestic output more when the shock is permanent.

Under the Bretton Woods system, a fall in export demand such as the one shown in Figure 19-1b would, if permanent, have led to a situation of "fundamental disequilibrium" calling for a devaluation of the currency or a long period of domestic unemployment as export prices fell. Uncertainty about the government's intentions would have encouraged speculative capital outflows, further worsening the situation by depleting central bank reserves and contracting the domestic money supply at a time of unemployment. Advocates of floating rates pointed out that the foreign exchange market would automatically bring about the required *real* currency depreciation through a movement in the nominal exchange rate. This exchange rate change would reduce or eliminate the need to push the price level down through unemployment, and because it would occur immediately there would be no risk of speculative disruption, as there would be under a fixed rate.

THE CASE AGAINST FLOATING EXCHANGE RATES

The experience with floating exchange rates between the world wars had left many doubts about how they would function in practice if the Bretton Woods rules were scrapped. Some economists were skeptical of the claims advanced by the advocates of floating and predicted instead that floating rates would have adverse consequences for the world economy. The case against floating rates rested on five main arguments:

1. *Discipline.* Central banks freed from the obligation to fix their exchange rates might embark on inflationary policies. In other words, the "discipline" imposed on individual countries by a fixed rate would be lost.

2. *Destabilizing speculation and money market disturbances.* Speculation on changes in exchange rates could lead to instability in foreign exchange markets, and this instability, in turn, might have negative effects on countries' internal and external balances. Further, disturbances to the home money market could be more disruptive under floating than under a fixed rate.

3. *Injury to international trade and investment.* Floating rates would make relative international prices more unpredictable and thus injure international trade and investment.

4. *Uncoordinated economic policies.* If the Bretton Woods rules on exchange rate adjustment were abandoned, the door would be opened to competitive currency practices harmful to the world economy. As happened during the interwar years, countries might adopt policies without considering their possible beggar-thy-neighbor aspects. All countries would suffer as a result.

5. *The illusion of greater autonomy.* Floating exchange rates would not really give countries more policy autonomy. Changes in exchange rates would have such pervasive macroeconomic effects that central banks would feel compelled to intervene heavily in foreign exchange markets even without a formal commitment to peg.

Thus, floating would increase the uncertainty in the economy without really giving macroeconomic policy greater freedom.

DISCIPLINE

Proponents of floating rates argue they give governments more freedom in the use of monetary policy. Some critics of floating rates believed that floating rates would lead to license rather than liberty: Freed of the need to worry about losses of foreign reserves, governments might embark on overexpansionary fiscal or monetary policies, falling into the inflation bias trap discussed in Chapter 16 (p. 460). Factors ranging from political objectives (such as stimulating the economy in time to win an election) to simple incompetence might set off an inflationary spiral. In the minds of those who made the discipline argument, the German hyperinflation of the 1920s epitomized the kind of monetary instability that floating rates might allow.

The pro-floaters' response to the discipline criticism was that a floating exchange rate would bottle up inflationary disturbances within the country whose government was misbehaving; it would then be up to its voters, if they wished, to elect a government with better policies. The Bretton Woods arrangements ended up imposing relatively little discipline on the United States, which certainly contributed to the acceleration of worldwide inflation in the late 1960s. Unless a sacrosanct link between currencies and a commodity such as gold were at the center of a system of fixed rates, the system would remain susceptible to human tampering. As discussed in Chapter 17, however, commodity-based monetary standards suffer from difficulties that make them undesirable in practice.

DESTABILIZING SPECULATION AND MONEY MARKET DISTURBANCES

An additional concern arising out of the experience of the interwar period was the possibility that speculation in currency markets might fuel wide gyrations in exchange rates. If foreign exchange traders saw that a currency was depreciating, it was argued, they might sell the currency in the expectation of future depreciation regardless of the currency's longer-term prospects; and as more traders jumped on the bandwagon by selling the currency the expectations of depreciation would be realized. Such **destabilizing speculation** would tend to accentuate the fluctuations around the exchange rate's long-run value that would occur normally as a result of unexpected economic disturbances. Aside from interfering with international trade, destabilizing sales of a weak currency might encourage expectations of future inflation and set off a domestic wage-price spiral that would encourage further depreciation. Countries could be caught in a "vicious circle" of depreciation and inflation that might be difficult to escape.

Advocates of floating rates questioned whether destabilizing speculators could stay in business. Anyone who persisted in selling a currency after it had depreciated below its long-run value or in buying a currency after it had appreciated above its long-run value was bound to lose money over the long term. Destabilizing speculators would thus be driven from the market, the pro-floaters argued, and the field would be left to speculators who had avoided long-term losses by speeding the adjustment of exchange rates *toward* their long-run values.

Proponents of floating also pointed out that capital flows could behave in a destabilizing manner under fixed rates. An unexpected central bank reserve loss might set up expectations of a devaluation and spark a reserve hemorrhage as speculators dumped domestic

FIGURE 19-2

A Rise in Money Demand Under a Floating Exchange Rate

A rise in money demand (the shift from AA^1 to AA^2) works exactly like a fall in the money supply, causing the currency to appreciate to E^2 and output to fall to Y^2. Under a fixed exchange rate the central bank would prevent AA^1 from shifting by purchasing foreign exchange and thus automatically expanding the money supply to meet the rise in money demand.

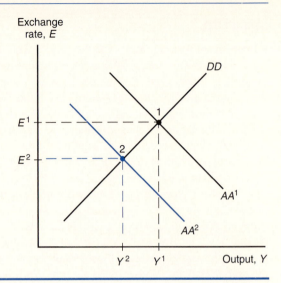

currency assets. Such capital flight might actually force an unnecessary devaluation if government measures to restore confidence proved insufficient.

A more telling argument against floating rates is that they make the economy more vulnerable to shocks coming from the domestic money market. Figure 19-2 uses the *DD-AA* model to illustrate this point. The figure shows the effect on the economy of a rise in real domestic money demand (that is, a rise in the real balances people desire to hold at each level of the interest rate and income) under a floating exchange rate. Because a lower level of income is now needed (given E) for people to be content to hold the available real money supply, AA^1 shifts leftward to AA^2: Income falls from Y^1 to Y^2 as the currency appreciates from E^1 to E^2. The rise in money demand works exactly like a fall in the money supply, and if it is permanent it will lead eventually to a fall in the home price level. Under a fixed exchange rate, however, the change in money demand does not affect the economy at all. To prevent the home currency from appreciating, the central bank buys foreign reserves with domestic money until the real money supply rises by an amount equal to the rise in real money demand. This intervention has the effect of keeping AA^1 in its original position, preventing any change in output or the price level.

A fixed exchange rate therefore automatically prevents instability in the domestic money market from affecting the economy. This is a powerful argument in favor of fixed rates *if* most of the shocks that buffet the economy come from the home money market (that is, if they result from shifts in *AA*). But as we saw in the previous section, fixing the exchange rate will worsen macroeconomic performance on average if output market shocks (that is, shocks involving shifts in *DD*) predominate.

INJURY TO INTERNATIONAL TRADE AND INVESTMENT

Critics of floating also charged that the inherent variability of floating exchange rates would injure international trade and investment. Fluctuating currencies make importers more uncertain about the prices they will have to pay for goods in the future and make exporters more uncertain about the prices they will receive. This uncertainty, it was claimed, would make it costlier to engage in international trade, and as a result trade volumes—and with them the gains countries realize through trade—would shrink. Similarly, greater uncertainty about the payoffs on investments might interfere with productive international capital flows.

Supporters of floating countered that international traders could avoid exchange rate risk through transactions in the forward exchange market (see Chapter 13), which would grow in scope and efficiency in a floating-rate world. The skeptics replied that forward exchange markets would be expensive to use and that it was doubtful that forward transactions could be used to cover all exchange-rate risks.

At a more general level, opponents of floating rates feared that the usefulness of each country's money as a guide to rational planning and calculation would be reduced. A currency becomes less useful as a unit of account if its purchasing power over imports becomes less predictable.

UNCOORDINATED ECONOMIC POLICIES

Some defenders of the Bretton Woods system felt that its rules had helped promote orderly international trade by outlawing the competitive currency depreciations that occurred during the Great Depression. With countries once again free to alter their exchange rates at will, they argued, history might repeat itself. Countries might again follow self-serving macroeconomic policies that hurt all countries and, in the end, helped none.

In rebuttal, the pro-floaters replied that the Bretton Woods rules for exchange rate adjustment were cumbersome. In addition, the rules were inequitable because, in practice, it was deficit countries that came under pressure to adopt restrictive macroeconomic policies or devalue. The fixed-rate system had "solved" the problem of international cooperation on monetary policy only by giving the United States a dominant position that it ultimately abused.

THE ILLUSION OF GREATER AUTONOMY

A final line of criticism held that the policy autonomy promised by the advocates of floating rates was, in part, illusory. True, a floating rate could in theory shut out foreign inflation over the long haul and allow central banks to set their money supplies as they pleased. But, it was argued, the exchange rate is such an important macroeconomic variable that policymakers would find themselves unable to take domestic monetary policy measures without considering their effects on the exchange rate.

Particularly important to this view was the role of the exchange rate in the domestic inflation process. A currency depreciation that raised import prices might induce workers to demand higher wages to maintain their customary standard of living. Higher wage settlements would then feed into final goods prices, fueling price level inflation and further wage hikes. In addition, currency depreciation would immediately raise the prices of imported goods used in the production of domestic output. Therefore, floating rates could be expected to quicken the pace at which the price level responded to increases in the money supply. While floating rates implied greater central bank control over the nominal money supply, M^s, they did not necessarily imply correspondingly greater control over the policy instrument that affects employment and other real economic variables, the *real* money supply, M^s/P. The response of domestic prices to exchange rate changes would be particularly rapid in economies where imports make up a large share of the domestic consumption basket: In such countries, currency changes have significant effects on the purchasing power of workers' wages.

The skeptics also maintained that the insulating properties of a floating rate are very limited. They conceded that the exchange rate would adjust *eventually* to offset foreign price inflation due to excessive monetary growth. In a world of sticky prices, however, countries are nonetheless buffeted by foreign monetary developments, which affect real interest rates and real exchange rates in the short run. Further, there is no reason, even in theory, why one country's fiscal policies cannot have repercussions abroad.

Critics of floating thus argued that its potential benefits had been oversold relative to its costs. Macroeconomic policymakers would continue to labor under the constraint of avoiding excessive exchange rate fluctuations. But by abandoning fixed rates, they would have forgone the benefits for world trade and investment of predictable currency values.

CASE STUDY

EXCHANGE RATE EXPERIENCE BETWEEN THE OIL SHOCKS, 1973–1980

Which group was right, the advocates of floating rates or the critics? In this Case Study and the next we survey the experience with floating exchange rates since 1973 in an attempt to answer this question. To avoid future disappointment, however, it is best to state up front that, as is often the case in economics, the data do not lead to a clear verdict. Although a number of predictions made by the critics of floating were borne out by subsequent events, it is also unclear whether a regime of fixed exchange rates would have survived the series of economic storms that has shaken the world economy since 1973.

The First Oil Shock and Its Effects, 1973–1975

As the industrialized countries' exchange rates were allowed to float in March 1973, an official group representing all IMF members was preparing plans to restore world monetary order. Formed in the fall of 1972, this group, called the Committee of Twenty, had been assigned the job of designing a new system of fixed exchange rates free of the asymmetries of Bretton Woods. By the time the committee issued its final "Outline of Reform" in July 1974, however, an upheaval in the world petroleum market had made an early return to fixed exchange rates unthinkable.

Energy Prices and the 1974–1975 Recession.   In October 1973 war broke out between Israel and the Arab countries. To protest support of Israel by the United States and the Netherlands, Arab members of the Organization of Petroleum Exporting Countries (OPEC), an international cartel including most large oil producers, imposed an embargo on oil shipments to those two countries. Fearing more general disruptions in oil shipments, buyers bid up market oil prices as they tried to build precautionary inventories. Encouraged by these developments in the oil market, OPEC countries began raising the price they charged to their main customers, the large oil companies. By March 1974 the oil price had quadrupled from its prewar price of $3 per barrel to $12 per barrel.

The massive increase in the price of oil raised the energy prices paid by consumers and the operating costs of energy-using firms and also fed into the prices of nonenergy petroleum products, such as plastics. To understand the impact of these price increases, think of them as a large tax on oil importers imposed by the oil producers of OPEC. The oil shock had the same macroeconomic effect as a simultaneous increase in consumer and business taxes: Consumption and investment slowed down everywhere, and the world economy was thrown into recession.

Because the price increase raised the import bills of oil importers, it worsened the current account deficits of many countries. The overall current account balance of the industrialized countries, taken as a group, went from $14.1 billion in 1973 to −$21.4 billion in 1974, while the overall current account of the less-developed countries that were not major oil exporters moved from −$3.5 billion to −$21.8 billion. The increased current account deficits of these two groups corresponded to a greater current account surplus for the main oil exporters. The total current account surplus of those countries rose from $6.8 billion to $65.2 billion between 1973 and 1974. (Data on 1973–1986 current account balances for the three major groups of countries described here are given in Table 22-2, p. 698.)[3]

The Acceleration of Inflation.

The model we developed in Chapters 13 through 17 predicts that inflation tends to rise in booms and fall in recessions. As the world went into deep recession in 1974, however, inflation accelerated in most countries. Table 19-1 shows how inflation in the seven largest industrial countries spurted upward in that year. In a number of these countries inflation rates came close to doubling even though unemployment was rising.

What happened? An important contributing factor was the oil shock itself: By directly raising the prices of petroleum products and the costs of energy-using industries, the increase in the oil price caused price levels to jump upward. Further, the worldwide inflationary pressures that had built up since the end of the 1960s had become entrenched in the wage-setting process and were continuing to contribute to inflation in spite of the deteriorating employment picture. The same inflationary expectations that were driving new wage contracts were also putting additional upward pressure on commodity prices as speculators built up stocks of commodities whose prices they expected to rise.

Finally, the oil crisis, as luck would have it, was not the only supply shock troubling the world economy at the time. From 1972 on, a coincidence of adverse supply disturbances pushed farm prices upward and thus contributed to the general inflation. These supply disturbances included poor harvests in the United

---

[3]The fall in the U.S. current account surplus, from $9.1 billion in 1973 to $7.6 billion in 1974, was relatively minor. This was because the United States, itself an oil producer, was less dependent on oil imports than were many other countries. In contrast, Japan, which is heavily dependent on energy imports, moved from a surplus of $0.1 billion to a deficit of $4.5 billion.

TABLE 19-1

Inflation Rates in Major Industrialized Countries, 1973–1980 (percent per year)

Country	1973	1974	1975	1976	1977	1978	1979	1980
United States	6.2	11.1	9.1	5.7	6.5	7.6	11.3	13.5
Britain	9.2	16.0	24.2	16.5	15.8	8.3	13.4	18.0
Canada	7.6	10.9	10.8	7.5	8.0	8.9	9.2	10.2
France	7.3	13.7	11.8	9.6	9.4	9.1	10.8	13.6
Germany	6.9	7.0	6.0	4.5	3.7	2.7	4.1	5.5
Italy	10.8	19.1	17.0	16.8	17.0	12.1	14.8	21.2
Japan	11.7	24.5	11.8	9.3	8.1	3.8	3.6	8.0

Source: Organization for Economic Cooperation and Development. *Economic Outlook: Historical Statistics, 1960–1986.* Paris: OECD, 1987. Figures are percentage increases in each year's average consumer price index over the average consumer price index for the previous year.

States and the Soviet Union; shortages of sugar and cocoa; and the mysterious disappearance of the Peruvian anchovies from their customary feeding grounds. Although you may think anchovies are important only to consumers of pizza and Caesar salad, they are also important to farmers since they are used in the fish meal that is fed to livestock. The precipitous drop in the anchovy catch led to sharp increases in the prices of competing feed grains (mainly corn and soybeans).

Stagflation. To describe the unusual macroeconomic conditions of 1974–1975, economists coined a new word that has since become commonplace: **stagflation,** a combination of stagnating output and high inflation. Stagflation was the result of two factors:

1. Increases in commodity prices that directly raised inflation while at the same time depressing aggregate demand and supply.
2. Expectations of future inflation that fed into wages and other prices in spite of recession and rising unemployment.

Even before the oil shock hit, the move to floating rates had allowed the industrialized countries to adopt more restrictive monetary and fiscal policies aimed at restraining the accelerating inflation. The slowdown in money growth was most dramatic in Germany, whose Bundesbank used its new-found control over the money supply to reduce its annual monetary growth rate from 14.7 percent in 1972 to a mere 2.6 percent in 1973. A significant monetary slowdown also took place in the United States, where the Fed allowed the money supply to grow by only 5.6 percent in 1973 and 4.4 percent in 1974, as compared with 9.2 percent in 1972. These initially restrictive policies helped deepen the 1974–1975 slump.

Regaining Internal and External Balance. The commodity shocks left most oil-importing countries further from both internal and external balance than they were when floating began in 1973. Countries were in no position to give up the expenditure-switching advantages of exchange rate flexibility and burden monetary policy with the job of defending a fixed rate. No commitment to fixed rates would have been credible in a period when countries were experiencing such different inflation rates and suffering shocks that permanently altered production costs. The speculative attacks that had brought the fixed-rate system down would have quickly undermined any attempt to fix parities anew.

How did countries use their policy tools to regain internal and external balance? As the recession deepened over 1974 and early 1975, most governments shifted to expansionary fiscal and monetary policies. In the seven largest industrial countries, monetary growth rates rose between 1974 and 1975 as central banks reacted to rising unemployment. As a result of these policy actions, a strong output recovery was underway in most industrialized countries by the second half of 1975. At the same time inflation was falling (see Table 19-1). Unfortunately, however, the unemployment rates of industrialized countries failed to return to prerecession levels even as output recovered.

The 1974 current account deficit of the industrial countries, taken as a group, turned to a surplus in 1975 as spending fell, and was near zero in 1976. The OPEC countries, which could not raise spending quickly enough to match their increased income, were running a substantial current account surplus in 1975 and 1976, but this was matched by the deficit of the oil-importing developing countries. Because the non-oil-developing countries did not cut their spending as sharply as industrial countries, GNP growth in developing countries as a group did not become negative in 1975, as it did in many developed countries. The developing countries financed their oil deficits in part by borrowing funds that the OPEC countries had deposited in the industrial countries' financial centers.

Most economists and policymakers viewed the international adjustment to the first oil shock as a success for floating exchange rates. Freed of the need to defend a fixed exchange rate, each government had chosen the monetary and fiscal response that best suited its goals. The United States and Germany had even been able to relax the capital controls they had set up before 1974. This relaxation eased the adjustment problem of the developing countries, which were able to borrow more easily from developed country financial markets to maintain their own spending and economic growth. In turn, the relative strength of the developing world's demand for industrial country exports helped mitigate the severity of the 1974–1975 recession.

Revising the IMF's Charter, 1975–1976

Because floating rates had seemed to function well in conditions of adversity, the governments of the industrialized countries acknowledged late in 1975 that they were prepared to live with floating exchange rates for the indefinite future. Meeting at the Château de Rambouillet, near Paris, in the first of a series of annual economic summit meetings, leaders of the main industrial countries called on the IMF to revise its Articles of Agreement to take account of the reality of floating exchange rates. The participating governments committed themselves to countering "erratic fluctuations" in exchange rates but made no provision for a return to fixed parities.

In response to the Rambouillet decisions, the IMF's directors met at Kingston, Jamaica, in January 1976 to approve a revision of the fourth IMF Article of Agreement, which covered exchange rate arrangements. The new Article IV implicitly endorsed floating rates by freeing each member country to choose any exchange rate system it preferred. Governments were urged to follow macroeconomic policies that would promote price stability and growth, and they were to avoid "manipulating exchange rates . . . to gain an unfair competitive advantage over other members." But more detailed restrictions were not placed on IMF members' policies.

The amended Article IV called on the IMF to monitor members' exchange rate policies to ensure compliance with the new guidelines. Although this "surveillance" of exchange rate policies went beyond IMF conditionality in that it applied even to countries not borrowing from the Fund, no mechanism was created to give the Fund clout in influencing nonborrowers' policies. In practice, therefore, the new article did no more than sanction what had already existed for nearly three years: a scheme of decentralized policy-making in which each country pursued what it perceived as its own interest.

The Weak Dollar, 1976–1979

As the recovery from the 1974–1975 recession slowed in late 1976 and unemployment remained persistently high, the United States urged the two other industrial giants, Germany and Japan, to join it in adopting expansionary policies that would pull the world economy out of its doldrums. Only at the Bonn economic summit of July 1978 did Germany and Japan, less fearful of inflation than they had been two years earlier, agree to join the United States as "locomotives" of world economic growth. Until then, the United States had been attempting to go it alone, and its policies, while causing a sharp drop in the U.S. unemployment rate (to 6.0 percent in 1978 from a recession high of 8.3 percent in 1975), had reignited inflation and pushed the U.S. current account into deficit. In contrast, inflation in Germany and Japan had reached relatively low levels by 1978 (see Table 19-1).

The result of this policy imbalance—vigorous expansion in the United States unmatched by expansion abroad—was a steep depreciation of the dollar starting in 1976. The depreciation of the dollar in these years is evident in Figure 19-3, which shows both **nominal and real effective exchange rate indexes** of the dollar. These indexes measure, respectively, the price of a dollar in terms of a basket of foreign currencies and the price of U.S. output in terms of a basket of foreign outputs. Thus, a rise in either index is a (nominal or real) dollar appreciation, while a fall is a depreciation.

International investors had little confidence in the dollar's future value in view of the widening gap between U.S. and foreign inflation rates. In addition, the weakening dollar helped fuel U.S. inflation by raising import prices and the inflation expectations of wage setters. To restore confidence in the dollar, President Carter appointed a new Federal Reserve Board chairman with broad experience in international financial affairs, Paul A. Volcker. The dollar remained weak in the foreign exchange market until October 1979, when Volcker announced a tightening of U.S. monetary policy and the adoption by the Fed of more stringent procedures for controlling money supply growth.

FIGURE 19-3

Nominal and Real Effective Dollar Exchange Rate Indexes, 1975–1994

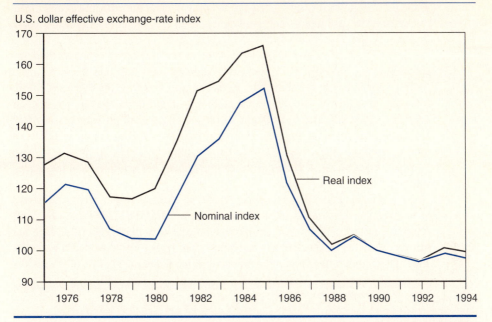

U.S. dollar effective exchange-rate index

The indexes are measures of the nominal and real value of the U.S. dollar in terms of a basket of 15 industrial-country currencies. An increase in the indexes is a dollar appreciation, a decrease a dollar depreciation. For both indexes, the 1990 value is 100.

Source: International Monetary Fund, *International Financial Statistics Yearbook,* 1991, 1995.

The sharp U.S. monetary turnaround of 1979 illustrated the truth of one point made by the critics of floating exchange rates. Governments could not be indifferent to the behavior of exchange rates and inevitably surrendered some of their policy autonomy in other areas to prevent exchange rate movements they viewed as harmful to their economies.

The Second Oil Shock, 1979–1980

The fall of the Shah of Iran in 1979 sparked a second round of oil price increases by disrupting oil exports from that country. Oil prices rose from around $13 per barrel in 1978 to nearly $32 per barrel in 1980. As they had after the 1973–1974 episode, oil-importing economies faced stagflation. Table 19-1 shows that inflation accelerated sharply in all the industrialized economies between 1978 and 1980. Output growth generally slowed and unemployment generally rose, but the effects were neither as uniform nor as dramatic as those of the first oil shock. Oil-importing developing countries, like the developed countries, experienced higher inflation coupled with slower growth.

As in the earlier oil shock, the industrial countries as a group ran a current account deficit that then declined, while the non-oil-producing developing countries ran persistent high deficits rather than adjusting spending downward (see Table 22-2, p. 698). But in contrast to what happened after the first round of oil price hikes, the developing world's deficit caused serious problems for the world financial system later in the 1980s.

In 1975 macroeconomic policymakers in the industrial countries had responded to the first oil shock with expansionary monetary and fiscal policies. They responded very differently to the second oil shock. Over 1979 and 1980, monetary growth was actually *restricted* in most major industrial countries in an attempt to offset the rise in inflation accompanying the oil price increase. After struggling to reduce the higher inflation of the early 1970s, central banks were now worried that the 1978–1980 upswing in inflation might be hard to reverse later if it were allowed to be built into inflationary expectations and the wage-setting process.

The fight against inflation had a high price in terms of employment and output. Unemployment appeared to take a ratchet step upward by 1981 (see Table 19-2), and restrictive macroeconomic policies blocked a decisive output recovery. In fact, the recovery from the oil shock barely had time to start up before the world economy, in 1981, plunged into the deepest recession since the Great Depression of the 1930s.

TABLE 19-2

Unemployment Rates in Major Industrialized Countries, 1979–1994 (percent of labor force)

Year	United States	Britain	Canada	France	Germany	Italy	Japan
1979	5.8	5.0	7.4	5.8	3.2	7.6	2.1
1980	7.0	6.4	7.5	6.2	2.9	7.5	2.0
1981	7.5	9.8	7.5	7.4	4.2	7.8	2.2
1982	9.5	11.3	10.9	8.1	5.9	8.4	2.4
1983	9.5	12.4	11.9	8.3	7.7	8.8	2.6
1984	7.4	11.7	11.2	9.7	7.1	9.4	2.7
1985	7.1	11.2	10.5	10.2	7.1	9.6	2.6
1986	6.9	11.2	9.5	10.4	6.4	10.5	2.8
1987	6.1	10.3	8.8	10.5	6.2	10.9	2.8
1988	5.4	8.6	7.7	10.0	6.2	11.0	2.5
1989	5.2	7.2	7.5	9.4	5.6	10.9	2.3
1990	5.4	6.9	8.1	8.9	4.8	10.3	2.1
1991	6.6	8.8	10.3	9.4	4.2	9.9	2.1
1992	7.3	10.1	11.3	10.4	4.6	10.5	2.2
1993	6.7	10.5	11.2	11.6	6.1	10.2	2.5
1994	6.0	9.6	10.3	12.5	6.9	--	2.9

Source: Organization for Economic Cooperation and Development. *OECD Economic Outlook* 57 (June 1995), Annex Table 22. Data for Germany do not include the former East Germany.

A Two-Country Model of Macroeconomic Interdependence Under a Floating Rate

Before discussing macroeconomic interactions between the United States and the rest of the world in the 1980s and 1990s, we will develop a model to analyze the transmission of policies between countries linked by a floating exchange rate. The model is applied to the short run in which output prices can be assumed to be fixed.

Imagine a world of two countries, Home and Foreign. In previous models the home country's current account balance has been written as a function of its real exchange rate and its income. In reality, however, the level of GNP abroad influences foreign demand for the home country's exports and therefore the home current account balance. The model of Chapters 16 and 17 implicitly assumed the home country was too small to influence foreign income, the level of which we took as fixed. The model cannot adequately illuminate the macroeconomic interdependence of national economies unless it is extended to apply to large countries like the United States.

As the first step in this extension, we now assume that Home's current account is a function of the real exchange rate, EP^*/P, its own disposable income, $Y - T$, and Foreign's disposable income, $Y^* - T^*$, where Y^* denotes Foreign's output and T^* Foreign's taxes. E is the Home currency price of Foreign's currency and EP^*/P is the real exchange rate, the price of Foreign output in terms of Home output. Home's current account is therefore

$$CA = CA(EP^*/P, Y - T, Y^* - T^*).$$

A real depreciation of Home's currency (a rise in EP^*/P) is assumed to cause an increase in its current account balance, while a rise in Home disposable income leads to a fall. Our previous model ignored the effect of Foreign disposable income on Home's current account, but in a model of two interacting economies we must ask how a rise in $Y^* - T^*$ affects CA. Because a rise in Foreign disposable income raises Foreign spending on Home products, it raises Home exports. *A rise in Foreign disposable income therefore causes an increase in Home's current account balance.*

Aggregate demand for Home output is, as always, the sum of Home's total spending, $C + I + G$, and its current account, CA. Aggregate supply and demand are therefore equal in Home when

$$Y = C(Y - T) + I + G + CA(EP^*/P, Y - T, Y^* - T^*). \qquad (19\text{-}1)$$

Foreign's current account, CA^*, also depends on the relative price of Home and Foreign products, EP^*/P, and on disposable income in the two countries. In fact, in a world of two countries, Home's current account surplus must exactly equal Foreign's current account deficit when both balances are measured in terms of a common unit. Since Home exports are Foreign imports and Home imports are Foreign exports, any Home export surplus is necessarily matched by a corresponding Foreign import surplus. In terms of Foreign output, Foreign's current account is

$$CA^* = -CA(EP^*/P, Y - T, Y^* - T^*) \div (EP^*/P).$$

CA is divided by the real exchange rate EP^*/P, the price of Foreign output in terms of Home output, to convert it into the Foreign output units used to measure CA^*.

Clearly, a rise in Home income, by worsening Home's current account *CA,* improves *CA**; in the same way, a rise in Foreign income worsens *CA**. Although the effect of a change in *EP*/P* on *CA** is more complicated, we assume that a rise in *EP*/P* (a relative cheapening of Home output) causes *CA** to fall at the same time it causes *CA* to rise.[4] In the Foreign output market supply equals demand when Foreign output, *Y**, equals total Foreign spending, *C* + I* + G**, less the value of Home's current account balance measured in terms of Foreign output, *(P/EP*) × CA:*

$$Y^* = C^*(Y^* - T^*) + I^* + G^* - (P/EP^*) \times CA(EP^*/P, Y - T, Y^* - T^*). \quad (19\text{-}2)$$

Assuming temporarily that the real exchange rate *EP*/P* is constant at a given level, Figure 19-4 shows how the Home and Foreign output levels are determined. The *HH* schedule shows the Home and Foreign output levels at which aggregate demand equals aggregate supply *in Home. HH* slopes upward because a rise in *Y** increases Home exports, raising aggregate demand and calling forth a higher level of Home output, *Y.* The *FF* schedule shows the Home and Foreign output levels at which aggregate demand equals aggregate supply *in Foreign.* Like *HH, FF* has a positive slope, and for the same reason: A rise in *Y* raises demand for Foreign exports, and Foreign output, *Y**, must rise to meet this increase in aggregate demand. At the intersection of *HH* and *FF* (point 1), aggregate demand and supply are equal in *both* countries, given the real exchange rate.

Notice that *HH* is drawn to be steeper than *FF.* The slopes of the two schedules differ in this way because a rise in a country's output has a greater effect on its own output market than on the foreign one. Along *HH,* then, a large increase in *Y** is needed to remove the excess supply of Home output caused by a rise in *Y.* Likewise, along *FF,* a large increase in *Y* is needed to restore balance in the Foreign output market after a rise in *Y**.[5]

Changes in fiscal policy at home or abroad shift the schedules by altering government purchases, *G* and *G**, and net taxes, *T* and *T**. In addition, fiscal policies affect *HH* and *FF* by altering the exchange rate, *E* (Chapter 16). Home fiscal expansion causes *E* to fall (an

---

[4]The complication behind this assumption is related to the one behind the Marshall-Lerner condition (see Chapter 16, Appendix III). We have already assumed that a rise in *EP*/P* causes *CA* to rise. But this is not always sufficient to imply that *CA** falls at the same time, because *CA* = −CA ÷ (EP*/P).* For example, if Home has a current account surplus *(CA > 0),* a rise in *EP*/P* pushes *CA* further away from zero. This tends to make *CA** more negative than it was, but at the same time it pushes *CA** closer to zero by increasing the denominator of *−CA ÷ (EP*/P)*—that is, by making Foreign's exports more expensive relative to its imports from Home. These two effects work in opposite directions, but the second will be small if current accounts are initially near zero.

[5]More formally, let *s* be the fraction of any increase in Home income that goes into saving and *m* the fraction that is spent on imports from Foreign. Let *s** and *m** denote the corresponding fractions for Foreign. Then an increase *ΔY* in Home output leads to an excess supply *(s + m)ΔY* in Home's output market, which must be matched by an increase in Foreign demand equal to *(EP*/P)m*ΔY** along *HH.* The slope of *HH* is therefore *ΔY*/ΔY = (s + m)/[(EP*/P)m*].* An identical argument shows that the slope of *FF* is *ΔY*/ΔY = m/[(EP*/P)(s* + m*)].* From these equations, the slope of *HH* is greater than that of *FF* when *(s + m)/m* > m/(s* + m*),* that is, when *(s + m)(s* + m*) > mm*.* This last inequality is always true, however, when none of the fractions that appear in it is a negative number.

The dependence of each country's equilibrium output on foreign output (for a given real exchange rate) is called the *export multiplier effect,* because changes in the demand for a country's exports can have an effect on its output several times as large. Using the formulas just given for the slopes of *HH* and *FF,* you can check that a unit increase in Foreign demand for Home exports raises Home output by *1/(s + m).* Similarly, Foreign's export multiplier is *1/(s* + m*).* Both numbers are likely to exceed 1.

FIGURE 19-4

Output Determination in a Two-Country World

For a given real exchange rate, the inter-section of *HH* (along which the Home output market clears) and *FF* (along which the Foreign output market clears) determines short-run equilibrium output levels in the two countries.

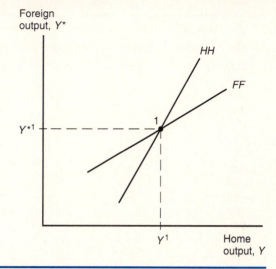

appreciation of Home currency against Foreign currency), while Foreign fiscal expansion causes *E* to rise (a depreciation of Home currency against Foreign currency). Monetary policies can also move the two schedules by influencing the exchange rate. Both monetary and fiscal policies are at the heart of exchange rate experience after 1980, and we now apply our two-country framework to these events.

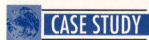

CASE STUDY

DISINFLATION, SLUMP, AND RECOVERY, 1980–1995

The years after 1980 brought a number of dramatic changes in the world econ-omy. On the positive side, inflation rates throughout the industrialized world fell to levels even below those of the Bretton Woods years (see Table 19-3). At long last, price stability seemed to have been restored. But the negative events of the period were so severe that they threatened the relatively open world trading and financial system that had been built up so laboriously after World War II. At times, the international community seemed on the verge of replaying the eco-nomic tragedy of the interwar years. Many economists and policymakers began to see floating exchange rates as a major cause of the world economy's problems and urged a return to more limited exchange rate flexibility.

TABLE 19-3

Inflation Rates in Major Industrialized Countries, 1981–1994, and 1961–1971 Average (percent per year)

Year	United States	Britain	Canada	France	Germany	Italy	Japan
1981	10.4	11.9	12.5	13.4	6.3	19.5	4.9
1982	6.1	8.6	10.8	11.8	5.3	16.5	2.7
1983	3.2	4.6	5.8	9.6	3.3	15.0	1.9
1984	4.3	5.0	4.3	7.4	2.4	10.6	2.2
1985	3.5	6.1	4.0	5.8	2.2	8.6	2.0
1986	1.9	3.4	4.2	2.7	−0.1	6.1	0.6
1987	3.7	4.1	4.4	3.1	0.2	4.6	0.1
1988	4.1	4.9	4.0	2.7	1.3	5.0	0.7
1989	4.8	7.8	5.0	3.6	2.8	6.6	2.3
1990	5.4	9.5	4.8	3.4	2.7	6.1	3.1
1991	4.2	5.9	5.6	3.2	3.5	6.4	3.3
1992	3.0	1.7	1.5	2.4	4.0	5.1	1.7
1993	3.0	1.3	1.9	2.1	4.1	4.2	1.3
1994	2.5	0.7	0.2	1.7	3.0	3.9	0.7
1961–71 average	3.1	4.6	2.9	4.3	3.0	4.2	5.9

Source: Organization for Economic Cooperation and Development. *Main Economic Indicators,* various issues. Figures are percentage increases in each year's average consumer price index over the average consumer price index for the previous year.

Disinflation and the 1981–1983 Recession

In October 1979, Federal Reserve Chairman Volcker announced an abrupt change in U.S. monetary policy aimed at fighting domestic inflation and stemming the dollar's fall. Volcker's monetary slowdown convinced the foreign exchange market that the Fed chairman would make good his promise to wring inflation out of the American economy. With the November 1980 election of President Reagan, who had campaigned on an anti-inflation platform, the dollar's value soared. Between the end of 1979 and the end of 1981, the dollar appreciated against the DM by 23.2 percent. U.S. interest rates also rose sharply late in 1979; by 1981, short-term interest rates in the United States were nearly double their 1978 levels.

Figure 19-5, which shows the effect of a Home monetary slowdown in the two-country model, will help you understand the effects of the Volcker policy change both in the United States (Home) and abroad (Foreign). By pushing up the U.S. interest rate and causing investors to expect a stronger dollar in the future, the U.S. action led to an immediate appreciation of the dollar. This appreciation made U.S. (Home) goods more expensive relative to Foreign goods, thereby raising the level of Foreign output, Y^*, needed to maintain the demand for Home output at any given level Y. Figure 19-5 shows this change as an upward shift of HH^1 to HH^2. The appreciation of the dollar (the Home currency) affects Foreign's out-

FIGURE 19-5

Monetary Contraction in Home

Monetary contraction in Home (shown in the shift of HH^1 to HH^2), by appreciating its currency relative to Foreign's (indicated by the shift of FF^1 to FF^2), causes Home output to fall (from Y^1 to Y^2) and Foreign output to rise (from Y^{*1} to Y^{*2}).

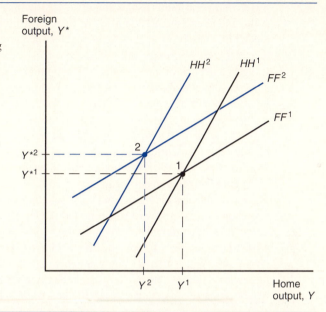

put market as well; since Foreign output becomes relatively cheaper, FF^1 shifts leftward, to FF^2.

As a result of the two shifts, Home output falls, Foreign output rises, and the world economy moves from its initial equilibrium at point 1 to a new equilibrium at point 2. It may seem surprising at first that monetary contraction at Home raises output abroad, since the fall in Home output causes a direct reduction in Home's demand for imports. This last reduction in Home's import demand is, however, a secondary effect of the initial switch in world spending from Home to Foreign goods.[6]

---

[6]You may be wondering if it can ever happen that Home output *rises,* which is what would occur if the upward shift of HH^1 were less than that of FF^1. To prove that this outcome is impossible, let Z (a positive quantity measured in Home output units) equal the switch in aggregate demand from Home to Foreign products caused by the Home currency's appreciation and recall the notation introduced in the last footnote. If Foreign demand for Home goods rises by $Z = (EP^*/P)m^*\Delta Y^*$ (where EP^*/P is the new real exchange rate), Home output Y does not change. The upward shift of HH^1 is therefore $Z/[(EP^*/P)m^*]$. How must Y^* change to maintain goods market equilibrium in Foreign, given Y? Since world demand for Foreign products rises by $Z/(EP^*/P)$, a Foreign output increase given by

$$Z/(EP^*/P) + (1 - s^* - m^*)\Delta Y^* = \Delta Y^*$$

leaves aggregate demand and supply equal in Foreign for a given value of Y. The solution of this last equation is $\Delta Y^* = Z/[(EP^*/P)(s^* + m^*)]$, which equals the upward shift of FF^1. This number is smaller than the upward shift of HH^1. Thus, Home monetary contraction must cause a fall in Home's output.

A similar argument shows that the leftward shift of FF^1 always exceeds that of HH^1, so that Foreign output always rises. (See problem 6 at the end of this chapter.) The model's predictions would be somewhat more complicated if real interest rates influenced spending decisions (as in Chapter 16, Appendix I).

As the model suggests, the Fed's monetary slowdown did have a negative effect on America's output and employment. The dollar's appreciation was not welcomed abroad, however, even though it may have lent foreign economies some positive stimulus in a period of slow growth. The reason was that a stronger dollar hindered foreign countries in their own fights against inflation, both by raising the import prices they faced and by encouraging higher wage demands by their workers. A stronger dollar had the opposite effect in the United States, hastening the decline of inflation there. The tight U.S. monetary policy therefore had a beggar-thy-neighbor effect on foreign economies, in that it lowered American inflation in part by exporting inflation to foreign economies.

Foreign central banks responded by intervening in the foreign exchange market to slow the dollar's rise. Through the process of selling dollar reserves and buying their own currencies, some central banks reduced their monetary growth rates for 1980 and 1981, driving interest rates upward.

Synchronized monetary contraction in the United States and abroad, following fast on the heels of the second oil shock, threw the world economy into a deep recession, the most severe since the Great Depression of the 1930s. Table 19-2 shows how unemployment moved in the major industrial countries. In 1982 and 1983 unemployment throughout the world rose to levels unprecedented in the post-World War II period. You can appreciate the severity of the unemployment rates shown in the table by comparing them with the average unemployment rate for the same seven countries over the years 1963–1972 (3.2 percent). As Table 19-3 shows, however, monetary contraction and the recession it brought quickly led to a dramatic drop in the inflation rates of industrialized countries.

Fiscal Policies, the Current Account, and the Resurgence of Protectionism

During his election campaign, President Reagan had promised to lower taxes and balance the federal budget. He made good on the first of these promises in 1981 when Congress approved legislation lowering personal taxes and providing fiscal investment incentives to businesses. At the same time, the Reagan administration pushed for an acceleration of defense spending, accompanied by cuts in government spending on domestic programs. The net result of these and subsequent congressional actions was a ballooning U.S. government budget deficit and a sharp fiscal stimulus to the economy.

Figure 19-6 illustrates the effects of a Home fiscal expansion in the two-country model. Because fiscal expansion by Home causes its currency (the dollar) to appreciate, Foreign products become relatively cheap and world demand for them rises. Foreign output, Y^*, therefore must rise for every level of Home output, Y, as represented by the upward shift of FF^1 to FF^2. Since Home is a large country, the impact of its fiscal expansion on the aggregate demand for its output is positive, in spite of the domestic currency's appreciation, and so Y must rise for every value of Y^*. This rise in Home aggregate demand implies that HH^1 shifts rightward to HH^2. Output goes up both in Home and in Foreign as the world economy moves to point 2 from its initial position at point 1.

An analysis of U.S. fiscal moves is complicated because the fiscal policy mandated in 1981 was a phased one that began only in 1982, and whose expansionary impact was probably not felt fully until 1983. The *anticipation* of future fiscal expansion in 1981 would simply have appreciated the dollar, shifting FF^1

FIGURE 19-6

Fiscal Expansion in Home

A Home fiscal expansion, which shifts HH^1 to HH^2, raises output at home as well as abroad. The shift from FF^1 to FF^2 is caused by the appreciation of Home's currency against Foreign's.

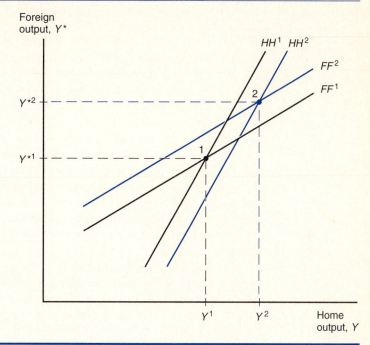

up as shown in Figure 19-6 but shifting the other schedule left rather than right. These changes would have tended to deepen the early stages of the 1981–1983 recession in the United States, while giving less stimulus abroad than Figure 19-6 suggests. Only by late 1982 or 1983 is Figure 19-6 an accurate portrayal of the global effects of U.S. fiscal policy.

All along, however, the U.S. fiscal stance encouraged continuing dollar appreciation (see Figure 19-3), as did the contractionary fiscal policies pursued at the time by Germany and Japan. By February 1985 the dollar's cumulative appreciation against the DM since the end of 1979 was 47.9 percent. The recession reached its low point in the United States in December 1982, and output began to recover both there and abroad as the U.S. fiscal stimulus was transmitted to foreign countries through the dollar's steady appreciation. Also contributing to the recovery was a looser Federal Reserve monetary policy.

Foreign central banks remained fearful of encouraging inflation through expansionary policies of their own. As easier U.S. money brought dollar interest rates down in the second half of 1982, however, some foreign central banks began to feel they could ease their monetary policies without causing their currencies to depreciate too sharply. By early 1984 U.S. unemployment had fallen and U.S. output was growing rapidly. Unemployment remained high in other industrialized countries, however, and the growth of output abroad was slow by historical standards.

While the U.S. fiscal expansion contributed to world recovery, growing federal budget deficits raised serious worries about the future stability of the world economy. Increasing government deficits were not met with offsetting increases in private saving or decreases in investment, so the American current account balance deteriorated sharply (recall Chapter 12's Case Study of the link between the government deficit and the current account, pp. 313–315). By 1987 the United States had become a net debtor to foreign countries and its current account deficit was at the postwar record level of 3.6 percent of GNP. Some analysts worried that foreign creditors would lose confidence in the future value of the dollar assets they were accumulating and sell them, causing a sudden, precipitous dollar depreciation.

Equally worrisome was the strong dollar's impact on the distribution of income within the United States. The dollar's appreciation had reduced U.S. inflation and allowed consumers to purchase imports more cheaply, but those hurt by the terms of trade change were better organized and more vocal than those who had benefited. Persistently poor economic performance in the 1980s had led to increased pressures on governments to protect industries in the exporting and import-competing sectors. As the U.S. recovery slowed late in 1984, protectionist pressures snowballed.

The Reagan administration had, from the start, adopted a policy of "benign neglect" toward the foreign exchange market, refusing to intervene except in unusual circumstances (for example, after a would-be assassin shot President Reagan). By 1985, however, the link between the strong dollar and the gathering protectionist storm became impossible to ignore.

From the Plaza to the Louvre and Beyond: Trying to Manage Exchange Rates

Faster U.S. monetary growth in 1985 brought some dollar depreciation but failed to head off congressional sentiment in favor of import restrictions. Fearing a disaster for the international trading system, economic officials of the Group of Five (G-5) countries—the United States, Britain, France, Germany, and Japan—announced at New York's Plaza Hotel on September 22, 1985, that they would jointly intervene in the foreign exchange market to bring about a dollar depreciation. The dollar dropped sharply the next day and continued to decline through 1986 and early 1987 as the United States maintained its loose monetary policy and pushed dollar interest rates down relative to foreign currency rates. (See Figure 19-3.)

The G-5 Plaza announcement represented a sharp change in the policy of the Reagan administration, a reversal of its opposition to foreign exchange intervention. The Plaza communiqué indicated growing dissatisfaction in government circles with the performance of floating exchange rates and marked the start of a period in which countries including the United States readily intervened, sometimes massively and in a cooperative fashion, to influence exchange rates.

By the end of 1986, the dollar's exchange rate had become a focus of disagreement among governments. The United States still had a large current account deficit. Faced with foreign reluctance to adopt expenditure-changing policies, American leaders pushed to restore external balance through the expenditure-switching policy of further dollar depreciation. Leaders of other industrial countries, however, felt the appreciation of their currencies had gone far enough. Their own tradables industries were finding it difficult to meet foreign competition, and so the expenditure change of a U.S. fiscal and monetary contraction appeared preferable to them.

A renewed effort to cooperate on exchange rates followed a meeting at the Louvre in Paris on February 22, 1987. Finance ministers and central bank governors from the G-5 countries plus Canada issued a statement pledging to stabilize nominal exchange rates around the levels then prevailing, which the officials viewed as "broadly consistent with underlying economic fundamentals," including the requirement of generalized external balance. The Louvre accord was far more, however, than a mere verbal pronouncement on exchange rates. In an unpublished agreement, governments set up target zones for exchange rates and agreed to defend them by intervening in the foreign exchange market. While these target zones were not made public, observers believe the Louvre accord called for bands of plus or minus 5 percent around the rates of DM 1.8250 per dollar and ¥ 153.50 per dollar. (In contrast, exchange rates in the weeks after the Plaza announcement were in the neighborhood of DM 2.750 per dollar and ¥ 250 per dollar.)

After adjusting the range for the yen/dollar rate in April 1987, the industrial countries succeeded in maintaining their new exchange rate bands for several months. The U.S. external deficit remained high, however, and the dollar stayed under heavy selling pressure; the bands thus could be maintained only with the help of slow U.S. money supply growth and a steadily rising interest difference favoring dollar assets. Market participants wondered whether the U.S. economy would be thrown into recession to enforce nominal exchange rate targets that seemed increasingly inconsistent with current account equilibrium, given output prices in the United States and abroad.

In October 1987 the brief period of exchange stability ended abruptly when the U.S. stock market dropped and then crashed following American criticism of a German interest rate hike. Major stock markets around the world followed Wall Street's dizzying plunge. In the United States, a more general economic crisis was turned aside by the new Federal Reserve chairman, Alan Greenspan, who announced the Fed's readiness to provide liquidity to a troubled financial system. Governors of foreign central banks acted similarly and interest rates throughout the world declined. In the process, however, U.S. authorities allowed the dollar to depreciate far beyond its Louvre limits.

New exchange rate zones were subsequently established, but these apparently have been changed on several occasions, never with on-the-record public acknowledgment. By 1993 any pretense of zones had been abandoned. Figure 19-7 gives an overview of exchange rate movements after the Louvre accord. Skeptics argue that the implicit zones for exchange rates had no real force and that the authorities' reluctance to announce the zones, rather than keeping the market guessing, served mainly to cover repeated official failures to stand up to market pressures. Supporters argue that exchange rates would have moved even more than they did had zones not been adopted. What seems clear is that official attempts to influence exchange rates have been successful only when backed up by changes in monetary or fiscal policy rather than the milder expedient of sterilized

FIGURE 19-7

Exchange Rate Changes Since the Louvre Accord

$/¥ and $/DM exchange rates
(percent changes relative to rates at end of February 1987)

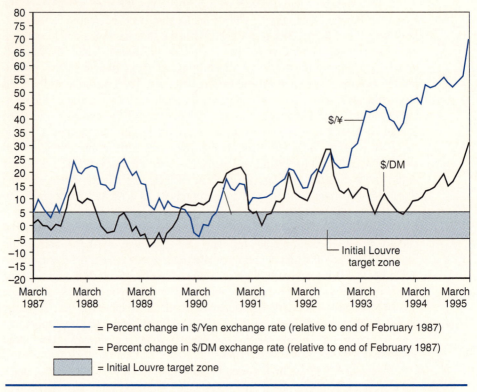

= Percent change in $/Yen exchange rate (relative to end of February 1987)

= Percent change in $/DM exchange rate (relative to end of February 1987)

= Initial Louvre target zone

The dollar prices of the DM and yen took wide swings after the February 1987 Louvre meeting despite an initial international agreement to keep those exchange rates within bands 10 percent wide.

Source: OECD, *Main Economic Indicators.*

intervention (which at times has been heavy). Authorities have thus faced genuine and sometimes painful trade-offs between internal balance and exchange stability, as the United States did in October 1987, and none of them has shown that in a crunch, exchange stability is the more important of these two goals.

Global Slump Once Again

Toward the end of the 1980s inflationary pressures reappeared in the main industrial countries (see Table 19-3). Inflation was the result of national developments rather than a global shock, and it emerged with different timing and force in each country.

In the United States, rapid monetary growth in 1985 and 1986 helped push inflation upward by 1987 and 1988. The Federal Reserve responded with exceptionally tight monetary policy, which tilted the U.S. economy into a prolonged economic downturn by the summer of 1990. Economic stagnation in the United States was a major reason for President George Bush's defeat in his 1992 reelection attempt. But even as Bush went down to defeat, the U.S. economy was starting to rebound.

Loose monetary policy in Britain in 1988 similarly contributed to higher inflation there by 1989 (Table 19-3). Despite this inflation, Britain entered the European Monetary System exchange rate mechanism in October 1990, agreeing to peg the pound sterling to the European Currency Unit at an exchange rate that probably made British exports too expensive relative to foreign goods. This was the same mistake Britain had made in returning to the gold standard in 1925, and, as Table 19-2 shows, British unemployment quickly began to rise. Only after freeing its exchange rate in 1992 did Britain begin to recover.

Japan's inflation picked up in 1989, possibly the result of a relatively loose monetary policy over 1986–1988. Two very visible symptoms of these pressures were skyrocketing prices for Japanese real estate and stocks. The Bank of Japan's strategy of puncturing these asset price bubbles through restrictive monetary policy and high interest rates succeeded well, and Tokyo's Nikkei stock price index lost more than half its value between 1990 and 1992. Unfortunately, the sharp fall in asset prices threw Japan's banking system into crisis and the economy into recession by early 1992. By 1995 the banking crisis was still intensifying.

The German economy faced a unique situation as the 1990s began. Starting in 1989 countries throughout Eastern Europe, including the eastern portion of Germany occupied by Soviet forces at the end of World War II, shook off communist rule and began the painful task of moving from centrally planned to market economies. (See Chapter 23 for further discussion.) West and East Germany rushed to reunite, with economic unification coming on July 1, 1990, even before political unification. One element of the unification agreement required much of the East German money supply to be converted to DM at an exchange rate of DM 1 per East German mark, despite the latter currency's much lower black-market value and purchasing power. This move, which was approved by West Germany's government over the vigorous opposition of the German Bundesbank, led to a 29.6 percent growth in Germany's DM money supply over 1990.

Money supply growth was only one of several factors contributing to higher German inflation after 1990. The federal German government began a program of massive fiscal expansion to finance infrastructure investment and transfer payments (largely unemployment compensation) in the former East Germany. That area's residents, starved for the high-quality consumer goods denied them under communism, spent heavily on imports from the West. Finally, Germany's labor unions, facing the unexpectedly high tax bill for reunification, mounted a wage offensive. The results were inflationary pressure, rising government debt, and a current account deficit. As we see in the next chapter, the Bundesbank's tight money response to the inflationary pressure caused grave difficulties for its EMS partners, with dramatic consequences for the stability of the system's fixed exchange rates.

WHAT HAS BEEN LEARNED SINCE 1973?

The first two sections of this chapter outlined the main elements of the cases for and against floating exchange rates. Having examined the events of the recent floating-rate period, we now compare experience with the predictions made before 1973 by the proponents and opponents of floating and ask whether recent history supports a definitive judgment about reforming the current exchange rate system.

MONETARY POLICY AUTONOMY

There is no question that floating gave central banks the ability to control their money supplies and to choose their preferred rates of trend inflation. A comparison of Tables 19-1 and 19-3 (which show inflation rates over the floating-rate period) with Table 18-1 and Figure 18-3 (which apply to the fixed-rate period) shows that floating rates allowed a much larger international divergence in inflation rates. Did exchange depreciation offset inflation differentials between countries over the floating-rate period? Figure 19-8 compares domestic currency depreciation against the dollar with the difference between domestic and

---

FIGURE 19-8

Exchange Rate Trends and Inflation Differentials, 1973–1993

Over the floating-rate period as a whole, higher inflation has been associated with greater currency depreciation. The exact relationship predicted by relative PPP, however, has not held for most countries. The inflation difference on the horizontal axis is calculated as $(\pi - \pi_{us}) \div (1 + \pi_{us}/100)$ using the exact relative PPP relation given in footnote 1 on p. 402.

Source: OECD, *Main Economic Indicators.*

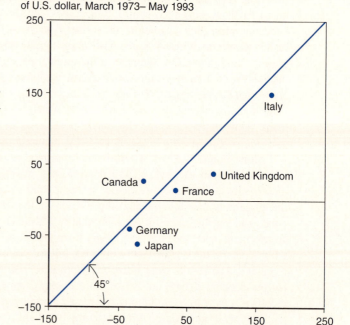

Percent change in foreign-currency price of U.S. dollar, March 1973– May 1993

Percent change in foreign price level less percent change in U.S. price level, March 1973– May 1993

U.S. inflation for the six largest industrial market economies outside the United States. The PPP theory predicts that the points in the figure should lie along the 45-degree line, indicating proportional exchange rate and relative price level changes, but this is not exactly the case. While Figure 19-8 therefore confirms the lesson of Chapter 15 that PPP has not held closely, it does show that on balance, high-inflation countries have tended to have weaker currencies than their low-inflation neighbors. Furthermore, most of the difference in depreciation rates is due to inflation differences, making PPP the major factor behind long-run nominal exchange-rate variability.

While the inflation insulation part of the policy autonomy argument is broadly supported as a *long-run* proposition, economic analysis and experience both show that in the short run, the effects of monetary as well as fiscal changes are transmitted across national borders under floating rates. The two-country macroeconomic model developed earlier, for example, shows that monetary policy affects output in the short run both at home and abroad as long as it alters the real exchange rate. The critics of floating were therefore right in claiming that floating rates would not insulate countries completely from foreign policy shocks.

Experience has also given dramatic support to the skeptics who argued that no central bank can be indifferent to its currency's value in the foreign exchange market. After 1973 central banks intervened repeatedly in the foreign exchange market to alter currency values, and even the Reagan administration's laissez-faire policy on exchange rates was abandoned when the G-5 Plaza initiative of September 1985 was launched. The post-1973 floating of exchange rates is often characterized as a "dirty float" rather than a "clean float" because central banks intervened on a discretionary basis and continued to hold foreign exchange reserves (Chapter 17). Advocates of floating had argued that central banks would not need to hold foreign reserves, but between 1972 and November 1994, the international reserves of the industrial countries rose in value from $113 billion to $461 billion.

Why did central banks continue to intervene even in the absence of any formal obligation to do so? As we saw in the example of a change in domestic money demand, intervention to fix the exchange rate can stabilize output and the price level when certain disturbances occur, and central banks sometimes felt that exchange rate movements were due to such factors. But even in the presence of output market disturbances, central banks wanted to slow exchange rate movements to prevent sharp changes in the international competitiveness of their tradable goods sectors. Such changes, if reversed later, might generate excessive sectoral employment fluctuations, and they might also lead to pressures for protection. Finally, central banks worried that even temporary exchange rate shifts might have medium-term inflationary effects that would be hard to wring out of the economy.

Those skeptical of the autonomy argument had also predicted that while floating would allow central banks to control nominal money supplies, their ability to affect output would still be limited by the price level's tendency to respond more quickly to monetary changes under a floating rate. This prediction was partially borne out by experience. Monetary changes clearly had a much greater short-run effect on the *real* exchange rate under a floating nominal exchange rate than under a fixed one, increasing the immediate influence of money on output in some countries. In many cases, however, this influence turned out to be short-lived. The quick response of the exchange rate to money supply changes affected import prices and wage settlements, shortening the time span over which money could alter real economic activity without changing nominal output prices. The link between exchange depreciation and inflation was illustrated by the U.S. experience of 1976–1979 and by the rapid inflation that resulted from attempts by Britain, France, and Italy, at various times, to spur output growth through monetary expansion. The U.S. disinflation after 1979 illustrated that a floating rate could also speed the translation of monetary contraction into lower inflation.

SYMMETRY

Because central banks continued to hold dollar reserves and intervene, the international monetary system did not become symmetric after 1973. The DM and the yen gained importance as international reserve currencies (and the British pound declined), but the dollar remained the primary component of most central banks' official reserves.

Economist Ronald McKinnon of Stanford University has argued that the current floating-rate system is similar in some ways to the asymmetric reserve currency system underlying the Bretton Woods arrangements.[7] He suggests that changes in the world money supply would have been dampened under a more symmetric monetary adjustment mechanism. Intervention outside the United States to slow the dollar's rise after 1979, for example, led to monetary contraction abroad with no symmetric increase in the U.S. money supply. The resulting world monetary crunch was harsher because of this asymmetry, which therefore helped deepen the recession that followed.

THE EXCHANGE RATE AS AN AUTOMATIC STABILIZER

The world economy has undergone major structural changes since 1973. Because these shifts changed relative national output prices (Figure 19-8), it is doubtful that any pattern of fixed exchange rates would have been viable without some significant parity changes. The industrial economies certainly wouldn't have weathered the two oil shocks as well as they did while defending fixed exchange rates. In the absence of capital controls, speculative attacks similar to those that brought down the Bretton Woods system would have occurred periodically, as the recent experience of the European Monetary System has shown (Chapter 20). Under floating, however, many countries were able to relax the capital controls put in place earlier. The progressive loosening of controls spurred the rapid growth of a global financial industry and allowed countries to realize greater gains from intertemporal trade.

The effects of the U.S. fiscal expansion after 1981 illustrate the stabilizing properties of a floating exchange rate. As the dollar appreciated, U.S. inflation was slowed, American consumers enjoyed an improvement in their terms of trade, and economic recovery was spread abroad.

The dollar's appreciation after 1981 also illustrates a problem with the view that floating rates can cushion the economy from real disturbances such as shifts in aggregate demand. Even though *overall* output and the price level may be cushioned, some sectors of the economy may be hurt. For example, while the dollar's appreciation helped transmit U.S. fiscal expansion abroad in the 1980s, it worsened the plight of American agriculture, which did not benefit directly from the higher government demand. Real exchange rate changes can do damage by causing excessive adjustment problems in some sectors and by generating calls for increased protection.

---

[7]Ronald I. McKinnon, *An International Standard for Monetary Stabilization,* Policy Analyses in International Economics 8 (Washington, D.C.: Institute for International Economics, 1984).

Permanent changes in goods market conditions require eventual adjustment in real exchange rates that can be speeded by a floating-rate system. Foreign exchange intervention to peg nominal exchange rates cannot prevent this eventual adjustment because money is neutral in the long run and thus is powerless to alter relative prices permanently. The events of the 1980s show, however, that if it is costly for factors of production to move between sectors of the economy, there is a case for pegging rates in the face of temporary output market shocks. Unfortunately, this lesson leaves policymakers with the difficult task of determining which disturbances are temporary and which are permanent.

An indictment of floating exchange rates is sometimes based on the poor economic growth performance of industrial countries in the 1970s and 1980s compared with the 1950s and 1960s. As noted above, unemployment rates in industrial countries rose sharply after the 1960s; in addition, labor productivity and real GNP growth rates dropped. These adverse developments followed the adoption of floating dollar exchange rates, but this coincidence does not prove that floating rates were their cause. Although economists have not yet fully explained the growth slowdown or the rise in unemployment rates, the likely culprits are structural changes that had little to do with floating rates. Examples include the oil price shocks, restrictive labor market practices, and worker displacement caused by the emergence of several developing countries as major exporters of manufactured goods. Much of the international trade of the European Monetary System has taken place at fixed exchange rates, yet the record of EMS countries in generating jobs and keeping down unemployment has not been superior to that of the United States or Japan.

DISCIPLINE

Did countries abuse the autonomy afforded by floating rates? Inflation rates did accelerate after 1973 and remained high through the second oil shock. But the concerted disinflation in industrial countries after 1979 proved that central banks could resist the temptations of inflation under floating rates. On several occasions, voters in industrial countries showed that they viewed a weak currency as a sign of economic mismanagement. For this reason, currency depreciation sometimes brought sharp changes in monetary policies, as in the United States in 1979.

The system placed fewer obvious restraints on unbalanced fiscal policies, for example, the high U.S. government budget deficits of the 1980s. While some observers felt that fixed rates would have forced a more moderate American fiscal stance, their arguments were not compelling. In the late 1960s, fixed rates had failed to restrain the Johnson administration's fiscal expansion, a policy move that contributed to the collapse of the Bretton Woods system, nor did the EMS restrain Germany in the early 1990s.

DESTABILIZING SPECULATION

Floating exchange rates have exhibited much more day-to-day volatility than the early advocates of floating would have predicted, but as we saw in Chapter 13, exchange rates are asset prices, and so considerable volatility is to be expected. The asset price nature of exchange rates was not well understood by economists before the 1970s.

Even with the benefit of hindsight, however, short-term exchange rate movements can be quite difficult to relate to actual news about economic events that affect currency values. Part of the difficulty is that government officials often try to influence exchange rates by hinting at intended policy changes, thus making expectations about future macroeconomic policies volatile. The question of whether exchange rate volatility has been "excessive" relative to the theoretical determinants of exchange rates is a controversial one and provides an active research area for academic economists (Chapter 21).

Over the longer term, however, exchange rates have roughly reflected fundamental changes in monetary and fiscal policies, and their broad movements do not appear to be the result of destabilizing speculation. The decline of the dollar in the late 1970s (Figure 19-3) coincides with loose U.S. monetary policies, while its steep ascent between 1980 and 1985 occurred as the United States embarked on disinflation and a fiscal expansion of a size unprecedented in peacetime. While most economists agree that the direction of these exchange rate swings was appropriate, there is continuing debate about their magnitude. Some feel the foreign exchange market overreacted to government actions and that more systematic foreign exchange intervention would have been beneficial.

The experience with floating rates has not supported the idea that arbitrary exchange rate movements can lead to "vicious circles" of inflation and depreciation. Britain, Italy, and, to a lesser extent, France experienced inflationary spirals similar to those predicted by the vicious circle theory. But the currency depreciation that accompanied these spirals was not the arbitrary result of destabilizing exchange rate speculation. As Figure 14-10 (page 387) shows, industrial countries with poor inflation performances under floating exchange rates have also tended to have relatively rapid rates of monetary growth.

INTERNATIONAL TRADE AND INVESTMENT

Critics of floating had predicted that international trade and investment would suffer as a result of increased uncertainty. The prediction was certainly wrong with regard to investment, for international financial intermediation expanded strongly after 1973 as countries lowered barriers to capital movement (see Chapter 21).

There is controversy about the effects of floating rates on international trade. The use of forward markets expanded dramatically, just as advocates of floating had foreseen, and innovative financial instruments were developed to help traders avoid exchange rate risk. But some economists contend that the costs of avoiding exchange rate risk have had an effect similar to increased international transport costs in reducing the available gains from trade. They argue that as a result of these costs, international trade has grown more slowly than it would have under a hypothetical fixed exchange rate regime.

A very crude but direct measure of the extent of a country's international trade is the average of its imports and exports of goods and services, divided by its output. Figure 19-9 plots this number for six of the main industrial market economies over the period from the mid-1950s to the mid-1990s. For most countries, the extent of trade shows a rising trend over the whole period, with no marked slowdown in trend after the move to floating. The figure probably exaggerates the growth of world trade in the decade after 1973 because a number of factors (notably the two OPEC shocks) caused the prices of tradable goods to rise relative to the prices of those that do not enter trade. Even after correcting for the resulting bias, however, it is difficult to make a strong case that the volume of world trade has grown more slowly over the entire period since the move to floating exchange rates. Further, to compare world trade growth before and after the early 1970s is to stack the deck against floating rates, because while the 1950s and 1960s were periods of dra-

FIGURE 19-9

Trade in Goods and Services as a Proportion of the Output of Major Industrial Countries, 1956–1994

Floating exchange rates do not appear to have reduced the trend growth rate of world trade.

Source: IMF, *International Financial Statistics.*

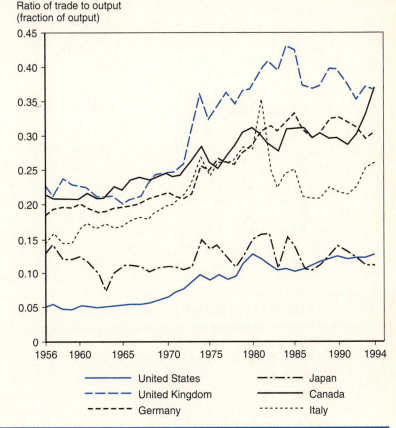

matic trade liberalization, the 1970s and 1980s were marked by a surge in nontariff barriers to trade.[8]

Evaluation of the effects of floating rates on world trade is complicated further by the activities of multinational firms, many of which expanded their international production operations in the years after 1973. Facing a more turbulent economic environment, multinationals may have spread their activities over more countries in the hope of reducing their dependence on any individual government's economic policies. Because trade and capital movements can substitute for each other, however, the displacement of some trade

---

[8]There is a large econometric literature that studies how exchange rate volatility affects trade growth, and some authors reach conclusions different from those in the preceding paragraph. Unfortunately, various researchers differ in terms of their measures of trade volume, definitions of exchange rate volatility, and choices of estimation period, so it is difficult to draw unambiguous conclusions from this body of work. A recent study pointing to negative effects of exchange rate variability is Paul De Grauwe, "Exchange Rate Variability and the Slowdown in Growth of International Trade," *International Monetary Fund Staff Papers* 35 (March 1988), pp. 63–84.

by multinational firms' overseas production does not necessarily imply that welfare-improving trade gains have been lost.[9]

International trade has recently been threatened by the resurgence of protectionism, a symptom of slower economic growth and wide swings in real exchange rates, which have been labeled *misalignments*. (The dollar's misalignment of the mid-1980s, shown in Figure 19-3, is a leading example.) It is possible, however, that similar pressures to limit trade would have emerged under fixed exchange rates. Misalignments have had an especially severe impact on those who lose jobs as a result and have few other financial resources.

POLICY COORDINATION

Floating exchange rates themselves have not promoted international policy coordination. On several occasions, for example, during the disinflation of the early 1980s, industrial countries as a group could have attained their macroeconomic goals more effectively by negotiating a joint approach to common objectives. The appendix to this chapter presents a formal model that illustrates how all countries can gain through international policy coordination.

While beggar-thy-neighbor policies sometimes have been a problem, critics of floating have not made a strong case that the problem would disappear under an alternative currency regime. Under fixed rates, for example, countries can always devalue their currencies unilaterally to attain nationalistic goals. The results of the informal target zone arrangements set up by the Louvre accord illustrate the wide gap between agreeing on exchange rates and true policy coordination.

Governments, like people, often are motivated by their own interest rather than that of the community. Legal penalties discourage antisocial actions by individuals, but it is a more difficult matter to design sanctions that bind sovereign governments. It seems doubtful that an exchange rate system alone can restrain a government from following its own perceived interest when it formulates macroeconomic policies.

DIRECTIONS FOR REFORM

The experience with floating exchange rates since 1973 shows that neither side in the debate over floating was entirely right in its predictions. The floating-rate system has not been free of serious problems, but neither has it been the fiasco its opponents predicted it would be.

An important lesson of this chapter and the previous one is that no exchange rate system works well when countries "go it alone" and follow narrowly perceived self-interest. The Bretton Woods system functioned reasonably well until the United States unilaterally adopted overexpansionary policies under President Johnson. The EMS experience sur-

---

[9]A study documenting the growth of U.S. multinationals' foreign exporting activities is Robert E. Lipsey and Irving B. Kravis, "The Competitiveness and Comparative Advantage of U.S. Multinationals, 1957–1984," *Banca Nazionale del Lavoro Quarterly Review* (June 1987), pp. 147–165.

veyed in the next chapter provides another example. Similarly, the worst problems of the floating-rate system occurred when countries failed to take coordinated action on common macroeconomic problems. Globally balanced and stable policies are a prerequisite for the successful performance of any international monetary system.

Current proposals to reform the international monetary system run the gamut from a more elaborate system of target zones for the dollar to the resurrection of fixed rates to the introduction of a single world currency. Because countries seem unwilling to give up the autonomy floating dollar rates have given them, it is unlikely that any of these changes is in the cards.[10] Since the Plaza announcement of September 1985, however, the United States has tended to show a greater awareness of its interdependence with other industrial economies. Although this development has not prevented serious international disagreement over policies, it certainly is a positive step toward improving the existing system.

With greater policy cooperation among the main players, there is no reason why floating exchange rates should not function tolerably well in the future. International policy cooperation is not unprecedented, as the GATT rounds of tariff reduction and the founding of the IMF, World Bank, and WTO indicate. Events of the last few years suggest, however, that cooperation should be sought as an end in itself and not as the indirect result of exchange rate rules that eventually are discredited through repeated amendment or violation.

Summary

1. The weaknesses of the Bretton Woods system led many economists to advocate floating exchange rates before 1973. They made three main arguments in favor of floating. First, they argued that floating rates would give national macroeconomic policymakers greater autonomy in managing their economies. Second, they predicted that floating rates would remove the asymmetries of the Bretton Woods arrangements. Third, they pointed out that floating exchange rates would quickly eliminate the "fundamental disequilibriums" that had led to parity changes and speculative attacks under fixed rates.

2. Critics of floating rates advanced several counterarguments. Some feared that floating would encourage monetary and fiscal excesses and beggar-thy-neighbor policies. Other lines of criticism asserted that floating rates would be subject to *destabilizing speculation* and that uncertainty over exchange rates would retard international trade and investment. Finally, a number of economists questioned whether countries would be willing in practice to disregard the exchange rate in formulating their monetary and fiscal policies. The exchange rate, they felt, was an important enough price that it would become a target of macroeconomic policy in its own right.

---

[10]An extended target zone proposal is outlined in John Williamson and Marcus H. Miller, *Targets and Indicators: A Blueprint for the International Coordination of Macroeconomic Policies,* Policy Analyses in International Economics 22 (Washington, D.C.: Institute for International Economics, 1987). McKinnon, op. cit., presents a program for reestablishing fixed rates for the dollar, yen, and DM. The case for a single currency for the industrialized democracies is made by Richard N. Cooper, "A Monetary System for the Future," *Foreign Affairs* 63 (1984), pp. 166–184.

3. Between 1973 and 1980 floating rates seemed on the whole to function well. In particular, it is unlikely that the industrial countries could have maintained fixed exchange rates in the face of the *stagflation* caused by two oil shocks. The dollar suffered a sharp depreciation after 1976, however, as the United States adopted macroeconomic policies more expansionary than those of other industrial countries.

4. A sharp turn toward slower monetary growth in the United States, coupled with a rising U.S. government budget deficit, contributed to massive dollar appreciation between 1980 and early 1985. Other industrial economies pursued disinflation along with the United States, and the resulting worldwide monetary slowdown, coming soon after the second oil shock, led to the deepest recession since the 1930s. As the recovery from the recession slowed in late 1984 and the U.S. current account began to register record deficits, political pressure for wide-ranging trade restrictions gathered momentum in Washington. The drive for protection was slowed (but not defeated) by the September 1985 decision of the Group of Five countries to take concerted action to bring down the dollar. An experiment with vaguely defined exchange rate target zones, initiated by the Louvre accord of February 1987, had mixed success in promoting more stable currency values. Exchange rate stability was downplayed as a prime policy goal in the early 1990s. Instead, governments struggled to restrain domestic inflation while restoring economic growth.

5. The experience of floating does not fully support either the early advocates of that exchange rate system or its critics. One unambiguous lesson of experience, however, is that no exchange rate system functions well when international economic cooperation breaks down. Severe limits on exchange rate flexibility are unlikely to be reinstated in the near future. But increased consultation among policymakers in the industrial countries should improve the performance of floating rates.

Key Terms

destabilizing speculation, p. 577

nominal and real effective exchange
rate indexes, p. 584

stagflation, p. 582

Problems

1. Use the *DD-AA* model to examine the effects of a one-time rise in the foreign price level, P^*. If the expected future exchange rate E^e rises immediately in proportion to P^* (in line with PPP), show that the exchange rate will also appreciate immediately in proportion to the rise in P^*. If the economy is initially in internal and external balance, will its position be disturbed by such a rise in P^*?

2. Analyze a transitory increase in the foreign interest rate, R^*. Under which type of exchange rate is there a smaller effect on output—fixed or floating?

3. Suppose now that R^* rises permanently. What happens to the economy, and how does your answer depend on whether the change reflects a rise in the foreign real interest rate or in foreign inflation expectations (the Fisher effect)?

4. If the foreign *inflation rate* rises permanently, would you expect a floating exchange rate to insulate the domestic economy in the short run? What would hap-

pen in the long run? In answering the latter question, pay attention to the long-run relationship between domestic and foreign nominal interest rates.

5. Imagine that domestic and foreign currency bonds are imperfect substitutes and that investors suddenly shift their demand toward foreign currency bonds, raising the risk premium on domestic assets (Chapter 17). Which exchange rate regime minimizes the effect on output—fixed or floating?

6. In the two-country model of this chapter, show that Foreign output must rise as a result of monetary contraction in Home.

7. How would you analyze the use of monetary and fiscal policy to maintain internal and external balance under a floating exchange rate?

8. The chapter described how the United States tried after 1985 to reduce its current account deficit by accelerating monetary growth and depreciating the dollar. Assume that the United States was in internal balance but external balance called for an expenditure-reducing policy (a cut in the government budget deficit) as well as the expenditure switching caused by currency depreciation. How would you expect the use of monetary expansion alone to affect the U.S. economy in the short and long runs?

9. After 1985 the United States asked Germany and Japan to adopt fiscal and monetary expansion as ways of increasing foreign demand for U.S. output and reducing the American current account deficit. Would fiscal expansion by Germany and Japan have accomplished these goals? What about monetary expansion? Would your answer change if you thought different German and Japanese policies might facilitate different U.S. policies?

10. A high volume of foreign exchange intervention occurred in 1987 in connection with the Louvre accord. What data might allow you to tell whether a large portion of this intervention was sterilized? Try to find the relevant data for Germany and Japan in back issues of the IMF's *International Financial Statistics*.

11. Suppose the U.S. and Japanese governments both want to depreciate their currencies to help their tradables industries but fear the resulting inflation. The two policy choices available to them are (1) expansionary monetary policy and (2) no change in monetary policy. Develop an analysis like the one in the appendix to show the consequences of different policy choices. Can Japan and the United States do better by cooperating than by acting individually?

Further Reading

Ralph C. Bryant. *International Coordination of National Stabilization Policies.* Washington, D.C.: Brookings Institution, 1995. Examines the interaction among national economic policies and the scope for international coordination.

Martin S. Feldstein. "Distinguished Lecture on Economics in Government: Thinking About International Economic Coordination." *Journal of Economic Perspectives* 2 (Spring 1988), pp. 3–13. The case *against* international macroeconomic policy coordination.

Milton Friedman. "The Case for Flexible Exchange Rates," in *Essays in Positive Economics.* Chicago: University of Chicago Press, 1953, pp. 157–203. A classic exposition of the merits of floating exchange rates.

Morris Goldstein. *The Exchange Rate System and the IMF: A Modest Agenda.* Policy Analyses in International Economics 39. Washington, D.C.: Institute for International Economics, 1995. An analysis of the roles of international coordination and the IMF in the present exchange-rate system.

Harry G. Johnson. "The Case for Flexible Exchange Rates, 1969." *Federal Reserve Bank of St. Louis Review* 51 (June 1969), pp. 12–24. An influential statement of the case for replacing the Bretton Woods system by floating rates.

Charles P. Kindleberger, "The Case for Fixed Exchange Rates, 1969," in *The International Adjustment Mechanism,* Conference Series 2. Boston: Federal Reserve Bank of Boston, 1970, pp. 93–108. Prescient analysis of problems with a floating-rate system.

Michael Mussa. "Macroeconomic Interdependence and the Exchange Rate Regime," in Rudiger Dornbusch and Jacob A. Frenkel, eds. *International Economic Policy.* Baltimore: Johns Hopkins University Press, 1979, pp. 160–204. Analyzes macroeconomic policy interactions under fixed and floating exchange rates.

Maurice Obstfeld. "International Currency Experience: New Lessons and Lessons Relearned." *Brookings Papers on Economic Activity* 1:1995, pp. 119–220. A broad overview of exchange rates and policy-making since the onset of floating rates.

Robert Solomon. *The International Monetary System, 1945–1981.* New York: Harper & Row, 1982. Chapters 15–19 cover the early years of floating exchange rates.

John Williamson. *The Exchange Rate System,* 2nd edition. Policy Analyses in International Economics 5. Washington, D.C.: Institute for International Economics, 1985. An indictment of floating exchange rates and a case for target zones.

Appendix to Chapter 19

International Policy Coordination Failures

This appendix illustrates the importance of macroeconomic policy coordination by showing how all countries can suffer as a result of self-centered policy decisions. The phenomenon is another example of the Prisoner's Dilemma of game theory (Chapter 9). Governments can achieve macroeconomic outcomes that are better for all if they choose policies cooperatively.

These points are made using an example based on the disinflation of the early 1980s. Recall that contractionary monetary policies in the industrial countries helped throw the world economy into a deep recession in 1981. Countries hoped to reduce inflation by slowing monetary growth, but the situation was complicated by the influence of exchange rates on the price level. A government that adopts a less restrictive monetary policy than its neighbors is likely to face a currency depreciation that partially frustrates its attempts to disinflate.

Many observers feel that in their individual attempts to resist currency depreciation, the industrial countries as a group adopted overly tight monetary policies that deepened the recession. All governments would have been happier if everyone had adopted looser monetary policies, but given the policies that other governments did adopt, it was not in the interest of any individual government to change course.

The argument above can be made more precise with a simple model. There are two countries, Home and Foreign, and each country has two policy options, a very restrictive monetary policy and a somewhat restrictive monetary policy. Figure 19A-1, which is similar to a diagram we used to analyze trade policies, shows the results in Home and Foreign

FIGURE 19A-1

Hypothetical Effects of Different Monetary Policy Combinations on Inflation and Unemployment

Monetary policy choices in one country affect the outcomes of monetary policy choices made abroad.

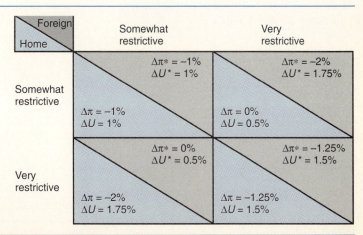

of different policy choices by the two countries. Each row corresponds to a particular monetary policy decision by Home and each column to a decision by Foreign. The boxes contain entries giving changes in annual inflation rates ($\Delta\pi$ and $\Delta\pi^*$) and unemployment rates (ΔU and ΔU^*). Within each box, lower-left entries are Home outcomes and upper-right entries are Foreign outcomes.

The hypothetical entries in Figure 19A-1 can be understood in terms of this chapter's two-country model. Under somewhat restrictive policies, for example, inflation rates fall by 1 percent and unemployment rates rise by 1 percent in both countries. If Home suddenly shifts to a very restrictive policy while Foreign stands pat, Home's currency appreciates, its inflation drops further, and its unemployment rises. Home's additional monetary contraction, however, has two effects on Foreign. Foreign's unemployment rate falls, but because Home's currency appreciation is a currency *depreciation* for Foreign, Foreign inflation goes back up to its predisinflation level. In Foreign, the deflationary effects of higher unemployment are offset by the inflationary impact of a depreciating currency on import prices and wage demands. Home's sharper monetary crunch therefore has a beggar-thy-neighbor effect on Foreign, which is forced to "import" some inflation from Home.

To translate the outcomes in Figure 19A-1 into policy payoffs, we assume each government wishes to get the biggest reduction in inflation at the lowest cost in terms of unemployment. That is, each government wishes to maximize $-\Delta\pi/\Delta U$, the inflation reduction per point of increased unemployment. The numbers in Figure 19A-1 lead to the payoff matrix shown as Figure 19A-2.

How do Home and Foreign behave faced with the payoffs in this matrix? Assume each government "goes it alone" and picks the policy that maximizes its own payoff given the other player's policy choice. If Foreign adopts a somewhat restrictive policy, Home does better with a very restrictive policy (payoff = $^8/_7$) than with a somewhat restrictive one (payoff = 1). If Foreign is very restrictive, Home still does better by being very restrictive (payoff = $^5/_6$) than by being somewhat restrictive (payoff = 0). So no matter what Foreign does, Home's government will always choose a very restrictive monetary policy.

FIGURE 19A-2

Payoff Matrix for Different Monetary Policy Moves

Each entry equals the reduction in inflation per unit rise in the unemployment rate (calculated as $-\Delta\pi/\Delta U$). If each country "goes it alone," they both choose very restrictive policies. Somewhat restrictive policies, if adopted by both countries, lead to an outcome better for both.

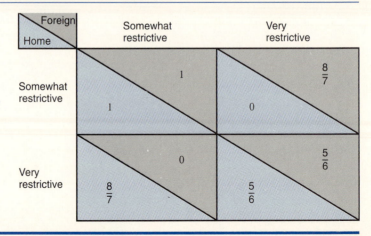

Foreign finds itself in a symmetric position. It, too, is better off with a very restrictive policy regardless of what Home does. The result is that both countries will choose very restrictive monetary policies, and each will get a payoff of $^5/_6$.

Notice, however, that *both* countries are actually better off if they simultaneously adopt the somewhat retrictive policies. The resulting payoff for each is 1, which is greater than $^5/_6$. Under this last policy configuration, inflation falls less in the two countries, but the rise in unemployment is far less than under very restrictive policies.

Since both countries are better off with somewhat restrictive policies, why aren't these adopted? The answer is at the root of the problem of policy coordination. Our analysis assumed that each country "goes it alone" by maximizing its own payoff. Under this assumption, a situation where both countries were somewhat restrictive would not be stable: Each country would want to reduce its monetary growth further and use its exchange rate to hasten disinflation at its neighbor's expense.

For the superior outcome in the upper-left corner of the matrix to occur, Home and Foreign must reach an explicit agreement, that is, they must *coordinate* their policy choices. Both countries must agree to forgo the beggar-thy-neighbor gains offered by very restrictive policies, and each country must abide by this agreement in spite of the incentive to cheat. If Home and Foreign can cooperate, both end up with a preferred mix of inflation and unemployment.

The reality of policy coordination is more complex than in this simple example because the choices and outcomes are more numerous and more uncertain. These added complexities make policymakers less willing to commit themselves to cooperative agreements and less certain that their counterparts abroad will live up to the agreed terms.

20 Optimum Currency Areas and the European Experience

Between the first oil shock in 1973–1974 and the late 1980s, Europe's macroeconomic performance lagged behind that of other industrial regions in terms of job creation and output growth. Europe's lackluster record was widely blamed on "Eurosclerosis"—a pattern of social legislation and market rigidities that blocked the flow of labor and capital to their most productive uses. Hoping to revitalize their economies, European Union (EU) leaders set out in the mid-1980s to remove the bewildering array of government regulations and trade restrictions that continued to harm economic efficiency despite the process of mutual trade liberalization the EU countries had begun in 1957. The initial success of this program and its apparent acceptance by the public encouraged EU heads of state to agree in December 1991 to a more radical step toward a unified European market: a timetable for replacing the individual national currencies in Europe with a single EU currency by January 1, 1999, at the latest.

Only a year later, this bold plan appeared to be in disarray. Facing domestic recession and waning voter support for further European unification, EU members were trying desperately to stay on the road toward a single currency. Meanwhile, the European Monetary System (EMS) of fixed EU exchange rates was being battered by the most violent speculative attacks on industrial country currencies since the Bretton Woods system's final collapse 20 years earlier. The result was a partial dismantling of the EMS's fixed exchange rates, a situation that left many observers wondering whether any of the larger EU members will achieve monetary unification before the century's end.

This chapter focuses on Europe's recent plans for monetary union to illustrate the economic benefits and costs of fixed exchange rate agreements and more comprehensive currency unification schemes. As we see in Europe's experience, the effects of joining a fixed exchange rate agreement are complex and depend crucially on microeconomic *and* macroeconomic factors. Our discussion of Europe will throw light not only on the forces promoting greater unification of national economies but also on the forces that make a country think twice before giving up completely its control over domestic monetary policy.

WHY HAS EUROPE FAVORED MUTUALLY FIXED EXCHANGE RATES?

The Bretton Woods system (which fell apart in 1973) fixed every member country's exchange rate against the U.S. dollar and as a result also fixed the exchange rate between every pair of nondollar currencies. Earlier chapters described the reasons for the Bretton Woods system's breakdown and how countries hoped to free their monetary policies by changing from fixed dollar exchange rates to floating rates. While allowing their currencies to float against the dollar, however, EU countries have tried progressively to narrow the extent to which they let their currencies fluctuate against each other. As a result, many EU currencies until recently took part in a concerted float against the dollar and therefore rose or fell against the U.S. currency by more or less equal percentages.

Even before 1973 EU members were examining ways to coordinate their monetary policies more closely and to reduce the limited intra-European exchange rate fluctuations allowed under Bretton Woods. These initiatives, which continued and gathered momentum after dollar exchange rates began to float in 1973, illustrate the economic and political forces behind the most recent plans for monetary unification in Europe.

EUROPEAN CURRENCY REFORM INITIATIVES, 1969–1978

European leaders meeting at The Hague in December 1969 initiated the drive toward European monetary unification. They appointed Pierre Werner, prime minister and finance minister of Luxembourg, to head a committee that would outline concrete steps for eliminating intra-European exchange rate movements, centralizing EU monetary policy decisions, and lowering remaining trade barriers within Europe. The Werner report, adopted by the EU in March 1971, proposed a three-phase program that, when completed, would result in locked EU exchange rates and the integration of the individual national central banks into a federated European system of banks.

What prompted the EU countries to seek closer coordination of monetary policies and greater exchange rate stability in the late 1960s? There were three main motives, one reflecting political changes in the world economy, one reflecting hopes for the evolution of the EU, and one reflecting the administrative problems that exchange rate changes caused for the EU:

> 1. *To enhance Europe's role in the world monetary system.* The currency crises of 1969 were accompanied by declining European confidence in the readiness of the United States to place its international monetary responsibilities ahead of its national interests (Chapter 18). By speaking with a single voice on monetary issues, EU countries hoped to defend more effectively their economic interests in the face of an increasingly self-absorbed United States.

TABLE 20-1

A Brief Glossary of Euronyms

CAP	Common Agricultural Policy
ECU	European Currency Unit
EMS	European Monetary System
EMU	Economic and Monetary Union
ERM	Exchange Rate Mechanism
EU	European Union

2. *To turn the European Union into a truly unified market.* Even though the 1957 Treaty of Rome founding the EU had established a customs union, significant official barriers to the movements of goods and factors within Europe remained. A consistent goal of EU members has been to eliminate all such barriers and transform the EU into a huge unified market on the model of the United States. European officials believed, however, that exchange rate uncertainty, like official trade barriers, was a major factor reducing trade within Europe. In their view, a truly unified European market could never be achieved unless mutual European exchange rates were fixed.

3. *To avoid disrupting the Common Agricultural Policy.* Perhaps the most pressing motive of all was the tremendous difficulty of adjusting the EU's Common Agricultural Policy (CAP) to exchange rate changes (recall our discussion of the economic inefficiency of the CAP in Chapter 8).

The CAP guarantees EU farmers minimum support prices for their products. Wishing to treat all EU farmers symmetrically, the CAP specifies its support prices in terms of a basket of EU currencies that since 1979 has been called the *European Currency Unit (ECU)*.

This mode of quoting agricultural support prices leads immediately, however, to a problem: When exchange rates within Europe are realigned, some countries' farmers find that the real value of their support prices has risen, while others are in the opposite position.

A simple example illustrates this effect. If the EU support price for wheat is 10 ECUs per bushel and an ECU is worth FFr 5, French wheat growers receive FFr 50 per bushel (= FFr 5 per ECU × 10 ECU/bushel). If, at the same time, an ECU is worth 3 DM, German farmers will get DM 30 per bushel of wheat (= DM 3 per ECU × 10 ECU/bushel).

Suppose now that there is a currency realignment, so that France devalues its currency to FFr 6 per ECU, while Germany revalues its currency to DM 2 per ECU.[1] What effect does this change have on the domestic currency prices received by French and German wheat growers? The price the French grower receives for wheat rises from FFr 50 to FFr 60 per bushel (= FFr 6 per ECU × 10 ECU/bushel), while the price the German grower receives *falls* from DM 30 to DM 20 per bushel (= DM 2 per ECU × 10 ECU per bushel). Clearly, the currency realignment increases the French farmer's income and reduces the German farmer's income.

---

[1]Remember that because the ECU is a *basket* of EU currencies, a depreciation of the franc against the ECU, other things equal, automatically results in an appreciation of the DM against the ECU.

Such redistributions have always provoked political outcry, and the European Union therefore was forced to adopt complex and costly administrative measures to offset them.[2] A desire to avoid the financial contortions needed to prevent sharp variations in farmers' incomes is one of the main factors behind EU policymakers' dislike of variable exchange rates. (Of course the first-best policy, were it politically possible, would be to scrap the CAP.)

The considerations leading EU policymakers to favor mutual currency stability have changed little since the late 1960s. The Werner committee's vision was, however, ahead of its time. Faced with the economic turbulence surrounding the 1971–1973 dollar crises, most European leaders did not want to give up completely the ability to direct domestic monetary policy toward domestic goals. Instead, Germany, the Netherlands, Belgium, and Luxembourg—joined for periods by other European countries—participated in an informal joint float against the dollar known as the "snake." French, Italian, and British participation in the snake arrangements of the 1970s was brief and sporadic; nonetheless, the snake served as a prologue to the more comprehensive European Monetary System.

THE EUROPEAN MONETARY SYSTEM: FROM 1979 TO THE PRESENT

The eight original participants in the European Monetary System's exchange rate mechanism—France, Germany, Italy, Belgium, Denmark, Ireland, Luxembourg, and the Netherlands—began operating a formal network of mutually pegged exchange rates in March 1979. In Chapter 17 we described how EMS intervention arrangements work to restrict the exchange rates of participating currencies within specified fluctuation margins.[3]

When the EMS was founded on the initiative of France and Germany, skeptics predicted that the system would do no better than its predecessor the snake: Speculative attacks would soon shatter its parities, forcing France, Italy, and some of the smaller countries out. The prospects for a successful fixed-rate area Europe seemed bleak indeed in early 1979, when recent yearly inflation rates ranged from Germany's 2.7 percent to Italy's 12.1 percent (see Table 19-1). Through a mixture of policy cooperation and realignment, however, the EMS fixed exchange rate club survived and even grew, adding Spain to its ranks in 1989, Britain in 1990, and Portugal early in 1992. Only in September 1992 did this growth suffer a sudden setback when Britain and Italy left the EMS exchange rate mechanism at the start of an ongoing European currency crisis that forced the remaining members within a year to retreat to very wide exchange rate margins. We discuss the causes and effects of this crisis later in this chapter.

---

[2]Specifically, the EU required that the *domestic currency* prices of agricultural products be held constant during a transition period following realignments—in our example, at FFr 50 per bushel of wheat in France and at DM 30 per bushel of wheat in Germany. Notice, though, that at these old domestic currency prices, but at the *new* exchange rates, wheat is priced at 8.33 ECU/bushel in France (= 1/6 ECU/franc × FFr 50 per bushel) and at 15 ECU/bushel (= 1/2 ECU/DM × DM 30 bushel) in Germany. How could the EU prevent people from buying wheat in France and selling it in Germany, thereby making arbitrage profits on the price difference? The EU prevented arbitrage by setting up a tax on French wheat exports and a subsidy on German wheat exports. These taxes and subsidies on agricultural trade within Europe, called *Monetary Compensation Amounts (MCAs),* were among the many trade regulations scheduled for removal by the EU 1992 project (see pp. 620–624). For a more detailed discussion of MCAs, see the book by Giavazzi and Giovannini listed in Further Reading.

[3]As a technical matter, all EU members are members of the EMS, but only those EMS members who enforce the fluctuation margins belong to the EMS *exchange rate mechanism (ERM).*

The EMS's operation has been aided by several safety valves that initially helped reduce the frequency of such crises. Most exchange rates "fixed" by the EMS until August 1993 actually could fluctuate up or down by as much as 2.25 percent relative to an assigned par value. Spain's peseta and Portugal's escudo had bands of $\pm$ 6 percent, as did the British pound until its recent float against EMS currencies started in September 1992. The Italian lira likewise had a 6 percent band until January 1990, when Italy adopted the standard narrow band. Inflationary instability was common in Italy during the 1970s, and the country's special exchange rate band was meant to give it a greater latitude than other exchange rate mechanism members to choose monetary policies. Similarly, the more recent members, Spain, Portugal, and Britain, desired greater room for maneuver during their initiation periods and therefore also chose to start out with wide bands. In August 1993 all EMS bands (other than that between the DM and Dutch guilder) were widened to $\pm$ 15 percent under the pressure of speculative attacks.

As another crucial safety valve, the EMS developed generous provisions for the extension of credit from strong- to weak-currency members. If the French franc depreciates too far against the DM, for example, Germany's central bank, the Bundesbank, is expected to lend the Bank of France DM that can be sold for francs in the foreign exchange market.

Finally, during the system's initial years of operation several members (notably France and Italy) reduced the possibility of speculative attack by maintaining exchange controls that directly limited domestic residents' sales of home for foreign currencies. All French, Italian, Danish, and Belgian controls were dismantled in a series of stages completed in 1990. At the time of the crisis of September 1992, when several EMS members backtracked and tightened their exchange controls, the remaining restrictions on payments within the EU had been scheduled to be scrapped within a few years.

The EMS has always gone through periodic currency realignments. In all, 11 realignments occurred between the start of the EMS in March 1979 and January 1987. Exchange controls played the important role of shielding members' reserves from speculators during these adjustments.

Starting in 1987, the phased removal of exchange controls increased the possibility of speculative attacks and thus reduced governments' willingness openly to consider devaluing or revaluing. At the same time the countries that dismantled controls sharply reduced their power to reach national employment or inflation goals through domestic monetary policy (recall the monetary policy ineffectiveness result of Chapter 17). Freedom of payments and capital movements within the EU has always been a key element of EU countries' plan to turn Europe into a unified single market. By agreeing to remove exchange controls, EU governments were saying that it was less important to use monetary and exchange rate policy for domestic purposes than to speed up progress toward a single European market.

For a period of five and a half years after January 1987, no adverse economic event was able to shake the EU's commitment to its single-market plan, and the EMS thus was free of serious currency crises. As we discuss below, however, domestic macroeconomic problems became more urgent late in 1992; as a result, the system's fixed exchange rates gave way.

Figure 20-1 shows the London *Financial Times'* weekly capsule summary of currencies' positions within the EMS.[4] As we discuss in the box on p. 621, these graphs give a

---

[4]Luxembourg is not shown separately because its franc is equivalent to Belgium's franc as the result of a currency union between the two countries.

FIGURE 20-1

The EMS Currency Grid

(a)

European Monetary System: The D-Mark remains at the top of the grid, following Friday's poor employment figures in the U.S. which triggered heavy investment in the German currency. The D-Mark, the hardest currency in Europe, is normally at the center of the table, allowing the monetary policies and exchange rates of other currencies to be altered around it. Its strong position is putting pressure on other member currencies, with sterling still firmly at the bottom of the table. But the U.K. government's decision last week to buy pounds on the foreign exchanges by means of an Ecu10bn ($14.3bn) loan has eased the pound's differential against the strongest currencies in the system.

(b)

European Monetary System: The spread between the strongest and weakest currencies in the EMS grid narrowed by more than one percentage point last week. The French franc rallied, despite a cut by the Bank of France in one of its key interest rates. There was no change to the order of the currencies.

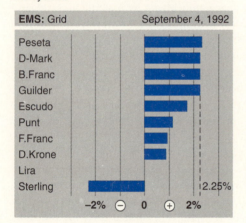

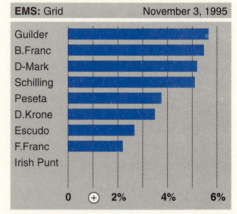

The chart shows the member currencies of the exchange rate mechanism measured against the weakest currency in the EMS's narrow 2.25 percent fluctuation band. In practice, currencies in the EMS narrow band cannot rise more than 2.25 percent from the weakest currency in that part of the system. Sterling, the Spanish peseta and the Portuguese escudo operate with 6 percent fluctuation bands.

The chart shows the member currencies of the exchange rate mechanism measured against the weakest currency in the system. Most of the currencies are permitted to fluctuate within 15 percent of agreed central rates against the other members of the mechanism. The exceptions are the D-Mark and the guilder which move in a 2.25 percent band.

The grid shows the relative positions of EMS currencies within their permitted fluctuation bands. The first of the two grids, shown in panel (a), dates from shortly before the onset of the autumn 1992 currency crisis. In mid-September 1992 Britain and Italy withdrew their currencies from the EMS exchange rate mechanism. In August 1993 most remaining ERM currencies moved to ±15 percent exchange rate bands. Panel (b) shows the state of play late in 1995, by which time Austria's schilling had joined the ERM.

Source: *Financial Times*, September 7, 1992, page 1, and November 6, 1995, page 1.

snapshot of currencies' relative positions within their EMS bilateral exchange rate bands. The two summaries we have selected—one from early September 1992 and one from November 1995—also illustrate the strains and setbacks that the system suffered during 1992 and 1993.

GERMAN MONETARY DOMINANCE AND THE CREDIBILITY THEORY OF THE EMS

Earlier we identified three main reasons why the European Union sought to fix exchange rates through the EMS: a desire to defend Europe's economic interests more effectively on the world stage, the ambition to achieve greater internal economic unity, and the complexity of adjusting the Common Agricultural Policy to intra-European currency realignments.

Europe's experience with inflation in the 1970s suggests an additional explanation for the EMS's existence. By fixing their exchange rates against the DM, the other EMS countries in effect imported the German Bundesbank's credibility as an inflation fighter and thus discouraged the development of inflationary pressures at home—pressures they might otherwise have been tempted to accommodate through monetary expansion. This view, the **credibility theory of the EMS,** is a variant of the "discipline" argument against floating exchange rates (Chapter 19): The political costs of violating an international exchange rate agreement can restrain governments from depreciating their currencies to gain the short-term advantage of an economic boom at the long-term cost of higher inflation.

To evaluate the credibility theory, we need first to understand how the German Bundesbank gained its low-inflation reputation. Germany's experiences with hyperinflation in the 1920s and again after World War II left its electorate with a deeply rooted fear of inflation. For this reason, the law establishing the Bundesbank singled out the defense of the DM's real value as the central bank's primary goal. Consistent with this goal, the bank's governing council has powers and membership rules that make it unusually independent of pressures from the politicians who run the rest of the German government.[5]

The way EMS intervention practices have evolved since the mid-1980s supports the view that Germany's EMS partners have sought to import its anti-inflation credibility. Increasingly, EMS countries other than Germany have come to hold DM in their reserves and to use these as an intervention medium when their exchange rates get too far from the official DM parity. (Germany also carries out some interventions in EMS currencies, especially during turbulent periods, but it instantly sterilizes any effects that these interventions might have on Germany's money supply.) The result is a system that functions very much in the asymmetric way the Bretton Woods system did under U.S. dominance. In practice, the EMS's *N*th currency problem (Chapter 17) has been solved by having Germany set the system's monetary policy while the other countries peg their currencies' DM exchange rates.

Policymakers in inflation-prone EMS countries, such as Italy, clearly gained credibility by placing monetary policy decisions in the hands of the German central bank. Devaluation was still possible, but only subject to EMS restrictions. Because politicians also fear

---

[5]Two interesting studies show that central bank independence appears to be associated with lower inflation. See Vittorio Grilli, Donato Masciandaro, and Guido Tabellini, "Political and Monetary Institutions and Public Financial Policies in the Industrial Countries," *Economic Policy* 13 (October 1991), pp. 341–392; and Alberto Alesina and Lawrence H. Summers, "Central Bank Independence and Macroeconomic Performance: Some Comparative Evidence," *Journal of Money, Credit and Banking* 25 (May 1993), pp. 151–162.

with other EMS countries, a small increase in Finland's price level, combined with some movement of foreign capital and labor into Finland, quickly eliminates the excess demand for Finnish products.[14]

An additional consideration that we have not yet discussed strengthens the argument that the economic stability loss to Finland from joining the EMS is lower when Finland and the EMS engage in a large volume of trade. Since imports from the EMS make up a large fraction of Finnish workers' consumption in this case, changes in the markka/ECU exchange rate may quickly affect nominal Finnish wages, reducing any impact on employment. A depreciation of the markka against the ECU, for example, causes a sharp fall in Finns' living standards when imports from the EMS countries are substantial; workers are likely to demand higher nominal wages from their employers to compensate them for the loss. In this situation the additional macroeconomic stability Finland gets from a floating exchange rate is small, so the country has little to lose by joining the EMS.

We conclude that *a high degree of economic integration between a country and the fixed exchange rate area that it joins reduces the resulting economic stability loss due to output market disturbances.*

The *LL* schedule shown in Figure 20-4 summarizes this conclusion. The figure's horizontal axis measures the joining country's economic integration with the fixed exchange rate area, the vertical axis the country's economic stability loss. As we have seen, *LL* has a negative slope because the economic stability loss from pegging to the area's currencies falls as the degree of economic interdependence rises.

FIGURE 20-4

The *LL* Schedule

The downward sloping *LL* schedule shows that a country's economic stability loss from joining a fixed exchange rate area falls as the country's economic integration with the area rises.

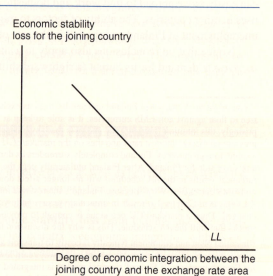

Economic stability loss for the joining country

LL

Degree of economic integration between the joining country and the exchange rate area

---

[14]The preceding reasoning applies to other economic disturbances that fall unequally on Finland's output market and those of its exchange rate partners. A problem at the end of this chapter asks you to think through the effects of an increase in demand for EMS exports other than Finland's.

THE DECISION TO JOIN A CURRENCY AREA: PUTTING THE *GG* AND *LL* SCHEDULES TOGETHER

Figure 20-5 combines the *GG* and *LL* schedules to show how Finland should decide whether to join the EMS. The figure implies that Finland should join if the degree of economic integration between Finnish and markets and those of the EMS is at least equal to θ_1, the integration level determined by the intersection of *GG* and *LL* at point 1.

Let's see why Finland should join the EMS if its degree of economic integration with EMS markets is at least θ_1. Figure 20-5 shows that for levels of economic integration below θ_1 the *GG* schedule lies below the *LL* schedule. Thus, the loss Finland would suffer from greater output and employment instability after joining exceeds the monetary efficiency gain, and the country would do better to stay out.

When the degree of integration is θ_1 or higher, however, the monetary efficiency gain measured by *GG* is greater than the stability sacrifice measured by *LL*, and joining the EMS results in a net gain for Finland. Thus the intersection of *GG* and *LL* determines the minimum integration level (here, θ_1) at which Finland will desire to peg its currency to the ECU.

The *GG-LL* framework has important implications about how changes in a country's economic environment affect its willingness to peg its currency to an outside currency area. Consider, for example, an increase in the size and frequency of sudden shifts in the demand for the country's exports. As shown in Figure 20-6, such a change pushes LL^1 upward to LL^2: At any level of economic integration with the currency area, the extra output and unemployment instability the country suffers by fixing its exchange rate is now greater. As a result, the level of economic integration at which it becomes worthwhile to join the currency area rises to θ_2 (determined by the intersection of *GG* and LL^2 at point 2).

FIGURE 20-5

Deciding When to Peg the Exchange Rate

The intersection of *GG* and *LL* at point 1 determines a critical level of economic integration θ_1 between a fixed exchange rate area and a country considering whether to join. At any level of integration above θ_1, the decision to join yields positive net economic benefits to the joining country.

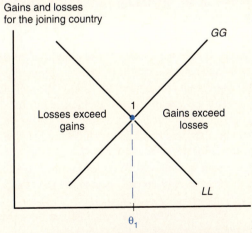

Gains and losses for the joining country

Losses exceed gains

Gains exceed losses

θ_1

Degree of economic integration between the joining country and the exchange rate area

FIGURE 20-6

An Increase in Output Market Variability

A rise in the size and frequency of country-specific disturbances to the joining country's product markets shifts the LL schedule upward from LL^1 to LL^2 because for a given level of economic integration with the fixed exchange rate area the country's economic stability loss from pegging its exchange rate rises. The shift in LL raises the critical level of economic integration at which the exchange rate area is joined to θ_2.

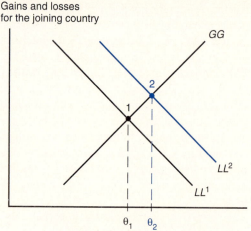

Gains and losses for the joining country

Degree of economic integration between the joining country and the exchange rate area

Other things equal, increased variability in their product markets makes countries less willing to enter fixed exchange rate areas—a prediction that helps explain why the oil price shocks after 1973 made countries unwilling to revive the Bretton Woods system of fixed exchange rates (Chapter 19). As we see later in this chapter, the same reasoning also explains some of the bumps and potholes on the road to European monetary unification.

WHAT IS AN OPTIMUM CURRENCY AREA?

The *GG-LL* model we have developed suggests a theory of the optimum currency area. *Optimum currency areas* are groups of regions with economies closely linked by trade in goods and services and by factor mobility. This result follows from our finding that a fixed exchange rate area will best serve the economic interests of each of its members if the degree of output and factor trade among the included economies is high.

This perspective helps us understand, for example, why it may make sense for the United States, Japan, and Europe to allow their mutual exchange rates to float. Even though these regions trade with each other, the extent of that trade is modest compared with regional GNPs and interregional labor mobility is low. In 1990, for example, U.S. merchandise trade with Western Europe (measured as the average of imports and exports) amounted to only about 2 percent of U.S. GNP; U.S. merchandise trade with Japan was even smaller.

The more interesting question, and the critical one for judging the economic success of the EMS, is whether Europe itself makes up an optimum currency area. We take up this topic next.

CASE STUDY

Is Europe an Optimum Currency Area?

The theory of optimum currency areas gives us a useful framework for thinking about the considerations that determine whether a group of countries will gain or lose by fixing their mutual exchange rates. A nation's gains and losses from pegging its currency to an exchange rate area are hard to measure numerically, but by combining our theory with information on actual economic performance we can evaluate the claim that Europe is an optimum currency area.

The Extent of Intra-European Trade

Our earlier discussion suggested that a country is more likely to benefit from joining a currency area if the area's economy is closely integrated with its own. The overall degree of economic integration can be judged by looking at the integration of product markets, that is, the extent of trade between the joining country and the currency area, and at the integration of factor markets, that is, the ease with which labor and capital can migrate between the joining country and the currency area.

Most EU members export from 10 to 20 percent of their output to other EU members. These numbers are larger than those for EU-U.S. trade, which is only around 2 percent of U.S. GNP and an even smaller percentage of EU GNP, but much smaller than the amount of trade between regions of the United States. If we take trade relative to GNP as a measure of economic integration, the *GG-LL* model of the last section suggests that a joint float of Europe's currencies against the rest of the world is a better strategy for EU members than a fixed dollar-ECU exchange rate would be. The extent of intra-European trade is not large enough, however, to give us an overwhelming reason for believing the European Union itself is an optimum currency area.

To some degree intra-EU trade may have been artificially limited until now by trade restrictions that the 1992 reforms largely removed. Evidence supporting the idea that restrictions seriously limited trade comes from comparisons of prices for similar products sold in different EU countries. As late as the end of 1992, for example, a can of Coca Cola cost twice as much in Ireland as in France, while a box of Kellogg's cornflakes was nearly 2.5 times more expensive in Italy than in Britain.[15] It is still too early to tell how effective the 1992 measures will be in bringing Europe closer to being an optimum currency area.

How Mobile Is Europe's Labor Force?

Earlier we mentioned that the European Union did not succeed in removing internal passport checks by the original deadline of January 1, 1993. The main barriers

---

[15]See "Whither the Cross-Border Cornflake?" *Financial Times*, January 4, 1993, p. 7.

to labor mobility within Europe are probably not due to border controls, however. Differences in language and culture discourage labor movements between European countries to a greater extent than is true, for example, between regions of the United States. In one econometric study comparing unemployment patterns in U.S. regions with those in EU countries, Barry Eichengreen of the University of California at Berkeley found that differences in regional unemployment rates are smaller and less persistent in the United States than are differences between national unemployment rates in the European Union.[16]

Even *within* European countries labor mobility appears limited, partly because of government regulations. For example, the requirement in some countries that workers establish residence before receiving unemployment benefits makes it harder for unemployed workers to seek jobs in regions that are far from their current homes. Table 20-2 presents evidence on the frequency of regional labor movement in the largest EU countries, as compared with Japan and the United States. Although these data must be interpreted with caution because the definition of "region" differs from country to country, they do suggest that in a typical year Japanese and Americans were significantly more footloose than Europeans.

Other Considerations

While the *GG-LL* model is useful for organizing our thinking about optimum currency areas, it is not the whole story. At least two other elements affect our evaluation of the EMS currency area's past and prospective performance.

Similarity of Economic Structure. The *GG-LL* model tells us that extensive trade with the EMS makes it easier for a member to adjust to output market disturbances that affect it and its EMS partners differently. But it does not tell us what factors will reduce the frequency and size of member-specific product market shocks.

A key element in minimizing such disturbances is similarity in economic structure, especially in the types of products produced. EMS countries are not entirely dissimilar in manufacturing structure, as evidenced by the very high volume of *intraindustry trade*—trade in similar products—within Europe (see Chapter 6). There are also important differences, however: The countries of northern Europe are better endowed with capital and skilled labor than the countries in Europe's South, and EU products that make intensive use of low-skill labor thus are likely to come from Portugal, Spain, Greece, or southern Italy. It is not yet clear whether completion of the single European market will remove these differences by redistributing capital and labor across Europe or increase them by encouraging regional specialization to exploit economies of scale in production.

Fiscal Federalism. Another consideration in evaluating the EMS is the European Union's ability to transfer economic resources from members with

---

[16]See Eichengreen, "One Money for Europe? Lessons of the U.S. Currency Union," *Economic Policy* 10 (April 1990), pp. 118–166. Further study of the U.S. labor market has shown that regional unemployment is eliminated almost entirely by worker migration rather than by changes in regional real wages. This pattern of labor market adjustment is unlikely to be possible in Europe in the near future. See Olivier Jean Blanchard and Lawrence F. Katz, "Regional Evolutions," *Brookings Papers on Economic Activity* 1:1992, pp. 1–75.

TABLE 20-2

People Changing Region of Residence in 1986 (percent of total population)

Britain	France	Germany	Italy	Japan	United States
1.1	1.3	1.1	0.6	2.6	3.0

Source: Organization for Economic Cooperation and Development. *OECD Employment Outlook.* Paris: OECD, July 1990, Table 3.3.

healthy economies to those suffering economic setbacks. In the United States, for example, states faring poorly relative to the rest of the nation automatically receive support from Washington in the form of welfare benefits and other federal transfer payments that ultimately come out of the taxes other states pay. Such **fiscal federalism** can help offset the economic stability loss due to fixed exchange rates, as it does in the United States. Unfortunately, its limited taxation powers allow the European Union to practice fiscal federalism only on a very small scale (see the box on p. 635).

Summing Up

How should we judge the EMS in light of the theory of optimum currency areas? On balance, there is little evidence that Europe's product and factor markets are sufficiently unified to make it an optimum currency area. Trade with EU partners typically is less than a quarter of each member's GNP, and while capital moves with little interference, labor mobility is nowhere near the high level countries would need to adjust smoothly to product market disturbances through labor migration.

The "1992" drive toward economic liberalization moved the European Union closer to being an optimum currency area in some respects, but it has done very little to promote labor mobility within Europe. Because labor income makes up around two-thirds of GNP in the European Union and the hardships of unemployment are so severe, the low labor mobility between and within EU countries implies that the economic stability loss from EMS membership is high. Evidence of such losses is provided by the persistently high unemployment rates in some EMS countries (see Table 19-3).

The European Union's current combination of rapid capital migration with limited labor migration may actually *raise* the cost of adjusting to product market shocks without exchange rate changes. If the Netherlands suffers an unfavorable shift in output demand, for example, Dutch capital can flee abroad, leaving even more unemployed Dutch workers behind than if government regulations were to bottle the capital up within national borders. Severe and persistent regional depressions could result, worsened by the likelihood that the relatively few workers who did successfully emigrate would be precisely those who are most skilled, reliable, and enterprising. Given that labor remains relatively immobile within Europe, the European Union's success in liberalizing its capital flows may have worked perversely to worsen the economic stability loss due to fixed EMS exchange rates. This possibility is an-

ners' interests. The European Central Bank that would replace the German Bundesbank under EMU would have to be more considerate of other countries' problems.

3. All of the EU countries' leaders hoped the Maastricht Treaty's provisions would guarantee the *political* stability of western Europe. Beyond its purely economic functions, the single EU currency was intended as a potent symbol of Europe's desire to place cooperation ahead of the national rivalries that often had led to war in the past.

The Maastricht Treaty's critics denied that EMU would have these positive effects and opposed the treaty's provisions for vesting stronger governmental powers with the European Union. To these critics, EMU was symptomatic of a tendency for the European Union's central institutions to ignore local needs, meddle in local affairs, and downgrade prized symbols of national identity (including, of course, national currencies).

Despite the optimistic atmosphere at Maastricht, the treaty soon was in trouble, in large part because of economic developments that led many Europeans to question whether their countries would be wise to sacrifice any more control over national economic policies.

 **CASE STUDY**

How European Macroeconomic Tensions Helped Derail Maastricht

The Maastricht Treaty could not come into force until all EU members had ratified it through national referendum or parliamentary vote. EU leaders were stunned in June 1992 when the treaty, in its very first electoral test, was narrowly rejected by Danish voters. Prospects for EMU worsened later in 1992. In September EMS parities were hit by speculative attacks that reversed much of the European Union's progress in completing stage 1 of the 1989 Delors plan for monetary unification, on which the treaty was based. In August 1993 speculators forced another retreat, this time to very wide exchange rate bands. How could EMU now go forward?

At the time of writing, the future of EMU remains somewhat in doubt. The economic stresses that produced the EMS's worst speculative crisis and slowed the drive toward European integration were not accidental, however. These stresses were the direct result of two features of the EMS discussed earlier in this chapter: the high economic stability losses members could suffer by holding exchange rates fixed and Germany's dominance over EMS monetary policy.

German Reunification

The reunification of East and West Germany in 1990 was an economic disturbance that the EMS was poorly designed to handle. As we see below, Germany's EMS partners very quickly felt the effects of the internal German policy decisions that accompanied unification.

The East German revolution of 1989—symbolized by the fall of the Berlin Wall—allowed the two parts of Germany, divided since the end of World War II, again to become a single country. Economic reunification commenced on July 1,

1990, when East Germans traded in their holdings of East German currency for DM (recall Chapter 19).

East German wages, initially far below those in the West, jumped upward as East German workers demanded parity with workers elsewhere in the country. This development was surprising because demand for the inferior products manufactured in the East was low, and many East German workers lacked the training, diligence, and modern equipment of those in the West. Furthermore, hoped-for flows of private investment to modernize eastern Germany didn't materialize. The result was high unemployment in the East (the measured unemployment rate was around 15 percent in 1992) and a dizzying fall in East Germany's output.[17] The eastern Germans' richer western cousins soon found themselves making massive payments to the East—to support and retrain unemployed workers, to renovate the East's antiquated capital stock, and to clean up its polluted environment. Because the German government borrowed much of this money rather than raising taxes, the public fiscal deficit widened sharply. This fiscal stimulus added to demand pressures that had been building up even before 1990.

Disillusion in the West and resentment in the East contributed to aggressive union wage demands and strikes. Additional inflationary pressure came from the liberal spending of the East Germans, who used many of the DM they received from the West to buy the high-quality consumer durables they had been denied under communism. To halt rising prices, Germany's Bundesbank hit its monetary brakes in 1992 and pushed interest rates to historically high levels.

At the time, however, the European economies other than Germany's had been weakening for more than a year. One factor behind this weakness may have been the German aggregate demand expansion itself, which had already raised interest rates in Germany and throughout the EMS. (The appendix to this chapter shows how an increase in aggregate demand in Germany can depress the economies of countries that peg their currencies to the DM.)

Germany's decision to tighten its monetary policy sharply therefore placed Britain, France, and Germany's other EMS partners in a dilemma: Should they tighten their own monetary policies in tandem with Germany's to maintain EMS exchange rates, or should they devalue their currencies against the DM as a way of stimulating international demand for their products? You will recognize this dilemma as exactly the type of situation that imposes economic stability losses in a multiregion currency area. While criticizing Germany's tight monetary policy, its EMS partners allowed their own interest rates to rise in order to resist devaluation. With EMU seemingly within reach, governments wanted to avoid being forced into realignment.

Unfortunately, the defense of EMS exchange parities deepened the European downturn outside of Germany. Germany denied any responsibility for Europe's macroeconomic problems and refused to make substantial policy changes.

---

[17]The number cited in the text is an underestimate of actual unemployment, since many workers with jobs (at least 5 percent of the labor force) were on "short time," working fewer hours than they would have liked. For a detailed analysis of the internal economic impact of German reunification, see George A. Akerlof, Andrew K. Rose, Janet L. Yellen, and Helga Hessenius, "East Germany in from the Cold: The Economic Aftermath of Currency Union," *Brookings Papers on Economic Activity* 1:1991, pp. 1–105.

Public Opinion and the Maastricht Treaty

The lesson of this policy conflict was not lost on European voters and legislatures. Europeans outside Germany feared that a European central bank would not be much better than the Bundesbank at meeting the monetary policy needs of individual countries; they also feared that a powerful, reunited Germany would have the decisive voice in running EMU. The Germans themselves worried that a European central bank would be less zealous than their own Bundesbank in fighting inflation. With unemployment on the rise everywhere, Europeans became more willing to believe EMU opponents who blamed job losses on the European Union's liberalized internal trade and migration policies. Public disaffection with the Maastricht Treaty increased, and in June 1992 Denmark, the first country to vote on the accord, rejected it by a small margin. The Danish rejection raised a serious legal problem because amendments to the Treaty of Rome require the unanimous approval of all EU members.

As EU lawyers and diplomats searched for a way around this problem, the treaty ran into unexpected trouble in France, where a referendum was scheduled for September 20. Public opinion polls taken in August showed that French voters, angry at their government over its management of the economy, were equally divided between supporters and opponents of the treaty. Rejection by France would have killed the treaty and possibly weakened the determination of EMS countries to maintain their fixed exchange rates.

Black Wednesday

The prospect of a French refusal to ratify the Maastricht Treaty encouraged foreign exchange market participants to gamble that weak currencies would be devalued. The first currencies to be hit by all-out speculative attacks were the Finnish markka and the Swedish krona. Neither country belonged to the EU at the time, but both desired membership and had pegged their currencies to the ECU to prove they were ready for admission. Finland gave up its fight quickly, letting the markka depreciate steeply against the ECU on September 8. Sweden was temporarily successful in defending the krona, but speculation died down only after its central bank, the Riksbank, allowed interest rates on overnight loans to reach 500 percent per annum (roughly 1.4 percent *per day*). At the same time, the British and Italian governments were struggling to keep their currencies above the floors of their EMS bands.

Pressure on the pound and lira continued during the week. By the evening of Friday, September 11, the Bundesbank had spent DM 24 billion (roughly $16 billion) in following EMS intervention rules and supporting the lira. The Bundesbank was reluctant to spend any more, however, and over the weekend the EMS agreed to let Italy devalue its currency by 7 percent against the ECU. The lira's parity change was the first EMS realignment under market pressure since January 1987, and it signaled to participants in the foreign exchange market that attacks on other EMS currencies might succeed.

On September 16, a day now known as "Black Wednesday" because of the damage done to the EMS, the pound was allowed to float after the Bank of England lost billions of dollars defending it. This action followed repeated pledges by the British government not to realign. Despite having devalued only two days before, Italy took the lira out of the EMS exchange rate mechanism rather than lose more reserves. Spain devalued its peseta and reimposed exchange controls to slow its own reserve losses.

Even the French franc came under attack, despite a French inflation rate lower than Germany's (see Figure 20-1). Heavy and prolonged intervention by the Bank of France and the Bundesbank, coupled with a sharp rise in French interest rates, eventually pried the franc from the bottom of its DM band. After the most turbulent week in EMS history, French voters narrowly approved the Maastricht Treaty on September 20 and thereby gave EMU another chance to stumble ahead.

Continuing Crisis

Currency turmoil continued in Europe through 1992 and into the spring of 1993. Later in 1992 the Portuguese escudo was devalued, the Spanish peseta devalued again, and the Swedish krona set afloat. In the first half of 1993, the Irish punt was devalued, the escudo devalued a second time, and the Spanish peseta devalued a third time. The French franc and Danish krone remained under periodic speculative pressure. The backdrop for these events was deepening recession in the EMS economies, coupled with the Bundesbank's insistence on making only gradual cuts in German interest rates.

In the spring of 1993 Denmark held a second referendum on Maastricht after other EU countries gave Denmark the right to refuse participation in the common monetary and defense institutions the treaty would create. This time the Danes went along, and Britain's Parliament followed suit by narrowly voting for ratification. By November 1993 the Maastricht Treaty had been adopted. At that time the group of 12 countries previously known as the European Community became the European Union.

The plan's vision of monetary union by the end of the century seemed increasingly out of touch, however, with the realities of EMS policy-making. At the end of July 1993 speculators attacked the French franc and other EMS currencies with unprecedented fury after a new disagreement over interest rates between Germany and other EMS members. On Friday, July 30, alone, the Bundesbank sold DM 50 billion (nearly $30 billion) to help prop up the French franc, while the Bank of France itself used up all of its foreign reserves. The following Monday, August 2, EMS exchange rates (other than the DM/Dutch guilder rate) were floating within drastically widened bands of ±15 percent around the existing central parities. This change in EMS rules was the only scheme EU ministers could find that let France's government avoid a formal devaluation of the franc (a step it had pledged to avoid at all costs) while leaving the Bundesbank free to lower German interest rates slowly.

Since 1993 interest rates have come down in Europe and its recession has eased, although unemployment remains very high. In 1995 Austria, Finland, and Sweden joined the EU (Norway's voters earlier declined to join in a national referendum). EU leaders insist that EMU will go ahead, and, in line with the Maastricht blueprint, have created the European Monetary Institute, an embryonic or transitional central bank currently lacking any monetary policy powers.

Many observers are skeptical that the amended EMS can be transformed into EMU in the space of only a few years, unless EMU initially consists of Germany and some smaller countries (for example, Austria and the Netherlands), with larger countries such as France initially pegging to the core group's currency. The

Maastricht Treaty specified that countries joining the EMU should have fiscal deficits below 3 percent of GDP and ratios of public debt to GDP below 60 percent, or at the least, be well on the way to meeting those targets. As of this writing few EMS members qualify, and it will not be politically easy for them to meet the Maastricht targets. France's efforts to trim its budget deficit, for example, set off a paralyzing general strike late in 1995.

Furthermore, currency-market tensions remain. The Spanish peseta and Portuguese escudo were forced into realignment early in 1995, and the French franc also came under pressure that year. Political cohesion within the EU was undermined further by the group's inability to formulate an effective joint policy in the face of the savage Bosnian civil war of the mid-1990s.

The dramatic economic events of 1992 and 1993 convinced many Europeans that the EMS was flawed; a good number were skeptical that a move to EMU would be an improvement. Considerable uncertainty remains about both the eventual shape of EMU and the path that will lead there from the current broadband EMS. These uncertainties are likely to unsettle the foreign exchange markets as the January 1, 1999, Maastricht deadline for EMU approaches.

DESIGNING AND NAMING A NEW CURRENCY

Among the least of the obstacles to achieving the comprehensive monetary union envisaged in the Maastricht Treaty are the choices of a look and a name for the new single European currency. Nonetheless, agreement has been hard to reach.

Some European leaders would like to retain a national symbol on bills they issue, although the national bills would circulate throughout Europe in the same way that U.S. dollar bills bearing the imprint of the Federal Reserve Bank of Chicago, for example, may turn up in New Yorkers' wallets. The British, in particular, insist that their monarch appear on their banknotes, regardless of what the rest of Europe does. A generic European note might portray the EU flag (a circle of 12 yellow stars on a field of dark blue), but there are more exotic proposals, for example, notes carrying Michelangelo's *David* or the Phoenecian princess Europa who, in Greek mythology, was carried off to Crete by the god Zeus (who took the form of a bull for the occasion).

The new currency's name was another problem until "Euro" was chosen in December 1995. The Maastricht Treaty refers to the single currency as the ECU, but most European leaders thought it would be misleading to adopt the name of a preexisting currency basket—and one that has depreciated sharply against the DM at that. A further problem was German chancellor Kohl's reported objection that in German *"ein ECU"* sounds like *"eine Kuh,"* German for "a cow."* Other proposed names included the franken and the shilling.

For some, christening the new currency "Euro" was a reluctant compromise. Britain's prime minister complained that the name Euro didn't send the blood coursing through his veins (unlike pound, presumably). The Greeks noted that Euro sounds like their word for urine.[†] Nonetheless, Euro it will be.

*See "What Fits in Europe's Wallet?" *New York Times,* July 11, 1995, p. C1.

[†]"Europeans Agree on New Currency," *New York Times,* December 16, 1995, p. 1.

Summary

1. European Union countries have three reasons for favoring mutually fixed exchange rates: They believe monetary cooperation will give them a heavier weight in international economic negotiations; they view fixed exchange rates as a complement to EU initiatives aimed at building a common European market; and fixed rates simplify the administration of the European Union's Common Agricultural Policy.

2. The European Monetary System was inaugurated in March 1979 and originally included Belgium, Denmark, France, Germany, Ireland, Italy, Luxembourg, and the Netherlands. Until 1992–1993 these countries all maintained their mutual exchange rates within a band of ±2.25 percent. Austria, Britain, Portugal, and Spain joined much later. Capital controls were an essential ingredient in maintaining the system until the mid-1980s, but since then many controls have been abolished as part of the European Union's wider "1992" program of market unification. During the currency crisis that broke out in September 1992, however, Britain and Italy allowed their currencies to float and several countries reimposed or tightened controls over international payments. In August 1993 most EMS currency bands were widened to ±15 percent in the face of continuing speculative attacks.

3. In practice all EMS currencies are pegged to the DM. As a result Germany is able to set monetary policy for the EMS, just as the United States did in the Bretton Woods system. The *credibility theory of the EMS* holds that participating governments profit from the German Bundesbank's reputation as an inflation fighter when they peg their currencies to the DM. In fact, inflation rates in EMS countries have tended to converge around Germany's generally low inflation rate. Critics of Germany charge, however, that on occasion it has abused its dominant position by neglecting the effects its policies have on other EMS countries.

4. The theory of *optimum currency areas* implies that countries will wish to join fixed exchange rate areas closely linked to their own economies through trade and factor mobility. A country's decision to join an exchange rate area is determined by the difference between the *monetary efficiency gain* from joining and the *economic stability loss* from joining. The *GG-LL* diagram relates both of these factors to the degree of economic integration between the joining country and the larger fixed exchange rate zone. Only when economic integration passes a critical level is it beneficial to join.

5. The European Union does not appear to satisfy all of the criteria for an optimum currency area. Although 1992 removed many barriers to market integration within the European Union, intra-EU trade still is not very extensive. In addition, labor mobility between and even within EU countries appears more limited than within other large currency areas, such as the United States. Finally, the level of *fiscal federalism* in the European Union is too small to cushion member countries from adverse economic events. Between 1985 and the early 1990s, however, good economic performance within the EMS allowed EU leaders to seek greater economic and monetary unity without significant voter opposition.

6. EU leaders currently hope to replace the EMS by an *economic and monetary union (EMU)*. EMU would imply a single European currency issued by a Euro-

pean System of Central Banks under a governing European Central Bank. In December 1991 EU heads of state signed the *Maastricht Treaty,* and agreed to seek approval from their electorates for concrete plans that would make EMU a reality by the start of 1999.

7. After public opposition to the Maastricht Treaty grew in the summer of 1992, the EMS was hit by a currency crisis that left its exchange rate mechanism in disarray. By November 1993 all current EU members had nonetheless ratified the treaty. Continuing economic and political tensions in Europe make it unlikely, however, that the ambitious goal of comprehensive EMU will be reached anytime soon.

Key Terms

credibility theory of the EMS, p. 619

economic stability loss, p. 626

economic and monetary union (EMU), p. 634

fiscal federalism, p. 633

Maastricht Treaty, p. 634

monetary efficiency gain, p. 625

optimum currency areas, p. 624

Problems

1. Why might EMS provisions for the extension of central bank credits from strong- to weak-currency members increase the stability of EMS exchange rates?

2. In the EMS before September 1992 the lira/DM exchange rate could fluctuate by up to 2.25 percent up *or* down. Assume that the lira/DM central parity and band are set in this way and cannot be changed. What is the maximum possible difference between the interest rates on *one-year* lira and DM deposits? What is the maximum possible difference between the interest rates on *six-month* lira and DM deposits? On three-month deposits? Do the answers surprise you? Give an intuitive explanation.

3. Continue with the assumptions of the last question. In Italy the interest rate on five-year government bonds is 11 percent per annum; in Germany the rate on five-year government bonds is 8 percent per annum. What are the implications for the credibility of the current lira/DM exchange parity?

4. Do your answers to the last two questions require an assumption that interest rates and expected exchange rate changes are linked by interest parity? Why or why not?

5. Finland joins the EMS, but soon after the EMS benefits from a favorable shift in the world demand for non-Finnish EMS exports. What happens to the exchange rate of the Finnish markka against non-EMS currencies? How is Finland's output affected? How does the size of this effect depend on the volume of trade between Finland and the other EMS economies?

6. Use the *GG-LL* diagram to show how an increase in the size and frequency of unexpected shifts in a country's money demand function affects the level of economic integration with a currency area at which the country will wish to join.

7. During the speculative pressure on the EMS exchange rate mechanism (ERM) shortly before Britain allowed the pound to float in September 1992, the *Economist,* a London weekly news magazine, opined as follows:

   The [British] government's critics want lower interest rates, and think this would be possible if Britain devalued sterling, leaving the ERM if necessary. They are wrong. Quitting the ERM would soon lead to higher, not lower, interest rates, as British economic management lost the degree of credibility already won through ERM membership. Two years ago British government bonds yielded three percentage points more than German ones. Today the gap is half a point, reflecting investors' belief that British inflation is on its way down—permanently. (See "Crisis? What Crisis?" *Economist,* August 29, 1992, p. 51.)

   a. Why might the British government's critics have thought it possible to lower interest rates after taking sterling out of the ERM? (Britain was in a deep recession at the time the article appeared.)
   b. Why did the *Economist* think the opposite would occur soon after Britain exited the ERM?
   c. In what way might ERM membership have gained credibility for British policymakers? (Britain entered the ERM in October 1990.)
   d. Why would a high level of British nominal interest rates relative to German rates have suggested an expectation of high future British inflation? Can you think of other explanations?
   e. Suggest two reasons why British interest rates might have been somewhat higher than German rates at the time of writing, despite the alleged "belief that British inflation is on the way down—permanently."

8. Imagine that the EMS becomes a monetary union with a single currency but that it creates no European Central Bank to manage this currency. Instead, the task is left to the various national central banks, each of which is allowed to issue as much of the European currency as it likes, and to conduct open-market operations. What problems could you foresee arising from such a scheme?

9. Why would the failure to create a unified EU labor market be particularly harmful to the prospects for a smoothly functioning EMU?

10. In the model of this chapter's appendix, what happens to Britain's output and interest rate if foreign exchange market participants decide the pound will be devalued against the DM in the future? What is the effect on Germany's economy? You should reach the conclusion that EMS currency crises harm all member countries.

Further Reading

Charles R. Bean. "Economic and Monetary Union in Europe." *Journal of Economic Perspectives* 6 (Fall 1992), pp. 31–52. Overview of the debate over European monetary unification, written just before the currency crisis in the autumn of 1992.

Paul De Grauwe. "Towards European Monetary Union Without the EMS." *Economic Policy* 18 (April 1994), pp. 147–185. Outlines a radical strategy for attaining EMU.

Barry Eichengreen and Charles Wyplosz. "The Unstable EMS." *Brookings Papers on Economic Activity* 1:1993, pp. 51–143. Detailed postmortem on the 1992 EMS currency collapse.

Martin Feldstein. "Does One Market Require One Money?" in *Policy Implications of Trade and Currency Zones.* Kansas City: Federal Reserve Bank of Kansas City, 1991, pp. 77–84. A prominent U.S. economist marshals the arguments against EMU.

Francesco Giavazzi and Alberto Giovannini. *Limiting Exchange Rate Flexibility: The European Monetary System.* Cambridge, MA: MIT Press, 1989. A comprehensive and fascinating account of EMS institutions and experience.

Peter B. Kenen. *Economic and Monetary Union in Europe.* Cambridge, U.K.: Cambridge University Press, 1995. A thorough economic analysis of the Maastricht Treaty's vision of EMU and of practical difficulties in the transition to EMU.

David Marsh. *The Bundesbank: The Bank That Rules Europe.* London: Heinemann, 1992. A journalist's account of the German central bank's role in formulating national and European economic policy.

Edward Tower and Thomas D. Willett. *The Theory of Optimal Currency Areas and Exchange Rate Flexibility,* Princeton Special Papers in International Economics 11. International Finance Section, Department of Economics, Princeton University, May 1976. Surveys the theory of optimum currency areas.

Appendix to Chapter 20

How German Reunification May Have Deepened the European Recession of the Early 1990s

The chapter described how the German aggregate demand expansion that followed the country's reunification in 1990 possibly depressed the economies of its EMS partners. It may surprise you that under fixed exchange rates a boom in one country can push its trading partners into a slump. This appendix explains the economic forces that can bring about this result.

To understand the effects of German reunification on the EMS, we must use the *IS-LM* model developed in Appendix I to Chapter 16. The *DD-AA* model is inappropriate for our purpose because it does not take into account the negative effects of higher real interest rates on consumption and investment. As we see below, these interest rate effects on aggregate demand are central to the analysis.

For simplicity imagine that the EMS consists of two countries, Germany and the United Kingdom. Germany has an independent monetary policy, but U.K. monetary policy is devoted completely to maintaining the pound/DM exchange rate at the fixed level $E^0_{\text{£/DM}}$. (To avoid unimportant complications we ignore the EMS exchange rate bands.)

The equation for Britain's *IS* curve takes the form

$$Y_{\text{UK}} = D_{\text{UK}}(E^0_{\text{£/DM}}P_G/P_{\text{UK}}, Y_{\text{UK}} - T_{\text{UK}}, Y_G - T_G, R_£ - \pi^e_{\text{UK}}, G_{\text{UK}}). \qquad (20A\text{-}1)$$

As in the two-country model of Chapter 19 [recall equations (19-1) and (19-2)], we recognize that an increase in German disposable income, $Y_G - T_G$, raises the aggregate demand for British goods and services by raising Germany's demand for imports. We also take notice in (20A-1) of the effect of U.K. government purchases on aggregate demand for British output. Germany's *IS* curve has a form similar to Britain's,

$$Y_G = D_G(P_{\text{UK}}/E^0_{\text{£/DM}}P_G, Y_G - T_G, Y_{\text{UK}} - T_{\text{UK}}, R_{\text{DM}} - \pi^e_{\text{UK}}, G_G). \qquad (20A\text{-}2)$$

Figure 20A-1 shows both of these *IS* curves as downward sloping schedules (recall Appendix I to Chapter 16).

The U.K. and German money market equilibrium conditions are $M^s_{\text{UK}}/P_{\text{UK}} = L_{\text{UK}}(Y_{\text{UK}}, R_£)$ and $M^s_G/P_G = L_G(Y_G, R_{\text{DM}})$. The *LM* curves along which national money markets clear also are shown in Figure 20A-1. The key point to remember about EMS monetary arrangements is that Germany has the power to manage its money supply as it wishes.

Because the United Kingdom pegs its currency to the DM, however, it must passively adjust its own money supply to maintain equilibrium in the foreign exchange market.

Assume that participants in the foreign exchange market don't expect the fixed exchange rate $E^0_{£/DM}$ to be changed.[18] Then the nominal sterling interest rate must equal the nominal DM interest rate:

$$R_£ = R_{DM}. \tag{20A-3}$$

Equation (20A-3) is the equilibrium condition for the foreign exchange market. Britain's intervention to peg the pound/DM exchange rate has the effect of shifting its *LM* curve so that (20A-3) always holds true.

Figure 20A-1 shows that Germany and Britain are initially at points 1 and 1', respectively, where both countries' output and money markets *and* the foreign exchange market are in equilibrium.

What happens when Germany reunifies and its private and government spending both rise? In Germany the *IS* curve shifts to the right and determines a new equilibrium (point 2) at which German output and interest rates are higher. Germany's *LM* curve does *not* shift because Germany has not changed its money supply. Because the DM is in practice the reserve currency of the EMS, Germany's EMS partners have to adjust their own money supplies to maintain their currencies' DM exchange rates.

This adjustment can be seen by looking at the United Kingdom's position after Germany's economic expansion. As you see in the diagram, two things happen in the United Kingdom:

1. The increase in Germany's income increases German demand for British exports and thereby moves Britain's *IS* curve to the right.
2. To keep its exchange rate fixed despite Germany's higher interest rate, Britain must intervene in the foreign exchange market, buying pounds with DM. The result is a leftward shift in Britain's *LM* curve that maintains equality between British and German interest rates.

As a result of these two shifts, Britain's new equilibrium is at point 2' and its output there is below its original level.

The result that Britain's output falls is true in Figure 20A-1, but it is not impossible that Y_{UK} rises as a result of Germany's spending increase. To get this alternative outcome, we would simply need a larger rightward shift of Britain's *IS* curve. The fall in British output shown in the figure will occur when trade between Britain and Germany is too limited for German income shifts to have a very strong effect on aggregate demand in Britain. Limited trade between Britain and Germany does not, however, weaken the impact of the German interest rate on the British interest rate and on the British economy. Even when Anglo-German trade is small, Britain must fully match German interest rate changes to maintain the fixed exchange rate of the pound against the DM.

Many economists believe that intra-EU trade is still too limited for German reunification to have produced a positive stimulus for the economies of its larger EMS partners. The argument that German reunification had a depressing effect elsewhere in Europe is not universally accepted, however. The Bundesbank has argued that the positive output effects of

---

[18]A problem at the end of this chapter asks you to study the effects of expectations that the pound will be devalued.

FIGURE 20A-1

The Effects of German Reunification on an EMS Partner's Economy

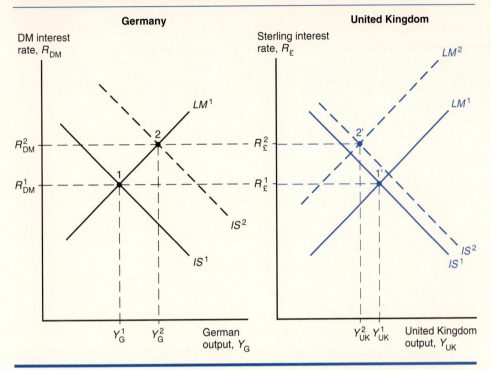

The rise in German spending and income raises the demand for U.K. exports and shifts the U.K.'s *IS* curve to the right. In addition, however, the United Kingdom must reduce its money supply to match the rise in German interest rates and hold the pound/DM exchange rate steady. This reduction in money supply shifts the U.K. *LM* curve to the left. The net effect on Britain is likely to be a fall in its output from Y^1 to Y^2.

Germany's increased import demand outweighed the negative effects of higher interest rates, that is, that German reunification had a net positive effect on output in other EMS countries.[19]

As the chapter discussed, reunification led to inflationary pressures within Germany that the Bundesbank resisted in 1992 through a tighter monetary policy. This change would be shown in Figure 20A-1 as a leftward shift of Germany's *LM* curve, which Britain must match to hold the pound/DM exchange rate fixed. Monetary tightening in Germany worsens the slump in the United Kingdom and, if taken too far, can also throw Germany into recession. This description of German monetary policy and its effects elsewhere in the EMS fits the European Union's predicament at the end of 1992 and in 1993.

---

[19]See "The Impact of the German Unification Process on Economic Trends in Germany's European Partner Countries," *Monthly Report of the Deutsche Bundesbank* 44 (July 1992), pp. 21–27.

21

The Global Capital Market: Performance and Policy Problems

If a financier named Rip van Winkle had gone to sleep in the early 1960s and awakened three decades later, he would have been shocked by changes in both the nature and the scale of international financial activity. In the early 1960s, for example, most banking business was purely domestic, involving the currency and customers of the bank's home country. Two decades later many banks were deriving a large share of their profits from international activities. To his surprise, Rip would have found that he could locate branches of Citibank in São Paulo, Brazil, and branches of Britain's National Westminster Bank in New York. He would also have discovered that by the early 1980s, it had become routine for a branch of an American bank located in London to accept a deposit denominated in Japanese yen from a Swedish corporation, or to lend Swiss francs to a Dutch manufacturer.

The market in which residents of different countries trade assets is called the **international capital market.** The international capital market is not really a single market; it is a group of closely interconnected markets in which asset exchanges with some international dimension take place. International currency trades take place in the foreign exchange market, which is an important part of the international capital market. The main actors in the international capital market are the same as those in the foreign exchange market (Chapter 13): commercial banks, large corporations, nonbank financial institutions, central banks, and other government agencies. And, like the foreign exchange market, the international capital market's activities take place in a network of world financial centers linked by sophisticated communications systems. The assets traded in the international capital market, however, include different countries' stocks and bonds in addition to bank deposits denominated in their currencies.

This chapter discusses three main questions about the international capital market. First, how has this well-oiled global financial network enhanced countries' gains from international trade? Second, what caused the rapid growth in international financial activity that has occurred since the early 1960s? And third, how can policymakers minimize the problems raised by a worldwide capital market without sharply reducing the benefits it provides?

THE INTERNATIONAL CAPITAL MARKET AND THE GAINS FROM TRADE

In earlier chapters, the discussion of gains from international trade concentrated on exchanges involving goods and services. By providing a worldwide payments system that lowers transaction costs, banks active in the international capital market enlarge the trade gains that result from such exchanges. But most deals that take place in the international capital market result in exchanges of assets between residents of different countries, for example, the exchange of a share of IBM stock for some British government bonds. Although such asset trades are sometimes derided as unproductive "speculation," they do, in fact, lead to gains from trade that can make consumers everywhere better off.

THREE TYPES OF GAIN FROM TRADE

All transactions between the residents of different countries fall into one of three categories: trades of goods or services for goods or services, trades of goods or services for assets, and trades of assets for assets. At any moment, a country is generally carrying out trades in each of these categories. Figure 21-1 (which assumes that there are two countries, Home and Foreign) illustrates the three types of international transaction, each of which involves a different set of possible gains from trade.

So far in this book we have discussed two types of trade gain. Chapters 2 through 6 showed that countries can gain by concentrating on the production activities in which they are most efficient and using some of their output to pay for imports of other products from abroad. This type of trade gain involves the exchange of goods or services for other goods or services. The top horizontal arrow in Figure 21-1 shows exchanges of goods and services between Home and Foreign.

A second set of trade gains results from *intertemporal* trade, which is the exchange of goods and services for claims to future goods and services, that is, for assets (Chapters 7 and 18). When a developing country borrows abroad (that is, sells a bond to foreigners) so that it can import materials for a domestic investment project, it is engaging in intertemporal trade. The borrowing country gains from this trade because it can carry out a project that it could not easily finance out of its domestic savings alone; the lending country gains because it gets an asset that yields a higher return than is available at home. The diagonal arrows in Figure 21-1 indicate trades of goods and services for assets. If Home has a current account deficit with Foreign, for example, it is a net exporter of assets to Foreign and a net importer of goods and services from Foreign.

The bottom horizontal arrow in Figure 21-1 represents the last category of international transaction, trades of assets for assets, such as the exchange of real estate located in France for U.S. Treasury bonds. In Table 12-2, which shows the 1994 U.S. balance of payments accounts, you will see under the capital account both a $125.7 billion purchase of foreign assets by U.S. residents (a capital outflow) and a $314.6 billion purchase of U.S. assets by foreign residents (a capital inflow). So while the United States could have financed its $155.7 billion current account deficit for 1994 simply by selling to foreigners

FIGURE 21-1

The Three Types of International Transaction

Residents of different countries can trade goods and services for other goods and services, goods and services for assets (that is, for future goods and services), and assets for other assets. All three types of exchange lead to gains from trade.

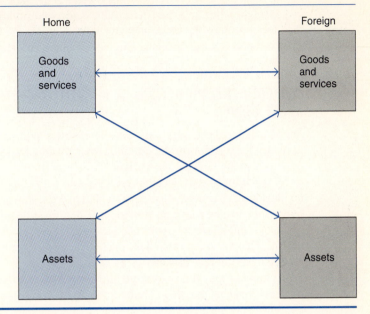

$155.7 billion worth of assets, U.S. and foreign residents also engaged in a considerable volume of pure asset swapping. Such a large volume of trade in assets between countries occurs because international asset trades, like trades involving goods and services, can yield benefits to all the countries involved.

RISK AVERSION

When individuals select assets, an important factor in their decisions is the riskiness of each asset's return (Chapter 13). Other things equal, people dislike risk. Economists call this property of peoples' preferences **risk aversion.** Chapter 17 showed that risk-averse investors in foreign currency assets base their demand for a particular asset on its riskiness (as measured by a risk premium) in addition to its expected return.

An example will make the meaning of risk aversion clearer. Suppose you are offered a gamble in which you win $1000 half the time but lose $1000 half the time. Since you are as likely to win as to lose the $1000, the average payoff on this gamble—its *expected value*—is $(^1/_2) \times (\$1000) + (^1/_2) \times (-\$1000) = 0$. If you are risk averse, you will not take the gamble because, for you, the possibility of losing $1000 outweighs the possibility that you will win, even though both outcomes are equally likely. Although some people (called risk lovers) enjoy taking risks and would take the gamble, there is much evidence that risk-averse behavior is the norm. For example, risk aversion helps explain the profitability of insurance companies, which sell policies that allow people to protect themselves or their families from the financial risks of theft, illness, and other mishaps.

If people are risk averse, they value a collection (or portfolio) of assets not only on the basis of its expected return but also on the basis of the riskiness of that return. Under risk aversion, for example, people may be willing to hold bonds denominated in several different currencies, even if the interest rates they offer are not linked by the interest parity condition, if the resulting portfolio of assets offers a desirable combination of return and risk. In general, a portfolio whose return fluctuates wildly from year to year is less desirable than one that offers the same average return with only mild year-to-year fluctuations. This observation is basic to understanding why countries exchange assets.

PORTFOLIO DIVERSIFICATION AS A MOTIVE FOR INTERNATIONAL ASSET TRADE

International trade in assets can make both parties to the trade better off by allowing them to reduce the riskiness of the return on their wealth. Trade accomplishes this reduction in risk by allowing both parties to diversify their portfolios—to divide their wealth among a wider spectrum of assets and thus reduce the amount of money they have riding on each individual asset. The economist James Tobin of Yale University, an originator of the theory of portfolio choice with risk aversion, has described the idea of **portfolio diversification** as: "Don't put all your eggs in one basket." When an economy is opened to the international capital market, it can reduce the riskiness of its wealth by placing some of its "eggs" in additional foreign "baskets." This reduction in risk is the basic motive for asset trade.

A simple two-country example illustrates how countries are made better off by trade in assets. Imagine that there are two countries, Home and Foreign, and that residents of each own only one asset, domestic land yielding an annual harvest of kiwi fruit.

The yield of the land is uncertain, however. Half the time, Home's land yields a harvest of 100 tons of kiwi fruit at the same time as Foreign's land yields a harvest of 50 tons. The other half the time the outcomes are reversed: The Foreign harvest is 100 tons, but the Home harvest is only 50. On average, then, each country has a harvest of $(1/2) \times (100) + (1/2) \times (50) = 75$ tons of kiwi fruit, but its inhabitants never know whether the next year will bring feast or famine.

Now suppose the two countries can trade shares in the ownership of their respective assets. A Home owner of a 10 percent share in Foreign land, for example, receives 10 percent of the annual Foreign kiwi fruit harvest, and a Foreign owner of a 10 percent share in Home land is similarly entitled to 10 percent of the Home harvest. What happens if international trade in these two assets is allowed? Home residents will buy a 50 percent share of Foreign land, and they will pay for it by giving Foreign residents a 50 percent share in Home land.

To understand why this is the outcome, think about the returns to the Home and Foreign portfolios when both are equally divided between titles to Home and Foreign land. When times are good in Home (and therefore bad in Foreign), each country earns the same return on its portfolio: half of the Home harvest (100 tons of kiwi fruit) plus half of the Foreign harvest (50 tons of kiwi fruit), or 75 tons of fruit. In the opposite case—bad times in Home, good times in Foreign—each country *still* earns 75 tons of fruit. If the countries hold portfolios equally divided between the two assets, therefore, each country earns a *certain* return of 75 tons of fruit—the same as the average harvest each faced before international asset trade was allowed.

Since the two available assets—Home and Foreign land—have the same return on average, any portfolio consisting of those assets yields an expected (or average) return of 75 tons of fruit. Since people everywhere are risk averse, however, all prefer to hold the 50-50 portfolio described above, which gives a sure return of 75 tons of fruit every year. After trade is opened, therefore, residents of the two countries will swap titles to land until the 50-

50 outcome is reached. Because this trade eliminates the risk faced by both countries without changing average returns, both countries are clearly better off as a result of asset trade.

The above example is oversimplified because countries can never really eliminate *all* risk through international asset trade. (Unlike the model's world, the real world is a risky place even in the aggregate!) The example does demonstrate that countries can nonetheless *reduce* the riskiness of their wealth by diversifying their asset portfolios internationally. A major function of the international capital market is to make this diversification possible.[1]

THE MENU OF INTERNATIONAL ASSETS: DEBT VERSUS EQUITY

International asset trades can be exchanges of many different types of assets. Among the many assets traded in the international capital market are bonds and deposits denominated in different currencies, shares of stock, and more complicated financial instruments such as stock or currency options. A purchase of foreign real estate and the direct acquisition of a factory in another country are other ways of diversifying abroad.

In thinking about asset trades it is frequently useful to make a distinction between **debt instruments** and **equity instruments.** Bonds and bank deposits are debt instruments, since they specify that the issuer of the instrument must repay a fixed value (the sum of principal plus interest) regardless of economic circumstances. In contrast, a share of stock is an equity instrument: It is a claim to a firm's profits, rather than to a fixed payment, and its payoff will vary according to circumstance. Similarly, the kiwi fruit shares traded in our example are equity instruments. By choosing how to divide their portfolios between debt and equity instruments, individuals and nations can arrange to stay close to desired consumption and investment levels despite the different eventualities that could occur.

The dividing line between debt and equity is not a neat one in practice. Even if an instrument's money payout is the same in different states of the world, its *real* payout in a particular state will depend on national price levels and exchange rates. In addition, the payments that a given instrument promises to make may not occur in cases of bankruptcy, government seizure of foreign-owned assets, and so on. Assets like low-grade corporate bonds, which superficially appear to be debt, may in reality be like equity in offering payoffs that depend on the doubtful financial fortunes of the issuer. The same has turned out to be true of the debt of many developing countries, as we will see in Chapter 22.

INTERNATIONAL BANKING AND THE INTERNATIONAL CAPITAL MARKET

The Home-Foreign kiwi fruit example above portrayed an imaginary world with only two assets. Since the number of assets available in the real world is enormous, specialized institutions have sprung up to bring together buyers and sellers of assets located in different countries.

---

[1] The Mathematical Postscript to this chapter develops a detailed model of international portfolio diversification. You may have noticed that in our example, countries could reduce risk through transactions other than the asset swap we have described. The high-output country could run a current account surplus and lend to the low-output country, for example, thereby partially evening out the cross-country consumption difference in every state of the world economy. The economic functions of intertemporal trades and of pure asset swaps thus can overlap. To some extent, trade over time can substitute for trade across states of nature, and vice versa, simply because different economic states of the world occur at different points in time. But, in general, the two types of trade are not perfect substitutes for each other.

THE STRUCTURE OF THE INTERNATIONAL CAPITAL MARKET

As we noted above, the main actors in the international capital market include commercial banks, corporations, nonbank financial institutions (such as insurance companies and pension funds), central banks, and other government agencies.

1. *Commercial banks.* Commercial banks are at the center of the international capital market, not only because they run the international payments mechanism but because of the broad range of financial activities they undertake. Bank liabilities consist chiefly of deposits of various maturities, while their assets consist largely of loans (to corporations and governments), deposits at other banks (interbank deposits), and bonds. Multinational banks are also heavily involved in other types of asset transaction. For example, banks may *underwrite* issues of corporate stocks and bonds by agreeing, for a fee, to find buyers for those securities at a guaranteed price. One of the key facts about international banking is that banks are often free to pursue activities abroad that they would not be allowed to pursue in their home countries. This type of regulatory asymmetry has spurred the growth of international banking over the last 30 years.

2. *Corporations.* Corporations—particularly those with multinational operations—routinely finance their investments by drawing on foreign sources of funds. To obtain these funds, corporations may sell shares of stock, which give owners an equity claim to the corporation's assets, or they may use debt finance. Debt finance often takes the form of borrowing from and through international banks or other institutional lenders; when longer-term borrowing is desired, firms may sell corporate debt instruments in the international capital market. Corporations frequently denominate their bonds in the currency of the financial center in which the bonds are being offered for sale. Increasingly, however, corporations have been pursuing novel denomination strategies that make their bonds attractive to a wider spectrum of potential buyers.

3. *Nonbank financial institutions.* Nonbank institutions such as insurance companies, pension funds, and mutual funds have become important players in the international capital market as they have moved into foreign assets to diversify their portfolios. Of particular importance are *investment banks* such as First Boston Corporation, Goldman Sachs, and Lazard Frères, which are not banks at all but specialize in underwriting sales of stocks and bonds by corporations and (in some cases) governments. In 1933 U.S. commercial banks were barred from investment banking activity within the United States (and from most other domestic transactions involving corporate stocks and bonds), although the U.S. government is in the process of easing some of these barriers. But U.S. commercial banks have long been allowed to participate in investment banking activities overseas, and such banks as Citicorp, Morgan Guaranty, and Bankers Trust have competed vigorously with the more specialized investment banks. Figure 21-2 shows how an international consortium of underwriters announced the Spanish government's arrangements for a line of credit denominated in European Currency Units.

4. *Central banks and other government agencies.* Central banks are routinely involved in the international financial markets through foreign exchange intervention. In addition, other government agencies frequently borrow abroad. Developing country governments and state-owned enterprises have borrowed substantially from foreign commercial banks. Even the governments of some Eastern European countries such as Poland and Hungary, which once had communist regimes, are heavily indebted to Western capitalist bankers.

FIGURE 21-2

Government Borrowing in the International Capital Market

In the summer of 1995 a consortium of international underwriters helped Spain's government keep its lines of foreign credit open.

Source: Financial Times, July 19, 1995, p. 13.

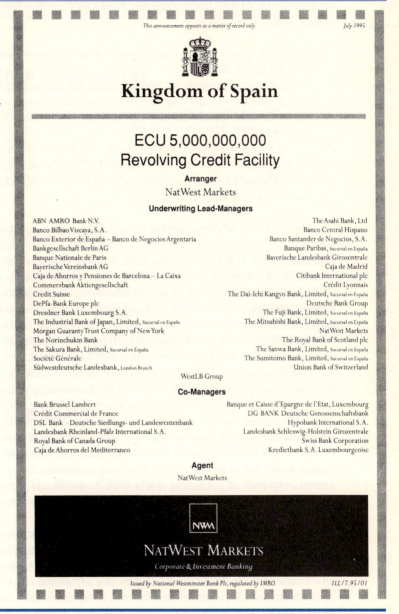

This announcement appears as a matter of record only.   July 1995

Kingdom of Spain

ECU 5,000,000,000
Revolving Credit Facility

Arranger
NatWest Markets

Underwriting Lead-Managers

ABN AMRO Bank N.V.	The Asahi Bank, Ltd
Banco Bilbao Vizcaya, S.A.	Banco Central Hispano
Banco Exterior de España – Banco de Negocios Argentaria	Banco Santander de Negocios, S.A.
Bankgesellschaft Berlin AG	Banque Paribas, Sucursal en España
Banque Nationale de Paris	Bayerische Landesbank Girozentrale
Bayerische Vereinsbank AG	Caja de Madrid
Caja de Ahorros y Pensiones de Barcelona – La Caixa	Citibank International plc
Commerzbank Aktiengesellschaft	Crédit Lyonnais
Credit Suisse	The Dai-Ichi Kangyo Bank, Limited, Sucursal en España
DePfa-Bank Europe plc	Deutsche Bank Group
Dresdner Bank Luxembourg S.A.	The Fuji Bank, Limited, Sucursal en España
The Industrial Bank of Japan, Limited, Sucursal en España	The Mitsubishi Bank, Limited, Sucursal en España
Morgan Guaranty Trust Company of New York	NatWest Markets
The Norinchukin Bank	The Royal Bank of Scotland plc
The Sakura Bank, Limited, Sucursal en España	The Sanwa Bank, Limited, Sucursal en España
Société Générale	The Sumitomo Bank, Limited, Sucursal en España
Südwestdeutsche Landesbank, London Branch	Union Bank of Switzerland

WestLB Group

Co-Managers

Bank Brussel Lambert	Banque et Caisse d'Epargne de l'Etat, Luxembourg
Crédit Commercial de France	DG BANK Deutsche Genossenschaftsbank
DSL Bank - Deutsche Siedlungs- und Landesrentenbank	Hypobank International S.A.
Landesbank Rheinland-Pfalz International S.A.	Landesbank Schleswig-Holstein Girozentrale
Royal Bank of Canada Group	Swiss Bank Corporation
Caja de Ahorros del Mediterraneo	Kredietbank S.A. Luxembourgeoise

Agent
NatWest Markets

NWM
NATWEST MARKETS
Corporate & Investment Banking

Issued by National Westminster Bank Plc, regulated by IMRO.   ILL/7.95/01

OFFSHORE BANKING AND OFFSHORE CURRENCY TRADING

One of the most pervasive features of the commercial banking industry in the 1990s is that banking activities have become globalized as banks have branched out from their home countries into foreign financial centers. In 1960 only eight American banks had branches

Balance Sheet of Deutsche Bank, London

Change in assets		*Change in liabilities*	
Deposits at Bankers Trust	+$35,000	Customers' deposits (Philips account)	+$35,000

Balance Sheet of Bankers Trust, New York

Change in assets		*Change in liabilities*	
Reserves at Fed	+$35,000	Customers' deposits (Deutsche Bank account)	+$35,000

In this case, the supply of Eurodollars rises by $75,000—the $40,000 deposited at Barclays by Daimler-Benz plus the $35,000 deposited at Deutsche Bank by Philips. As before, the U.S. monetary base is unaffected: The net result of the long chain of transactions is simply a transfer of reserves from Citibank's Fed account (which falls by $40,000) to those of Chase and Bankers Trust (which rise by $5000 and $35,000, respectively). Obviously, the process can continue further if Deutsche Bank lends out part of the $35,000 deposited by Philips rather than holding it all in its Bankers Trust account in New York. The $40,000 paid out by the U.S. auto buyer who initiates all this, however, always finds its way back to the U.S. banking system. Once again, the expansion in the volume of Eurodollars can occur without any dollars ever having to "leave" the United States.[3]

Eurodollars and the U.S. Balance of Payments.   Another assertion often made about Eurodollars is that growth in the Eurodollar supply requires continuing U.S. balance of payments deficits. The example shows that this statement is also incorrect. The $40,000 paid to import a car from Germany enters the U.S. current account as a debit. Offsetting this debit is a capital account credit of $40,000, which reflects the $5000 deposit at Chase acquired by Barclays and the $35,000 deposit at Bankers Trust acquired by Deutsche Bank. The net effect on the U.S. balance of payments is nil, even though the Eurodollar supply rises by $75,000.

---

[3]There is a slight inaccuracy in the preceding example due to the technicalities of measuring the U.S. money supply. Deposits by foreign banks in U.S. banks are *not* counted by the Fed as part of the U.S. money supply, so when our imaginary American buys his Mercedes, extinguishing his own $40,000 deposit at Citibank and (indirectly) creating a $40,000 deposit at Chase owned by Barclays Bank, the measured U.S. money supply drops by $40,000. However, the monetary base doesn't change, and it is still true that the *second* round of Eurocurrency creation analyzed above (which occurs after Barclays lends $35,000 to Philips) raises the Eurodollar supply by $35,000 with no change in any U.S. monetary aggregate. So it might be more accurate to say that Eurodollar expansion never affects the U.S. monetary base and need not affect the U.S. money supply. The first part of our example shows an instance in which Eurodollar transactions alter the money multipliers linking the base to broader monetary aggregates. We return to this issue in a moment.

THE GROWTH OF EUROCURRENCY TRADING

Earlier we outlined the main reasons for the growth of offshore banking activities: (1) the growth of world trade; (2) government financial regulations (including taxes); and (3) political considerations. The growth of Eurocurrency trading illustrates the importance of all three of these factors in the internationalization of banking.

Eurodollars were born in the late 1950s, a response to the needs generated by a growing volume of international trade. European firms involved in trade frequently wished to hold dollar balances or to borrow dollars. In many cases, banks located in the United States could have served these needs, but Europeans often found it cheaper and more convenient to deal with local banks familiar with their circumstances. As currencies other than the dollar became increasingly convertible after the late 1950s, offshore markets for them sprang up also.

While the convenience of dealing with local banks was a key factor inspiring the invention of Eurodollars, the growth of Eurodollar trading was encouraged at an early stage by both of the two other factors we have mentioned: official regulations and political concerns.

In 1957, at the height of a balance of payments crisis, the British government prohibited British banks from lending pounds to finance non-British trade. This lending had been a highly profitable business, and to avoid losing it British banks began financing the same trade by attracting dollar deposits and lending dollars instead of pounds. Because stringent financial regulations prevented the British banks' nonsterling transactions from affecting Britain's domestic asset markets, the government was willing to take a laissez-faire attitude toward foreign currency activities. As a result, London became—and has remained—the leading center of Eurocurrency trading.

The political factor stimulating the Eurodollar market's early growth was a surprising one—the Cold War between the United States and the U.S.S.R. During the 1950s the Soviet Union acquired dollars (largely through sales of gold and other raw materials) so that it could purchase goods such as grains from the West. The Soviets feared the United States might confiscate dollars placed in American banks if the Cold War were to heat up. So instead, Soviet dollars were placed in European banks, which had the advantage of residing outside America's jurisdiction. Indeed, the folklore of international banking has it that the term *Eurobank* originated as the telex code of a Soviet-controlled Paris bank.

The Eurodollar system mushroomed in the 1960s as a result of new U.S. restrictions on capital outflows and U.S. banking regulations. As America's balance of payments weakened in the 1960s, the Kennedy and Johnson administrations imposed a series of measures to discourage American lending abroad. The first of these was the Interest Equalization Tax of 1963, which discouraged Americans from buying foreign assets by taxing those assets' returns. Next, in 1965, came "voluntary" guidelines on the amounts U.S. commercial banks could lend abroad, followed three years later by a set of wide-ranging mandatory controls. All these measures increased the demand for Eurodollar loans by making it harder for would-be dollar borrowers located abroad to obtain the funds they wanted in the United States.

Federal Reserve regulations on U.S. banks also encouraged the creation of Eurodollars—and new Eurobanks—in the 1960s. The Fed's Regulation Q (which was phased out after 1980) placed a ceiling on the interest rates U.S. banks could pay on time deposits. When U.S. monetary policy was tightened at the end of the 1960s to combat rising inflationary pressures (see Chapter 18), market interest rates were driven above the Regulation Q ceiling and American banks found it impossible to attract time deposits for relending.

The banks got around the problem by borrowing funds from their European branches, which faced no restriction on the interest they could pay on Eurodollar deposits and were able to attract deposits from investors who might have placed their funds with U.S. banks in the absence of Regulation Q. Many American banks that had previously not had foreign branches established them in the late 1960s so that they could end-run Regulation Q.

With the move to floating exchange rates in 1973, the United States and other countries began to dismantle controls on capital flows across their borders, removing an important impetus to the growth of Eurocurrency markets in earlier years. But at that point, the political factor once again came into play in a big way. Arab members of OPEC accumulated vast wealth as a result of the oil shocks of 1973–1974 and 1979–1980 but were reluctant to place most of their money in American banks for fear of possible confiscation. Instead, these countries placed funds with Eurobanks. (In 1979 Iranian assets in U.S. banks and their European branches were frozen by President Carter in response to the taking of hostages at the American embassy in Teheran. A similar fate befell Iraq's U.S. assets after that country invaded neighboring Kuwait in 1990.)

THE IMPORTANCE OF REGULATORY ASYMMETRIES

The history of Eurocurrencies shows how the growth of world trade, financial regulations, and political considerations all helped form the present system. The major factor behind the continuing profitability of Eurocurrency trading is, however, regulatory: In formulating bank regulations, governments in the main Eurocurrency centers discriminate between deposits denominated in the home currency and those denominated in others and between transactions with domestic customers and those with foreign customers. Domestic currency deposits are heavily regulated as a way of maintaining control over the domestic money supply, while banks are given much more freedom in their dealings in foreign currencies. Domestic currency deposits held by foreign customers may receive special treatment, however, if regulators feel they can insulate the domestic financial system from shifts in foreigners' asset demands.

The example of U.S. *reserve requirements* shows how regulatory asymmetries can operate to enhance the profitability of Eurocurrency trading. Every time a U.S. bank operating onshore accepts a deposit, it must place some fraction of that deposit in a non-interest-bearing account at the Fed as part of its required reserves.[4] The British government imposes reserve requirements on *pound sterling* deposits within its borders, but it does not impose reserve requirements on *dollar* deposits within its borders. Nor are the London branches of U.S. banks subject to U.S. reserve requirements on dollar deposits, provided those deposits are payable only outside the United States. A London Eurobank therefore has a competitive advantage over a bank in New York in attracting dollar deposits: It can pay more interest to its depositors than the New York bank while still covering its operating costs. The Eurobank's competitive advantage comes from its ability to avoid a "tax" (the reserve requirement) that the Fed imposes on domestic banks' dollar deposits.

To understand this competitive advantage, suppose the New York bank faces a 10 percent reserve requirement. If the bank receives a $100 deposit, it can relend at most $90 and is obliged to place $10 in its Fed account, which pays no interest. Suppose the bank has an-

---

[4]Alternatively, the bank could add the same amount to its holdings of vault cash, which also pay no interest. The discussion assumes the bank holds reserves at the Fed.

nual operating costs equal to $1 per $100 of deposits and the interest rate on bank loans is 10 percent per year. Then the New York bank can offer its depositors an interest rate of at most 8 percent and still cover its costs. At that deposit rate, the bank pays the owner of the $100 dollar deposit $0.08 \times $100 = $8, while earning $0.10 \times $90 = $9 on the fraction of the deposit it can relend. So the bank is just able to cover its $1 operating expense out of the difference between what it gets from the borrower and what it pays to the depositor.

In contrast, a Eurobank can offer a higher interest rate on dollar deposits than the New York bank. The Eurobank, which faces no reserve requirement, can lend *all* of a $100 deposit, and therefore it can earn $0.10 \times $100 = $10 at a loan rate of 10 percent. If the Eurobank pays its depositors interest of 9 percent, the owner of a $100 deposit gets $9, and the difference, $10 - $9 = $1, just covers the bank's operating cost. Because the Eurobank faces no reserve requirement, it is able to offer its depositors an interest rate that is a full percentage point higher than what the New York bank can offer. Interest rates on Eurodollar deposits are always higher than rates on comparable time deposits located in the United States (in fact as well as in theory), and many depositors have been lured to the Eurocurrency markets by the higher interest rates Eurobanks offer.

Eurobanks can compete with onshore banks on the loan side also by offering lower interest rates to borrowers, but competition in the loan market tends to drive all banks' loan charges to approximate equality. Why are any depositors willing to hold onshore time deposits when they offer lower yields than Eurocurrency deposits? Part of the reason is that the regulations faced by onshore banks make domestic deposits less susceptible to the risk of bank failure. The risk that depositors' claims will not be honored is greater in the unregulated Eurocurrency market, and the higher deposit rates paid there compensate depositors for bearing this risk.

Freedom from reserve requirements is probably the most important regulatory factor that makes Eurocurrency trading attractive to banks and their customers, but there are others. For example, Eurodollar deposits are available in shorter maturities than the corresponding time deposits banks are allowed to issue in the United States. Regulatory asymmetries like these explain why those financial centers whose governments impose the fewest restrictions on foreign currency banking have become the main Eurocurrency centers. London is the leader in this respect, but it has been followed by Luxembourg, Bahrain, Hong Kong, and other countries that have competed for international banking business by lowering restrictions and taxes on foreign bank operations within their borders.

Neither the United States nor Germany has attracted a significant share of the world's Eurocurrency business because both countries apply fairly uniform regulations to all domestic deposits, regardless of their currency of denomination. Recently, however, the U.S. government has tried to help the American banking industry get more of the action. In 1981, the Fed allowed resident banks to set up **international banking facilities (IBFs)** in the United States for the purpose of accepting time deposits and making loans to foreign customers. IBFs are not subject to reserve requirements or interest rate ceilings, and they are exempt from state and local taxes. But an IBF is prohibited from accepting deposits from or lending money to U.S. residents (other than the establishing bank or another IBF). Before 1981, much of the business currently carried out by IBFs was done less efficiently through "shell" branch offices located in the Caribbean.

Technically speaking, a dollar deposit in an IBF is not a Eurodollar because the IBF resides physically within the United States. U.S. regulators have imposed rules, however, that fence off IBFs from onshore banks as effectively as if the IBF were overseas. IBFs provide an excellent example of how countries have lured lucrative international banking

face rules against lending too large a fraction of their assets to a single private customer or to a single foreign government borrower.

4. *Bank examination.* The Fed, the FDIC, and the Office of the Comptroller of the Currency all have the right to examine a bank's books to ensure compliance with bank capital standards and other regulations. Banks may be forced to sell assets that the examiner deems too risky or to adjust their balance sheets by writing off loans the examiner thinks will not be repaid.

5. *Lender of last-resort facilities.* U.S. banks can borrow from the Fed's discount window. While discounting is a tool of monetary management, the Fed can also use discounting to prevent bank panics. Since the Fed has the ability to create currency, it can lend to banks facing massive deposit outflows as much as they need to satisfy their depositors' claims. When the Fed acts in this way, it is acting as a **lender of last resort (LLR)** to the bank. When depositors know the Fed is standing by as the LLR, they have more confidence in the bank's ability to withstand a panic and are therefore less likely to run if financial trouble looms. The administration of LLR facilities is complex, however. If banks think the central bank will *always* bail them out, they will take excessive risks. So the central bank must make access to its LLR services conditional on sound management. To decide when banks in trouble have not brought it on themselves through unwise risk taking, the LLR must be involved in the bank examination process.

The banking safeguards listed above are interdependent: Laxness in one area may cause other safeguards to backfire. Deposit insurance alone, for example, may encourage bankers to make risky loans because depositors no longer have any reason to withdraw their funds even from carelessly managed banks. The recent U.S. S&L crisis is a case in point. In the early 1980s, the U.S. deregulated the S&Ls. Before deregulation, S&Ls had largely been restricted to home mortgage lending; after, they were allowed to make much riskier loans, for example, loans on commercial real estate. At the same time this deregulation was occurring, bank examination was inadequate for the new situation and depositors, lulled by government-provided insurance, had no reason to be vigilant about the possibility that S&L managers might finance foolish ventures. The result was a wave of S&L failures that left taxpayers holding the bill for the insured deposits.

The U.S. commercial bank safety net worked reasonably well until the late 1980s, but as a result of deregulation, the 1990–1991 recession, and a sharp fall in commercial property values, bank closings rose dramatically and the FDIC insurance fund was depleted. The U.S. government is currently in the process of overhauling its system of banking safeguards. Like the United States, other countries that deregulated domestic banking in the 1980s—including Japan, the Scandinavian countries, the United Kingdom, and even Switzerland—faced serious problems a decade later.

DIFFICULTIES IN REGULATING INTERNATIONAL BANKING

Banking regulations of the type used in the United States and other countries become even less effective in an international environment where banks can shift their business among different regulatory jurisdictions. A good way of seeing why an international banking system is harder to regulate than a national one is to look at how the effectiveness of the U.S. safeguards just described is reduced as a result of offshore banking activities.

1. Deposit insurance is essentially absent in international banking. National deposit insurance systems may protect domestic and foreign depositors alike, but the amount of insurance available is invariably too small to cover the size of deposit usual in international banking. In particular, interbank deposits are unprotected.

2. The absence of reserve requirements has been a major factor in the growth of Eurocurrency trading. While Eurobanks derive a competitive advantage from escaping the required reserve tax, there is a social cost in terms of the reduced stability of the banking system. No country can solve the problem single-handedly by imposing reserve requirements on its own banks' overseas branches. Concerted international action is blocked, however, by the political and technical difficulty of agreeing on an internationally uniform set of regulations and by the reluctance of some countries to drive banking business away by tightening regulations.

3. and 4. Bank examination to enforce capital requirements and asset restrictions becomes more difficult in an international setting. National bank regulators usually monitor the balance sheets of domestic banks and their foreign branches on a consolidated basis. But they are less strict in keeping track of banks' foreign subsidiaries and affiliates, which are more tenuously tied to the parent bank but whose financial fortunes may affect the parent's solvency. Banks have often been able to take advantage of this laxity by shifting risky business that home regulators might question to regulatory jurisdictions where fewer questions are asked. Further, it is often unclear which group of regulators has responsibility for monitoring a given bank's assets. Suppose the London subsidiary of an Italian bank deals primarily in Eurodollars. Should the subsidiary's assets be the concern of British, Italian, or American regulators?

5. There is uncertainty over which central bank, if any, is responsible for providing LLR assistance in international banking. The problem is similar to the one that arises in allocating responsibility for bank supervision. Let's return to the example of the London subsidiary of an Italian bank. Should the Fed bear responsibility for saving the subsidiary from a sudden drain of dollar deposits? Should the Bank of England step in? Or should the Banca d'Italia bear the ultimate responsibility? When central banks provide LLR assistance they increase their domestic money supplies and may compromise domestic macroeconomic objectives. In an international setting, a central bank may also be providing resources to a bank located abroad whose behavior it is not equipped to monitor. Central banks are therefore reluctant to extend the coverage of their LLR responsibilities. The problems surrounding the 1982 failure of Italy's Banco Ambrosiano, discussed in the box on page 670, illustrate how international banking can lead to gaps in LLR coverage.

INTERNATIONAL REGULATORY COOPERATION

The internationalization of banking has weakened national safeguards against banking collapse, but at the same time it has made the need for effective safeguards more urgent. Offshore banking involves a tremendous volume of interbank deposits—roughly 80 percent of all Eurocurrency deposits, for example, are owned by private banks. A high level of interbank depositing implies that problems affecting a single bank could be highly contagious and could spread quickly to banks with which it is thought to do business. Through this ripple effect, a localized disturbance could, conceivably, set off a banking panic on a global scale.

This nightmarish scenario has haunted central bankers and other government officials since offshore banking began to grow rapidly in the 1960s. Little was done, however, until 1974. In that year a number of banks failed as a result of foreign exchange losses, among them the Franklin National Bank in the United States and Germany's Bankhaus I. D. Herstatt. The failures sent tremors through the international financial markets, and the volume of international lending dropped sharply.

In response to the 1974 banking crises, central bank heads from 11 industrialized countries set up a group called the **Basle Committee** whose job was to achieve "a better co-ordination of the surveillance exercised by national authorities over the international banking system. . . ." (The group was named after Basle, Switzerland, the home of the central bankers' meeting place, the Bank for International Settlements.) The Basle Committee remains the major forum for cooperation among bank regulators from different countries.

In 1975 the Committee reached an agreement, called the Concordat, which allocated responsibility for supervising multinational banking establishments between parent and

THE BANCO AMBROSIANO COLLAPSE

The collapse of Italy's most important private bank in June 1982 is a vivid illustration of how the intricate cross-border links between financial institutions can frustrate bank supervisors and cause financial crises. The Banco Ambrosiano failure is notorious, however, because of the bank president's close connections with a subversive political group and with the Vatican. Roberto Calvi, the president of Banco Ambrosiano, stood at the center of a vast international financial network spanning Europe, the Caribbean, and South America. In 1981 Calvi was convicted of violating Italian foreign exchange regulations. At the same time, government investigators obtained the membership roster of a secret lodge of right-wing freemasons known as Propaganda-2 (or P-2). P-2 numbered Calvi and many other influential Italians among its members, including two cabinet ministers. The government of Prime Minister Arnaldo Forlani was forced to resign, and P-2 was outlawed.

Because Banco Ambrosiano had become the object of such close scrutiny by the government and the press, it soon became known that some of the bank's loans were weak. This revelation led to a deposit run. Italy's central bank, the Banca d'Italia, set up a con-sortium of Italy's major banks that took over many of Banco Ambrosiano's assets and liabilities and established a new bank, Nuovo Banco Ambrosiano.

The Banca d'Italia exercised its LLR function by ensuring that Nuovo Banco Ambrosiano repaid domestic and foreign residents who had placed deposits with Banco Ambrosiano itself. The central bank did not, however, guarantee the liabilities of Banco Ambrosiano's foreign subsidiaries. Banco Ambrosiano and its subsidiaries allegedly had extensive financial connections with the Catholic Church's Institute for Religious Works (sometimes called the "Vatican bank"). As a result of the many claims raised by Banco Ambrosiano's failure, the Vatican bank's finances came under investigation.

Calvi himself never saw the ramifications of his bank's collapse. In mid-June 1982 he disappeared from Italy. Shortly afterward he was found dead, hanging from Blackfriars Bridge in London, his pockets stuffed with rocks. It has never been determined if he died by suicide or murder.[*]

[*]For a lively account of the Banco Ambrosiano scandal and its background, see Rupert Cornwell, "God's Banker" (New York: Dodd, Mead & Company, 1984). The 1991 film *The Godfather, Part III* derived part of its plot from the Ambrosiano affair.

host countries. (A revised Concordat was issued in 1983.) In addition, the Concordat called for the sharing of information about banks by parent and host regulators and for "the granting of permission for inspections by or on behalf of parent authorities on the territory of the host authority."[8] In further work the Basle Committee has located loopholes in the supervision of multinational banks and brought these to the attention of national authorities. The Committee has recommended, for example, that regulatory agencies monitor the assets of banks' foreign subsidiaries as well as their branches. Much of the group's work has been devoted to developing better data on the balance sheets of multinational banks, a prerequisite to more effective supervision.

A major step toward reconciling countries' supervisory practices was taken in January 1988 when the Basle Committee agreed to a set of common standards for assessing bank capital adequacy. These standards require international banks to hold capital equal to at least 8 percent of their risk-weighted assets plus off-balance-sheet commitments. This 8 percent requirement is high by historical standards for some banks (for example, Japan's). But the narrow escape from financial crisis during the worldwide stock market crash of October 1987 presented the Committee with a persuasive case for tough standards.

While the work of the Basle Committee has improved the supervision of multinational banks, little has been done to clarify the division of LLR responsibilities among countries. Following the 1974 bank failures, central bankers discussed the provision of international LLR facilities but declined to announce any definite agreement. There is speculation that such an agreement exists but that central bankers have kept it secret to avoid suggesting an automatic bailout for banks that take unwise risks and get into trouble.

The international activities of nonbank financial institutions are another potential trouble spot. International cooperation in bank supervision has come a long way since the early 1970s, but regulators are just starting to grapple with the problems raised by nonbank financial firms. Their task is, however, an important one. The failure of a major securities house, for example, like the failure of a bank, could seriously disrupt national payments and credit networks. Increasing **securitization** (in which bank assets are repackaged in readily marketable forms) has made it harder for regulators to get an accurate picture of global financial flows by examining bank balance sheets alone. As a result, the need for authorities to collect and pool data on internationally active nonbanks has become acute. In 1992 the European Union moved to impose uniform capital requirements on securities firms and on banks' trading operations.

How Well Has the International Capital Market Performed?

The present structure of the international capital market involves risks of financial instability that can be reduced only through the close cooperation of bank supervisors in many countries. But the same profit motive that leads multinational financial institutions to innovate their way around national regulations can also provide important gains for consumers. As we have seen, the international capital market allows residents of different countries to diversify their portfolios by trading risky assets. Further, by ensuring a rapid international flow of information about investment opportunities around the world, the market can help allocate the world's savings to their most productive uses. How well has the international capital market performed in these respects?

---

[8]The Concordat was summarized in these terms by W. P. Cooke of the Bank of England, then chairman of the Basle Committee, in "Developments in Co-operation Among Banking Supervisory Authorities," *Bank of England Quarterly Bulletin* 21 (June 1981), pp. 238–244.

THE EXTENT OF INTERNATIONAL PORTFOLIO DIVERSIFICATION

Since accurate data on the overall portfolio positions of a country's residents are often impossible to assemble, it is not feasible to gauge the extent of international portfolio diversification by direct observation. Nonetheless, some U.S. data can be used to get a rough idea about changes in international diversification in recent years.

In 1970 the foreign assets held by U.S. residents were equal in value to 6.2 percent of the U.S. capital stock. Foreign claims on the United States amounted to 4.0 percent of its capital stock (including residential housing). By 1993, U.S.-owned assets abroad equaled 13.2 percent of U.S. capital, while foreign assets in the United States had risen to 15.7 percent of U.S. capital.

These percentages seem small; with full international portfolio diversification, we would expect them to reflect the size of the U.S. economy relative to that of the rest of the world. Thus, in a fully diversified world economy, something like 70 percent of the U.S. capital stock would be owned by foreigners, while U.S. residents' claims on foreigners would equal around 70 percent of the value of the U.S. capital stock. What makes the apparently low extent of international portfolio diversification even more puzzling is the presumption most economists would make that the potential gains from diversification are large. An influential study by the French financial economist Bruno Solnik, for example, estimated that a U.S. investor holding only American stocks could more than halve the riskiness of her portfolio by further diversification into stocks from European countries.[9]

The data do show, however, that diversification has increased substantially as a result of the growth of the international capital market since 1970. Further, international asset holdings are large in absolute terms. At the end of 1993, for example, U.S. claims on foreigners were about $2.6 trillion, equal to 41.7 percent of the U.S. GNP in that year, while foreign claims on the United States were about $3.2 trillion, or 49.7 percent of U.S. GNP. Stock exchanges around the world are establishing closer communication links, and companies are showing an increasing readiness to sell shares on foreign exchanges. Japan (as noted above) began a gradual but continuing opening of its financial markets in the late 1970s; Britain removed restrictions barring its public from international asset trade in 1979; and the European Union embarked in the late 1980s on a broad program of market unification meant to integrate its financial markets more fully into the global capital market.

The seemingly low extent of international portfolio diversification attained so far is not a strong indictment of the world capital market. The market has certainly contributed to a rise in diversification since the early 1970s, despite some remaining impediments to international capital movement. Further, there is no foolproof measure of the socially optimal extent of diversification; in particular, the existence of nontraded products can cut down significantly the gains from international asset trade. What seems certain is that asset trade will continue to expand as barriers to the international flow of capital are progressively dismantled.

THE EXTENT OF INTERTEMPORAL TRADE

An alternative way of evaluating the performance of the world capital market has been suggested by the economists Martin Feldstein and Charles Horioka. Feldstein and Horioka

---

[9]See Solnik, "Why Not Diversify Internationally Rather than Domestically?" *Financial Analysts Journal* (July-August 1974), pp. 48–54.

FIGURE 21-3

Saving and Investment Rates for 22 Industrial Countries, 1982–1991 Averages

Industrial countries' saving and investment ratios to GNP tend to be positively related.

Source: OECD, *National Income Accounts.*

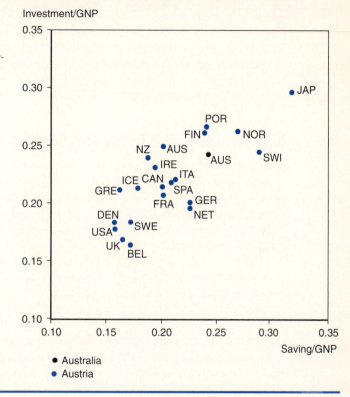

pointed out that a smoothly working international capital market allows countries' domestic investment rates to diverge widely from their saving rates. In such an idealized world, saving seeks out its most productive uses worldwide, regardless of their location; at the same time, domestic investment is not limited by national saving because a global pool of funds is available to finance it.

For many countries, however, differences between national saving and domestic investment rates (that is, current account balances) have not been large since World War II: countries with high saving rates over long periods also have high investment rates, as Figure 21-3 illustrates. Feldstein and Horioka concluded from this evidence that cross-border capital mobility is low, in the sense that most of any sustained increase in national saving will lead to increased capital accumulation at home. The world capital market, according to this view, does not do a good job of helping countries reap the long-run gains from intertemporal trade.[10]

The main problem with the Feldstein-Horioka argument is that it is impossible to gauge whether the extent of intertemporal trade is deficient without knowing if there are

---

[10]See Martin Feldstein and Charles Horioka, "Domestic Savings and International Capital Flows," *Economic Journal* 90 (June 1980), pp. 314–329.

unexploited trade gains, and knowing this requires more knowledge about actual economies than we generally have. For example, a country's saving and investment may usually move together simply because the factors that generate a high saving rate (such as rapid economic growth) also generate a high investment rate. In such cases, the country's gain from intertemporal trade may simply be small. An alternative explanation of high saving-investment correlations is that governments have tried to manage macroeconomic policy to avoid large current account imbalances. In any case, events appear to be overtaking this particular debate. For industrialized countries, the empirical regularity noted by Feldstein and Horioka seems to have weakened recently in the face of the historically high external imbalances of the United States, Germany, and Japan.

ONSHORE-OFFSHORE INTEREST DIFFERENTIALS

A quite different barometer of the international capital market's performance is the relationship between onshore and offshore interest rates on similar assets denominated in the same currency. If the world capital market is doing its job of communicating information about global investment opportunities, these interest rates should move closely together and not differ too greatly. Large interest rate differences would be strong evidence of unrealized gains from trade.

Figure 21-4 shows data from a 1982 study of the interest rate difference between two comparable dollar bank liabilities, three-month Eurodollar deposits and certificates of deposit issued in the United States. As we saw earlier, these rates should differ mainly by the required reserve "tax" on domestic banks, provided Eurobanks are competitive and efficient. The black line (showing the difference between the offshore and onshore rates) confirms that Eurodollar interest rates are always higher than the corresponding domestic rates, as our theory predicts. The colored line (which adjusts the interest rate difference to account for the required reserve tax) shows that the adjusted differential typically was low after the mid-1970s. Thus, these data provide no indication of large unexploited gains.

Studies of Germany and the Netherlands, countries with open capital markets, also show an approximate equality between onshore and offshore interest rates. The same equality has held for Japan since it completed a major step in its program of phased capital account liberalization in December 1980. France and Italy maintained capital controls until the late 1980s, but onshore and offshore rates, which had tended to move in tandem even before, converged quickly after those countries began dismantling the restrictions.[11]

THE EFFICIENCY OF THE FOREIGN EXCHANGE MARKET

The foreign exchange market is a central component of the international capital market, and the exchange rates it sets help determine the profitability of international transactions

---

[11]On the European countries, see Francesco Giavazzi and Marco Pagano, "Capital Controls and the European Monetary System" in *Capital Controls and Foreign Exchange Legislation,* Occasional Paper 1. Milan, Italy: Euromobiliare, June 1985, pp. 19–38. The Japanese case is investigated by Takatoshi Ito, "Capital Controls and Covered Interest Parity," *Economic Studies Quarterly* 37 (September 1986), pp. 223–241. A detailed study on the United States is in Lawrence L. Kreicher, "Eurodollar Arbitrage," *Federal Reserve Bank of New York Quarterly Review* 7 (1982), pp. 10–21. An examination of Germany between 1970 and 1974, when capital controls were in effect, found large differences between onshore and offshore DM interest rates. See Michael P. Dooley and Peter Isard, "Capital Controls, Political Risk, and Deviations from Interest-Rate Parity," *Journal of Political Economy* 88 (April 1980), pp. 370–384. A recent overview is contained in the paper by Obstfeld in Further Reading.

FIGURE 21-4

Comparing Eurodollar and Onshore Interest Rates

When adjusted for the required reserve "tax," the difference between the Eurodollar interest rate and the domestic U.S. certificate of deposit rate is usually very close to zero.

Source: Edward J. Frydl, "The Eurodollar Conundrum," *Federal Reserve Bank of New York Quarterly Review* 7 (Spring 1982), p. 13.

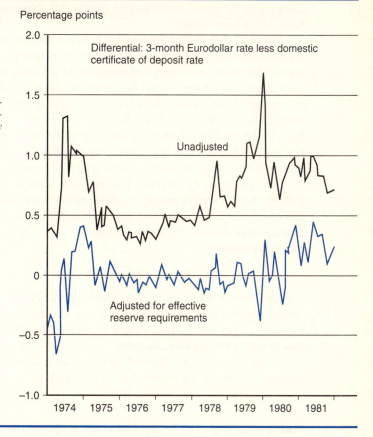

Percentage points

Differential: 3-month Eurodollar rate less domestic certificate of deposit rate

Unadjusted

Adjusted for effective reserve requirements

of all types. Exchange rates therefore communicate important economic signals to households and firms engaged in international trade and investment. If these signals do not reflect all available information about market opportunities, a misallocation of resources will result. Studies of the foreign exchange market's use of available information are therefore potentially important in judging whether the international capital market is sending the right signals to markets.

Studies Based on Interest Parity. The interest parity condition that was the basis of the discussion of exchange rate determination in Chapter 13 has also been used to study whether market exchange rates incorporate all available information. Recall that interest parity holds when the interest difference between deposits denominated in different currencies is the market's forecast of the percentage by which the exchange rate between those two currencies will change. More formally, if R_t is the date-t interest rate on home currency deposits, R_t^* the interest rate on foreign currency deposits, E_t the exchange rate (defined as the home-currency price of foreign currency), and E_{t+1}^e the exchange rate market participants expect when the deposits paying interest R_t and R_t^* mature, the interest parity condition is

$$R_t - R_t^* = (E_{t+1}^e - E_t)/E_t. \tag{21-1}$$

(see Chapter 17). In this case, the interest difference is not necessarily the market's forecast of future depreciation. Thus, under imperfect asset substitutability, the empirical results just discussed cannot be used to draw inferences about the foreign exchange market's efficiency in processing information.

Because people's expectations are inherently unobservable, there is no simple way to decide between equation (21-4) and the interest parity condition, which is the special case that occurs when ρ_t is always zero. Several econometric studies have attempted to explain departures from interest parity on the basis of particular theories of the risk premium, but none has been entirely successful.[14]

The mixed empirical record leaves the following two possibilities: Either risk premiums are important in exchange rate determination, or the foreign exchange market has been ignoring the opportunity to profit from easily available information. The second alternative seems unlikely in light of foreign exchange traders' powerful incentives to make profits. The first alternative, however, awaits solid statistical confirmation. It is certainly not supported by the evidence reviewed in Chapter 17, which suggests that sterilized foreign exchange intervention has not been an effective tool for exchange rate management. More sophisticated theories show, however, that sterilized intervention may be powerless even under imperfect asset substitutability. Thus, a finding that sterilized intervention is ineffective does not necessarily imply that risk premiums are absent.

Tests for Excessive Volatility.   One of the most worrisome findings is that statistical forecasting models of exchange rates based on standard "fundamental" variables like money supplies, government deficits, and output perform badly—even when *actual* (rather than predicted) values of future fundamentals are used to form exchange rate forecasts! Indeed, in a famous study, Richard A. Meese of the University of California at Berkeley and Kenneth Rogoff of Princeton University showed that a naive "random walk" model, which simply takes today's exchange rate as the best guess of tomorrow's, does better. Some have viewed this finding as evidence that exchange rates have a life of their own, unrelated to the macroeconomic determinants we have emphasized in our models. More recent research has confirmed, however, that while the random walk outperforms more sophisticated models for forecasts up to a year away, the models do better at horizons longer than a year and have considerable explanatory power for long-run exchange rate movements.[15]

An additional line of research on the foreign exchange market examines whether exchange rates have been excessively volatile, perhaps because the foreign exchange market "overreacts" to events. A finding of excessive volatility would prove that the foreign exchange market is sending confusing signals to traders and investors who base their decisions on exchange rates. But how volatile must an exchange rate be before its volatility becomes excessive? As we saw in Chapter 13, exchange rates *should* be volatile, because to send the correct price signals they must move swiftly in response to economic news. It is possible, though, that exchange rates are substantially more volatile than the underlying

---

[14]For recent surveys see Charles Engel, "The Forward Discount Anomaly and the Risk Premium: A Survey of Recent Evidence," *Journal of Empirical Finance,* 1996; and Karen Lewis, "Puzzles in International Finance," in Gene M. Grossman and Kenneth Rogoff, *Handbook of International Economics,* vol. 3 (Amsterdam: North-Holland, 1996).

[15]The original Meese-Rogoff study is "Empirical Exchange Rate Models of the Seventies: Do They Fit out of Sample?" *Journal of International Economics* 14 (February 1983), pp. 3–24. On longer-run forecasts, see Menzie D. Chinn and Richard A. Meese, "Banking on Currency Forecasts: How Predictable Is Change in Money?" *Journal of International Economics* 38 (February 1995), pp. 161–178; and Nelson C. Mark, "Exchange Rates and Fundamentals: Evidence on Long-Horizon Predictability," *American Economic Review* 85 (March 1995), pp. 201–218.

factors that move them—such as money supplies, national outputs, and fiscal variables. Attempts to compare exchange rates' volatility with those of their underlying determinants have, however, produced inconclusive results.[16] A basic problem underlying tests for excessive volatility is the impossibility of quantifying exactly all the variables that convey relevant news about the economic future. For example, how does one attach a number to a political assassination attempt or a major bank failure?

The Bottom Line.   The ambiguous evidence on the foreign exchange market's performance warrants an open-minded view. Such a view is particularly advisable because the statistical methods that have been used to study exchange rates are very imperfect. A judgment that the market is doing its job well would support a laissez-faire attitude by governments and a continuation of the present trend toward increased cross-border financial integration in the industrial world. A judgment of market failure, on the other hand, might imply a need for increased foreign exchange intervention by central banks and a reversal of the trend toward capital account liberalization. The stakes are high, and more research and experience are needed before a firm conclusion can be reached.

Summary

1. When people are *risk averse,* countries can gain through the exchange of risky assets. The gains from trade take the form of a reduction in the riskiness of each country's consumption. International *portfolio diversification* can be carried out through the exchange of *debt instruments* or *equity instruments.*

2. The *international capital market* is the market in which residents of different countries trade assets. One of its important components is the foreign exchange market. Banks are at the center of the international capital market, and many operate offshore, that is, outside the countries where their head offices are based.

3. Regulatory and political factors have encouraged *offshore banking.* The same factors have encouraged *offshore currency trading,* that is, trade in bank deposits denominated in currencies of countries other than the one in which the bank is located. Such *Eurocurrency* trading has received a major stimulus from the absence of reserve requirements on deposits in *Eurobanks.*

4. Creation of a Eurocurrency deposit does not occur because that currency leaves its country of origin; all that is required is that a Eurobank accept a deposit liability denominated in the currency. Eurocurrencies therefore pose no threat for central banks' control over their domestic monetary bases. Fears that *Eurodollars,* for example, will some day come "flooding in" to the United States are misplaced. Eurocurrency creation can add significantly to the broader monetary aggregates, however, and may complicate central bank monetary management by shifting money multipliers unpredictably.

5. Offshore banking is largely unprotected by the safeguards national governments have imposed to prevent domestic bank failures. In addition, the opportunity banks have to shift operations offshore has undermined the effectiveness of national bank

---

[16]See, for example, Richard A. Meese, "Testing for Bubbles in Exchange Markets: A Case of Sparkling Rates?" *Journal of Political Economy* 94 (April 1986), pp. 345–373; and Kenneth D. West, "A Standard Monetary Model and the Variability of the Deutschemark-Dollar Exchange Rate," *Journal of International Economics* 23 (August 1987), pp. 57–76.

The chapter also reviews the history of relations between developed and developing countries during the twentieth century. That history culminated in 1982 in a sharp decade-long contraction of rich country lending to poorer countries—an international debt crisis. Below, we apply what we learn about developing country macroeconomics to examine the causes and effects of the debt crisis and the factors that have helped to bring it under control.

INCOME AND WEALTH IN THE WORLD ECONOMY

Compared with industrialized countries, developing countries are poor in the factors of production essential to modern industry: capital and skilled labor. The relative scarcity of these factors contributes to low levels of per capita income and often prevents developing countries from realizing economies of scale from which many richer nations benefit. Political instability and misguided economic policies frequently have made matters worse.

The world's economies can be divided into four main categories according to per capita income levels: low-income economies (including mainland China, India, and much of sub-Saharan Africa); lower-middle-income economies (including the smaller Latin American and Caribbean countries, the Philippines, Thailand, most former Soviet bloc countries, and most of the remaining African countries); upper-middle-income economies (including the largest Latin American countries, Korea, Malaysia, and the poorer west European countries); and high-income economies (including the rich industrial market economies and a handful of exceptionally fortunate developing countries such as Singapore and Israel). The first three categories consist mainly of countries at a backward stage of development relative to the industrial economies. Table 22-1 shows 1992 average per capita income levels (measured in dollars) for these country groups, together with another indicator of economic well-being, average life expectancy at birth.[1]

Table 22-1 illustrates the sharp disparities in international income levels. Average per capita annual GNP in the richest economies is 57 times that of the poorest developing countries. Even the upper-middle-income countries enjoy only one-sixth of the annual per capita GNP of the industrial group. The life expectancy figures generally reflect international differences in income levels: Average life spans fall as relative poverty increases.

MACROECONOMIC FEATURES OF DEVELOPING COUNTRIES

While there are many economic features that differentiate developing from developed countries, five are particularly important for macroeconomic analysis. These features apply to a majority of developing countries, but not to all, and several are shared by some in-

---

[1]Chapter 15 showed that an international comparison of *dollar* incomes will portray relative welfare levels inaccurately because countries' price levels measured in terms of a common currency (here U.S. dollars) generally differ. An additional problem with dollar income comparisons is that some developing countries have multiple exchange rates for current account transactions. A detailed description of how the numbers in Table 22-1 were constructed and adjusted is given in their source, the World Bank's *World Development Report 1994*. More reliable real output estimates are reported by Robert Summers and Alan Heston, "The Penn World Table (Mark 5): An Expanded Set of International Comparisons, 1950–1988," *Quarterly Journal of Economics* 106 (May 1991), pp. 327–368. The alternative estimates, like those in Table 22-1, show that real output per capita differs widely among countries.

TABLE 22-1

Indicators of Economic Welfare in Four Groups of Countries, 1992

Income group	GNP per capita (U.S. dollars)	Life expectancy (years)
Low-income	390	56*
Lower-middle-income	1,590†	67
Upper-middle-income	4,020	69
High-income	22,160	77

*Excluding China (average life expectancy, 69) and India (61).
†1991 GNP per capita.
Source: World Bank, *World Development Report 1994.* The ex-communist countries of Eastern Europe are included with lower- and upper-middle-income developing countries. The World Bank classifies Hong Kong, Singapore, Kuwait, the United Arab Emirates, and Israel as high-income developing countries.

dustrialized economies. Nonetheless, a broad description of a "typical" developing economy's structure is essential to understanding macroeconomic relationships between the developed and less-developed parts of the world economy. This description also will help you to understand the steps many developing countries currently are taking to reform their economies.

1. Financial markets in developing countries are limited in extent and subject to heavy official control. Governments often keep interest rates below the level that would equalize demand and supply for loans, so loans tend to be rationed.
2. Direct government involvement in the economy extends beyond the financial markets. Governments own a significant portion of the economy's firms, and government spending is a very high percentage of GNP.
3. The government finances a large fraction of its outlays by printing money. This practice results in high average inflation rates and, sometimes, the indexation of wages, loan contracts, and other money prices to the general price level.
4. Exchange rates are set by the government rather than determined in the foreign exchange market. Private international borrowing and lending are heavily restricted, and the government may allow residents to purchase foreign exchange only for certain purposes. In some countries different exchange rates apply to different categories of transaction.
5. Natural resources or agricultural commodities make up an important share of exports for many developing countries.

UNDEVELOPED FINANCIAL MARKETS

On the whole, developing countries lack the broad and rapidly adjusting financial markets characteristic of the main industrial countries. Stock markets are usually rudimentary or nonexistent, as are markets for long-term debt. Bank lending to businesses and the farm sector is tightly controlled by the government, which often decrees artificially low interest rates.

Developing country governments sometimes exercise direct control over credit markets because it is one way of channeling funds at reduced interest rates to favored industries or sectors of the economy. Governments often find this method of helping selected industries preferable to outright subsidization because subsidies would show up in the government's budget as an increase in its measured deficit. Thus, credit diversion by the government to favored sectors results in an implicit subsidy to those who get artificially cheap loans. At the same time, it results in an implicit tax on the banking system, which could earn higher profits in a less heavily regulated national capital market. Low domestic interest rates also help the government finance its budget deficit.

The absence of the higher-yielding assets available in industrial economies means that the few assets that are available to developing country savers are not very attractive as stores of wealth. Government controls often aim to prevent domestic savers from holding foreign assets, so the main financial assets available are money and time deposits. Partly as a result, saving rates have tended to be low in some developing regions. Much of the private saving flow that is available ends up financing government activities, and fragmented capital markets make it costly to funnel the rest into private corporate investment.

Wealthier savers in developing countries can sometimes get around government controls and acquire high-yielding assets located abroad. Such outflows of domestic savings make it harder to finance domestic investment. *Capital flight*—a flow of private funds into foreign assets, prompted by domestic economic instability—is common, and provides a clear illustration of how developing country residents often try to shield their wealth by moving it abroad and out of the domestic government's reach.

In many developing countries an informal "curb market" for loans conducts small-scale lending at market-determined interest rates. The supply side of the curb market includes individual moneylenders, pawnbrokers, merchant trade credit, and private saving associations; the demand side includes households and small farms and businesses. Some developing countries are building on these informal financial markets in broader programs of financial market restructuring.

GOVERNMENT'S PERVASIVE ROLE

To a greater extent than in most industrial countries, developing country governments are involved in the day-to-day management of the economy. Government regulations abound, and many firms are state companies run directly by the government. (Brazil's state companies, for example, produce half the country's recorded GNP.) In recent years there has been more **privatization** in the developing world, with some governments selling state-owned enterprises to trim public deficits. Because underdeveloped financial markets have difficulty pricing and absorbing such government divestments, however, it has not always been easy for governments to sell them to private domestic owners. Successful privatization thus may depend on capital inflows from abroad. Fierce political opposition from those who stand to lose comfortable jobs at inefficient public firms often stalls the privatization process. In a few developing countries privatization efforts have brought a qualitative change in the government's central economic role, but not in most.[2]

INFLATION AND THE GOVERNMENT BUDGET

When domestic financial markets are underdeveloped, governments find it difficult to finance their deficits through domestic bond issues. This difficulty has resulted in extensive

---

[2]For a clear account see Eliana A. Cardoso, "Privatization Fever in Latin America," *Challenge* (September/October 1991), pp. 35–41. Similar but even more severe privatization problems have arisen in Eastern Europe and the former Soviet Union, where most or all of the economy had to be privatized. See David Lipton and Jeffrey Sachs, "Privatization in Eastern Europe: The Case of Poland," *Brookings Papers on Economic Activity* 2:1990, pp. 293–341. We discuss problems of that region in Chapter 23.

direct government borrowing from foreigners. Developing country governments are also led to rely on an additional instrument of public finance: They run the printing press and use newly created money to purchase goods and services.

The real output that a government obtains by printing money and spending it is called **seigniorage.** Seigniorage is a component of government revenue everywhere, but it is particularly important in the finances of developing country governments.

Money creation leads to inflation, which erodes the real value of nominal money holdings. This "inflation tax" paid by moneyholders is one component of the real resources the government obtains by printing money. The inflation rates attained by some developing countries seem spectacular compared with the low (usually less than double-digit) rates seen recently in industrial economies. Such rapid rates of price increase reflect continuing attempts by governments to extract seigniorage from their economies by printing money.

As a result of chronically high inflation, nominal wages are sometimes indexed to the price level. When wages are indexed, they are adjusted frequently in response to inflation rather than set, once and for all, until the next contract negotiation. This procedure is meant to prevent the large fluctuations in workers' real wages that would otherwise occur over the life of a labor contract.

Wage indexation has two major drawbacks that have contributed to macroeconomic instability in developing countries. First, changes in real wages are sometimes necessary to maintain full employment, but indexation makes these changes difficult if not impossible to achieve. If real wages do not fall when the terms of trade deteriorate, for example, export industries are forced to lay off workers and shut down plants.

The second problem with indexation is that wages are often linked to *past* price level increases. If a government decides to reduce a rapid inflation rate, for example, real wages may rise for a time as nominal wages continue to be adjusted upward to compensate for earlier inflation. Rising real wages, however, lead to layoffs and put additional upward pressure on product prices. A government that contemplates disinflation may therefore be discouraged by the prospect of a long and painful adjustment to a lower inflation rate. Developing country governments have recently coupled disinflation programs with direct wage controls, but such "incomes policies" are politically unpopular and cannot be sustained unless the government's program improves economic conditions very quickly.[3]

PEGGED EXCHANGE RATES, EXCHANGE CONTROLS, AND INCONVERTIBLE CURRENCIES

Most developing countries set exchange rates and strictly control financial transactions involving foreign currencies. Foreign exchange controls prevent residents from legally purchasing foreign currencies without government permission; at the same time, someone who earns foreign currency abroad may be required to sell it to the government for domestic currency. Foreigners holding a developing country's currency are not generally able to exchange it for foreign currencies with the country's central bank or residents. Thus, developing country currencies are often *inconvertible,* even for current action transactions.

Why do most developing countries peg exchange rates and supervise foreign transactions? One main reason is the government's desire to use exchange rate arrangements as a

---

[3]Some industrial countries that experienced double-digit inflation, such as Italy, also indexed wages. Developing country governments sometimes index their bonds by adjusting interest and principal payments upward in line with domestic inflation. Once again, some industrial countries (such as Britain) also issue indexed government debt.

period London, the hub of the gold standard system, was the main international financial center. Many developing countries borrowed by selling bonds in London, usually through syndicates of London financial brokers and banks.

From the vantage point of an international economy shattered by World War I, the pre-1914 period appeared to be a paradise for international investors. The international capital market centered in London certainly did thrive up to 1914, but conditions were not as tranquil as nostalgic descriptions penned during the interwar period (and after) might lead you to believe. As we saw in Chapter 18, economic fluctuations were severe under the gold standard, and fluctuations in Europe had a major impact on the prosperity of developing borrowers. Faced with sudden declines in export earnings, debtor countries were sometimes forced to suspend payments of interest and principal on their debt. In addition, domestic economic mismanagement sometimes contributed to the interruption of payments to foreign creditors.

A loan is said to be in **default** whenever the borrower does not make the payments specified in the loan contract. Defaults by less-developed debtors were not at all uncommon before 1914—in fact, several American states defaulted on foreign loans in that period. The losers in cases of default were the individual lenders. Even though a defaulting borrower sometimes resumed payments after its economic circumstances had improved, the immediate effect of default was a sharp fall in the value of its outstanding bonds, and therefore a sharp capital loss for bondholders. Private bondholders generally could do little to prevent developing country governments from defaulting.

Why did international capital flows to developing countries thrive before 1914 despite the very real possibility of default? Three factors appear to have been particularly important:

1. Foreign investment opportunities appeared very profitable. Resource-rich areas were relatively unexploited, and the payoffs expected from building factories, railways, and utilities were immense.

2. Countries like the United States, Canada, Argentina, and Australia, which absorbed most of the funds lent by Europe before 1914, had low population densities and were therefore attracting a large immigration of Europeans, including skilled workers and entrepreneurs. In a famous article, Ragnar Nurkse of Columbia University pointed out that flows of labor and capital from Europe were mutually reinforcing. European lenders felt confident that European immigrants moving to "regions of recent settlement" would successfully transplant the achievements of the Industrial Revolution, and a shared cultural heritage made the negotiation of international loans easier. European countries invested in more densely populated tropical areas too, but largely by acquiring direct investments in mines, plantations, or other resource-based ventures. Unlike bond lending, direct investments run by European managers could be profitable even in the absence of local entrepreneurial talent.[6]

3. Britain's leadership of the world economy played a key role in promoting a hospitable environment for international investment. As a champion of free trade and capital movements, Britain provided a ready source of savings for the rest of the world and a ready market in which developing exporters could earn the money needed to

---

[6]See Nurkse, "International Investment Today in the Light of Nineteenth-Century Experience," *Economic Journal* 64 (1954), pp. 134–150.

meet foreign debt payments. Because investment opportunities within Britain appeared relatively sparse by the end of the nineteenth century, anywhere from 25 to 40 percent of Britain's savings flowed abroad between 1870 and 1914. London's financial houses therefore had strong incentives to seek investment opportunities overseas, and foreign investment made up a large part of their activities. In addition, British loans to developing countries allowed the borrowers to import machinery and other goods from Britain. Recognizing foreign lending as crucial to domestic prosperity, the British government played an active role in assuring that defaults were settled quickly and did not lead to a breakdown of international lending and trade.

THE INTERWAR PERIOD AND ITS AFTERMATH: 1918–1972

London lost its position as the world's leading financial center after World War I and the United States emerged as the major lender to the less-developed world. Britain and France had incurred large war debts to the United States, while Germany was saddled with reparations. None of these European countries, which had been the main foreign lenders before 1914, was now in a position to play a major role in development lending. To bolster its weak balance of payments, Britain prohibited foreign lending by its residents at several points during the interwar years.

During the 1920s, many developing countries floated bonds in the United States and experienced growing inflows of American direct investment. No developing country governments defaulted in the 1920s, but signs of trouble appeared as the decade drew to a close. After the mid-1920s, world prices for agricultural products, a main source of export revenue in much of the developing world, declined. And after 1928, U.S. lending abroad fell as Americans diverted their savings from foreign investments to the booming New York stock market.

The New York stock market crash of October 1929 and the ensuing worldwide depression caused foreign finance to dry up almost entirely. No longer able to borrow abroad, developing countries were forced to cut imports, a move that accentuated the decline in aggregate demand facing the developed world. As industrialized countries erected higher barriers to imports, it became nearly impossible for international debtors to earn the export revenues needed to meet debt payments. Bolivia defaulted on January 1, 1931, and was followed, within three years, by almost every other country in Latin America. Most of these countries simultaneously left the gold standard, adopted floating exchange rates, and pursued expansionary monetary and fiscal policies to combat the effects of the depression.

The United States was not in a position to avert the worldwide financial collapse, as Britain might have been before 1914. Only a small fraction of U.S. saving was lent abroad and exports were a relatively small part of U.S. GNP. Therefore, the American government and financial community did not perceive a well-functioning international trade and financial system as really crucial to U.S. economic health.

Also in contrast to Britain before 1914, the United States failed to shoulder its responsibility as an international creditor of providing a ready market for debtor exports. As countries throughout the world raised tariffs in the early 1920s to combat recession or protect new industries that had grown up during World War I, the United States, rather than setting an example of free trade, enacted the Fordney-McCumber tariff in 1922. Many economists think the subsequent Smoot-Hawley tariff of 1930 was particularly damaging to the world economy (Chapters 9 and 18). That measure aggravated the plunge in developing country agricultural export prices at the beginning of the Great Depression.

While debt defaults had occurred in the years before 1914, the widespread and synchronized default of the early 1930s was unprecedented. The nearly universal developing country default was accompanied by that of a major developed country, Germany, after Adolf Hitler's accession to power. Under the pressure of these shocks, the flow of international lending that had encouraged world economic growth during the 1920s shrank to a trickle in the 1930s. Before 1914, individual countries in default generally were able to resume borrowing once their economic prospects brightened and their previous foreign debts were settled. After the defaults of the 1930s, however, the international capital market showed no such resilience. The generalized nature of the interwar debt crisis helped deepen the Great Depression. The Depression and the trade restrictions it inspired, in turn, encouraged default and discouraged a return to normal international lending. At the outbreak of World War II, developing countries remained largely shut out of the international capital market; private lending to them on the scale seen before the Depression did not revive until the 1970s.

From 1945 to the early 1970s, most capital flows to developing countries took one of three forms: official lending, short-term trade credit granted by foreign exporters, or direct foreign investment. Many trade-related loans to developing countries became official loans when lender governments guaranteed them as a way of indirectly subsidizing their countries' exports. Because individual borrowers sometimes encountered difficulties in paying their debts during this period, governments and international lending institutions established the **Paris Club** in 1956 as a framework for rescheduling debts to official creditors (see the box below). **Debt rescheduling** occurs when payments on the debt are postponed, subject to the provision that interest is charged on the postponed payments.

THE PARIS CLUB

In 1956, Argentine debt difficulties prompted the formation of the Paris Club, a forum for negotiations on countries' debts to government creditors. The club has no set membership. Instead, the participants in any Paris Club negotiation are the debtor government and its creditors, who traditionally meet under the chairmanship of a senior French treasury official.

An important principle governing Paris Club rescheduling negotiations is the symmetric treatment of all creditors. Prior to the conclusion of an agreement, debtor countries approaching the Paris Club are usually required to conclude an agreement with the International Monetary Fund providing for an IMF loan together with an IMF-approved program of economic policy measures. The IMF adjustment program, an example of Fund conditionality, is typically aimed at restricting aggregate demand in the debtor country and raising its exports. Creditors view the IMF stabilization package as essential for attaining a current account path that allows the debtor to resume payment on its foreign debt.*

Commercial banks faced with the need to reschedule a country's debt to them take their cues from the Paris Club. These private creditors negotiate through a newer institution, the London Club.

*Brazil, which concluded a Paris Club negotiation in 1986 *without* agreeing to an IMF program, is one exception. By early 1987, however, Brazil's domestic economic problems had led it temporarily to suspend interest payments on its foreign commercial bank debt.

Direct investments were subject to a threat different from default: the threat of nationalization (that is, expropriation) by the host government. The period following World War II was one of rising nationalism as former colonial territories became independent. In this environment, some governments did not stop at taxing the profits of foreign-owned firms but instead simply seized their assets. Disputes over compensation for such seizures were resolved on a case-by-case basis, but companies whose assets were seized usually had little power over the outcome. In spite of the risk of nationalization or heavy taxation, direct investment flows to developing countries grew quickly in the 1950s and 1960s, in part because many of them offered abundant supplies of valuable raw materials.

BORROWING AFTER 1973: OIL SHOCKS AND FLOATING INTEREST RATES

The OPEC oil shock of 1973–1974 marked the beginning of a surge in private commercial bank lending to developing countries. Banks in the industrialized world had not previously played a dominant role in such lending, but the huge OPEC current account surplus that followed the rise in oil prices had to be "recycled" to finance the current account deficit of the rest of the world. OPEC countries lent their surplus funds to developed countries, and banks in those countries found it profitable to relend the funds to developing borrowers.

Table 22-2 shows the global pattern of current account balances for the period between 1973 and 1994. An immediate effect of the oil price rise was a tenfold increase in the current account surplus of the major oil exporters between 1973 and 1974. These countries could not raise their spending quickly enough in the short run to keep pace with their skyrocketing export earnings, so they ran large but declining surpluses until 1978, when their expenditure finally caught up with their income. As a group, the industrial countries ran a short-lived deficit after the first OPEC shock. In contrast, the current account deficits of the nonoil developing countries rose sharply in 1974 and remained high through 1978. Why did nonoil developing countries fail to adjust their current accounts quickly to the oil shock? As the industrial countries slipped into the recession of 1974–1975, developing country governments adopted and maintained expansionary policies that spurred investment and helped keep their output growth rates high relative to those in the industrialized world. The cost of these measures was a large and persistent deficit: Developing countries were borrowing heavily abroad and building up foreign debt to maintain spending levels in excess of their incomes.

In most of the years between 1974 and 1978, the deficits of the nonoil developing countries shown in Table 22-2 correspond closely to the surpluses of the major oil producers. Oil producers were not lending directly to other developing countries but instead were lending whatever oil earnings they could not spend to industrial countries, whose banks in turn lent these funds to developing borrowers. Why was this recycling necessary? Oil exporters did not want to assume the risks of direct lending to developing countries but preferred to acquire safer assets located in industrial economies. At the same time, banks in developed countries faced interest rates that were low; in fact, when measured in real terms, that is, in terms of output, interest rates in developed countries were negative.[7] It is

---

[7]In 1976, for example, the interest rate on three-month U.S. Treasury bills averaged 4.9 percent per year, while the consumer price index rose by 6.7 percent over the same year. These figures tell us that a U.S. bank lending domestically in 1976 would have earned an average real rate of return of $4.9 - 6.7 = -1.8$ percent over the year. Econometric studies suggest that *expected* as well as realized U.S. real interest rates were negative in the mid-1970s.

TABLE 22-2

Current Account Balances of Major Oil Exporters, Other Developing Countries, and Industrial Countries, 1973–1994 (billions of dollars)

Year	Major oil exporters	Other developing countries	Industrial countries
1973	6.82	−3.46	14.09
1974	65.17	−21.77	−21.37
1975	34.13	−31.08	11.11
1976	31.15	−17.87	−8.57
1977	20.74	−13.03	−12.86
1978	−4.53	−21.20	20.33
1979	53.07	−32.12	−16.25
1980	92.84	−53.21	−45.81
1981	32.15	−70.45	−2.34
1982	−17.86	−60.07	−26.72
1983	−16.97	−41.24	−19.17
1984	−5.23	−27.77	−56.61
1985	−0.70	−25.21	−65.87
1986	−36.84	−10.09	−34.27
1987	−10.51	5.78	−67.01
1988	−29.10	4.21	−57.01
1989	−10.71	−6.20	−84.13
1990	1.13	−12.73	−110.10
1991	−76.57	−11.38	−32.14
1992	−46.92	−20.19	−43.21
1993	−48.46	−56.16	12.14
1994	−47.37	−58.84	7.79

Source: International Monetary Fund. Global current accounts may not sum to zero because of errors, omissions, and the exclusion of some countries (for example, members of the former Soviet bloc).

no wonder that when faced with negative real interest rates at home, developed country banks were eager to lend to developing country borrowers, who were willing to pay somewhat higher rates than the banks' local customers. Even after the addition of a borrowing premium, developing countries faced historically low real interest charges for foreign loans, which naturally encouraged them to borrow abroad.

The second oil shock brought a renewed surge in the current account surpluses of the main oil exporters in 1979; at the same time, it worsened the deficits of other countries. Oil producers' earnings were once again recycled to developing borrowers, but while the industrial countries as a group were close to current account balance by 1981, the nonoil developing countries borrowed over $70 billion in that year to finance their overall current account deficit. By 1982, however, the oil exporters were themselves running a deficit and therefore were not providing the funds to finance the still large deficit of the other developing countries. As a result, less-developed debtors were encountering increased difficulty in borrowing from developed country banks even before the debt crisis erupted in the second half of 1982.

The severity of the debt crisis is closely tied to a key institutional feature of bank lending to developing countries in the late 1970s: the use of loan contracts with adjustable interest rates, called **floating-rate loan contracts.** Under a floating-rate loan contract, the lender is allowed to change the interest rate the borrower pays on the loan as market interest rates change. As an example, suppose you borrow from a bank for a year at a rate of 5 percentage points above the rate on U.S. Treasury bills, adjustable every six months. If the Treasury bill rate is 5 percent per annum when you take out your loan, you pay interest at a rate of 10 percent during the loan's first six months; but if the Treasury bill rate rises to 9 percent within the first six months, you must pay interest at a rate of 14 percent for the next six months. Typically, the interest charged on floating-rate dollar loans from banks to developing countries was tied to the London Interbank Offered Rate (LIBOR), the interest rate London commercial banks charge each other for dollar loans.

Banks favored the use of floating-rate contracts because adjustable interest rates protected them from being "locked in" to low-interest rate loans when the interest rates they themselves had to pay to depositors rose. By the late 1970s, a large portion of developing country debt (particularly that of Latin American countries) carried floating interest rates. Heavy borrowing on a floating-rate basis left developing countries exposed to the danger that a sharp rise in U.S. interest rates would increase their interest burden dramatically. Such an increase did occur in the late 1970s, and that increase, together with the events that accompanied it, set the stage for a widespread developing country debt crisis comparable only with that of the 1930s.

THE DEVELOPING COUNTRY DEBT CRISIS OF THE 1980s

In the years 1981–1983, the world economy suffered the worst recession since the 1930s. Just as the Great Depression made it hard for developing countries to make payments on their foreign loans—quickly causing an almost universal default—the great recession of the 1980s also sparked a crisis over developing country debt.

LEADING UP TO THE CRISIS

Chapter 19 described how the U.S. Federal Reserve in 1979 adopted a tough anti-inflation monetary policy that helped push the world economy into recession by 1981. Even before the recession hit, however, the U.S. monetary shift had direct adverse effects on developing countries' real incomes.

Adverse effects came through two principal channels, U.S. interest rates and the dollar's exchange rate. The Fed's monetary changes were followed by sharp rises in dollar interest rates and in the dollar's foreign exchange market value. LIBOR, to which interest rates on many developing country loans are tied, rose sharply in 1979 (Figure 22-1a).[8] This rise in LIBOR made new borrowing more expensive, and because much developing country debt had been contracted at floating interest rates, the interest payments due on previous loans also rose. The developing world's foreign interest burden therefore took an immediate upward jump.

The interest rate effect was reinforced by the behavior of the dollar. Since much developing country debt is denominated in dollars, the dollar's appreciation increased the

---

[8]Through asset market arbitrage, LIBOR is determined mainly by interest rates on dollar assets located in the United States. The shift in U.S. monetary policy in 1979 therefore had a direct and immediate impact on LIBOR.

FIGURE 22-1

LIBOR and Developing Country Nonoil Commodity Export Prices, 1978–1991

In 1981, dollar interest rates reached a historic high point, worsening developing country debt service burdens. At the same time, the prices of developing country commodity exports (and with them, the terms of trade) plunged. In 1985, the favorable effect of lower dollar interest rates on debt service burdens was offset by another decline in commodity export prices.

Source: (a) International Monetary Fund, *International Financial Statistics*, various issues. (b) International Monetary Fund, *World Economic Outlook*, various issues, Table A29.

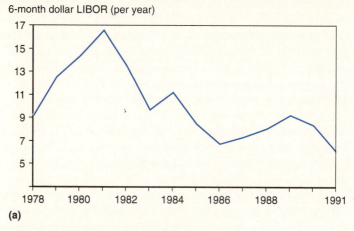

6-month dollar LIBOR (per year)

(a)

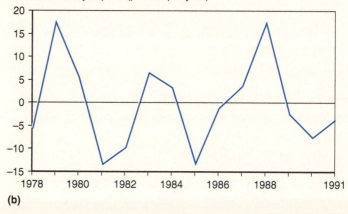

Growth in dollar prices of developing country nonoil commodity exports (percent per year)

(b)

real value of **debt service**—the flow of interest payments and principal to foreign creditors. Table 22-3 shows a measure of the dollar value of developing country debt service payments from 1977 to 1985. In reading this table, keep in mind that the dollar's real appreciation after 1980 caused the real value of these payments to rise by more than their dollar value. Thus, the rise in dollar payments after 1980 understates the increase in the real interest burden of developing countries.

The developing countries' reaction to the adverse movements in interest rates and debt burdens helped set the stage for the crisis to follow. The rise in nonoil developing country borrowing after 1978 (Table 22-2) resulted not only from the oil shock but also from the simultaneous rise in real debt service burdens. Developing countries viewed both setbacks as partially temporary and hoped to soften their impact by borrowing abroad and maintaining domestic demand until better conditions allowed them to repay their loans. Interest rates did not, however, return quickly to pre-1979 levels.

TABLE 22-3

Debt Service Payments of Developing Debtors, 1977–1985 (billions of dollars)

1977	1978	1979	1980	1981	1982	1983	1984	1985
39.5	57.2	83.8	102.6	124.1	135.9	132.5	124.0	129.0

Source: International Monetary Fund, *World Economic Outlook,* 1985–1991. The debt service payments reported here include all interest payments plus principal payments on debt with a maturity exceeding one year. These figures exclude Eastern Europe and the former Soviet Union.

As the world economy slid into recession in 1981, developing countries therefore were carrying an unprecedented external debt burden. U.S. interest rates were at a peak, and these rates were reflected in payments on both new borrowing and older floating-rate debt (Figure 22-1a). Much of the short-term borrowing of the immediately preceding years was coming due, and countries faced the choice of repaying these loans or refinancing them at historically high interest rates. As Table 22-2 shows, the overall current account surplus of the oil exporters turned to a deficit between 1981 and 1982, so the ready supply of "petrodollars" that had financed developing country borrowing in earlier years was disappearing. And with inflation falling throughout the industrialized world (see Table 19-4), commercial banks in the developed countries found they could now earn high real returns by lending at home. As a result, developing debtors were finding it increasingly hard to borrow from the banks that had eagerly financed their earlier current account deficits.

DEVELOPING COUNTRIES IN THE WORLDWIDE RECESSION

The 1981–1983 growth slowdown in industrial countries had two immediate effects on developing country incomes. First, as growth slowed in the industrialized world, developing countries began to face diminished demand for their exports. This fall in aggregate demand directly reduced the growth rate of output in developing countries. Second, the reduction in demand for developing country exports tended to lower their prices. As noted earlier, many less-developed countries depend on exports of agricultural products or raw materials, whose prices are sensitive to demand conditions in world markets. Developing countries' real incomes therefore declined not only because output growth slowed but also because the prices of the primary commodities they export fell relative to the prices of their imports. A further negative factor was increased protectionist pressure in a number of industrialized countries, which made it harder to sell in industrial country markets.

The effect of the world recession on the dollar prices of nonoil primary commodities can be seen in Figure 22-1b. After rising fairly steadily from the mid-1960s to 1980, commodity prices plunged dramatically in 1981 and 1982. The fall in prices was not entirely due to the fall in worldwide aggregate demand. The dollar's appreciation also put downward pressure on dollar commodity prices.[9]

---

[9]The fall in commodity prices was mirrored in the behavior of the developing countries' terms of trade. The terms of trade of indebted developing countries fell by 3.3 percent in 1981 and by 2.7 percent in 1982. See International Monetary Fund, *World Economic Outlook,* April 1985, Table 27.

TABLE 22-4

Growth Rates of Output for Developed and Selected Developing Countries, 1971–1980 Average and 1981–1994 (percent per year)

Country group	1971–1980 average	1981	1982	1983	1984	1985	1986	1987	1988	1989	1990	1991	1992	1993	1994
Industrial countries	3.2	1.5	−0.3	2.8	4.5	3.3	2.8	3.2	4.4	3.3	2.4	0.8	1.5	1.1	3.1
Developing countries	5.5	1.9	2.2	2.2	4.5	4.4	3.8	5.7	5.2	4.2	4.0	4.9	5.9	6.1	6.2
Africa	3.8	1.9	2.5	−0.9	1.4	4.1	1.7	1.6	3.6	3.4	2.1	1.7	0.7	0.8	2.6
Asia	5.3	5.9	5.4	7.8	8.4	6.7	6.7	8.1	9.1	6.0	5.7	6.4	8.2	8.7	8.5
Western Hemisphere	5.9	0.3	−0.8	−2.7	3.6	3.4	4.3	3.4	1.1	1.6	0.6	3.5	2.7	3.3	4.6

Source: International Monetary Fund, *World Economic Outlook*, 1989–1995. Developing countries exclude Eastern Europe and the former Soviet Union.

Table 22-4 shows recent output growth rates for developed and developing countries. The table indicates a marked reduction in industrial country growth rates during the early 1980s, with GNP growth actually turning negative in 1982, the low point of the 1981–1983 recession. Developing countries exhibit a similar fall in growth rates during the early 1980s. However, the numbers for developing countries as a group conceal important regional differences.

In Asian countries such as South Korea and Taiwan the recession had little effect on growth, which soon reached levels far exceeding those of the previous decade. Many of these countries (with the exception of the Philippines) had relatively low debt levels and had been promoting vigorous manufacturing export sectors for some time.

Countries in Africa and the Western Hemisphere did not fare so well (and their growth rates have generally remained at levels well below those of the 1970s). The group of Western Hemisphere developing countries, which includes Latin America, was especially hard hit, with an output growth rate of only 0.3 percent in 1981 and *negative* 0.8 percent in 1982. The staggering −2.7 percent growth rate these countries suffered in 1983 was a direct result of the debt crisis, which started in August 1982.

THE BEGINNING OF THE CRISIS

On August 12, 1982, Mexico notified foreign financial officials that its central bank had nearly run out of reserves and that it could no longer meet previously scheduled payments on its foreign debt. That debt, amounting to more than $80 billion at the time, made Mexico, after Brazil, the world's largest developing debtor. Mexico requested a loan from foreign governments and central banks, a moratorium on payments of principal to commercial banks, and a rescheduling of the principal on debt due to mature in coming months. At the same time, Mexican officials approached the International Monetary Fund with a request for a loan and an IMF-sponsored macroeconomic stabilization plan.

Even as Mexico began its long and complex debt negotiations, other debtors in Latin America, for example, Brazil (with a 1982 debt of close to $88 billion) and Argentina (with a 1982 debt near $40 billion), found themselves unable to take out additional foreign loans or even refinance maturing short-term debt. Bankers saw similarities in the economic circumstances of all the Latin American debtors, and they feared that if Mexico defaulted other countries might follow its example, as happened in the 1930s. Banks scrambled to reduce their risks by refusing to extend new credits or renew old ones. By the end of 1986, more than forty countries in Latin America, Africa, and elsewhere had encountered severe external financing problems. Countries in East Asia (other than the Philippines) maintained high growth rates throughout the recession and avoided the need to reschedule their debts (see Table 22-4).

Much of the debt of African nations was owed to official agencies and governments; the Paris Club therefore provided a ready-made forum for the resolution of African debt issues. A framework for rescheduling Latin America's massive debts to commercial banks, however, did not yet exist. Hundreds of banks around the world had claims on Latin America, and American giants like Citicorp, Bank of America, and Manufacturers Hanover had invested significant portions of their loan portfolios in the region. A widespread Latin American default would have threatened the viability of the large banks and some of the smaller banks, endangering the world financial system. The Fed and foreign central banks therefore viewed the task of averting default, even by a single country, as crucial. A Brazilian default, say, could have set off a chain reaction of bank failures involving many countries. No one wanted a replay of the widespread banking crisis that occurred at the beginning of the Great Depression.

MANAGING THE DEBT CRISIS

By late 1982 individual banks in the industrial world wanted not only to avoid additional lending to developing countries, but also to reduce their overall holdings of those countries' liabilities. A single bank can reduce its holdings of developing country loans by refusing to renew existing loans or by selling them off; *all* banks can do so at the same time, however, only if developing countries rapidly achieve a current account surplus large enough to reduce substantially their aggregate bank debt. Developing countries generally had current account deficits in 1982 and would have preferred to default on their debts rather than adopt the politically unacceptable fiscal measures that would have been needed to generate the repayment banks wanted.

The 1982 debt panic raised a coordination problem similar to the one that arises when individual depositors attempt to withdraw deposits during a bank run (Chapter 21). Each individual depositor finds it in her interest to withdraw her money from the bank, even though the joint action of *all* depositors forces the bank to close and prevents *anyone* from getting money out. Similarly, individual banks, in pursuing their own interests, collectively risked causing sovereign defaults that would leave all parties worse off.

Deposit insurance and last-resort lending by central banks discourage panics in domestic banking systems, but no similar institutions back up the obligations of sovereign debtors. The task facing international policymakers was somehow to generate enough new lending to deter immediate default, even though individual banks preferred to reduce their exposure to developing borrowers.

When the Mexican crisis began, Mexico and the United States organized a meeting between Mexican financial officials and representatives of the hundreds of banks with claims on the country. A bank advisory committee of the largest banks was set up to represent all banks and to keep them informed about the progress of negotiations. This advisory committee system turned into a model for the numerous debt problems that arose after the Mexican case. One purpose of the advisory committees was to help coordinate continued lending. The banks on a country advisory committee had lent too much to the country to stop lending without provoking an immediate default; these large banks, joined by industrial country governments and the IMF, provided new credits and coaxed (or pressured) smaller banks into continued lending.

Bank lending under these arrangements is known as *concerted lending,* a polite term for lending that in many cases was involuntary! Under concerted lending, banks are supposed to contribute new funds in proportion to their loan exposure at the beginning of the debt crisis. Continued bank lending to developing countries has taken two forms, rescheduling and extension of new credits. Rescheduling is one way of refinancing maturing debts: Principal payments are postponed, but they are due with additional interest, so that short-term debts are changed into longer-term debts. But if lenders only reschedule principal on maturing debts, a debtor's net foreign liabilities cannot increase. Thus, its current account must be balanced or in surplus and the net resources it transfers to creditors (its trade balance surplus) must equal or exceed the entire interest bill on its debt. Banks initially provided some additional loans to help finance debtors' (much-reduced) current account deficits. The banks' reluctance to provide money grew, however, as the years passed and the debt crisis refused to go away.

Policymakers had hoped that appropriate adjustments of debtor policies and quicker economic growth in the industrial world would promote an early return to "spontaneous" or voluntary capital flows to developing countries. Concerted lending was intended as a stopgap measure, meant to buy time while banks reduced developing country exposure and while developing countries reduced their debt-output ratios. The hope in official circles was that eventually debtors would be able and willing to repay creditors in full. But this hoped-for outcome did not come to pass.

The Brady Plan.   The persistence of the debt problem led the U.S. government to advance a bold debt initiative, the Brady Plan, in March 1989. Named after U.S. Treasury Secretary Nicholas Brady, the plan recognized implicitly that full repayment was no longer a reasonable goal. The plan put pressure on banks to concede some form of debt relief, and also called for an expansion in secondary market transactions aimed at debt reduction, such as debtor buybacks of their own debts at bargain basement prices.

More specifically, the Brady Plan had three major parts:

1. Commercial banks were urged "to work with debtor nations to provide a broader range of alternatives for financial support, including greater efforts to achieve both debt and debt service reduction and to provide new lending." The syndication agreements governing commercial bank lending to debtor countries contain "sharing" and "negative pledge" clauses that prevent individual syndicate members from making mutually advantageous financial deals with the debtor. Brady called for a temporary waiver of the clauses to allow debtors and individual banks to settle debts.
2. The IMF and World Bank were urged to provide funding "for debt or debt service reduction purposes." In practice, the international institutions might guarantee new bonds issued by a debtor in exchange for existing debt or might provide loans "to replenish [debtor] reserves following a cash buyback" of debt on the secondary market.
3. The IMF was urged to modify its practice of delaying its own disbursements to debtors until commercial bank creditors had agreed on their own lending commitments. The original rationale for this IMF practice was the institution's desire to overcome a market coordination problem and push banks into concerted lending, but by 1989 IMF delays had turned into a bargaining chip used by the banks against debtors.

The Brady Plan clearly had features that would seriously reduce the cohesiveness of the banks as a negotiating group. It thus represented a "tilt" in U.S. government policy toward the debtors. What had persuaded the United States to get tough on the banks? Most important, the debt crisis seemed to be undermining political stability in Latin America. In addition, however, banks had strengthened their balance sheets sufficiently over the past seven years that even substantial losses on developing country debt no longer posed the threat to world financial stability they had posed in 1982.

The Brady Plan's authors believed direct negotiations between debtors and individual banks would promote a process of "voluntary" debt reduction that might place developing debtors on the path to economic growth. By implication, the United States had served notice that it would not act as a collection agency for the banks: They would now be on their own in reaching some mutually agreeable deal with debtors.

Mexico provided the first test case for the Brady Plan when it asked its commercial bank creditors for debt reduction. Under the package eventually offered by the banks in February 1990, the face value of Mexico's debt was reduced by about 12 percent.

TABLE 22-5

Debt Effects of the First Six Brady Plan Packages

	Mexico	Philippines	Costa Rica	Venezuela	Uruguay	Niger
Net effective debt reduction (as percent of public sector debt to banks)	11.9	4.7	47.1	9.9	18.8	100.0

Source: Alessandro Leipold et al., *International Capital Markets: Developments and Prospects.* Washington, D.C.: International Monetary Fund, May 1991, Table 15.

Mexico holds special strategic importance for the United States, and it also had been the "model" debtor, meeting its rescheduled obligations promptly and moving aggressively to reform its economy by reducing the government's role. Within a year, however, commercial bank debt reduction agreements were negotiated by the Philippines, Costa Rica, Venezuela, Uruguay, and Niger. (Table 22-5 shows IMF estimates of the effective debt reduction achieved in the first six Brady Plan agreements.) When Argentina and Brazil reached preliminary relief agreements with their creditors in 1992, it looked as if all the major debtors, along with a number of smaller countries, had at last put the debt crisis behind them.

RENEWED CAPITAL INFLOWS

The early 1990s saw an apparent renewal of private capital flows into some highly indebted countries. As Table 22-2 shows, the foreign borrowing of the developing countries was able to expand sharply in 1993 and 1994.

It is unlikely that the Brady Plan itself was the major catalyst for this renewed private lending. As you can see in Table 22-5, the debt relief negotiated in the initial round of Brady deals amounted to a very large fraction of outstanding commercial bank debt only for the tiny nations of Costa Rica and Niger. While the Brady Plan may have removed some uncertainties for investors, its quantitative effects seem too small to have substantially improved the creditworthiness of the larger debtor countries.

More significant was the sharp decline in U.S. interest rates after 1990 (Figure 22-1a), which both lowered debtors' interest burdens and induced American capital to seek higher returns in the developing world.

An additional important factor was the decisive move toward deregulation, privatization, trade liberalization, and inflation stabilization in several developing countries. Brazil, Mexico, Chile, Argentina, Peru, and Colombia are among the Latin American countries engaged in wide-ranging restructuring. In 1987 Mexico made a significant commitment to free trade by entering the GATT, and it joined the United States and Canada in the North American Free Trade Area in 1994.[10]

---

[10]On Mexico's reform efforts, see Nora Lustig, *Mexico: The Remaking of an Economy* (Washington, D.C.: Brookings Institution, 1992).

Capital inflows to Latin America and other developing regions faltered in 1994–1995 as U.S. interest rates rose and countries' macroeconomic stabilization programs showed signs of strain. Understanding these strains and their implications for continued access to world capital markets requires a close look at the history of inflation stabilization in developing countries.

TRYING TO TAME INFLATION IN THE DEVELOPING WORLD

As mentioned earlier, developing countries as a group did not generally move to floating exchange rates when the industrial countries did in 1973. Often, however, developing country governments devalued their currencies frequently to head off the real currency appreciation that domestic inflation otherwise would have caused.

Deprived of any discipline that the fixed exchange rates of the Bretton Woods system had provided (see Chapter 19), countries throughout the developing world lapsed into chronic inflation, financing growing public budget deficits through seigniorage. Inflation jumped especially dramatically in Latin America (although some countries there, notably Brazil, had suffered from high inflation even in the 1960s). Often the resulting economic dislocation helped military dictatorships come to power.

THE LATIN AMERICAN *TABLITAS* OF THE LATE 1970S

In 1978 Chile, Uruguay, and Argentina all turned to a new exchange rate strategy in the hope of taming inflation. In Spanish the approach was called the *tablita:* a preannounced schedule (or "little table") of declining rates of domestic currency depreciation against the U.S. dollar. The *tablita* thus was a crawling peg system, in which the rate of crawling depreciation against the dollar was supposed to fall over time, bringing inflation down with it. The basic philosophy motivating the *tablita* was the same as that underlying the "credibility theory of the EMS" (Chapter 20): Tying the domestic currency to a stable foreign currency would reduce the inflation bias in policy, while dampening inflation directly by limiting increases in the prices of tradable goods. All three countries simultaneously undertook trade reforms, allowed more freedom to banks and other financial institutions, and opened up their economies to private capital flows.

Inflation did not fall into line with the *tablitas'* declining depreciation rates, however. In Chile, for example, inflation was still running at 2.5 percent *per month* when the country went so far as to fix its exchange rate against the dollar in June 1979. With domestic inflation way above U.S. inflation and their currencies depreciating by far less than the difference, Argentina, Chile, and Uruguay all experienced massive real currency appreciations and growing current account deficits during their 1978–1980 *tablita* experiments. (Data from Argentina and Chile are shown in panels (a) and (b) of Figure 22-2, in which a move upward along the left-hand axis is a rise in the current account *deficit* and a move upward along the right-hand axis is a real *appreciation* of domestic currency against the U.S. dollar.)

Over the course of 1981–1982, with interest rates at historic highs in the industrial world, the appreciated currencies and large current account deficits in Latin America's "Southern Cone" became impossible to sustain. All three inflation stabilization programs collapsed in the midst of speculative attacks on exchange rates and runs on the recently liberalized domestic financial institutions. Chronic inflation returned with renewed force, just as the developing country debt crisis broke out.

episodes of *default* and sharp international business fluctuations, the international capital market thrived until the outbreak of World War I. This was in part a result of London's leadership of the world economy—its commitment to free trade and its flexibility in accommodating the temporary difficulties of less-developed debtors. In the interwar period, most developing country loans originated in the United States. When the Great Depression began, there was no internationally recognized authority prepared to support free trade and ensure a continuing flow of credit to the developing world. As a result, most countries there defaulted on their foreign debts. Private lending to developing countries on the scale of the 1920s did not resume until the early 1970s.

5. Bank lending to developing countries after 1973 was stimulated by negative real interest rates in industrialized countries and the need to recycle OPEC's current account surplus. By borrowing abroad, developing countries were able to sustain high growth rates of spending and output through the 1970s. Heavy borrowing after the second oil shock led to trouble, however, as disinflation in the industrial economies raised interest rates and drove the world into recession. In August 1982, Mexico's announcement that it could no longer meet scheduled payments to creditors sparked a generalized slowdown in lending to developing countries.

6. The world macroeconomic disturbances of the early 1980s created circumstances in which developing countries might well have defaulted had governments, banks, and the IMF not joined to ensure a continuing flow of loans through debt rescheduling and concerted lending. Coordinated collective action initially prevented the complete halt in lending that might have occurred if each bank, acting in its own self-interest, had attempted to reduce its holdings of loans to developing countries.

7. The Brady Plan of March 1989 hoped to encourage debt reduction on terms agreeable to debtors and creditors alike. Coordinated debt relief following the model of Mexico's 1989 agreement with creditors seems to have provided a more solid basis for renewed growth in some heavily indebted economies. New private capital flows to developing debtors did accelerate in the early 1990s. A key factor behind this renewed lending is the ability of several countries to mount wide-ranging programs of economic liberalization and inflation reduction against a background of political stability. The main elements of the reform programs have been trade liberalization, extensive *privatization* of state-owned enterprises, market deregulation, moderate monetary growth, and low government budget deficits.

8. Many developing-country efforts to tame inflation have ended in crisis followed by even higher inflation. Often countries have tried to reduce inflation by slowing the depreciation rates of their currencies. Invariably such exchange rate–based stabilization plans lead to a real appreciation of the domestic currency and a current account deficit, factors that may ultimately undermine the plan's success. The successful stabilization programs have been those which have used exchange rate flexibility to avoid drastic real appreciation (perhaps after a temporary period of fixing the exchange rate). Success also requires a sharp and permanent reduction in the government's budgetary deficit and vigilant regulation of the domestic banking system.

Key Words

crawling peg, p. 688

debt rescheduling, p. 696

debt service, p. 700

default, p. 694

floating-rate loan contracts, p. 699

Paris Club, p. 696

privatization, p. 686

seigniorage, p. 687

Problems

1. Can a government always collect more seigniorage simply by letting the money supply grow faster? Explain your answer.

2. Assume that a country's inflation rate was 100 percent per year in both 1980 and 1990 but that inflation was falling in the first year and rising in the second. Other things equal, in which year was seigniorage revenue greater? (Assume that asset holders correctly anticipated the path of inflation.)

3. The table in the box on measuring seigniorage (p. 689) shows that Brazil's government, through an average inflation rate of 147 percent per year, got only 1.0 percent of output as seigniorage, while Sierra Leone's government got 2.4 percent through an inflation rate less than a third as high. Can you think of differences in financial structure that might partially explain this contrast? (Hint: In Sierra Leone the ratio of currency to nominal output averaged 7.7 percent; in Brazil it averaged only 1.4 percent.)

4. How does an artificially low domestic interest rate help a developing country government finance its budget deficit?

5. Suppose an economy open to international capital movements has a crawling peg exchange rate under which its currency is continuously devalued at a rate of 10 percent per year. How would the domestic nominal interest rate be related to the foreign nominal interest rate?

6. The external debt buildup of some developing countries (such as Argentina) is in large part due to (legal or illegal) capital flight in the face of expected currency devaluation. (Governments and central banks borrowed foreign currencies to prop up their exchange rates, and these funds found their way into private hands and into bank accounts in New York and elsewhere.) Since capital flight leaves a government with a large debt but creates an offsetting foreign asset for citizens who take money abroad, the consolidated net debt of the country as a whole does not change. Does this mean that countries whose external government debt is largely the result of capital flight face no debt problem?

7. Much developing country borrowing was carried out by state-owned companies. In some of these countries there have been moves to privatize the economy by selling state companies to private owners. Would the countries have borrowed more or less if their economies had been privatized earlier?

8. How might a developing country's decision to reduce trade restrictions such as import tariffs affect its ability to borrow in the world capital market?

9. Given output, a country can improve its current account by either cutting investment or cutting consumption (private or government). After the debt crisis began, many developing countries achieved improvements in their current accounts by cutting investment. Is this a sensible strategy?

10. During the 1980s debt crisis, economist Peter B. Kenen of Princeton University suggested the creation of a government-sponsored International Debt Discount Corporation (IDDC) that would issue its own long-term bonds to banks in exchange for their loans to developing countries. How might an IDDC have facilitated debt relief for developing countries? What problems can you see in operating such a facility? (For a symposium on these and related questions, see the Winter 1990 issue of the *Journal of Economic Perspectives*.)

Further Reading

Bela Balassa. "Adjustment Policies in Developing Countries: A Reassessment." *World Development* 12 (September 1984), pp. 955–972. A review of trade and macroeconomic policies in developing countries after 1973.

Michael Bruno et al., eds. *Inflation Stabilization: The Experience of Israel, Argentina, Brazil, Bolivia, and Mexico.* Cambridge, MA: MIT Press, 1988. A collection of case studies of stabilization programs in developing countries.

Michael Bruno et al., eds. *Lessons of Economic Stabilization and Its Aftermath.* Cambridge, MA: MIT Press, 1991. A valuable sequel to the preceding book.

Guillermo A. Calvo, Leonardo Leiderman, and Carmen M. Reinhart. "Inflows of Capital to Developing Countries in the 1990s." *Journal of Economic Perspectives* 10 (Spring 1996), pp. 123–139. Discusses the causes and effects of renewed lending to developing counyries.

Susan M. Collins. "Multiple Exchange Rates, Capital Controls, and Commercial Policy," in Rudiger Dornbusch and F. Leslie C. H. Helmers, eds. *The Open Economy: Tools for Policymakers in Developing Countries.* New York: Oxford University Press (for the World Bank), 1988. Describes how developing country governments have regulated trade and capital flows to achieve policy goals.

Carlos F. Díaz-Alejandro. "Good-bye Financial Repression, Hello Financial Crash." *Journal of Development Economics* 19 (September-October 1986), pp. 1–24. Discusses linkages among financial liberalization, macroeconomic policy, and external debt problems.

Rudiger Dornbusch and Sebastian Edwards, eds. *Reform, Recovery, and Growth: Latin America and the Middle East.* Chicago: University of Chicago Press, 1995. Case studies on recent policy reforms in developing countries.

Sebastian Edwards. *Crisis and Reform in Latin America: From Despair to Hope.* Oxford, U.K.: Oxford University Press, 1995. A comprehensive account of the background and progress of recent economic reform efforts in Latin America.

Albert Fishlow. "Lessons from the Past: Capital Markets During the 19th Century and the Interwar Period." *International Organization* 39 (Summer 1985), pp. 383–439. Historical review of international borrowing experience, including comparisons with the post-1982 debt crisis.

Jeffrey D. Sachs, ed. *Developing Country Debt and the World Economy.* Chicago: University of Chicago Press, 1989. Useful surveys of recent debt problems and individual country experiences.

23 International Economic Problems of Former Communist Countries

At the beginning of 1989 more than 400 million people, producing about 12 percent of the world's output, lived in **centrally planned economies**—that is, economies in which decisions about production and employment were made by government officials rather than by private firms. In spite of some efforts at reform, the Soviet Union and the Eastern European governments installed by Soviet forces after World War II still ran their economies mostly by central directive rather than through a decentralized market mechanism.

By the end of 1991, however, the situation had changed dramatically. Communist governments had abdicated or been overthrown throughout the former Soviet empire, and the Soviet Union itself had broken apart into its separate republics. Most of the Eastern European nations and the largest of the former Soviet republics had launched economic reforms intended to transform themselves into Western-style market economies. The formerly centrally planned economies are generally referred to as the **transition economies**—that is, they are in the process of transition to a market system.

Few economists doubted that in the long run the turn to market economics would raise productivity and living standards. It was widely believed that central planning had proved to be a much less efficient system than a private market economy. Some parts of Eastern Europe, such as the Czech Republic and East Germany, had been advanced industrial regions before falling under communist rule. When the Iron Curtain lifted they were revealed to have antiquated factories, low-quality goods and services, and crippling environmental problems. The return to the market offered the hope of rapid growth in these once-prosperous areas, perhaps even of an "economic miracle" comparable to the recovery of Western Europe after World War II.

But while there were high hopes for economic performance in the long run, the immediate effects of the breakup of the economic system centered on the Soviet Union were far less positive. As Table 23-1 shows, the years after 1989 were marked by severe declines in output and high inflation both in the nations of Eastern Europe and in the newly independent republics that were formed out of the wreckage of the Soviet Union. (Notice that in 1993 Czechoslovakia broke into the separate Czech and Slovak republics). In the Eastern European nations that broke away from Soviet rule in 1989, there were signs of recovery by 1994, and there were some signs at least of stabilization in the former Soviet Union. The process of transition, however, has proved far more difficult than many had expected.

Why has transition been so difficult? This question is a subject of considerable dispute, but economic analysis can shed some light on the problem, particularly on the special role played by international trade and finance. In this chapter we first review some features of the precollapse international trading system in Eastern Europe and the Soviet Union that helped make transition difficult. We then turn to some of the reasons why output declined so much, before turning finally to the special international financial problems that have arisen in Russia and some other former Soviet republics.

TABLE 23-1

Economic Developments in Transition Economies

A. GDP Growth

	1990	1991	1992	1993	1994
Bulgaria	−9.1	−11.7	−5.7	−4.2	0
Czechoslovakia	−0.4	−15.9	−8.5	—	—
Czech Republic	—	—	—	−0.9	2.6
Slovak Republic	—	—	—	−4.1	5.3
Hungary	−3.5	−11.9	−4.3	−2.3	2.6
Poland	−11.6	−7.0	2.6	3.8	6.0
Romania	−5.6	−12.9	−10.1	1.3	3.4
Russia	—	−13.0	−19.0	−12.0	−15.0
Ukraine	—	−11.9	−17.0	−17.1	−23.0

B. Inflation

	1990	1991	1992	1993	1994
Bulgaria	23.9	333.5	82.0	72.8	96.0
Czechoslovakia	10.8	59.0	11.0	—	—
Czech Republic	—	—	—	20.8	10.0
Slovak Republic	—	—	—	23.1	13.4
Hungary	29.0	34.2	23.0	22.5	18.8
Poland	585.8	70.3	43.0	35.3	32.2
Romania	4.7	161.1	210.3	256.0	137.0
Russia	—	92.7	1353.0	896.0	302.0
Ukraine	—	91.2	1209.7	4734.9	891.2

Source: International Monetary Fund, *World Economic Outlook,* May 1995. Numbers for 1994 are preliminary estimates.

TRADE IN EASTERN EUROPE BEFORE 1989

After its victory in the Russian Civil War of 1917–1921, the Communist Party of the Soviet Union experimented briefly with a market economy. This experiment was abandoned, however, when Joseph Stalin took power after the death of Lenin. In 1928 Stalin imposed full-scale central planning, in which factories and farms were required to meet production targets set by government officials. Between then and World War II, he followed a strategy of industrialization aimed, among other things, at making the nation highly self-sufficient. After the war, as pro-Soviet governments took power in Eastern Europe, those nations were integrated into the Soviet system. Formally, trade among Soviet-bloc nations was supposed to be governed by a body known as the **Council for Mutual Economic Assistance;** the Soviet-centered economic zone is therefore often referred to as the CMEA. Its members are shown in Figure 23-1.

CMEA TRADE UNDER COMMUNISM

Viewed as a unit, the CMEA was largely shut off from external trade. In 1980 the combined output of the CMEA was estimated at about 50 percent that of either the European Community (as the European Union was then called) or the United States. Yet EC exports to the rest of the world were $412 billion, compared with only $84 billion for the CMEA. Broadly speaking, the CMEA nations tried to make for themselves anything they could, and their low-quality manufactured goods had little market in the Western world; thus their trade consisted largely of an exchange of raw materials, especially Soviet oil, for sophisticated Western products that they were unable to produce (such as the machinery in the Italian-built factory that in turn manufactured more than half of Soviet automobiles in 1989).

While the CMEA nations traded little with the outside world, however, they traded extensively with each other. Soviet central planners and their Eastern European students believed strongly in the advantages of specialization, especially to achieve economies of scale. Thus they tended to favor geographical concentration of many kinds of industrial production, often building huge plants to supply goods to enormous market areas. For example, most tractors for Eastern Europe were produced at one huge Polish tractor factory, most buses at one large Hungarian plant. The Russian steel plant at Magnetogorsk, with 60,000 employees, produced half the steel the Soviet Union used to fight World War II. Even in 1991, a single plant in Belarus (the world's largest) produced 90 percent of the Soviet Union's polyester and a single plant in Russia produced 58 percent of the Union's automobiles.

As a result of this policy of specialization, trade as a share of national income was quite large for many Eastern European nations. Figure 23-2 illustrates this point. Figure 23-2 shows ratios of exports to GNP for the Eastern European nations (excluding the Soviet Union) and for developing countries elsewhere in the world. The figure shows that in 1984, the typical Eastern European nation exported about 27 percent of its output, compared with only 25 percent for the typical developing market economy. That is, the Eastern European countries were actually somewhat more open to trade until the plunge at the end of the 1980s. The reason is that while the planned economies did very little trade with the West, they made up for it by doing much more than one might have expected with each other.

The high degree of *interdependence* among Eastern European nations was matched or exceeded by the degree of interdependence among the republics of the Soviet Union. The

keep Trabants in production.) Terms of trade were also highly politicized. Most notably, after world oil prices surged in the 1970s one might have expected the Soviet Union, the supplier of most Eastern European oil, to demand more manufactured goods in return. It did not do so, however, for two reasons. First, the idea that the terms of trade among "fraternal socialist nations" should be sharply affected by a rise in the price that Saudi Arabia charged the United States for oil seemed to conflict with the whole ideology of communism, which denounced the arbitrary and unequal distribution of income created by free markets. Second, the Soviet Union was reluctant to impose new economic burdens on its Eastern European allies at a time when the people of these countries were becoming increasingly discontented with communist rule. A foretaste of the 1989 collapse came in 1981, when a Polish austerity program led to a wave of strikes that nearly forced the government to appeal for Soviet help to hold on to power. (The labor movement that emerged in 1981—Solidarity—survived underground and took power in 1989, setting in motion the whole process of communist collapse.)

The combination of a lack of clear standards for, and the politicization of, trade prices meant that trade between CMEA nations took place at prices that were very different from world market prices. In particular, manufactured goods were generally overvalued given their poor quality, while raw materials—especially oil—were priced well below world levels. In effect, raw material exporters—which included, above all, the Soviet Union itself—were subsidizing the exporters of manufactured goods.

Similar but probably much larger deviations of trading prices from world levels characterized internal trade within the Soviet Union. Regions with relatively advanced manufacturing, such as the Baltic republics of Lithuania, Latvia, and Estonia, had captive markets for their rather shoddy products, while raw materials were made available at very low prices.

In summary, then, the trading system in the CMEA differed from what would have happened under free markets in two main ways:

1. The *direction* of trade was distorted, with CMEA nations trading much more with each other and much less with the West than they would have under a free market system.
2. The *prices* at which trade took place were very far from world prices.

Given the distorted nature of this trading system, it was inevitable that its breakup would be traumatic. In particular, former communist countries faced two kinds of problem. Throughout Eastern Europe, they faced the **problem of adjustment,** that is, of reorienting their economies in the face of new competition for their exports and much higher prices for many of their imports. Within the Soviet Union this problem was compounded by a collapse of **coordination:** The centralized control that enforced at least some rationality in interrepublic trade was gone, but a functioning market system had not yet taken its place.

THE ADJUSTMENT PROBLEM IN EASTERN EUROPE

During the first half of the 1990s the economies of Eastern Europe found themselves with a novel set of problems. For more than forty years these had been shortage economies—places where shops were often empty of useful merchandise and where standing on long lines was part of daily experience. On the other hand, they had virtually full employment. As the economies were liberalized, the shops began to fill with high-quality merchandise and the lines disappeared—but so did many of the jobs. For the first time since the 1940s, Eastern Europe found itself in a severe Western-style recession.

While the causes of this recession are a matter of considerable dispute, two important factors stand out. First, the breakdown of the CMEA trading system led to a decline in exports. Second, two major sources of domestic demand under central planning—investment in heavy industry and military spending—virtually collapsed.

THE DECLINE IN INTRA-CMEA EXPORTS

As we pointed out above, before 1989 the CMEA nations engaged in relatively little trade with the outside world but were highly dependent on each other. Once communist rule had collapsed, this special trading relationship broke down. Poland no longer felt obliged to buy Hungarian buses, but was prepared to buy, say, more reliable and fuel-efficient Volvo buses from Sweden instead. Hungary, conversely, might choose to stop buying Polish tractors and instead buy the superior products of America's Caterpillar or Japan's Komatsu. These reasonable decisions by individual countries had a sharply contractionary effect on the Eastern European economy as a whole.

To see why, we can return to the simple analysis of interdependence developed in Chapter 19 (pp. 587–589). In that analysis, we considered two countries, each of whose income depends in part on the value of exports to the other. To think about the Eastern European situation, let us imagine a world of *three* countries: call them Czechoslovakia (C), Hungary (H), and Western Europe (W). Countries C, H, and W all export to each other. Suppose, however, that W's economy is much larger than C's or H's, so that we can treat its output as unaffected by developments in the other two countries.

In the model developed in Chapter 19, we showed how output in two countries can be interdependent. That is, if either country's output rises, it will import more from the other country, which will stimulate output in that country as well. We reproduce that analysis in Figure 23-3, which is essentially the same as Figure 19-4 (p. 589). On the axes of the figure are the outputs of Czechoslovakia and Hungary, Y_C and Y_H, respectively. The curve HH^1 shows how Hungarian output is affected by Czech output. It is upward sloping because an increase in Y_C will lead to an increase in Czech imports from Hungary, which will lead to an expansion of Hungarian output. Similarly, CC^1 shows how Czech output is affected by Hungarian output. As explained in Chapter 19, we can normally assume that HH^1 is flatter than CC^1, implying that point 1 is a stable equilibrium.

Now suppose that after the breakup of the CMEA, each country shifts away from its traditional Eastern European suppliers toward suppliers in the West. This means that at any given level of Hungarian output, Hungary will import less from Czechoslovakia. Because Hungary will be importing less, Czech output will be less than it would otherwise have been. So the curve determining Czech output shifts left, to CC^2. Similarly, at any given level of Czech output, Hungarian exports to Czechoslovakia are lower, so the curve determining Hungarian output shifts down to HH^2. The equilibrium shifts from point 1 to point 2: Each country's decision to buy less from its neighbor and more from the West leads to a fall in output in both countries.

A rough look at the experience of the Eastern European nations during the first two years after the end of communism suggests that the decline of trade within the CMEA was a major factor in their output slump. Table 23-3 compares the initial declines in output for Eastern European countries with the declines in their exports to other CMEA nations. It

FIGURE 23-3

The Adjustment Problem When Special Trading Relationships End

The economies of Czechoslovakia and Hungary are linked by their imports from each other. The higher each country's output is, the higher the other country's exports and output. If each country shifts to buying from other sources, equilibrium moves from 1 to 2: Output in both countries falls.

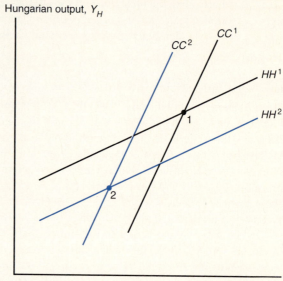

Hungarian output, Y_H

CC^2 CC^1

HH^1

HH^2

Czech output, Y_C

shows that the declines in traditional trade were very large and could indeed have been a significant part of the explanation of output decline.

DECLINES IN DOMESTIC DEMAND

While the decline of trade was probably a major factor in output decline, an even more important factor in the slump was the collapse of two related components of the communist system: massive military expenditures and massive investment in heavy industry.

TABLE 23-3

Trade and Output Declines

Country	Decline in output, 1989–1991 (percent)	Change in exports to other CMEA nations (as percentage of initial output)
Romania	−19	−10
Czechoslovakia	−17	−9
Hungary	−12	−8
Poland	−20	−4
Soviet Union	−17	−4

Source: Stanley Fischer, "Stabilization and Economic Reform in Russia," *Brookings Papers on Economic Activity* 1:1992, pp. 77–126.

Prior to 1989 the Soviet Union maintained armed forces that were roughly comparable in size and equipment to those of the United States, even though the Soviet economy was far smaller. It is difficult to be sure how large a share of GDP this effort represented, but many estimates exceed 15 percent. (In contrast, defense spending is less than 5 percent of U.S. GDP.) The breakup of the Soviet Union meant a virtual end to this spending, and many factories both in the former Soviet Union and elsewhere in Eastern Europe that had been devoted to military production lost their main businesses.

The pre-1989 system had also been characterized by a very high rate of investment, much of it going into heavy industries such as steel, which were, in turn, viewed as essential to the military buildup. As late as 1990 the CMEA area devoted more than 30 percent of its GDP to investment, a much higher fraction than in advanced economies other than Japan. After the fall of communism, investment fell by more than 50 percent, for at least two reasons. First, even before the collapse of the system the rate of return on investment seems to have been very low. Second, demand for the output of the industries that had been receiving large investment declined sharply (for example, steel demand dropped off once Russia stopped building large numbers of tanks).

In the first few years after the end of the communist system, then, the demand for many of the goods that system had been producing effectively vanished. It is worth pointing out that much of this was output of little value—weapons that were no longer needed, machinery that would have had very low marginal productivity, and so on. (It is also true that the goods that CMEA economies imported from each other were often dispensable, especially because of their low quality.) Thus the huge decline in output in the transition economies was not matched by a comparable fall in overall living standards. In Russia, for example, the International Monetary Fund estimates that real GDP fell at least 30 percent between 1989 and 1993, but real consumption fell little if at all.

While the standard of living may not have fallen nearly as much as one might have expected, however, output declines were accompanied by large-scale unemployment. The troubling question is why this happened. Even though many old sources of employment, such as exporting to other CMEA countries or building military hardware, were no longer viable, why couldn't labor and other productive resources be absorbed into new activities?

THE EMPLOYMENT PROBLEM

Standard macroeconomic analysis, of the kind we developed in Chapters 16 and 17, would seem to suggest an easy answer to the demand declines that took place in the CMEA economies after 1989: offset them with devaluation and/or expansionary monetary policies, so that the workers and other resources displaced from traditional employment could become employed in new jobs—exporting to the West, producing consumer goods and services, and so on. Why didn't this happen?

The short answer is that it did happen to some extent but that the ability of CMEA nations to expand demand was limited by their problems with inflation. As part B of Table 23-1 indicates, the first few years of transition were marked by very high rates of inflation, in some cases threatening to break out into full hyperinflation. Under those circumstances countries were of necessity more concerned with reducing the rate of growth of the money supply than with increasing it in order to increase employment.

But this leads to a further question: Why didn't the existence of unemployed resources restrain inflation? The main answer seems to be that these resources were not in a position to help satisfy consumer demand. The idle workers and excess capacity were concentrated in large enterprises, most of which remained under government ownership, designed to produce such goods as steel, heavy machinery, and weapons. Meanwhile, what the market wanted were consumer goods and services, products best supplied by small private sector firms. In fact, throughout the transition economies' output and employment were growing in the private sector even as they fell in the traditional sectors. As late as 1996, however, the old state enterprises still employed far more workers than the new private firms in most transition economies—in Russia, for example, the private sector employed only one worker in five. The private sector simply could not expand rapidly enough to absorb the massive layoffs in the state-owned sector.

One would expect that over time this problem would ease, as the continuing growth of private-sector capacity began to make a sufficient number of new jobs available. And indeed some of the transition economies—such as the Czech Republic and the Baltic nations (Lithuania, Latvia, and Estonia)—appeared to be staging strong recoveries by 1996. In other places, however, notably Russia, the stresses of the adjustment problem appeared to be producing a political backlash that could undermine the transition itself.

RUSSIA'S OIL MESS

The difficulties Russia has experienced in attracting foreign investment in its oil industry offer a good illustration of the way in which political uncertainty has impeded economic transition.

Foreign investment in Russia's oil industry offers clear opportunities for mutual gains. Russia's huge resources already make it the world's second largest oil producer (after Saudi Arabia), and it could produce far more if its industry had adequate capital, better management, and up-to-date technology. Western oil companies are in a position to supply all three. Industry experts unanimously agree that the improvements in production efficiency that Western companies could achieve would allow them to earn a healthy profit even while paying the Russian government much more in royalties than it currently earns from oil exports. Yet by 1996 the Russian oil industry had attracted only modest foreign investments; tens of billions of dollars in potential investment were reported by indus-

try sources to have been put on hold, out of fear that at some later date nationalist politicians would accuse them of stealing the nation's resources and expropriate their investments.

Early in 1996 the Duma, Russia's legislature, passed a new law regarding foreign investment in oil that seemed to confirm these fears. The law required that any new investment be specifically approved by the legislature; it limited the right of foreign oil companies to appeal to international courts to adjudicate any contract disputes; and it reserved the right of the Russian government to renegotiate the terms of its contracts if the world price of oil should increase. In effect, the Duma seemed to be saying that if foreign investments in the oil industry should turn out to be especially profitable, the Russian government would step in and seize the extra profits.

At the time of writing, it seemed as if the political risks had stalled any prospect for extensive foreign investment in Russian oil.

FINANCIAL AND BALANCE OF PAYMENTS ISSUES

The difficulties of the transition economies were to some extent aggravated by some special financial and balance of payments problems. Russia in particular suffered from unusually large problems with capital flight and dollarization.

DEBT, FOREIGN INVESTMENT, AND CURRENT ACCOUNTS IN TRANSITION ECONOMIES

In the aftermath of the fall of communism, it was widely expected that the transition economies would attract large inflows of capital from the rest of the world. Indeed, many observers worried that these inflows would be so large that they would create a global capital shortage. The case for large capital flows into Eastern Europe rested on two points. First, while the CMEA countries had had high rates of investment before 1989, the bulk of this investment had (as we pointed out earlier) gone into heavy industry and defense-related sectors, which were not likely to be where the comparative advantage of these countries would lie in the future. Second, the labor forces of the CMEA countries were not only large but well-educated—the former Soviet Union, in particular, had trained large numbers of engineers and other technical workers whose skills are highly regarded in the West. (For example, there are many excellent Russian computer programmers, whose talents were frustrated by the lack of access to modern hardware.) It seemed reasonable to suppose, then, that the transition economies would offer foreign investors a high expected rate of return, and that these economies would pass through an extended period of substantial current account deficits financed by foreign investments and loans (see Chapter 12, pp. 308–310 to review balance of payment accounting relationships).

The actual size of capital flows has fallen far short of expectations. Table 23-4 shows the current account balances of the Eastern European nations and of the Russian republic over the three years 1992–1994, and compares them with the current account balance of Mexico over the same period. As the data show, Mexico alone attracted more net capital inflows in each year than the combined flow to *all* transition economies over the whole period. Moreover, a significant part of the financing that did take place came from loans from official institutions such as the IMF and the World Bank. Foreign direct investment was negligible in most transition economies (with the exception of Hungary, which attracted $5 billion over the period).

TABLE 23-4

Current Account Balances in Selected Countries ($ billion)

	Eastern Europe	Russia	Mexico
1992	−0.5	−4.2	−24.8
1993	−8.0	2.8	−23.4
1994	−7.5	−1.0	−29.5

Source: International Monetary Fund, *World Economic Outlook,* May 1995, pp. 92, 156.

THE BACKLASH AGAINST REFORM

By 1995 economic difficulties had led to a startling development in several transition economies: Communists had reemerged as a major political force, this time via democratic elections. In 1995 a communist candidate was elected president of Poland, defeating Lech Walensa, the leader of the 1981 uprising (although the new president resigned shortly after his election, as evidence that he had been a Soviet agent came to light). And in December 1995 the reconstituted Communist party was the largest vote-getter in Russia's parliamentary elections, although it was far short of receiving a majority. At least as of early 1996 it seemed quite possible that communists—perhaps in coalition with nationalists—would soon once again be running Russia.

Would this turn of political events lead to a return to the old system of central planning? Most observers regarded this as unlikely. Not only would reconstructing that system require a huge effort, too many people—including many former communists—had grown rich under the new regime for it to be easy to contemplate returning all property to the state. Nonetheless, the evident public dissatisfaction with the results of economic reform was already leading to some backsliding. Early in 1996 Russian President Boris Yeltsin dismissed the remaining advocates of a free-market system from his government, replacing them with men who had served as economic officials under the old Soviet regime.

Why have the former communist countries had so much difficulty attracting foreign investment? The most important answer is probably political uncertainty. Foreign investors were, understandably, cautious about committing funds to countries that had so suddenly turned to market economies. This caution was reinforced as the difficulty of the transition process became apparent, and investors began to worry about the risks of a backlash.

While nervousness on the part of foreign investors was the main reason that transition economies were not able to finance large current account deficits, however, an important contributory factor was the export of capital by domestic residents.

CASE STUDY

THE ESTONIAN SUCCESS STORY

While many transition economies have had great difficulty resuming economic growth, a few appear to be over the hump. One of the biggest success stories is the tiny Baltic nation of Estonia, a former Soviet Republic, which by the mid-1990s was growing at a 6 percent annual rate.

Estonia's success has been based on developing close economic ties to the nearby Scandinavian countries, especially Finland and Sweden. Since Estonian wages are only about one-tenth those in Scandinavia, companies in Sweden and

Finland have increasingly begun to subcontract labor-intensive work to Estonian subsidiaries. The attraction of Estonia arises in part from its geographical location and partly from its traditional cultural ties with its Western neighbors. The political environment has also been helpful. Estonia began privatizing much of its industry in 1993, and allowed foreigners to bid on more or less the same terms as domestic residents. Estonia also imposes few restrictions on foreign investors, allowing them to enter most industries freely and to send profits home at will. Less easy to document, but surely an important factor, is the fact that most Estonians have little nostalgia for the former Soviet Union: They always regarded themselves less as part of that union than as a nation occupied by Russia. Thus the risk of a nationalist backlash against foreign investors is less in Estonia than elsewhere.

The result of this combination of factors has been very large per capita foreign investment compared with other transition economies. At the end of 1994 Estonia, with only 1.6 million people, had already attracted $470 million in direct investments—about as much as Ukraine, with a population of 52 million, and 20 times as much per capita as Russia.

CAPITAL FLIGHT AND DOLLARIZATION

Table 23-5 shows the foreign debt of Eastern Europe and of Russia (that is, to briefly recap what foreign debt is, money owed to foreigners or owed to Eastern Europeans and Russians *by* foreigners) from the end of 1991 to the end of 1994. There is a somewhat puzzling lack of congruence between these figures and the current account numbers in the previous table. The current account plus the capital account (which includes foreign debt) must always sum to zero; a country that is running a current account surplus must have an equal capital account deficit and vice versa. But the inflows of capital represented by the increase in the foreign debt of the former communist countries were much larger than the current account deficits of these countries. This was especially true in the case of Russia, which ran only a small current account deficit ($2.4 billion) over the whole three-year period, yet saw its foreign debt increase by more than $26 billion. The puzzle is slightly deepened by the fact that Russia also attracted more than $2 billion in foreign direct investment, enough by itself to cover the current account deficit. Where did all the borrowed money go?

Some of it simply left the country again, in the form of **capital flight:** residents of Russia moving funds out of the country. Capital flight may have been motivated in part by the same political uncertainty that limited foreign investment. To an unknown extent, capital flight also reflected an attempt by Russians who had acquired wealth in questionable or

TABLE 23-5

External Debt of Transition Economies (end of year, $ billion)

	1991	1992	1993	1994
Eastern Europe	101.6	113.6	119.8	125.1
Russia	67.0	77.7	83.7	93.4

Source: International Monetary Fund, *World Economic Outlook,* May 1995.

downright illegal fashion to put that wealth out of the reach of the local authorities. (The breakdown of the Soviet system unfortunately led to a surge in organized crime.)

It is generally believed, however, that most of the apparent discrepancy between capital inflows and a nearly balanced current account was due to the rapid accumulation of foreign currency, mainly dollars, within Russia. According to some estimates, by 1995 approximately $20 billion of foreign currency was being used both as a store of wealth and, in many cases, as a medium of exchange. In fact, the value of foreign currency circulating in Russia was estimated as being substantially more than the domestic (ruble) monetary base, perhaps even twice as large.

This phenomenon, called **dollarization,** raises two questions: Why is it happening, and what will be its impact?

The Causes of Dollarization.   The widespread use of dollars within Russia is not a unique phenomenon. At various times in the past 15 years dollars have temporarily come to play a major role in the economies of Israel, Argentina, Mexico, and a number of other countries.

What do these episodes have in common? In all cases the countries were experiencing rapid inflation, a situation that led to an unwillingness of local residents to hold domestic currency (see the discussion of hyperinflation in Chapter 14). One way to hold less domestic currency is to use the currency of a less inflationary foreign country to make payments instead. Because the U.S. dollar is a familiar "brand name," and also because the United States has no controls on the dollar's use, in the modern world when people abandon the use of their home currency they usually turn to the dollar instead.

Inflation does not, however, always lead to dollarization. The main obstacle is that in many cases it is illegal to use dollars or any other foreign currency as a substitute for local money. Indeed, countries suffering from high inflation have a strong incentive to limit the use of foreign money in order to protect their seignorage (see below). Thus episodes of widespread dollarization require more than the incentive provided by high inflation; they also depend on a situation in which the government is unwilling or unable to force people to continue to use domestic currency.

The special feature of the Russian situation is that inflation is occurring at a time when the enforcement ability of the government is particularly weak—as evidence by the rise of large-scale organized crime. Under these conditions there has been nothing to stop a large part of the economy from shifting from a ruble to a dollar basis.

Consequences of Dollarization.   The growing use of dollars in Russia has two main consequences for the economy. First, it is a form of capital outflow: Some Russian savings are used to finance investment not in Russia, but in other countries. Second, by substituting for domestic currency the stock of dollars reduces the ability of the government to collect seignorage.

It may at first seem confusing to describe the hoarding of dollars by Russian residents as a capital outflow. However, consider the following two actions:

1. A Russian resident opens a bank account in New York, and deposits $10,000.
2. A Russian resident places $10,000 in cash in a Moscow vault.

It might seem that in the first case a Russian has acquired an overseas asset, while in the second he or she has a local asset. However, a bank account is nothing but a promise on the bank's part to pay dollars on demand, while dollars in Moscow are valuable only because they can ultimately be spent in the United States. That is, in each case, the basic point is that a Russian resident has acquired a $10,000 claim on the United States.[3]

Such claims do not come for free. In order to increase their claims on the United States, whether bank accounts or actual dollar notes, Russian residents must sell something in return. That is why Russia, despite extensive borrowing from abroad, has not run current account deficits: The sale of assets (bank loans) to foreigners has been used to finance purchases of other assets (dollars and bank accounts) rather than imports.

Dollarization has involved a fairly serious diversion of resources. Dollar bills do not yield any return, not even interest. Meanwhile, the $20 billion or so of foreign currency that Russians have acquired represents resources that could have been used for productive investment in Russian enterprises.

To this cost of dollarization one should also add the problems it creates for the finances of a government that, like Russia in the mid-1990s, depends to a considerable extent on seignorage to cover its deficits. (See the discussion of seignorage on pp. 686–687.) Suppose that dollars take the place of half of the monetary base that would otherwise be in circulation. Then a given rate of increase of the ruble supply will produce only half as much seignorage as it would if dollarization had not taken place. If the government responds by increasing the rate at which it prints money, it will produce a higher inflation rate—which further increases the incentive to shift to dollars. In Israel in the mid-1980s a runaway cycle of inflation and dollarization briefly threatened to push the country into hyperinflation. At the time of writing Russia appeared to have pulled back from that brink, but few observers were willing to declare the danger over.

The process of dollarization in Russia, then, has been a contributory factor (though far from the sole or even the main cause) of the country's economic difficulties. It has diverted resources that might have been used for productive investment into unproductive accumulation of dollar bills. And it has aggravated the country's problems with both budget deficits and inflation.

PROSPECTS FOR THE FUTURE

The process of transition to a market economy in the former communist countries has been far more difficult than anyone anticipated. Nonetheless, there are already enough clear success stories—economies like Estonia that have already achieved a dramatic economic turnaround based on close links with the world economy, larger countries like Poland and the Czech Republic that seem to have finally begun to deliver convincing growth—to show that there is light at the end of the tunnel. Given time and a favorable political environment, the transition economies clearly can achieve a higher standard of living than anything they achieved under central planning.

Nonetheless, some analysts now fear that the transition might fail in at least some of the former communist countries—including the biggest nation, Russia itself. The scenario for failure involves a vicious circle of economic difficulties and political backsliding. As the prolonged transition brings unemployment and declining living standards for many

---

[3]A bizarre qualification to this statement was the fact that an unknown fraction of the dollars circulating in Russia may be counterfeits. At the time of writing, someone—probably in Iran—was producing large numbers of extremely good reproductions of $100 bills, using plates stolen from the U.S. Treasury. Many of these bogus notes were alleged to be ending up in Russia.

people, the idea of a market economy comes under increasing attack, leading to growing political interference both with domestic markets and with international trade and investment. This government intervention in turn discourages entrepreneurs from creating the kind of private sector growth that is needed to convince the public that a market economy is really in its interest, reinforcing the political doubts, and so on.

This scenario does not have to happen. It is equally possible that there will be a virtuous circle of improving economic performance and growing political confidence. Indeed, this already seems to be happening in some countries. And even serious backsliding from economic reforms need not be a permanent setback. As we discussed in Chapter 10, after decades of protectionist policies many developing countries have moved decisively toward outward-looking trade policies; this shows that economic reform should never be dismissed as politically impossible.

However it turns out, the great experiment in economic transition in Eastern Europe and the former Soviet Union is a dramatic lesson in the importance of economics in general, and international economics in particular, to the great political events of our time.

Summary

1. The fall of communism from 1989 to 1991 led to the breakup of a once tightly unified economic zone. Before communism's fall, the Soviet Union and Eastern Europe were joined in the Council for Mutual Economic Assistance (CMEA), and the various republics of the Soviet Union were part of a single planning mechanism. These nations, now known as transition economies, have faced difficult problems of adjustment, in which the collapse of the CMEA and the breakup of the Soviet Union have played major roles.

2. The CMEA formed a largely self-sufficient unit, in which member countries did little trade with the rest of the world, but a large amount of trade with each other. After the fall of communism, this trade fell sharply, as former CMEA economies shifted to imports from the West. This shift exerted a contractionary impact on the transition economies. Other factors, notably a sharp drop in investment and the end of massive military spending, also led to large declines in output. The result was a severe recession throughout the region.

3. The transition economies could not easily offset the contractionary effects of reduced demand via devaluation or monetary expansion because they were also suffering from high inflation. The excess capacity created by the decline in investment and military spending did not restrain inflation because it was concentrated in the wrong sectors.

4. Although many observers expected the transition economies to attract large inflows of capital, in practice the first several years after the end of communism were marked by only small inflows, in large part because of political uncertainty. Furthermore, in some transition economies—especially Russia—inflows of foreign capital were used to finance capital flight and dollarization and not current account deficits.

5. Dollarization has happened in a number of countries, although never before on quite the scale of the recent Russian experience. It reflects both the desire of indi-

viduals to avoid holding domestic currency in a period of high inflation and the inability of the government to enforce the use of national currency.

6. Dollarization has made the transition to market economies more difficult, both by diverting resources that might otherwise have been used to finance productive investment and by reducing the government's ability to collect seignorage.

Key Terms

Problems

1. In the text we showed that the CMEA economies as a group were relatively closed to outside trade, but that they did a great deal of trade with each other. To illustrate the effects of the CMEA's inward orientation, imagine a simplified world in which there are only two CMEA economies, Poland and Hungary, and only two goods, buses and tractors. Furthermore, the world is Ricardian: As in the models we studied in Chapter 2, labor is the only factor of production. Each country has 1 million units of labor. We assume that it takes 5 units of either country's labor to produce a tractor, but that it takes either 6 units of Hungarian labor or 8 units of Polish labor to produce a bus.

   Suppose initially that both countries operate free-market economies, and that they trade freely on a world market in which both tractors and buses sell for $30,000 each.
   a. Describe the pattern of specialization and trade.
   b. Determine real wages in each country in terms of both goods.
   c. Suppose that each country spends half its income on tractors, the other half on buses. What are the shares of exports in each country's GDP? What is the share of exports to the outside world in the combined GDP of the region?

2. Maintaining the assumptions of problem 1, now suppose that Poland and Hungary cut themselves off from trade with the rest of the world, but maintain trade with each other. Ignore the fact that these are planned economies, and ask what would happen under free markets.
   a. Determine the pattern of specialization and trade.
   b. What is the share of exports in each country's GDP? Compare with the results under (c) of question 1, and explain.
   c. Determine real wages in each country, and compare with the results when the region is open to trade.

3. One country that was never communist has nonetheless suffered serious difficulties as a result of the turmoil among former communist nations. Before 1991 manufactured goods from Finland, a market economy but a politically neutral neighbor of the Soviet Union, had a privileged position in Soviet markets. Finland is now in a severe recession and has devalued its currency, the markka.

Place Finland in the context of the analysis of the adjustment problem in Eastern Europe. How is it the same, how different from the Eastern European nations?

4. Another country that has been battered by political events is Cuba. Before 1991 the Soviet Union bought most of Cuba's sugar crop (its main export) at prices above world market levels, and sold it oil at less than world market prices. It also provided a significant amount of direct aid. Now all of that is gone.

   a. Compare the Cuban situation with that of East European nations. Is the *mix* of shocks any different?

   b. Suppose that you headed the first post-communist government of Cuba. What international trade strategy might you follow? (There is no single right answer.)

5. One reason why there may have been so much trade between Soviet republics was that under the Soviet system transportation prices were set very low, well below the true costs of shipping goods. Why would low transport charges encourage the construction of very large plants? What would be the economic inefficiency involved in doing so?

6. If all goes well, sometime in the early years of the next decade many European countries will abandon their national currencies and replace them with a European currency, the *Euro*. Will this process produce the same problems that Russia has experienced from dollarization? Why or why not?

7. Suppose that we suspect that several billion "dollars" circulating in Russia are really counterfeits printed in the Middle East. Should the Russian government cooperate with the United States in its efforts to detect these counterfeits and remove them from circulation? (Think about this carefully—there may be several levels to the answer.)

Further Reading

Susan M. Collins and Dani Rodrik. *Eastern Europe and the Soviet Union in the World Economy.* Washington, D.C.: Institute for International Economics, 1991. Written just before the Soviet breakup, this study remains useful as an attempt to chart the likely changes in East European trade.

Padma Desai. *Perestroika in Perspective: The Design and Dilemmas of Soviet Reform.* Princeton: Princeton University Press, 1989. Books on the Soviet Union have quickly become out of date, but this volume remains a useful survey of the difficulties that brought the Soviet system down.

Stanley Fischer. "Economic Reform in the USS and the Role of Aid." *Brookings Papers on Economic Activity* 2:1991, pp. 289–302. A good discussion of the economic crisis just following the breakup of the Soviet Union.

International Monetary Fund. *World Economic Outlook,* May 1994 and May 1995. Both issues contain extensive articles on the problems of transition economies, together with data and useful bibliographies.

Gerlinde Sinn and Hans-Werner Sinn. *Jumpstart: The Economic Unification of Germany.* Cambridge, MA: MIT Press, 1992. Analyzes the special problems of merging a former communist economy with an advanced market economy.

Mathematical Postscripts

Postscript to Chapter 3

The Specific Factors Model

In this postscript we set out a formal mathematical treatment for the specific factors model of production explained in Chapter 3. The mathematical treatment is useful in deepening understanding of the model itself, and it also provides an opportunity to develop concepts and techniques that apply to subsequent models. In particular it is a good place to introduce an extremely useful tool of analysis, the so-called hat algebra.

FACTOR PRICES, COSTS, AND FACTOR DEMANDS

The specific factors model has two sectors: manufactures and food. In each sector, two factors of production are employed: capital and labor in manufactures, land and labor in food. Before turning to the full model, let us examine in general how costs and the demand for factors of production are related to the prices of factors when producers employ two factors.

Consider the production of some good that requires capital and labor as factors of production. Provided the good is produced with constant returns to scale, the technology of production may be summarized in terms of the *unit isoquant* (*II* in Figure 3P-1), a curve showing all the combinations of capital and labor that can be used to produce one unit of the good. Curve *II* shows that there is a trade-off between the quantity of capital used per unit of output, a_K, and the quantity of labor per unit of output, a_L. The curvature of the unit isoquant reflects the assumption that it becomes increasingly difficult to substitute capital for labor as the capital-labor ratio increases, and conversely.

In a competitive market economy, producers will choose the capital-labor ratio in production that minimizes their cost. Such a cost-minimizing production choice is shown in Figure 3P-1 as point *E*. It is the point at which the unit isoquant *II* is tangent to a line whose slope is equal to minus the ratio of the price of labor, *w,* to the price of capital, *r.*

The actual cost of production is equal to the sum of the cost of capital and labor inputs,

$$C = a_K r + a_L w, \qquad (3P\text{-}1)$$

where the input coefficients, a_K and a_L, have been chosen to minimize C.

FIGURE 3P-1

Efficient Production

The cost-minimizing capital-labor ratio depends on factor prices.

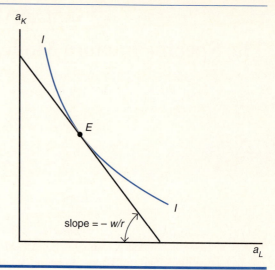

Because the capital-labor ratio has been chosen to minimize costs, it follows that a change in that ratio cannot reduce costs. Costs cannot be reduced by increasing a_K while reducing a_L, nor conversely. It follows that an infinitesimal change in the capital-labor ratio from the cost-minimizing choice must have no effect on cost. Let da_K, da_L be small changes from the optimal input choices. Then

$$rda_K + wda_L = 0 \tag{3P-2}$$

for any movement along the unit isoquant.

Consider next what happens if the factor prices r and w change. This alteration will have two effects: It will change the choice of a_K and a_L, and it will change the cost of production.

First, consider the effect on the relative quantities of capital and labor used to produce one unit of output. The cost-minimizing labor-capital ratio depends on the ratio of the price of labor to that of capital:

$$\frac{a_K}{a_L} = \Phi\left(\frac{w}{r}\right). \tag{3P-3}$$

The cost of production will also change. For small changes in factor prices dr and dw, the change in production cost is

$$dC = a_K dr + a_L dw + rda_K + wda_L. \tag{3P-4}$$

From equation (3P-2), however, we already know that the last two terms of equation (3P-4) sum to zero. Hence the effect of factor prices on cost may be written

$$dC = a_K dr + a_L dw. \tag{3P-4'}$$

It turns out to be very convenient to derive a somewhat different equation from equation (3P-4′). Dividing and multiplying some of the elements of the equation, a new equation can be derived that looks as follows:

$$\frac{dC}{C} = \left(\frac{a_K r}{C}\right)\left(\frac{dr}{r}\right) + \left(\frac{a_L w}{C}\right)\left(\frac{dw}{w}\right). \tag{3P-5}$$

The term dC/C may be interpreted as the *percentage change* in C, and may conveniently be designated as $\hat{C}$; similarly, let $dr/r = \hat{r}$ and $dw/w = \hat{w}$. The term $a_K r/C$ may be interpreted as the *share of capital in total production costs;* it may be conveniently designated θ_K. Thus equation (3P-5) can be compactly written

$$\hat{C} = \theta_K \hat{r} + \theta_L \hat{w}, \tag{3P-5′}$$

where

$$\theta_K + \theta_L = 1.$$

This is an example of "hat algebra," an extremely useful way to express mathematical relationships in international economics.

The relationship between factor prices and the capital-labor ratio can also be expressed in hat algebra. A rise in the price of labor relative to the price of capital lowers the ratio of labor to capital; this statement may be written

$$\hat{a}_L - \hat{a}_K = -\sigma(\hat{w} - \hat{r}), \tag{3P-6}$$

where σ is the percentage change in the labor-capital ratio that results from a 1 percent change in the ratio of factor prices, and is known as the *elasticity of substitution.*

FACTOR PRICE DETERMINATION IN THE SPECIFIC FACTORS MODEL

The specific factors model has two sectors, each of which is like that just described. Manufactures are produced using capital (the specific factor) and labor:

$$Q_M = Q_M(K, L_M). \tag{3P-7}$$

Food is produced using the specific factor land and labor:

$$Q_F = Q_F(T, L_F). \tag{3P-8}$$

The supplies of capital and land to each sector are simply whatever they are. Labor, however, can be allocated to either sector:

$$L_M + L_F = \bar{L}, \tag{3P-9}$$

where $\bar{L}$ is the economy's total supply of labor.

In a perfectly competitive economy, the price of each good must just equal its cost of production. In manufactures, then,

$$P_M = a_{KM} r_K + a_{LM} w, \tag{3P-10}$$

where r_K is the price of capital, w the wage rate of labor, and a_{KM} and a_{LM} the unit input coefficients. Using the notation introduced in equation (3P-6), it follows that

$$\hat{P}_M = \theta_{KM} \hat{r}_K + \theta_{LM} \hat{w}, \tag{3P-11}$$

or

$$\hat{r}_K = \left(\frac{1}{\theta_{KM}}\right)(\hat{P}_M - \theta_{LM}\hat{w}) = \hat{P}_M + \left(\frac{\theta_{LM}}{\theta_{KM}}\right)(\hat{P}_M - \hat{w}). \tag{3P-12}$$

Similarly, with parallel notation, in the food sector

$$\hat{r}_T = \left(\frac{1}{\theta_{TF}}\right)(\hat{P}_F - \theta_{LF}\hat{w}) = \hat{P}_F + \left(\frac{\theta_{LF}}{\theta_{TF}}\right)(\hat{P}_F - \hat{w}). \tag{3P-13}$$

Equations (3P-12) and (3P-13) allow derivation of the change in the prices of capital and land, given the changes in the prices of manufactures, food, and labor. The next step is to derive the change in the wage rate, which we do by examining the demand and supply for labor.

Notice first that

$$K = a_{KM}Q_M \tag{3P-14}$$

and

$$L_M = a_{LM}Q_M. \tag{3P-15}$$

It follows that

$$L_M = \left(\frac{a_{LM}}{a_{KM}}\right)K. \tag{3P-16}$$

Because the supply of the specific factor capital is fixed, employment of labor in the production of manufactures can change only through changes in the capital-labor ratio. Using the hat notation, the following can be derived:

$$\hat{L}_M = \hat{a}_{LM} - \hat{a}_{KM} = -\sigma(\hat{w} - \hat{r}_K). \tag{3P-17}$$

From equation (3P-12), it can be shown that

$$\hat{r}_K - \hat{w} = \left(\frac{1}{\theta_{KM}}\right)(\hat{P}_M - \hat{w}). \tag{3P-18}$$

Hence,

$$\hat{L}_M = \sigma_M\left(\frac{1}{\theta_{KM}}\right)(\hat{P}_M - \hat{w}), \tag{3P-19}$$

where σ_M is the elasticity of substitution in manufactures and, by analogy,

$$\hat{L}_F = \sigma_F\left(\frac{1}{\theta_{TF}}\right)(\hat{P}_F - \hat{w}). \tag{3P-20}$$

Now turn to the full-employment condition for labor, equation (3P-9). If total employment is to remain unchanged, an increase in one sector's employment must be offset by a decline in the other sector:

$$dL_M + dL_F = 0. \tag{3P-21}$$

As before, this expression can be transformed into one that uses the hat algebra:

$$\left(\frac{dL_M}{L_M}\right)\left(\frac{L_M}{L}\right) + \left(\frac{dL_F}{L_F}\right)\left(\frac{L_F}{L}\right) = 0 \tag{3P-22}$$

or

$$\alpha_M \hat{L}_M + \alpha_F \hat{L}_F = 0, \tag{3P-22$'$}$$

where $\alpha_M = L_M/L$ is the share of the labor employed in manufactures in the economy's total labor supply.

The last step is to substitute the labor-demand equations (3P-19) and (3P-20) into equation (3P-22$'$):

$$(\alpha_M \sigma_M/\theta_{KM})\hat{P}_M + (\alpha_F \sigma_F/\theta_{TF})\hat{P}_F = [(\alpha_M \sigma_M/\theta_{KM}) + (\alpha_F \sigma_F/\theta_{TF})]\hat{w} \tag{3P-23}$$

or

$$\hat{w} = \frac{[(\alpha_M \sigma_M/\theta_{KM})\hat{P}_M + (\alpha_F \sigma_F/\theta_{TF})\hat{P}_F]}{[(\alpha_M \sigma_M/\theta_{KM}) + (\alpha_F \sigma_F/\theta_{TF})]} \tag{3P-23$'$}$$

That is, the rise in the wage rate is a weighted average of the increases in the prices of manufactures and food.

EFFECTS OF A CHANGE IN RELATIVE PRICES

Suppose the price of manufactures rises relative to that of food; that is, $\hat{P}_M > \hat{P}_F$. Then, because the change in the wage rate is a weighted average of the change in the two goods prices,

$$\hat{P}_M > \hat{w} > \hat{P}_F.$$

The effect on the allocation of labor is apparent from equations (3P-19) and (3P-20): Because $\hat{P}_M > \hat{w}$, $\hat{L}_M > 0$; since $\hat{P}_F < \hat{w}$, $\hat{L}_F < 0$. Employment in manufactures rises and employment in food falls.

The effects on the prices of capital and land may be seen from equations (3P-12) and (3P-13). Again, because $\hat{P}_M > \hat{w}$, r_K must rise by *more* than P_M, while conversely r_T rises by less than P_F. Thus the overall description of the relation of goods price and factor price changes is

$$\hat{r}_K > \hat{P}_M > \hat{w} > \hat{P}_F > \hat{r}_T. \tag{3P-24}$$

Because the price of capital rises in terms of both goods, someone who derived his or her income entirely from capital would be unambiguously better off. Because the price of land falls relative to both goods, someone deriving his or her income entirely from land would be unambiguously worse off. Someone deriving income from labor would find that the purchasing power of that income had risen in terms of food and fallen in terms of manufactures.

Postscript to Chapter 4

The Factor Proportions Model

The factor proportions model with flexible coefficients is very similar to the specific factors model: It has two sectors, each of which uses two factors of production. The only difference is that these are the *same* factors of production, so that both labor and the other factor (land in this example) can be allocated across sectors.

THE BASIC EQUATIONS IN THE FACTOR PROPORTIONS MODEL

Suppose a country produces two goods, X and Y, using two factors of production, land and labor. Assume that X is land intensive. The price of each good must equal its production cost:

$$P_X = a_{TX}r + a_{LX}w, \tag{4P-1}$$

$$P_Y = a_{TY}r + a_{LY}w, \tag{4P-2}$$

where a_{TX}, a_{LX}, a_{TY}, a_{LY} are the cost-minimizing input choices given the price of land, r, and labor, w.

Also, the economy's factors of production must be fully employed:

$$a_{TX}Q_X + a_{TY}Q_Y = T, \tag{4P-3}$$

$$a_{LX}Q_X + a_{LY}Q_Y = L, \tag{4P-4}$$

where T, L, are the total supplies of land and labor.

The factor price equations (4P-1) and (4P-2) imply equations for the rate of change for factor prices, just as in the specific factors model:

$$\hat{P}_X = \theta_{TX}\hat{r} + \theta_{LX}\hat{w}, \tag{4P-5}$$

$$\hat{P}_Y = \theta_{TY}\hat{r} + \theta_{LY}\hat{w}, \tag{4P-6}$$

where θ_{TX} is the share of land in the production cost of X, etc. $\theta_{TX} > \theta_{TY}$, and $\theta_{LX} < \theta_{LY}$, because X is more land intensive than Y.

The quantity equations (4P-3) and (4P-4) must be treated more carefully. The unit inputs a_{TX}, etc. can change if factor prices change. If goods prices are held constant, however, then factor prices will not change. Thus for *given* prices of X and Y, it is also possible to write hat equations in terms of factor supplies and outputs:

$$\alpha_{TX}\hat{Q}_X + \alpha_{TY}\hat{Q}_Y = \hat{T}, \qquad (4P\text{-}7)$$

$$\alpha_{LX}\hat{Q}_X + \alpha_{LY}\hat{Q}_Y = \hat{L}, \qquad (4P\text{-}8)$$

where α_{TX} is the share of the economy's land supply that is used in production of X, etc. $\alpha_{TX} > \alpha_{LX}$, and $\alpha_{TY} < \alpha_{LY}$, because of the greater land intensity of X production.

GOODS PRICES AND FACTOR PRICES

The factor price equations (4P-5) and (4P-6) may be solved together to express factor prices as the outcome of goods prices (these solutions make use of the fact that $\theta_{LX} = 1 - \theta_{TX}$ and $\theta_{LY} = 1 - \theta_{TY}$):

$$\hat{r} = \left(\frac{1}{D}\right)[(1 - \theta_{TY})\hat{P}_X - \theta_{LX}\hat{P}_Y], \qquad (4P\text{-}9)$$

$$\hat{w} = \left(\frac{1}{D}\right)[\theta_{TX}\hat{P}_Y - \theta_{TY}\hat{P}_X], \qquad (4P\text{-}10)$$

where $D = \theta_{TX} - \theta_{TY}$ (implying that $D > 0$). These may be arranged in the form

$$\hat{r} = \hat{P}_X + \left(\frac{\theta_{LX}}{D}\right)(\hat{P}_X - \hat{P}_Y), \qquad (4P\text{-}9')$$

$$\hat{w} = \hat{P}_Y - \left(\frac{\theta_{TY}}{D}\right)(\hat{P}_X - \hat{P}_Y). \qquad (4P\text{-}10')$$

Suppose that the price of X rises relative to the price of Y, so that $\hat{P}_X > \hat{P}_Y$. Then it follows that

$$\hat{r} > \hat{P}_X > \hat{P}_Y > \hat{w}. \qquad (4P\text{-}11)$$

That is, the real price of land rises in terms of both goods, while the real price of labor falls in terms of both goods. In particular, if the price of X were to rise with no change in the price of Y, the wage rate would actually fall.

FACTOR SUPPLIES AND OUTPUTS

As long as goods prices may be taken as given, equations (4P-7) and (4P-8) can be solved, using the fact that $\alpha_{TY} = 1 - \alpha_{TX}$ and $\alpha_{LY} = 1 - \alpha_{LX}$, to express the change in output of each good as the outcome of changes in factor supplies:

$$\hat{Q}_X = \left(\frac{1}{\Delta}\right)[\alpha_{LY}\hat{T} - \alpha_{TY}\hat{L}], \qquad (4P\text{-}12)$$

$$\hat{Q}_Y = \left(\frac{1}{\Delta}\right)[-\alpha_{LX}\hat{T} + \alpha_{TX}\hat{L}], \qquad (4P\text{-}13)$$

where $\Delta = \alpha_{TX} - \alpha_{LX}$, $\Delta > 0$.

These equations may be rewritten

$$\hat{Q}_X = \hat{T} + \left(\frac{\alpha_{TY}}{\Delta}\right)(\hat{T} - \hat{L}), \tag{4P-12$'$}$$

$$\hat{Q}_Y = \hat{L} - \left(\frac{\alpha_{LX}}{\Delta}\right)(\hat{T} - \hat{L}). \tag{4P-13$'$}$$

Suppose that P_X and P_Y remain constant, while the supply of land rises relative to the supply of labor—$\hat{T} > \hat{L}$. Then it is immediately apparent that

$$\hat{Q}_X > \hat{T} > \hat{L} > \hat{Q}_Y. \tag{4P-14}$$

In particular, if T rises with L remaining constant, output of X will rise more than in proportion while output of Y will actually fall.

Postscript to Chapter 5

The Trading World Economy

SUPPLY, DEMAND, AND EQUILIBRIUM

WORLD EQUILIBRIUM

Although for graphical purposes it is easiest to express world equilibrium as an equality between relative supply and relative demand, for a mathematical treatment it is preferable to use an alternative formulation. This approach is to focus on the conditions of equality between supply and demand of either one of the two goods, cloth and food. It does not matter which good is chosen because equilibrium in the cloth market implies equilibrium in the food market and vice versa.

To see this condition, let Q_C, Q_C^* be the output of cloth in Home and Foreign respectively, D_C, D_C^* the quantity demanded in each country, and corresponding variables with an F subscript refer to the food market. Also, let p be the price of cloth relative to that of food.

In all cases world expenditure will be equal to world income. World income is the sum of income earned from sales of cloth and sales of food; world expenditure is the sum of purchases of cloth and food. Thus the equality of income and expenditure may be written

$$p(Q_C + Q_C^*) + Q_F + Q_F^* = p(D_C + D_C^*) + D_F + D_F^*. \tag{5P-1}$$

Now suppose that the world market for cloth is in equilibrium; that is,

$$Q_C + Q_C^* = D_C + D_C^*. \tag{5P-2}$$

Then from equation (5P-1) it follows that

$$Q_F + Q_F^* = D_F + D_F^*. \tag{5P-3}$$

That is, the market for food must be in equilibrium as well. Clearly the converse is also true: If the market for food is in equilibrium, so too is the market for cloth.

It is therefore sufficient to focus on the market for cloth to determine the equilibrium relative price.

PRODUCTION AND INCOME

Each country has a production possibility frontier along which it can trade off between producing cloth and food. The economy chooses the point on that frontier which maximizes the value of output at the given relative price of cloth. This value may be written

$$V = pQ_C + Q_F.$$ (5P-4)

As in the cost-minimization cases described in earlier postscripts, the fact that the output mix chosen maximizes value implies that a small shift in production along the production possibility frontier away from the optimal mix has no effect on the value of output:

$$pdQ_C + dQ_F = 0.$$ (5P-5)

A change in the relative price of cloth will lead to both a change in the output mix and a change in the value of output. The change in the value of output is

$$dV = Q_C \, dp + pdQ_C + dQ_F;$$ (5P-6)

however, because the last two terms are, by equation (5P-5), equal to zero, this expression reduces to

$$dV = Q_C \, dp.$$ (5P-6′)

Similarly, in Foreign,

$$dV^* = Q_C^* \, dp.$$ (5P-7)

INCOME, PRICES, AND UTILITY

Each country is treated as if it were one individual. The tastes of the country can be represented by a utility function depending on consumption of cloth and food:

$$U = U(D_C, D_F).$$ (5P-8)

Suppose a country has an income I in terms of food. Its total expenditure must be equal to this income, so that

$$pD_C + D_F = I.$$ (5P-9)

Consumers will maximize utility given their income and the prices they face. Let MU_C, MU_F be the marginal utility that consumers derive from cloth and food; then the change in utility that results from any change in consumption is

$$dU = MU_C \, dD_C + MU_F \, dD_F.$$ (5P-10)

Because consumers are maximizing utility given income and prices, there cannot be any affordable change in consumption that makes them better off. This condition implies that at the optimum,

$$\frac{MU_C}{MU_F} = p.$$ (5P-11)

Now consider the effect on utility of changing income and prices. Differentiating equation (5P-9) yields

$$pdD_C + dD_F = dI - D_C \, dp.$$ (5P-12)

But from equations (5P-10) and (5P-11),

$$dU = MU_F[pdD_C + dD_F].$$ (5P-13)

Thus

$$dU = MU_F[dI - D_C dp]. \tag{5P-14}$$

It is convenient to introduce now a new definition: The change in utility divided by the marginal utility of food, which is the commodity in which income is measured, may be defined as the change in *real income,* and indicated by the symbol *dy:*

$$dy = \frac{dU}{MU_F} = dI - D_C dp. \tag{5P-15}$$

For the economy as a whole, income equals the value of output: $I = V$. Thus the effect of a change in the relative price of cloth on the economy's real income is

$$dy = [Q_C - D_C]dp. \tag{5P-16}$$

The quantity $Q_C - D_C$ is the economy's exports of cloth. A rise in the relative price of cloth, then, will benefit an economy that exports cloth; it is an improvement in that economy's terms of trade. It is instructive to restate this idea in a slightly different way:

$$dy = [p(Q_C - D_C)]\left(\frac{dp}{p}\right). \tag{5P-17}$$

The term in brackets is the value of exports; the term in parentheses is the percentage change in the terms of trade. The expression therefore says that the real income gain from a given percentage in terms of trade change is equal to the percentage change in the terms of trade multiplied by the initial value of exports. If a country is initially exporting $100 billion and its terms of trade improve by 10 percent, the gain is equivalent to a gain in national income of $10 billion.

SUPPLY, DEMAND, AND THE STABILITY OF EQUILIBRIUM

In the market for cloth, a change in the relative price will induce changes in both supply and demand.

On the supply side, a rise in p will lead both Home and Foreign to produce more cloth. We will denote this supply response as s, s^* in Home and Foreign, respectively, so that

$$dQ_C = s\, dp, \tag{5P-18}$$
$$dQ_C^* = s^*\, dp, \tag{5P-19}$$

The demand side is more complex. A change in p will lead to both *income* and *substitution* effects. These effects are illustrated in Figure 5P-1. The figure shows an economy that initially faces a relative price indicated by the slope of the line VV^0. Given this relative price, the economy produces at point Q^0 and consumes at point D^0. Now suppose the relative price of cloth rises to the level indicated by the slope of VV^2. If there were no increase in utility, consumption would shift to D^1, which would involve an unambiguous fall in consumption of cloth. There is also, however, a change in the economy's real income; in this case, because the economy is initially a net exporter of cloth, real income rises. This change leads to consumption at D^2 rather than D^1, and this income effect tends to raise consumption of cloth. Analyzing the effect of change in p on demand requires taking account of both the substitution effect, which is the change in consumption that would take place if real income were held constant, and the income effect, which is the additional change in consumption that is the consequence of the fact that real income changes.

FIGURE 5P-1

Consumption Effects of a Price Change

A change in relative prices produces both income and substitution effects.

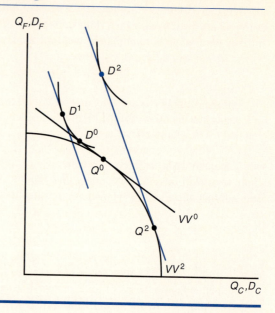

Let the substitution effect be denoted by $-e\,dp$; it is always negative. Also, let the income effect be denoted by $n\,dy$; as long as cloth is a normal good, for which demand rises with real income, it is positive if the country is a net exporter of cloth, negative if it is a net importer.[1] Then the total effect of a change in p on Home's demand for cloth is

$$dD_C = -e\,dp + n\,dy$$
$$= [-e + n(Q_C - D_C)]dp. \tag{5P-20}$$

The effect on Foreign's demand similarly is

$$dD_C^* = [-e^* + n^*(Q_C^* - D_C^*)]dp. \tag{5P-21}$$

Because $Q_C^* - D_C^*$ is negative, the income effect in Foreign is negative.

The demand and supply effect can now be put together to get the overall effect of a change in p on the market for cloth. The *excess supply* of cloth is the difference between desired world production and consumption:

$$ES_C = Q_C + Q_C^* - D_C - D_C^*. \tag{5P-22}$$

The effect of a change in p on world excess supply is

$$dES_C = [s + s^* + e + e^* - n(Q_C - D_C) - n^*(Q_C^* - D_C^*)]dp. \tag{5P-23}$$

If the market is initially in equilibrium, however, Home's exports equal Foreign's imports, so that $Q_C^* - D_C^* = -(Q_C - D_C)$; the effect of p on excess supply may therefore be written

---

[1] If food is also a normal good, n must be less than $1/p$. To see this effect, notice that if I were to rise by dI without any change in p, spending on cloth would rise by $np\,dI$. Unless $n < 1/p$, then, more than 100 percent of the increase in income would be spent on cloth.

$$dES_C = [s + s^* + e + e^* - (n - n^*)(Q_C - D_C)]dp. \qquad (5P\text{-}23')$$

Suppose the relative price of cloth were initially a little higher than its equilibrium level. If the result were an excess supply of cloth, market forces would push the relative price of cloth down and thus lead to restoration of equilibrium. On the other hand, if an excessively high relative price of cloth leads to an excess *demand* for cloth, the price will rise further, leading the economy away from equilibrium. Thus equilibrium will be *stable* only if a small increase in the relative price of cloth leads to an excess supply of cloth; that is, if

$$\frac{dES_C}{dp} > 0. \qquad (5P\text{-}24)$$

Inspection of equation (5P-23′) reveals the factors determining whether or not equilibrium is stable. Both supply effects and substitution effects in demand work toward stability. The only possible source of instability lies in income effects. The net income effect is of ambiguous sign: It depends on whether $n > n^*$; that is, on whether Home has a higher marginal propensity to consume cloth when its real income increases than Foreign does. If $n > n^*$, the income effect works against stability, while if $n < n^*$, it reinforces the other reasons for stability.

In what follows it will be assumed that equation (5P-24) holds, so that the equilibrium of the world economy is in fact stable.

EFFECTS OF CHANGES IN SUPPLY AND DEMAND

THE METHOD OF COMPARATIVE STATICS

To evaluate the effects of changes in the world economy, a method known as *comparative statics* is applied. In each of the cases considered in the text, the world economy is subjected to some change, which will lead to a change in the world relative price of cloth. The first step in the method of comparative statics is to calculate the effect of the change in the world economy on the excess supply of cloth *at the original p*. This change is denoted by $dES|_p$. Then the change in the relative price needed to restore equilibrium is calculated by

$$dp = \frac{-dES|_p}{(dES/dp)}, \qquad (5P\text{-}25)$$

where dES/dp reflects the supply, income, and substitution effects described earlier.

The effects of a given change on national welfare can be calculated in two stages. First there is whatever direct effect the change has on real income, which we can denote by $dy|_p$; then there is the indirect effect of the resulting change in the terms of trade, which can be calculated using equation (5P-16). Thus the total effect on welfare is

$$dy = dy|_p + (Q_C - D_C)dp. \qquad (5P\text{-}26)$$

ECONOMIC GROWTH

Consider the effect of growth in the Home economy. As pointed out in the text, by growth we mean an outward shift in the production possibility frontier. This change will lead to changes in both cloth and food output at the initial relative price p; let dQ_C, dQ_F be these changes in output. If growth is strongly biased, one or the other of these changes may be negative, but because production possibilities have expanded, the value of output at the initial p must rise:

$$dV = p \, dQ_C + dQ_F = dy|_p > 0. \qquad (5P\text{-}27)$$

At the initial p the supply of cloth will rise by the amount dQ_C. The demand for cloth will also rise, by an amount $n\,dy|_p$. The net effect on world excess supply of cloth will therefore be

$$dES|_p = dQ_C - n(p\,dQ_C + dQ_F). \tag{5P-28}$$

This expression can have either sign. Suppose first that growth is biased toward cloth, so that while $dQ_C > 0$, $dQ_F \leq 0$. Then demand for cloth will rise by

$$dD_C = n(p\,dQ_C + dQ_F) \leq np\,dQ_C < dQ_C.$$

(See footnote 1.)

Thus the overall effect on excess supply will be

$$dES|_p = dQ_C - dD_C > 0.$$

As a result, $dp = -dES|_p/(dES/dp) < 0$: Home's terms of trade worsen.

On the other hand, suppose that growth is strongly biased toward food, so that $dQ_C \leq 0$, $dQ_F > 0$. Then the effect on the supply of cloth at the initial p is negative, but the effect on the demand for cloth remains positive. It follows that

$$dES|_p = dQ_C - dD_C < 0,$$

so that $dp > 0$. Home's terms of trade improve.

Growth that is less strongly biased can move p either way, depending on the strength of the bias compared with the way Home divides its income at the margin.

Turning next to the welfare effects, the effect on Foreign depends only on the terms of trade. The effect on Home, however, depends on the combination of the initial income change and the subsequent change in the terms of trade, as shown in equation (5P-26). If growth turns the terms of trade against Home, this condition will oppose the immediate favorable effect of growth.

But can growth worsen the terms of trade sufficiently to make the growing country actually worse off? To see that it can, consider first the case of a country that experiences a biased shift in its production possibilities that raises Q_C and lowers Q_F while leaving the value of its output unchanged at initial relative prices. (This change would not necessarily be considered growth, because it violates the assumption of equation (5P-27), but it is a useful reference point.) Then there would be no change in demand at the initial p, while the supply of cloth rises; hence p must fall. The change in real income is $dI|_p - (Q_C - D_C)dp$; by construction, however, this is a case in which $dI|_p = 0$, so dy is certainly negative.

Now this country did not grow, in the usual sense, because the value of output at initial prices did not rise. By allowing the output of either good to rise slightly more, however, we would have a case in which the definition of growth is satisfied. If the extra growth is sufficiently small, however, it will not outweigh the welfare loss from the fall in p. Therefore, sufficiently biased growth can leave the growing country worse off.

THE TRANSFER PROBLEM

Suppose Home makes a transfer of some of its income to Foreign, say as foreign aid. Let the amount of the transfer, measured in terms of food, be da. What effect does this alteration have?

At unchanged relative prices there is no effect on supply. The only effect is on demand. Home's income is reduced by da, while Foreign's is raised by the same amount. This adjustment leads to a decline in D_c by $-n\,da$, while D_c^* rises by a n^*da. Thus

$$dES\big|_p = (n - n^*)da \qquad (5\text{P-}29)$$

and the change in the terms of trade is

$$dp = -da\frac{(n - n^*)}{(dES/dp)}. \qquad (5\text{P-}30)$$

Home's terms of trade will worsen if $n > n^*$, which is widely regarded as the normal case; they will, however, improve if $n^* > n$.

The effect on Home's real income combines a direct negative effect from the transfer and an indirect terms of trade effect that can go either way. Is it possible for a favorable terms of trade effect to outweigh the income loss? In this model it is not.

To see the reason, notice that

$$
\begin{aligned}
dy &= dy\big|_p + (Q_c - D_c)dp \\
&= -da + (Q_c - D_c)dp \\
&= -da\left\{1 + \frac{(n - n^*)(Q_c - D_c)}{s + s^* + e + e^* - (n - n^*)(Q_c - D_c)}\right\} \\
&= -da\frac{(s + s^* + e + e^*)}{[s + s^* + e + e^* - (n - n^*)(Q_c - D_c)]} < 0. \qquad (5\text{P-}31)
\end{aligned}
$$

Similar algebra will reveal correspondingly that a transfer cannot make the recipient worse off.

An intuitive explanation of this result is the following. Suppose p were to rise sufficiently to leave Home as well off as it would be if it made no transfer and to leave Foreign no better off as a result of the transfer. Then there would be no income effects on demand in the world economy. But the rise in price would produce both increased output of cloth and substitution in demand away from cloth, leading to an excess supply that would drive down the price. This result demonstrates that a p sufficiently high to reverse the direct welfare effects of a transfer is above the equilibrium p.

In the text we mention that recent work shows how perverse effects of a transfer are nonetheless possible. This work depends on relaxing the assumptions of this model, either by breaking the assumption that each country may be treated as if it were one individual or by introducing more than two countries.

A Tariff

Suppose Home places a tariff on imports, imposing a tax equal to the fraction t of the price. Then for a given world relative price of cloth p, Home consumers and producers will face an internal relative price $\bar{p} = p/(1 + t)$. If the tariff is sufficiently small, the internal relative price will be approximately equal to

$$\bar{p} = p - pt. \qquad (5\text{P-}32)$$

In addition to affecting p, a tariff will raise revenue, which will be assumed to be redistributed to the rest of the economy.

At the initial terms of trade, a tariff will influence the excess supply of cloth in two ways. First, the fall in the relative price of cloth inside Home will lower production of cloth and induce consumers to substitute away from food toward cloth. Second, the tariff may affect Home's real income, with resulting income effects on demand. If Home starts with no tariff and imposes a small tariff, however, the problem may be simplified, because the tariff will have a negligible effect on real income. To see this relation, recall that

$$dy = p \, dD_C + dD_F.$$

The value of output and the value of consumption must always be equal at world prices, so that

$$p \, dD_C + dD_F = p \, dQ_C + dQ_F$$

at the initial terms of trade. But because the economy was maximizing the value of output before the tariff was imposed,

$$p \, dQ_C + dQ_F = 0.$$

Because there is no income effect, only the substitution effect is left. The fall in the internal relative price $\bar{p}$ induces a decline in production and a rise in consumption:

$$dQ_C = -sp \, dt, \tag{5P-33}$$
$$dD_C = ep \, dt, \tag{5P-34}$$

where dt is the tariff increase. Hence

$$dES\big|_p = -(s + e)p \, dt < 0, \tag{5P-35}$$

implying

$$dp = \frac{-dES\big|_p}{(dES/dp)}$$

$$= \frac{p \, dt(s + e)}{[s + s^* + e + e^* - (n - n^*)(Q_C - D_C)]} > 0. \tag{5P-36}$$

This expression shows that a tariff unambiguously improves the terms of trade of the country that imposes it.

Can a tariff actually improve the terms of trade so much that the internal relative price of the imported good falls and the internal price of the exported good rises? The change in $\bar{p}$ is

$$d\bar{p} = dp - p \, dt, \tag{5P-37}$$

so that this paradoxical result will occur if $dp > p \, dt$.

By inspecting equation (5P-36) it can be seen that this result, the famous Metzler paradox, is indeed possible. If $s^* + e^* - (n - n^*)(Q_C - D_C) < 0$, there will be a Metzler paradox; this need not imply instability, because the extra terms s and e help give the denominator a positive sign.

Postscript to Chapter 6

The Monopolistic Competition Model

We want to consider the effects of changes in the size of the market on equilibrium in a monopolistically competitive industry. Each firm has the total cost relationship

$$C = F + cX, \tag{6P-1}$$

where c is marginal cost, F a fixed cost, and X the firm's output. This implies an average cost curve of the form

$$AC = C/X = F/X + c. \tag{6P-2}$$

Also, each firm faces a demand curve of the form

$$X = S[1/n - b(P - \bar{P})], \tag{6P-3}$$

where S is total industry sales (taken as given), n is the number of firms, and $\bar{P}$ is the average price charged by other firms (which each firm is assumed to take as given).

Each firm chooses its price to maximize profits. Profits of a typical firm are

$$\pi = PX - C = PS[1/n - b(P - \bar{P})] - F - cS[1/n - b(P - \bar{P})]. \tag{6P-4}$$

To maximize profits, a firm sets the derivative $d\pi/dP = 0$. This implies

$$X - SbP + Sbc = 0. \tag{6P-5}$$

Since all firms are symmetric, however, in equilibrium $P = \bar{P}$ and $X = S/n$. Thus (6P-5) implies

$$P = 1/bn + c, \tag{6P-6}$$

which is the relationship derived in the text.

Since $X = S/n$, average cost is a function of S and n,

$$AC = Fn/S + c. \tag{6P-7}$$

In zero-profit equilibrium, however, the price charged by a typical firm must also equal its average cost. So we must have

$$1/bn + c = Fn/S + c, \tag{6P-8}$$

which in turn implies

$$n = \sqrt{S/bF} .\tag{6P-9}$$

This shows that an increase in the size of the market, S, will lead to an increase in the number of firms, n, but not in proportion—for example, a doubling of the size of the market will increase the number of firms by a factor of approximately 1.4.

The price charged by the representative firm is

$$P = 1/bn + c = c + \sqrt{F/Sb} ,\tag{6P-10}$$

which shows that an increase in the size of the market leads to lower prices.

Finally, notice that the sales per firm, X, equal

$$X = S/n = \sqrt{SbF} .\tag{6P-11}$$

This shows that the scale of each individual firm also increases with the size of the market.

Postscript to Chapter 21

Risk Aversion and International Portfolio Diversification

This postscript develops a model of international portfolio diversification by risk-averse investors. The model shows that investors generally care about the risk as well as the return of their portfolios. In particular, people may hold assets whose expected returns are lower than those of other assets if this strategy reduces the overall riskiness of their wealth.

A representative investor can divide her real wealth, W, between a Home asset and a Foreign asset. Two possible states of nature can occur in the future, and it is impossible to predict in advance which one it will be. In state 1, which occurs with probability q, a unit of wealth invested in the Home asset pays out H_1 units of output and a unit of wealth invested in the Foreign asset pays out F_1 units of output. In state 2, which occurs with probability $1 - q$, the payoffs to unit investments in the Home and Foreign assets are H_2 and F_2, respectively.

Let α be the share of wealth invested in the Home asset and $1 - \alpha$ the share invested in the Foreign asset. Then if state 1 occurs, the investor will be able to consume the weighted average of her two assets' values,

$$C_1 = [\alpha H_1 + (1 - \alpha)F_1] \times W. \qquad (21P\text{-}1)$$

Similarly, consumption in state 2 is

$$C_2 = [\alpha H_2 + (1 - \alpha)F_2] \times W. \qquad (21P\text{-}2)$$

In any state, the investor derives utility $U(C)$ from a consumption level of C. Since the investor does not know beforehand which state will occur, she makes the portfolio decision to maximize the average or *expected* utility from future consumption,

$$qU(C_1) + (1 - q)U(C_2).$$

AN ANALYTICAL DERIVATION OF THE OPTIMAL PORTFOLIO

After the state 1 and 2 consumption levels given by (21P-1) and (21P-2) are substituted into the expected utility function above, the investor's decision problem can be expressed as follows: Choose the portfolio share α to maximize expected utility,

$$qU\{[\alpha H_1 + (1 - \alpha)F_1] \times W\} + (1 - q)U\{[\alpha H_2 + (1 - \alpha)F_2] \times W\}.$$

This problem is solved (as usual) by differentiating the expected utility above with respect to α and setting the resulting derivative equal to 0.

Let $U'(C)$ be the derivative of the utility function $U(C)$ with respect to C; that is, $U'(C)$ is the *marginal utility* of consumption. Then α maximizes expected utility if

$$\frac{H_1 - F_1}{H_2 - F_2} = -\frac{(1 - q)U'\{[\alpha H_2 + (1 - \alpha)F_2] \times W\}}{qU'\{[\alpha H_1 + (1 - \alpha)F_1] \times W\}}. \tag{21P-3}$$

This equation can be solved for α, the optimal portfolio share.

For a risk-averse investor, the marginal utility of consumption, $U'(C)$, falls as consumption rises. Declining marginal utility explains why someone who is risk averse will not take a gamble with an expected payoff of zero: The extra consumption made possible by a win yields less utility than the utility sacrificed if the gamble is lost. If the marginal utility of consumption does not change as consumption changes, we say the investor is *risk neutral* rather than risk averse. A risk neutral investor is willing to take gambles with a zero expected payoff.

If the investor is risk neutral, however, so that $U'(C)$ is constant for all C, equation (21P-3) becomes

$$qH_1 + (1 - q)H_2 = qF_1 + (1 - q)F_2,$$

which states that *the expected rates of return on Home and Foreign assets are equal.* This result is the basis for the assertion in Chapter 13 that all assets must yield the same expected return in equilibrium when considerations of risk (and liquidity) are ignored. Thus, the interest parity condition of Chapter 13 is valid under risk-neutral behavior, but not, in general, under risk aversion.

For the analysis above to make sense, neither of the assets can yield a higher return than the other in *both* states of nature. If one asset did dominate the other in this way, the left-hand side of equation (21P-3) would be positive while its right-hand side would be negative (because the marginal utility of consumption is usually assumed to be positive). Thus, (21P-3) would have no solution. Intuitively, no one would want to hold a particular asset if another asset that *always* did better were available. Indeed, if anyone did, other investors would be able to make riskless arbitrage profits by issuing the low-return asset and using the proceeds to purchase the high-return asset.

To be definite, we therefore assume that $H_1 > F_1$ and $H_2 < F_2$, so that the Home asset does better in state 1 but does worse in state 2. This assumption is now used to develop a diagrammatic analysis that helps illustrate additional implications of the model.

A DIAGRAMMATIC DERIVATION OF THE OPTIMAL PORTFOLIO

Figure 21P-1 shows indifference curves for the expected utility function described by $qU(C_1) + (1 - q)U(C_2)$. The points in the diagram should be thought of as contingency plans showing the level of consumption that will occur in each state of nature. The preferences represented apply to these contingent consumption plans rather than to consumption of different goods in a single state of nature. As with standard indifference curves, however, each curve in the figure represents a set of contingency plans for consumption with which the investor is equally satisfied.

To compensate the investor for a reduction of consumption in state 1 (C_1), consumption in state 2 (C_2) must rise. The indifference curves therefore slope downward. Each curve becomes flatter, however, as C_1 falls and C_2 rises. This property of the curves reflects the property of $U(C)$ that the marginal utility of consumption declines when C rises. As C_1 falls, the investor can be kept on her original indifference curve only by successively greater increments in C_2: Additions to C_2 are becoming less enjoyable at the same time as subtractions from C_1 are becoming more painful.

Equations (21P-1) and (21P-2) imply that by choosing the portfolio division given by α, the investor also chooses her consumption levels in the two states of nature. Thus, the

FIGURE 21P-1

Indifference Curves and Budget Line for the Portfolio-Selection Problem

The indifference curves are sets of state-contingent consumption plans with which the individual is equally happy. The budget line describes the trade-off between state 1 and state 2 consumption that results from portfolio shifts between Home and Foreign assets.

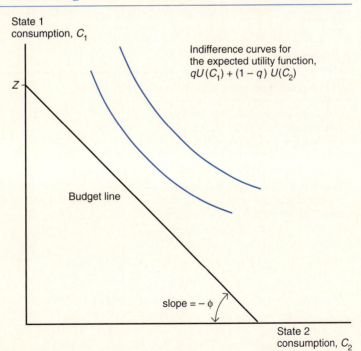

problem of choosing an optimal portfolio is equivalent to one of optimally choosing the contingent consumption levels C_1 and C_2. Accordingly, the indifference curves in Figure 21P-1 can be used to determine the optimal portfolio for the investor. All that is needed to complete the analysis is a budget line showing the trade-off between state 1 consumption and state 2 consumption that the market makes available.

This trade-off is given by equations (21P-1) and (21P-2). If equation (21P-2) is solved for α, the result is

$$\alpha = \frac{F_2 W - C_2}{F_2 W - H_2 W}.$$

After substitution of this expression for α in (21P-1), the latter equation becomes

$$C_1 + \phi C_2 = Z, \tag{21P-4}$$

where $\phi = (H_1 - F_1)/(F_2 - H_2)$ and $Z = W \times (H_1 F_2 - H_2 F_1)/(F_2 - H_2)$. Notice that be-cause $H_1 > F_1$ and $H_2 < F_2$, both ϕ and Z are positive. Thus, equation (21P-4) looks like the budget line that appears in the usual analysis of consumer choice, with ϕ playing the role of a relative price and Z the role of income measured in terms of state 1 consumption. This budget line is graphed in Figure 21P-1 as a straight line with slope $-\phi$ intersecting the vertical axis at Z.

To interpret ϕ as the market trade-off between state 2 and state 1 consumption (that is, as the price of state 2 consumption in terms of state 1 consumption), suppose the investor shifts one unit of her wealth from the Home to the Foreign asset. Since the Home asset has

FIGURE 21P-2

Solving the International Investor's Problem

To maximize expected utility, the in-vestor makes the state-contingent con-sumption choices shown at point 1, where the budget line is tangent to the highest attainable indifference curve, II_1. The optimal portfolio share, α, can be calculated as $(F_2 W - C_2^1) \div (F_2 W - H_2 W)$.

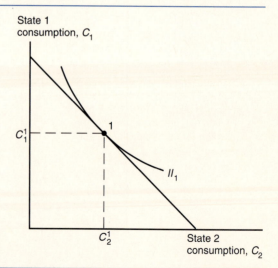

the higher payoff in state 1, her net loss of state 1 consumption is H_1 *less* the Foreign asset's state 1 payoff, F_1. Similarly, her net gain in state 2 consumption is $F_2 - H_2$. To obtain additional state 2 consumption of $F_2 - H_2$, the investor therefore must sacrifice $H_1 - F_1$ in state 1. The price of a single unit of C_2 in terms of C_1 is therefore $H_1 - F_1$ divided by $F_2 - H_2$, which equals ϕ, the absolute value of the slope of budget line (21P-4).

Figure 21P-2 shows how the choices of C_1 and C_2—and, by implication, the choice of the portfolio share α—are determined. As usual, the investor picks the consumption levels given by point 1, where the budget line just touches the highest attainable indifference curve, II_1. Given the optimal choices of C_1 and C_2, α can be calculated using equation (21P-1) or (21P-2). As we move downward and to the right along the budget constraint, the Home asset's portfolio share, α, falls. (Why?)

For some values of C_1 and C_2, α may be negative or greater than 1. These possibilities raise no conceptual problems. A negative α, for example, means that the investor has "gone short" in the Home asset, that is, issued some positive quantity of state-contingent claims that promise to pay their holders H_1 units of output in state 1 and H_2 units in state 2. The proceeds of this borrowing are used to increase the Foreign asset's portfolio share, $1 - \alpha$, above 1.

Figure 21P-3 shows the points on the investor's budget constraint at which $\alpha = 1$ (so that $C_1 = H_1W$, $C_2 = H_2W$) and $\alpha = 0$ (so that $C_1 = F_1W$, $C_2 = F_2W$). Starting from $\alpha = 1$, the investor can move upward and to the left along the constraint by going short in the Foreign asset (thereby making α greater than 1 and $1 - \alpha$ negative). She can move downward and to the right from $\alpha = 0$ by going short in the Home asset.

FIGURE 21P-3

Nondiversified Portfolios

When $\alpha = 1$, the investor holds all her wealth in the Home asset. When $\alpha = 0$ she holds all her wealth in the Foreign asset. Moves along the budget constraint upward and to the left from $\alpha = 1$ correspond to short sales of the Foreign asset, which raise α above 1. Moves downward and to the right from $\alpha = 0$ correspond to short sales of the Home asset, which push α below 0.

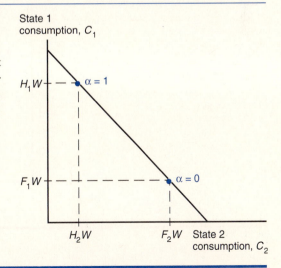

THE EFFECTS OF CHANGING RATES OF RETURN

The diagram we have developed can be used to illustrate the effect of changes in rates of return under risk aversion. Suppose, for example, the Home asset's state 1 payoff rises while all other payoffs and the investor's wealth, W, stay the same. The rise in H_1 raises ϕ, the relative price of state 2 consumption, and therefore steepens the budget line shown in Figure 21P-3.

We need more information, however, to describe completely how the position of the budget line in Figure 21P-3 changes when H_1 rises. The following reasoning fills the gap. Consider the portfolio allocation $\alpha = 0$ in Figure 21P-3, under which all wealth is invested in the Foreign asset. The contingent consumption levels that result from this investment strategy, $C_1 = F_1W$, $C_2 = F_2W$, do not change as a result of a rise in H_1, because the portfolio we are considering does not involve the Home asset. Since the consumption pair associated with $\alpha = 0$ does not change when H_1 rises, we see that $C_1 = F_1W$, $C_2 = F_2W$ is a point on the new budget constraint: After a rise in H_1, it is still feasible for the investor to put all of her wealth into the Foreign asset. It follows that the effect of a rise in H_1 is to make the budget constraint in Figure 21P-3 pivot clockwise around the point $\alpha = 0$.

The effect on the investor of a rise in H_1 is shown in Figure 21P-4, which assumes that initially $\alpha > 0$ (that is, the investor initially owns a positive amount of the Home asset).[1]

FIGURE 21P-4

Effects of a Rise in H_1 on Consumption

A rise in H_1 causes the budget line to pivot clockwise around $\alpha = 0$, and the investor's optimum shifts to point 2. State 1 consumption always rises; in the case shown, state 2 consumption falls.

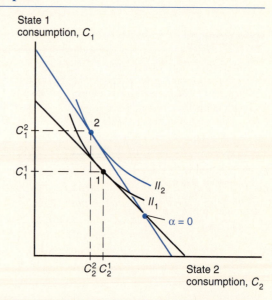

[1]The case in which $\alpha < 0$ initially is left as an exercise.

FIGURE 21P-5

Effects of a Rise in H_1 on Portfolio Shares

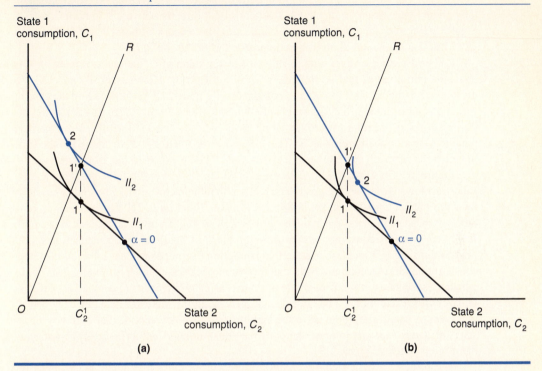

(a)

(b)

Panel (a): If the investor is not too risk averse, she shifts her portfolio toward the Home asset, picking a C_1/C_2 ratio greater than the one indicated by the slope of OR. Panel (b): A very risk-averse investor might increase state 2 consumption by shifting her portfolio toward the Foreign asset.

As usual, both a "substitution" and an "income" effect influence the shift of the investor's contingent consumption plan from point 1 to point 2. The substitution effect is a tendency to demand more C_1, whose relative price has fallen, and less C_2, whose relative price has risen. The income effect of the rise in H_1, however, pushes the entire budget line outward and tends to raise consumption in *both* states (as long as $\alpha > 0$ initially). Because the investor will be richer in state 1, she can afford to shift some of her wealth toward the Foreign asset (which has the higher payoff in state 2) and thereby even out her consumption in the two states of nature. Risk aversion explains the investor's desire to avoid large consumption fluctuations across states. As Figure 21P-4 suggests, C_1 definitely rises while C_2 may rise or fall. (In the case illustrated, the substitution effect is stronger than the income effect and C_2 falls.)

Corresponding to this ambiguity is an ambiguity concerning the effect of the rise in H_1 on the portfolio share, α. Figure 21P-5 illustrates the two possibilities. The key to understanding this figure is the observation that if the investor does *not* change α in response to the rise in H_1, her consumption choices are given by point 1', which lies on the new budget constraint vertically above the initial consumption point 1. Why is this the case? Equation (21P-2) implies that $C_2^1 = [\alpha H_2 + (1 - \alpha)F_2] \times W$ doesn't change if α doesn't change; the new, higher value of state 1 consumption corresponding to the original portfolio choice is then given by the point on the new budget constraint directly above C_2^1. In both panels of Figure 21P-5, the slope of the ray OR connecting the origin and point $1'$ shows the ratio C_1/C_2 implied by the initial portfolio composition after the rise in H_1.

It is now clear, however, that to shift to a lower value of C_2 the investor must raise α above its initial value, that is, shift the portfolio toward the Home asset. To raise C_2, she must lower α, that is, shift toward the Foreign asset. Figure 21P-5a shows again the case in which the substitution effect outweighs the income effect. In that case, C_2 falls as the investor shifts her portfolio toward the Home asset, whose expected rate of return has risen relative to that on the Foreign asset. This case corresponds to those we studied in the text, in which the portfolio share of an asset rises as its relative expected rate of return rises.

Figure 21P-5b shows the opposite case, in which C_2 rises and α falls, implying a portfolio shift toward the Foreign asset. You can see that the factor giving rise to this possibility is the sharper curvature of the indifference curves II in Figure 21P-5b. This curvature is precisely what economists mean by the term *risk aversion*. An investor who becomes more risk averse regards consumptions in different states of nature as poorer substitutes, and thus requires a larger increase in state 1 consumption to compensate her for a fall in state 2 consumption (and vice versa). Note that the paradoxical case shown in Figure 21P-5b, in which a rise in an asset's expected rate of return can cause investors to demand *less* of it, is unlikely in the real world. For example, an increase in the interest rate a currency offers, other things equal, raises the expected rate of return on deposits of that currency in all states of nature, not just in one. The portfolio substitution effect in favor of the currency therefore is much stronger.

The results we have found are quite different from those that would occur if the investor were risk neutral. A risk-neutral investor would shift all of her wealth into the asset with the higher expected return, paying no attention to the riskiness of this move.[2] The greater the degree of risk aversion, however, the greater the concern with the riskiness of the overall portfolio of assets.

---

[2] In fact, a risk-neutral investor would always like to take the maximum possible short position in the low-return asset and, correspondingly, the maximum possible long position in the high-return asset. It is this behavior that gives rise to the interest parity condition.

Index

Note: Page numbers followed by *t* and *f* indicate tables and figures, respectively.